AN ANALYTICAL APPROACH TO

Investments, Finance, and Credit

AN ANALYTICAL APPROACH TO

Investments, Finance, and Credit

First Edition

Chris Droussiotis

Columbia University

cognella® ACADEMIC PUBLISHING

3970 Sorrento Valley Blvd., Ste. 500, San Diego, CA 92121

Bassim Hamadeh, CEO and Publisher
John Remington, Executive Editor
Gem Rabanera, Senior Project Editor
Abbey Hastings, Production Editor
Emely Villavicencio, Senior Graphic Designer
Trey Soto, Licensing Specialist
Jaye Pratt, Interior Designer
Natalie Piccotti, Director of Marketing
Kassie Graves, Vice President of Editorial
Jamie Giganti, Director of Academic Publishing

Printed in the United States of America.

cognella® ACADEMIC PUBLISHING
3970 Sorrento Valley Blvd., Ste. 500, San Diego, CA 92121

ACTIVE LEARNING

This book has interactive activities available to complement your reading.

Your instructor may have customized the selection of activities available for your unique course. Please check with your professor to verify whether your class will access this content through the Cognella Active Learning portal (http://active.cognella.com) or through your home learning management system.

cognella® | ACTIVE LEARNING content

I dedicate this book to our dog Chester. Chester, who sat next to me while I was writing this book in the wee hours, passed this year while I was finishing chapter 13; I still feel his presence as I am writing this dedication. I miss you buddy.

BRIEF CONTENTS

About the Author xix

Acknowledgments xxi

PART I INVESTMENT & PORTFOLIO RETURN ANALYSIS

1 Risk-and-Return Analysis 3

2 Covariance, Correlation, and Efficient Frontiers 33

3 Beta Coefficient, R-Squared, and Regression Analysis 49

4 Sharpe Ratio, CAPM, Jensen's Alpha, Treynor Measure, and M-Square 64

PART II PRIMARY MARKETS: CAPITAL MARKETS AND CAPITAL RAISING

5 Equity Markets: Raising Equity for Private Companies 88

6 Equity Markets: Initial Public Offering (IPO) and other Transactions for Publicly Traded Companies 106

7 Debt Markets: Issuing Corporate Bonds, 144As, and Private Placements 132

8 Debt Markets: Issuing Bank Loans, Private Loans, and Loan Syndication 158

9 Transaction Analysis: LBOs, M&As, and other Capital Market Deals 180

PART III SECONDARY MARKETS: INVESTMENTS AND DERIVATIVES

10 Stock Investments, Analysis, and Valuation 209

11 Corporate Bond Investments, Analysis, and Valuation 233

12 Credit and Alternative Investments: Leveraged Loans, CLOs, and Structured Finance 257

13 Derivative Investments: Option Strategies, Analysis, and Valuation 273

14 Derivative Investments: Futures, Forwards, Swaps, Swaptions, CDAs, FRAs, and Other Derivatives 313

PART IV COMPANY-SPECIFIC ANALYSIS: CORPORATE FINANCE, VALUATIONS, AND CREDIT ANALYSIS

15 Financial Statement Analysis 341

16 Projections Analysis 373

17 Valuation Analysis 407

18 Credit Risk Analysis and Debt-Capacity Analysis 431

PART V FINANCIAL MODELS AND CASE STUDY

References 459

DETAILED CONTENTS

About the Author xix

Acknowledgments xxi

PART I **INVESTMENT & PORTFOLIO RETURN ANALYSIS**

1 Risk-and-Return Analysis 3

Learning Objectives 3

Rates of Return Overview 4

Time Value of Money 6

Measuring Return and Return Expectation 9

Measuring Return and Quantifying Risk 14

Case Study 20

Problems 29

Online Templates & Case Studies 32

2 Covariance, Correlation, and Efficient Frontiers 33

Learning Objectives 33

Covariance and Correlation Overview 34

Investment Return and Risk Efficiency 35

Case Study 45

Problems 48

Online Templates & Case Studies 48

3 Beta Coefficient, R-Squared, and Regression Analysis 49

Learning Objectives 49

Regression Analysis: An Analytical Introduction 50

Introduction to Linear Regression and Beta Coefficient 51

Case Study 59

Problems 62

Online Templates & Case Studies 63

4 Sharpe Ratio, CAPM, Jensen's Alpha, Treynor Measure, and M-Square 64

Learning Objectives 64

Portfolio Management Performance Measurement: An Overview 64

Setting Up the Basis for Portfolio Measurement: Re-Introduction to Basic Return Characteristics 66

Setting Up the Basis for Portfolio Measurement: Re-Introduction to Basic Volatility Characteristics 68

From Portfolio Efficiency to Optimization 68

Sharpe Ratio 70

Capital Asset Pricing Model (CAPM) 71

Jensen's Alpha Ratio 72

Treynor Ratio 73

M-Square Ratio 74

Other Useful Portfolio Analysis Ratios 76

Case Study 79

Problems 81

Online Templates & Case Studies 83

PART II PRIMARY MARKETS: CAPITAL MARKETS AND CAPITAL RAISING

5 Equity Markets: Raising Equity for Private Companies 88

Learning Objectives 88

Raising Equity: An Overview 89

The Life Cycle of the Company 90

Getting Ready to Go to Market 95

Case Study 99

Problems 103

Online Templates 105

6 Equity Markets: Initial Public Offering (IPO) and other Transactions for Publicly Traded Companies 106

Learning Objectives 106
Initial Public Offering: An Overview 107
The Life Cycle of the Public Company 109
Syndication of Securities Offerings 115
Merger and Acquisition Transaction 121
Case Study 128
Problems 130
Online Templates 131

7 Debt Markets: Issuing Corporate Bonds, 144As, and Private Placements 132

Learning Objectives 132
Corporate Debt: An Overview 133
Corporate Bonds: An Overview 135
Rating Corporate Bonds 138
Terms and Conditions of Corporate Bonds (Money and Non-Money Terms) 143
Going to Market to Raise Corporate Bonds 143
Rating Agency Methodology 149
Bond Investment Concepts 153
Case Study 155
Problems 157
Online Templates 157

8 Debt Markets: Issuing Bank Loans, Private Loans, and Loan Syndication 158

Learning Objectives 158
Corporate Loans: An Overview 159
Corporate Loans 160
Rating Corporate Loans 168

Types of Loan Syndication 170

The Loan Syndication Process 171

Typical Internal Analysis Process by Each Bank 173

Terms and Conditions of Corporate Loans (Money and Non-Money Terms) 174

Problems 179

Online Templates 179

9 Transaction Analysis: LBOs, M&As, and other Capital Market Deals 180

Learning Objectives 180

Transaction Analysis: An Overview 180

One Transaction, Multiple Expectations: The Analysis 182

Case Study 186

Online Templates 205

PART III SECONDARY MARKETS: INVESTMENTS AND DERIVATIVES

10 Stock Investments, Analysis, and Valuation 209

Learning Objectives 209

Trading Stocks: An Overview 210

Secondary Trading Markets: An Overview 212

How to Trade Stocks 214

Trading Strategies 216

Stock Analysis 220

Stock Valuation 226

Case Study 227

Problems 232

Online Templates 232

11 Corporate Bond Investments, Analysis, and Valuation 233

Learning Objectives 233

Trading Bonds: An Overview 233

Secondary Bond Markets: An Overview 235
Bond Investment Concepts: Reintroduced 238
Bond Investment Valuation Concepts 249
Case Study 252
Problems 256
Online Templates 256

12 Credit and Alternative Investments: Leveraged Loans, CLOs, and Structured Finance 257

Learning Objectives 257
Secondary Loan Markets—An Overview 258
Case Study 267
Problems 271
Online Templates 272

13 Derivative Investments: Option Strategies, Analysis, and Valuation 273

Learning Objectives 273
Option Markets: Overview 273
Option Markets 275
Uncovered (Naked) Option Trading Strategy Contracts 276
Covered Option Trading Strategy Contracts 282
Advanced Option Trading Strategies 285
Option Valuation Methods 291
Case Study 308
Problems 310
Online Templates 312

14 Derivative Investments: Futures, Forwards, Swaps, Swaptions, CDAs, FRAs, and Other Derivatives 313

Learning Objectives 313
Forwards, Futures Swap Contracts: Overview 314
Forwards, Futures Swap Contracts 316

Other Derivatives 329

Pricing and Valuation of FRAs (VFRA) 332

Case Study 334

Problems 336

Online Templates 337

PART IV COMPANY-SPECIFIC ANALYSIS: CORPORATE FINANCE, VALUATIONS, AND CREDIT ANALYSIS

15 Financial Statement Analysis 341

Learning Objectives 341

Financial Statements Overview 341

Understanding Financial Statements 343

Financial Ratio Analysis 356

Case Study 363

Problems 367

Online Templates 372

16 Projections Analysis 373

Learning Objectives 373

Projections Overview 374

Projections—Building the Financial Model 375

Building the What-if Scenario Cases 387

Case Study 394

Problems 403

Online Templates 406

17 Valuation Analysis 407

Learning Objectives 407

Valuation Overview 407

Valuation Methods 409

Methods 1–6: Valuation of Public Traded Companies 409

Case Study 426

Problems 429
Online Templates 430

18 Credit Risk Analysis and Debt-Capacity Analysis 431

Learning Objectives 431
Credit Analysis Overview 432
Review of financial statements and application of credit-related ratios 433
Debt-Capacity Analysis 437
Risk and Credit Restructure Analysis 438
Corporate Credit and Recovery Scores by Rating Agencies and Others 442
Case Study 448
Problems 452
Online Templates 454

PART V FINANCIAL MODELS AND CASE STUDY

References 459

About the Author

Chris Droussiotis's training and expertise is in the area of investment banking. Possessing over 30 years of experience by working for numerous corporations in various executive management positions at Bank of America Merill Lynch, CIBC Oppenheimer, Mizuho Financial Group, Bank of Tokyo-Mitsubishi Trust UFJ, Sumitomo Mitsui Banking Corporation, and Mitsui Nevitt Banking Corporation.

He is a former managing director, general manager and head of the Leverage Finance, Private Equity Sponsor Group & Structured Finance Department at Sumitomo Mitsui Banking Corporation (SMBC) where he managed a loan portfolio of over $8 billion of large cap and middle-market leveraged loans, as well as investments in SPV funds, CLOs and BDCs that are backed by leveraged loans, and high-yield bonds. He left SMBC recently to join, as a senior managing partner, Kinisis Ventures Limited (www.kinisisventures.com), a business accelerator company that helps international company start-ups expand in U.S. markets. At Kinisis Ventures he leads the firm's deal-flow review, valuations, and strategic capital-raising team.

ACADEMIC EXPERIENCE

Droussiotis has been adjunct professor for Columbia University's School of Professional Studies, Enterprise Risk Management; Fordham University's Gabelli School of Business; Baruch College's Economics and Finance Department in New York; Baruch College's Continuing and Professional Studies (CAPS); Stillman School of Business at Seton Hall; and Fairleigh Dickinson University's International School of Hospitality and Tourism Management in New Jersey. Courses he has taught include Quantitative Analysis in Business, Investment Analysis, Managerial Finance, Commercial Credit Banking, Debt and Fixed Income Markets, Derivative Strategies, Business Statistics, Equity Valuation, and Advanced New Venture Management.

Professor Droussiotis coauthored *Merges and Acquisitions: A Practitioner's Guide to Successful Deals*.

Professor Droussiotis has also given lectures and attended many panels on various subjects including fin tech, clean tech, health tech, mergers and acquisitions, leveraged buyouts, credit markets, loan syndications, and capital markets at Baruch College, Bank of China, Cendant Corporation, China Construction Bank, Wyndham Worldwide, Travelport and the Industrial Bank of Japan, among others.

Credit

Acknowledgments

I would like to acknowledge with gratitude Niki Maroulakos for her love, support, guidance, and of course her 120 words-per-minute typing skills. Similarly, I would like to thank my children Amanda, Christopher, Alec, and Troy for their support and enthusiasm. My Cypriot-American friends at Leschi ("Club" in Greek), Andreas Panayi, George Kokkinos, Chris Demetriou, Chris Christoforou, Chris Koutsokoumnis, Peter Ioannou, Savvas Zachariades, Michael Hadjiloukas, Mike Franjeskos, Andreas Frangoudis, and Nicos Nicolaou encouraged me to write this textbook, so thank you; of course playing friendly card games with them taught me that that the markets are not as efficient as many of my scholars write in their finance text books.

This book could have not been completed without the help of one of my top students and mentees, Jason Uliano, who spend countless hours on the computer assisting me with the write-up, analytics, and format of this book. Thank you, Jason. I will also want to thank Theano Paterakis, another student of mine from Fordham University who helped me with the original research with this book and the previous book that I coauthored regarding leveraged buyouts. Also, my nephew Alexandros Tsouloftas has helped tremendously with brilliant IT ideas that can complement this book with an electronic training platform for an ultimate learning experience—to be available soon.

Last, I must acknowledge the many mentors and support groups throughout my life and career as a banker and a professor: Dr. Harvey Poniachek, my professor and life mentor; Stuart Shelly, who was my very first colleague when I started at Bank of America back in the late 80s, someone who taught me accounting, finance, and financial modeling in one afternoon; my recent bank colleagues who stuck with me all these years at SMBC, Andrei Eftimie, Eric Planey, Lindsay Drogin, Sofia Ghaiti, Heather Buhman, Nick Karsiotis, Irina Popova, Nick Sanders, Jane Zhang, Waki Iwayama, Tatiana Nepotu, and Andreas Panteli; all of my hundreds of students over the last 15 years at Baruch College, Columbia University, Fordham University, Seton Hall University, and Fairleigh Dickinson University, thanks for all of your inspiration; and last but not least, my father Spyros Droussiotis and sisters Isabella and Sharon and brother Spyros, as well as my nephews and nieces George, Alex, Electra, Imogen and Cassandra who are my greatest fans and support group.

Professor Droussiotis and Cognella gratefully acknowledge the contributions of the following reviewers:

Miriam Tsymuk
Professor of Global Finance and Economics
Baruch College

George Kokkinos
Chief Financial Officer
Eckler Industries, Inc.

Jason Uliano Analyst
Goldman Sachs

PART I

Investment & Portfolio Return Analysis

CHAPTER 1
Risk-and-Return Analysis

CHAPTER 2
Covariance, Correlation, and Efficient Frontiers

CHAPTER 3
Beta Coefficient, R Squared, and Regression Analysis

CHAPTER 4
Sharpe Ratio, CAPM, Jensen's Alpha, Treynor Measure, and M Squared

PART I of the textbook is designed to introduce investment concepts and various tools used to access the performance of these investments. They say, "A picture is worth a thousand words." The following chart gives a bird's eye view of the investing environment. Every investor's original expectation looks like the 45-degree blue line shown in this chart. The premium, which is the difference between risk-free investment, such as buying treasuries, and the investment expectation brings along risk and uncertainty. The investor may achieve the expectation that was originally set but expect the line not to be as smooth as the original 45-degree blue line. The line could look like the red dotted line in the chart. "Buckle up before we ride the rollercoaster." Can the investor stay the course with such volatility and doubt? That is the question.

CUMULATIVE INVESTMENT RETURN EXPECTATION

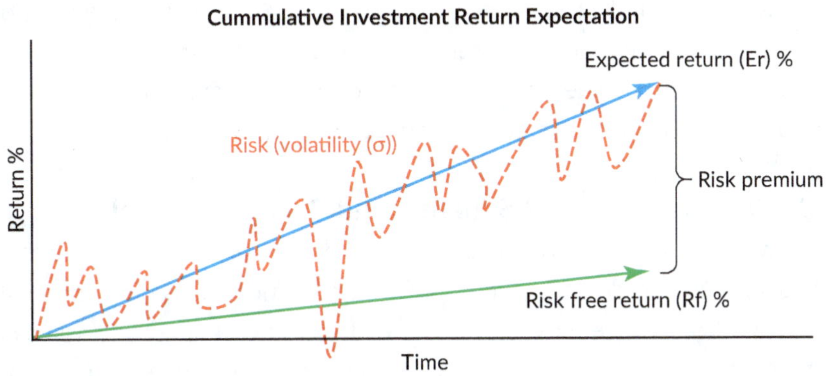

Part I will dive into concepts such as volatility, beta, alpha, delta, risk premium, and other Greek characters that measure performance. Starting with the basics, I will say that before someone is looking to invest in stocks, bonds, or any other asset class, he or she needs to consider the four following factors:

1. Measuring the expected return of the investment
2. Quantifying the risk of such investment
3. Setting the time to exit the investment
4. Exploring ways to allocate to achieve portfolio risk diversification, investment efficiency, and optimization

Part I will address these factors for various asset classes, such bonds and stocks, and educate the reader on how to build a portfolio of investments. The line-up and brief description of Part I's chapters are as follows:

Chapter 1: Risk-and-Return Analysis

This chapter will introduce time value of money and cover the basic concepts of risk and return and what constitutes a satisfactory investment portfolio. The chapter will also examine return expectation for specific asset classes such as stocks and bonds and walk the reader through how to use the two different analytical approaches to determine the risk-return balance, through fundamental and technical analysis.

Chapter 2: Covariance, Correlation, and Efficient Frontier

This chapter will continue to focus on return, risk, and their respective relationship and allocation but demonstrate that the correlation between two assets can be used to achieve higher portfolio efficiency. The covariance and correlation analysis are the factors that contribute to a minimum variance and achieve an efficient frontier.

Chapter 3: Beta Coefficient, R Squared, and Regression Analysis

This chapter will specifically focus on the comparative analysis of a portfolio versus the market. Stocks go up and down based on information such as earnings or technical data such as the 200-day average movement of the stock. This chapter will assess the risk or volatility of a portfolio of stocks to understand such movements versus market movements and the relationship versus the movements of the market.

Chapter 4: Sharpe Ratio, CAPM, Jensen's Alpha, Treynor Measure, and M Squared

This chapter will re-emphasize these comparisons by introducing other ways to compare results via performance measurements ratios such as the Sharpe ratio, Jensen's alpha, M-squared, and the Treynor measure, among others that are used extensively on Wall Street to gain valuable insight using comparisons.

CHAPTER 1

Risk-and-Return Analysis

This chapter will introduce time value of money and cover the basic concepts of risk and return and what constitutes a satisfactory investment portfolio. The chapter will also examine return expectation for specific asset classes such as stocks and bonds and walk the reader through how to use the two different analytical approaches to determine the risk-return balance, through fundamental and technical analysis.

LEARNING OBJECTIVES

After reading this chapter, students will be able to do the following:

- Understand the component that make time value of money (TVM) including the calculations of present value (PV), future value (FV), interest rate (i) and time (t) for a one-time investment, annuity or uneven cash receipts
- Compute various measures to calculate the historical and expected returns on many asset classes such as equities and bonds
- Quantify the risk on these asset classes by calculating the variance and standard deviation
- Understand how to measure past performances of stocks and bonds using both historical analysis and scenario analysis to determine the expected risk/return going forward
- Construct a portfolio of investments consisting of stocks, bonds, and risk-free investments such as cash, money market, or treasury bills and the impact of diversification
- Understand portfolio optimization and efficiency based on asset allocation between stock, bonds, and cash

RATES OF RETURN OVERVIEW

If you invest $100 today and receive $120 next year, the $20 gain on your investment represents the return on your initial $100 investment, or 20% (20/100). Basically, the return is the growth rate of your initial investment growing from $100 to $120 calculated at $120/100 − 1 = 0.20 or 20%. The rate of return calculation is the first performance measurement ratio of any investment. After someone adds the time or period of the investment, such as a month or a year, then the rate of return can be compared to other periods. The chapter will describe various methods of calculating the rate of return compared to other rates of return, such as to the market, to another portfolio, or to another stock for the same period.

AUTHOR'S NOTES

A joke that I heard many years ago makes a perfect introduction to investment return expectation and it goes like this: John woke up one morning and looked at the clock and it was 7:07a.m. Then he looked at the calendar and the day was July 7 (7/7). He noticed that the 7s could be the theme of the day. As he was running out of the door he stopped at his mailbox and he opened an envelope with his weekly paycheck that had a check for $777.77. As he was crossing the road, he almost got hit by a car that stopped inches short of his body. The car's license number was GGG 777; "Very strange," he moans, considering that G is also the seventh letter of the alphabet. He looked up and saw that the seven bus was approaching the station. So, he had to get on it. He was sure that this was a sign. He asked the bus driver when the next station was, and the bus driver replied: "The seventh station." He said to himself, "I need to get off the bus at the next station." After he got off the bus he looked up and saw a building in front of him; "77 on 7th Avenue" was posted on top of the door. He walked into the building as he was sure by now that this was a sign. In the lobby of the building there was an off-track betting (OTB) store where patrons can bet on horse races without being at the racetrack. John walked in and asked when the next race was. He was told that the next race was the seventh race and he had exactly 7 minutes before post time. He then asked how many horses were in this seventh race. "Seven horses!" someone replied. He then asked what are the odds that the horse with number 7 will win. "Don't bother" somebody shouted, "This is a long shot ... 77 to 1 to win." John thought to himself: "This is it." He approached the betting window and said, "Here is my paycheck of $777.77. Put it all for 7 to win ... I am feeling it he shouted!" Of course, with 77 to 1 odds, his payoff would be huge, making approximately

$60,000 on a $777.77 bet if the number 7 horse won. The race was over—and the number 7 horse came in seventh.

You see, this is a funny way of explaining the investment expectation based on trends; of course, this bet, or investment is all based on emotions and behavioral return expectation, which is very difficult to predict since there was no mathematical basis. Such behavioral analysis, which in many cases dictates why someone buys or sells the stock, won't be covered in this chapter. There are many books written on behavioral finance that discusses various interesting observations that challenge the traditional analytical tools of risk-and-return analysis. The other measurements of risk-and-return expectations that this chapter and this unit will cover are through fundamental and technical analyses.

KEY TAKEAWAYS

- Before investing, the investor needs to consider the following four factors:
    1. Measurement of the expected return (Er)
    2. Quantification of the risk (σ)
    3. How to allocate the investments to achieve efficiency and optimization (A for Allocation)
    4. Time to determine the exit strategy or realization of the investment (t)
- To determine the return expectation or predict the investment payoff, and quantify the risk to achieve such expectation, the analyst can use fundamental analysis, technical analysis and/or behavioral analysis. The chapter will focus on the first two analytical approaches.
- By allocating the investments across different asset classes including stocks, bonds, and cash, the investors can diversify their risk and achieve portfolio efficiency, which is the point where you attain the highest possible return at the lowest possible risk.
- The analyst can also determine the future risk/return expectation by analyzing the historical trends and applying various economic scenarios based on probability outcomes such as expected performance under recessionary or economic boom environment.

TIME VALUE OF MONEY

Before introducing the risk-return relationship, which this chapter and unit is mostly focused on, it is important to discuss the fundamental concept of time value of money. This concept states that a dollar in hand today is worth more than a dollar received in the future, because if you have that dollar today you could invest it, earn interest, and receive more than a dollar in the future. The relationship between cash flow, or profits, from the investment, rate of return on the investment, and time to realize the investment are the basic variables in calculating time value of money. Time value calculations are addressed in the following three concepts: (a) calculating a one-time investment; (b) ongoing receipt of even annual cash flows from the investment, called annuities; and (c) ongoing receipt of uneven annual cash flows from the investment.

ONE-TIME INVESTMENT

The cash flow that is expected to be received in the future based on an investment made today is referred to as the future value (FV). For example, if an investor invests $100 today and expects the investment will grow 10% by next year, the future value of his or her investment will be $110, calculated as $100 (1 + 0.10) = 100 × 1.10 = $110. If the investment continues for another year and earns the same growth of 10%, then the future value will grow to $121, calculated as 100 (1 + 1.10) (1 + 1.10) = 100 (1.10) (1.10) = 100 $(1.10)^2$ = 121. If the investment is realized the third year then the calculation becomes 100 $(1.10)^3$ or $133.10. Therefore, the formula for future value is expressed as follows:

$$\mathbf{FV} = \mathbf{PV}(1 + i)^t$$

where FV is the future value of the investment, PV is the present value of the investment or the initial investment, i is the expected interest rate or rate of return of the investment, and t is time to realize such investment.

If the investor sets a future target for an expected return to be realized at a certain date, then he or she can calculate how much to invest today. The formula to calculate the present value of the investment derived by the FV formula above is as follows:

$$\mathrm{FV} = \mathrm{PV}(1+i)^t, \text{ then } \mathrm{PV} = \frac{\mathrm{FV}}{(1+i)^t}$$

As an example, assuming the investor targets an investment that is expected to receive $133.10 in 3 years, representing a 10% interest or expected return (sometimes referred to as the discount rate), the investment required today will be calculated as follows:

$$\mathrm{PV} = \frac{\mathrm{FV}}{(1+i)^t} = \frac{133.10}{(1+.10)^3} = \frac{133.10}{1.331} = 100$$

If the investor knows the amount they are planning to invest today, and targets a specific investment payoff at a set time in the future, then the investor can rearrange the formula to calculate the interest (i) or discount rate that he or she will earn, as follows:

Starting at $FV = (1 + i)^t$, then $(1 + i)^t = \frac{FV}{PV}$, and

$$i = \left(\frac{FV}{PV}\right)^{\frac{1}{t}} - 1$$

As an example, let's assume the investor invests $100 today and targets an investment that expects to receive $133.10 in 3 years. What will the annual rate of return be on such an investment?

$$i = \left(\frac{FV}{PV}\right)^{\frac{1}{t}} - 1 = \left(\frac{133.10}{100}\right)^{\frac{1}{3}} - 1 = (1.331)^{\frac{1}{3}} - 1 = 1.10 - 1 = 0.10 = 10\%$$

If the investor knows the amount that they are planning to invest today, then sets a target payoff amount in the future and assumes a given rate of return, then he or she can calculate how long it will take to achieve the target. The time (t) to realize the targeted return is calculated by rearranging the formula as follows:

Starting at $FV = PV\,(1 + i)^t$, then $(1 + i)^t = \frac{FV}{PV}$, then adding ln on both sides, you get

$\ln\,(1 + i)^t = \ln\left(\frac{FV}{PV}\right)$, $t[\ln(1 + i)] = \ln\left(\frac{FV}{PV}\right)$, and

$$t = \frac{\ln\left(\frac{FV}{PV}\right)}{\ln(1 + i)}$$

As an example, assume the investor invests $100 today and wants to find out how long it will take for the investment to reach $133.10 if invested at an annual rate of return of 10%. The time to reach the targeted future value of such investment is calculated as follows:

$$t = \frac{\ln\left(\frac{FV}{PV}\right)}{\ln\,(1 + i)} = \frac{\ln\left(\frac{133.10}{100}\right)}{\ln\,(1 + 0.10)} = \frac{\ln\left(\frac{133.10}{100}\right)}{\ln\,(1 + 0.10)} = \frac{\ln\,(1.331)}{\ln\,(1.100)} = \frac{0.2859}{0.0953} = 3 \text{ years}$$

ANNUITIES OR EVEN ANNUAL CASH FLOWS

As mentioned earlier, the initial investment, the return on the investment, and the time to realize the investment are the basic variables in calculating time value of money. If the investment expected to produce the same annual cash flow for the investor, called payments, for a set time, using the same expected rate of return, then this type of investment is called annuities investment. The basic formula flow is the expected cash flow to be received in the future, referred to the future value (FV). Assuming a timeline, the formula to calculate the future value annuity (FVA) will be as follows:

$$FVA = CF + CF(1+i) + CF(1+i)(1+i), \text{ or } FVA = CF\left(\frac{(1+i)^t - 1}{i}\right)$$

For example, if an investor invests $100 per year for 3 years and expects a 10% rate of return, then the value of such investment when it is cashed out in 3 years will be calculated as follows:

$$FVA = CF\left(\frac{(1+i)^t - 1}{i}\right) = 100\left(\frac{(1+0.10)^3 - 1}{.10}\right) = 100\left(\frac{(1.10)^3 - 1}{.10}\right) = 100\left(\frac{1.331 - 1}{.10}\right) = 331.00$$

The present value of an annuity (PVA) can be calculated as follows:

$$PVA = \frac{CF}{(1+i)^1} + \frac{CF}{(1+i)^2} + \frac{CF}{(1+i)^3} + \ldots + \frac{CF}{(1+i)^n}, \text{ or } PVA = CF\left[\frac{1 - \frac{1}{(1+i)^t}}{i}\right]$$

For example, if an investor expects to receive $100 per year for 3 years, then what is the present value for an investment if the investor expects to receive a 10% annual rate of return? The calculation of the present value of such an investment is as follows:

$$PVA = CF\left[\frac{1 - \frac{1}{(1+i)^t}}{i}\right] = 100\left[\frac{1 - \frac{1}{(1+.10)^3}}{.10}\right] = 100\left[\frac{1 - \frac{1}{1.331}}{.10}\right] = 248.69$$

UNEVEN ANNUAL CASH FLOWS

If the investment expected to produce uneven annual cash flows to the investor, called payments, for a set time, using the same expected rate of return, then the investment is calculated differently. The present value of such cash flows is the sum of all the future cash flows discounted back at a given expected rate of return, as follows:

$$PV = \frac{CF_1}{(1+i)^1} + \frac{CF_2}{(1+i)^2} + \frac{CF_3}{(1+i)^3} + \ldots \frac{CF_t}{(1+i)^t} \ldots\; PV = \sum \frac{CF_t}{(1+i)^t}$$

For example, if an investor expects to receive $95 the first year, $92 the second year, and $105 the third year, what is the present value for such an investment if the investor expects a 10% annual rate of return? The calculation of the present value of such investment is as follows:

$$PV = \frac{CF_1}{(1+i)^1} + \frac{CF_2}{(1+i)^2} + \frac{CF_3}{(1+i)^3} = \frac{95}{(1+0.10)^1} + \frac{92}{(1+1.10)^2} + \frac{105}{(1+1.10)^3}$$

$$= 86.36 + 76.03 + 78.89 = 241.28$$

Excel formulas for calculating all five variables including the present value, future value, rate of return, time and cash flows or payments (represent set additional payments received during the investment):

= PV (rate, years, payment, future value) or *=pv(rate,nper,pmt,fv)*

= FV (rate, years, payment, -present value) or *=fv(rate,nper,pmt,pv)*

= Rate (years, payment, -present value, future value) or *=rate(nper,pmt,pv,fv)*

= Nper (rate, payment, -present value, future value) or *=nper(rate,pmt,pv,fv)*

= Pmt (rate, years, -present value, future value) or *=pmt(rate,nper,pv,fv)*

MEASURING RETURN AND RETURN EXPECTATION

Before you invest your money in any securities or any businesses, **it's extremely important to consider and must measure the following four factors:**

1. **Return expectation**
2. **Risk**
3. **Allocation**
4. **Time**

Every factor is essential to estimate investment return expectation. The investor needs to determine return expectation first. Without any measuring such as expectation the investor should not proceed with the investment. Any investment expectation comes with risk appetite of the individual investor. The expectation needs to be set before the investor adjusts based on the risk that he or she is willing to take. The basic premise, of course, is that the higher the risk the higher the return expectation. This and the following chapters will discuss this relationship in depth. We will examine a possibility that when the investor allocates his or her investments across different assets, he or she will not only diversify the risk but can also achieve efficiency or attempt to better balance the risk with the return. One of the most important components of achieving this measurement is to have an exit strategy or set the time when the investor can realize the investment.

OBJECTIVE OF RETURN AND RETURN EXPECTATION

As discussed previously, it is essential to measure the historical returns of a particular asset class and then set an expectation going forward based on various methods that we will examine in this section. The return analysis objectives are as follows:

- **Trend Analysis:** To compare the return analysis to historical trends of the particular investment, project the trend going forward, and adjust such trends based on views for driving such investment
- **Comparative Analysis:** To compare it to other asset classes and/or the market, and/or the risk-free rate.
- **Expectation Analysis:** To compare it to last year's expectations and continue to test the performance versus expectation

If all three objectives are met, then the assessment is completed. For example, just giving a rate-of-return number of 10% without comparing such rate to historical trends, to the market or other asset classes and to what was expected is not enough. Though 10% return in a year seems like a good return, if it was achieved in April of 1979, for example, that rate of return would have been terrible since the risk-free 3-month treasury rate and inflation were 9.8% and 11.35%, respectively, only 0.2% higher than the risk free rate and 1.35% lower than inflation.

RATES OF RETURN: HOLDING PERIOD RETURN (HPR)

The first basic measurement of return does not consider the length of time that the return was achieved and is called the holding period return (HPR). HPR is focused on what the net return over the investment life. It measures the rate of return from the time the investor initiated the investment until the investment was realized, basically the rate of return for the holding period whether it is 1 month or 5 years. The ratio in its most basic form is

$$\text{HPR} = \frac{\text{CF}}{\text{I}}$$

where CF is the cash flow (inflow and outflow) during the investment period and I is the initial investment. For example, if an investor buys the stock for $100 and sells it for $120 and during the investment he or she received $2 in dividends, then the cash flow on the numerator is $120 of proceeds for selling the stock plus $2 of cash dividends received (cash inflow) minus the initial investment of $100 (cash outflow), and the net cash flow is $22 = ($120 + $2 - $100). The HPR will be then be calculated by dividing the net cash flow of $22 by the initial investment of $100 resulting in a 22% return:

$$\frac{(120-100+2)}{100}=\frac{22}{100}=0.22=22\%$$

For a quick analysis of expected return, the HPR ratio, which represents the relationship between cash flow to the initial investment, can be found in many applications on various asset classes. For example, let's assume the investor is interested in buying a bond that has an 8% per-year coupon rate, or annual interest income of $80 on a $1,000 bond, and the secondary market price of the bond is 95% of par, or $950. To calculate the expected return or the current yield (CY) in bond talk, the numerator of $80, representing the annual expected payment or cash flow, and the denominator of $950, representing the purchase price of the bond or initial investment, will calculate the expected annual return of 8.42%:

$$CY=\frac{CF}{I}=\frac{\text{Annual Coupon Payment}}{\text{Market Price of the Bond}}=\frac{80}{950}=0.0842=8.42\%$$

In many cases an expected return (discussed in depth later) that the investor sets as a target before making the investment determines the initial investment needed to achieve the expected cash flow. Using the bond example, the annual coupon payment of $80 is already set based on the bond agreement (indenture), but in this case the investor desires a 10.0% return based on new measured risk assessment of this bond; then to achieve 10.0% the numerator will be $80 divided by the expected return of 0.10 or 10.0%, calculating the initial investment needed $800.00 by solving for investment (I):

$$\text{since } CY=\frac{CF}{I}\text{, then } CF=(CY).(I)\text{ and } I=\frac{CF}{CY}=\frac{80}{.10}=\$800.00$$

When trying to calculate the annual rate instead of the total rate of return for the entire investment hold period, then this rate is referred to as the internal rate of return, or IRR, covered in the next section.

RATES OF RETURN: ANNUAL RATE OF RETURN (ROR) AND INTERNAL RATE OF RETURN (IRR)

The concept of time value of money is mostly used for calculating the annual rate of return as the basis of comparing such return to other years, or to the risk-free rate to establish the risk premium, explained in later chapters. The relationship between today's investment to future expectation for given years will result in an annual rate of return.

Starting with the basic time value of money formula of present value, the formula is

$$PV = \frac{FV}{(1+i)^t} \text{ in future year t}$$

where it calculates the initial investment needed to achieve at a set future payoff in year "t" at the annual rate of return (ROR) or "i." For example, what do you need to invest today to receive $100 in 5 years at 5% return per year? Based on the calculation, you need to invest $78.35:

$$PV = \frac{\$100}{(1+0.05)^5} = \frac{100}{1.2763} = \$78.35$$

If we know what we need to invest today at an annual rate "i", and we are trying to calculate what the investment will be "t" years, then the formula is

$$FV = PV(1+i)^t$$

For example, if you invest $100 today for 5 years and expect 5% return per year, your investment will be calculated to grow to $127.63:

$$Fv = \$100(1+0.05)^5 = \$100(1.2763) = \$127.63$$

To then reverse this formula to calculate the annual rate of return (ROR) the formula is

$$(1+i)^t = \frac{FV}{PV}, \text{ then } i = \left(\frac{FV}{PV}\right)^{\frac{1}{t}} - 1$$

For example, if you invest $100 today and expect in 5 years a payoff of $127.63, what is the rate of return per year? The calculation shows 5.0% annual return:

$$i = 5127.63100\, i = \left(\frac{127.63}{100.00}\right)^{\frac{1}{5}} - 1 = 1.05 - 1 = 0.05 = 5\%$$

For an investment where the investor receives annual cash flows during the investment period, the ROR or IRR calculation is a little more challenging than a one-time payment in the future. If the cash flows from the investment are the exact same amount for every year, then the annual cash flows over the investment represent the annual return, including the original investment amount, similar to a bond investment where the investor receives annual or semi-annual fixed payments and a one-time principal payment at maturity of the bonds or early repayment (sometimes referred to as redemption).

For example, if we invest $100 to an investment that pays $5 fixed per year for 5 years plus, receiving the initial investment of $100 in year 5, then the annual (ROR) will be 5%.

The Present Value or your initial investment when such investment will yield future cash flows can be calculated as follows.

For even Cash Flows per year the formula is:

$$PV = CF\left[\frac{1-\dfrac{1}{(1+i)^t}}{i}\right]$$

where the first formula represents expected future even cash flows for the investment and the second formula represents the even cash flows to grow at annual growth rate (g).

For example, an investment that pays $100 fixed per year for 5 years with an interest rate of 10.0% per year, then the Present Value of the investment annual will calculate as follows:

$$PV = 100\left[\frac{1-\dfrac{1}{(1+0.10)^5}}{0.10}\right] = 378.88$$

For uneven Cash Flows per year the formula is:

$$PV = \frac{CF_1}{(1+i)^1} + \frac{CF_2}{(1+i)^2} + \frac{CF_3}{(1+i)^3} + \ldots \frac{CF_n}{(1+i)^t} \text{ or } PV = \sum \frac{CF}{(1+r)^t}$$

where CF is the expected future uneven cash flows for the investment.

For example, an investment that expect to pay $100 the first year, 105 the second year, 95 the third year with an expected return 0.0% per year, then the Present Value of the investment annual will calculate as follows:

$$PV = \frac{CF_1}{(1+i)^1} + \frac{CF_2}{(1+i)^2} + \frac{CF_3}{(1+i)^3}$$

$$PV = \frac{100}{(1+0.10)^1} + \frac{105}{(1+0.10)^2} + \frac{95}{(1+0.10)^3} = 90.91 + 86.78 + 71.43 = 249.12$$

The more challenging calculation is if the payment is different every year, so the annual rate of return must be weighted based on size and the year paid sometime referred to as dollar weighted return. This type of rate return method is the internal rate of return. It's challenging because each year the investment would have different payoffs and sometimes negative numbers. The best approach to calculate the IRR is using spreadsheet analysis. The formula that will be used throughout this book is = $IRR(CF_0, CF_1, CF_2, CF_3 \ldots CF_t)$.

FIGURE 1.1 INTERNAL RATE OF RETURN (IRR)

Dollar Weighted Return (Even Annual Payments)

	0	1	2	3	4
Net CF ($)	-100	5	5	5	105

EXCEL

	A	B	C	D	E	F
10	IRR	0	1	2	3	4
11	5.00%	-100	5	5	5	105

=IRR(B11:F11)

Dollar Weighted Return (Uneven Annual Payments)

	0	1	2	3	4
Net CF ($)	-100	-9	-5	26	110

1 = + (-0.1 / (1+IRR) + (-0.5 / (1+ IRR) ^2 + (0.8 / (1+ IRR)^3) + (1.0 / (1+IRR)^4

EXCEL

	A	B	C	D	E	F
10	IRR	0	1	2	3	4
11	4.96%	-100	-9	-5	26	110

=IRR(B11:F11)

MEASURING RETURN AND QUANTIFYING RISK

The expected return on a risky asset depends on the asset's systematic risk because any idiosyncratic risk can be diversified away—a phenomenon that will be measured later. The risk of a standalone asset class, such stocks or bonds, could be driven by systematic risk, where the overall market goes up and down, and/or by idiosyncratic risk referred to as "firm specific" risk, or the standalone risk. The standalone risk is measured by using the standard deviation (σ) or volatility of the expected return. They are other risks, such as relevant risk, that also need to be considered when assessing any investment. The relevant risk is the risk that remains once the stock is in a diversified portfolio—measured later in this chapter.

RATE OF RETURN: AVERAGE ANNUAL RATE OF RETURN

The average annual rate of return can be calculated by looking at 5 to 10 years of historical returns and averaging them to represent the annual return. It gives the investor an indication what to expect on an average. This method is used for comparing to other investments that were calculated the same way and by taking this number to the next level of assessment of volatility in the return as compared to the average on a given year.

RATE OF RISK: STANDARD DEVIATION OF PERIODIC RETURNS

The expected return on a risky asset such stocks and bonds depend on systematic risk, such as the overall market movements, and unsystematic risk or portfolio-specific risk. We will examine later in detail how the unsystematic or idiosyncratic risk can be minimized or eliminated through diversification. First, it's important to examine the relationship between the rate of return and risk such as volatility, or the standard deviation of these returns. There are two methods of calculating the risk-return: historical analysis and scenario analysis.

Historical Analysis Method

The most used method of assessing the risk and return of an investment or a portfolio of investments is to look at the historical annual performance and use conventional averages and standard deviation to determine the annual risk and return. Though not perfect, the historical average shows how the investment performs through the years, which includes all the high points, low points, and positive and negative points. **The deviation from the average, called standard deviation, represents how risky the return could be. When two portfolios have the same average return, the one that is less risky is the one with the lower standard deviation.** Figure 1.2 shows that both 10-year average returns for portfolios A and B is 9.92%, but portfolio B is riskier with standard deviation of 11.21% versus 10.92% of portfolio A. In this and follow-on chapters, we will examine this relationship closer and how we can compare it to the market or other asset classes.

Scenario Analysis Method

The previous section showed the performance of the portfolio by calculating the historical average returns, variance, and standard deviations. This section will calculate the expected return, variance, and standard deviation based on the probability of various economic scenarios. This method can be used to recalculate the expected return, variance, and standard deviation when two or more asset classes are combined. Depending

FIGURE 1.2 HISTORICAL RETIURN ANALYSIS (PORTFOLIO A AND PORTFOLIO B)

PORTOLIO A

Year	ROR	Deviation to return (X-Avg(X))	SQR Deviation
1	12.9%	3.0%	0.089%
2	31.3%	21.4%	4.571%
3	5.0%	-4.9%	0.242%
4	-2.0%	-11.9%	1.421%
5	2.0%	-7.9%	0.627%
6	22.0%	12.1%	1.459%
7	12.0%	2.1%	0.043%
8	12.0%	2.1%	0.043%
9	-5.0%	-14.9%	2.226%
10	9.0%	-0.9%	0.008%
Total	99.2%		10.730%

Observations=	10	n
Average =	**9.920%**	Total ROR / n
Variance =	1.192%	Sqr Dev/ (n - 1)
Standard Dev.=	**10.92%**	

PORTOLIO B

Year	ROR	Deviation to return (X-Avg(X))	SQR Deviation
1	19.9%	10.0%	0.996%
2	15.0%	5.1%	0.258%
3	8.0%	-1.9%	0.037%
4	-11.0%	-20.9%	4.376%
5	7.0%	-2.9%	0.085%
6	14.0%	4.1%	0.166%
7	24.0%	14.1%	1.982%
8	20.0%	10.1%	1.016%
9	-5.4%	-15.3%	2.347%
10	7.7%	-2.2%	0.049%
Total	99.2%		11.314%

Observations=	10	n
Average =	**9.920%**	Total ROR / n
Variance =	1.257%	Sqr Dev/ (n - 1)
Standard Dev.=	**11.21%**	

on the correlation between the performance of different asset classes such as stocks and bonds, the analysis should demonstrate that the portfolio can achieve both efficiency and optimization. **The efficiency, called efficient frontier, which represents the highest possible return with the lowest possible risk, could be achieved by trading partially by selling stocks and buying bonds and vice versa.** After the efficiency is achieved, then the portfolio manager will look to optimize the portfolio. The optimization can be achieved by moving from the efficiency position to a position where the analyst is seeking additional return with minimum additional risk to the point that the risk will catch up to the return. This optimization, measured by a ratio called Sharpe ratio, will be described in this chapter and more detailed in the following chapters in this unit.

Let's assume that we examined a given stock portfolio and determined the different holding period returns achieved during different economic cycles including recession, boom, and normal years. Figure 1.3 shows that during the recession the stock portfolio showed 12% negative return, during normal years it had positive 14%, and during boom years it achieved positive 28%. Using scenario analysis, the expected average return will be calculated based on the probability expectation. In other words, let's assume we asked 100 analysts what they believe the next year will bring and from our survey 25 of them (25%) said that they expect a recession, 45 of them (45%) expect that the economy will stay at a normal stage, and the remaining 30 analysts (30%) expect that we will have a boom year. We categorize their response as the probability to determine the expected weighted average return. Figure 1.3 shows that the expected return is calculated to be 11.70%. The variance and standard deviation using these probabilities are calculated at 222.51% or 2.225x and 14.92%, respectively.

Let's assume that we also looked at a different portfolio that include only bonds. Figure 1.4 shows that the bond portfolio during the same economic periods as the historical return during the recession was 14.0%, during normal years, 5%, and during boom

FIGURE 1.3 SCENARIO PORTFOLIO ANALYSIS (STOKS)

		Stocks (s)				
Scenario (s)	Probability (p)	ROR % (rs)	p * rs %	Deviation for Exp. Ret. (Dev.)	Square Deviation (SD) Dev^2	p * SD
Recession (Sr)	**25.0%**	**-12.00**	-3.00	-23.70	561.69	140.42
Normal (Sn)	**45.0%**	**14.00**	6.30	2.30	5.29	2.38
Boom (Sb)	**30.0%**	**28.00**	8.40	16.30	265.69	79.71
	100.0%		**11.70** %		**Variance=**	**222.51**
					SD =	**14.92** %

FIGURE 1.4 SCENARIO PORTFOLIO ANALYSIS (BONDS)

		Bonds (b)				
Economic Scenario (s)	Probability (p)	ROR % (r_b)	p * r_b %	Deviation for Exp. Ret. (Dev.)	Square Deviation (SD) Dev^2	p * SD
Recession	25.0%	14.00	3.50	9.75	95.06	23.77
Normal	45.0%	5.00	2.25	0.75	0.56	0.25
Boom	30.0%	-5.00	-1.50	-9.25	85.56	25.67
	100.0%		4.25 %		Variance=	49.69
					SD =	7.05 %

years, −5.0%. Just eyeballing the differences with the stocks portfolio during this year we can easily see that the returns for the recession and boom years are moving in opposite direction; where the stocks are showing positive return, the bonds show negative. We will later discuss that important relationship called correlation. Figure 1.4 shows that the expected average return using the same probability numbers, as the equity is 4.25%. The variance and standard deviation are calculated at 49.69% or 0.4969x and 7.05%, respectively.

RETURN, RETURN EXPECTATION, RISK AND ALLOCATION

Once the return and risk are determined by asset class, the investor can achieve efficiencies and optimization (discussed in the following chapters) by allocating his or her investment across asset classes. Using the example of the stock portfolio that had return and standard deviation of 11.7% and 14.92%, respectively, and the bond portfolio that had return and standard deviation of 4.25% and 7.05%, respectively, when combined at different holding levels, this can achieve efficiency. For argument sake, let's assume that we decided to invest 60% of our money into the stock portfolio shown in figure 1.3 and 40% of our money in the bond portfolio shown in figure 1.4. Then the combined portfolio shown in figure 1.5 consisting of 60% stock and 40% bonds shows an expected combined return, variance, and standard deviation of 8.72%, 38.99% or .39x, and 6.24%, respectively. As expected, as we moved from the stock portfolio of 100% to a portfolio of 60% stock and 40% bonds, the return is calculated at 8.72% measured as

$$(Ws \cdot Rs) + (Wb \cdot Rb) = (.60)\,(11.70\%) + (.40)\,(4.25\%) = 7.02\% + 1.7\% = 8.72\%$$

The surprising part of this is that the standard deviation of the combined portfolio that is made of 60% stocks and 40% bonds is calculated at 6.24%, which is lower that the stand-alone stock or bond portfolio's standard deviation of 14.92% and 8.23%, respectively, shown in figure 1.5. In other words, in moving from an all-bond portfolio to partial stock and bonds portfolio we achieved a greater efficiency. This phenomenon is achieved

FIGURE 1.5 PORTFOLIO ANALYSIS (ASSET ALLOCATION)

Asset Allocation	Weights (W%)
Stocks (Ws) =	60%
Bonds (Wb) =	40%

(Ws * rs) + (Wb * rb)

Scenario (s)	Probability (p)	ROR % (rs)	p * rs %	Deviation for Exp. Ret. (Dev.)	Square Deviation (SD) Dev^2	p * SD
Recession (Sr)	25.0%	-1.6	-0.40	-10.32	106.50	26.63
Normal (Sn)	45.0%	10.4	4.68	1.68	2.82	1.27
Boom (Sb)	30.0%	14.8	4.44	6.08	36.97	11.09
	100.0%		8.72 %		Variance=	38.99
					SD =	6.24 %

due to correlation, which is basically comparing the direction of the two standard deviations. The negative correlation between the two portfolios (shown in figure 1.6) causes the combined portfolio to have a lower standard deviation as the positive movement of the stock is offset by the negative movement of the bond, resulting in lower combined variance and standard deviation.

Of course, we arbitrarily picked the 60% stock and 40% bonds that resulted in a more efficient combined portfolio. If we continue to move the percentages around of bonds and stocks, we can eventually find the highest point of efficiency, known as the efficient frontier. This point is examined in chapter 2 using the same example at different correlation points. Figure 1.6 shows the actual correlation between the stock and bond portfolios, calculated at -0.97, given the standard deviations of each of the portfolios. To calculate the covariance between two asset classes shown at -102.23 in figure 1.6 is to first use the deviation points from the mean information for each scenario for each asset class and

FIGURE 1.6 COVARIANCE & CORRELATION

Scenario (S)	Probability (p)	Stocks (Deviation from the mean)	Bonds (Deviation from the mean)	Ds * Db	Covariance [p * (Ds*Db)
Recession (Sr)	25.0%	-23.70	9.75	-231.08	-57.77
Normal (Sn)	45.0%	2.30	0.75	1.73	0.78
Boom (Sb)	30.0%	16.30	-9.25	-150.78	-45.23
	100.0%			Covariance=	-102.23
				Correlation Coefficient =	-0.97

multiply to each other and by the probability. The covariance is the sum of these amounts illustrated below:

$$Cov = \sum[((Ds1 \,.\, Db1)p1) + ((Ds2 \,.\, Db2)p2) + ((Ds3 \,.\, Db3)p3)]$$

where Ds1, Ds2 and Ds3 are the deviation points from the mean for the stock during the recession, normal and boom years, respectively; where the Db1, Db2 and Db3 are the deviation points from the mean for the bonds during the recession, normal and boom years; where the p1, p2 and p3 are the probabilities set for expecting a recession, normal and boom outcome, respectively. Please note that the deviation amounts are taken from figures 1.3 and 1.4 representing the information of the stock portfolio and bond portfolio, respectively.

The calculation of correlation shown in figure 1.6 is illustrated below:

$$\text{Cor} = \frac{\text{Cov}}{\sigma \text{s} \cdot \sigma \text{b}}$$

where Cov is the covariance calculated previously, σs is the standard deviation of the stock portfolio (14.92%) and σb is the standard deviation of the bond portfolio (7.05%).

CASE STUDY

SETTING UP A PORTFOLIO OF STOCKS AND BONDS

Assume an asset management firm raises a new $200-million fund called Zeus Fund I, which will be set up to buy stock and corporate bonds. In this and in the next four chapters we will be using the Zeus Fund I as a case study, applying all the tools that the portfolio analyst needs. We will also assume that the fund is leveraged at 50%; in other words, the $200-million fund is financed by $100 million of a loan and $100 million of newly raised equity. Figure 1.7 shows the transaction sources and uses of the fund. The loan is structured as 5 years, $100 million, with a 5% fixed interest rate. At closing (June 1), the $200 million fund is used for purchasing $82.6 million in stocks and $96.65 million in bonds. The manager has kept about $20 million or 10% in cash for liquidity, earning 1.5% of annual interest income. The balance is used to pay accrued interest on the bonds which represents the additional upfront cost the investor needs to pay for buying bonds in between coupon payments—discussed in later chapters.

Figure 1.8 shows a 7-month cash flow of Zeus Fund I portfolio that includes all the trades, dividends received, coupon payments received, payment to service the loan, and accrued interest paid and received due to trades in between coupon dates and interest income from the cash that is deposited at the bank. Latter figures show the details of such activity.

From the cash flow trading activity of this portfolio shown on figure 1.8, the analyst can calculate the monthly IRR, shown at 2.86%. The other return that was discussed earlier in the chapter is the holding period return (HPR). For this portfolio, the HPR is a levered HPR because 50% of capital used to finance the portfolio is by debt. The levered 7-month HPR, which is HPR = $\frac{CF}{I}$, is calculated as follows (amounts in $000 s):

$$\frac{(-100{,}000+3{,}242-1{,}019-831-145+513+3{,}277+116{,}347)}{100{,}000}=0.214=21.4\%$$

FIGURE 1.7 ZEUS FUND I (TOTAL SOURCES & USES)

PORTFOLIO OF STOCKS AND BONDS

TOTAL SOURCES & USES (June 1, 20xx)			
SOURCES ($ 000's)	**Amount**	**% Cap**	**Interest Rate**
Portfolio Loan	100,000	50.0%	5.00%
Investor's Cash	100,000	50.0%	
Total Sources	**200,000**	**100.0%**	

USES ($ 000's)	**Amount**	**% Cap**	**Interest Rate**
Stock Purchase	$ 82,600	409.5%	
Bond Purchase	95,650	474.1%	
Accrued Interest	1,577	7.8%	
Cash	$ 20,173	100.0%	1.50%
Total Uses	**$ 200,000**	**991.4%**	

FIGURE 1.8 ZEUS FUND I (PORTFOLIO STOCK & BONDS - CASH FLOW)

PORTFOLIO OF STOCKS AND BONDS

CASH FLOWS		ENTRY							EXIT
		0	1	2	3	4	5	6	7
	MONTHLY IRR	June 1 20x1	July 1 20x1	Aug 1 20x1	Sep 1 20x1	Oct 1 20x1	Nov 1 20x1	Dec 1 20x1	Jan 2 20x2
Beginning Cash		100,000	20,173	23,415	22,396	21,564	21,420	21,932	25,210
Buy/Sell Stock		$ (82,600)	$ -	$ 1,550	$ 2,300	$ -	$ -	$ -	$ 92,600
Buy/Sell Bonds		$ (95,650)	$ 2,875	$ (2,880)	$ (4,075)	$ -	$ 865	$ 3,550	$ 97,000
Stock Dividends			$ 93	$ 90	$ 150	$ 245	$ 63	$ -	$ -
Bond Coupon Received		$ -	$ 875	$ 594	$ 1,344	$ -	$ -	$ -	$ -
Acrued Interest (paid)/Received		$ (1,577)	$ (209)	$ 14	$ (161)	$ -	$ (25)	$ 117	$ 1,927
Loan Principal Increase/Decrease		$ 100,000							$(100,000)
Loan Interest Payment			$ (417)	$ (417)	$ (417)	$ (417)	$ (417)	$ (417)	$ (417)
Cash Balance Interest Income			$ 25	$ 29	$ 28	$ 27	$ 27	$ 27	$ 27
Cash		$ (20,173)							$ 25,210
Total Cash Flows (Levered)	2.86%	$ (100,000)	$ 3,242	$ (1,019)	$ (831)	$ (145)	$ 513	$ 3,277	$ 116,347
Use of cash		$ 20,173	$ -	$ -	$ -	$ -	$ -	$ -	$ (25,210)
Total Cash Flows		20,173	23,415	22,396	21,564	21,420	21,932	25,210	116,347
% of Cash to total Value		10.2%	11.8%	11.0%	10.4%	10.2%	10.4%	11.7%	

HPR (Levered) = 21.4%

	0	1	2	3	4	5	6	7
Unlevered Return Calculation:	June 1 20x1	July 1 20x1	Aug 1 20x1	Sep 1 20x1	Oct 1 20x1	Nov 1 20x1	Dec 1 20x1	Jan 2 20x2
Total Cash Flows (Levered)	$ (100,000)	$ 3,242	$ (1,019)	$ (831)	$ (145)	$ 513	$ 3,277	$ 116,347
Addback Loan Principal	(100,000)	-	-	-	-	-	-	100,000
Addback Loan Interest	-	417	417	417	417	417	417	417
Unlevered Cash Flow	$ (200,000)	$ 3,658	$ (603)	$ (415)	$ 272	$ 929	$ 3,694	$ 216,764

HPR (UnLevered) = 12.2%

The unlevered 7-month HPR is calculated as follows (amounts in $000s):

$$\frac{(-200{,}000+3{,}658-603-415+272+929+3{,}694+216{,}764)}{100{,}000}=0.122=12.2\%$$

Figures 1.9 shows the breakout of the initial purchases that includes 10 stock positions for $82.6 million and four bond positions for $96.65 million.

FIGURE 1.9 ZEUS FUND I (STOCK & BONDS NAMES)

STOCK PORTFOLIO

Stock Prices

Symbol	Company Name	Industry	June 1 20x1
ABC	ABC Chem Inc	Chemicals	23.00
BCD	BCD Precision Inc	Industrial	12.00
CDE	CDE Inc	Publishing	18.00
DEF	DEF Inc	Hospitality	40.00
EFG	Effective Inc	TV/Cable	52.00
FGH	FGH Inc	Techonlogy	31.00
GHI	General HI	Service	15.00
HIK	Hicks Kental Inc	Retail	8.00
IKL	IKL Inc	Pharmaceutical	15.00
KLM	KLM Health	Healthcare	25.00

Number of Shares own (000's)

Symbol	Company Name	Industry	June 1 20x1
ABC	ABC Chem Inc	Chemicals	400
BCD	BCD Precision Inc	Industrial	350
CDE	CDE Inc	Publishing	300
DEF	DEF Inc	Hospitality	300
EFG	Effective Inc	TV/Cable	200
FGH	FGH Inc	Techonlogy	400
GHI	General HI	Service	600
HIK	Hicks Kental Inc	Retail	1000
IKL	IKL Inc	Pharmaceutical	300
KLM	KLM Health	Healthcare	300

Total Stock Value ($000's)

Symbol	Company Name	Industry	June 1 20x1
ABC	ABC Chem Inc	Chemicals	9,200
BCD	BCD Precision Inc	Industrial	4,200
CDE	CDE Inc	Publishing	5,400
DEF	DEF Inc	Hospitality	12,000
EFG	Effective Inc	TV/Cable	10,400
FGH	FGH Inc	Techonlogy	12,400
GHI	General HI	Service	9,000
HIK	Hicks Kental Inc	Retail	8,000
IKL	IKL Inc	Pharmaceutical	4,500
KLM	KLM Health	Healthcare	7,500
Total Value			82,600

BOND PORTFOLIO

Bond Prices

Symbol	Company Name	Industry	June 1 20x1
AAA	Alpha Inc.	Healthcare	890.00
BBB	Beta Inc.	Retail	910.00
CCC	CC Corporation	Industrial	790.00
DDD	Delta D Inc.	Hospitality	1010.00

Bonds Own (000's)

Symbol	Company Name	Industry	June 1 20x1
AAA	Alpha Inc.	Healthcare	15
BBB	Beta Inc.	Retail	20
CCC	CC Corporation	Industrial	30
DDD	Delta D Inc.	Hospitality	40

Total Bond Value ($000's)

Symbol	Company Name	Industry	June 1 20x1
AAA	Alpha Inc.	Healthcare	13,350
BBB	Beta Inc.	Retail	18,200
CCC	CC Corporation	Industrial	23,700
DDD	Delta D Inc.	Hospitality	40,400
Total Value			95,650

Figure 1.10 shows the information of the bonds, including two more that the manager is looking to buy in the future. The bond information includes the maturity date, the external corporate ratings, the coupon dates, and payments.

FIGURE 1.10 ZEUS FUND I (BONDS INFO)

BOND PORTFOLIO

BOND INFORMATION

Symbol	Company	Industry	Face Value	Maturity Date	S&P Rating	Moody's Rating	Coupon Rate	First Coupon Payment	Second Coupon Payment	Annual Coupon Payment
AAA	Alpha Inc.	Healthcare	1000	15-Aug-23	BB-	Ba2	5.2500%	15-Feb-17	15-Aug-17	52.50
BBB	Beta Inc.	Retail	1000	1-Jul-20	BB+	Ba1	4.5000%	1-Jan-17	1-Jul-17	45.00
CCC	CC Corpor	Industrial	1000	15-Sep-25	B	B2	7.0000%	15-Mar-17	15-Sep-17	70.00
DDD	Delta D Inc	Hospitality	1000	15-Jul-19	BBB	Baa2	3.5000%	15-Jan-17	15-Jul-17	35.00
EEE	Epsilon Inc	Technology	1000	1-Oct-26	BB	Ba3	4.7500%	1-Apr-17	1-Oct-17	47.50
FFF	Fusbol For	Retail	1000	15-Aug-26	CCC+	Caa1	8.0000%	15-Feb-17	15-Aug-17	80.00

Figures 1.11 and 1.12 show the value of the stock portfolio that includes all the trades during the hold period, as well as all the dividends received during this period. For argument's sake, let's assume the manager sets up only a 7-month trading portfolio, and in order to realize return liquidates the entire portfolio 7 months after the initial investment (Jan 2).

FIGURE 1.11A ZEUS FUND I (STOCK PRICES & INFO)

STOCK PORTFOLIO

Stock Prices

			0	1	2	3	4	5	6	7
Symbol	**Company Name**	**Industry**	**June 1 20x1**	**July 1 20x1**	**Aug 1 20x1**	**Sep 1 20x1**	**Oct 1 20x1**	**Nov 1 20x1**	**Dec 1 20x1**	**Jan 2 20x2**
ABC	ABC Chem Inc	Chemicals	23.00	24.00	22.50	25.00	26.00	27.00	28.00	31.00
BCD	BCD Precision Inc	Industrial	12.00	10.00	12.00	12.00	15.00	18.00	19.50	22.00
CDE	CDE Inc	Publishing	18.00	19.00	18.00	19.00	21.00	20.00	19.00	21.00
DEF	DEF Inc	Hospitality	40.00	42.00	43.00	45.00	45.00	45.00	46.00	48.00
EFG	Effective Inc	TV/Cable	52.00	60.00	60.00	60.00	62.00	62.00	61.00	63.00
FGH	FGH Inc	Techonlogy	31.00	20.00	25.00	26.00	20.00	22.00	24.00	25.00
GHI	General HI	Service	15.00	16.00	17.00	18.00	19.00	19.00	18.00	20.00
HIK	Hicks Kental Inc	Retail	8.00	9.50	10.50	11.00	11.50	12.00	14.00	14.50
IKL	IKL Inc	Pharmaceutical	15.00	13.00	12.00	14.00	15.00	18.00	22.00	20.00
KLM	KLM Health	Healthcare	25.00	26.00	26.00	26.00	26.00	26.00	27.00	20.00
LMN	LMN Hotel & Resorts	Hospitality	26.00	30.00	32.00	33.00	35.00	32.00	34.00	35.00
MNO	MNO Cable Inc	TV/Cable	19.00	20.00	19.00	18.00	18.00	16.00	20.00	18.00
NOP	Norton Optimum	Techonlogy	53.00	52.00	55.00	56.00	58.00	59.00	59.00	61.00
OPQ	Odyssea PQ Inc	Retail	11.00	8.50	11.00	11.00	11.00	11.00	11.50	12.00
PQR	PQR Chemicals	Chemicals	18.00	17.00	19.00	19.00	20.00	22.00	26.00	24.00

FIGURE 1.11B ZEUS FUND I (STOCK PRICES & INFO)

Number of Shares own (000's)

Symbol	Company Name	Industry	0 June 1 20x1	1 July 1 20x1	2 Aug 1 20x1	3 Sep 1 20x1	4 Oct 1 20x1	5 Nov 1 20x1	6 Dec 1 20x1	7 Jan 2 20x2
ABC	ABC Chem Inc	Chemicals	400	400	100	100	100	100	100	0
BCD	BCD Precision Inc	Industrial	350	350	50	50	50	50	50	0
CDE	CDE Inc	Publishing	300	300	200	200	200	200	200	0
DEF	DEF Inc	Hospitality	300	300	300	200	200	200	200	0
EFG	Effective Inc	TV/Cable	200	200	200	200	200	200	200	0
FGH	FGH Inc	Techonlogy	400	400	400	400	100	100	100	0
GHI	General HI	Service	600	600	600	600	600	600	600	0
HIK	Hicks Kental Inc	Retail	1000	1000	1000	1000	1000	1000	1000	0
IKL	IKL Inc	Pharmaceutical	300	300	300	300	300	300	300	0
KLM	KLM Health	Healthcare	300	300	300	300	300	300	300	0
LMN	LMN Hotel & Resorts	Hospitality		0	100	100	100	100	100	0
MNO	MNO Cable Inc	TV/Cable		0	100	100	100	100	100	0
NOP	Norton Optimum	Techonlogy		0	100	100	100	100	100	0
OPQ	Odyssea PQ Inc	Retail		0	0	200	200	200	200	0
PQR	PQR Chemicals	Chemicals		0	0	0	300	300	300	0

Buy/Sell Stock (000's)

Symbol	Company Name	Industry	0 June 1 20x1	1 July 1 20x1	2 Aug 1 20x1	3 Sep 1 20x1	4 Oct 1 20x1	5 Nov 1 20x1	6 Dec 1 20x1	7 Jan 2 20x2
ABC	ABC Chem Inc	Chemicals			-300					-100
BCD	BCD Precision Inc	Industrial			-300					-50
CDE	CDE Inc	Publishing			-100					-200
DEF	DEF Inc	Hospitality				-100				-200
EFG	Effective Inc	TV/Cable								-200
FGH	FGH Inc	Techonlogy					-300			-100
GHI	General HI	Service								-600
HIK	Hicks Kental Inc	Retail								-1000
IKL	IKL Inc	Pharmaceutical								-300
KLM	KLM Health	Healthcare								-300
LMN	LMN Hotel & Resorts	Hospitality			100					-100
MNO	MNO Cable Inc	TV/Cable			100					-100
NOP	Norton Optimum	Techonlogy			100					-100
OPQ	Odyssea PQ Inc	Retail				200				-200
PQR	PQR Chemicals	Chemicals					300			-300

Symbol	Company Name	Industry	0 June 1 20x1	1 July 1 20x1	2 Aug 1 20x1	3 Sep 1 20x1	4 Oct 1 20x1	5 Nov 1 20x1	6 Dec 1 20x1	7 Jan 2 20x2
ABC	ABC Chem Inc	Chemicals	0	0	6,750	0	0	0	0	3,100
BCD	BCD Precision Inc	Industrial	0	0	3,600	0	0	0	0	1,100
CDE	CDE Inc	Publishing	0	0	1,800	0	0	0	0	4,200
DEF	DEF Inc	Hospitality	0	0	0	4,500	0	0	0	9,600
EFG	Effective Inc	TV/Cable	0	0	0	0	0	0	0	12,600
FGH	FGH Inc	Techonlogy	0	0	0	0	6,000	0	0	2,500
GHI	General HI	Service	0	0	0	0	0	0	0	12,000
HIK	Hicks Kental Inc	Retail	0	0	0	0	0	0	0	14,500
IKL	IKL Inc	Pharmaceutical	0	0	0	0	0	0	0	6,000
KLM	KLM Health	Healthcare	0	0	0	0	0	0	0	6,000
LMN	LMN Hotel & Resorts	Hospitality	0	0	-3,200	0	0	0	0	3,500
MNO	MNO Cable Inc	TV/Cable	0	0	-1,900	0	0	0	0	1,800
NOP	Norton Optimum	Techonlogy	0	0	-5,500	0	0	0	0	6,100
OPQ	Odyssea PQ Inc	Retail	0	0	0	-2,200	0	0	0	2,400
PQR	PQR Chemicals	Chemicals	0	0	0	0	-6,000	0	0	7,200
Total Sale/Purchases Cash Flow			**0**	**0**	**1,550**	**2,300**	**0**	**0**	**0**	**92,600**

FIGURE 1.11C ZEUS FUND I (STOCK PRICES & INFO)

Total Value ($000's)

Symbol	Company Name	Industry	0 June 1 20x1	1 July 1 20x1	2 Aug 1 20x1	3 Sep 1 20x1	4 Oct 1 20x1	5 Nov 1 20x1	6 Dec 1 20x1	7 Jan 2 20x2
ABC	ABC Chem Inc	Chemicals	9,200	9,600	2,250	2,500	2,600	2,700	2,800	0
BCD	BCD Precision Inc	Industrial	4,200	3,500	600	600	750	900	975	0
CDE	CDE Inc	Publishing	5,400	5,700	3,600	3,800	4,200	4,000	3,800	0
DEF	DEF Inc	Hospitality	12,000	12,600	12,900	9,000	9,000	9,000	9,200	0
EFG	Effective Inc	TV/Cable	10,400	12,000	12,000	12,000	12,400	12,400	12,200	0
FGH	FGH Inc	Techonlogy	12,400	8,000	10,000	10,400	2,000	2,200	2,400	0
GHI	General HI	Service	9,000	9,600	10,200	10,800	11,400	11,400	10,800	0
HIK	Hicks Kental Inc	Retail	8,000	9,500	10,500	11,000	11,500	12,000	14,000	0
IKL	IKL Inc	Pharmaceutical	4,500	3,900	3,600	4,200	4,500	5,400	6,600	0
KLM	KLM Health	Healthcare	7,500	7,800	7,800	7,800	7,800	7,800	8,100	0
LMN	LMN Hotel & Resorts	Hospitality	0	0	3,200	3,300	3,500	3,200	3,400	0
MNO	MNO Cable Inc	TV/Cable	0	0	1,900	1,800	1,800	1,600	2,000	0
NOP	Norton Optimum	Techonlogy	0	0	5,500	5,600	5,800	5,900	5,900	0
OPQ	Odyssea PQ Inc	Retail	0	0	0	2,200	2,200	2,200	2,300	0
PQR	PQR Chemicals	Chemicals	0	0	0	0	6,000	6,600	7,800	0
Total Value			**82,600**	**82,200**	**84,050**	**85,000**	**85,450**	**87,300**	**92,275**	**0**

FIGURE 1.12 ZEUS FUND I (DIVIDENDS)

STOCK PORTFOLIO

Dividends

Symbol	Company Name	Industry	0 June 1 20x1	1 July 1 20x1	2 Aug 1 20x1	3 Sep 1 20x1	4 Oct 1 20x1	5 Nov 1 20x1	6 Dec 1 20x1	7 Jan 2 20x2
ABC	ABC Chem Inc	Chemicals		$ 0.10				$ 0.10		
BCD	BCD Precision Inc	Industrial		$ 0.15				$ 0.15		
CDE	CDE Inc	Publishing								
DEF	DEF Inc	Hospitality			$ 0.30					
EFG	Effective Inc	TV/Cable				$ 0.30				
FGH	FGH Inc	Techonlogy								
GHI	General HI	Service				$ 0.15				
HIK	Hicks Kental Inc	Retail					$ 0.20			
IKL	IKL Inc	Pharmaceutical					$ 0.15			
KLM	KLM Health	Healthcare						$ 0.15		
LMN	LMN Hotel & Resorts	Hospitality								
MNO	MNO Cable Inc	TV/Cable								
NOP	Norton Optimum	Techonlogy								
OPQ	Odyssea PQ Inc	Retail								
PQR	PQR Chemicals	Chemicals								

Dividends ($ 000's)

Symbol	Company Name	Industry	0 June 1 20x1	1 July 1 20x1	2 Aug 1 20x1	3 Sep 1 20x1	4 Oct 1 20x1	5 Nov 1 20x1	6 Dec 1 20x1	7 Jan 2 20x2
ABC	ABC Chem Inc	Chemicals		40	0	0	0	10	0	0
BCD	BCD Precision Inc	Industrial		53	0	0	0	8	0	0
CDE	CDE Inc	Publishing		0	0	0	0	0	0	0
DEF	DEF Inc	Hospitality		0	90	0	0	0	0	0
EFG	Effective Inc	TV/Cable		0	0	60	0	0	0	0
FGH	FGH Inc	Techonlogy		0	0	0	0	0	0	0
GHI	General HI	Service		0	0	90	0	0	0	0
HIK	Hicks Kental Inc	Retail		0	0	0	200	0	0	0
IKL	IKL Inc	Pharmaceutical		0	0	0	45	0	0	0
KLM	KLM Health	Healthcare		0	0	0	0	45	0	0
LMN	LMN Hotel & Resorts	Hospitality		0	0	0	0	0	0	0
MNO	MNO Cable Inc	TV/Cable		0	0	0	0	0	0	0
NOP	Norton Optimum	Techonlogy		0	0	0	0	0	0	0
OPQ	Odyssea PQ Inc	Retail		0	0	0	0	0	0	0
PQR	PQR Chemicals	Chemicals		0	0	0	0	0	0	0
		Total Dividends		93	90	150	245	63	0	0

Figures 1.13 and 1.14 show the value of the bond portfolio that includes all the trades during the hold period, including paid accrued interest as well as all the coupon payment received during this period. For argument sake, let's assume the manager sets up only a 7-month trading portfolio and in order to realize return liquidates the entire portfolio 7 months after the initial investment (Jan 2).

FIGURE 1.13 ZEUS FUND I (BONDS INFO)

BOND PORTFOLIO

Bond Prices

			0	1	2	3	4	5	6	7
Symbol	**Company Name**	**Industry**	**June 1 20x1**	**July 1 20x1**	**Aug 1 20x1**	**Sep 1 20x1**	**Oct 1 20x1**	**Nov 1 20x1**	**Dec 1 20x1**	**Jan 2 20x2**
AAA	Alpha Inc.	Healthcare	890	893	895	905	910	912	915	910
BBB	Beta Inc.	Retail	910	925	915	925	915	922	935	930
CCC	CC Corporation	Industrial	790	800	810	815	820	822	815	800
DDD	Delta D Inc.	Hospitality	1010	1015	1020	1022	1026	1025	1020	1027
EEE	Epsilon Inc	Technology	950	965	975	980	982	995	1000	1010
FFF	Fusbol For Friends	Retail	640	680	687	695	710	720	710	700
			5190	5278	5302	5342	5363	5396	5395	5377

Bonds Own

			0	1	2	3	4	5	6	7
Symbol	**Company Name**	**Industry**	**June 1 20x1**	**July 1 20x1**	**Aug 1 20x1**	**Sep 1 20x1**	**Oct 1 20x1**	**Nov 1 20x1**	**Dec 1 20x1**	**Jan 2 20x2**
AAA	Alpha Inc.	Healthcare	15	15	15	15	15	15	15	0
BBB	Beta Inc.	Retail	20	8	0	0	0	0	0	0
CCC	CC Corporation	Industrial	30	30	30	35	35	40	40	0
DDD	Delta D Inc.	Hospitality	40	40	50	50	50	50	50	0
EEE	Epsilon Inc	Technology	0	5	5	5	5	0	0	0
FFF	Fusbol For Friends	Retail	0	5	5	5	5	5	0	0

Buy/Sell

Symbol	**Company Name**	**Industry**	**June 1 20x1**	**July 1 20x1**	**Aug 1 20x1**	**Sep 1 20x1**	**Oct 1 20x1**	**Nov 1 20x1**	**Dec 1 20x1**	**Jan 2 20x2**
AAA	Alpha Inc.	Healthcare	15							-15
BBB	Beta Inc.	Retail	20	-12	-8					0
CCC	CC Corporation	Industrial	30			5		5		-40
DDD	Delta D Inc.	Hospitality	40		10					-50
EEE	Epsilon Inc	Technology	0	5				-5		0
FFF	Fusbol For Friends	Retail	0	5					-5	0

Buy/Sell

Symbol	**Company Name**	**Industry**	**June 1 20x1**	**July 1 20x1**	**Aug 1 20x1**	**Sep 1 20x1**	**Oct 1 20x1**	**Nov 1 20x1**	**Dec 1 20x1**	**Jan 2 20x2**
AAA	Alpha Inc.	Healthcare		-	-	-	-	-	-	13,650
BBB	Beta Inc.	Retail		11,100	7,320	-	-	-	-	-
CCC	CC Corporation	Industrial		-	-	(4,075)	-	(4,110)	-	32,000
DDD	Delta D Inc.	Hospitality		-	(10,200)	-	-	-	-	51,350
EEE	Epsilon Inc	Technology		(4,825)	-	-	-	4,975	-	-
FFF	Fusbol For Friends	Retail		(3,400)	-	-	-	-	3,550	-
Total Buy/Sale Proceeds			-	2,875	(2,880)	(4,075)	-	865	3,550	97,000

Value of Bonds

Symbol	**Company Name**	**Industry**	**June 1 20x1**	**July 1 20x1**	**Aug 1 20x1**	**Sep 1 20x1**	**Oct 1 20x1**	**Nov 1 20x1**	**Dec 1 20x1**	**Jan 2 20x2**
AAA	Alpha Inc.	Healthcare	13,350	13,395	13,425	13,575	13,650	13,680	13,725	-
BBB	Beta Inc.	Retail	18,200	7,400	-	-	-	-	-	-
CCC	CC Corporation	Industrial	23,700	24,000	24,300	28,525	28,700	32,880	32,600	-
DDD	Delta D Inc.	Hospitality	40,400	40,600	51,000	51,100	51,300	51,250	51,000	-
EEE	Epsilon Inc	Technology	-	4,825	4,875	4,900	4,910	-	-	-
FFF	Fusbol For Friends	Retail	-	3,400	3,435	3,475	3,550	3,600	-	-
Total Value			95,650	93,620	97,035	101,575	102,110	101,410	97,325	-

Figure 1.14 also includes current yield and duration calculation, discussed in more detail in latter chapters.

Further analysis on Zeus Fund I portfolio will be shown in following chapters on this unit including the standard deviation, beta coefficient regression analysis calculations, Sharpe ratio, Jensen's alpha, M square, and Treynor measures. The following chapters will also show how to achieve efficiency and optimization by trading out stocks into bonds due to correlation, as discussed earlier in this chapter.

FIGURE 1.14A ZEUS FUND I (BONDS PRICE & INFO)

Coupon Payment

Symbol	Coupon Dates		01-Jun-18	01-Jul-18	01-Aug-18	01-Sep-18	01-Oct-18	01-Nov-18	01-Dec-18	01-Jan-19	WA 9/17
AAA	15-Feb-17	15-Aug-17				26.25					3.508
BBB	1-Jan-17	1-Jul-17			22.50						0.000
CCC	15-Mar-17	15-Sep-17					35.00				9.829
DDD	15-Jan-17	15-Jul-17			17.50						8.804
EEE	1-Apr-17	1-Oct-17					23.75				1.146
FFF	15-Feb-17	15-Aug-17				40.00					1.368
			0.00	0.00	40.00	66.25	58.75	0.00	0.00	0.00	24.655
										Annual	49.310

Coupon Payment

			0	1	2	3	4	5	6	7
Symbol	Coupon Dates		01-Jun-18	01-Jul-18	01-Aug-18	01-Sep-18	01-Oct-18	01-Nov-18	01-Dec-18	01-Jan-19
AAA	15-Feb-17	15-Aug-17		$ -	$ -	$ 393.75	$ -	$ -	$ -	$ -
BBB	1-Jan-17	1-Jul-17		$ -	$ -	$ -	$ -	$ -	$ -	$ -
CCC	15-Mar-17	15-Sep-17		$ -	$ -	$ -	$ 1,225.00	$ -	$ -	$ -
DDD	15-Jan-17	15-Jul-17		$ -	$ 875.00	$ -	$ -	$ -	$ -	$ -
EEE	1-Apr-17	1-Oct-17		$ -	$ -	$ -	$ 118.75	$ -	$ -	$ -
FFF	15-Feb-17	15-Aug-17			$ -	$ 200.00	$ -	$ -	$ -	$ -
Total Value				$ -	$ 875.00	$ 593.75	$ 1,343.75	$ -	$ -	$ -

Days Since Coupon Paid

Symbol	Coupon Dates		01-Jun-18	01-Jul-18	01-Aug-18	01-Sep-18	01-Oct-18	01-Nov-18	01-Dec-18	01-Jan-19
AAA	15-Feb-17	15-Aug-17	105	135	165	15	45	75	105	135
BBB	1-Jan-17	1-Jul-17	150	0	30	60	90	120	150	0
CCC	15-Mar-17	15-Sep-17	76	106	136	166	16	46	76	106
DDD	15-Jan-17	15-Jul-17	136	166	16	46	76	106	136	166
EEE	1-Apr-17	1-Oct-17	60	90	120	150	0	30	60	90
FFF	15-Feb-17	15-Aug-17	105	135	165	15	45	75	105	135

Acrued Interest calculated

Symbol	Coupon Dates		01-Jun-18	01-Jul-18	01-Aug-18	01-Sep-18	01-Oct-18	01-Nov-18	01-Dec-18	01-Jan-19
AAA	15-Feb-17	15-Aug-17	-15.31	-19.69	-24.06	-2.19	-6.56	-10.94	-15.31	-19.69
BBB	1-Jan-17	1-Jul-17	-18.75	0.00	-3.75	-7.50	-11.25	-15.00	-18.75	0.00
CCC	15-Mar-17	15-Sep-17	-14.78	-20.61	-26.44	-32.28	-3.11	-8.94	-14.78	-20.61
DDD	15-Jan-17	15-Jul-17	-13.22	-16.14	-1.56	-4.47	-7.39	-10.31	-13.22	-16.14
EEE	1-Apr-17	1-Oct-17	-7.92	-11.88	-15.83	-19.79	0.00	-3.96	-7.92	-11.88
FFF	15-Feb-17	15-Aug-17	-23.33	-30.00	-36.67	-3.33	-10.00	-16.67	-23.33	-30.00

Acrued Interest

Symbol	Coupon Dates		01-Jun-18	01-Jul-18	01-Aug-18	01-Sep-18	01-Oct-18	01-Nov-18	01-Dec-18	01-Jan-19
AAA	15-Feb-17	15-Aug-17	(229.69)	-	-	-	-	-	-	295.31
BBB	1-Jan-17	1-Jul-17	(375.00)	-	30.00	-	-	-	-	-
CCC	15-Mar-17	15-Sep-17	(443.33)	-	-	(161.39)	-	(44.72)	-	824.44
DDD	15-Jan-17	15-Jul-17	(528.89)	-	(15.56)	-	-	-	-	806.94
EEE	1-Apr-17	1-Oct-17	-	(59.38)	-	-	-	19.79	-	-
FFF	15-Feb-17	15-Aug-17	-	(150.00)	-	-	-	-	116.67	-
Total Accrued Interest			(1,576.91)	(209.38)	14.44	(161.39)	-	(24.93)	116.67	1,926.70

FIGURE 1.14B ZEUS FUND I (BONDS PRICE & INFO)

Symbol	Coupon Annual Payments	01-Jun-18	01-Jul-18	01-Aug-18	01-Sep-18	01-Oct-18	01-Nov-18	01-Dec-18	01-Jan-19
AAA	$ 52.50	5.899%	5.879%	5.866%	5.801%	5.769%	5.757%	5.738%	5.769%
BBB	$ 45.00	4.945%	4.865%	4.918%	4.865%	4.918%	4.881%	4.813%	4.839%
CCC	$ 70.00	8.861%	8.750%	8.642%	8.589%	8.537%	8.516%	8.589%	8.750%
DDD	$ 35.00	3.465%	3.448%	3.431%	3.425%	3.411%	3.415%	3.431%	3.408%
EEE	$ 47.50	5.000%	4.922%	4.872%	4.847%	4.837%	4.774%	4.750%	4.703%
FFF	$ 80.00	12.500%	11.765%	11.645%	11.511%	11.268%	11.111%	11.268%	11.429%

Remaining Years to Maturity

Symbol	Maturity	01-Jun-18	01-Jul-18	01-Aug-18	01-Sep-18	01-Oct-18	01-Nov-18	01-Dec-18	01-Jan-19
AAA	15/08/23	5.21	5.13	5.04	4.96	4.87	4.79	4.71	4.62
BBB	01/07/20	2.08	2.00	1.92	1.83	1.75	1.67	1.58	1.50
CCC	15/09/25	7.30	7.21	7.13	7.04	6.96	6.88	6.79	6.71
DDD	15/07/19	1.12	1.04	0.95	0.87	0.79	0.70	0.62	0.53
EEE	01/10/26	8.34	8.26	8.17	8.09	8.01	7.92	7.84	7.75
FFF	15/08/26	8.21	8.13	8.04	7.96	7.88	7.79	7.71	7.62

Duration

Symbol		01-Jun-18	01-Jul-18	01-Aug-18	01-Sep-18	01-Oct-18	01-Nov-18	01-Dec-18	01-Jan-19	WA Duration 9/17
AAA	15/08/23	4.54	4.46	4.38	4.41	4.33	4.24	4.16	4.08	0.54
BBB	01/07/20	1.98	1.93	1.85	1.77	1.68	1.60	1.52	1.47	0.00
CCC	15/09/25	5.65	5.57	5.50	5.42	5.54	5.46	5.37	5.28	1.48
DDD	15/07/19	1.10	1.01	0.95	0.86	0.78	0.70	0.61	0.53	0.27
EEE	01/10/26	6.91	6.83	6.75	6.67	6.74	6.66	6.58	6.50	0.31
FFF	15/08/26	5.68	5.66	5.58	5.78	5.71	5.64	5.55	5.45	0.19
										2.79

PROBLEMS

1. What is the future value of $2,000 after 2 years if the interest rate is 10% compounded annually?
2. Suppose your grandfather deposited $1,000 at 5% interest into a savings account 100 years ago. How much would the investment be worth today?
3. A company just reported revenues and profits of $100 million and $10 million, respectively. If revenues increase 5% and profits increase 10% each year, how much revenue and profit will the company report 10 years from now?
4. You borrow $40,000 in student loans your freshman year, at an annual interest rate of 4% per year. If you don't service the debt while you are attending college, and start paying back the loan the day you graduate, how much money do you owe 4 years later?
5. If the stock price of Facebook is $200 and it is expected to have an 8% return per year, how much will it be worth in 3 years?
6. What is the PV of $100 due in 5 years, if the discount rate is 5%?
7. How much money must you invest in an account that earns 10% today if you want to have $10,000 in 5 years?
8. How much money must you invest today if you can earn 10% and you would like to have $100,000 in 10 years?
9. Suppose you buy Facebook stock for $180 and sell it for $220 at the end of the year. How much gain did you earn in amount and rate?
10. You are looking at an investment that will pay $10,000 in 5 years if you invest $6,000 today. What is the rate of return of this investment?
11. Suppose you buy a home for $400,000 and sell it 5 years later for $500,000. What yearly interest rate did you earn?
12. If you buy a stock for $65 and sell it for $70 one year later, what yearly interest rate did you earn?
13. You buy a stock for $30, which you expect to grow at a rate of 7% each year. How long will it be before the stock is worth $60?
14. If you can earn 10% annual interest, how long does it take for your investment to double?
15. How much will an ordinary annuity be worth in 3 years, if it pays $100 per year and earns 10% annual interest?
16. You decide that, starting when you are 20 years old, you will save $5 a day for retirement. At the end of the year, you invest the accumulated savings ($1,825) in a brokerage account with an expected annual return of 8%. If you continue the practice every year until you are 65, how much money will you have?

17. If you would like to have $120,000 in your child's college account in 18 years and you can earn 5% per year, how much must you invest each year?
18. How much money do you need to save each year to be a millionaire by the time you are 65 if you can earn an interest rate of 8% and you start saving when you are 45? 30? 20? When you are born?
19. What interest rate must you earn to have $500,000 in a savings account in 20 years if you contribute $2,500 per year?
20. How large a mortgage can you get if you can afford payments of $24,000 per year for the next 30 years and the interest rate is 3.5%?
21. After you retire, you want to withdraw $80,000 a year from your savings account, which earns 5% annual interest for 25 years. How much money do you need in your savings account when you retire?
22. At retirement you have $750,000 in your savings account. You intend to withdraw $65,000 per year. What interest rate must you earn to make your money last for the next 30 years?
23. Run the average historical return and standard deviation of a portfolio if the portfolio had the following historical annual returns:

YEAR	RATE OF RETURN %
1	11.0
2	12.0
3	-6.0
4	-5.0
5	6.0
6	2.0
7	5.0

24. Run the average historical return and standard deviation of XYZ's stock price:

YEAR	STOCK PRICE
1	110
2	121
3	105
4	140
5	165
6	135
7	145

25. Run the average historical return and standard deviation of ABC's stock price that also pays annual dividends:

YEAR	STOCK PRICE	DIVIDENDS
1	100	3.50
2	115	4.10
3	95	4.10
4	110	4.10
5	125	4.60
6	120	5.00
7	140	5.20

26. Run the scenario analysis average return and standard deviation of following portfolio:

ECONOMIC SCENARIO	PROBABILITY %	RATE OF RETURN %
Recession	25	-10
Normal	50	12
Boom	25	25

27. Run the scenario analysis average return and standard deviation of following company that pays dividends:

ECONOMIC SCENARIO	PROBABILITY %	AVERAGE STOCK PRICE $	AVERAGE DIVIDENDS $
Recession	20	25	1.00
Normal	50	36	2.40
Boom	30	56	3.00

28. Start constructing a portfolio (called your Portfolio Project) in Excel and complete it after you have studied all of Part 1 of this textbook.

FINAL EXCEL PROJECT

Construct a $200,000 portfolio of stocks, corporate bonds, and cash (in Excel) using the following information:

1. Initial capital $100,000 (equity)
2. Additional $100,000 loan for 5% interest per annum
3. Starting date (Year 0)—closing stock and bond prices for that day (Go back and get the historical prices.)
4. Value date (Year 5)
5. Maintain diversification discipline.*
6. Always maintain at least 10% cash. Cash interest income is 1.5% per annum.

7. You must trade stocks or bonds at least five times during this period. (Five initial stock and bond positions need to be replaced during this period.)
8. Assume no trading costs or any additional expenses (except interest on the margin loan).

You spreadsheet should include the following:

1. Initial transaction sources and uses (Jan 1, Year 0)
2. List of stocks and corporate bonds
3. Business description and industry categorization for each stock and S&P, and Moody's rating of each bond
4. Monthly cash flow, which will include any dividends, coupon payments, gains and losses on trades, interest payments, and interest income of cash balance
5. Overall monthly performance (including a graph)
6. S&P 500 Index on the end of Year 1, 2, 3, 4, and 5 (using closing) to compare to your stock portfolio

At value date calculate the following:

1. Total portfolio HPR for stock, bond, and combined portfolio (levered and unlevered)
2. Bond portfolio duration (no need for convexity)
3. Covariance and correlation of bond and stock portfolios
4. Sharpe ratios, Treynor, Jensen, and M^2 measurement for equity portfolio
5. Sharpe ratios, standard deviation, HPR, and average monthly returns for entire portfolio
6. Portfolio performance as compared (including a graph) to S&P 500 Index during this period (beta coefficient calculation, regression analysis between stock portfolio and S&P 500, bond portfolio and bond benchmark, and combined portfolio and weighted benchmarks of stocks and bonds)

***Diversification discipline:**

- There must be no fewer than 10 stocks in the portfolio at all times.
- Each stock value cannot represent more than 20% of the total portfolio.
- Each industry value cannot represent more than 25% of the total portfolio.
- **Portfolio must be across eight different industry sectors. One of the industry sectors should have at least two companies.**

ONLINE TEMPLATES & CASE STUDIES

The Excel spreadsheets used in the chapter can be accessed online via Cognella Active Learning platform.

CHAPTER 2

Covariance, Correlation, and Efficient Frontiers

The last chapter did establish the basics for measuring risk and quantifying the expected return, as well as introduced a few ways to get increased efficiency out of this relationship through allocation and diversification. This chapter will continue to focus on return, risk, and their respective relationship and allocation but demonstrate that the correlation between two assets can be used to achieve higher portfolio efficiency. The covariance and correlation analysis are the factors that contribute to a minimum variance and achieve an efficient frontier.

LEARNING OBJECTIVES

After reading this chapter, students will be able to do the following:

- Compute the covariance and correlation between two asset classes such as stocks and bonds
- Understand diversification benefits and explain how the correlation in a two-asset portfolio affects the such diversification benefits
- Quantify the weights between two asset classes, such as stock and bonds, to achieve the efficient frontier
- Understand the sensitivity of a combined portfolio at different correlation levels between minus 1.0 and positive 1.0
- Use a sample portfolio example that consists of stocks and bonds to show how the standard deviation of this combined portfolio changes at different correlations

COVARIANCE AND CORRELATION OVERVIEW

After reviewing the risk and return independently for each asset, the next step for an investor is to analyze a potential portfolio that combines all asset classes and apply the same measurement of return and calculation of risk. The risk and return of the combined portfolio can be significantly different when compared to each individual asset calculated separately. The covariance and correlation calculation represent the relationship of the risk between two or more asset classes. This an important step towards building a combined portfolio that achieves efficiency.

AUTHOR'S NOTES

Correlation between two unrelated events or two independent objects has been a focus for a lot of scientists, statisticians, and others who try to find common ground to justify their dependence or non-dependence. It does remind me of a story that I heard long time ago. The story goes like this: The Native American chief of a tribe somewhere in upstate Massachusetts, in preparation for the upcoming winter and planning how much wood the tribe needed to collect, approached the tribe's wise man to ask him what his prediction on the coming winter. For the first time the wise man was not getting any signs using his intuition to make such a prediction. The chief then, for the first time, called the American Meteorological Association to find out if they had run studies to predict the temperatures for the upcoming winter. According to them they were predicting colder-than-usual temperatures. The chief then asked all the tribesmen to start gathering wood. A week later, to make sure, the chief called again, and they said that the new prediction is that this winter will definitely be colder than past winters. The chief then asked his staff to go back and cut more wood. After a week, the chief made one more call to make sure what they were predicting was right. He asked them what measurement methods they were using to predict such low temperatures. Someone from the American Meteorological Society said, "Well, it will be the coldest winter ever; you should see how much wood the natives are gathering this year." Of course, this is a funny way of addressing correlation. It highlights when each event depends on another to the point that the self-prophecy will end up happening. It is felt that is always the case between the Federal Reserve Board of Governors (Fed) raising rates and the stock market. The stock market reacts to the Fed's comments of increasing or decreasing rates but sometimes the chairman of the Fed, based on human nature, influences the decision based on how the market will react. Therefore, the market reaction is not unexpectedly surprising that can trigger volatility.

KEY TAKEAWAYS

- Covariance and correlation between two assets is measured between minus 1 and positive 1. This is the cause of how two standalone portfolios with historical risks and returns, when combined, can achieve better-than-average risk.
- Perfect positive correlation—basically positive 1—between two asset classes or two portfolios will not allow for any efficiencies if the investor combines these assets or portfolios since the risk and return are moving in the same direction.
- Perfect negative correlation—basically negative 1—between two asset classes or two portfolios will almost definitely allow for efficiencies if the investor combines these assets or portfolios. In this case, the investor could benefit from the average return between the two asset classes or portfolios and at the same time minimize the standalone standard deviations to a lower combined one.
- The relationship between average return and combined standard deviation is the basis for introducing the concept of the Sharpe ratio that will be discussed in later chapters.

INVESTMENT RETURN AND RISK EFFICIENCY

As it was mentioned in the first chapter, the four factors that an investor needs to consider before investing is to ***first*** measure the return expectation; ***second***, quantify the risk or the probability to achieve such expectation; ***third*** seek the right allocation of investments to various asset classes, not only to diversify the risk, but also to possibly achieve higher efficiencies; and ***fourth*** set the time to achieve such goals or establish the exit strategy. The previous chapter touched on the first two factors. This chapter and many chapters to follow will continue to emphasize the first two factors and the importance of the relationship between risk and return. This chapter will focus more on the third and fourth factors. All four factors are essential to build expectation. The investor needs to determine return expectation first. Without any expectations the investor should not proceed with the investment. The expectation comes with risk appetite. The basic premise, of course, is that the higher the risk the higher the return expectation. We will examine a possibility that when the investor allocates his or her investments across different assets, he or she will not only diversify the risk, but can also achieve efficiency or attempt to better balance the risk with the return.

The investment thesis is based on the idea that by diversifying or allocating your investments to various assets classes you can achieve higher efficiency. This is the point where the investment has the highest possible return at the lowest possible risk or volatility. The single biggest factor that drives such efficiency is correlation. The key assessment of portfolio risk is the measurement of if the returns on two asset classes or more move in tandem or opposite directions. Portfolio risk depends on the correlation between the returns of the investments in the portfolio.

To construct a portfolio of risky assets, the portfolio manager needs to understand how the uncertainties can affect the returns of these assets. Starting with the example in chapter 1, the figure 2.1 shows that the standard deviation of the combined portfolio that has 60% stocks and 40% bonds of 6.24% which is lower than an all-bond portfolio of 7.05%. This phenomenon is credited to the negative correlation shown in figure 2.1 of −0.97.

COVARIANCE AND CORRELATION CALCULATIONS: THE SPECIFICS

Let's compare two asset classes such as stocks and bonds, as illustrated in figure 2.1. After we calculate each deviation from their respective mean for each economic scenario and apply the probability, we will then calculate the covariance (Cov) (Rs, Rb) for stock and bonds, which is the sum of these deviations. **The correlation is calculated as follows:**

$$\rho = \frac{\text{cov}(R_s R_b)}{\sigma s \cdot \sigma_b}$$

where cov is the covariance of the combined portfolio of returns over the standard deviation of each asset class

FIGURE 2.1 PORTFOLIO ANALYSIS (ASSET ALLOCATION)

SCENARIO PERFROMANCE ANALYSIS

Scenario (S)	Probability (p)	Stocks (s): ROR % (rs)	p * rs %	Deviation for Exp. Ret. (Dev.)	Square Deviation (SD) Dev^2	p * SD	Bonds (b): ROR % (rb)	p * rb %	Deviation for Exp. Ret. (Dev.)	Square Deviation (SD) Dev^2	p * SD
Recession (Sr)	25.0%	-12.00	-3.00	-23.70	561.69	140.42	14.00	3.50	9.75	95.06	23.77
Normal (Sn)	45.0%	14.00	6.30	2.30	5.29	2.38	5.00	2.25	0.75	0.56	0.25
Boom (Sb)	30.0%	28.00	8.40	16.30	265.69	79.71	-5.00	-1.50	-9.25	85.56	25.67
	100.0%		11.70 %		Variance=	222.51		4.25 %		Variance=	49.69
					SD =	14.92 %				SD =	7.05 %

PORTFOLIO ANALYSIS (Asset Allocation)

Asset Allocation	Weights (W%)
Stocks (Ws) =	60%
Bonds (Wb) =	40%

(Ws * rs) + (Wb * rb)

Scenario (S)	Probability (p)	ROR % (rs)	p * rs %	Deviation for Exp. Ret. (Dev.)	Square Deviation (SD) Dev^2	p * SD
Recession (Sr)	25.0%	-1.6	-0.40	-10.32	106.50	26.63
Normal (Sn)	45.0%	10.4	4.68	1.68	2.82	1.27
Boom (Sb)	30.0%	14.8	4.44	6.08	36.97	11.09
	100.0%		8.72 %		Variance=	38.99
					SD =	6.24 %

COVARIANCE & CORRELATION

Stocks (Deviation from the mean)	Bonds (Deviation from the mean)	Ds * Db	Covariance [p * (Ds*Db)]
-23.70	9.75	-231.08	-57.77
2.30	0.75	1.73	0.78
16.30	-9.25	-150.78	-45.23
		Covariance=	-102.23
		Correlation Coefficient =	-0.97

THE BASICS OF RISK-RETURN (MEAN-VARIANCE) ANALYSIS

Though the risk-return relationship will be discussed in depth later in this chapter and unit, it is necessary to establish a basis for choosing the right portfolio. **The mean-variance portfolio theory provides the theoretical foundation for assessing the risk-return relationship when selecting a portfolio**. Mean-variance portfolio risk theory is based on the concept that the value of a specific investment can be measured in terms of mean return and variance return. The analysis first assumes that the investor will always seek higher return at lower risk (taking out the behavioral aspect of investing), as we discussed in chapter 1 and further prove in this chapter. Also, the analysis assumes that the expected return, variance, and covariances are already quantified based on historical information. Once the information is understood and accepted as the basis of historical assessment, the analysis will then use that to build the investment expectation and run various sensitivities to identify the efficient and optimum levels.

THE IMPACT OF CORRELATION TO PORTFOLIO EFFICIENCY: ACHIEVING MINIMUM VARIANCE

When combining two asset classes in one portfolio, the combined return, variance, and standard deviation can be achieved as follows:

Mean return (average return)

$$R_p = (w_s \cdot R_s) + (w_b \cdot R_b)$$

where R_p is the return of the combined portfolio, R_s is the return of the stock portfolio, R_b is the return of the bond portfolio, and w_s and w_b are the percentage weights of stock and bonds, respectively.

Variance and standard deviation

$$\sigma_P^2 = w_s^2\sigma_s^2 + w_b^2\sigma_b^2 + 2w_s\sigma_s w_b\sigma_b\rho$$

$$\sigma_P = \sqrt{w_s^2\sigma_s^2 + w_b^2\sigma_b^2 + 2w_s\sigma_s w_b\sigma_b\rho}$$

where σ_P^2 is the variance of the combined portfolio, w_s and w_b are the percentage weights of stocks and bonds, respectively, σ_s and σ_b are the standard deviation of the stocks and bonds, respectively, and ρ is the correlation.

Correlation, expressed with the Greek rho (ρ), can significantly change the portfolio's variance and standard deviation.

Before we examine the impact of correlation to portfolio efficiency, let's discuss efficiency and express the concept by using an example of two portfolios. As shown figure 2.1, by trading out 100% bonds to 60% stocks and 40% bonds, the bond portfolio's standard

FIGURE 2.2 FINDING RISK RETURN EFFICIENCY (EFFICIENT FRONTIER)

Portfolio A

E (rs) =	11.700
E (rb) =	4.250
σs =	14.917
σb =	7.049
Correlation=	-0.972

Minimum Variance - Efficient Frontier

W% Stock	W% bond	σ %	E(r) %
31.9%	68.1%	1.12759	6.62655

Correlation =			PORTF. A CORRELATION -0.972	
Portfolio Weights			Risk	Return
W% stocks	W% bonds		σ %	E(r) %
0%	100%		7.05	4.25
10%	90%		4.91	5.00
20%	80%		2.83	5.74
30%	70%	Efficiency	1.20	6.49
40%	60%		2.10	7.23
50%	50%		4.12	7.98
60%	40%		6.24	8.72
70%	30%		8.40	9.47
80%	20%		10.57	10.21
90%	10%		12.74	10.96
100%	0%		14.92	11.70

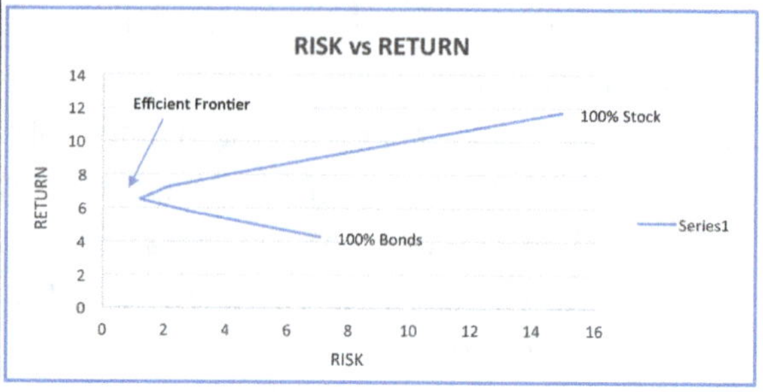

deviation has improved from 7.05% to 6.24%. Figure 2.2 shows the capital allocation line as you move from 100% bonds to 100% stock, traveling left before the line turns right toward the stock portfolio. **The most northwestern point of the map just before the turn is the efficient frontier. This is the point with the highest possible return at the lowest possible risk, measured by the standard deviation.** Figure 2.2 calculates that the lowest possible variance is estimated at 31.9% Stocks and 68.1% bonds achieving a minimum standard deviation of 1.12759 and weighted average return of 6.62655%.

EFFICIENT FRONTIER AT DIFFERENT CORRELATION LEVELS

Let's assume that we take the portfolio example of risk-return characteristics and use different levels of correlation between negative (−1) to positive (+1). The portfolio efficiency dramatically changes from the highest level of efficiency to no efficiency. **A portfolio with perfect positive correlation (+1) does not yield any efficiency as the portfolio manager shifts the investment portfolio from bonds to stock.** A portfolio with perfect negative correlation (−1) could yield the maximum efficiency, conceivably eliminating any risk as the portfolio trades out of a heavily concentrated bond portfolio to a higher concentration of stock portfolio. At zero correlation the portfolio continues to be tested for any efficiencies. Figure 2.3 shows all three possibilities (−1, 0, and +1) and as compared to the portfolio example.

Figures 2.4, 2.5 and 2.6 show the two-asset class capital allocation line from the extreme bend to the left, representing the perfect negative correlation between bonds and stocks to a straight line representing no efficiency; **basically, as the portfolio manager trades out of bonds and substitutes it with equity to achieve a higher return, since the correlation between these two assets are a perfect 1, the additional return will come with the exact linear additional risk.**

FIGURE 2.3 FINDING RISK RETURN EFFICIENCY (EFFICIENT FRONTIER)

Portfolio A
E (rs) = 11.700
E (rb) = 4.250
σs = 14.917
σb = 7.049
Correlation= -0.972

			ZERO CORRELATION		POSITIVE CORRELATION		NEGATIVE CORRELATION		PORTF. A CORRELATION	
Correlation =			0.000		1.000		-1.000		-0.972	
Portfolio Weights			Risk	Return	Risk	Return	Risk	Return	Risk	Return
W% stocks	W% bonds		σ %	E(r) %	σ %	E(r) %	σ %	E(r) %	σ %	E(r) %
0%	100%		7.05	4.25	7.05	4.25	7.05	4.25	7.05	4.25
10%	90%	Efficiency	6.52	5.00	7.84	5.00	4.85	5.00	4.91	5.00
20%	80%		6.38	5.74	8.62	5.74	2.66	5.74	2.83	5.74
30%	70%		6.66	6.49	9.41	6.49	0.46	6.49	1.20	6.49
40%	60%		7.31	7.23	10.20	7.23	1.74	7.23	2.10	7.23
50%	50%		8.25	7.98	10.98	7.98	3.93	7.98	4.12	7.98
60%	40%		9.38	8.72	11.77	8.72	6.13	8.72	6.24	8.72
70%	30%		10.65	9.47	12.56	9.47	8.33	9.47	8.40	9.47
80%	20%		12.02	10.21	13.34	10.21	10.52	10.21	10.57	10.21
90%	10%		13.44	10.96	14.13	10.96	12.72	10.96	12.74	10.96
100%	0%		14.92	11.70	14.92	11.70	14.92	11.70	14.92	11.70

FIGURE 2.4 FINDING RISK RETURN EFFICIENCY (EFFICIENT FRONTIER)

Portfolio A
E (rs) = 11.700
E (rb) = 4.250
σs = 14.917
σb = 7.049
Correlation= 0.000

			ZERO CORRELATION	
Correlation =			0.000	
Portfolio Weights			Risk	Return
W% stocks	W% bonds		σ %	E(r) %
0%	100%		7.05	4.25
10%	90%		6.52	5.00
20%	80%	Efficiency	6.38	5.74
30%	70%		6.66	6.49
40%	60%		7.31	7.23
50%	50%		8.25	7.98
60%	40%		9.38	8.72
70%	30%		10.65	9.47
80%	20%		12.02	10.21
90%	10%		13.44	10.96
100%	0%		14.92	11.70

Minimum Variance - Efficient Frontier

W% Stock	W% bond	σ %	E(r) %
18.3%	81.7%	6.37319	5.61335

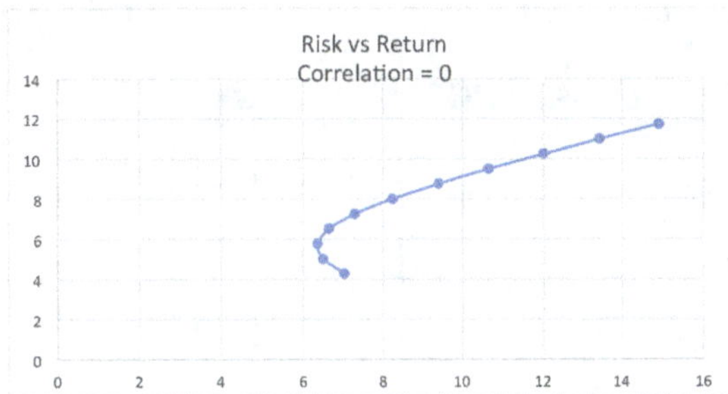

Scenario Analysis Example

Figure 2.4 shows that our portfolio (portfolio A) with an assumed zero correlation. The efficiency can be achieved around 10%–20% stock allocation, showing that the standard deviation at these levels is reduced from 7.05% (all bonds) to 6.52% at 10% stock and continues to reduce to 6.38% at 20% stock before the standard deviation increases again around 30%, showing a standard deviation of 6.66%. The lowest possible standard deviation representing the efficient frontier is calculated at 18.3% stocks and 81.7% bonds calculating a 6.637319% and 5.61335% standard deviation and combined portfolio return, respectively.

FIGURE 2.5 FINDING RISK RETURN EFFICIENCY (EFFICIENT FRONTIER)

Portfolio A

E (rs) =	11.700
E (rb) =	4.250
σs =	14.917
σb =	7.049
Correlation=	1.000

Minimum Variance - Efficient Frontier

W% Stock	W% bond	σ %	E(r) %
0.0%	100.0%	7.04894	4.25000

Correlation =		POSITIVE CORRELATION 1.000	
Portfolio Weights		Risk	Return
W% stocks	W% bonds	σ %	E(r) %
0%	100%	7.05	4.25
10%	90%	7.84	5.00
20%	80%	8.62	5.74
30%	70%	9.41	6.49
40%	60%	10.20	7.23
50%	50%	10.98	7.98
60%	40%	11.77	8.72
70%	30%	12.56	9.47
80%	20%	13.34	10.21
90%	10%	14.13	10.96
100%	0%	14.92	11.70

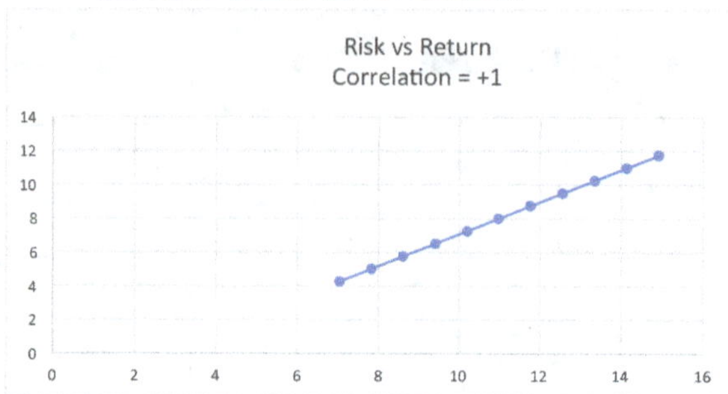

FIGURE 2.6 FINDING RISK RETURN EFFICIENCY (EFFICIENT FRONTIER)

Portfolio A

E (rs) =	11.700
E (rb) =	4.250
σs =	14.917
σb =	7.049
Correlation=	-1.000

Minimum Variance - Efficient Frontier

W% Stock	W% bond	σ %	E(r) %
32.1%	67.9%	0.00206	6.64145

Correlation =			NEGATIVE CORRELATION -1.00000	
Portfolio Weights			Risk	Return
W% stocks	W% bonds		σ %	E(r) %
0%	100%		7.04894	4.25000
10%	90%		4.85237	4.99500
20%	80%		2.65580	5.74000
30%	70%	Efficiency	0.45922	6.48500
40%	60%		1.73735	7.23000
50%	50%		3.93392	7.97500
60%	40%		6.13049	8.72000
70%	30%		8.32706	9.46500
80%	20%		10.52363	10.21000
90%	10%		12.72020	10.95500
100%	0%		14.91677	11.70000

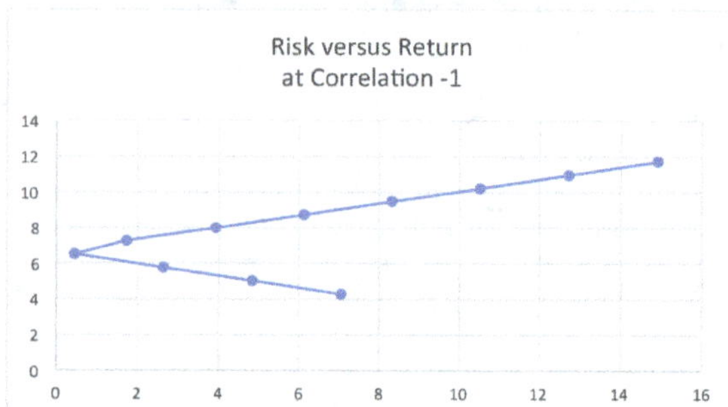

Figure 2.5 shows our portfolio's (portfolio A) risk-versus-return allocation line assuming a perfect positive +1 correlation. At a +1 correlation there is no efficiency. As the portfolio moves from all bonds to all stock, the line is at 45-degree angle, showing that the risk continues to increase at the same pace as the portfolio manager is seeking higher returns.

Figure 2.6 shows our portfolio (portfolio A) with perfect negative −1 correlation. At −1 correlation, since the two assets held at the portfolio are moving in the opposite way from each other, the risk can be offset as the portfolio manager is moving from an all-bond portfolio to all stock portfolio. The chart shows that the efficient frontier, which is the point where the combined portfolio of bonds and stocks have the highest possible return at the lowest possible risk, can be achieved around 30% stock and 70% bonds, showing a combined return of 6.49% at 0.46% standard deviation. The lowest possible standard deviation with negative −1 correlation representing the efficient frontier is calculated at 32.1% stocks and 67.9% bonds calculating a 0.00206% and 6.64145% standard deviation and combined portfolio return, respectively.

Historical Analysis Example

Figure 2.7 shows a portfolio consisting of 12-year historical information of stocks and bonds. The average return and standard deviation for the stocks are 11.68% and 19.20%, respectively. The bonds have 2.08% average return and 4.97% standard deviation. The covariance and correlation between stocks and bonds is at -70.05 and negative −0.73x, respectively (please note that the average variance is calculated by 11 observations and not 12, hence the denominator is n-1 rather n). This is because the deviations are calculated based on estimated average return for that year instead of the true expected return. In statistics, this adjustment, called "degrees of freedom," is to accommodate for any unknown errors in the information. In Excel, the function is =stdev.s for the n-1 instead of the Excel function of =stdev.p or =stdev, which is divided by n observations. We also run a combined portfolio with 30% stocks and 70% bonds, showing a higher return and lower standard

FIGURE 2.7 HISTORICAL ANALYSIS

	Returns		**Deviations from Average Return**		**Standard Deviation Calculation**		**Product from Deviation**
	Stocks %	**Bonds %**	**Stocks (Ds)**	**Bonds (Db)**	**Stocks**	**Bonds**	**Ds . Db**
Year -12	-6.50	3.10	-18.18	1.02	330.33	1.03	-18.48
Year -11	-13.20	5.20	-24.88	3.12	618.77	9.71	-77.53
Year -10	-8.90	7.90	-20.58	5.82	423.33	33.83	-119.68
Year -9	25.00	6.10	13.33	4.02	177.56	16.13	53.52
Year -8	48.50	-9.50	36.83	-11.58	1356.08	134.17	-426.56
Year -7	37.60	-2.50	25.93	-4.58	672.11	21.01	-118.82
Year -6	10.50	2.50	-1.18	0.42	1.38	0.17	-0.49
Year -5	7.20	1.50	-4.48	-0.58	20.03	0.34	2.61
Year -4	-5.60	3.40	-17.28	1.32	298.43	1.73	-22.75
Year -3	17.50	-3.20	5.83	-5.28	33.93	27.91	-30.78
Year -2	21.50	3.50	9.83	1.42	96.53	2.01	13.92
Year -1	6.50	7.00	-5.18	4.92	26.78	24.17	-25.44

	Stocks	Bonds
Average Return	**11.68**	**2.08**
Standard Deviation	19.20	4.97
Covariance	-70.04	
Correlation	-0.73	

	Stocks	Bonds		
Total	**4055.24**	**272.24**		**-770.47**
Average (use n-1)	368.66	24.75	Cov=	-70.04
Standard Deviation	19.20	4.97	Correl=	-0.73

Combinced Portfolio at 30% Stocks and 70% Bonds	
Average Return	**4.96**
Standard Deviation	**3.99**

deviation 4.96% and 3.99%, respectively, as compared to an all-bond portfolio with return and standard deviation of 2.08% and 4.97%.

> **Excel formulas for average, standard deviation, covariance, and correlation:**
> =Average(number1, number2, ...): highlight information range
> =Stdev.p(number1, number 2, ...) for n observations, =stdev.s for n-1 observations
> =Covar(aray1, array2): highlight each comparative range
> =Correl(array1, array2): highlight each comparative range

Allocating various percentages between stocks and bonds can achieve efficiency. Figure 2.8 shows that the efficiency (lowest possible combined standard deviation) is between the 10–30% stocks and 70–90% bonds. The lowest possible standard deviation representing the efficient frontier is calculated at 17.8% stocks and 82.2% bonds, calculating a 2.81182% and 3.79065% standard deviation and combined portfolio return, respectively.

EXTENSION TO THE THREE-ASSET CASE

Earlier in this chapter we discussed how to form a two-asset class portfolio consisting of stocks and bonds and how to allocate these assets so the investor can achieve efficiency. Let's assume that the investor is now seeking to continue maximizing the expected return with the lowest possible minimum volatility by adding another asset class in the portfolio.

FIGURE 2.8 HISTORICAL ANALYSIS

Portfolio Consruction

	W% Stocks	W% Bonds		WeightedA verage St. Dev.	Weighted Average Return
	0%	100%		4.97	2.08
Efficiency	10%	90%		3.34	3.04
Efficiency	20%	80%		2.86	4.00
Efficiency	30%	70%		3.99	4.96
	40%	60%		5.85	5.92
	50%	50%		7.96	6.88
	60%	40%		10.15	7.84
	70%	30%		12.39	8.80
	80%	20%		14.65	9.76
	90%	10%		16.92	10.72
	100%	0%		19.20	11.68
Efficiency	17.8%	82.2%		2.81182	3.79065

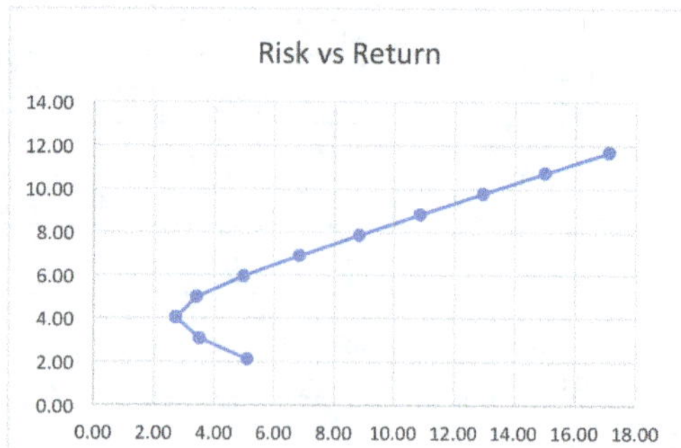

The question is how the investor could improve the trade-off between risk and return by adding a new asset class in the portfolio. Figure 2.9 shows the existing portfolio from figure 2.7, which consists of large-cap stocks and corporate bonds and trade out of these to buy a portfolio consisting of small-cap stocks.

FIGURE 2.9 THREE ASSET CASE

Achieving efficiency by adding a third asset class

	Returns		
	Large-Cap Stocks %	**Bonds %**	**Small-Cap Stocks %**
Year -12	-6.50	3.10	-7.80
Year -11	-13.20	5.20	-16.00
Year -10	-8.90	7.90	-11.00
Year -9	25.00	6.10	21.00
Year -8	48.50	-9.50	57.00
Year -7	37.60	-2.50	49.00
Year -6	10.50	2.50	16.50
Year -5	7.20	1.50	9.00
Year -4	-5.60	3.40	-9.60
Year -3	17.50	-3.20	15.00
Year -2	21.50	3.50	27.00
Year -1	6.50	7.00	7.80
Average Return	**11.68**	**2.08**	**13.16**
Standard Deviation	**19.20**	**4.97**	**23.18**
% Holdings before Extension	30.0%	70.0%	
% Holdings including new Extension	10.0%	50.0%	40.0%

Correlation	
Large-Cap Stocks and Bonds	-0.733
Small Cap-Stocks and Large Cap Stocks	0.987
Bond and Small Cap-Stocks	-0.738

Portfolio Results	
Return for 2-Asset Holdings	4.96
Standard Deviation for 2-Asset Holdings	**3.99**
Return for 2-Asset Holdings	7.47
Standard Deviation for 3-Asset Holdings	**2.00**

Figure 2.9 shows that the investor first holds 30% large-cap stocks and 70% bonds that achieve a more efficient portfolio than if the investor had only bonds. As expected, the return goes up from 2.08% at 100% bonds to 4.96% at 30% stock and 70% bonds. Despite the increase in return, by adding stock to the portfolio of bonds the standard deviation goes down from 4.97% at 100% bonds to 3.99% at 30% stocks and 70% bonds. Now, let's add a third asset class such as small-cap stocks where the 12-year average return and standard deviation is at 13.16% and 23.18%, respectively. Obviously, the initial expectation is that adding a more volatile asset class at 23.18% will increase the risk for the two-asset class even if we are bringing a much higher return performance from the small-cap stocks. At 10% large-caps stocks, 50% bonds and 40% small-caps stocks, as expected, the return goes up to 7.47%, but the standard deviation goes down even further than holding all bonds at 2.0%, achieving further efficiency.

$$Two-asset\ mean\ return: R_p = (W_s \cdot R_s) + (W_b \cdot R_b)$$

$$Three-asset\ mean\ return: R_p = (W_{s1} \cdot R_{s1}) + (W_b \cdot R_b) + (W_{s2} \cdot R_{s2})$$

$$Two-asset\ standard\ deviation: \sigma_p = \sqrt{(W_s^2\sigma_s^2 + W_b^2\sigma_b^2 + 2W_s\sigma_s W_b\sigma_b W\rho_{sb})}$$

$$Three-asset\ standard\ deviation:$$

$$\sigma_p = \sqrt{\begin{array}{l}(W_{s1}^2\sigma_{s1}^2 + W_b^2\sigma_b^2 + W_{s2}^2\sigma_{s2}^2 + 2W_{s1}\sigma_{s1}W_b\sigma_b \cdot \rho_{s1b} + 2W_{s2}\sigma_{s2}W_b\sigma_b \cdot \rho_{s2b} \\ +2W_{s2}\sigma_{s2}W_{s1}\sigma_{s1} \cdot \rho_{s1s2}\end{array}}$$

Where σ_p is the standard deviation of the combined portfolio, W_{s1}, W_{s2}, W_b are the percentage weights of large-cap stocks, small-cap stocks, and bonds, respectively; σ_{s1}, σ_{s2}, and σ_b are the standard deviations of large-cap stocks, small-cap stocks, and bonds, respectively; and ρ_{s1b}, ρ_{s2b} and ρ_{s1s2} are the correlations between the asset classes.

CASE STUDY

PORTFOLIO OF STOCKS AND BONDS: ZEUS FUND I CASE STUDY

The previous chapter described the initial capital raised to fund a newly established $200-million fund called Zeus Fund I. Zeus Fund I is set up to buy stock and corporate bonds, as shown chapter 1, figure 1.7.

Figures 1.11 and figures 1.12 from chapter 1 shows all the stock and bond trades over 7 months. Figure 2.10 calculates the average monthly changes of the Zeus Fund I portfolio of stocks and bonds (please note that the blue information represents the input into the model and the dark information represents the calculated formulas.

Figure 2.11 shows the overall combined stock/bond 7-month performance of the Zeus Fund I portfolio. The average portfolio made of 46.4% stocks and 53.6% bonds yields an average rate or return (ROR) of 1.86% per month with 1.1415% volatility. The correlation

FIGURE 2.10A ZEUS FUND I

Stock Prices		0	1	2	3	4	5	6	7
Symbol	Company Name	June 1 20x1	July 1 20x1	Aug 1 20x1	Sep 1 20x1	Oct 1 20x1	Nov 1 20x1	Dec 1 20x1	Jan 2 20x2
ABC	ABC Chem Inc	23.00	24.00	22.50	25.00	26.00	27.00	28.00	31.00
BCD	BCD Precision Inc	12.00	10.00	12.00	12.00	15.00	18.00	19.50	22.00
CDE	CDE Inc	18.00	19.00	18.00	19.00	21.00	20.00	19.00	21.00
DEF	DEF Inc	40.00	42.00	43.00	45.00	45.00	45.00	46.00	48.00
EFG	Effective Inc	52.00	60.00	60.00	60.00	62.00	62.00	61.00	63.00
FGH	FGH Inc	31.00	20.00	25.00	26.00	20.00	22.00	24.00	25.00
GHI	General HI	15.00	16.00	17.00	18.00	19.00	19.00	18.00	20.00
HIK	Hicks Kental Inc	8.00	9.50	10.50	11.00	11.50	12.00	14.00	14.50
IKL	IKL Inc	15.00	13.00	12.00	14.00	15.00	18.00	22.00	20.00
KLM	KLM Health	25.00	26.00	26.00	26.00	26.00	26.00	27.00	20.00
LMN	LMN Hotel & Resorts	26.00	30.00	32.00	33.00	35.00	32.00	34.00	35.00
MNO	MNO Cable Inc	19.00	20.00	19.00	18.00	18.00	16.00	20.00	18.00
NOP	Norton Optimum	53.00	52.00	55.00	56.00	58.00	59.00	59.00	61.00
OPQ	Odyssea PQ Inc	11.00	8.50	11.00	11.00	11.00	11.00	11.50	12.00
PQR	PQR Chemicals	18.00	17.00	19.00	19.00	20.00	22.00	26.00	24.00

Stock Prices Monthly %		0	1	2	3	4	5	6	7	
Symbol	Company Name	June 1 20x1	July 1 20x1	Aug 1 20x1	Sep 1 20x1	Oct 1 20x1	Nov 1 20x1	Dec 1 20x1	Jan 2 20x2	Total
ABC	ABC Chem Inc		4.3%	-6.3%	11.1%	4.0%	3.8%	3.7%	10.7%	31.5%
BCD	BCD Precision Inc		-16.7%	20.0%	0.0%	25.0%	20.0%	8.3%	12.8%	69.5%
CDE	CDE Inc		5.6%	-5.3%	5.6%	10.5%	-4.8%	-5.0%	10.5%	17.1%
DEF	DEF Inc		5.0%	2.4%	4.7%	0.0%	0.0%	2.2%	4.3%	18.6%
EFG	Effective Inc		15.4%	0.0%	0.0%	3.3%	0.0%	-1.6%	3.3%	20.4%
FGH	FGH Inc		-35.5%	25.0%	4.0%	-23.1%	10.0%	9.1%	4.2%	-6.3%
GHI	General HI		6.7%	6.3%	5.9%	5.6%	0.0%	-5.3%	11.1%	30.2%
HIK	Hicks Kental Inc		18.8%	10.5%	4.8%	4.5%	4.3%	16.7%	3.6%	63.2%
IKL	IKL Inc		-13.3%	-7.7%	16.7%	7.1%	20.0%	22.2%	-9.1%	35.9%
KLM	KLM Health		4.0%	0.0%	0.0%	0.0%	0.0%	3.8%	-25.9%	-18.1%
LMN	LMN Hotel & Resorts		15.4%	6.7%	3.1%	6.1%	-8.6%	6.3%	2.9%	31.9%
MNO	MNO Cable Inc		5.3%	-5.0%	-5.3%	0.0%	-11.1%	25.0%	-10.0%	-1.1%
NOP	Norton Optimum		-1.9%	5.8%	1.8%	3.6%	1.7%	0.0%	3.4%	14.4%
OPQ	Odyssea PQ Inc		-22.7%	29.4%	0.0%	0.0%	0.0%	4.5%	4.3%	15.6%
PQR	PQR Chemicals		-5.6%	11.8%	0.0%	5.3%	10.0%	18.2%	-7.7%	32.0%
Average Return			-1.0%	6.2%	3.5%	3.5%	3.0%	7.2%	1.2%	23.6%
Standard Deviation			15.2%	11.4%	5.2%	9.6%	8.9%	9.4%	10.4%	23.2%

FIGURE 2.10B ZEUS FUND I

BOND PORTFOLIO

Bond Prices

		0	1	2	3	4	5	6	7
Symbol	**Company Name**	**June 1 20x1**	**July 1 20x1**	**Aug 1 20x1**	**Sep 1 20x1**	**Oct 1 20x1**	**Nov 1 20x1**	**Dec 1 20x1**	**Jan 2 20x2**
AAA	Alpha Inc.	890	893	895	905	910	912	915	910
BBB	Beta Inc.	910	925	915	925	915	922	935	930
CCC	CC Corporation	790	800	810	815	820	822	815	800
DDD	Delta D Inc.	1010	1015	1020	1022	1026	1025	1020	1027
EEE	Epsilon Inc	950	965	975	980	982	995	1000	1010
FFF	Fusbol For Friends	640	680	687	695	710	720	710	700

Bond Prices Monthly %

		0	1	2	3	4	5	6	7	
Symbol	**Company Name**	**June 1 20x1**	**July 1 20x1**	**Aug 1 20x1**	**Sep 1 20x1**	**Oct 1 20x1**	**Nov 1 20x1**	**Dec 1 20x1**	**Jan 2 20x2**	**Total**
AAA	Alpha Inc.		0.34%	0.22%	1.12%	0.55%	0.22%	0.33%	-0.55%	2.23%
BBB	Beta Inc.		1.65%	-1.08%	1.09%	-1.08%	0.77%	1.41%	-0.53%	2.22%
CCC	CC Corporation		1.27%	1.25%	0.62%	0.61%	0.24%	-0.85%	-1.84%	1.30%
DDD	Delta D Inc.		0.50%	0.49%	0.20%	0.39%	-0.10%	-0.49%	0.69%	1.68%
EEE	Epsilon Inc		1.58%	1.04%	0.51%	0.20%	1.32%	0.50%	1.00%	6.16%
FFF	Fusbol For Friends		6.25%	1.03%	1.16%	2.16%	1.41%	-1.39%	-1.41%	9.21%
Average Return			1.93%	0.49%	0.78%	0.47%	0.64%	-0.08%	-0.44%	3.80%
Standard Deviation			2.19%	0.86%	0.40%	1.04%	0.62%	1.02%	1.12%	3.18%

COMBINED PORTFOLIO

Symbol	**Company Name**	**June 1 20x1**	**July 1 20x1**	**Aug 1 20x1**	**Sep 1 20x1**	**Oct 1 20x1**	**Nov 1 20x1**	**Dec 1 20x1**	**Jan 2 20x2**	**Total**
Weightts										
Stocks (Weights)		45.6%	46.3%	46.8%	46.4%	45.6%	45.6%	46.3%	48.7%	46.4%
Bonds (Weights)		54.4%	53.7%	53.2%	53.6%	54.4%	54.4%	53.7%	51.3%	53.6%
Portfolio Measurement										
Average Return			0.6%	3.2%	2.0%	1.8%	1.7%	3.3%	0.4%	13.0%
Standard Deviation			6.5%	5.1%	2.3%	4.1%	3.9%	4.1%	4.8%	10.0%
Correlation										-0.521x

is calculated at −0.521. Finding the efficiency based on the historical performance is approximately 10–20% stocks and 80–90% bonds. At these levels the standard deviation is lower than an all-bond portfolio.

NEXT: FROM EFFICIENCY TO OPTIMIZATION

EFFICIENT FRONTIER → $\frac{\Delta_r}{\Delta\sigma} > 1$ → OPTIMIZATION

To review this chapter and set the basis for the following chapters, the concept of the efficient frontier will be taken to another level of portfolio assessment. The efficient frontier works as the starting point of choosing the right investment that enjoys high returns and

FIGURE 2.11 ZEUS FUND I

STOCK AND BOND PORTFOLIO

Performance	0	1	2	3	4	5	6	7
Symbol		July 1 20x1	Aug 1 20x1	Sep 1 20x1	Oct 1 20x1	Nov 1 20x1	Dec 1 20x1	Jan 2 20x2
Stocks		-1.0%	6.2%	3.5%	3.5%	3.0%	7.2%	1.2%
Bonds		1.9%	0.5%	0.8%	0.5%	0.6%	-0.1%	-0.4%
Total Stock Value	81,757	82,600	82,200	84,050	85,000	85,450	87,300	92,275
Total Bonds Value	97,495	95,650	93,620	97,035	101,575	102,110	101,410	97,325
Total Portfolio Value	179,253	178,250	175,820	181,085	186,575	187,560	188,710	189,600
Portfolio % change		-0.6%	-1.4%	3.0%	3.0%	0.5%	0.6%	0.5%
Cummulative % Change		-0.6%	-1.9%	1.1%	4.1%	4.6%	5.2%	5.7%
Stocks (Weights)	45.6%	46.3%	46.8%	46.4%	45.6%	45.6%	46.3%	48.7%
Bonds (Weights)	54.4%	53.7%	53.2%	53.6%	54.4%	54.4%	53.7%	51.3%

7-month Portfolio Performance

STOCKS		BONDS		COMBINED PORTFOLIO	
Average	3.3777%	Average	0.5428%	Average	1.8581%
Standard Deviation	2.7976%	Standard Deviation	0.7477%	Variance	0.0130%
Average % of Portfolio	46.3954%	Average % of Portfolio	53.6046%	Standard Deviation	1.1415%

Covariance (Portfolio)	0.000
Correlation (Portfolio)	-0.521

Finding Efficiency in the Portfolio

						Current Position						
Stocks	0.000%	10.000%	20.000%	30.000%	40.000%	46.395%	50.000%	60.000%	70.000%	80.000%	90.000%	100.000%
Bonds	100.000%	90.000%	80.000%	70.000%	60.000%	53.605%	50.000%	40.000%	30.000%	20.000%	10.000%	0.000%
Average Return	0.5428%	0.8263%	1.1098%	1.3933%	1.6768%	1.8581%	1.9603%	2.2438%	2.5273%	2.8107%	3.0942%	3.3777%
Standard Deviation	0.7477%	0.5787%	0.5674%	0.7214%	0.9645%	1.1415%	1.2455%	1.5439%	1.8513%	2.1639%	2.4797%	2.7976%

HIGHEST EFFICIENCY

lowest possible risk. The portfolio manager does not end the search there for building a more effective portfolio. After achieving an efficient portfolio using historical and/or scenario analysis, the next move is to go from efficiency to optimization. The optimization, discussed in depth in the following chapters, can be achieved by moving from the efficient frontier to seek additional return at minimum rate of change of risk. As discussed, the efficient frontier is the point where the portfolio manager enjoys the highest possible return to the lowest possible risk. From that point the portfolio analyst is seeking to achieve an even a higher return delta (rate of change), but as we discussed it will also come with higher risk. The optimization point is where additional return, or the rate of change going from bonds to stocks, should be lower than the rate of change of the additional risk—basically, higher return delta at lower risk delta. That achievement is called the optimum point and is the basis of the Sharpe ratio, which is discussed in the next few chapters.

PROBLEMS

1. Use the scenario analysis of the following portfolio to answer questions a to g by using the excel spreadsheet template on Active Learning

SCENARIO	PROBABILITY	STOCK FUND RATE OF RETURN	BOND FUND RATE OF RETURN
Recession	0.35	-9.0%	5.0%
Normal	0.40	6.0%	7.5%
Boom	0.25	28.0%	-6.5%

   a. Determine the **mean return** for the stock fund
   b. Determine the **mean return** for the bond fund.
   c. Find the **standard deviation** of returns on the stock fund
   d. Find the **standard deviation** of returns bond fund.
   e. Determine the **mean return** on a combined portfolio (stocks "s" and bonds "b") that consists of 50% in the stock fund and 50% in the bond fund.
   f. Calculate the **standard deviation** of the combined portfolio
   g. Calculate the **correlation** of the combined portfolio

2. Use the following portfolio information to answer questions a to d:

ASSETS	PORTFOLIO ALLOCATION %	EXPECTED RATE OF RETURN	EXPECTED STANDARD DEVIATION
Risk-Free Assets			
T-Bills	20%	2.0%	0
Risky Assets			
Bonds	50%	6.0%	10%
Stocks	30%	20.0%	34%

   a. Assuming the correlation between stocks and bonds is 0.30, compute the standard deviation of the **combined risky portfolio** (use % and three decimals)
   b. If you had $100,000 to invest in this portfolio, based on the allocation above—including cash—compute the expected $ profit amount. (use two decimals)
   c. If you had $100,000 to invest in this portfolio, based on the allocation above—including cash—compute the expected HPR% (use % and two decimals).
   d. Assuming the correlation between stocks and bonds is negative (-1), compute the standard deviation of the **combined risky portfolio** (use % and two decimals)

ONLINE TEMPLATES & CASE STUDIES

The Excel spreadsheets used in the chapter can be accessed online via Cognella Active Learning platform.

CHAPTER 3

Beta Coefficient, R-Squared, and Regression Analysis

Regression is a powerful tool for forecasting. Economists using it successfully predicted ten out of the last two recessions.

—*Anonymous*

The last two chapters covered the risk and return characteristics of the portfolio over time and over various economic scenarios, as well as how they compared to other asset classes or portfolios of assets. The next level of analysis is to assess the portfolio as compared to other bench markets such as the market. This chapter will specifically focus on the comparative analysis of a portfolio versus the market. Stocks go up and down based on information such as earnings or technical data such as the 200-day average movement of the stock. This chapter will assess the risk or volatility of a portfolio of stocks in order to understand such movements versus market movements and the relationship versus the movements of the market as a whole.

LEARNING OBJECTIVES

After reading this chapter, students will be able to do the following:

- Calculate the beta and understand how these betas are used for quantifying return expectations
- Use regression analysis to compare a given portfolio of stocks as compared to the market
- Understand how to use historical data to assess if the movement of asset values are caused by other factors
- Understand how to differentiate between dependent and independent variables in a linear regression in order to set the return expectation

- Explain the assumptions underlying a linear regression and the regression coefficients and discuss the limitations of regression analysis
- Understand the use of analysis of variance (ANOVA) in regression analysis, interpret ANOVA results, and calculate and interpret F-statistic

REGRESSION ANALYSIS: AN ANALYTICAL INTRODUCTION

Regression analysis is one of the most fundamental methods used by statisticians to compare the movement of one or many variables to each other. This is different than correlation that also calculates periodic change of one value to another. Where the correlation measured from negative −1 to positive 1 designating the direction of the one value to another the beta coefficient is different. Beta measures the sensitivity of the movement of the value or the portfolio of stocks to another value such as the benchmark or a market index.

AUTHOR'S NOTES

We love to compare everything. It's our nature. It puts things in perspective. I once asked an analyst who worked for me at the bank if he would be happy if I awarded him a $1-million bonus. Of course, only 1 year out of college, who would not be? He said, "Are you serious?" I said, "Let's assume I gave you a $1-million bonus, but then how would you feel if I told you I gave everyone else at your level $2 million?" This is the point: He would usually be ecstatic to get such a large and unexpected sum of money as his first-year bonus. In his mind, he compared it to his very low expectation of what a first-year analyst, just out of school, should receive. Once, however, I introduced the fact that his $1 million would have been the lowest bonus paid compared to what his colleagues were receiving, his excitement and expectation automatically changed dramatically. I was trying to show that analysts, statisticians, physicists, chemists, mathematicians, and even Albert Einstein talked about relativity and the comparison of one event to another. Therefore, statisticians began providing methods to predict if the movement of one element is dependent on the movement of another element and to what extent. I always wondered if I ran a regression analysis of my employees' productivity and bonus received and ran another after their expectation changed what the results would be. This mathematical formula was developed in the early 1800s from one of my favorite mathematicians, Carl Friedrich Gauss. Gauss was brilliant. He introduced the method called least of squares, which is used extensively by investment bankers today to calculate the market beta coefficient.

KEY TAKEAWAYS

- A portfolio analyst often needs to examine the relationship between two or more variables.
- A regression analysis is used for estimating when one variable causes the other or when one is dependent on the other. Such an estimate can be useful for predicting investment value of one variable based on the value of the other variable such as the market.
- At perfect negative correlation - basically negative 1 - between two asset classes or two portfolios there will almost definitely be opportunities for efficiencies if the investor combines these assets or portfolios. In this case, the investor could benefit from the average return between the two asset classes or portfolios and at the same time minimize the standalone standard deviations to a lower combined one therefore reducing risk.
- The relationship between average return and combined standard deviation is the basis for introducing the concept of the Sharpe Ratio that will be discussed in later chapters.

INTRODUCTION TO LINEAR REGRESSION AND BETA COEFFICIENT

The objective for using a linear regression model in statistics is to analyze the straight-line relationship between two variables. The relationship can be explained as follows:

$$y = \beta_0 + \beta_1 x + e$$

where y is the dependent variable or response variable, x is the independent variable or explanatory variable, and β_0 is the y-intercept. The y-intercept is the value of y when x = 0, and β_1 is the slope of the line. β_1 gives the amount of change in y for every unit change in x. Finally, e is the random error. The random error is included under the premise that analysts are never perfectly precise in their analyses of predicting future outcomes. Many financial models that use regression analysis to predict future values or returns do not include the error calculation. The regression analysis on Excel uses the statistical concept of least squares, a method that seeks the coefficients β_0 and β_1 such as that

$$y = \beta_0 + \beta_1 x.$$

The regression analysis estimates the average value of the dependent variable (*y*), such as the value of the portfolio when the independent variable (*x*), such as the market index, is

FIGURE 3.1 GRAPHS OF VARIOUS BETA (β) LEVELS

fixed. Let's say that the average market index had a monthly average return of 1% and you are convinced that the market movements, up or down, affect the value of the portfolio, which is usually explained as a multiple. Let us assume 2%, which means that every time the market goes up or down by 1.0%, the value of the portfolio or the specific stock moves twice that amount in the same direction (a multiple 2.0x). We will run a regression analysis to calculate first if there is indeed a strong dependent relationship and then attempt to estimate how much of is affected by what is called the beta (β_1). The beta coefficient (β_1), called in statistics the slope, can be calculated by using linear regression.

Figure 3.1 demonstrates the relationship of various portfolios of stocks as compared to the market index. At beta 1, the portfolio moves exactly at the same pace as the market. Portfolios of stocks that have beta of 2 are moving up and down twice as much as the market. High beta portfolios or individual stocks could be technology companies that have higher volatility than the market. Companies with high beta expect to give you higher return than the market but they carry higher risk. Portfolios with 0.5 beta are less volatile than the market by half. Stocks with less than 1 beta include utility companies, which will not move as much as the market will and are viewed as more conservative investments. Portfolios of beta of zero (0) are usually are investments that, no matter the volatility of the market, could offer a return at a fixed rate, such as treasury bonds. Portfolios or stocks with negative beta (−1) or (−2) represent investments with contrarian views against the market. Examples of negative beta could be investments in gold, which acts as a hedge against inflation, or investments that will benefit if the market drops.

An example of a historical performance of a stock as compared to the performance of the stock market, using the S&P 500 Index, is demonstrated in Figure 3.2.

BLOOMBERG DEFINITION OF BETA

Adjusted beta vs. raw beta: The beta of a stock can be presented as either an adjusted beta or a raw beta. A raw beta is obtained from the linear regression of a stock's historical data. Raw beta, also known as historical beta, is based on the observed relationship between the security's return and the returns of an index.

The adjusted beta is an estimate of a security's future beta. Adjusted beta is initially derived from historical data but modified by the assumption that a security's true beta will move toward the market average of 1 over time. The formula used to adjust beta is (0.67) x raw beta + (0.33) x 1.0.

Bloomberg equity codes:

- BETA: Historical beta
- COMP: Comparative total returns

REGRESSION ANALYSIS, R-SQUARED, AND THE ANALYSIS OF VARIANCE (ANOVA) USING EXCEL

Figure 3.2 shows the regression analysis using Excel for comparing the portfolio returns versus the market index returns, as illustrated previously in figure 3.1. The Excel regression analysis yields three-part outputs:

1. **Regression statistics:** R-squared and the standard error.
2. **Analysis of variance (ANOVA) between the two variables.** The ANOVA shows the degrees of freedom (df), calculates the sum of squares (SS), the mean squares, the F statistic, and significance F. The ANOVA shows whether there are any statistically significant differences between the means of two or more variables.

FIGURE 3.2 HISTORICAL ANALYSIS

	Returns		Deviations from Average Return		Product from Deviation	Product from Return
	[?]	[?]	y−y	x−x	(y−y)·(x−x)	(x−x)↑2
	Stocks %	S&P Index %	Stocks %	S&P Index %	%	%
Year -12	-6.50	-4.60	-18.18	-9.82	178.42	96.37
Year -11	-13.20	-11.30	-24.88	-16.52	410.85	272.80
Year -10	-8.90	-5.00	-20.58	-10.22	210.21	104.38
Year -9	25.00	12.00	13.33	6.78	90.39	46.01
Year -8	48.50	23.00	36.83	17.78	654.87	316.25
Year -7	37.60	25.00	25.93	19.78	512.88	391.38
Year -6	10.50	1.00	-1.18	-4.22	4.95	17.78
Year -5	7.20	4.50	-4.48	-0.72	3.21	0.51
Year -4	-5.60	1.00	-17.28	-4.22	72.84	17.78
Year -3	17.50	3.00	5.83	-2.22	-12.91	4.91
Year -2	21.50	12.00	9.83	6.78	66.65	46.01
Year -1	6.50	2.00	-5.18	-3.22	16.65	10.35
					2209.01	1324.54
Average Return	**11.68**	**5.22**				
Standard Deviation	19.20	10.97			Beta (β)	**1.6678**

Σ↑▒[(y−y)·(x−x)]

EXCEL FORMULAS

Slope (β)=	*1.6678*	*Relationship between Dependent Y with Indepent X*
Forecast =	*4.6426*	*Predicts value of y given a value of x=1%*
Standard Error =	*6.0923*	*Predicts the standard error y-value for each x in the regression*

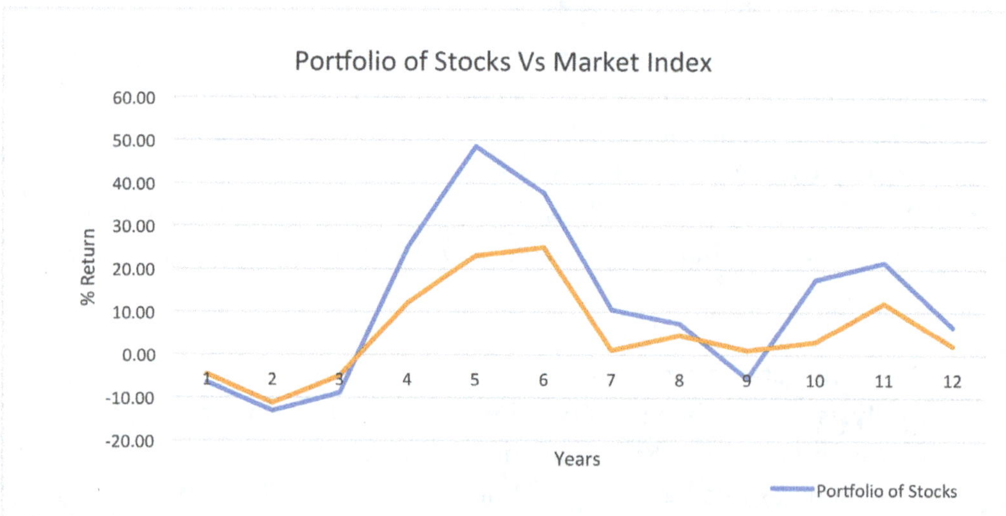

FIGURE 3.3 REGRESSION SUMMARY ANALYSIS

Regression Statistics	
Multiple R	0.953139
R Square	0.908474
Adjusted R Square	0.899322
Standard Error	6.092286
Observations	12

Analysis of Variance (ANOVA)	*df*	*SS*	*MS*	*F*	*Significance F*
Regression	1	3684.083055	3684.083055	99.25877166	1.64467E-06
Residual	10	371.1594445	37.11594445		
Total	11	4055.2425			

Slope (beta)	*Coefficients*	*Standard Error*	*t-Stat*	*P-value*	*Lower 95%*	*Upper 95%*	*Lower 95.0%*	*Upper 95.0%*
Intercept	2.974868822	1.963560699	1.515037871	0.160712968	-1.40021706	7.349954704	-1.40021706	7.349954704
X Variable 1 (Beta Slope)	1.667756775	0.167397229	9.96286965	1.64467E-06	1.294772505	2.040741046	1.294772505	2.040741046

3. **Regression coefficients:** The slope or beta coefficient, the t test and upper/lower 95% limits "within" the group variability and "between" the group variability. The t test is another measurement for comparing the samples. The t test is more effective if there is a comparison of two variables.

Regression Statistics

***Multiple R*: The multiple R, which is measured between 0 to 1, reflects the correlation coefficient of the two variables. It tells the analyst how strong the linear regression is**. Figure 3.3 shows a relatively strong correlation between the portfolio and the market index at 0.95. Value 1 represents a perfect correlation and a value of zero means no relationship at all.

R-squared: R-squared (r^2), also called coefficient of determination, measures how many points fall on the regression line between the two variables. Figure 3.3 shows $r^2 = 0.908$. This means that approximately 91% of the variation of the portfolio values (y values) can be explain by the market index (x-values). The r^2 is relatively strong at 90% because it means that more than 90% of the data fits the model—one of the first numbers the analyst looks at to determine if the data can be compared more accurately. A low r^2 might make the regression analysis irrelevant, so using a beta to determine the expected return, for example, could cause a problem for the analyst. R-Squared can also be calculated by squaring correlation result of two variables ($Correl^2$).

Adjusted R-squared: This number reflects a more accurate r^2 if the number of variables used are more than one.

Standard error: The standard error in a regression analysis measures how precise the regression coefficient is. In other words, it tells the analyst how spread out the y variables are around the mean (average). Looking at the standard error in figure 3.3, it reflects that the data is widely spread, showing that the average deviation from the regression line is estimated at 6.1%. The smaller the standard error, the closer the values are to the regression line.

Observations: Number of observations in the analysis. Figure 3.3 shows 12 representing the 12 years of historical performance for both the portfolio and market index annual returns.

ANOVA

Degrees of freedom (df): When calculating historical data, the average standard deviation of each of the variables is based on the number of observations minus one (n – 1).

Between-group variability and sum of squares: When looking for comparing two samples—in this case, the portfolio value and market index—there could be an overlap in the date. This is where the portfolio could have had the same returns as the index at a few specific times. If the analyst plots the data into a normal distribution and compares each variable to the grand mean between the two variables (the average of both variables), it could calculate the between-group variability, which is the distance between the two means as illustrated in figure 3.3.

Within-group variability and mean squares: If the analyst plots the data into a normal distribution and compares each variable to the grand mean within the two variables it could calculate the within-group variability, which is the distance between the two means, as illustrated in figure 3.4.

F statistic or significance F: The F statistic or significance F and sometimes called the F ratio, is the number that measures if the means of different samples are significantly different. The lower the number, the more similar the sample means are. Figure 3.3 and figure 3.4 show that the between-group variability is smaller than within-group variability by a factor of 10x (37.1 versus 371.2), making the F ratio smaller. The 99.25 shown previously in figure 3.3 does not mean much unless you had to compare this portfolio to another portfolio and then compare each to stock market index (independent variable). This will give the analyst a reference on how close the average return performance of each portfolio is to the average market return performance. Unlike the t distribution (explained later), the F distribution does not have any negative values because between- and within-group variability are always positive because both are squared.

FIGURE 3.4 ANALYSIS OF VARIANCE (ANOVA)

Returns		Sorted	
[?]	[?]	[?]	[?]
Stocks %	S&P Index %	Stocks %	S&P Index %
-6.50	-4.60	-13.20	-11.30
-13.20	-11.30	-8.90	-5.00
-8.90	-5.00	-6.50	-4.60
25.00	12.00	-5.60	1.00
48.50	23.00	6.50	1.00
37.60	25.00	7.20	2.00
10.50	1.00	10.50	3.00
7.20	4.50	17.50	4.50
-5.60	1.00	21.50	12.00
17.50	3.00	25.00	12.00
21.50	12.00	37.60	23.00
6.50	2.00	48.50	25.00
11.68	5.22	Average Return	
19.20	10.97	Standard Deviation	

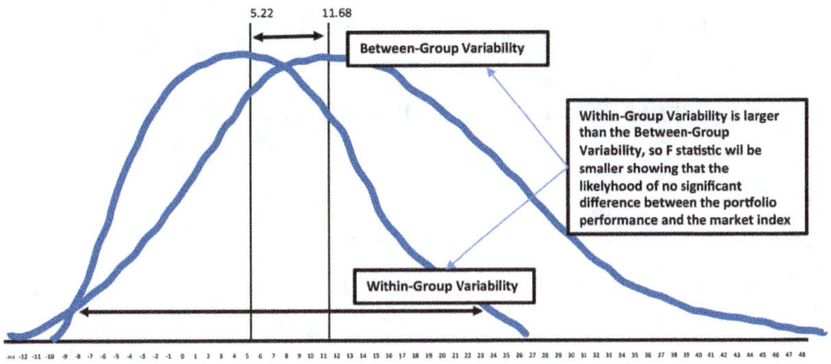

Regression Coefficients

Beta coefficient (slope): As mentioned, the linear regression analysis is basically the linear relationship between the independent (x) and dependent (y) variables expressed in the equation $y = \alpha + \beta x$, called the regression line. The first calculation coefficient is beta coefficient (β), also known as the slope. In both figures 3.1 and 3.2, the beta (β) shown is calculated at 1.66x. Assuming x represents the market index return and assuming the constant alpha coefficient (α) is zero, then the beta (β) represents the multiplier effect that calculates the portfolio or company-specific expected return (y). The beta (β) results from the regression analysis can be used to predict the portfolio's expected return. The following chapter will closely examine this model for predicting return expectation, the capital asset pricing model (CAPM). Though CAPM measures a slightly different result, it uses the same regression line concept to predict the expected return of a specific stock or a portfolio of stocks.

Standard error: The standard error is similar to standard deviation measuring the spread or the deviation from the data's average. Though both are calculated the same, the standard error uses smaller statistical sample data, and the standard deviation uses the entire population data (aka parameters) to calculate the difference from the average.

t test: The t test or t statistic is used when the analyst decides to accept or reject the null hypothesis—basically that the movements or performance of the dependent variable (y) do depend on the movement of the independent variable (x). In our example, the portfolio value is looking to see if there is systemic risk. The t test is used for a small sample and is more effective if it compares two variables. The higher the t, the more evidence the analyst must show that there is significant difference between the combined average of the two variables.

***p* value:** The p value, or probability value, is expressed from 0–1 and it measures the percentage difference in the combined average of the variables. Figure 3.2 shows 0.16 or 16.0% variation, relatively small percentage.

Lower and upper 95% confidence intervals: The confidence intervals are expressed as a percentage, in this case 95%. It means that the results are expected to match 95% of the time. In a normal distribution, the performance of the portfolio that is based on historical returns is predicted to stay within 95% of the range. The upper represents the positive or right side of the normal distribution graph and the lower represents the negative or the left side of the normal distribution graph (see figure 3.5).

FIGURE 3.5 NORMAL DISTRIBUTION GRAPH

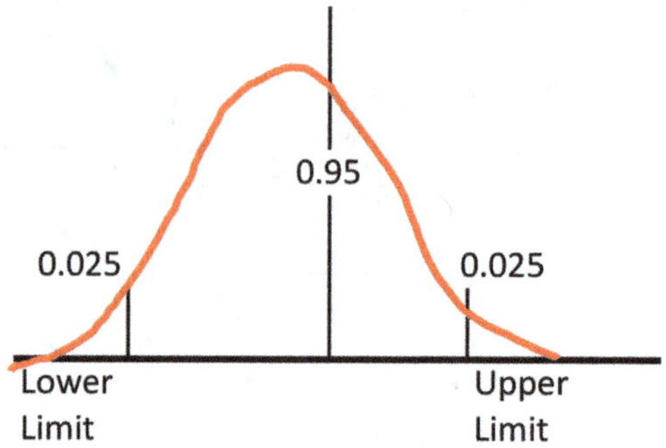

EXCEL FORMULAS REVIEWED

1. Annual rate of return: = IRR (Range of cash flows including the initial investment as negative)
2. Average of returns: = AVERAGE (Range of periodic returns)
3. Variance: VAR (Range of data)
4. Standard deviation: STDEV (Range of data)
5. Covariance: COVARIANCE.P (Range 1, Range 2)
6. Correlation: = CORREL (Range 1, Range 2)
7. R-squared: = RSQ (Range 1, Range 2)

Analysis of Variance (ANOVA) and Regression Analysis Using Excel:
Data tab/Analysis group, click Data Analysis/Regression Analysis, then select the INPUT Y Range (Dependent Variables) and INPUT X Range (Independent Variable)

CASE STUDY

PORTFOLIO OF STOCKS AND BONDS: ZEUS FUND I CASE STUDY

The previous two chapters focused primarily on the risk and return of the Zeus Fund I portfolio, which includes stocks and bonds and how each of these asset classes have performed against each other. It also attempted to find the right mix in order to achieve efficiency and optimization based on the correlational phenomenon. This chapter will take the Zeus Fund I performance and compare each asset class to the equivalent index such as the S&P 500 Index for stocks and the Bloomberg Barclays U.S. Aggregate Bond Index (Bloomberg Bond Index) for bonds. This comparative analysis should establish the beta coefficient (β) for each asset class. This beta (β) will then be used for basic portfolio analysis in later chapters. Figure 3.6 shows the 7-month performance of each of the stocks and bonds, as well as the historical return of the stock index benchmark (S&P 500) and bond index benchmark (Bloomberg Bond Index).

Figure 3.7 shows the betas between the stock portfolio versus the stock market benchmark, the bond portfolio versus the bond market benchmark, and the combined Zeus Fund I portfolio of stocks and bonds versus the weighted benchmark of the stock and bond index.

FIGURE 3.6 ZEUS FUND I

STOCK AND BOND PORTFOLIO

Performance	0	1	2	3	4	5	6	7
Symbol		July 1 20x1	Aug 1 20x1	Sep 1 20x1	Oct 1 20x1	Nov 1 20x1	Dec 1 20x1	Jan 2 20x1
Stocks		-1.0%	6.2%	3.5%	3.5%	3.0%	7.2%	1.2%
Bonds		1.9%	0.5%	0.8%	0.5%	0.6%	-0.1%	-0.4%
Total Stock Value	81,757	82,600	82,200	84,050	85,000	85,450	87,300	92,275
Total Bonds Value	97,495	95,650	93,620	97,035	101,575	102,110	101,410	97,325
Total Portfolio Value	179,253	178,250	175,820	181,085	186,575	187,560	188,710	189,600
Portfolio % change		-0.6%	-1.4%	3.0%	3.0%	0.5%	0.6%	0.5%
Cummulative % Change		-0.6%	-1.9%	1.1%	4.1%	4.6%	5.2%	5.7%
Bench Mark: S&P 500	2,430.1	2,429.0	2,476.4	2,476.6	2,529.1	2,579.4	2,644.2	2,644.2
% Increase / Decrease		0.0%	1.9%	0.0%	2.1%	2.0%	2.5%	0.0%
Bench Mark: Bloomberg Barclays US Aggreagate Bond Index	2,021.6	2,041.8	2,034.8	2,044.5	2,039.5	2,039.5	2,042.8	2,042.8
% Increase / Decrease		1.0%	-0.3%	0.5%	-0.2%	0.0%	0.2%	0.0%
Weighted Combined Index	2,207.9	2,221.2	2,241.2	2,245.0	2,262.6	2,285.5	2,321.0	2,335.5
% Increase / Decrease		0.6%	0.9%	0.2%	0.8%	1.0%	1.6%	0.6%
Stocks (Weights)	45.6%	46.3%	46.8%	46.4%	45.6%	45.6%	46.3%	48.7%
Bonds (Weights)	54.4%	53.7%	53.2%	53.6%	54.4%	54.4%	53.7%	51.3%

7-month Portfolio Performance

STOCKS		BONDS		COMBINED PORTFOLIO	
Average	3.3777%	Average	0.5428%	Average	1.8613%
Standard Deviation	2.7976%	Standard Deviation	0.7477%	Variance	0.0185%
Average % of Portfolio	46.5076%	Average % of Portfolio	53.4924%	Standard Deviation	1.3612%

7-month Benchmark Performance

STOCK INDEX BENCHMARK		BOND INDEX BENCHMARK		WEIGHTED INDEX BENCHMARK	
Average	1.2197%	Average	0.1506%	Average	0.8069%
Standard Deviation	1.1664%	Standard Deviation	0.4614%	Standard Deviation	0.4268%
Average % of Portfolio	46.5076%	Average % of Portfolio	53.4924%	Average % of Portfolio	100.0000%

FIGURE 3.7 ZEUS FUND I

Beta (β) Coefficient Analysis

STOCK AND BOND PORTFOLIO

STOCK PORTFOLIO						
	y	x	[y - Avg(y)]	[x-Avg(x)]	[y-Avg(y)].[x- Avg(x)]	[x-Avg(x)]^2
	Portfolio	S&P Index	Portfolio	S&P Index	Product Deviation	Product Deviation
Month 1	-1.0%	0.0%	-4.4%	-1.3%	0.05554%	0.01595%
Month 2	6.2%	1.9%	2.9%	0.7%	0.02086%	0.00532%
Month 3	3.5%	0.0%	0.1%	-1.2%	-0.00133%	0.01468%
Month 4	3.5%	2.1%	0.1%	0.9%	0.00076%	0.00816%
Month 5	3.0%	2.0%	-0.3%	0.8%	-0.00265%	0.00588%
Month 6	7.2%	2.5%	3.8%	1.3%	0.04966%	0.01677%
Month 7	1.2%	0.0%	-2.1%	-1.2%	0.02615%	0.01488%
Mean Avg=	3.4%	1.2%			0.14898%	0.08162%
Stand. Dev.=	2.8%	1.2%			**Beta=**	**1.8251175**

BOND PORTFOLIO						
	y	x	[y - Avg(y)]	[x-Avg(x)]	[y-Avg(y)].[x- Avg(x)]	[x-Avg(x)]^2
	Bonds	Bond Index	Bonds	Bond Index	Product Deviation	Product Deviation
Month 1	1.9%	1.0%	1.4%	0.8%	0.01178%	0.00721%
Month 2	0.5%	-0.3%	-0.1%	-0.5%	0.00025%	0.00244%
Month 3	0.8%	0.5%	0.2%	0.3%	0.00079%	0.00109%
Month 4	0.5%	-0.2%	-0.1%	-0.4%	0.00028%	0.00158%
Month 5	0.6%	0.0%	0.1%	-0.1%	-0.00015%	0.00022%
Month 6	-0.1%	0.2%	-0.6%	0.0%	-0.00008%	0.00000%
Month 7	-0.4%	0.0%	-1.0%	-0.2%	0.00148%	0.00023%
Mean Avg=	0.5%	0.2%			0.01435%	0.01277%
Stand. Dev.=	0.7%	0.5%			**Beta=**	**1.12381**

COMBINED PORTFOLIO						
	y	x			y . x	x^2
Portfolio Weight Stocks	Combined Portfolio	Weighted Benchmark	Combined Portfolio	Weighted Benchmark	Product Deviation	Product Deviation
45.6%	0.6%	0.6%	-1.3%	-0.2%	0.00259%	0.00041%
46.3%	3.2%	0.9%	1.3%	0.1%	0.00120%	0.00009%
46.8%	2.0%	0.2%	0.2%	-0.6%	-0.00117%	0.00404%
46.4%	1.9%	0.8%	0.0%	0.0%	0.00000%	0.00001%
45.6%	1.7%	1.0%	-0.1%	0.2%	-0.00027%	0.00042%
46.3%	3.3%	1.6%	1.4%	0.8%	0.01072%	0.00563%
48.7%	0.4%	0.6%	-1.5%	-0.2%	0.00273%	0.00034%
Mean Avg=	1.9%	0.8%			0.01581%	0.01093%
Stand. Dev.=	1.1%	0.4%			**Beta=**	**1.4463175**

FIGURE 3.8 INTERNAL

Regression Analysis

STOCK PORTFOLIO

Regression Statistics	
Multiple R	0.693441209
R Square	0.48086071
Adjusted R Square	0.377032852
Standard Error	0.005901349
Observations	7

ANOVA

	df	SS	MS	F	Significance F
Regression	1	0.00016129	0.00016129	4.631326501	0.084026789
Residual	5	0.00017413	3.48259E-05		
Total	6	0.00033542			

	Coefficients	Standard Error	t Stat	P-value	Lower 95%	Upper 95%	Lower 95.0%	Upper 95.0%
Intercept	0.003735656	0.002365108	1.579486358	0.17505993	-0.002344048	0.009815361	-0.002344048	0.009815361
X Variable 1	1.123811607	0.522204745	2.152051696	0.084026789	-0.218558425	2.466181638	-0.218558425	2.466181638

BOND PORTFOLIO

Regression Statistics	
Multiple R	0.760919562
R Square	0.578998579
Adjusted R Square	0.494798295
Standard Error	0.019884755
Observations	7

ANOVA

	df	SS	MS	F	Significance F
Regression	1	0.00271897	0.00271897	6.876444478	0.046967403
Residual	5	0.001977017	0.000395403		
Total	6	0.004695988			

	Coefficients	Standard Error	t Stat	P-value	Lower 95%	Upper 95%	Lower 95.0%	Upper 95.0%
Intercept	0.0115171	0.011337785	1.015815743	0.356323521	-0.017627604	0.040661804	-0.017627604	0.040661804
X Variable 1	1.825117514	0.695999395	2.622297557	0.046967403	0.035994111	3.614240916	0.035994111	3.614240916

COMBINED PORTFOLIO

Regression Statistics	
Multiple R	0.547926404
R Square	0.300223344
Adjusted R Square	0.160268013
Standard Error	0.010324207
Observations	7

ANOVA

	df	SS	MS	F	Significance F
Regression	1	0.000228649	0.000228649	2.145136893	0.202908038
Residual	5	0.000532946	0.000106589		
Total	6	0.000761595			

	Coefficients	Standard Error	t Stat	P-value	Lower 95%	Upper 95%	Lower 95.0%	Upper 95.0%
Intercept	0.00696525	0.008872453	0.785042187	0.467976732	-0.015842116	0.029772615	-0.015842116	0.029772615
X Variable 1	1.446317549	0.987497829	1.464628585	0.202908038	-1.092126434	3.984761531	-1.092126434	3.984761531

Figure 3.8 shows the regression analysis, ANOVA, and regression coefficient. Figure 3.8 demonstrates that the betas on a standalone basis are 1.12 and 1.82 for the stock and bond portfolios, as compared with their corresponding benchmarks. By combining the portfolio and adjusting for the weights, the beta is at 1.44—basically the weighted average of betas between stocks and bonds. The R squares are relatively low, below 60%, suggesting that the analyst should be warned that the data could be not as effective.

PROBLEMS

1. Stock A has a beta of 1.5 and Stock B has a beta of 0.8. Which of the following statements must be true about these securities? (Assume the market is in equilibrium.)
   a. When held in isolation, Stock A has greater risk than Stock B.
   b. Stock B would be a more desirable addition to a portfolio than Stock A.
   c. Stock A would be a more desirable addition to a portfolio than Stock B.
   d. The expected return on Stock A will be greater than that on Stock B.
   e. The expected return on Stock B will be greater than that on Stock A.

2. Calculate the **beta** given the data below (use Figure 3.7 as a spreadsheet to calculate Beta)—(use 4 decimals and round up/down):

YEARS	ABC INC. STOCK CHANGE %	S&P INDEX CHANGE %
1	12.0%	10.0%
2	22.0%	18.0%
3	15.0%	10.0%
4	-15.0%	-12.0%
5	7.0%	4.0%
6	13.0%	9.0%
7	-8.0%	-5.0%
8	22.0%	17.0%
9	35.0%	19.0%
10	19.0%	10.0%

3. Calculate the **beta** given the data below (use 4 decimals and round up/down):

YEARS	XYZ INC. STOCK	S&P 500 INDEX
1	$35.50	2,525
2	$32.25	2,415
3	$42.50	2,700
4	$45.00	2,710
5	$32.00	2,385
6	$46.00	2,825
7	$57.00	2,925
8	$51.00	2,625

4. Run an ANOVA, calculate the **R-squared value**, and perform a regression analysis using Excel, given the following information (use 4 decimals and round up/down):

YEARS	CDE INC. % CHANGE	S&P 500 INDEX % CHANGE
1	5.0%	-1.0%
2	4.0%	-1.0%
3	-4.0%	-2.0%
4	3.0%	3.0%
5	-2.0%	-1.0%
6	12.0%	4.0%
7	22.0%	8.0%
8	26.0%	3.0%
9	-26.0%	-2.0%
10	-5.0%	2.0%

ONLINE TEMPLATES & CASE STUDIES

The Excel spreadsheets used in the chapter can be accessed online via Cognella Active Learning platform.

CHAPTER 4

Sharpe Ratio, CAPM, Jensen's Alpha, Treynor Measure, and M-Square

This chapter continues to emphasize the risk-and-return relationship. In previous chapters, the risk-and-return characteristics of a given portfolio were measured in comparison to both to other asset classes and the market benchmarks. This chapter will re-emphasize these comparisons by introducing other ways to compare results via performance measurements ratios such as the Sharpe ratio, Jensen's Alpha, M-square, and the Treynor measure, among others that are used extensively on Wall Street to gain valuable insight using comparisons.

LEARNING OBJECTIVES

After reading this chapter, students will be able to do the following:

- Calculate and use various methods for evaluating investment performance
- Determine which performance ratios are appropriate in a variety of investment situations
- Apply various analytical tools to identify portfolio strategy and measure expectations
- Understand how to differentiate between dependent and independent variables in a linear regression and use them to set return expectation
- Determine how to allocate various assets classes within a portfolio to achieve portfolio optimization

PORTFOLIO MANAGEMENT PERFORMANCE MEASUREMENT: AN OVERVIEW

There are many ways to measure the performance of a portfolio. The most common method is to compare the performance against last year or against last few years, often called trend analysis. Investors will always ask how the portfolio returns are performing from year to year. However, displaying the trend analysis to an investor who is in the process of deciding whether to come into the fund is not enough. The investor will demand a comparative analysis of portfolio performance against other portfolios, or against other asset classes, or the market. These comparative measures include ratios such as the Sharpe ratio, CAPM, Jensen's Alpha, and Treynor measure—all these are ratios that give the investor comfort about how the portfolio performed against the market or other assets.

AUTHOR'S NOTES

In the spring of 2006, just 2 years before the worst financial crisis the United States has faced since the 1930s, I visited a few European countries to promote a new investment opportunity for managers who only invested in stocks, bonds, and real estate. The new investment opportunity, already established in the United States, was to invest equity in various U.S. collateral loan obligations (CLO). The most difficult task for me was to convince these asset managers to accept an average 10–12% annual returns when their portfolios, that already consisted of stocks, bonds, and real estate holdings, enjoyed returns in excess of 30% per year for the last 3–4 years. I was told that it was too much work for them to include a new opportunity that would give returns three times lower than their existing portfolios. My marketing pitch of course was that CLOs had an unlevered return of approximately 6%, with a standard deviation measuring volatility of 2.0%. The relationship between return and risk was among the best compared to their holdings. I was also showing very low correlations with other asset classes such as stock, bonds, gold and other commodity investing, which of course can help any portfolio achieve higher efficiency (additional return with lower risk). I am not sure if it was just the timing of my marketing pitch, or if it was behavioral factors or how the managers got paid their bonuses, driven by total return, but I failed to convince them to invest in my product. I failed to convince them to diversify a portion of their portfolio into a lower volatility asset class in case the markets turned south. Just two years later, these managers had the worst performance ever contacting me to reintroduce the CLO opportunity which on a relative basis did much better during the crisis. Evaluating performance of the portfolio based on average return alone is not very useful. These returns need to be adjusted for risk. This relationship between return and volatility, explained in previous chapters, is the basis for introducing other ratios, such as the Sharpe ratio or Jensen's alpha.

KEY TAKEAWAYS

1. A portfolio analyst needs to value the portfolio based on trends, market benchmarks, and expectations.
2. Evaluating performance of the portfolio based on an average return alone is not that useful. The analyst needs to adjust such returns to risk before they can be meaningfully compared.
3. Many portfolio value measurement ratios are set up to give you a comprehensive understanding of the security's performance as follows:
   - The Sharpe ratio measures the excess return to standard deviation
   - The Treynor ratio measures the excess return beta
   - Jensen's alpha is the excess return over the market index
   - M-square focuses on total volatility as a measured of adjusted risk compared to the market benchmark

SETTING UP THE BASIS FOR PORTFOLIO MEASUREMENT: RE-INTRODUCTION TO BASIC RETURN CHARACTERISTICS

Repeating what was discussed in chapter 1, it is important to mention the conventional theories that measure performance returns as a basis for introducing other ratios.

AVERAGE RATE OF RETURN

The first ratio introduced was the holding period return (HPR). In its simplest form it is the best approach to calculate the ongoing return of any asset class or portfolio. **The numerator represents all the cash activity of an investment, including the trading cash inflows and outflows, any dividends received minus any taxes paid, and any hedging/additional costs over the denominator, representing the initial investment as follows:**

$$\text{HPR} = \frac{\text{CF}}{\text{I}}$$

where **CF** is the net cash flow (inflow and outflow) during the investment period and I is the initial investment. For example, an investor buys the stock for $100 and sells it for $120 while also receiving a $2 dividend per share during the holding period. The cash flow in the numerator will be $120 of proceeds for selling the stock, plus $2 of the cash dividend received (cash inflow) minus the initial investment of $100 (cash outflow). The net cash flow will be $22 ($120 + $2 − $100). The HPR can then be calculated by dividing the net cash flow of \$22 by the initial investment of \$100, resulting in a 22% return or HPR:

$$\frac{(120-100+2)}{100}=\frac{22}{100}=0.22=22\%$$

For a quick analysis of expected return, the HPR ratio, which represents the relationship between cash flow and initial investment, can be found in many applications on various asset classes as described in chapter 1.

The next average return measurement introduced in chapter 1 is annual return. This is partly due to portfolio managers having access to annual returns when comparing investments to the market benchmark and them being readily available for trend analysis. Additionally, because many portfolios can be levered and include margin loans of debt funds that are structured with set annual costs, it becomes easier to compare portfolios on an annual basis. In turn, we use the internal rate of return (IRR). The IRR method adds all annual HPRs that account for each annual activity found in the numerator to different annual investment activities in the denominator and is then weighted by year to represent an average annual return, as shown in figure 4.1.

However, simply comparing two asset classes to each other or to the bench mark using the average return does not tell the whole story about how these asset classes have performed. To create a more effective comparison, they need to be adjusted for

FIGURE 4.1 INTERNAL RATE OF RETURN

Dollar Weighted Return (Even Annual Payments)

	0	1	2	3	4
Net CF ($)	-100	5	5	5	105

Excel		B	C	D	E	F
10	IRR	0	1	2	3	4
11	5.00%	-100	5	5	5	105

=IRR(B11:F11)

Dollar Weighted Return (Uneven Annual Payments

	0	1	2	3	4
Net CF ($)	-100	-9	-5	26	110

1 = + (-0.1 / (1+IRR) + (-0.5 / (1+ IRR) ^2 + (0.8 / (1+ IRR)^3) + (1.0 / (1+IRR)^4

Excel		B	C	D	E	F
10	IRR	0	1	2	3	4
11	4.96%	-100	-9	-5	26	110

=IRR(B11:F11)

risk or volatility. Also, these returns need to be calculated after subtracting the risk-free rate. Comparing absolute returns between one year and another will not always reflect a true comparison, as the risk-free rate changes from one year to another. The difference between the absolute return and risk-free rate is called the risk-premium return, which is the basis for many portfolio performance ratios discussed later in this chapter.

SETTING UP THE BASIS FOR PORTFOLIO MEASUREMENT: RE-INTRODUCTION TO BASIC VOLATILITY CHARACTERISTICS

Again, repeating what was discussed in chapter 1, it is important to re-introduce the conventional theories of measuring portfolio performance returns and how they relate to their volatility—the basic measurement of risk. Two portfolios with the same average return do not necessarily make these portfolios equally successful. Take the following two stocks shown in figure 4.2; they are sorted by minimum to maximum values. Both stocks average $40, but stock A had a larger variance in prices ranging from $20 to $60 as compared to stock B that had prices stay between $30 and $50.

FROM PORTFOLIO EFFICIENCY TO OPTIMIZATION

Chapter 2 covered the process by which the portfolio manager finds the point of efficiency, or efficient frontier. This represents the point with the highest possible return and the lowest possible risk. Once that point is determined, the portfolio manager's next task is to move from efficiency to optimization. Optimization can be achieved by moving from the efficient frontier and seeking additional return with a minimum rate of change in risk. From

FIGURE 4.2 COMPARING STOCKS

Same average return with different variance

	Stock A $ price	Stock B $ price
Range	$ 20.00	$ 30.00
	$ 30.00	$ 35.00
	$ 40.00	$ 40.00
	$ 50.00	$ 45.00
	$ 60.00	$ 50.00
Average	$ 40.00	$ 40.00
$ Variance (max-min)	$40.00	$20.00
Avg/$Variance	1.00x	2.00x

EFFICIENT FRONTIER → $\frac{\Delta_r}{\Delta\sigma} > 1$ → OPTIMIZATION

the point of efficiency, the portfolio manager is seeking to achieve an even a higher return delta (rate of change), but as discussed, it will also come with higher risk. The optimization point is where the additional return, or the rate of change going from bonds to stocks, is lower than the rate of change of additional risk—basically, higher return delta at a lower risk delta. That achievement is called the optimum point and is the basis of the Sharpe ratio. Figure 4.3 shows a basic illustration of the optimization process.

Figure 4.3 shows that the efficient frontier is achieved at 14% return (R) and 6.0% risk (σ), as the analyst trades out of 100% bonds that have a risk and return of 6% and 8%, respectively, to buy additional stocks. As the analyst trades out of bonds and into stocks, the return is increasing, and the risk is decreasing to the point that the slope of the graph shifts toward higher risk. After achieving the efficient frontier, assuming 60% bonds and 40% stocks, the analyst wants to continue to buy stock and sell bonds in order to seek higher returns. The optimization point is where the rate of change (ΔR) of return is higher than the rate of change (Δσ) of the risk. In this case, a 2.0% higher rate of return is achieved

FIGURE 4.3 FROM EFFICIENCY TO OPTIMIZATION

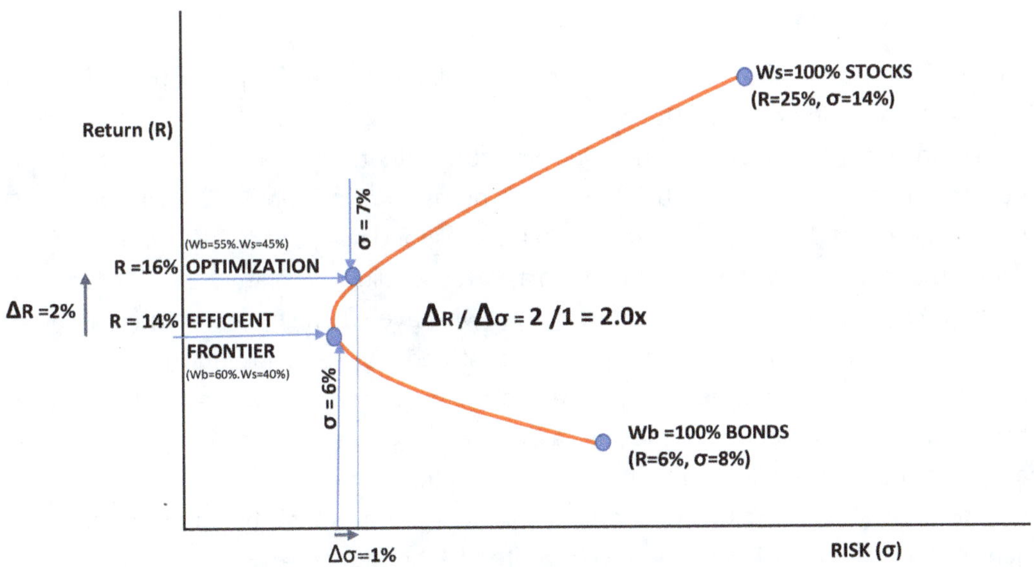

by only giving up 1.0% of standard deviation and is calculated as $\Delta R/\Delta\sigma = 2/1 = 2.0x$, assuming 55% of bonds and 45% of stocks.

The following ratios are the most common ratios used when measuring the performance of a given portfolio. It's important to note, emphasized in chapter 1, that the best way to assess or analyze any asset, in this case the portfolio, is for the analyst to keep answering the following three questions:

1. **How well is the portfolio performing versus last year or the years before?**
2. **How well is the portfolio performing versus other portfolios or the market benchmark?**
3. **How well is the portfolio performing versus expectation given various scenarios?**

SHARPE RATIO

The Sharpe ratio is named after the American economist William Sharpe, a man who devoted all of his adult life to analyzing the relationship between risk and return among various asset classes and compared to their respective markets. The Sharpe ratio, in its basic form, is the relationship between return (numerator) and risk (denominator). The numerator is adjusted to reflect the risk premium, done by taking the absolute rate of return and subtracting the risk-free rate, which, by definition, has little to no risk for the given period. The denominator representing the risk is measured by the volatility of the investment return or the standard deviation of the asset class for the same time period. The Sharpe ratio formula is as follows:

$$SR = \frac{R_P - Rf}{\sigma_P}$$

where, R_P is the absolute return of a given portfolio, Rf is the risk-free rate, and σ_P is the standard deviation of the portfolio.

The resulting number from this Sharpe ratio reflects the relationship between the numerator and denominator, the return and the risk. For example, a Sharpe ratio of 0.5 shows that every 1% of return comes with a corresponding 2% of risk. A Sharpe ratio of 2 shows that every 2% of return comes with a corresponding risk of only 1%. The higher the ratio, the higher the comfort level the analyst will have when seeking additional returns. Of course, even with the result giving a quantified risk-return relationship, it is more important to apply the three-questions assessment rule to determine a better framework for the analysis. This generally includes assessments of this ratio versus years in the past and other portfolios, and if the ratio beat expectation.

The illustration expressed previously in figure 4.3 shows that the optimization point is achieved when the portfolio is broken down to 55% bonds and 45% stocks, thus achieving a 16% return with a 7% standard deviation. Assuming a 3.0% risk-free rate that has a 0% standard deviation, the Sharpe ratio is calculated as follows:

$$\text{at optimization point, } SR = \frac{R_P - Rf}{\sigma_P} = \frac{16-3}{7} = 1.86$$

The calculation shows that every 1.86% increase in return comes with an equivalent 1% of risk. The optimization point is the point with the highest possible Sharpe ratio. Using the same illustration (figure 4.3) to calculate the Sharpe ratio using the efficient frontier risk and return points, the ratio calculates as follows:

$$\text{at efficiency point, } SR = \frac{R_P - Rf}{\sigma_P} = \frac{14-3}{6} = 1.83$$

showing that every 1.83% increase in return has an equivalent 1% of risk even though the efficient frontier, which represents the highest possible return with the lowest possible risk ($R = 14\%$, $\sigma = 6\%$), it does not appear to be the case when introducing the risk-free rate. After the risk premium is calculated, the optimization point has a higher Sharpe Ratio than the efficient frontier.

CAPITAL ASSET PRICING MODEL (CAPM)

Another concept that was extensively developed by William Sharpe in the early 1960s is the capital asset pricing model (CAPM). The CAPM is a formula that was developed to calculate the expected return of any risky asset class (ER_i) as compared to the systematic market risk. This formula will be used extensively in later chapters, not only for portfolio management applications, but also as a discount rate for determining the present value of the equity invested in a firm. The formula is as follows:

$$ER_i = R_f + \beta(ER_m - R_f)$$

where, R_f is the risk-free rate, β is the beta, and ER_m is the expected market return.

If the investor's expectation is risk free, then the formula will be $ER_i = R_f$. If the investor anticipates taking additional risk, then we add the second part of the equation $\beta(ER_m - R_f)$ as it represents the risk premium return, the return above the risk-free rate. This risk premium is adjusted by the beta (β), which represents the multiples of risk as compared to the market. As described in earlier chapters, if the beta (β) equals 1, then the investor expects the set market premium return. If a certain stock is trading at beta (β) of 2, then the expected premium return will be adjusted to be twice as much as the market premium return expectation. If the beta (β) is less than 1, then that specific stock premium return is anticipated to be less than the market premium return.

The objective of CAPM is set as the basis for evaluating if the stock is fairly valued as compared to the market. For example, let's assume that the investor is looking to buy XYZ Inc.'s stock that has a beta (β) of 1.5x, which means that the volatility of such stock is 1.5x the volatility of the total equity market index. If the market is anticipated to grow 10% this year, then the return of such investment should grow at 15% (1.5 x 10%). The CAPM formula adjusts for risk-free rate after establishing the market risk premium return ($ER_m - R_f$) or (10% – R_f), so the expected risk premium return for such stock is 1.5x the market premium. Assuming the risk-free rate is 2%, the expected investment return is calculated at 14% as follows:

$$ER_i = R_f + \beta(ER_m - R_f) = 2\% + 1.5(10\% - 2\%) = 2\% + 12\% = 14\%$$

CAPM is used as the basis for the minimum expectation of an investor who is seeking to evaluate a portfolio of stocks or a single stock adjusted to market fluctuations. Later we will discuss that when valuating investments in specific companies the CAPM is used as a first guideline for the minimum required return before deciding to invest. Any additional return over the calculated CAPM expectation is considered return in excess of the minimum required return. It is an indicator to move forward with the investment, as it highlights an investment with returns in excess of what is readily available in the market. In portfolio theory, this excess is called Jensen's alpha and is covered more in depth in the next section.

JENSEN'S ALPHA RATIO

Jensen's alpha, developed by mutual fund manager Michael Jensen in the late 1960s, **is a formula that determines the average return over (positive alpha) or below (negative alpha) the expectation calculated by the CAPM.** As mentioned previously, CAPM represents the minimum expected return of a portfolio or single stock adjusted to the market expectation. Jensen's alpha, or simply alpha (α), if positive, represents the excess return over CAPM. The formula is as follows:

$$\alpha = R_i - [R_f + \beta(R_m - R_f)] \text{ or } \alpha = R_i - \text{CAPM}$$

where, R_i is the realized return on the investment of the portfolio, R_f is the risk-free rate, β is beta, and R_m is the market index return.

To analyze the performance of an asset manager as compared to other asset managers, the analyst must not only look at the actual portfolio returns but the alpha (α) that managers are generating for their respective portfolio. For example, if two portfolios of investments such as a mutual funds generate 20% return, the next question the analyst will ask these asset managers is what their risk-adjusted return is against the market and whether that return has exceeded the market-adjusted return. Jensen's alpha is one number that could be used to compare these two portfolios. First, if the value is positive, this demonstrates that the analyst beat the market-expected return. The analyst must then figure out who beat the market more efficiently. Using the 20% example, let's assume portfolio Z had beta (βz) of 1.3 and portfolio X had beta (βx) of 1.5. Let's assume the overall market returned 10% and the risk-free rate is 2.0% for that period. The following formulas calculates the alphas for portfolio Z (αz) and portfolio X (αx):

$$\alpha z = R_i - [R_f + \beta(R_m - R_f)] = 20\% - [2\% + 1.3(10\% - 2\%)] = 7.6\%$$

$$\alpha z = 7.6\%$$

$$\alpha x = R_i - [R_f + \beta(R_m - R_f)] = 20\% - [2\% + 1.5(10\% - 2\%)] = 6.0\%$$

$$\alpha x = 6.0\%$$

The alpha for portfolio Z at 7.6% is higher than portfolio X of 6.0%, demonstrating that despite both having beat the market showing positive alpha (α), portfolio Z had a better performance when adjusting for risk, which is determined by the lower beta (β). Let's use another example where portfolio Z shows 19% return and portfolio X shows 20%. By just looking at the total returns, it's obvious at first to conclude that portfolio X has slightly outperformed portfolio Z (20% versus 19%). When calculating the alphas though, we can see that portfolio Z has better performance metrics despite the lower overall return after adjusting for risk, as follows:

$$\alpha z = R_i - [R_f + \beta(R_m - R_f)] = 19\% - [2\% + 1.3\ (10\% - 2\%)] = 6.6\%$$

$$\alpha z = 6.6\%$$

$$\alpha x = R_i - [R_f + \beta(R_m - R_f)] = 20\% - [2\% + 1.5\ (10\% - 2\%)] = 6.0\%$$

$$\alpha x = 6.0\%$$

The cliché "seeking alpha" is a statement that most asset managers like to say when pitching their investment thesis and one number that they represent historically to show their ability to meet or exceed such expectations.

TREYNOR RATIO

Both the Sharpe ratio and Treynor ratio measure the relationship between risk and return. In turn, both ratios have the same numerator but different denominators. The numerator represents premium return (R_p - Rf) and the denominator, though similarly addressing the risk, has slightly a different objective. The Sharpe ratio focuses on the relationship between the portfolio risk premium return and the standard deviation of the portfolio that is expressed as a deviation percentage (0 - 1) from the portfolio mean (average). **The Treynor ratio focuses on the relationship between the portfolio risk premium return**

and the beta (β) of the portfolio. It is expressed in factors (positive or negative) or as a multiple of the market premium risk. The formula is as follows:

$$T = \frac{R_P - Rf}{\beta_P}$$

Jack Treynor, an American economist who is credited with the equation and was awarded for many finance and portfolio management concepts in his career, presented this specific ratio with the objective to measure performance that would be applicable for all investors regardless of their personal risk appetite. In many of his papers, he made suggestions that there were in fact two types of volatility risks: stock market risk and the individual risk of the portfolio or a specific stock, measured by beta (β). The beta coefficient, discussed in previous chapters, is simply the volatility or the line's slope (steepness) of a portfolio compared to the market itself. The higher the line's slope or steepness, the better the risk-return tradeoff.

The Treynor ratio, also known as the reward-to-volatility ratio, is designed to assess the portfolio's performance against the benchmark. Instead of measuring a portfolio return only against the risk-free rate, the ratio examines how well a portfolio outperforms the market. Using the previous example, let's assume the market benchmark had a 10% return, which represents beta (β = 1), and portfolio Z and portfolio X returned 19% and 20%, respectively. Portfolios Z and X had betas (β) of 1.30 and 1.50, respectively. Also, let's assume the risk-free rate (treasury bills) is 2%. The Treynor value of each is calculated as follows:

$$\text{Market: } Tm = \frac{R_m - Rf}{\beta_m} = \frac{.10 - .02}{1} = .080 = 8.000\%$$

$$\text{Portfolio Z: } Tz = \frac{R_z - Rf}{\beta_z} = \frac{.19 - .02}{1.3} = .1307 = 13.077\%$$

$$\text{Portfolio X: } Tx = \frac{R_x - Rf}{\beta_x} = \frac{.20 - .02}{1.5} = .120 = 12.000\%$$

The higher the Treynor ratio (T), the more efficient the portfolio. Like the Sharpe ratio, if the analyst was only evaluating the portfolio on return performance alone, he or she may have recognized that portfolio X returns the best results. The Treynor ratio is adjusted to reflect the risk adjusted to the market.

M-SQUARE RATIO

Like the Treynor ratio, M-square (M^2) is another ratio that measures the risk-adjusted return of the portfolio relative to the market benchmark. M^2 measures the difference between the excess return of the portfolio over the market. Unlike the Sharpe ratio that is measured in units of return versus risk, M^2 is expressed as a percentage return, making it easier for the investor to read when analyzing a portfolio. M^2 is one of the newest modern portfolio measurement methods, only developed in 1997 by the Nobel Prize winner Franco Modigliani and his granddaughter Leah Modigliani, hence the concept of M-square. The formula is as follows:

$$M^2 = SR \cdot \sigma_m + R_f$$

where SR is the Sharpe ratio of the risky portfolio, σ_m is the market benchmark standard deviation, and R_f is the risk-free rate. The M^2 ratio can be written also as follows:

$$M^2 = \frac{R_p - R_f}{\sigma_p} \cdot \sigma_m + R_f$$

where R_p is the portfolio return, σ_p is the portfolio's standard deviation, σ_m is the market benchmark standard deviation, and R_f is the risk-free rate. Rearranging the formula will yield

$$M^2 = RPRp \,.\frac{\sigma_m}{\sigma_p} + R_f$$

where RPR_p is the portfolio risk premium return, σ_p is the portfolio's standard deviation, σ_m is the market benchmark standard deviation, and R_f is the risk-free rate.

Let's use the same information to compare portfolio Z to portfolio X in order to measure their M^2s. Let's assume portfolio Z had returns of 19% with standard deviation of 26%, and portfolio X had returns of 20% with standard deviation of 36%. The market benchmark had return of 10% with standard deviation of 18%. The risk-free rate had a return of 2.0%. The M^2s for these portfolios are calculated as follows:

$$M_z^2 = (Rz - Rf) \,.\frac{\sigma_m}{\sigma_z} + R_f = (19\% - 2\%)\frac{18\%}{26\%} + 2\% = 13.769\%$$

$$M_x^2 = (Rx - Rf) \,.\frac{\sigma_m}{\sigma_x} + R_f = (20\% - 2\%)\frac{18\%}{36\%} + 2\% = 11.000\%$$

From the calculations the analyst can conclude that despite the absolute return for portfolio X, 20%, being higher than portfolio Z's, 19.0%, portfolio Z has a significant higher M^2 of 13.769% versus 11%.

Figure 4.4 compares the measurements of portfolio Z to portfolio X and as compared to the stock market benchmark. Looking at the performance metrics in figure 4.4 it appears that portfolio X has higher return (20%) than portfolio Z (19%) before the risk parameters are observed such as standard deviations and betas. Both portfolios have done much

FIGURE 4.4 PORTFOLIO PERFORMANCE RATIO ANALYSIS

	Description	Symbol	Calculation	Stock Portfolio Z	Stock Portfolio X	Stock Benchmark Market (m)
INPUT	Average Return	R		19.00%	20.00%	10.00%
	Risk Free Return	Rf		2.00%	2.00%	2.00%
	Standard Deviation	σ		26.00%	36.00%	18.00%
	Beta	β		1.300x	1.500x	1.000x
OUTPUT	Risk Premium Return	RPR	R - Rf	17.00%	18.00%	8.00%
	Market Premium	Pm	Rm - Rf	8.00%	8.00%	8.00%
	Capital Asset Pricing Model	CAPM	Rfr + β. Pm	12.40%	14.00%	10.00%
	Sharpe Ratio	SR	RPR / σ	0.654	0.500	0.444
	Jensen's Alpha	α	R - CAPM	6.600%	6.000%	0.000%
	Treynor Measure	T	RPR / β	13.077%	12.000%	8.000%
	M-Square	M^2	((σm/σp)*P)+Rf	13.769%	11.000%	10.000%

better than the stock benchmark market on absolute basis before adjusting for risk. Portfolios Z and X performed at 19% and 20% as compared to the market benchmark at 10%. Adjusting for the betas to calculate the risk adjusted return as compared to the market the portfolio manager uses first the CAPM approach. Figure 4.4 shows that the return when adjusting for betas should have been 12.4% and 14.0% as compared to the absolute of 19% and 20% for portfolio X and Z respectively showing clearly that both portfolio beat the market on a risk adjusted basis against the market's risk as illustrated by looking at Jensen's alpha of 6.6% and 6.0% for portfolio Z and X respectively. Just comparing the Jensen's alpha between portfolio Z and X it's clear that portfolio Z beat the market at a 0.6% higher than portfolio X (6.6% – 6.0%). Also, the Treynor's measure ratio comparison between portfolios shows a stronger argument that portfolio Z versus portfolio X have performed better as compare to the market (13.077% versus 12.000%). The better comparison of the performance between the portfolio Z and X are to review other ratios such as the Sharpe Ratio showing that Portfolio Z has a stronger performance than Portfolio X (0.654 versus 0.500) representing the ratio of 1% unit of premium return to 1.% unit of volatility or risk. M-square is another measurement that shown portfolio Z performed better than portfolio X (13.769% versus 11.000%).

OTHER USEFUL PORTFOLIO ANALYSIS RATIOS

There are other useful ratios portfolio managers around the world use to measure their portfolio performance.

BURKE RATIO BASED ON DRAWDOWNS INSTEAD OF STANDARD DEVIATION

The Burke ratio, also referred to as a sharper Sharpe ratio, is similar to the Sharpe ratio in that it also measures the risk-adjusted performance of the portfolio. It uses

the same numerator of Rp - Rf, but instead of using the portfolio's standard deviation as the denominator, the Burke ratio uses the concept of drawdowns. The concept of drawdowns (D) is used primarily by hedge fund managers to calculate how long it takes an investment to recover from a temporary decline in value. It's expressed as a percentage from the previous peak value, measuring the downside risk. The drawdown (D) is the difference between the current value and the peak value is divided by the peak value in order to determine the percentage drop from the highest value D = min [0, (Pt - Pmax)/ Pmax]. The Burk Ratio formula is as follows:

$$BR = \frac{Rp - R_f}{\dot{D}^2}$$

where R_p is the portfolio return, R_f is the risk-free return, and D is the drawdown.

OMEGA RATIO BASED ON MIN/MAX VARIANCE INSTEAD OF STANDARD DEVIATION

The omega ratio (Ω) is another risk-adjusted measurement of return. **This ratio is similar to the Sharpe ratio in that it compares the return to volatility. The Omega ratio, however, uses the higher points of distribution, arguing that these points could show a better assessment of volatility. It is done to combat the tendency of a distribution to be asymmetric with tail risk or negative skewness;** it is basically the probability-weighted ratio of gains versus loses for a given return. The formula is a little complex but is written as follows:

$$\Omega = \frac{\int_{ERp}^{\infty} (1 + F(x))dx}{\int_{-\infty}^{ERp} F\,(x)dx}$$

where F(x) is the cumulative probability distribution function of the returns, in other words, the probability that the return is less than x. ERp is the expected or target return threshold selected by the investor, which is used as the basis to compare all the points of gain versus all the points of loss. A higher result shows that the portfolio had more gains than losses compared to the rate of return threshold represented by ERp. To summarize, the commonly used Sharpe ratio measures the average of only two points of the return distribution over the measurement of volatility based on a normal distribution whereas the omega ratio considers all the points including the mean, max/min variance, skew, and kurtosis. The best way to calculate the omega ratio is through Excel with a matrix formula. The analyst needs a column of historical returns and a set of threshold return (not the average). The numerator will consist of an "=*if*" statement that takes the sum of all these historical returns minus the threshold. The numerator in the formula will consist of an Excel "=if" statement that takes only the sum of all the historical returns minus the threshold that results in a positive number. The sum of these positive numbers will then be divided by the denominator, as stated in the formula—basically measuring the negative difference between the sum of these investments and the threshold. (Please note that the matrix formula can be run by CNTRL+SHIFT+Return.)

SORTINO RATIO BASED ON LOSSES INSTEAD OF STANDARD DEVIATION

The Sortino ratio is a ratio that adjusts for trading losses. Using the standard deviation, the basis of calculating the Sharpe ratio, the measure is penalized by both downside and upside volatility. Sometimes investors like to show the sudden uptick in their portfolio based on decisions they've made and using the Sharpe ratio might not make this as obvious as one might desire. This is due to the fact that it is offset by the series of historical downsides and upsides equally. The Sortino ratio, on the other hand, only penalizes downside risk. The formula is as follows:

$$SoR = \frac{ER_p - Rf}{\sigma_d}$$

where ER_p is the expected return of the portfolio, Rf is the risk-free rate, and σ_d is the standard deviation of negative asset returns (downside risk). The downside risk is calculated as follows:

$$\sigma_d = \sqrt{\frac{\sum (R_p - ER_p)^2 f(t)}{n}}$$

where R_p are the historical returns of the portfolio, ER_p is expected return (threshold), n is the number of years or observations, and f(t) represents the arguments (expressed as 1 or 0) that are tested if the returns are higher or lower than the expected return (ER_p). For example, f(t) = 1 when total returns are higher than the target return (ER_p) and f(t) = 0 if the historical returns are equal to zero or higher than the target return of (ER_p).

CASE STUDY

PORTFOLIO OF STOCKS AND BONDS: ZEUS FUND I CASE STUDY

The previous three chapters focused primarily on the risk and return of the Zeus Fund I portfolio, which includes stocks and bonds and how each of these asset classes have performed against each other and the market. This chapter will follow up on these comparisons and set out to test more ratios that a portfolio manager would need in order to better understand the performance of the Zeus Fund I portfolio. Figure 4.5 shows the Sharpe ratio for the combined portfolio on a total holding period return basis for both a levered and unlevered adjusted portfolio. It's worth noting that the standard deviation of the portfolio needs to be adjusted in order to account for leverage. Despite the clear advantage of leverage in that the absolute return of the portfolio increased

FIGURE 4.5 ZEUS FUND I

PORTFOLIO OF STOCKS AND BONDS

CASH FLOWS		ENTRY 0	1	2	3	4	5	6	EXIT 7
	MONTHLY IRR	June 1 20x1	July 1 20x1	Aug 1 20x1	Sep 1 20x1	Oct 1 20x1	Nov 1 20x1	Dec 1 20x1	Jan 2 20x2
Beginning Cash		100,000	20,173	23,415	22,396	21,564	21,420	21,932	25,210
Buy/Sell Stock		$ (82,600)	$ -	$ 1,550	$ 2,300	$ -	$ -	$ -	$ 92,600
Buy/Sell Bonds		$ (95,650)	$ 2,875	$ (2,880)	$ (4,075)	$ -	$ 865	$ 3,550	$ 97,000
Stock Dividends			$ 93	$ 90	$ 150	$ 245	$ 63	$ -	$ -
Bond Coupon Received		$ -	$ 875	$ 594	$ 1,344	$ -	$ -	$ -	$ -
Acrued Interest (paid)/Received		$ (1,577)	$ (209)	$ 14	$ (161)	$ -	$ (25)	$ 117	$ 1,927
Loan Principal Increase/Decrease		$ 100,000							$ (100,000)
Loan Interest Payment			$ (417)	$ (417)	$ (417)	$ (417)	$ (417)	$ (417)	$ (417)
Cash Balance Interest Income			$ 25	$ 29	$ 28	$ 27	$ 27	$ 27	$ 27
Cash		$ (20,173)							$ 25,210
Total Cash Flows (Levered)	2.86%	$ (100,000)	$ 3,242	$ (1,019)	$ (831)	$ (145)	$ 513	$ 3,277	$ 116,347
Use of cash		$ 20,173	$ -	$ -	$ -	$ -	$ -	$ -	$ (25,210)
Total Cash Flows		20,173	23,415	22,396	21,564	21,420	21,932	25,210	116,347
% of Cash to total Value		10.2%	11.8%	11.0%	10.4%	10.2%	10.4%	11.7%	

HPR (Levered) Rp= 21.38%

Risk Free Rate (Rfr) = 1.00% (7-month Interpolated Treasury Bill)

Portfolio Standard Deviation (σp)= 17.57% (Levered adjusted for 7 months)

Sharpe Ratio (SR) = 1.16

Unlevered Return Calculation:	0 June 1 20x1	1 July 1 20x1	2 Aug 1 20x1	3 Sep 1 20x1	4 Oct 1 20x1	5 Nov 1 20x1	6 Dec 1 20x1	7 Jan 2 20x2
Total Cash Flows (Levered)	$ (100,000)	$ 3,242	$ (1,019)	$ (831)	$ (145)	$ 513	$ 3,277	$ 116,347
Addback Loan Principal	(100,000)	-	-	-	-	-	-	100,000
Addback Loan Interest	-	417	417	417	417	417	417	417
Unlevered Cash Flow	$ (200,000)	$ 3,658	$ (603)	$ (415)	$ 272	$ 929	$ 3,694	$ 216,764

HPR (UnLevered) = 12.15%

Risk Free Rate (Rfr) = 1.00% (7-month Interpolated Treasury Bill)

Portfolio Standard Deviation (σp)= 9.98%

Sharpe Ratio (SR) = 1.12

from 12.2% to 21.4%, the Sharpe ratio does not change due to leverage. Figure 4.5 shows a slight change in the Sharpe ratios between the levered and unlevered adjusted portfolio due to moving averages, but it is negligible. The levered standard deviation is adjusted as follows:

σ (Levered) = σ (Unlevered) × (Rl/Ru)

where σ is standard deviation, Rl is the levered return, and R is the unlevered return. The calculation using the funds figures is

σ (Levered) = 9.98% × (12.15%/21.38%) = 1.16.

Figure 4.6 shows all performance ratios discussed earlier in this chapter for Zeus Fund I.

FIGURE 4.6 ZEUS FUND I

Portfolio Perfromance Ratio Analysis (Monthly)

	Description	Symbol	Zeus Stock Portfolio	Stock Benchmark Market (m)	Zeus Bond Portfolio	Bonds Benchmark Market (m)	Zeus Combined Portfolio	Weighted Benchmark Market (m)
INPUT	Average Montly Return	*R*	3.38%	1.22%	0.54%	0.15%	1.86%	0.81%
	Risk Free Return (Monthly)	*Rf*	0.14%	0.14%	0.14%	0.14%	0.14%	0.14%
	Standard Deviation	*σ*	2.80%	1.17%	0.75%	0.46%	0.02%	0.43%
	Beta	*β*	1.825x	1.000x	1.124x	1.000x	1.446x	1.000x
OUTPUT	Risk Premium Return	*RPR*	3.23%	1.08%	0.40%	0.01%	1.72%	0.66%
	Market Premium	*Pm*	1.08%	1.08%	0.01%	0.01%	0.66%	0.66%
	Capital Asset Pricing Model	*CAPM*	2.11%	1.22%	0.15%	0.15%	1.10%	0.81%
	Sharpe Ratio	*SR*	1.156	0.923	0.535	0.017	92.745	1.556
	Jensen's Alpha	*α*	1.270%	0.000%	0.391%	0.000%	0.758%	0.000%
	Treynor Measure	*T*	1.772%	1.077%	0.356%	0.008%	1.188%	0.664%
	M-Square	M^2	1.492%	1.220%	0.390%	0.151%	39.728%	0.807%

Portfolio Perfromance Ratio Analysis (Annualized)

	Description	Symbol	Zeus Stock Portfolio	Stock Benchmark Market (m)	Zeus Bond Portfolio	Bonds Benchmark Market (m)	Zeus Combined Portfolio	Weighted Benchmark Market (m)
INPUT	Average Annualized Return	*R*	40.53%	14.64%	6.51%	1.81%	22.34%	9.68%
	Risk Free Return (Annualized)	*Rf*	1.71%	1.71%	1.71%	1.71%	1.71%	1.71%
	Standard Deviation	*σ*	33.57%	14.00%	8.97%	5.54%	0.22%	5.12%
	Beta	*β*	1.825x	1.000x	1.124x	1.000x	1.446x	1.000x
OUTPUT	Risk Premium Return	*RPR*	38.82%	12.92%	4.80%	0.09%	20.62%	7.97%
	Market Premium	*Pm*	12.92%	12.92%	0.09%	0.09%	7.97%	7.97%
	Capital Asset Pricing Model	*CAPM*	25.30%	14.64%	1.82%	1.81%	13.24%	9.68%
	Sharpe Ratio	*SR*	1.156	0.923	0.535	0.017	92.745	1.556
	Jensen's Alpha	*α*	15.235%	0.000%	4.695%	0.000%	9.096%	0.000%
	Treynor Measure	*T*	21.269%	12.922%	4.271%	0.093%	14.258%	7.969%
	M-Square	M^2	3.063%	2.791%	1.961%	1.722%	41.300%	2.378%

PROBLEMS

1. In one sentence, explain what an efficient frontier is.
2. Explain the difference between an efficient portfolio and an optimum portfolio.
3. Define CAPM and explain its use.
4. Define Sharpe ratio and explain its use.
5. You purchased 100 shares in the JZ Growth mutual fund one month ago for $13.00. Today the share is worth $19.00. During the month you received total dividends of $50 and capital gains distribution per share of $0.10. What was your $ profit amount and holding period rate of return on your investment? (Ignore taxes and fees.)
6. Define each portfolio performance measurement, including Jensen's Alpha, Treynor measure, and M-square, and describe its use.
7. Calculate the Sharpe measures for the following portfolios, if the risk-free rate of return is 1.5%. **Circle** the portfolio with the most favorable Sharpe measure. (4 points)

PORTFOLIO	EXPECTED PORTFOLIO RETURN %	PORTFOLIO STANDARD DEVIATION %	SHARPE RATIO
A	9	6	
B	12	15	
C	25	20	
D	33	45	

8. The following data represents the probability distribution of the holding period returns for an investment in Celerity Tech Inc. (CTI) stock. (8 points)

STATE OF THE ECONOMY	SCENARIO #	PROBABILITY, P(S)	HPR
Boom	1	0.30	16.00%
Normal Growth	2	0.50	4.50%
Recession	3	0.20	11.00%

a. What is the expected return on CTI?
b. What is the standard deviation of the returns on CTI?

9. Calculate the portfolio ratio analysis of the two portfolios and the stock benchmark, and explain in which portfolio the investor should invest.

DESCRIPTION	STOCK PORTFOLIO Z	STOCK PORTFOLIO X	STOCK BENCHMARK MARKET (M)
Average Return	15.00%	18.00%	9.00%
Risk-Free Return	1.50%	1.50%	1.50%
Standard Deviation	22.00%	33.00%	16.00%
Beta	1.250x	1.400x	1.000x
Output			
Risk Premium Return			
Market Premium			
Capital Asset Pricing Model			
Sharpe Ratio			
Jensen's Alpha			
Treynor Measure			
M-Square			

10. Finish constructing your Portfolio Project, now that you have studied all of Part 1 of this textbook.

FINAL EXCEL PROJECT

Construct a $200,000 portfolio of stocks, corporate bonds, and cash (in Excel) using the following information:

1. Initial capital $100,000 (equity)
2. Additional $100,000 loan for 5% interest per annum
3. Starting date (Year 0)—closing stock and bond prices for that day (Go back and get the historical prices.)
4. Value date (Year 5)
5. Maintain diversification discipline.*
6. Always maintain at least 10% cash. Cash interest income is 1.5% per annum.
7. You must trade stocks or bonds at least five times during this period. (Five initial stock and bond positions need to be replaced during this period.)
8. Assume no trading costs or any additional expenses (except interest on the margin loan).

You spreadsheet should include the following:

1. Initial transaction sources and uses (Jan 1, Year 0)
2. List of stocks and corporate bonds
3. Business description and industry categorization for each stock and S&P, and Moody's rating of each bond

4. Monthly cash flow, which will include any dividends, coupon payments, gains and losses on trades, interest payments, and interest income of cash balance
5. Overall monthly performance (including a graph)
6. S&P 500 Index on the end of Year 1, 2, 3, 4, and 5 (using closing) to compare to your stock portfolio

At value date calculate the following:

1. Total portfolio HPR for stock, bond and combined portfolio (levered and unlevered)
2. Bond portfolio duration (no need for convexity)
3. Covariance and correlation of bond and stock portfolios
4. Sharpe ratios, Treynor, Jensen, and M^2 measurement for equity portfolio
5. Sharpe ratios, standard deviation, HPR, and average monthly returns for entire portfolio
6. Portfolio performance as compared (including a graph) to S&P 500 Index during this period (beta coefficient calculation, regression analysis between stock portfolio and S&P 500, bond portfolio and bond benchmark, and combined portfolio and weighted benchmarks of stocks and bonds).

***Diversification discipline:**

- There must be no fewer than 10 stocks in the portfolio at all times.
- Each stock value cannot represent more than 20% of the total portfolio.
- Each industry value cannot represent more than 25% of the total portfolio.
- **Portfolio must be across eight different industry sectors. One of the industry sectors should have at least two companies.**

ONLINE TEMPLATES & CASE STUDIES

The Excel spreadsheets used in the chapter can be accessed online via Cognella Active Learning platform.

PART II

Primary Markets: Capital Markets and Capital Raising

CHAPTER 5
Equity Markets: Raising Equity for Private Companies

CHAPTER 6
Equity Markets: Initial Public Offering (IPO) and Publicly Traded Companies

CHAPTER 7
Debt Markets: Issuing Corporate Bonds, 144As, and Private Placements

CHAPTER 8
Debt Markets: Issuing Bank Loans, Private Loans, and Loan Syndication

CHAPTER 9
Transaction Analysis: LBOs, M&As, and other Capital Market Deals

PART II of the textbook introduces ways that a company will go about raising capital. Depending where the company is in its business development cycle, the capital raising can vary from raising early seed money to raising private equity, to getting ready to go public via initial public offering. The last two chapters of Part II walk the reader through the process of accessing the debt markets including the public bond and private loan markets. The image provided below illustrates the evolution of the company's capital raising. Part II will give an overview of all the options a company or an investor has to raise capital.

RAISING CAPITAL THROUGH THE COMPANY'S BUSINESS CYCLE

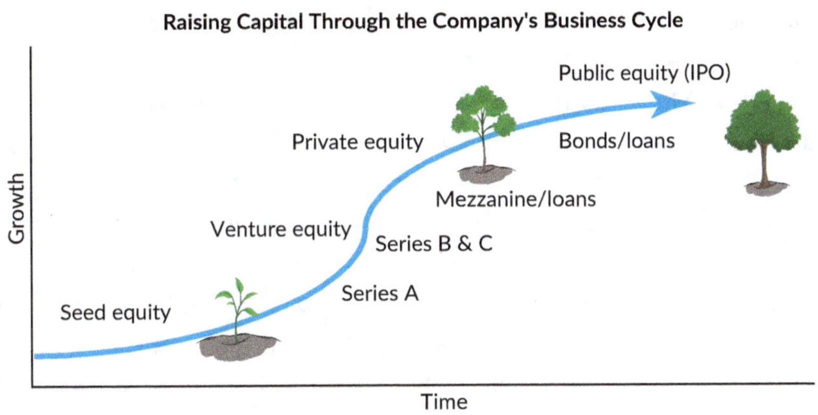

The line-up and brief description of Part II's chapters are as follows:

Chapter 5: Equity Markets: Raising Equity for Private Companies

This chapter will summarize the main approaches through which a company can access equity capital. The book first covers an overview of the life cycle of the company while privately owned and describe all the financing options available to business owners throughout the growth process, from start-up to eventually going public. An investment advisor needs to understand the company's capital structure as well as the types of financing available to the company. This is largely based on where it is in its growth and development. This chapter will cover the capital accessibility vehicles available to private companies including the process of raising equity from private placement markets. Equity return expectations, debt capacity requirements, relevant regulatory framework, and continuously changing market dynamics are some of the factors that will be discussed when the company is in the process of raising capital in the private placement markets.

Chapter 6: Equity Markets: Initial Public Offering (IPO) and Publicly Traded Companies

This chapter will cover in detail the last stage of a company's maturity and development: an initial public offering (IPO). Once the company becomes public, the chapter will then describe the precedent of an M&A transaction and the tender offer procedures involved, starting from the bidding stage to the closing and funding stage. The analytical approach for valuing the company in order to raise capital will be described in more detail in other parts of the books including chapters 9 and 17. This chapter gives an introduction to the process of raising capital with which the reader should follow up with a valuation analysis of pricing the company for M&A and M&A accretion/dilution as well as going from public to private via a leveraged buyout (LBO) and recapitalization financing.

Chapter 7: Debt Markets: Issuing Corporate Bonds, 144As, and Private Placements

This chapter will summarize the various approaches through which a company can access the bond markets. The chapter will outline the process by which a company can raise debt publicly or privately and walk the reader through the vehicles a company issues when looking to raise capital in the form of debt. Throughout this chapter it is key that students keep in mind the double-edged sword that comes with acquiring leverage, especially in large quantities. It is imperative students understand that while helping maximize returns for companies and investment portfolios alike, leverage, like other long-term liabilities, can add a substantial financial burden in times of economic hardship and greatly increase the risk profile of the associated assets. The chapter will then give an overview of the analysis that S&P and Moody's go through to grade the risk and recovery of bonds. The rating process helps members of the public make informed decisions and protect them from unwarranted investment risk.

Chapter 8: Debt Markets: Issuing Bank Loans, Private Loans, and Loan Syndication

This chapter will summarize various approaches through which a company can access the loan markets. The chapter will outline the process and various best practices a company will go through when raising corporate loans from the syndicate, club, or private markets. Throughout this chapter, it's important that students continue to understand the various types of loans offered and how they are syndicated. It is also important for students to take into account the primary risk of default when assessing credit worthiness and grading comparisons.

Chapter 9: LBOs, M&As, and other Capital Market Deals

This chapter will introduce substantive case studies that will highlight the application of different approaches to raising capital in the primary market. Many of the methods covered are outlined in the earlier chapters of this unit. The case studies include a public-to-private leveraged buyout (LBO); private-to-private leveraged buyout; a merger between two strategic companies, both a stock purchase and an asset purchase; a buyout of a distressed company; and a private-to-public initial public offering (IPO).

Credit

CHAPTER 5

Equity Markets: Raising Equity for Private Companies

This chapter will summarize the main approaches through which a company can access equity capital. The book first covers an overview of the life cycle of the company while privately owned and describe all the financing options available to business owners throughout the growth process, from start-up to eventually going public (figure 5.1). An investment advisor needs to understand the company's capital structure as well as the types of financing available to the company. This is largely based on where it is in its growth and development. This chapter will cover the capital accessibility vehicles available to private companies including the process of raising equity from private placement markets. Equity return expectations, debt capacity requirements, relevant regulatory framework, and continuously changing market dynamics are some of the factors that will be discussed when the company is in the process of raising capital in the private placement markets.

LEARNING OBJECTIVES

After reading this chapter, students will be able to do the following:

- Understand the private placement market for equity investments
- Evaluate the various financing options available in the market
- Prepare the company to "go to market" by determining the capital needs and expectations
- Know how to balance the equity return expectation and debt capacity requirement
- Understand the relevant elements of raising capital including a time requirement, associated costs, dilution of ownership, and pressure for results
- Implement a due diligence check list and business/market validation processes

RAISING EQUITY: AN OVERVIEW

A well-established private company that has been in the business for years and early founders that have just established their new company both have the same objective: raising capital, and specifically raising equity to develop and grow their business. Of course, early-stage companies are more likely to approach private equity than well-established larger companies that have more choices, including going public or IPO. The investor, private or public, representing the equity contribution or buy-in will do their own valuation analysis based on their return expectation, adjusted for risk and probability of success.

AUTHOR'S NOTES

The transaction sources and uses is the first section that shows up on any financial model. It determines how much capital the company needs, what type of capital, and how it is to be applied. I still remember a specific instructor in the credit training program I attended as an entry-level analyst at Bank of America in the late 80s in San Francisco. He constantly challenged us to build the transaction's sources and uses of capital for a specific transaction we had been working on. One of his famous stories went like this: "On a heavily rainy night, three men were driving in a car on a highway. With such bad weather, they were desperately looking for a motel to stay the night. Unsure if they would approach one sooner rather than later, they pulled into one that had the sign "NO VACANCIES." Though the motel manager waved them away, signaling his motel was fully booked, the three men insisted they needed a place to stay. They argued and pleaded with the manager, even suggesting staying a few hours in the lobby until the rain slowed down. The manager, feeling bad for the men, mentioned that he had one room left available. However, he explained that a customer had stayed there the night before and just left, leaving him no time to clean the room. He asked if they wanted stay in the dirty room anyway and offered to only charge them $30 for the night. The three men agreed and each paid $10 to the manager. After opening the door to the room, they saw that the room was unbearably dirty. They called the manger and asked if anyone was available to clean the room and if not to have new sheets and towels so they could clean it themselves. The manager said that he would have his wife come up and clean up a little. He agreed he had not realized the true state of the room and stated he would charge them only $25 for the night, basically reimbursing them $5. The lady came up with the $5 (all singles) as reimbursement. Because it is difficult to divide $5 into 3, they each got $1 and gave the lady the other $2 as a tip. The question is this: Since each paid $9 for the room ($10 – $1), which makes

$27 (3 x 9), plus $2 to the manager's wife, which makes $29, where is the other dollar—since we started at $30? Of course, this story is very tricky, and it requires a little logical thinking to find the flaw in the story. Someone needs to separate the payers and the receivers of the cash, or the sources and uses of the cash. Clearly the three men paid net $27 and they were the payors, or the SOURCE of cash. The other side are the receivers, or the USE of cash that clearly received $27 made up of $25 for the room and $2 for the service (manager's wife's tip since she is part of the establishment). By adding her with the men there was a flaw in our thinking since she received money, but the men paid money. Our credit training instructor was trying to teach us that we needed to think as accountants to determine the transaction sources and uses. First the analyst needs to determine the use of capital to calculate the financing needs and then build the source of capital to match those capital needs.

KEY TAKEAWAYS

- To provide advice, investment bankers need to understand a company's corporate structure and the types of financing that are available to their client companies.
- Companies in the market for raising equity need to understand that fundamentals are more important than technical characteristics. Having a good product, good management, and feasibility in their future are more important characteristics than aiming at financial engineering or taking advantage of overenthusiastic markets.
- Valuations are very subjective given all the methods to derive them, but at the end of the day, the actual value of the company is the price that someone is willing to pay for it.
- In preparing to go to market, the company must determine the capital needed by running a full financial model showing all the cash flow needs that are in line with their growth expectations.

THE LIFE CYCLE OF THE COMPANY

SEED CAPITAL

Many of the large companies today like Apple and Microsoft started in the founder's garage. The first financing founders are said to receive is usually from the three Fs: friends, family, and fools (fools being investors giving you money that are not your friends or your family);

FIGURE 5.1 RAISING CAPITAL THROUGH THE COMPANY'S BUSINESS CYCLE

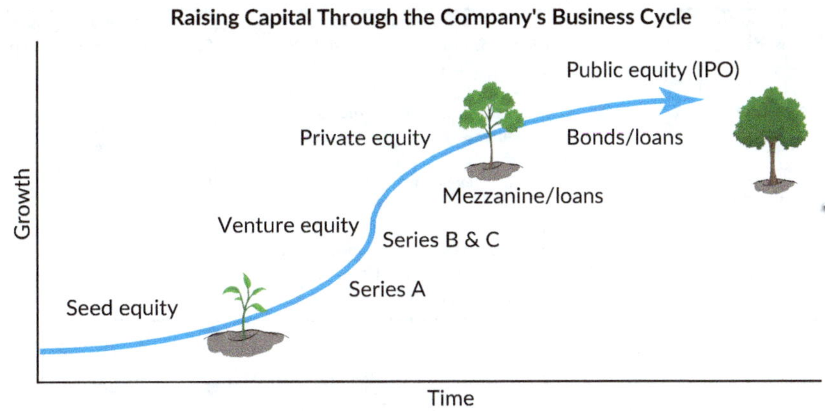

or FFM: friends, family and Mastercard. Once the founder has created a new idea and is able to represent it in a sound business plan that solves a specific problem or enhances an existing process, he or she generally should conduct an extensive research and feasibility study. After figuring out the achievability and possible cost of production of the new product or service, the owner can then access certain investors called "seed" or "angel" investors. These investors are often successful entrepreneurs on their own; they share a company's vision and are more interested in the timing of launch and funding needed to achieve the go-to market strategy rather than intermediate valuation fluctuations or initial stability of cash flows. **These "angel" investors are willing to take tremendous risk, as the idea they are risking their money on is often not yet tested.** Angel investors typically ask for 20–50% equity ownership in the company. With this ownership value defined, their investment generally establishes the first level of valuation. For example, if the angel investor invests $500,000 for 50% of the company, the value of the company is then set at $1 million. Given the startup nature of the company, the return expectation for angel investing is very high—typically five to 10 times the initial investment. This is often balanced by a staggeringly high failure rate of many entrepreneurial endeavors that are undertaken. Knowing this, angel investors' aims are to increase the likelihood of success through active management and constant adjustment of the business plan to meet market demands and maximize revenue growth.

Sometimes new companies will look to establish a bank financing relationship even at this early stage of development. This method of financing is primarily used for working capital. These banks are generally willing to extend a line of credit to a new start-up if the owner provides a personal guarantee or if the loan is approved by the Small Business Administration (SBA), a government agency who offers several programs designed to assist start-ups with initial funding. The SBA's Venture Capital program specifically provides

FIGURE 5.2 SEED INVESTMENT

Investors	Purpose of Investment	What do you need
The 3 Fs (Family, Friends and Fools)	Hiring instumental team members	Support / share your vision
Angel Funds ($50,000 - $2 million)	Market testing ideas / product development	Business Plan / Preliminary Valuation
Government subsidies (Small Business Administration)	Further developing MVPs	Momentum
University grants	Iron out the kinks of business models and product-market fits – Checking your "gut feeling" re-adjusting the business	

venture capital to new businesses via the small business investment companies (SBIC). SBICs are privately owned investment funds that are licensed and regulated by the SBA. However, it is important to keep in mind the start-ups that receive approval for such funding are usually small companies with very little income or loss.

Figure 5.2 summarizes who these seed investors are, the purpose of their investment, and what you need to obtain such investment:

Valuations for early-stage investments are some of the most challenging since there is no history of revenue or cash flow. The best approach is to run a monthly cash-flow analysis to determine the initial and ongoing funding needs for the next 18 months. Please refer to chapter 17 where it introduces a valuation method for distressed or start-up companies. The basis for this type of valuation method is very similar to valuing an out-of-money call option using the Black-Scholes pricing model described in chapter 13. The model is basically based on the probability of success, valuing the cash needs during the initial stage (referred to as "Death Valley") and the velocity or acceleration of the profit in later years, as demonstrated in figure 5.3.

FIGURE 5.3 CASH FLOW NEEDS DURING EARLY STAGE OF COMPANY ("DEATH VALLEY") FUNDED BY THE ANGEL INVESTOR AND THE EXPECTED VELOCITY AND PROFIT ACCELERATION

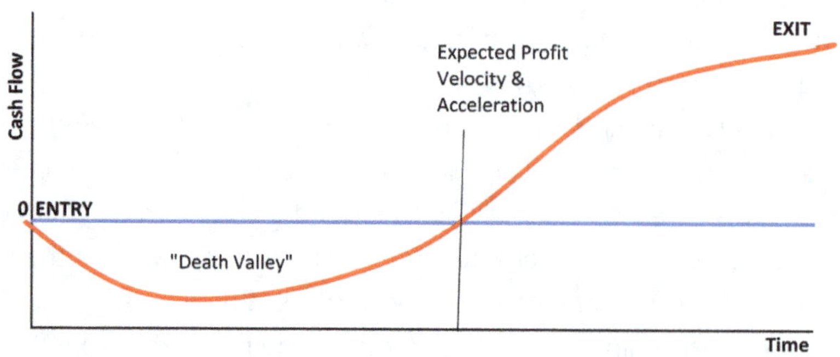

Angel investors are expected to be taken out by venture capitalists or private equity firms. Occasionally if the acceleration of the business happens much faster and the stock markets are very attractive, the angel investor might take the company public via an IPO to get the most value.

VENTURE CAPITAL

Venture capital is provided by private investment funds such as hedge funds, institutional investors, or industry-specific ventures that are specialized in start-up companies during their early stages of development. Venture capitalists are interested in companies that have developed a proven product, strategic patents, new technology, and intellectual property (IP) and that have achieved double-digit growing revenues. Venture capitalists also look for companies with strong management. These investors usually are very patient with their investment as the company develops their business and expansion plan. They take a long-term approach and thus do not demand liquidity or dividends. The founders and initial investors seeking venture capital investment will go through several rounds of venture capital raising (typically starting with Series A issuance and then Series B, C and many more if necessary) and various auctions. The main concern of the existing owners is in exchange for having new capital invested in their company what will they have to give up. In any transaction based predominantly on equity rather than debt, the concern is always ownership control—how much ownership (dilution) the owners and investors are willing give up for the right investment in the business. The timing of fund raising, revenue generation prospects, and expected terminal value are essential elements for the investor to establish the right valuation and pay an advantageous price for the expected return on investment. The financial analysis that is necessary to calculate the immediate cash needs or investments to cover these needs should also determine the value of the company, so the cash needs to the investment has the right balance. For example, raising excess funds to just have for rainy days might require unnecessarily giving higher ownership. On the other hand, raising lower funds than the cash needs in hopes that these needs will be covered by immediate revenues so the owners could avoid giving up equity could also be a problem. Though most of the investment raised is equity, if any debt financing is obtained to mitigate some of the dilution the debt investors often ask for warrants (conversion feature to owning stock) to leverage their upside.

Figure 5.4 summarizes who these venture capital investors are, the purpose of their investment, and what the owners need in order to obtain such investment.

Prior to a venture capital transaction, the founders will need to prepare a business plan while the investors will typically run a basic discount cash flow (DCF) method analysis. This analysis includes the future stream of cash flows from running the company, an estimated terminal value at an assumed exit year (typically 3–5 years) while

FIGURE 5.4 VENTURE CAPITAL

Investors	Purpose of Investment	What do you need
Series A ($2 mm - $10 million)	Revenue Growth (no necessarily income growth)	Exit Strategy
Hedge Funds	Market Share / Penetration	Business Plan
Institutional Investors (GP/LP structures)	Continue to develop the product	DCF Valuation
Industry Specific Venture Funds		

using an expected rate of return as a discount rate for the cash flows. The projections are also used to determine the cash flow needs of the company in the earlier years of the investment. Examples of DCF analysis are shown in chapter 9 and 17.

As the company grows and matures, the venture capital investors are expected to be taken out by other venture capital and private equity firms, as well as the larger IPO market if the stock markets are attractive to get the best value possible.

PRIVATE EQUITY CAPITAL

These investors are typically institutional investors with capital behind them from pension funds, banks, insurance companies, and high net-worth individuals. **A private equity (PE) firm is set up as a portfolio manager of funds that invests in these types of companies. The funds are set up as limited partnerships (LPs).** The LPs (investors in the fund) are passive in their investment—they have no influence over investment decisions. However, LPs can decide not to invest again if they are not satisfied with the fund's performance or the portfolio manager. Typically, the investments into a portfolio of companies range from $10 million to multiple billions of dollars. The focus of a PE firm is on the income, cash flow stability, and growth (with a special focus on EBITDA), as well as the attractiveness of their exit strategy. The PE firm will generally demand at least 2–3 years of historical financials to initiate their valuation process. These financial statements are used by PE analysts as a basis to run projections, develop their strategy, and establish an exit multiple. PE firms will also work on establishing a plan to enhance further profitability. This will include research and efforts toward cost cutting, cost efficiency, productivity enhancements, and plant implementation programs. PE firms also implement using leverage to enhance their returns (hence the name leveraged buyouts, emphasis on the word *leveraged*). Chapter 9 17 show the analysis (LBO analysis) that PE firms run to measure their expected return and that guides them toward what they are willing to pay for the company. Unlike venture capital firms, PE firms are known to bring their own management team in to run the company.

FIGURE 5.5 PRIVATE EQUITY CAPITAL

Investors	Purpose of Investment	What do you need
Large and Middle Market PE firms (Higher than $10 million)	Revenue & EBITDA Growth	2-3 Year Financial Statements
Institutional Investors (GP/LP structures)	Cost Efficiency and Plant implementation	Operational Data (supporting Revenue, Income and Cash Flow
Industry specific PE firms	Financial Engineering (using leverage)	Industry Consulting Reports
	Focus on Core Business	DCF Valuation and other Valuation Methods (Comparables)
		Exit Strategy and Estimated Terminal Values

Therefore, PE firms do not place as much weight on the existing senior management's strengths or weaknesses before making an investment.

Figure 5.5 summarizes who these private equity investors are, the purpose of their investment, and what you need to obtain such an investment.

Typical PE transactions include buyouts of public companies (public to private) or buyouts of private companies (private to private or secondary LBO). In some cases, the acquiring firm could have one of its existing portfolio companies buy or merge with the target company to achieve synergies.

PE firms look to hold investments in their portfolio for 3 to 5 years. The investments in these companies are typically replaced by larger sums from other PE firms or via the IPO market. IPOs are especially considered if the stock markets are very attractive in order to get the best value possible.

GETTING READY TO GO TO MARKET

Before the owners of the company go to the market to raise capital, they first need to evaluate if they are ready to do so. The strategy needs to be clear and the business model needs to be validated. The preliminary investor presentation, which will at some point become the information memorandum to attract investors, needs to answer the following questions:

- Who are we? The answer must include a description of the company, its management, and its stage of growth and development.
- Why invest in us? The answer should be the company's investment thesis including its target markets, product uniqueness, and the validation of its proposed technology.
- What is our strategy? A full-scope strategic plan identifies the problem, the need for a solution, why there's a substantial enough opportunity for profit, and how

this can become a business opportunity that sustains itself into the future, all of which encompass the characteristics that need to be considered in the final go-to-market strategy.

- How do we get there? The investors run a financial model that shows the expected revenue growth, the cash flow needs to support it, and a basic valuation of the company's enterprise value.
- What do we need to make that happen? Management must consider how much capital funding is reasonably attainable and sustainable. A capacity analysis will help curb and measure expectations of ongoing funding needs and capabilities.
- How much time will it take? The strategy needs to establish a set timeline that is in line with the company's growth and is attractive enough to investors that they anticipate receiving their intended return.

STEP I: GENERATING INTEREST

Typically, more mature companies in their development stage hire a financial advisor or an investment banker to assist the company with raising capital. The owners of these companies will call a few of these advisors and ask them to present their pitch on how they can assist the company with a successful fundraising execution. The importance of hiring an advisor is that they have the "rolodex" of contacts and can advise the company on who is the best fit as a source of capital. After the company chooses its advisor, they work together on creating an information memorandum or business plan.

STEP II: WRITING THE INFORMATION MEMORANDUM

The information memorandum (IM) is a document created by the business owners, assisted by the advisor, for prospective investors or buyers. The primary purpose of the IM is to motivate potential investment into the business.

The IM is the most effective way to summarize all the information about a company to give to investors. When preparing the IM, it is beneficial to look at it from the prospective of the buyer. This will help the company reflect on how to structure the IM. Sometimes, especially if the company is for sale, the advisor or bank will implement a staple financing package to attract investors. Because access to capital funding is already in place, investors are enticed to bid due to a smoother and quicker execution. Staple financing will include the potential selling price, any additional expenses, and how much equity the investor needs in conjunction with the debt financing. An example of staple financing is demonstrated in the next section of this chapter.

Figure 5.6 is an example checklist for an information memorandum.

FIGURE 5.6 CHECKLIST FOR INFORMATION MEMORANDUM

1. Executive Summary
- Company Overview ☐
- Key financials and company drivers ☐
- Transaction Key investment considerations ☐
- Investment considerations ☐

2. Company
- History ☐
- Legal structure ☐
- Business model and product information ☐
- Vision and strategy ☐

3. Business
- Segments, business units and markets ☐
- Description of products and services ☐
- Customers, references, and networks ☐

4. Resources
- Organization chart ☐
- Labor and operations ☐
- Infrastructure & manufacturing ☐

5. Operations
- Suppliers and procurement ☐
- Production and distribution ☐
- Management ☐
- Research and development ☐
- Systems and processes ☐
- Marketing and sales ☐

6. Customers
- Key customers ☐
- Customer concentration ☐
- Attrition trends and projections ☐
- Market share ☐

7. Industry
- Description of Industry and structure ☐
- Competitors ☐
- Competitive position ☐
- Strategic position ☐

8. Financials
- Financial overview ☐
- Income statement ☐
- Balance Sheet statement ☐
- Cash flow statement ☐

9. Outlook
- Summarize existing state of affairs ☐
- Highlight long and short term goals ☐
- Main strategies utilized in market trends ☐
- Main growth strategies ☐

STEP III: STAPLE FINANCING

The advisor will call few banks to secure staple financing commitments. Staple financing is a financing package arranged by a company for potential purchasers as part of an auction process. The staple financing package includes the amount of the loan, the maturity date, pricing such as interest and fees, and other terms such as loan covenants. The term *staple* comes from the fact that the bank commitment letter and term sheets are stapled to the back of the acquisition term sheet provided by the company that is interested in selling.

The purpose of staple financing is for quickening the bidding process. In doing so, the buyers do not have to go out and obtain their own debt financing, as the arrangement is already included as part of the deal. Due to a conflict of interest, the advisor may ask other banks to provide such financing instead of their own investment banking institution. Occasionally, though, the advisor may indeed ask his or her own investment bank to initiate the financing packages with the buyer, in addition to providing advisory services to the seller. In these cases, the investment bank is expected to create separate teams within the institution, called "trees," and confidentiality/separation between the teams is ensured.

The advisor representing the buyer is seeking the maximum available debt financing so the return on equity can be achieved. The bank providing such financing is trying to create a structure with the right amount of debt so that the company can comfortably service the loan and hopefully achieve the intended equity return expectation. Steps IV is better explained through an actual case study.

Credit

Fig. 5.1b: Copyright © 2015 Depositphotos/smokhov.

CASE STUDY

ALEXANDRIA HOTEL PROPERTY

The "Transaction Sources and Uses of Alexandria Hotel" shown in figure 5.7 is based on the comfort level of the banks attempting to provide the appropriate level of leverage. In this case, the comfort level of the bank loan is set at 3x senior loan to first-year's EBITDA, and the mezzanine is set at additional 1.5x mezzanine debt to first-year's EBITDA for a total leverage ratio of 5x. At this level of leverage and based on reasonable projections, the model will show that the equity return is higher than the expected equity returns of the 20% minimum expectation, as calculated by the capital asset pricing model (CAPM) (See figure 5.10 showing IRR of 28.77%).

Figure 5.7 shows that based on first-year's EBITDA of $20 million, the maximum level of debt for this specific single property hotel business is set at total debt to EBITDA ratio of 5x made of up the $60 million bank loan set at 3x leverage ratio and the mezzanine note of $40 million. Pricing for the bank loan and mezzanine note is the floating rate of LIBOR + 4% and 9% fixed, respectively. The after-tax weighted average cost of capital (WACC) between debt and expected equity return is calculated at 8.87% and the EBITDA acquisition multiple including $120 million for the purchase of the business and its existing assets, $10 million to renovate the property, and $3.6 million of transaction fees is at 6.7x. This will be the minimum suggested price that the seller is expected to receive though the returns are not usually shared with the buyer. The buyer will run his or her own projections based on the staple financing or other available financing.

The summary financing term sheets for both debt facilities are shown in figure 5.8.

FIGURE 5.7 ALEXANDRIA HOTEL PROPERTY LBO EQUITY ANALYSIS USING CAPM

LBO Equity Analysis using CAPM

TRANSACTION SOURCES & USES

Sources:	Debt Capacity (EBITDA x)	Amount	% Capital	Interest / Exp. Return	Interest/ Exp. Ret. (After Tax)	WACC (After Tax)	EBITDA Multiple
Bank Loan (LIBOR + 4.0% for 7 years)	3.0x	60,000,000	44.9%	7.359%	4.710%	2.12%	3.0x
Mezzanine Note (9.0% Fixed for 8 yrs)		40,000,000	29.9%	9.000%	5.760%	1.72%	2.0x
Total Debt	5.0x	100,000,000	74.9%			3.84%	**5.0x**
Private Equity		33,600,000	25.1%	**20.00%**	**20.00%**	5.03%	1.7x
Total Sources		133,600,000	100.0%			**8.87%**	**6.7x**

Uses:	1st Year's EBITDA Multiple	Amount ($)	% of Total Uses
Purchase of the business	6.0x	**120,000,000**	89.8%
Property Renovation		10,000,000	
Transaction Fees & Expenses	3.0%	3,600,000	2.7%
Total Uses		133,600,000	100.0%

Projected First Year's EBITDA	**20,000,000**
Tax Rate	**36.00%**

MINIMUM COST OF EQUITY CALCULATION USING CAPM (EXPECTED RETURN) $E(re) = rf + \beta . Pe + e$	
6-year Treasury Note [rf]	2.60%
Beta for Publicly Traded Hotel [β]	1.582x
Equity Premium [Pe]	11.00%
Firm Specific Risk Premium [e]	0.0%
Cost of Equity	**20.00%**

FIGURE 5.8 ALEXANDRIA HOTEL PROPERTY SUMMARY TERM SHEET FOR BANK LOAN AND MEZZANINE NOTE

Summary Term Sheets for Bank Loan and Mezzanine Note

DESCRIPTION	BANK LOAN	MEZZANINE
Borrower	Alexandria Hotel Property Inc.	Alexandria Hotel Property Inc.
Security	Perfected Pledge of (i) all of the Borrower's capital stock and (ii) substantially all assets of the Borrower	Unsecured
Facilities	Term Loan $60,000,000	Note $40,000,000
Initial Coupon	LIBOR + 400 bps	9.0% Fixed
Tenor	7 years	8 years
Scheduled Amortization	Year 1: $3mm, Year 2:$4mm, Year 3:$5mm, Year 4:$5mm, Year 5:$6mm, Year 6:$7mm, Year 7:$30mm	Year 1-7: $0 Year 8: $40mm
Mandatory Prepayments	100% non-ordinary course asset sales proceeds 100% net cash process from Debr issuances and 50% excess cash flow Change of Onwership Control	Change of Ownership Control
Financial Covenants	6..0x Total Debt Leverage	No Covenants

Applying the scheduled amortization shown on figure 5.8, the projected debt service is shown in figure 5.9. The model will also assume that LIBOR will start at 2.25% and increase by 0.5%, 0.5%, and 1% for years 1, 2, and 3, respectively. This projected debt service for both facilities is used to calculate the equity return for the buyer, shown in figure 5.10.

Figure 5.10 shows a 7-year projected cash flow based on reasonable assumptions including 6.5% revenue growth, 35% cost of revenue as a percentage of revenues, 15% operating costs as a percentage of revenues, and 3.0% capital expenditures as a percentage

FIGURE 5.9 ALEXANDRIA HOTEL PROPERTY DEBT SCHEDULE AND ASSUMPTIONS

Debt Schedule and Assumptions

DEBT ASSUMPTIONS & RETURN ANALYSIS										
Bank Loan Information	*Debt IRR*	Terms	2020	2021	2022	2023	2024	2025	2026	2027
Amount Outstanding (End of Year)		**60,000,000**	57,000,000	53,000,000	48,000,000	43,000,000	37,000,000	30,000,000	-	-
Schedule Principal Payments		**7 years**	3,000,000	4,000,000	5,000,000	5,000,000	6,000,000	7,000,000	30,000,000	-
Interest Payment (Calc based on last Year's Outs)		**7.36%**	3,750,000	3,847,500	3,842,500	3,960,000	3,547,500	3,052,500	2,475,000	-
Total Financing Payment	7.359%	(60,000,000)	6,750,000	7,847,500	8,842,500	8,960,000	9,547,500	10,052,500	32,475,000	-
LIBOR RATE		*2.25%*	*2.25%*	*2.75%*	*3.25%*	*4.25%*	*4.25%*	*4.25%*	*4.25%*	*104.25%*
LIBOR Rate Increase Assumptions			*0.00%*	*0.50%*	*0.50%*	*1.00%*	*0.00%*	*0.00%*	*0.00%*	*100.00%*
Interest Rate			*6.25%*	*6.75%*	*7.25%*	*8.25%*	*8.25%*	*8.25%*	*8.25%*	*108.25%*
Mezzanine Note										
Amount Outstanding		**40,000,000**	40,000,000	40,000,000	40,000,000	40,000,000	40,000,000	40,000,000	40,000,000	-
Schedule Principal Payments		**8 years**	-	-	-	-	-	-	-	40,000,000
Interest Payment (Calc based on last Year's Outs)		**9.00%**	3,600,000	3,600,000	3,600,000	3,600,000	3,600,000	3,600,000	3,600,000	3,600,000
Total Financing Payment	9.000%	(40,000,000)	3,600,000	3,600,000	3,600,000	3,600,000	3,600,000	3,600,000	3,600,000	43,600,000
Total Financing			10,350,000	11,447,500	12,442,500	12,560,000	13,147,500	13,652,500	36,075,000	43,600,000
Total Debt Outstanding			97,000,000	93,000,000	88,000,000	83,000,000	77,000,000	70,000,000	40,000,000	-

FIGURE 5.10 ALEXANDRIA HOTEL PROPERTY CASH FLOW PROJECTIONS AND EQUITY RETURN

Cash Flow Porjection and Equity Return

CASH FLOW & EQUITY RETURN ANALYSIS									Exit Year	
Company Projections	**Operating Assump.**		**Entry Year 2019**	Year 1 **2020**	Year 2 **2021**	Year 3 **2022**	Year 4 **2023**	Year 5 **2024**	Year 6 **2025**	**2026**
Revenues	6.50%	growth		40,000,000	42,600,000	45,369,000	48,317,985	51,458,654	54,803,467	58,365,692
Cost of Revenues	35.0%	% of Revenue		(14,000,000)	(14,910,000)	(15,879,150)	(16,911,295)	(18,010,529)	(19,181,213)	(20,427,992)
Operating Costs	15.0%	% of Revenue		(6,000,000)	(6,390,000)	(6,805,350)	(7,247,698)	(7,718,798)	(8,220,520)	(8,754,854)
EBITDA	50.0%			**20,000,000**	**21,300,000**	**22,684,500**	**24,158,993**	**25,729,327**	**27,401,733**	**29,182,846**
Less Depreciation	3.00%	% of Revenue		(1,200,000)	(1,278,000)	(1,361,070)	(1,449,540)	(1,543,760)	(1,644,104)	(1,750,971)
Less Amortization of Fees	7	years		(514,286)	(514,286)	(514,286)	(514,286)	(514,286)	(1,028,571)	
EBIT				18,285,714	19,507,714	20,809,144	22,195,167	23,671,282	24,729,058	27,431,875
Less Interest (Unlevered for DCF Analysis)				-	-	-	-	-	-	-
EBT				18,285,714	19,507,714	20,809,144	22,195,167	23,671,282	24,729,058	27,431,875
Less Taxes (adj out Interest Exp)	36.0%	% of EBT		(6,582,857)	(7,022,777)	(7,491,292)	(7,990,260)	(8,521,661)	(8,902,461)	(9,875,475)
Plus Depreciation & Amortization				1,714,286	1,792,286	1,875,356	1,963,825	2,058,045	2,672,675	1,750,971
Less Working Capital	0.00%	% of Revenue		-	-	-	-	-	-	-
Less Capex	2.00%	% of Revenue		(800,000)	(852,000)	(907,380)	(966,360)	(1,029,173)	(1,096,069)	(1,167,314)
Cash Flow Before Financing (CFBF)				**12,617,143**	**13,425,223**	**14,285,828**	**15,202,373**	**16,178,493**	**17,403,203**	**18,140,057**
Less Financing (P + I)				(10,350,000)	(11,447,500)	(12,442,500)	(12,560,000)	(13,147,500)	(13,652,500)	(36,075,000)
Equity Cash Flows				2,267,143	1,977,723	1,843,328	2,642,373	3,030,993	3,750,703	(17,934,943)
Terminal Value										
EBITDA Multiple Method (initial purchase multiple)			**6.7x**						183,043,578	
Perpetuity Method (using next year's CFBF and WACC)			**8.87%**						204,504,549	
Average Terminal Value									**193,774,064**	
Debt Outstanding									70,000,000	
Equity Value (TV - Debt)									123,774,064	
Equity Cash Flows			**(33,600,000)**	**2,267,143**	**1,977,723**	**1,843,328**	**2,642,373**	**3,030,993**	**127,524,767**	
				x	x	x	x	x	x	
$ 1 PV Table (Expected Equity Rate)			**20.00%**	*0.8333073*	*0.6944010*	*0.5786495*	*0.4821928*	*0.4018148*	*0.3348352*	
PV Table (Expected Equity Rate)			**49,521,010**	1,889,227	1,373,333	1,066,641	1,274,133	1,217,898	42,699,780	
Initial Investment			**(33,600,000)**							
NPV=			**15,921,010**							
IRR=			**28.77%**							

of revenues. The discount cash flow analysis shows that the expected equity return is at 28.77%, about 8.77% higher than the minimum return expectation (DCF analysis is explained in detailed on chapters 9 and 17).

STEP IV: EQUITY FINANCING AND RETURN ANALYSIS

Once the buyer receives the information on the company and the staple financing offer package, he or she runs his or her own analysis to derive a bidding price. The analysis of a private equity firm is based primarily on return expectation. Assuming the return expectation is 25%, the analysis will suggest a price that the buyer is willing to pay based on the financing available and using the same projected cash flows provided by management. Figure 5.11 shows that at 25% expected return, the maximum price the buyer is willing to pay for Alexandria Hotel Property stock is $125 million, plus the $10 million renovation and $3.75 million transactions fees.

STEP V: BIDDING PROCESS

The buyers or investors who are planning to buy the whole company or partially invest in the company are asked to put in a bid at a set date that includes the financing structure. Sometimes they are also asked to present their strategy with the operations and

FIGURE 5.11 ALEXANDRIA HOTEL PROPERTY LBO EQQUITY ANALYSIS USING CAMP

LBO Equity Analysis using CAPM

TRANSACTION SOURCES & USES

Sources:	Debt Capacity (EBITDA x)	Amount	% Capital	Expected Return	Expected Return (After Tax)	WACC (After Tax)	EBITDA Multiple
Bank Loan	3.0x	60,000,000	43.2%	7.359%	4.710%	2.04%	3.0x
Mezzanine Note		40,000,000	28.8%	9.000%	5.760%	1.66%	2.0x
Total Debt	5.0x	100,000,000	72.1%			3.70%	**5.0x**
Equity		38,750,000	27.9%	**20.00%**	**20.00%**	5.59%	1.9x
Total Sources		138,750,000	100.0%			**9.28%**	**6.9x**

Uses:	1st Year's EBITDA Multiple	Amount ($)	% of Total Uses
Purchase of the business	6.0x	**125,000,000**	90.1%
Property Renovation		10,000,000	
Transaction Fees & Expenses	3.0%	3,750,000	2.7%
Total Uses		138,750,000	100.0%

CASH FLOW & EQUITY RETURN ANALYSIS

Company Projections	Operating Assump.	Entry Year 2019	Year 1 2020	Year 2 2021	Year 3 2022	Year 4 2023	Year 5 2024	Exit Year 2025	2026
Revenues	6.50% growth		40,000,000	42,600,000	45,369,000	48,317,985	51,458,654	54,803,467	58,365,692
Cost of Revenues	35.0% % of Revenue		(14,000,000)	(14,910,000)	(15,879,150)	(16,911,295)	(18,010,529)	(19,181,213)	(20,427,992)
Operating Costs	15.0% % of Revenue		(6,000,000)	(6,390,000)	(6,805,350)	(7,247,698)	(7,718,798)	(8,220,520)	(8,754,854)
EBITDA	50.0%		**20,000,000**	**21,300,000**	**22,684,500**	**24,158,993**	**25,729,327**	**27,401,733**	**29,182,846**
Less Depreciation	3.00% % of Revenue		(1,200,000)	(1,278,000)	(1,361,070)	(1,449,540)	(1,543,760)	(1,644,104)	(1,750,971)
Less Amortization of Fees	7 years		(535,714)	(535,714)	(535,714)	(535,714)	(535,714)	(1,071,429)	
EBIT			18,264,286	19,486,286	20,787,716	22,173,739	23,649,853	24,686,201	27,431,875
Less Interest (Unlevered for DCF Analysis)			-	-	-	-	-	-	-
EBT			18,264,286	19,486,286	20,787,716	22,173,739	23,649,853	24,686,201	27,431,875
Less Taxes (adj out Interest Exp)	36.0% % of EBT		(6,575,143)	(7,015,063)	(7,483,578)	(7,982,546)	(8,513,947)	(8,887,032)	(9,875,475)
Plus Depreciation & Amortization			1,735,714	1,813,714	1,896,784	1,985,254	2,079,474	2,715,533	1,750,971
Less Working Capital	0.00% % of Revenue		-	-	-	-	-	-	-
Less Capex	2.00% % of Revenue		(800,000)	(852,000)	(907,380)	(966,360)	(1,029,173)	(1,096,069)	(1,167,314)
Cash Flow Before Financing (CFBF)			**12,624,857**	**13,432,937**	**14,293,542**	**15,210,087**	**16,186,207**	**17,418,632**	**18,140,057**
Less Financing (P + I)			(10,350,000)	(11,447,500)	(12,442,500)	(12,560,000)	(13,147,500)	(13,652,500)	(76,075,000)
Equity Cash Flows			2,274,857	1,985,437	1,851,042	2,650,087	3,038,707	3,766,132	(57,934,943)
Terminal Value									
EBITDA Multiple Method (initial purchase multiple)		**6.9x**						190,099,525	
Perpetuity Method (using WACC)		**9.28%**						195,392,351	
Average Terminal Value								**192,745,938**	
Debt Outstanding								70,000,000	
Equity Value (TV - Debt)								122,745,938	
Equity Cash Flows		**(38,750,000)**	**2,274,857**	**1,985,437**	**1,851,042**	**2,650,087**	**3,038,707**	**126,512,070**	
			x	x	x	x	x	x	
$ 1 PV Table (Expected Equity Rate)		**20.00%**	*0.8333073*	*0.6944010*	*0.5786495*	*0.4821928*	*0.4018148*	*0.3348352*	
PV Table (Expected Equity Rate)		**49,204,992**	1,895,655	1,378,690	1,071,105	1,277,853	1,220,997	42,360,693	
Initial Investment		**(38,750,000)**							
NPV=		**10,454,992**							
IRR=		**25.31%**							

management. Throughout the process of choosing the right investors, there are several bidding sessions that take place.

STEP VI: FILING REQUIREMENTS IF NECESSARY

The private target company is not required to publicly file documents with the SEC. When a public acquirer buys a private target, it may require filing certain disclosure documents, especially if they need to issue shares in excess of 20% of the pre-deal shares.

For leveraged buyouts (LBOs) that use high-yield bonds to finance private targets, purchasers need to file an S-4 with the SEC. The S-4 typically contains data on the purchase price and financial information on the target.

PROBLEMS

Construct the transaction sources and uses, calculate the WACC, and complete the debt schedules for the following case studies:

1. **Green Landscape Services LLP**

Transaction

Heinz Ward & Co. (HW), a private equity firm, signed an agreement to acquire Green Landscape Services LLP ("GLS") for an aggregate of $1.8 billion. The $1.8 billion acquisition includes (a) the purchase of all the company's 100 million shares at $13 per share, and (b) transaction expenses of $50 million and the balance of the $450 million to be applied to pay off the company's debt.

Use 22% tax rate.

Company Overview

GLS is a provider of residential landscape services in 30 states, primarily in the Northeast and Midwest. GLS served approximately 500,000 customers last year.

Capital Raising

HW is in the process of raising the necessary funds to cover the purchase price, refinance GLS's existing debt, and pay for transaction fees. The proposed structure is as follows.

Bank Debt Financing

Spring Bank approved a loan based on the company's next year EBITDA. The money terms were as follows:

AMOUNT	4.0 × LAST YEAR'S EBITDA
Interest	6% fixed
Term	5 years
Scheduled Payments	Year 1: 5%, Year 2: 5%, Year 3: 10%, Year 4: 10%, Year 5: 70%

Equity Financing

HW will invest the balance of the financing needed to acquire GLS. The expected equity return is based on a risk-free rate of 2.5%, 1.50× beta and 10% market premium.

EBITDA Assumptions

Average revenue per service (ARPS): $60

Average number of services per customer per year: 10 visits

Number of total customers: 500,000

Cost of revenue as 50% of revenue

Operating expenses as 20% of revenue

DO THE FOLLOWING (use template spreadsheet via Active Learning):

a. Construct the transaction sources and uses
b. Calculate the WACC
c. Prepare the Debt Schedule

2. **Colorado Dental LLP**

Transaction

Joseph & Clyde (J&C), a private equity firm, signed an agreement to acquire Colorado Dental LLP ("Colorado Dental") for an aggregate of $1.1 billion (before transaction expenses). The $1.1 billion acquisition includes a purchase of equity of $780 million and $320 million of refinancing of existing debt. Transaction fees are $50 million.

Use 22.0% Tax Rate

Company Overview

Colorado Dental operates 480 locations across 30 states, primarily in the Northeast and Midwest. The dentists supported by Colorado Dental last year 6 served 2 million patients.

Capital Raising

HW is in the process of raising the necessary funds to cover the purchase price, refinance Colorado Dental's existing debt, and pay for transaction fees. The proposed structure is as follows.

Equity

HW will invest $600 million of equity.

Bank Debt

Spring Bank approved a loan based on the company's last year EBITDA. The money terms were as follows:

REVOLVER: $100 million ($0 funded on day one)—assume no unfunded expense

TERM LOAN A

AMOUNT	180,000,000
Interest	LIBOR + 3.5%
Term	7 years
Scheduled Payments	Year 1: 5%, Year 2: 5%, Year 3: 8%, Year 4: 10%, Year 5: 12%, Year 6: 15%, Year 7: 45%

TERM LOAN B

AMOUNT	200,000,000
Interest	LIBOR + 4.0%
Term	7 years
Scheduled Payments	Year 1: 1%, Year 2: 1%, Year 3: 1%, Year 4: 1%, Year 5: 1%, Year 6: 1%, Year 7: 94%

Libor assumptions: Starting LIBOR at 0.60%, increase 0.5% in Year 1, increase 0.5% in Year 2, and increase 1.0% in Year 4

Senior Unsecured Notes

Morgan Stanley, an investment bank, managed to raise the senior unsecured notes. The money terms were as follows:

AMOUNT	THE BALANCE OF THE FINANCING (AFTER BANK LOANS AND EQUITY)
Interest	9.0%
Term	8 years
Scheduled Payments	Year 1–Year 7: 0%, Year 8: 100% (bullet payment)

DO THE FOLLOWING (use template spreadsheet via Active Learning):

a. Construct the transaction sources and uses
b. Calculate the WACC assuming the risk-free rate is 1.0%, Market Return is 10% and the beta is 2.0x
c. Prepare the Debt Schedule

ONLINE TEMPLATES

The Excel spreadsheets used in the chapter can be accessed online via Cognella Active Learning platform.

CHAPTER 6

Equity Markets: Initial Public Offering (IPO) and other Transactions for Publicly Traded Companies

This chapter will cover in detail the last stage of a company's maturity and development: an initial public offering (IPO). Once the company becomes public, the chapter will then describe the precedent of an M&A transaction and the tender offer procedures involved, starting from the bidding stage to the closing and funding stage. The analytical approach for valuing the company in order to raise capital will be described in more detail in chapters 9 and 17. This chapter gives an introduction to the process of raising capital with which the reader should follow up with a valuation analysis of pricing the company for M&A and M&A accretion/dilution, as well as going from public to private via a leveraged buyout (LBO) and recapitalization financing.

LEARNING OBJECTIVES

After reading this chapter, students will be able to do the following:

- Briefly understand the life cycle of a public company
- Understand how a company raises capital at various phases of its growth and development
- Understand the process of an initial public offering (IPO), follow-on offerings, and rights offerings

- Apply various analytical tools as an investment advisor to determine the best course of raising capital
- Understand how transactions are financed including mergers and acquisitions (M&A), takeovers, tender offers (TO), and leveraged buyouts (LBOs)

INITIAL PUBLIC OFFERING: AN OVERVIEW

Everyone knows what an IPO is. It is one of the most exciting milestones of a company. It validates that the company is already successful in what they are doing, and they are ready for the big league. A company that has successfully raised money via IPO has reached the last chapter of their early development and has proven that their product is in demand. Of course, not all IPOs have successful outcomes, but given the rigorous process required to go public, it feels like the company is already successful. It feels like graduation. It's one of the best feelings any student has after achieving such a milestone; but graduation is also the beginning of many more successes. Companies that achieve the milestone of going public are also in the beginning stage of many successful years to come. Accessing capital in the public markets gives a company more options to continue its growth by accessing more ongoing capital from equity investors and other types of investors, such bondholders.

AUTHOR'S NOTES

Companies that are interviewing various investment bankers advising them how to access the market and how much capital they should raise will conduct a "beauty contest" or "bake off." As futile as these cliché terms may sound, they are the best analogies for describing the environment investment bankers find themselves in. When participating in a beauty contest or bake off, investment bankers will do their best to show why they are the most qualified to lead the transaction. Their pitch includes the profiles of people on the team and why they are the best option among their compatriots; they will display their "tombstone" of transactions showing their successful track record; they will promote their industry team and how knowledgeable they are; they will show how active their trading platform is; and they will focus specifically on providing the most attractive valuation analysis of the company. I lived through this process and always smile about how much preparation each investment banker goes through to show his or her best during these periods. There is an old investment banker joke that goes like this: "An investment banker dies and goes to the 'waiting room' to find out if he will end up in heaven or hell. St. Peter was buffaloed that he was the first investment banker on the heaven list and gives him a choice. St. Peter tells him to spend one night in hell and one night in heaven and then report back with a decision on where he wants to spend the rest of the afterlife. Curiously, the investment banker takes the elevator down to hell to see what it's like. The elevator opens and to his surprise he sees all his colleagues who died before him hanging out at the bar and having a great time. Food and drinks were flowing, there was high level entertainment, and a display in the corner scattered with planned golf games for the morning. The next day the banker took the elevator going up to heaven. As the elevator opened, he walked into a well-lit library with wall-to-wall books, yoga mats, and a harper playing music. People were meditating and reading books; it was a very quiet place. After experiencing each place, he obviously decided to go to hell as he longed to have fun with his friends and colleagues. St. Peter scripted the contract; the man signed the agreement, and he jumped on the first elevator down to hell. When the elevator opened, the room was cold and dark with no one in sight. As he crept into the next room, he saw his friends kneeling and cleaning the floors with water and soap while others were digging holes outside. He approached one of his colleagues and asked what was going on. He said, 'I don't get it. Only yesterday we were having so much fun and today this?' His friend leaned over to him and whispered, 'Yesterday, you were a prospect. Today, you are a client.'"

I always visualize the capital markets as a place where the bankers seeking business put on their best behavior to entice clients to sign with them partly for the best execution and partly to show they are the best. I felt the pressure of putting on a show; I spent hours on preparation. While this is a known solicitation process for business, the investment bankers are often expected to provide a view on the likelihood of success for a particular transaction. On one end investment bankers are pressured to entice the client for more business, but at the same time they must be careful not to guarantee or otherwise make any binding commitments regarding the pricing, deal size, or the successful completion of the transaction. An investment banking pitch generally includes a book the banker uses to give a visible description of the transaction to the client. From a compliance perspective, bankers should use a basic pitch style template and have it reviewed by legal or tax professionals. They should never disclose any confidential information on other clients or transactions. Any estimates of transaction fees and expenses should be clearly identified as estimates and the valuation analysis should be unbiased.

KEY TAKEAWAYS

- The company's cash flow and corporate structure determines the types of financing needed.
- The companies that are in the market for raising equity need to understand that fundamentals are more important than technicals. Having a good product, good management, and feasibility in their future is more important than financial engineering and taking advantage of the overenthusiastic markets.
- Valuations are very subjective given all the methods to derive them, but at the end of the day the actual value of the company is the price that someone is willing to pay for it.
- Different cycles in the market or the economy can help or hinder access to equity financing.
- The Securities and Exchange Commission (SEC) is in place to make sure that any publicly traded companies that are in the market to raise capital go through a rigorous process to protect the investor.

THE LIFE CYCLE OF THE PUBLIC COMPANY

A company that decides to raise capital via an initial public offering is viewed as the last stage of the company's growth and development. It could be the last stage of development for the initial owners and subsequent private equity investors but is also the first stage of the life of the company as a public entity which its main goal is to continue to create value for the shareholders. The life cycle of a public company obviously starts with an IPO and continues to grow by accessing the capital markets either to acquire or merger with other companies and/or implement operating strategies to organically grow revenues and profit.

INITIAL PUBLIC OFFERING

A company will seek equity financing from the public markets through a process called an initial public offering (IPO). When the company is IPO ready (discussed next), it will choose to offer its equity to a large market of investors to meet the existing owner's following objectives:

- To provide liquidity for the founders and early private investors to sell their holdings to the public markets

FIGURE 6.1 INITIAL PUBLIC OFFERING

Investors	Purpose of Investment	What do you need
Public Investors - Institutional - Individual	Revenue & EBITDA Growth	- File with the Securities Exchange Commision (SEC) and prepare Prospectus and Information Memorandum - American Depository Receipt (ADR) Registration - SEC Regulation S & D Non-Exempt IssuersInformation Memorandum
	Product Growth Feasibility - Normalization	3 Year Audited Financials
	Back to Fundamentals (no need for financial engineering)	Proven Management / Anchor Investors
		Third Party Valuation Analysis

- To establish a broad-based valuation of the company by offering the stock to a large group of investors, hence increasing the existing value to the current owners who stay post-IPO
- To fund the company's ongoing needs and access follow-on financings
- To create stock that can be used to offer executives and employees retirement plans

Figure 6.1 summarizes who these IPO investors are, the purpose of investment for the public investor, and what the owners need in order to obtain such investment. (The IPO process is discussed in more detail later this chapter.)

The institutional and public investors investing in a new company during and post IPO are looking to enhance their returns through earnings growth and multiple expansion. If this becomes a reality, the broader market will gain confidence and drive the stock price up. It will also continue to increase in the future if expectations for these higher multiples of earnings (PE or EBITDA) are realized. Dividends can also be a source of income for these investors, though typically new IPO companies are still in a growth stage of their development and do not pay dividends.

Raising Common Stock in the Public Markets (Primary Market) and Post-IPO Shareholder Rights and Trading (Secondary Market)

Common stock is the most widely held equity security. Investors receive stock certificates that represent the company's ownership. The state that the company is incorporated in needs to approve the number of shares that will be issued, known as authorized stock or capital stock. These shares are referred to as outstanding shares once they are in the hands of the investors. If the company decides to buy back shares from the public, these shares that are purchased are called treasury shares and are valued and accounted for as a negative number on the balance sheet. When calculating the company's enterprise value these treasury shares are not included in the calculation.

The investors that buy these shares have the following rights:

- **Voting rights:** Holders of common stock exercise control by electing the board of directors that vote on corporate policy. Each share gives the shareholder a share of the vote that represents their percentage of ownership as a percentage of total shares outstanding. The voting can be carried out by either a statutory voting method or cumulative voting method. The statutory voting method is based on the stocks that the shareholders owns: one share = one vote. The cumulative voting method is based on allocating the shares that the shareholder owns to each candidate.
- **Financial reporting and company information:** Shareholders have the right to access certain financial information regarding the company including audited annual reports and quarterly financial statements.
- **Dividends:** There are two ways a shareholder can profit from buying stock: by capital gain, which is buying the stock at one price and selling it for a higher price, with the difference resulting as the return, or by receiving dividends. Shareholders always have the right to receive dividends when the company decides to pay them, something that is not always a guarantee. Companies are free to decide whether to payout their cash flow as dividends or to reinvest part or all the sum into the business. This is a decision that is at the discretion of the board of directors who will weigh future growth possibilities of the company and the capital requirements needed to achieve them. Companies, especially growth companies, may decide not to pay dividends and instead reinvest the profits to grow the company, resulting in a higher pay off in the future.
- **Preemptive rights:** When a company decides to raise additional common stock, the existing shareholders are occasionally given preemptive rights or the right to buy newly issued stock before the shares are sold to the public. This is mainly to give current shareholders the option to keep the same percentage of ownership, basically to prevent dilution. These rights are not common in the U.S. markets but are seen more in younger companies that are still in their growth stages.

Dividend Payment Process

The process of dividend payment is outlined by understanding a congregation of important dates:

1. **Declaration date:** This is the date by which the board of directors declares dividends. In their announcement they mention two other dates including the record date and the payable date.

2. **Record date:** This is the date the shareholder must register on or before to receive the dividend.
3. **Payable date:** This is the date that the dividend is paid to the shareholder on record.
4. **Ex-dividend date:** This is the date 2 business days prior to the record date. Any regular way trades of the stock take 3 days to settle (T+3), which will give the official title of the stock. The ex-dividend date is the first date a buyer can purchase the stock without receiving the dividend. Figure 6.2 gives an illustration of who receives it and when the dividend is paid. In this example, if the Record Date is Friday, the Ex-Dividend is Wednesday (2 business days). Any investor that bought the stock on Monday, Tuesday or even Wednesday are entitled to receive the dividend. If an investor bought the stock on Thursday or Friday, is not entitled to receive the dividend. Such dividend is paid to the seller of the stock.

Stock Splits

A stock split occurs when a company believes the price per share is too high to keep buyers interested in purchasing shares. This of course is due to the perception that the market of buyers shrinks once the stock price is too high, as the common unsophisticated investor looks for other cheaper stocks to purchase instead. For example, a two-for-one split of a stock that is trading at $50 will result in the stock trading at $25 ($50/2). Note that holders of the stock will double their shares at the time of the split, preventing dilution of current

FIGURE 6.2 EX-DIVIDEND DATE & RECORD DATE

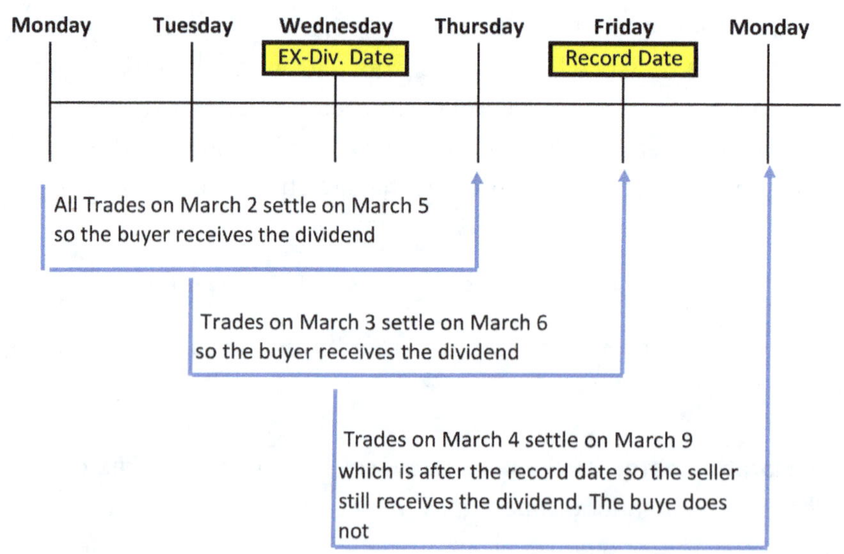

investors. A reverse split is when the stock price is too low, and the company decides to reduce the number of overall shares to increase the per unit price. For this to occur it usually indicates that current perception of the stock is weak and growing weaker, and the low per share price is contributing to that perception. For example, in a one-for-five reverse split, five \$5 shares become one \$25 share (5 x \$5).

Classifying Common Stock

Stocks are classified based on investment characteristics as follows:

Income stocks: These are stocks of companies that consistently pay dividends. When an investor purchases income stock he or she expects to receive dividends. Most of the return for such an investment is based on consistent dividends. Companies that are classified as having income stock are more mature companies with limited research and development and stable cash flows. There are two methods of calculating the dividend payout ratio:

$$\text{Dividend payout ratio} = \frac{\text{Annual dividend}}{\text{Net income}}$$

and per share,

$$\text{Dividend payout ratio} = \frac{\text{Annual dividend per share}}{\text{Earnings per share (EPS)}}$$

The dividend yield (δ) % per share is calculated as follows:

$$\text{Dividend yield } (\delta)\% = \frac{\text{Annual dividend per share}}{\text{Stock price}}$$

Growth stocks: These are stocks of companies that reinvest most of their income into their business. Investors buying these stocks expect a higher capital gain from growth in share price due to expanding earnings/revenue multiples. These stocks also commonly trade at higher multiples or price-to-earnings ratios (P/E). Since the expectation is for the company to grow, the stock is very sensitive if the expected growth (mainly quarterly/yearly earnings targets) is not met. This generally causes the stock to drop even if the profit grows incrementally year over year. Expectations and the potential to meet earnings and revenue targets are key when valuing growth stocks and their potential for capital gain. For tax purposes, note that investors pay less taxes on realized capital gain than on dividend income.

STOCK PRICES AND INVESTMENT OPPORTUNITIES: GROWTH STOCK VERSUS DIVIDEND STOCK

Let's assume that two companies, Cash-Is-King, Inc. (CIK) and Growth-Is-the-Only-Way, Inc. (GITOW), each have an expected net income of $10 per share. In principal, both companies could pay out all the income they've made to the current shareholders as dividends. If the capitalization rate (κ) is 10% (a valuation method discussed in later chapters), both companies would then be valued at D_1/κ = $10/10% = $100 per share. If all the profit was distributed to the shareholders instead of reinvested in the company, the company is not anticipated to grow.

Now suppose rather than paying it out as dividends, GITOW reinvests the profit into a project that generates 15% return on investment. You will notice this is greater than the capitalization rate (κ) of 10%. If that is the case, it would then not make sense to pay all the profit to the shareholders in the form of dividends. Given the good prospects of the project that should return 15%, GITOW decides to pay a much lower dividend in order to reinvest the other portion of the prior year's profit into the project—let's assume they pay out 50% of the profit instead of 100% of the profit. This is called the **payout ratio.** The maintaining of the other 50% is called the **plowback ratio.** In this case, GITOW will only pay $5 in dividends ($5/$10 = 50%) and reinvest the difference of $5 per share into the project that is expected to generate a 15% return.

Suppose GITOW's project costs $100 million and is entirely equity financed. Thus, with an expected return on investment of 15%, it will generate $15 million in income (15% x $100 million). Let's assume there are 3 million shares outstanding at $5.00 per share ($15 million/3 million shares) which would be all of the equity capital invested in the business (there is no debt). If 50% of the project's $15 million profit is reinvested, then the value of the company's stock should increase $7.5 million (50% x $15 million) or 7.5% ($7.5 million/$100 million project). With the 7.5% higher-invested capital, the company yields 7.5% more income and ultimately will pay a 7.5% higher dividend. This is due to the increase in price being that dividend payouts are expressed as a percentage of each share's current value (dividend yield). The 7.5% represents the company's growth rate on the underlying profit and thus the value of the stock will go up. Using the intrinsic value method (discussed in chapter 17) we value the new stock as follows:

$$\text{Price} = \frac{\text{D paid}}{\kappa - g} = \frac{\$5}{.10 - .075} = \$200$$

Notice $200 is twice the value of the $100 current value of CIK's stock, with 100% paid dividends and no growth $\left(\text{Price} = \frac{\text{D paid}}{\kappa - g} = \frac{\$10}{.10 - 0} = \$100\right)$.

It's important to note that the calculated $200 value of the stock for GITOW is based on an expectation that the company will return 15% on the project. The stock will be trading near $200 as the expectation is 100% that the project will be a success. If the realized return of the project is lower, then the stock will drop. The additional $100 ($200 value for GITOW; $100 value for CIK) is called present value of growth opportunities (PVGO).

PRIVATE PLACEMENTS AND PRIVATE INVESTMENT IN PUBLIC EQUITY (PIPES)

Another way of raising capital is through private placement. The company issues shares to accredited investors (instead of the public) under the Securities Exchange Commission's Regulation D. Private placements may be offered to an unlimited number of investors as long as they are accredited. The company prepares a private placement memorandum (PPM), which includes (a) the structure of the deal; (b) brief information about the issuer; (c) the issuer's management; (d) 2–3 years financial statements; (e) risks and other disclosures; (f) use of proceeds; and (g) the subscription agreement and sales contract. Private placement will be more thoroughly discussed in the next chapter.

SYNDICATION OF SECURITIES OFFERINGS

Raising funds including stocks or bonds in the primary markets is very complicated, especially if the funds are raised from the public markets that require an extensive filing process with the SEC. The companies seek supervision from investment bankers who are experienced not only with the process but the strength of their network of investors. Execution is very important.

INITIAL PUBLIC OFFERING (IPO)

An IPO is the company's first public sale of securities; it is essentially when a privately-owned company is going public to raise capital primarily to either fund operations and/or payout the existing owners. The IPO itself is a registered filing with the SEC, offering the sale of the company's stock to public investors. It involves choosing an investment advisor and underwriters to first determine the offering price and then secure potential investors. The success of an IPO is mainly dependent on favorable market conditions. The company also needs to have all the characteristics of an IPO including visibility of stable cash flows, a high probability of growth, and a demonstration of niche industry characteristics. Typically, the process takes 3–6 months depending on the condition of the market and size of the IPO.

Step 1: Selecting the Investment Company/Underwriter

The first step for a company in the IPO process is to choose an investment bank that is willing to underwrite the IPO. Before the IPO process officially starts, the underwriter will ask for a letter of intent (LOI) in order to have an understanding that the process will come underway. This is because the underwriter will usually incur a set of initial expenses. This agreement will typically, at a minimum, offer reimbursement for these expenses in case the company changes its mind with regards to registering for an IPO. Furthermore, the LOI binds the company to being cooperative in the disclosing of all requested financial information during the IPO process. The underwriter will agree to act as diligently as possible in completing the registration and the selling and distribution of the company's shares. The underwriting fees are also included in the LOI.

Step 2: Preparing the Documents for the IPO

The next step in the IPO process involves preparing all the necessary information including financial statements that will be disclosed for official registration. The Securities Exchange Commission (SEC) has a very specific criteria for filing. The SEC's duty is to make sure that the company adequately informs the prospective investors about the financial performance of the firm and the risk factors present. The document that includes all the information the SEC requires is referred to as the preliminary prospectus or the red hearings.

Step 3: SEC Registration and Approval

After the preliminary prospectus is filed with the SEC, the SEC makes an announcement that the registration is effective. The SEC will then continue to work with the underwriter to gain additional supplemental information and make the necessary corrections in order for the registration to be approved.

Step 4: Marketing the IPO

After official approval to solicit interest from the syndicate of investors, the next step in the IPO process involves marketing the strengths of the company and the investment considerations to these prospective investors. The marketing involves presentations and various pitches that are sent to large-scale investors such as financial institutions and corporations.

Step 5: Indication of Interest

Based on supply and demand the underwriter determines a market price for the IPO stock, the number of initial shares being offered, and the date open trading will begin. Additional details including the number of initial institutional investors, any price discounts, and modified market prices are filed as an amendment to the original registration.

Step 6: Closing, Funding, and Free to Trade

The underwriter then announces the price and determines that the trade process has been established. It takes approximately 3 days (T+3) for the IPO exchange to close. The stock is then delivered, and the company receives the proceeds (net of underwriting fees) from its sale. The underwriter's obligation is to monitor the stock's price for a few months post-IPO and exercise the right to purchase or sell shares to make sure the stock stabilizes.

TYPES OF UNDERWRITING COMMITMENTS

There are two types of underwriting commitments related to the stock in an IPO: firm commitment and best-effort commitment.

Firm Commitment

A firm commitment is a commitment from the underwriters that enables them to purchase all the shares that are offered in an IPO. The lead underwriter (referred to as "left lead" or "book-runner") is responsible to sell, through the syndicate (the other committed underwriters), all the shares to interested institutional and retail investors. If there is not enough demand to sell all the shares after the price is set, any unsold shares are to be distributed among the syndicate. Sometimes the agreement between the company and the underwriters includes provisions for additional shares that will be issued post-IPO. These shares could have preemptive rights. In this arrangement, the stocks that are offered as an addition are offered first to current shareholders 2 to 3 weeks prior to being offered to the public. This process is called a rights' offering. These shares are first offered to existing shareholders, then to the retail investors, and if there are remaining shares the syndicate purchases them, referred to as **standby commitments.**

Best-Effort Commitment

A best effort's underwriting agreement is an agreement in which the underwriters seek to sell all the shares to the interested investors but have no obligation to purchase any unsold shares. Typically, this agreement is for higher-risk issuers or tough IPO markets, as the underwriters do not want to take any market risk. Some best-efforts agreements are set as "all or none." This refers to a best-effort attempt to sell the shares. If they are short (undersubscribed) of selling 100% of the shares, the offering is cancelled within a specific timeframe (i.e., the IPO is postponed or cancelled).

CHOOSING AN UNDERWRITER (S)

For choosing the left lead underwriter or co-underwriters, the company will contact many investment bankers and ask them to give their proposal for a successful IPO offering. The company, in this case the issuer, will decide between the left lead underwriter and other

FIGURE 6.3 COMPONENTS OF THE UNDERWRITING SPREAD

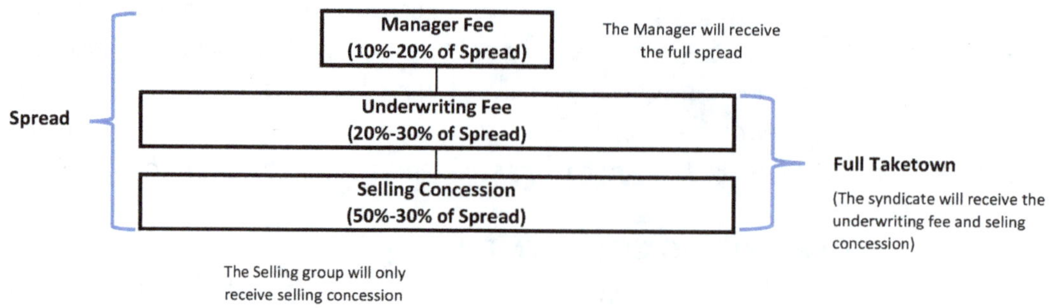

underwriters on who lead the offering. This is largely based on who they feel will provide a successful execution and stable process. For an IPO, typically, the competing process (called a bake-off) for choosing the left lead underwriter is through a negotiation process involving all the interested underwriters. Part of the underwriting agreement between the underwriter(s)—in a firm agreement—is the ability to purchase the shares from the issuer and sell them to the public at the offering price. The purchase of the shares from the issuer will run at a discount to the public offering price, representing the underwriter's fees, referred to as an underwriter's spread.

Underwriting spread (fees): The components of the spread include three types of fees: manager's fee, underwriting fee, and selling concession fee. The **manager's fee** is the fee that the left lead or the manager of the syndicate receives first. The **underwriting fee** is the fee that the syndicate of underwriters receives. The **selling concession** is the fee that the managing underwriter, the syndicate members, and the selling group receive based on the shares sold. Figure 6.3 shows the components of the underwriting spread.

Breaking down underwriting compensation: For small companies, a typical underwriting spread fee is around 12%, or a discount rate of 88% of the IPO proceeds raised from the offering. Figure 6.4 shows an example of a Celerity Technology Inc. IPO and the allocation of the spread compensation to the manager, the syndicate, and the selling groups.

BUILDING THE BOOK

The first responsibility of the left lead manager is to pre-market the offering to institutional investors (qualified investors). The other underwriters in the syndicate also start pre-marketing to their own investors. Before they start this process, called building the book, each underwriter of the syndicate is allocated shares by the left lead manager. The Celerity Technology IPO example (Figure 6.4) shows that the company or the issuer is planning to issue 15 million shares. The left lead manager keeps 9 million of the shares and the remaining 6 million are allocated pro-rata (equally) among the three underwriters.

FIGURE 6.4 CELERITY TECHNOLOGY INC. INITIAL PUBLIC OFFERING

Initial Public Offering

Shares Sold:	15,000,000

Transaction Sources & Uses:

Sources:		
Securities	**Amount $**	**% Capital**
Corporate Loan	-	0.0%
Corporate Bond	-	0.0%
Equity	600,000,000	100.0%
Total Sources:	600,000,000	100.0%

Uses:				
Allocation of Capital		**Per Share**	**Total Proceeds**	**% of Total**
IPO Porceeds to the Issuer		$37.60	564,000,000	94.0%
Gross Spread (Fee)	6.00%	$ 2.40	36,000,000	6.0%
Total Offering Price		$40.00	600,000,000	100.0%
Other Trans. Expenses			00	
Total Uses			600,000,000	

Syndication Analysis	Allocation	Shares Sold	Left-Lead Fees	U/W Fee	Selling Concession	Total Takedown	Total Spread
Percentage of Spread			**20%**	**30%**	**50%**	**80%**	**100%**
Per Share			**$0.48**	**$0.72**	**$1.20**	**$1.92**	**$2.40**
Left Lead Underwritter	9,000,000	8,000,000	7,200,000	6,480,000	9,600,000	16,080,000	23,280,000
Syndicate Member A	2,000,000	1,000,000		1,440,000	1,200,000	2,640,000	2,640,000
Syndicate Member B	2,000,000	1,000,000		1,440,000	1,200,000	2,640,000	2,640,000
Syndicate Member C	2,000,000	1,000,000		1,440,000	1,200,000	2,640,000	2,640,000
Selling Group (Total)		4,000,000			4,800,000	4,800,000	4,800,000
Total	15,000,000	15,000,000	7,200,000	10,800,000	18,000,000	28,800,000	36,000,000

These institutional investors who are interested in purchasing the stock will give an indication of interest (IOI). These IOIs will become orders on the effective day, though they are not obliged at this point to commit and are able to cancel any time before purchase. The syndicate, and other institutional investors are motivated to be part of the selling group so they can accumulate fees. Therefore, in the marketing stage, the involved investment banks are calling/presenting to groups of high-quality investors to get either verbal or written IOIs. Much larger investors will ask to meet management and view their presentations.

The building-the-book stage is probably one of the most important stages during the offering as the manager, syndicate, and selling group receive a lot of market feedback and evaluate the demand, which can be used as the basis to start the discussion on the offering price. The initial discussion on the offering price is usually a range. Using Celerity Technology's IPO example above (Figure 6.4) before it settled at $40, the range could have been $38–42. This range is not binding and the discussion with the investors during this period is to close in on a range based on strong or weak demand. If there is a strong demand at a certain price the underwriters may decide to increase the number of shares. Once all the investor demand is accounted for based on the range, the underwriters work with the syndicate and the selling group to allocate or "circle" shares. Technically, investors can change their minds and get out of their circle, but this practice is discouraged as it would be a devastating business blunder for the investor in case of future business with the syndicate group.

SETTING UP THE INVESTOR LIST BY UNDERWRITER (ALLOTMENT)

Before the building-the-book stage, which involves the pre-marketing of the offering, the list of investors could be allocated among the underwriters. This process, which is the preferred process in the United States, is called a **fixed-pot arrangement.** This arrangement is sometimes cleaner to execute since each underwriter focuses on his or her allocated list of investors and fees are shared across all, despite one underwriter doing better than the other. The **jump-ball arrangement** is basically an arrangement that the credit of circling investors is on a first-come-first-serve basis and the underwriters are paid based on how big a book they are building with IOIs.

PRICING

The left lead manager is untimely responsible for letting the issuer know about the success or failure of the book-building effort and the state of the market, including records of other IPOs that have already been priced. **The manager also confirms the final pricing and scheduling.** After looking at the final book with all the orders at different prices within the range, the manager sets the price and communicates it to the company. In the Celerity Technology IPO example, (Figure 6.4) the final price is $40, given that the total issuance represents 15 million shares and the total capital raised is calculated to be $600 million. After subtracting the gross fees, totaling 6% of the total capital raised, or $36 million are allocated, the net proceeds to the company are estimated to be $564 million before any other transaction expenses.

OTHER IPO TERMS, CONCEPTS, AND CONDITIONS

Over-Allotment Option (Green Shoe)

Many underwriting agreements may include a provision that the underwriter can exercise: the option to issue more shares than originally anticipated. This provision is called "Green Shoe" and is usually used when the orders from investors are higher than the original number of shares scheduled to be issued. The over-allotment option is known as a Green Shoe named after the Green Shoe Manufacturing Company was the first to issue this type of option some time ago. This is used to provide some price stability and helps balance volume and price when it is free to trade in the secondary exchange market. This option typically allows the underwriters to create and sell more shares (maximum allowed 15%). The actual percentage and terms are included in the prospectus that is filed with the SEC prior to the offering.

The decision to use the Green Shoe option is dependent on the market demand for the offering. If the IPO is a success and stock price increases after the IPO is priced, the underwriters can buy extra stock from the company at the IPO price and sell it in the market to record a profit. On the other hand, if the prices post-IPO closing decrease, they buy back from the market at a lower price to support their short position and support the price of the stock. Most issuers don't like this option in the agreement, especially if the proceeds of the IPO are used for a special project with a defined purpose.

Lock-Up Agreements

Since one of the underwriters' responsibilities is to stabilize the stock after the IPO is priced, the underwriters generally require the management of the issuer and large shareholders to enter a lock-up agreement. This agreement is meant to avoid a group of insiders such as management and large holders of stock dumping the stock after the IPO is priced and causing a steep price decline. The lock-up period is typically set at 180 days. This should be enough time to allow the stock to stabilize after the IPO.

MERGER AND ACQUISITION TRANSACTION

Specific transactions such a merger or an acquisition involves a process similar to raising capital discussed above, especially in the merger or the acquisition that involves publicly traded companies. The process could involve advisors, such as an investment banker, on both the buy side and sell side to make sure that the execution is successful at the best possible price for both the seller and buyer.

STEPS FOR THE TRANSACTION ANALYSIS

Prior to any transaction such as an initial public offering, merger and acquisition, or restructuring, the investment banker hired to assist with such transactions needs to conduct a preliminary analysis to determine the offering price range. This analysis involves multiple methods to derive a price range including trading comparable analysis, acquisition comparable analysis, and the discount cash flow method. Chapter 17 goes into an in-depth discussion on these and other methods that are used to value the company. The following shows the step-by-step approach to executing such pre-pricing transaction analysis.

Step 1: Select Comparable Acquisitions

The investment banker's job is first to identify the comparable companies to be used for trading comps. This is always very challenging. The investment banker finds him- or herself justifying ways that these companies are truly comparable to the target and its sector. The banker first searches his or her own database to see if a relevant set of comparable acquisitions exists. He or she then searches various M&A databases, merger proxies of comparable companies that include fairness opinions. It's important for the banker to learn as much as possible regarding the target company and all the circumstances surrounding the transaction.

FIGURE 6.5 COMPARABLE TRADING MULTIPLES

Comparable Trading Multiples

Company	Symbol	Stock Price	Stocks Outstanding ($000)	Equity Value ($000)	Debt (ST&LT) ($000)	Cash ($000)	Enterprise Value ($000)	EBITDA ($mm)	EBITDA Multiple
Choice Hotels International	CHH	$ 83.20	56,572	4,706,804	796,200	37,150	5,465,854	335,560	16.29x
Hilton Worldwide Holdings Inc.	HLT	$ 80.96	298,190	24,141,462	7,580,000	423,000	31,298,462	1,760,000	17.78x
Hyatt	HOT	$ 77.93	117,448	9,152,748	1,440,000	879,000	9,713,748	657,000	14.79x
Intercontinental Hotel	IHG	$ 62.58	190,000	11,890,200	2,040,000	233,000	13,697,200	843,000	16.25x
Marcus Corporation	MCS	$ 40.80	19,680	802,944	317,420	18,070	1,102,294	139,930	7.88x
Marriott International	MAR	$ 130.90	346,990	45,420,991	8,990,000	366,000	54,044,991	2,850,000	18.96x
Park Hotels & Resorts Inc.	PK	$ 32.89	201,180	6,616,810	3,080,000	421,000	9,275,810	734,000	12.64x
Wyndham Worldwide	WYN	$ 136.73	108,640	14,854,347	8,310,000	1,500,000	21,664,347	1,790,000	12.10x
								Average =	14.59x

Step 2: Find the Necessary Financial Information Related to the Transaction

Once the peer or comparable companies are identified, the banker gathers as much information as possible for these companies, including financial statements, related acquisitions, and press releases. Since the analysis needs to be publicly disclosed to justify the fairness opinion, it's important to note that the banker only discloses information that is publicly available. When using an M&A database that includes private companies, it is very difficult to obtain or disclose the information, if available.

Step 3: Review Key Multiples for Trading and Transaction Multiples

Once all the relevant information is screened and it is internally agreed that these publicly traded companies are truly comparable to the target, the banker then spreads all the information of these companies and determines the multiples ratios such as enterprise value to EBITDA, enterprise value to revenue, or even enterprise value to net income. Figure 6.5 shows a comprehensive trading comparable analysis in the hotel sector.

The next set of comparable analysis is to compare the target company to other acquisition-related transactions. For each comparable company, the banker writes a brief description of the acquisition that occurred and why it is relevant to the target company. Figure 6.6 shows recent acquisitions of hotel companies.

Step 4: Comparable and Benchmark Analysis

After the trading and acquisition comparable analytical methods are done and justified as truly comparable, the banker sets the average or the range of multiples that are used to value the target company. The average or range of multiples are used as an industry benchmark and the basis for analyzing the target company.

Step 5: Determine Valuation

The mean (averages) and median multiples for both analytical approaches are used to value the relevant target company. Figures 6.5 and 6.6 show that the averages of the hotels

FIGURE 6.6 COMPARABLE TRANSACTION MULTIPLES

Comparable Transaction Multiples

Target	Acquirer	Acquisition Price /Share	Shares Outstanding	Equity Value ($mm)	Total Net Debt ($mm)	Enterprise Value (EV)	EBITDA (last reported)	EBITDA Multiple
Hilton Hotels	Blackstone Group	$ 47.50	390,400,000	$ 18,544	$ 6,180	$ 24,724	$ 1,680	14.72x
Four Seasons*	Kingtom Hotels Int'l / Gates' Cascade	$ 82.00	33,078,000	$ 2,712	$ 279	$ 2,991	$ 94	31.90x
Fairmont/Rafles	Kingtom Hotels Int'l	$ 45.00	73,335,000	$ 3,300	$ 124	$ 3,424	$ 187	18.29x
Hilton International	Hilton Hotels Corp.			$ 5,578	$ -	$ 5,578	$ 504	11.07x
Starwood Hotels	Host Marriott					$ 4,096	$ 315	13.00x
La-Quinta Corp	Blackstone Group	$ 12.22	203,000,000	$ 2,481	$ 926	$ 3,406	$ 230	14.83x
Wynham Int'l	Blackstone Group	$ 1.15	172,053,000	$ 198	$ 2,682	$ 2,880	$ 275	10.47x
John Q. Hammons Hotels	JQH Acquisition LLC	$ 24.00	19,583,000	$ 470	$ 765	$ 1,235	$ 123	10.04x
Societe du Louvre	Starwood Capital					$ 1,029	$ 91	11.30x
Intercontinental Hotels	LRG					$ 981	$ 107	9.20x
Boca Resorts	Blackstone Group	$ 24.00	40,284,000	$ 967	$ 217	$ 1,184	$ 90	13.15x
Prime Hospitality	Blackstone Group	$ 12.25	44,808,000	$ 549	$ 244	$ 792	$ 55	14.38x
Extended Stay	Blackstone Group	$ 19.93	95,077,000	$ 1,895	$ 1,232	$ 3,126	$ 225	13.90x
							Average =	14.33x

sector for trading comparable and acquisition comparable are 14.6x and 14.3x EBITDA multiples, respectively. These multiples ranging from 14–15x EBITDA will then be used to calculate the relevant hotel company that is either an IPO or M&A candidate.

MERGERS AND ACQUISITIONS

The sale of a company, division, or business is a major event for its owners. It is an intense process with very high stakes. The seller spends time with its banker (sell-side advisor), examining various strategic alternatives, including selling all or part of the company, an initial public offering, or doing nothing. Once the decision is made to sell, the bankers seeks to achieve the perfect balance between high valuation and speedy execution. The banker's responsibility is to identify the process that suits the seller's priorities. Bankers run a **broad auction,** which is used to reach out to as many potential interested parties as possible, go to **targeted buyers,** or zero in on a specific buyer for a **negotiated sale.** From an analysis point of view, the sell-side assignment requires the team to run a comprehensive valuation of the target using the various methodologies that were discussed earlier in this chapter and that are discussed more expansively in chapter 17. The team also needs to run various scenarios depending on who the buyers are, including a private equity firm or another strategic entity. These valuations are used to establish the seller's price expectation, which should be in line with the buyer's expectations. Chapter 17 will run various valuation scenarios based on buyer expectation including an accretion/dilution analysis for publicly traded companies that buy other publicly traded companies.

The following outlines the process laid out by the Securities and Exchange Commission (SEC) of selling a publicly traded company:

First Round

Reaching out to prospective buyers: The banker contacts prospective buyers, which marks the official launch of the auction process. The sell-side banker will contact his or her network of investors with an accompanied one to two-page teaser and the confidentiality agreement (CA).

Execute the confidentiality agreement (CA): The CA is distributed to interested parties' legal counsel for their review. After going back and forth on comments and negotiations, the CA is then executed. Following the execution of the CA, the sell-side banker is allowed to distribute the confidential information memorandum (CIM) and a letter outlining the bidding process **(initial bid procedures letter).**

Distribution of CIM and initial bid procedures letter: Once the buyers receive the CIM, typically they have 3 to 4 weeks to review it before submitting their initial non-binding bid. Their review includes an analysis of the target and the industry sector that they are in. The buyer's team of analysts will also run a financial analysis focusing on their historical performance and lay out the other investment opportunities available to them. During this period, the sell-side banker is in constant communication with the prospective buyers to provide additional supporting information. Sometimes buyers, especially buyers who are very interested, will hire their own advisors (buy-side advisors) to assist them with the process, primarily with the valuations and how to access financing.

Initial Bid

The initial bid procedures letter includes the deadline for the buyers to submit their non-binding bid. **The letter also outlines the information that the buyers need to submit with their bid including their initial purchase price and the composition of payment such as all cash, stock, or a combination of the two.** They typically are also asked to show how they derived their bid price. The information provided should also include the structure (transaction sources and uses). The transaction sources and uses show how the target company will be purchased: debt and/or equity. Other information needed by the sell-side company are the buyer's business plan including the treatment of the management and employees, timing of completing the transaction, and additional diligence that needs to be performed. A timing sheet will also document other required approvals and timing of due diligence before the final bid is presented.

Preparation of management presentation: During this period, the sell-side management prepares a presentation—typically a PowerPoint slide show—outlining specific points of emphasis. Included are the (a) executive summary, (b) industry overview, (c) company overview, (d) operations overview, and (e) financial overview. This presentation is in line with the CIM provided earlier, but this time the management presents it in person or via conference call among their business associates.

Setting up the data room: The company will start to organize and set up the data room for buyers during the second round of bids. This is a hub for the buyers to access detailed data on the operations of the company.

Receive initial bids: The sell-side banker receives the initial indications of interest, accompanied by all the information that was stated in the initial bid procedures letter. Following the initial bids, the sell-side banker and the company will review all the bids received and their indicative purchase prices. The analysis will also include a discussion by the buyers that indicates how serious they are despite their initial bidding price. Once the analysis is completed, the company makes the final decision, which includes two or three buyers who proceed to the next round.

Second Round

The sell-side banker will send a letter to the few investors who are chosen to proceed to the second round. The letter will include a detailed timeframe that includes when the final bids need to be in. It could also include a calendar showing when the investors will attend the management presentations and visit the facility. Finally, it will have detailed information on how to gain access to the data room on further occasions.

Management presentations and site visit: This is the official start of the second round. Management gets a chance to present the company's operations, business strategy, industry information, and financial performance. The presentations, usually given by the CEO and CFOs, are followed by a Q&A session. The prospective buyers might bring their buy-side advisors and industry consultants to help them get a comprehensive outlook of the company in preparation for their final bid. Following the management presentation, the company will arrange site visits. These visits provide a firsthand view of the company's operations—an essential component of the buyer's due diligence. The scheduled tour of the facilities is generally led by the local manager. Given the sensitivity and confidentiality of buying the company, the investors do not reveal the purpose of their visit.

Data room: In addition to listening to management presentations and visiting the facilities, the company provides access to the data room. The data room includes detailed information on the company, including operational and manufacturing activity data, tax and accounting information, information technology, various tests, and environmental inspections and permits. The sell-side banker coordinates all the questions or additional requests from these investors.

Final bid procedure letter: Like the initial bid procedures letter in the first round, the final bid procedures letter includes the exact date and details for submitting a final bid. Unlike the initial bid, the final bid is legally binding. The details on the final bid procedures letter include the purchase price and the method of paying (cash and/or stock) and evidence of committed financing and who is financing (banks, financial institutions, and equity investors). In addition to the final bid procedures letter, a draft of the definitive agreement is distributed for review and it is ultimately expected for the buyer to sign. The letter will also include the timing and procedures after the final bid is granted by the buyer.

Definitive agreement: The definitive agreement, once signed, binds both the buyer(s) and seller to agreement of the purchase and sale of the company, respectively. Prior to the seller signing it, a draft of this agreement is sent to the final bidders toward the end of the due diligence process. The definitive agreement includes the transaction structure, representations and warranties, financing commitment, and the terms and conditions of the financing.

Final bid: At the conclusion of the second round, the prospective buyers submit their bid to the sell-side banker. These are expected to be the final bid with minimal conditions or "outs."

Negotiations

Evaluating final bids: The sell-side banker works with the company and legal counsel to review the conditions and potential outcomes of all the final bids including the price, structure, terms, and conditions. All these are important elements to making the final decision. For example, even if one bid price is higher than the others, the financing structure could be weak, or the terms and conditions could be prudish. Once the assessment is completed, the company selects the preferred buyer or buyers with whom to negotiate a definitive agreement.

Negotiate with the selected buyer: The sell-side banker communicates to the buyer that he or she is among the preferred bidders and needs to clarify a few terms that are included in the final bid letter. During these final negotiations, the banker makes sure that there are not any outstanding issues or requests that are subject to preventing the execution of the definitive agreement.

Select winning bidder: After the last round of negotiation with the winning bidder, the deal is presented to the company's board of directors for approval. The seller still reserves the right to reject the bid—basically becoming subject to further approvals. The buyer has some rights to withdraw from the process. It is rare, though it has happened in the past; this is commonly referred to as a "busted deal." In a busted deal, expect legal action by the buyer.

Board of directors' approval: For publicly traded companies the board of directors will ask for a fairness opinion on the valuation of the target company. This will be used comparatively with the offer price and could possibly become a reason to negotiate further about the proposed offer. The fairness opinion is a letter commenting on the overall "fairness" of the offer that is under consideration. It includes various valuation methods including comparable trading and acquisition multiples and a discounted cash flow analysis; these methods are explained in detail in chapter 9 and chapter 17. In a public transaction, the fairness opinion needs to be approved by the fairness opinion committee and disclosed through an SEC filing.

Closing

Prior to closing and funding, there are additional approvals needed to fully complete the transaction, including regulatory and shareholder approvals. The regulatory approvals required for M&A transactions involving publicly traded companies fall under the Hart-Scott-Rodino Antitrust Improvements Act of 1976. Under this regulation, every M&A transaction for publicly traded companies requires approval from the Federal Trade Commission (FTC) and Antitrust Division of the Department of Justice (DOJ). Following the execution of the definitive agreement, the company needs to file with these agencies. The approval process typically requires 30 days to issue confirmation of the transaction depending of the size of the company, its revenues, and its assets. These set amounts are constantly adjusted each year for inflation.

The shareholders also need to approve the transaction. Before a scheduled shareholder meeting is set for approval, a proxy statement is sent out to the shareholders describing the transaction, the fairness opinion, and parties involved. Shareholder approval is typically determined by majority vote (50.1%).

While the approvals are in the review process for both the government agency and shareholders, the investor buying the company proceeds to source the necessary capital to close and fund the transaction.

CASE STUDY

FUNKID TOY COMPANY

Funkid Toy Company ("FTC") is a private company owned solely by Mr. Michael Smith and his sons. Mr. Smith, the chairman of FTC, approached JS Investments Corporation ("JSIC") to advise him and the FTC board about the possibility of taking the company public. Mr. Smith is interested in selling up to 20% of the company. Seventy-five percent of the proceeds will be used to invest in new technology and the other 25% will be used to pay a dividend to the current owners.

As the lead manager, JSIC's first responsibility was to pre-market the offering to institutional investors (qualified investors). JSIC also approached other potential underwriters and asked them if they wanted to join in the syndicate; they could then start pre-marketing to their own investors after they accepted their designation as co-underwriters. Each signed co-underwriter of the syndicate is allocated shares by JSIC, who is designated as the left lead manager. FTC IPO example (Figure 6.7) shows that the company or the issuer is planning to issue 10 million shares. The left lead manager keeps 6 million of the shares and the remaining 4 million are allocated pro rata (equally) among the two other co-underwriters. These institutional investors who are interested in purchasing the stock will give an indication of interest (IOI). These IOIs will become orders on the effective day, though they are not obliged at this point to commit and are able to cancel any time before purchase.

FIGURE 6.7 FUNKID TOY COMPANY IPO

Initial Public Offering

Shares Sold: 10,000,000

Transaction Sources & Uses:

Sources:		
Securities	**Amount $**	**% Capital**
Corporate Loan	-	0.0%
Corporate Bond	-	0.0%
Equity	180,000,000	100.0%
Total Sources:	180,000,000	100.0%

Uses:				
Allocation of Capital		**Per Share**	**Total Proceeds**	**% of Total**
IPO Porceeds to the Issuer		$16.92	169,200,000	94.0%
Gross Spread (Fee)	6.00%	$ 1.08	10,800,000	6.0%
Total Offering Price		$18.00	180,000,000	100.0%
Other Trans. Expenses			00	
Total Uses			180,000,000	

Syndication Analysis	Allocation	Shares Sold	Left-Lead Fees	U/W Fee	Selling Concession	Total Takedown	Total Spread
Percentage of Spread			20%	30%	50%	80%	100%
Per Share			$0.22	$0.32	$0.54	$0.86	$1.08
Left Lead Underwritter	6,000,000	4,000,000	2,160,000	1,944,000	2,160,000	4,104,000	6,264,000
Syndicate Member A	1,333,333	1,000,000		432,000	540,000	972,000	972,000
Syndicate Member B	1,333,333	1,000,000		432,000	540,000	972,000	972,000
Selling Group (Total)		2,666,667			1,440,000	1,440,000	1,440,000
Total	8,666,667	8,666,667	2,160,000	3,240,000	5,400,000	7,488,000	10,800,000

The initial discussion on the offering price is usually a range. Using the FTC IPO example above (Figure 6.7), it settled at $18, giving a range based on their independent valuation of the company between $16 and $20. This range is not binding and the discussion with the investors during this period is to close in on a range based on strong or weak demand. Assuming an average price of $18, the final price for 10 million newly issued shares, representing 20% of the company, puts the overall valuation of the equity at $900 million, calculated as follows:

$18 per share × 10 million shares = $180 million representing 20% of the company

$180 million/0.20 = $900 million equity value

The $900 million total company valuation was based on comparable industry EBITDA multiple of 10× on $90 million reported EBITDA ($90 million × 10). (Valuation methods such this one will be discussed in later chapters.)

JSIC reported to FTC how the book-building effort was going and where the market thinks the value of the company is estimated, based primarily on other comparable companies in the toy industry, as well as the state of the market, including records of other IPOs that have already been priced. After subtracting the gross fees, totaling 6% of the total capital raised, or $10.8 million, which are allocated between the JSIC and the other co-underwriters, the net proceeds to the company are estimated to be $169.2 million before any other transaction expenses. The breakdown of the fees is $6,264,000 for JSIC, $972,000 for each of the co-underwriters, and $1,440,000 for the selling group that consisted of 15 other investment companies.

PROBLEMS

1. List at least three reasons why the company decided to raise capital through the IPO market.
2. What does the company have to have to execute a successful IPO?
3. Define "shares outstanding."
4. List all the rights of a shareholder.
5. Explain the process of dividend payment and define the various dates regarding dividends as follows:
   a. Declaration date
   b. Record date
   c. Payable date
   d. Ex-dividend date
6. Explain why a company would decide to do a stock split.
7. What's the difference growth and income stocks?
8. The company announced an annual dividend of $4 per share on 10 million shares, and the current stock price is $40. The company reported an annual net income of $100 million. Calculate the following:
   a. Dividend payout ratio
   b. Dividend payout ratio per share
   c. Dividend yield %
9. Assume that XYZ Inc. is looking to finance with all equity a new factory that will cost them $20 million. The company calculated that the new factory would bring an annual return of 20%. The company has 10 million of outstanding shares. If 50% of factory income is reinvested,
   a. What would the value of the company's stock increase by?
   b. Calculate the intrinsic value of the stock.
10. What is included in the private placement memorandum (PPM)?
11. List the six steps of underwriting the IPO and explain each step.
12. Who receives the manager fees, underwriting fees, and selling concession fees?

MULTIPLE CHOICE (from FINRA series 79 training manual):

13. All the following are classified as equity facilities except:
    a. Preferred stock
    b. Convertible bonds
    c. Warrants
    d. Common stock

14. The benefits of common stock ownership include all of the following except:
    a. The opportunity for capital appreciation
    b. The right to elect the company's board
    c. Preferred status in a corporate liquidation
    d. The right to receive dividends when declared
15. Common stock is most often purchased to satisfy which of the following investment objectives?
    a. Income
    b. Growth
    c. Participating protection
    d. Tax minimization
16. The right of shareholders to maintain their proportionate ownership interest in a corporation is known as:
    a. Subscription rights
    b. Liquidation rights
    c. Pre-emptive rights
    d. Conversion rights

ONLINE TEMPLATES

The Excel spreadsheets used in the chapter can be accessed online via Cognella Active Learning platform.

CHAPTER 7

Debt Markets: Issuing Corporate Bonds, 144As, and Private Placements

This chapter will summarize the various approaches through which a company can access the bond markets. The chapter will outline the process by which a company can raise debt publicly or privately and walk the reader through the vehicles a company issues when looking to raise capital in the form of debt. Throughout this chapter it is key that students keep in mind the double-edged sword that comes with acquiring leverage, especially in large quantities. It is imperative students understand that while helping maximize returns for companies and investment portfolios alike, leverage, like other long-term liabilities, can add a substantial financial burden in times of economic hardship and greatly increase the risk profile of the associated assets. The chapter will then give an overview of the analysis that S&P and Moody's go through to grade the risk and recovery of bonds. The rating process helps members of the public make informed decisions and protect them from unwarranted investment risk.

LEARNING OBJECTIVES

After reading this chapter, students will be able to do the following

- Understand the various types of corporate bonds offered in both the investment-grade and high-yield markets
- Recognize the difference between investment grade and high-yield bond issues and issuers

- Learn how the rating agencies, S&P, Moody's, and Fitch assign risk ratings to bonds in the market
- Prepare the company to go to market to raise public and private debt
- Understand the terms and conditions of bonds
- Know both the key elements at play when an investment bank approaches the primary market as an underwriter and the process of syndicating corporate bonds

CORPORATE DEBT: AN OVERVIEW

Corporate debt is by far one of the most preferred types of capital that a company seeks, assuming they qualify to raise such capital. As described in previous chapters, raising equity sometimes is the only available source of capital, especially for early-stage companies whose cash flows have not yet reached stability—a main requirement for bond holders. Raising equity, though, can be very expensive. Equity investors seek ownership in return, which results in diluting the existing ownership structure. Raising debt, on the other hand, allows companies to receive funds without the owners, with some exceptions, needing to give up ownership. Instead, they sign a contract. The contract, called bond indenture or loan agreement, requires the company to pay back such debt in the future plus a pre-determined interest payment, which represents the cost of borrowing. Though debt is the preferred source of capital, is not always available. The debt holders' or investors' objectives are different than equity investors. Where equity investors are betting that the company will do very well so they can benefit from the appreciation of their investment, debt holders are betting that the company has relatively strong income and cash flows to meet their debt obligations, which include both interest and principal payments.

AUTHOR'S NOTES

When someone analyzes the asset class of debt such as bonds and loans versus other asset classes, the first pieces of information that need to be laid out are the so-called money terms. They consist of four key items: the amount, interest rate, maturity/term, and fixed payment on the debt. These basic terms are the main characteristics of any debt instrument. For example, when my 25-year old son called me to let me know that he bought a car, the first thing I asked him was how he paid for it. Of course, I was very proud that he did it on his own, establishing his independence after landing a very good job out of college. I said, "Excellent! How did you pay for it?" He said that he put a down payment and got a car loan.

Then I asked him the four questions that in a sense describe the four money terms: How much was the loan? What is the interest payment that the bank is charging you? How long is the loan? and What is your total monthly payment? These four money terms are printed on the first few pages of any bond indenture or loan agreement: They are (1) the amount the company issued; (2) the coupon rate or interest rate the issuer is paying; (3) when the bond or loan matures; and (4) how the original amount issued (the principal) is paid back. Bonds can either hold a redemption price at the date of maturity (lump-sum payment) or have set yearly scheduled payments (amortizing loan and serial bond, respectively). These four items are referred to as money terms and are the most important characteristics of any bond indenture or loan agreement. All other terms, sometimes referred to as non-money terms, include other obligations the issuer needs to meet such as financial covenants, negative covenants, and affirmative covenants. ***Financial covenants*** *are specific financial thresholds that are designed to encourage the issuer to be disciplined and focus on meeting the financial plan. These covenants are mostly applied to corporate loans. You don't often see financial covenants for publicly traded bonds since the company is not required to provide projections.* ***Negative covenants*** *are a set of rules that restricts or limits the issuer to take certain business actions while the bond or the loan is in place. These restrictions include limitations put on the issuer when raising more debt, and/or paying dividends to shareholders, and/or selling assets.* ***Affirmative covenants*** *are set instructions for the issuer regarding the reporting of its quarterly and annual financial statements or other compliance certificates.*

KEY TAKEAWAYS

- Like the public equity markets, companies in the market for raising debt need to understand that fundamentals are more important than technical characteristics. Having a good product, good management, and feasibility in the future are more important characteristics than aiming at financial engineering or taking advantage of overenthusiastic markets.
- The debt markets are very large and liquid, but no one debt facility is the same as another, nor do they all serve the same strategic purpose for the issuer, borrower, or investor.
- A bond indenture is broken down into money terms and non-money terms, which are a set of rules surrounding the agreement that set the terms of the contract.

CORPORATE BONDS: AN OVERVIEW

Corporate bonds are issued by companies that need long-term capital without giving up ownership. The term *bond* usually applies to longer-term debt facilities with maturities of 10 years or more. The term *notes* refer to medium-term maturity facilities (1–8 years), and commercial paper has a maturity of 270 days or lower. Bonds may be backed by collateral or may be unsecured and backed by the "good faith" of the corporation. In a bankruptcy, bonds are viewed higher in the capital structure than stock. In this sense, they expect to recover higher amounts of their investment based on the priority of payments known commonly as the "waterfall." Figure 7.1 shows the priority of payment order ("waterfall").

UNSECURED BONDS

Unsecured bonds have a higher interest rate than secured ones given the risk of recovery in the case of bankruptcy. Some unsecured facilities are further broken down by senior unsecured and subordinated facilities. The holders of subordinated facilities, sometimes referred to as high-yield or junk bonds, have a lower priority claim in the case of bankruptcy. These bonds are typically used for leveraged buyout (LBO) transactions where

FIGURE 7.1 "WATERFALL"

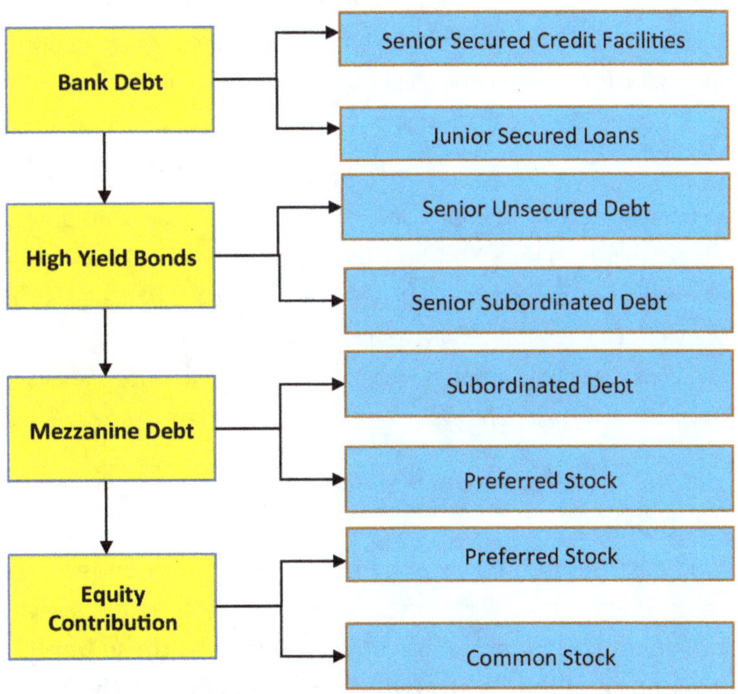

the target companies have very aggressive capital structures. The typical grading by S&P and/or Moody's is below B and B1, respectively. Some high-yield or junk bond issues could be graded CCC and Caa1 by S&P and Moody's, respectively. These grading levels are discussed in detail later in this chapter and in chapter 18.

SECURED BONDS

There are many types of secured bonds that are backed by collateral and offered in the public markets. These consist of mortgage bonds, collateral trust bonds, equipment trust obligations, and guarantee bonds.

> **Mortgage bonds** are corporate bonds backed by real estate assets. In a bankruptcy, holders of mortgage bonds can claim the underlying property listed in the bond agreement (indenture) and can sell it off to recover their investment.
>
> **Collateral trust bonds** are corporate bonds that are secured by financial assets or investments owned by the company such as stocks, bonds, or other investments. In a bankruptcy, collateral trust bondholders are entitled to the securities that are held with the trust. These securities will be delivered to the holders and are at their discretion if they want to liquidate these at the net asset value or market price.
>
> **Equipment trust obligations** are debt obligations that are secured by equipment or physical assets. These assets are listed in detail in the indenture, and the title of these assets are held at a trust until the bonds are paid off. Equipment or physical assets could be factory equipment, shipping containers, or trucks. Today these trust certificates are seen more in the transportation industries such as airline, trucking, and rail.
>
> **Guarantee bonds** are bonds where the interest and principal payments are guaranteed by a company other than the direct borrower of these bonds. Guarantee bonds are sometimes needed for borrowers who have very weak debt parameters such as weak cash and/or weak collateral. Typically, a subsidiary of a company will raise bonds and the parent company might guarantee those bonds in case the subsidiary cannot meet the obligations under the indenture.

CONVERTIBLE BONDS

This type of bond is structured so that the holders of these bonds have the option to convert their bonds (debt) to stock (equity). The terms and conditions regarding the conversion is imbedded in the indenture agreement. **Typically, these bonds carry a lower interest rate (coupon rate) than a straightforward bond given the conversion option**

the holder has. Therefore, convertible bonds tend to be offered by companies that are trying to have lower borrowing costs and are willing to give equity as the upside. From the investor prospective, convertible bonds are a safer bet, expecting a fixed income and enjoying the potential upside if the company has success. Stated in the convertible bond indenture is a mechanism of how and when the investor can convert his or her bonds to stock. The methodology for converting bonds to stock is based on a ratio between stocks and bonds called the convertible ratio.

The formula to calculate the conversion ratio is as follows:

$$\text{Conversion ratio} = \frac{\text{Par value}}{\text{Conversion price}}$$

No matter what the bond price is when traded in the secondary market (market price), the numerator is at par value or $1,000. The conversion price is stated in the convertible bond indenture. For example, let's assume the conversion price is $20 per share. Basically, the conversion ratio is calculated to be at 50 shares per one bond as follows:

$$\text{Conversion ratio} = \frac{\$1{,}000}{\$20} = 50 \text{ shares: } 1 \text{ bond}$$

Using the example, if the stock is trading at $25, the convertible bond holder will most likely convert from bonds to stock since the value of holding 50 shares (50 x $25 = $1,250) is higher than holding one bond valued at $1,000 par. The **conversion parity** is the point where the bond value is equal to the market value of the stock. Using the example, if the stock is traded at $25, the market value of the bond will be trading at premium of 125% of par to be in parity as follows:

$$\text{Parity price of the stock} = \frac{\text{Market value of the bond}}{\text{Conversion ratio}} = \frac{\$1{,}250}{50 \text{ shares}} = \$25$$

In other words, if the bond price has increased by 25% from $1,000 to $1,250, the stock price must also have appreciated by 25% over the conversion price of the stock to be in parity, in this case, from $20 to $25.

ZERO COUPON BONDS

This type of bond is structured so that the issuer does not have to pay any cash interest during the life of the bond. Instead, the interest on these bonds is added to the principal amount and gets paid at maturity. These bonds are issued at a deep discount from par value. The difference between the par value and the discount is the interest expense, compounded semiannually or annually to reach par value at maturity. Companies that issue zero bonds are companies that might have initial negative or light cash flow, and this is a way to normalize their projections in the near future without the burden of meeting their debt obligations.

PAID-IN-KIND (PIK) BONDS

Like zero coupon bonds that pay cash interest until maturity, paid-in-kind (PIK) bonds are structured as such that the interest payment is deferred for a certain number of years (PIKs are typically 3 years) and then the interest payment starts to be paid in cash. These bonds are structured in order to give the issuer additional breathing room for cash outlay. In essence, PIKs allow a company to borrow more money without having immediate concerns about cash flow. There are a few types of PIK bonds that are structured to partially pay cash and be partially deferred for certain years. Given the initial weak cash flow of the issuer and the increasing debt as the compounded interest is deferred and aggregated to later years, PIKs are considered high yield or speculative debt securities.

RATING CORPORATE BONDS

The companies issuing bonds in the public markets are required by the Securities and Exchange Commission (SEC) to be independently rated by at least two rating agencies before they are issued. Conceptually, the rating that is assigned to the firm issuing the bonds and the actual security is a proxy for the probability of default. The rating agencies' sole objective when measuring the risk of default for bonds is to protect the public investor who is not sophisticated enough to analyze the risk of the company raising debt nor measure the probability of default. The rating agencies such as Standard & Poor's (S&P), Moody's, and Fitch assign two to three separate ratings: One rating is for the company that is specifically issuing the bonds, one is for the bonds themselves, and in many cases the rating agency issues a rate for large syndicated bank loans who are being bought by an array of funds. These include collateralized loan obligation (CLO) funds that are set up to only purchase rated bank loans. All three rating measurements focus on the credit strength of the company and the likelihood that debts are paid. They are essentially woven into the ratings themselves and can affect access to corporate bond and bank loan opportunities. Figure 7.2 shows the corporate bond rating system and the symbols assigned and is broken down into five categories of risk described later in this chapter including AAA risk-free grade, investment-grade, non-investment grade, and distress and default grades. The initial issuance rating usually starts at investment grade or non-investment grade, and as the rating agency monitors these ratings frequently, they upgrade, or downgrade based on their ongoing credit risk.

After the initial rating is granted, the rating agencies will continue to monitor the bonds and issuers that they have rated. As the issuer releases their financials or announces major changes, the rating agencies may announce that they are reviewing the credit rating of

FIGURE 7.2 CORPORATE BOND RATING AGENCIES' SCALES

Description		Standard & Poor's	Moody's	Fitch
Highest Quality (Risk Free)	INVESTMENT GRADE	AAA	Aaa	AAA
High Quality		AA+ AA AA-	Aa1 Aa2 Aa3	AA+ AA AA-
Strong Payment Capacity		A+ A A-	A1 A2 A3	A+ A A-
Adequate Payment Capacity		BBB+ BBB BBB-	Baa1 Baa2 Baa3	BBB+ BBB BBB-
Likely to fullfill Obligations	NON-INVESTMENT GRADE (HIGH YEILD)	BB+ BB BB-	Ba1 Ba2 Ba3	BB+ BB BB-
High-risk Obligations		B+ B B-	B1 B2 B3	B+ B B-
Current Vulnarable to Default	DISTRESS	CCC+ CCC CCC- CC C	Caa	CCC
Default	DEFAULT	D	D	DDD,DD,D

the company. They may even go further and comment that they are in the process of downgrading or upgrading the rating. When such announcements are made by the rating agency, the issuer or issue (bonds and corporate loans) are said to be under credit watch. The description of each of the bonds and their respective markets by grade is next.

HIGHEST QUALITY RATING (RISK-FREE) (AAA)

The AAA, Aaa, and AAA ratings by Standard & Poor's (S&P), Moody's, and Fitch, respectively, are the highest ratings possible. Only a handful of companies have an AAA rating and it's not an active market for corporate entities since there is always some embedded risk of running a company. The AAA rating is assigned primarily to specific portfolio funds such as collateralized loan obligations (CLOs) that are protected by a well-structured portfolio of loans and ample cushion of capital below such security (discussed in detail in later chapters). Typical AAA issuers are wealthy countries who issue short and long-term securities such as U.S. treasury notes and bonds that are considered, at least from likelihood of default, risk-free investments.

INVESTMENT GRADE BONDS (BBB TO AA)

A bond is considered investment grade (IG) if the rating is BBB-, or Baa3 and higher, by S&P and Moody's, respectively. The designation of IG is sometimes a very important outcome for the companies that are in the process of raising bonds in the bond markets. Not only can the issuer's interest rate or coupon rate be substantially lower with a non-investment grade rating, but also certain capital structures could be more flexible as well as obtain less restricted terms and conditions of the bond indenture. Typical IG bonds will have more flexibility in terms of refinancing these bonds with no penalties, as exampled by various non-investment grade bonds that could include call prices. These call prices (discussed later in the chapter) are designed to disidentify the issuer for early repayment of the bonds, as these prices or redemption levels could be set at significantly higher-than-the-par value. For example, a call price or redemption price of 105 suggests that the issuer desires to repay or call the bonds; the repayment is set at 105% of par or 5% penalty—a very steep arrangement. Most IG bonds are not structured that way, giving flexibility to the issuer to refinance earlier if, for example, the rates drop or the issuer gets upgraded and can get a better coupon rate with a new bond. Another benefit IG issuers can enjoy is a more flexible covenant package, which are certain restrictions on business actions such as paying dividends to shareholders or structuring the bonds as unsecured (no pledge of collateral).

Typical IG bond structures include a "make-whole" call premium provision to address a situation where the issuer repays the bonds earlier than maturity. This feature allows an issuer to entirely avoid the call structure issue (which is typically included in non-investment grade structures; discussed in the next section). The make-whole premium is made up of penalty fees that the issuer pays over the market value of the bonds.

NON-INVESTMENT GRADE BONDS OR HIGH-YIELD BONDS (B– TO BB+):

Non-investment grade high-yield bonds are debt securities issued by corporations with ratings of BB- and Ba1 or lower by S&P and Moody's, respectively. High-yield bond are for companies that are seeking money for growth (i.e., M&A or LBO), working capital, recapitalization, refinancing existing debt, or other cash flow purposes.

Since these issuers are riskier given the low ratings, they must offer a higher interest rate and, in most cases, have additional investor-friendly structural features. The high-yield market was originally developed in the late 80s by Michael Milken, also referred to as the "junk bond king," while he was at Drexel Lambert, an investment bank. This type of corporate bond was developed to finance the mega leveraged buyout (LBO) deals in the 80s such as the KKR buyout of RJR Nabisco, illustrated in the satiric book and movie *Barbarians at the Gate* (Burrough & Helyar, 1990). Though these bonds are sometimes called junk bonds (typical B, B-, and CCC+ rated bonds) and have given the asset class some negative connotation over the years, this asset class has matured into a solid 25% of the overall corporate bond market, according to Bond Market Association estimates.

High-yield bond indentures typically include call protection limits or provisions. This gives the issuer the ability to call the bond for redemption. Typically, it is at the half term of the bonds. For example, 10-year bonds will carry five years of call protection. Using the 10-year example, the call prices or redemptions could be set at 105, 104, 103, 102, and 101 for years 1, 2, 3, 4, and 5 from issuance, respectively. That means if the issuer decides to call (refinance) the bonds by the third anniversary from the issuance, he or she needs to repay the bonds at 103% of par, representing a 3.0% penalty for early termination. Some high-yield bonds are structured as 7-year (non-call 3) paper or 8-year (non-call 5) bonds. These bonds are not callable, which means that if the issuer for some reason needs to terminate the bonds during the non-call period, he or she will have to pay all the future interest for the non-callable period. In this case the repayment amount is calculated by the present value of all future coupons that would have been paid through the non-call period.

Other terms that riskier high-yield bond structures could include in the indenture are equity claw backs, equity warrants, or escrow accounts.

> **Equity claw backs** are terms in the agreement that allow the issuer to repay a portion of the outstanding bonds with the proceeds from an equity offering. Generally, this is from financing instances called initial or follow-on offerings. A typical claw back found in a high-yield indenture would be for up to 35% of the outstanding bond issue at a level equal to par, plus the coupon. Company XYZ, for example, raises equity through an IPO and exercises a claw back for a portion of its 20% bonds at a repurchase price of 105% of par. This is an optional redemption for the issuer who is willing to reduce its debt at a premium to perhaps achieve an investment grade rating or better IPO pricing.
>
> **Equity warrants** are terms in the agreement negotiated by the investor making him or her stand to benefit from the equity upside of the issuer. The agreement will include a defined number of warrants to purchase equity in the company at a later date. Usually a bond carries warrants for ownership in 2–5% of the company.
>
> **Escrow accounts** are terms in the agreement that instruct the issuer to cover a specific number of interest payments. This feature is popular with companies that include a buildup phase where the issuer does not have cash to service the debt, such as the construction of a casino. Escrow accounts typically range from 18 to 36 months.

All these terms are added or taken out of the agreement based on the credit quality of the issuer. Other terms that the agreement could include are financial and non-financial covenants. High-yield bond issues are generally unsecured obligations of the company's assets, and the covenants are much looser than on bank loans (discussed in the next chapter). This provides the issuer with more operating flexibility and enables the company to avoid the need for compliance certification on a quarterly basis. Typical covenants that are in the structure (negative covenants) include limitations on raising additional debt, disbursement of dividends to shareholders, acquiring liens, and sale and leaseback transactions on mergers or consolidation. The other common covenant included in a high-yield bond indenture is change-of-control provision: If the company is sold and the new ownership is changed, it could trigger the refinancing of the bonds.

DISTRESS BONDS (C – CCC+)

These bonds are securities that a company will issue when experiencing financial and operational difficulties and is near or under bankruptcy. Many investors, primarily hedge funds or "vulture funds," buy these bonds because they believe their market value is lower than the ultimate price recovery after a restructuring. As such, it can also be the case that this reorganization can be done in or out of bankruptcy. The investment thesis of a distress bond buyer is that when the company enters a period of financial distress, the original investors often sell automatically at any price as part of their investment policy. Many funds such as collateralized debt obligations (CDOs) are structured to maintain consistent average credit for their portfolio, meaning when one of their portfolio holdings gets downgraded to CCC+, for example, the asset manager needs to sell immediately without necessarily analyzing the recovery values of these bonds. The company, "fighting for its life," will prefer bond holders that have the best interest of the company's future in mind post-bankruptcy. Therefore, the exchange of normal investors to distress buyers might impact their value expectation.

There is a large market of initial issuance rated CCC-/CCC/CCC+ bonds (typically deeply "subordinated" bonds) that investors have been supporting as they see value in these bonds for raising capital in a leveraged buyout (LBO). Despite the high probability of default, the investors feel comfortable with the risk/reward parameters and recovery after default. In an LBO structure the financing consists of the highest quality of debt, such as bank loans, and the lowest quality of bonds being subordinated debt. Both are still higher in the priority of payment than the equity. The equity below a CCC-rated bond is viewed as a cushion for equity investors and makes them very motivated to make the deal work, ultimately aiding the low-rated bonds have a higher chance of full repayment or high recovery.

DEFAULTED BONDS (D) AND SELECT DEFAULT BONDS (SD)

These are bonds where the issuer has failed to meet the debt obligation. Once the company fails to pay interest or principal payment of any debt, the rating agencies automatically downgrade the issuer and bonds. Sometimes the rating agencies, such as S&P, will give an "SD" or select default rating. This rating is assigned when the rating agency believes that the issuer has selectively defaulted on a specific debt facility but that it will continue to make payments on the other debt facilities.

TERMS AND CONDITIONS OF CORPORATE BONDS (MONEY AND NON-MONEY TERMS)

Bonds, notes, and debentures are governed by an indenture. The next chapter will introduce the corporate loan asset class that is governed by loan agreements. Both have similar money terms that covers the amount, the interest rate, the maturity/term, and the scheduled principal payments but differ substantially in non-money terms such as covenants and other terms.

Typically, prospective investors or underwriters receive a preliminary term sheet that includes all the basic terms and conditions. These are negotiated terms between the underwriter and the issuer before they go to market, so it is not uncommon to see changes of a few terms given by market feedback. These terms are listed in the preliminary prospectus, offering memorandum or offering circular, which is filed with the SEC.

Figure 7.3 shows a typical offering summary of the terms of the bonds.

MONEY TERMS

Money-terms include all relevant information in the debenture that describe the what, how, and when: What is the amount borrowed and at what coupon rate? How long will this be paid? and When will it be paid describing the coupon dates?

NON-MONEY TERMS

Non-money terms are terms in the indenture that are not related to the amount, price, and maturity of the bond. However, terms such as optional redemptions, for example, entail that the price of the bonds will be paid if the issuer exercises the option to repay the bond value earlier than maturity (call price at certain call dates). Other non-money terms include covenants, permissions, and restrictions of the issuer while the bonds are outstanding.

GOING TO MARKET TO RAISE CORPORATE BONDS

Similar to the IPO process described in the previous chapter, the following steps show a typical process of how a company approaches the bond markets to raise capital.

FIGURE 7.3 THE OFFERING

	Issuer	**Celerity Technology Inc.**
MONEY-TERMS	Notes Offered	$1,200,000,000 principal amount of 7.0% Senior Notes due 2029
	Coupon Rate	7.0%
	Maturity Dates	December 1, 2029
	Interest Payments	June 1 and December 1, beginning June 1, 2019 (Issuance Day)
NON-MONEY TERMS	Optional Redemption	The issuer may exercise the right to call the bonds to be redeemed all or part of the notes at any time before December 1, 2025 at a price based on the following redemption prices: Redeem on or before: December 1, 2020 105% of Principal Amount December 1, 2021 104% of Principal Amount December 1, 2022 103% of Principal Amount December 1, 2023 102% of Principal Amount December 1, 2024 101% of Principal Amount December 1, 2025 100% of Principal Amount
	Offer To Repurchase	If there is **change of control**, as defined in "Description of Notes – Definitions" the repurchase all or part of the notes will be available for purchase at price equal to 101% of their principal amount plus accrued and unpaid interest to the repurchase date. If we sell a portion, but less than all or substantially all, of our assets under certain circumstances, we will use the cash proceeds of such asset sale remaining after other permitted uses to offer to repurchase the notes at a price equal to 100% of their principal amount plus accrued and unpaid interest to the repurchase date. After a fall away event, as described below, these note repurchase obligations no longer apply.
	Permitted Spin-Off Transaction	The indenture governing the notes will permit a spin-off, split-up, split-off or other transaction involving the dividend, distribution or transfer by us of all or some portion of one or more of our business units. To make this dividend, distribution or transfer: • The company created by the spin-off must complete a registered exchange offer in which it offers holders of the notes the opportunity to exchange their notes for notes of the new company with terms substantially identical to those of the notes; • The company created by the spin-off must be able to incur at least $1.00 of additional debt pursuant to the fixed charge coverage ratio test set forth under "Description of Notes – Covenants – Incurrence of Indebtedness and Issuance of Preferred Stock" after giving pro forma effect to the spin-off transaction; • Each series of new notes issued in the exchange offer has ratings at least as high as the highest ratings given to the corresponding series of the notes in the one-year period immediately prior to the consummation of the spin-off transaction; • Immediately after such transaction, no default or event of default exists; • The company created by the spin-off assumes all obligations of the Company under the notes and the indenture pursuant to agreements reasonably satisfactory to the trustee, whereupon the company's obligation in respect to the notes exchanged for such notes of the new company shall be fully satisfied and discharged; and • We must offer to repurchase all of the notes at a price equal to 100% of the principal amount of the notes plus accrued and unpaid interest to the repurchase date.
	Covenants	Unless and until the notes receive an investment grade rating from two or more nationally recognized statistical rating organizations and other conditions are satisfied, which we refer to as a fall away event, the indenture will, among other things, limit our ability and the ability of our restricted subsidiaries to: • Pay dividends on our stock or repurchase our stock; • Make investments; • Borrow money and issue preferred stock; • Create liens; • Restrict the ability of our restricted subsidiaries to pay dividends or make other transfers to us; • Consolidate or merge with another person or sell all or substantially all of our assets and our restricted subsidiaries' assets to another person; • Engage in certain transactions with affiliates; • Enter into sale and leaseback transactions; and • Expand into unrelated businesses.
	Use of Proceeds	We intend to use the net proceeds of this offering to repay borrowings under our revolving credit agreement, to provide cash necessary for the transaction and for other general corporate purposes.

STEP I: SELECT THE INVESTMENT COMPANY/UNDERWRITER

In the last chapter, the step I process was discussed in detail for choosing the investment advisor and underwriting group for raising equity. The process for choosing the advisor and unwriting group for the bond issuance is the same. This section will purposely be repeated for a better flow of the steps. The types of commitments, such firm or best efforts are also the same as the equity markets.

Like the IPO process, the first step for a company to go to the bond market is to choose an investment bank that is willing to underwrite the bonds ahead of the market. For choosing the left lead underwriter or co-underwriters, the company will contact many investment bankers and ask them to give their proposal for a successful bond offering, typically in conjunction with an acquisition or a buyout for refinancing existing debt. The company, in this case the issuer, will decide between the left lead underwriter and other underwriters on who will lead the offering. This is largely based on who it feels will provide the most stable process and successful overall execution. For a bond offering, typically the competing process (called a bake-off) for choosing the left lead underwriter is through a negotiated method with each interested underwriter. Part of the underwriting agreement, called a firm agreement between the underwriter(s), is the ability to place these bonds or purchase them in case they fail to do so.

Before the bond offering process officially starts, the underwriter will ask for a letter of intent (LOI) in order to have an understanding that the process will definitely come underway. This is because the underwriter will usually incur a set of initial expenses. This agreement will typically, at a minimum, offer reimbursement for these expenses in case the company changes its mind with regards to registering the bonds for issuance. Furthermore, the LOI binds the company to being cooperative in the disclosing of all requested financial information during the offering period. The underwriter will agree to act as diligently as possible in completing the registration as well as selling and distributing of the company's bonds. The underwriting fees are also included in the LOI. The underwriter(s) will also outline their syndication strategy and qualifications, as well as their view as to where the securities being offered will be priced. Once the mandate is awarded the syndication process starts. They are two types of underwriting commitments by the underwriters.

Firm Commitment

A firm commitment is a commitment from the underwriters that enables them to purchase all the bonds that are offered in the market. The lead underwriter (referred to as "left lead" or "book-runner") is responsible to sell, through the syndicate (the other committed underwriters), all the bonds to interested institutional and retail investors. If there is not enough demand to sell all the bonds after the price is set, any unsold bonds are to be distributed among the syndicate.

Best-Effort Commitment

A best effort underwriting agreement is an agreement in which the underwriters seek to sell all the bonds to interested investors but have no obligation to purchase any unsold bonds. Typically, this agreement is for higher-risk issuers or tough bond markets, as the underwriter does not want to take any market risk. Some best-efforts agreements are set as "all or none." This refers to a best-effort attempt by the underwriter to sell all the shares. If they are short (undersubscribed) of selling 100% of the bonds, the offering is cancelled within a specific timeframe (i.e., the bond offering is postponed or cancelled).

STEP II: PREPARING THE DOCUMENTS FOR THE BOND OFFERING

The next step in the bond offering process involves preparing all the necessary information, including financial statements, that will be disclosed for official registration. The Securities Exchange Commission (SEC) has a very specific criteria for filing. The SEC's duty is to make sure that the company adequately informs the prospective investors about the financial performance of the firm and the risk factors present, hence the requirement of the prospective issuer to independently grade the bonds by at least two rating agencies. This registration document includes all the information that the SEC requires and is referred to as the indenture or preliminary information memorandum or prospectus.

In conjunction with the preparation for the information memorandum, the investment bank or the lead underwriter reaches out to the ratings agencies to start the process of rating the issuer and the securities. The rating agencies will have a chance to listen to management by setting up a one-to-one meeting and having discussions regarding their business and income stability. Typically, the rating agency gets back to the company and its advisor in about 10–15 days with the ratings. These ratings are then announced to the investors so they can adjust their own pricing expectations. The rating methodology the rating agencies use is described later in this chapter.

STEP III: SEC REGISTRATION AND APPROVAL

After the preliminary indenture or information memorandum is filed with the SEC (S4 registration), the SEC makes an announcement that the registration is effective. The SEC will then continue to work with the underwriter to gain additional supplemental information and make the necessary corrections for the registration to be approved.

Registration of high-yield bond offerings are not typically registered initially with the SEC. Most of these deals come to market under the exception of Rule 144A (private with rights for future registration). Smaller deals come to market as permanent 144A or private called "144A for life," meaning without registration rights. The rule 144A exception essentially modifies the SEC's requirement for investors to hold privately placed securities for at least 2 years. These buyers of bonds are defined under the SEC Rule 144A as "qualified institutional buyers" or QIBs. The investor list provided shows that these investors are financially sophisticated and legally recognized by securities regulators, who hence need less protection from sellers than most members of the public.

STEP IV: MARKETING THE BOND OFFERING

After official approval to solicit interest from the syndicate of investors, the next step in the bond-offering process involves marketing the company and the purpose of raising these bonds. The marketing involves presentations and various pitches that are sent to large-scale bond investors such as financial institutions. The offering memorandum (prospectus or red herring) that is drawn up by the underwriter(s) is sent ahead of these presentations. The offering memorandum typically will include an executive summary, investment considerations, an industry overview, and a financial model. The actual bond terms have not been finalized, but often pro forma coupon rates are described to help financial modeling. The syndicate desk likely will try to obtain feedback from potential investors regarding appetite for the deal. Once this intelligence has been gathered the agent will market the deal to potential investors.

The investors in the bond markets primarily are institutions seeking to earn fixed income rates. Investors investing in the high-yield bonds are seeking higher rates of return than their investment-grade corporate, government, and cash market counterparts. Other bond investors include hedge funds and individuals and arrangers of instruments that pool debt securities like CDOs and CLOs. Some common investor groups are the following:

- **Mutual funds** represent a large part of the investor pool. These institutional investors might be managing traditional, long-only bond funds or portfolios, specifically in investment grade or non-investment grade, or a combination of both. General fixed income mutual funds hold positions across corporate, government, and municipal securities segments.
- **Pension funds** are also active in the fixed income bond market for buying both high-yield and investment-grade bonds. These pension funds find bond investment ideal due to high return, fixed income, and long-term characteristics that match the long-term liabilities from retirees' investments.
- **Insurance companies** also invest their own capital in the bond market. Like pension funds, the insurance companies like the fixed income and long-term components of the bond market, though they are limited to how much risk they need to invest for the premiums, typically allocating a certain percentage for high-yield bonds.
- **Collateralized debt obligations, or CDOs**, are structured to specifically purchase bonds both investment grade and high yield. These packaged debt instruments invest in a pool of securities for a lower risk of default. Thus, the pool of bonds or basket of securities generally receive higher credit ratings. There are bond-only

instruments known as CBOs, loan-only instruments known as CLOs, and packages of both, which are generically described as CDOs.

- **Hedge funds** have had a growing presence in the bond market, primarily buying high-yield bonds given the high-interest fixed-income component that could compliment their portfolio.

For high-yield bond issuance the offering process is slightly different than an investment-grade bond offering. This involves the following:

1. Investment bankers draft the offering memorandum and negotiate conditions with potential investors.
2. Once the terms are finalized, the securities are allocated to bondholders.
3. The bonds then are available for purchase and sale in the aftermarket, or secondary, via broker/dealers.

The initial pricing of bonds is guided primarily by demand and supply based on the rating. In setting up the coupon rate, which is the interest rate of the cost of borrowing for the issuer, the investment advisor considers the following factors:

1. Risk-free rate or AAA rated bonds, which are used as the base.
2. Inflation price—this reflects what the market will be asking. In high inflation years, the bonds are priced higher than in low inflation years.
3. Maturity rate price—based on the term of the bonds. Typically, a 10-year bond is priced higher than a 7-year bond given the same rating.
4. Default rate—this is measured by the rating agencies and is communicated in the form of the grading system. BBB bonds are priced lower than BB bonds, since the risk is lower.
5. Liquidity—this is purely market driven. In high liquidity markets, bonds get priced more favorably, as the demand to invest in bonds is much higher. The price of bonds is compared to other bonds that trade in the secondary market given the same rating.

For example, a bond that is priced at 8% could be derived as follows:

$$Coupon\ rate = Rfr + IP + MRP + DRP + LP$$

where Rfr is the risk − free rate, IP is the inflation price, MRP is the maturity rate price, DRP is the default rate price, and LP is the liquidity price,

or

$$Coupon\ rate = 1.5\% + 2.0\% + 1.0\% + 3.0\% + 0.5\% = 8.0\%$$

STEP V: INDICATION OF INTEREST

Based on the expected rating by S&P and Moody's and the preliminary demand for the bonds, the underwriter determines a coupon payment market, which is usually set at a rate over the risk-free treasury rates. Additional details including the number of initial institutional investors, any price discounts, and modified market pricing, such as the coupon rate or the original issuance discount (OID), and any other amendments to the original registration, are also issued.

STEP VI: CLOSING, FUNDING, AND FREE TO TRADE

The underwriter then announces the price and determines that the trade process has been established. It takes approximately 3 days (T+3) for the bond offering to close. The bonds are then delivered, and the company receives the proceeds (net of underwriting fees and OID) from its sale. Depending on the type of underwriting, if the bonds are not sold to the syndicate, the underwriter is required to buy them and proceed with the funding unless it's a best effort underwriting.

RATING AGENCY METHODOLOGY

The corporate credit risk to determine the issuer-specific rating focuses on the following five areas of strength.

INDUSTRY RISK

Rating agencies such as S&P recognize that every industry is different and as compensation focus on how each industry has credit risk built into the company's business plan going forward. The industry drivers of revenue and cost are the focus points for calculating risk. Some companies are cyclical, some are seasonal, and others are stable. Some industries develop barriers to entry and others have fragmented.

Rating agencies characterize industries in five ways regarding the company's revenue drivers. The industry that the company competes in could be in a growth industry, a mature industry, a niche sector, a global business, or in a highly cyclical industry. Each characterization will have an impact on the way the rating agency interprets the credit quality of the industry and the companies that are part of it.

Industries that are *highly affected by economic changes* include chemical companies, paper and packaging, large-scale manufacturing such as auto and appliances, airlines, shipping, trucking, homebuilding and building materials, hotels, restaurants and retail. Industries that are *moderately affected* by economic changes include telecommunications, technology, broadcasting, and publishing. Industries slightly affected by economic changes include regulated utilities, government contracts, non-discretional consumer products, health care, and pharmaceuticals.

COMPANY-SPECIFIC BUSINESS RISKS

The rating agency spends most of its analytical work assessing the company's business. The analysis focuses on the company's market position in the industry, sales growth potential, strength and stability of cash flow, and how management's strategy will impact the company's credit strength.

The rating agencies start their analysis of what drives the revenues of the company and the likelihood of it getting affected by competition or new product innovation. A strong market share is an attractive consideration when the company is rated. The reality is that not every company can be the industry leader and the industry leader is not always guaranteed to be the most profitable. In many cases, the number two or number three company in an industry can be more successful than number one. Many companies that have the highest market share in terms of volume and sales can have lower income and cash flow than the ones with less market share. Another focus is the actual product and service and its differentiation from its competitors. Consistency in sales versus the economy is one measurement that the credit analyst must pay attention to. Consistent sales growth and pricing power are two of the areas of good credit, as well as strong liquidity.

MANAGEMENT FACTOR

The analyst of a rating agency assesses how management strategies affect the operational and financial success of the company. The assessment, which is more of a quality approach after all the quantitative factors are measured, is based on historical record and how management was able to manage the business through economic cycles. Also considered will be managements experience in running a company with high leverage while at the same time being able to successfully reduce that leverage. During the presentations between the management and the rating agencies, the analyst spends a lot of time assessing the management's confidence, company knowledge, and vision.

The integrity of management is most important. Management should be accessible to answer questions and answer these without deception. Being transparent and discussing their strategy and other activities openly builds necessary credibility with the rating agencies.

FINANCIAL RISK ANALYSIS

After the analyst spends most of the time assessing the company's business, the revenue and profit drivers, its position in the market place, and how management can positively or negatively affect the company's direction, then the analysis is concentrated on debt capacity and financial engineering. The amount of debt or equity support is very important when rating a company. Even if the company is successful with growing the sales and profit consistently over the years, the wrong amount of debt that requires heavy debt service could significantly impact the company's credit performance. A company with cyclical revenues is not ideal for making fixed debt obligations. The rating agency focuses on all three financial statements including the balance sheet and income and cash flow statements and then applies various ratios to measure the solvency, profitability, liquidity, and operational performance.

Chapter 17 discusses in detail the credit and ratio analysis approach, which is similar to the rating agency's financial risk analysis. The three solvency ratios that the agencies focus on are provided with explanations:

- **Loan-to-value or debt capitalization ratio:** One of the areas of credit analysis that establishes the position of debt in relationship to other capital raised, such as preferred and common equity. It analyzes the debt as percentage of the market and book value, enterprise value, and real assets, respectively. Figure 7.4 shows that the debt capitalization ratio starts at 35.4%, meeting Standard & Poor's BB- benchmark of 60%.

FIGURE 7.4 CELERITY TECHNOLOGY INC ("CTI") CREDIT RISK ANALYSIS

Credit Risk Analysis

	HISTORICAL		PROJECTED				
BASE CASE	**Year -1**	**Year 0**	**Year 1**	**Year 2**	**Year 3**	**Year 4**	**Year 5**
Revenues	960,000	1,110,000	1,228,140	1,344,200	1,442,919	1,529,268	1,605,161
Revenue Growth		15.6%	10.6%	9.5%	7.3%	6.0%	5.0%
EBITDA	385,000	433,000	493,561	547,928	592,424	629,659	660,688
EBITDA Margin							
Interest Expense			95,450	99,600	113,450	141,750	157,250
Tax Expense			129,769	147,070	156,960	158,461	162,851
Working Capital			(2,870)	4,548	3,869	3,384	2,974
Capex			138,304	151,374	162,491	172,215	180,761
Cash on Balance Sheet	45,000	65,800	118,577	179,246	236,183	267,484	278,544
Total Debt	1,220,000	1,190,000	1,160,000	1,130,000	1,090,000	1,030,000	950,000
Equity Ownerhip	1,746,000	1,919,800	2,114,453	2,335,059	2,570,498	2,808,190	3,052,467
Credit Risk Analysis							
1. Debt Capitalization			35.4%	32.6%	29.8%	26.8%	23.7%
2. Leverage Ratio : Total Debt / EBITDA			2.4x	2.1x	1.8x	1.6x	1.4x
3. Interest Ratio: EBITDA / Interest			5.2x	5.5x	5.2x	4.4x	4.2x
4. 30% EBITDA Haircut:	Haircut						
Total Debt / EBITDA (Leveraged Ratio)	30.0%		3.4x	2.9x	2.6x	2.3x	2.1x
EBITDA / Interest (Coverage Ratio)	30.0%		3.6x	3.9x	3.7x	3.1x	2.9x
Bench Mark (Target S&P BB- or higher):							
Debt Capitalization			60.0%	60.0%	60.0%	60.0%	60.0%
Total Debt / EBITDA (Leveraged Ratio)			4.0x	4.0x	4.0x	4.0x	4.0x
EBITDA / Interest (Coverage Ratio)			3.0x	3.0x	3.0x	3.0x	3.0x
5. Industry Designation (Industry Beta Sensitivity - needs to be less than 3x)							
Technology			2.5x	2.5x	2.5x	2.5x	2.5x
Credit Risk Benchmark			3.0x	3.0x	3.0x	3.0x	3.0x

- **Leverage ratio of debt to EBITDA: This solvency-type ratio, well known as the leverage ratio, is one of the most popular ratios to analyze the credit of a company.** Even few government agencies such as the board of governors of the Federal Reserve System (the "Fed Reserve"), the Federal Deposit Insurance Corporation (FDIC), and the Office of the Controller of Currency (OCC) are using this ratio to give guidance to banks to how much debt they should be advancing to companies in a new transaction, such as a leveraged buyout. On page 7 of the letter written on March 21, 2013 by the Federal Reserve, FDIC, and OCC with the subject *"Interagency Guidance on Leverage Lending"*, it states the following: "Credit agreement covenant protections, including financial performance (such as debt-to cash flow, interest coverage, or fixed charge coverage), reporting requirements, and compliance monitoring (are imperative). Generally, a leverage level after planned asset sales (that is, the amount of debt that must be serviced from operating cash flow) in excess of 6X Total Debt/EBITDA raises concerns for most industries." *(https://www.federalreserve.gov/supervisionreg/srletters/sr1303a1.pdf)*

  This ratio is also used by analysts to derive debt capacity and is incorporated in a lot of the credit agreements as a covenant ratio to measure ongoing performance of the borrower versus his or her projections. Figure 7.4 shows that the leverage ratio starts at 2.4x, meeting the Standard & Poor's BB- benchmark of 4.0x
- **Coverage ratios, including EBITDA/interest and cash flow to debt service:** While the two previous ratios focus on the debt as in relationship to value or other source of capital by setting up the initial debt as compared to current EBITDA and cash flow, the coverage ratios addresses the ongoing ability of the company to meet its annual debt obligations. These ratios, such as EBITDA to interest or EBITDA minus Capex-to-debt payments, are usually found in credit agreements as a covenant ratio. These ratios are very effective when running various sensitivity cases to test the ability of the company to pay its debt obligations. For example, if the starting EBITDA-to-interest ratio of a transaction is 3x, assuming EBITDA of $90 million and interest expense of $30 million, then even if EBITDA drops in half from $90 million to $45 million, the $30 million interest expenses can be covered, therefore significantly reducing the risk of the company not meeting these obligations. In this example, the credit agreement between the company and banks that have given the loan might have a covenant restriction of 2x, which means that at 1.5x the company will have a technical default. This technical default will give the bank a reason to increase its interest rate to reflect the new risk before approving to amend a new covenant level or waiving the current level. Figure 7.4 shows that the starting coverage ratio starts at 5.2x, meeting Standard & Poor's BB- benchmark of 3.0x.

Figure 7.4 is an example (Celerity Technology Inc.) of a few of the ratios the credit analyst uses to measure the financial risk of the company.

CASH FLOW FORECASTING AND MODELING

The rating agency will run various financial projection scenarios to measure the strength of the company's cash flows and its ability to pay its debt obligations. The company will give the rating agency the business plan, which will include financial projections before obtaining a bond and/or a loan. The analyst working for the rating agency that is in the process of rating the issuer and the bond will run various stress cases, including a case that adjusts down the top-line and bottom-line income and cash flow by 20–30% to test how the company can meet its debt obligations. The strength and stability of the cash flows based on the drivers are then compared with a benchmark of other issuers in the industry.

BOND INVESTMENT CONCEPTS

Bond analysis and valuation methods are further discussed in chapter 11, covering the secondary markets. There are also calculation references in Part I that cover investments and portfolio return investments. Here are some basic investment concepts and their brief explanations:

Yield to maturity (YTM): This is the interest rate that is equal to the present value of a bond's cash flow to its current price. YTM assumes that the bond will be held until maturity and that all coupon payments representing the cash flows of the bond investment will be reinvested at a rate equal to the yield to maturity.

Yield to call (YTC): This is the yield on a bond, assuming the bond is redeemed by the issuer at the first call date. Yield to call differs from yield to maturity in that yield to call uses a bond's call date as the final maturity date (most often, the first call date).

Yield to worst (YTW): After calculating the YTM and YTC, the YTW represents the lowest yield generated.

Current yield (CY): This measures a quick annual rate of return for the investor who is planning to buy the bond in the secondary market. The calculation is similar to the holding period return (HPR), which equals the expected cash flows from the investment divided by the initial investment. CY is calculated by dividing the annual interest earned on a bond by its current market price (not on its face or par value). For example, a $1,000 bond selling for $950 and paying a 7% coupon rate (or $70 per year) has a current yield of 7.37% (the quotient of $70 divided by $950). The coupon rate in this example is 7% (70/1,000).

Duration (D): This is a measurement the price sensitivity of the bond and/or bond funds to changes with interest rates. They are two types of duration measurement:

- The **Macaulay duration**, expressed in years, identifies how many years it will take to recover the initial investment (market value) by calculating the weighted average of each present value of future coupon payments using the yield as a discount rate times the payment year.
- The **modified duration**, expressed in percentages, measures the average percentage of movement of the bond price for every 1% movement of the interest rate. For example, the price of a bond with a duration of 2 would be expected to move 2% for every 1% move in interest rates.

Convexity (C): Like the modified duration, it measures the sensitivity of the bond price to 1% movement of the interest rates, but it's calculated on non-linear relationship. It is represented as a derivative to the duration.

CASE STUDY

EXAMPLE OF HIGH-YIELD ISSUANCE AND EXPLANATION OF THE "BOND TALK"

This is a sample announcement of a X Health Inc. high-yield transaction to tender and repay the existing outstanding notes. This announcement will be made by the lead underwriter to the investors and advise them that the bonds are now free to trade in the secondary market the day that the securities are processed (the names were changed):

> ***X Health*** *this afternoon completed its $1.5 billion note offer in two parts, pricing $500 million of senior secured notes due 2027 at 5.75%, the tight end of initial guidance, and $1 billion of add-on 8.5% senior notes due 2027 at 103.25, also the tight end of early guidance, according to sources. The add-on portion was upsized from $750 million. The offering via lead book-runner KP Investment Bank will fund tender offer and consent solicitation for the company's existing 5.625% senior notes due 2021, 5.5% senior notes due 2023, and 5.875% senior notes due 2023. The original offering of 8.5% senior notes due 2027 priced at par in May 2018; they were trading between 104.375 and 104.625 yesterday, yielding as much as 7.5%. The pharmaceutical concerns trades on the New York Stock Exchange with an $8.31 billion market capitalization.*

ISSUER:	**X HEALTH**
Notes	*$500 million*
Coupon Rate	*5.75% (T+314 bps) yield 5.75% senior notes*
Maturity	*August 15, 2027*
Price	*100*
Ratings	*Ba2/BB-*
Call Provision	*NC 3.5 @par +50% coupon*
Notes (Type)	*144A-life; 40% equity clawback option; talk 5.875% area*
Settlement	*03/08/19 (T+10)*
Book-runners	*KP/DDD/ABC/BCC/LLP*

ISSUER:	**X HEALTH**
Notes	*$1 billion*
Coupon rate	*8.75% (T + 516 bps) yield 7.75% senior notes*
Maturity	*January 31, 2027*
Price	*103.25*
Ratings	*B3/B-*
Call provision	*NC 3.5 @par +50% coupon*
Notes (type)	*144A-life; 40% equity clawback option; talk 103–103.25 area total deal size now $1.75B*
Settlement	*03/08/19 (T+10)*
Book-runners	*KP/DDD/ABC/BCC/LLP*

EXPLANATION OF THE "BOND TALK"

- X Health has priced two different notes for total proceeds of $1.5 billion: $500mm and $1 billion.
- Proceeds were used to repay the existing notes that are due in 2 years.
- The coupons were circled at 5.75% and 8.75% fixed, respectively.
- The coupons were set at approximately 10-year treasuries (T) of 2.61%, plus a premium (risk premium over risk free) of 315 and 516 basis points, respectively.
- The pricing (original issuance discount) is 100 (par) for the first note and the 103.25 (premium), calculating 5.75% yield and 7.75% yield (it makes sense that the yield is lower than the 8.75% coupon rate priced at premium), respectively.
- The ratings were Ba2/BB- and B3/B-, respectively; the 8.75% notes are rated much lower than the 5.75% notes (S&P three notches lower from BB- to B- and Moody's four notches lower from Ba2 to B3).
- Both have no call for 3.5 years and a make-whole (if the company refinance early) of par + 50% of the coupon.
- These notes have approximately 8- and 8.5-year terms (August 15, 2017 and January 31, 2027, respectively).
- The notes were not registered with the SEC since they were raised in 144A private market.
- The 144A-life means that the issuance will stay private, it does not have registration rights to convert to public bond.
- The settlement is T+10, which means the investors will own the bonds 10 business days since the trade (T) day.
- The book-runners of all these banks listed (KP/DDD/ABC/BCC/LLP) are the initial underwriters before the retail syndication.

PROBLEMS

1. Explain the meaning of the "waterfall" in the capital structure.
2. Why do the unsecured notes charge a higher interest rate than the secured notes?
3. What are mortgage bonds and the types of assets these bonds use as collateral?
4. What are the main characteristics of collateral trust bonds?
5. Explain the use of equipment trust obligations and who are typically the issuers of these trust obligations.
6. What are guarantee bonds and who is the typical issuer of these bonds?
7. Assume that the company's stock is trading at $30 and the convertible bonds have a conversion rate of 50 shares for one bond. Should the convertible bond holder convert from bonds to stock? Explain the reasoning.
8. What is conversion parity? If the conversion ratio is 1 bond to 10 shares, what will the stock be at parity?
9. What are zero coupon bonds and PIK bonds, and what do they have in common?
10. Explain why the company is required to rate the bonds of a new issue by rating agencies such as S&P and Moody's.
11. What bonds are considered investment grade and non-investment grade?
12. Explain what the call provisions in a bond indenture are.
13. What are equity claw backs, and what types of bonds are typically used in these equity claw backs?
14. What right does the bond holder have when owning bonds with equity warrants?
15. Given the high risk, who invests in CCC rated bonds, and why?
16. What is the difference between "D" rated bonds and "D selective" rated bonds?
17. In a bond indenture, what are considered money terms and not-money terms?
18. Explain the difference between firm commitment and best effort commitment regarding the syndication of a bond.
19. What are the five quantitative factors that the rating agency is using to determine the risk rating of the issuer of bond?

ONLINE TEMPLATES

The Excel spreadsheets used in the chapter can be accessed online via Cognella Active Learning platform.

CHAPTER 8

Debt Markets: Issuing Bank Loans, Private Loans, and Loan Syndication

This chapter will summarize various approaches through which a company can access the loan markets. The chapter will outline the process and various best practices a company will go through when raising corporate loans from the syndicate, club, or private markets. As descried in the last chapter, it is key that students keep in mind the double-edged sword that comes with acquiring leverage, especially in large quantities. It is imperative students understand that while helping maximize returns for companies and investment portfolios alike, leverage, like other long-term liabilities, can add a substantial financial burden in times of economic hardship and greatly increase the risk profile of the associated assets.

LEARNING OBJECTIVES

After reading this chapter, students will be able to do the following:

- Understand various types of corporate loans offered in both the investment-grade and leveraged loan markets
- Recognize the difference between investment-grade and leveraged loan issues and issuers
- Learn how the rating agencies S&P and Moody's assign risk ratings to corporate loans. These loans are usually syndicated by funds who are required to invest in rated securities

- Prepare the company for a go-to-market strategy to syndicate its primary as well as other private loans
- Understand the capital-raising process and the investors for these loans in the middle market and broadly syndicated loan (BSL) market
- Understand the various terms and conditions surrounding loan agreements
- Become familiar with how each bank does its own internal analysis and credit review for applying its own grading methodologies

CORPORATE LOANS: AN OVERVIEW

Unlike corporate bonds, corporate loans are issued by companies that need flexibility during the repayment process. These corporate loans are provided by banks and structured as floating rate loans based on an index, such as the London Inter Banking Offering Rate (LIBOR), plus a negotiated spread determined by the issuer's credit quality. These loans may be backed by collateral or be unsecured and backed by the "good faith" of the corporation. In a bankruptcy, corporate loans have the highest priority of payment.

AUTHOR'S NOTES

In 1988, only one year out of business school while working for Bank of America, I was assigned as the analyst to the largest leveraged buyout of the time ($31.5 billion): The acquisition of the RJR Nabisco by KKR, made into a book and later the satiric movie Barbarians at the Gate *(Burrough & Helyar, 1990). The bank loan consisted of $13.6 billion, with the biggest buyers becoming the Japanese banks; ironically, I worked on all of them in my later years. (In 1988 there were more than 10 Japanese banks; these were consolidated in the 1990s and early 2000s into three mega banks.) When the Japanese recession hit in the 1990s (commonly known as the lost decade), the result of this consolidation became clear. The truth was 50% of the buyers of these loans were no longer there; the market realized and thus predicted there would no longer be any large syndications similar to that of Nabisco since 50% of the investors are not there. However, the market consistently has a funny way of reinventing itself and making room for other players to step in and profit. No one exactly foresaw the early 2000s and the emergence of collateralized loan obligations (CLOs). The asset managers operating these vehicles would ultimately end up purchasing 70% of all syndicated loans. In February 2007, the LBO for TXU, a Texas utility company, surpassed the 1988 RJR Nabisco as the largest LBO to date ($37.9 billion financing), with the leverage loan* *being twice as much as the RJR Nabisco transaction ($26 billion versus $13 billion). Then the financial crisis came the next year and the CLO market went dead overnight. I remember there being reports that the mega LBOs were done and would never come again—deja vu of 1988 where the same comment was made when the Japanese banks got out of the leveraged market—and was the end of the mega LBO deals. I wonder who will be financing the next wave of mega deals ... but wait. The CLO market came back again, clipping the largest issuance of CLO financing ever in 2018 with $130 billion of issuance.*

KEY TAKEAWAYS

- Like any public or private capital raising, companies need to understand that fundamentals are more important than technical characteristics. Having a good product, good management, and feasibility in the future are more important characteristics than aiming at financial engineering or taking advantage of overenthusiastic markets.
- The loan markets are very large and liquid, but no one debt facility is the same as another.
- A loan agreement is broken down by money terms and non-money terms.

CORPORATE LOANS

There are many types of corporate loans depending on the company's purpose in raising such loans. The following represent the most common types of loans.

REVOLVING LOAN FACILITY (REVOLVER)

The revolving loan facility or revolver provided by a traditional commercial bank is a variable line of credit used by companies to primarily fund working capital needs. This revolver is one of the most flexible debt facilities that a company obtains from a bank. It can borrow and be repaid at any time and typically for any reason. It provides short-term liquidity and in many cases the company uses the revolver as a guarantee letter of credit for ordering their raw materials and supplies. The pricing is made up of two rates: an unfunded rate called a commitment fee, plus a funded interest rate based on the LIBOR, plus a negotiated spread based on the quality of the borrower. Commitment fees are calculated as a percentage of the unfunded portion of the facility, typically 0.35–0.50%.

The amount determined by the bank is based on the company's working capital needs and expected cash flow. This amount is often highly negotiated as the company is trying to obtain the best possible flexibility to fund its short-term cash flow setbacks. Seasonal companies, such as retailers that build up their inventory before the holidays in November and December, are heavy users of revolver credit. The rule of thumb for a traditional user of a revolver is for the amount to be set at 1.0x EBITDA.

Revolvers are also used as a measurement of liquidity for a trade before they advance any credit against the shipped supplies. In distressed times, the company uses the revolver to cover losses and can bridge the time until normalization. Given the revolving nature of the facility, it can range between a zero balance to potentially a full balance. It is important to remember that the marketability of these facilities in the secondary loan market is not ideal and is viewed by most investors as very difficult to price when a bank wants to trade. Revolvers are usually provided by traditional banks to investment-grade and non-investment-grade companies as a complimentary addition to other debt facilities that have better return characteristics such as term loans. A revolver, sometimes called relationship capital, is a banking product that left lead and co-arrangers of a syndicated transaction, such as for an LBO or M&A, are required to provide in addition to term loans and other financing.

ASSET-BASED LENDING FACILITY (ABL)

This type of revolver is structured based on the company's current assets such as accounts receivable and inventory. The lender has a priority of payment over the borrower's current assets. The term loans provided, also by the banks, have a second priority claim on these assets. The amount that can be drawn under this facility is based on a set advance rate against the pledged assets. Typically, accounts receivable, which has the highest liquidity after cash, draws advanced rates of 85%. Inventory typically carries 50% advance rates, but they can be dependent on the individual business and current situation. Since ABLs are directly secured by the most liquid collateral, the interest rate charged is significantly lower than bank revolvers and term loans (1–2% lower), which rely on the company's future cash flows for debt repayment.

TERM LOANS

Unlike the revolver, term loans are one-time loans provided by a traditional bank and are typically used for acquisitions, purchasing equipment, and real estate. A term loan typically carries a floating interest rate based on a benchmark like the U.S. prime rate or LIBOR plus a negotiated spread based on the quality of the borrower. The interest and principal payments for such loans are typically paid on a quarterly basis for 5–7 years. Throughout the years, terms loans have developed to be marketable in the secondary markets. This led to ratings being assigned to these loans, similar to bonds, by the rating agencies. Also, these term loans are sometimes structured in various tranches like term loan A and term loan B, or even term loan C or term loan D. Each tranche can be priced differently based on maturity and scheduled payments. Term loan B is one of the most marketable debt facilities that represents the loan secondary market, often called Term loan B markets. Most collateral loan obligations (CLOs) use term loan Bs in their portfolio and trade these securities frequently in the secondary market. The scheduled principal repayment for these term loan Bs are structured similar to that of bonds with most of the repayment being made at maturity (bullet payment). Typically, a 7-year term loan will have a scheduled amortization payment of 1–2% per year for the first 6 years with the balance (other 94%) being paid in the seventh year.

Pricing for term loan Bs are based on three sections: LIBOR or LIBOR floor, spread, and original issue discount (OID).

- **The LIBOR** is an index used as an initial rate benchmark. In years where the LIBOR was very low or close to zero, term loan agreements incorporated LIBOR floors that were higher than these benchmarks. This was to ensure that these facilities would be marketable in the secondary market. If a security is not marketable it carries significantly more risk for the bank to issue and hold. This is especially relevant for CLOs due to a higher cost of capital than traditional banks.
- **The spread** is the additional interest rate added to the LIBOR or LIBOR floor to complete the actual interest rate imposed on the loan and funding recipient. This interest rate is then used to calculate the interest expense charged as a result. The spread that is negotiated and stated in the agreement is based on the quality of the borrower's credit. Typically, it is set until maturity; however, there are certain agreements sometimes incorporated in these loans (covenants) that base the rate on certain financial ratios. This is largely to ensure the bank keeps the same probability of repayment. The ratios used as indicators measure the company's ability to service the debt such as the leverage ratio (i.e., total debt to EBITDA).
- **Original issuance discount (OID)** is the discount that the loan is priced at in the primary markets and represents the fee that the original investor in the term loan receives net of funding. For example, if the OID is set at $99, the net fee the investor receives is 1% of the investment. The OID is the original price of the loan before it trades in the secondary market.

To calculate the loan-yield the analyst needs all the sections of pricing, as described. The formula is as follows:

Annual loan yield = LIBOR or LIBOR floor + spread + (100 – OID)/4 years

For example, a term loan B is priced at LIBOR or LIBOR floor of 1% plus 4% spread and OID of 98. Assuming current LIBOR is 1.5%, the original issued yield is calculated as follows:

First, since LIBOR is higher than LIBOR floor (1.5% versus 1.0%), the LIBOR is used as the benchmark to calculate yield:

Annual loan yield (%) = 1.5 + 4.0 + (100 − 98)/4 = 5.5 + 2/4 = 5.5 + .5 = 6.0

Please note that the OID calculation is based on a 4-year time span as the conventional time period for these loans in the secondary market is 4 years. Therefore, we calculate and spread the fee as 100 − OID over 4 years to determine the annual yield.

Term loan A is typically a loan that traditional commercial banks feel comfortable but not excited about holding in their portfolio. The difference between term loan A and term loan B could be that the maturity is shorter (5 versus 7 years) and/or the repayment schedule is much heavier for term loan A compared to term loan B. Typically term loan A start with 5–10% scheduled payments that tend to escalate to 15–25% in later years.

Figure 8.1 shows Colorado Dental's scheduled principal and interest payments for both term loan A and term loan B based on an assumed increased LIBOR.

FIGURE 8.1 COLORADO DENTAL DEBT SCHEDULES

Colorado Dental

DEBT SCHEDULES								
($ 000's)	Historical	PROJECTED						
	Year 0	Year 1	Year 2	Year 3	Year 4	Year 5	Year 6	Year 7
Interest Rate Assumptions								
LIBOR Rate	2.50%	3.00%	3.50%	4.50%	4.50%	4.50%	4.50%	4.50%
LIBOR lincrease / Decrease		0.5%	0.5%	1.0%				
Term Loan A								
Outstanding	180,000	160,000	130,000	95,000	55,000	-	-	-
Increase / (Decrease)		20,000	30,000	35,000	40,000	55,000		
Interest Payment		11,700	11,200	10,400	7,600	4,400	-	-
Total Payment (Interest + Principal)	(180,000)	31,700	41,200	45,400	47,600	59,400	-	-
Spread		3.50%	3.50%	3.50%	3.50%	3.50%		
Interest rate		6.50%	7.00%	8.00%	8.00%	8.00%		
Schedule Repayment based on Percentage %		11.11%	16.67%	19.44%	22.22%	30.56%		
Term Loan B								
Outstanding	200,000	198,000	196,000	194,000	192,000	190,000	188,000	-
Increase / (Decrease)		2,000	2,000	2,000	2,000	2,000	2,000	188,000
Interest Payment		14,000	14,850	16,660	16,490	16,320	16,150	15,980
Total Payment (Interest + Principal)	(200,000)	16,000	16,850	18,660	18,490	18,320	18,150	203,980
Spread		4.00%	4.00%	4.00%	4.00%	4.00%	4.00%	4.00%
Interest rate		7.00%	7.50%	8.50%	8.50%	8.50%	8.50%	8.50%
Schedule Repayment based on Percentage %		1.00%	1.00%	1.00%	1.00%	1.00%	1.00%	94.00%

Figure 8.1 shows the annual payments of both term loan A and term loan B. The 5-year term loan A shows a much higher repayment schedule than a 7-year term loan B; as mentioned, this is designed based on the marketability of term loan Bs, which are sold to CLO funds. Because of the longer maturity, the term loan B's interest rate is higher than a term loan A. Also, this case shows that the analyst assumes that the LIBOR will increase in the next 3 years. Though this is not included in the credit agreement, this is a typical adjustment that credit analysts include in their analysis.

SECOND-LIEN TERM LOANS

Second-lien term loans are more popular in mid-cap LBO transactions. In the last few years there has been a shift in replacing unsecured bonds with second-lien term loans to provide the company and the private equity buying or owning the company with the flexibility of restructuring the debt in the future.

A second-lien term loan is a secured loan that has a subordinated or second lien claim to collateral pledged as a means of securing the term loan and revolver. In a bankruptcy that results in a forced liquidation, the second-lien term loan may receive proceeds from the sale of assets pledged to secure the loan, but only after senior term loan holders have been paid. Due to the second-lien nature of this loan, second liens carry more risk for lenders than senior-term loans. As a result, these loans usually have higher borrowing rates, typically 1–2% higher than term loans.

Analysts that attempt to weigh the default risk before approving a second-lien loan usually assess many of the same factors as first-lien lenders. This includes borrowers' leverage ratios such as total debt to EBITDA, total debt to total capitalization (total debt/(total debt + equity)), and credit ratings.

MEZZANINE LOANS AND NOTES

Mezzanine financing is placed between senior loans and equity, hence the name "mezzanine." A typical structure would be a hybrid of debt and equity financing that gives the lender the right to convert to an equity interest in the company in case of default on the loan. Given the financial risk, pricing is set much higher than on senior loans (12% to 20%). Mezzanine financing is structured to replace part of the capital equity investors would otherwise have to provide the company. For example, a company would seek financing for $20 million and put in $30 million of its own funds for the buyout (the purchased company's assets are generally placed as collateral for the loan). The mezzanine lenders will look to gain equity in the business through structured warrants allowing the purchase of equity later, sometimes at an agreed-on rate. Basically, mezzanines are structured originally as debt that entitles the issuer to receive interest payments with the upside of equity returns if the company succeeds.

FIGURE 8.2 COLORADO DENTAL TRANSACTION SOURCES & USES

Colorado Dental

TRANSACTION SOURCES & USES

Sources	Interest Rate	Term (Years)	Commited ($ 000's)	Funded ($ 000's)	% Cap	EBITDA x
Revolving Credit	0.50%/LIBOR+3.5%		100,000	-		
Term Loan A	LIBOR + 3.5%	5	180,000	180,000	18.4%	1.5x
Term Loan B	LIBOR + 4.0%	7	200,000	200,000	20.4%	1.7x
Total Bank Debt			480,000	380,000	38.8%	3.2x
Senior Unsecured / Subordinated Notes	10% FIXED		200,000	200,000	20.4%	1.7x
Total Debt			**680,000**	**580,000**	59.2%	4.8x
Cash Equity			400,000	400,000	40.8%	3.3x
Total Sources			**1,080,000**	**980,000**	100.0%	8.2x

Uses	Amount ($ 000's)
Cash	-
Purchase of Equity (100% shares	740,000
Refinance Existing Debt	220,000
Transaction Fees & Expenses	20,000
Total Uses	**980,000**

Acquisition Target EBITDA = **120,000**

The borrowers could prefer mezzanine debt instead of equity if there is enough support because the interest is tax deductible. Also, since the mezzanine investor has the best interest of the company in mind (potential equity ownership), he or she might be willing to amend certain terms to help the company through tough times.

Figure 8.2 shows an example of Colorado Dental LBO structure purchased by a private equity firm for $1.15 billion that includes bank loans, mezzanine notes, and equity.

UNITRANCHE TERM LOANS

Unitranche debt is a type of structured debt that combines senior and junior loans into one debt vehicle. These senior and junior loans are awarded different priority of payment or pricing in one loan agreement during the structuring of the security. This type of loan is obtained from one or multiple participants that are interested in the combination of the different term structures. It is typically arranged by financial institutions and not your traditional bank and allows the borrower to raise funds with a one-stop-shop arrangement that only requires one approval process. Combining different debt structures from different investors that have their own risk assessment and purposes allows the total debt package to be more comprehensive, tailored, and marketable in the secondary market. The borrower in this case will make one interest payment to one lender with the cost of the loan (interest rate) being a blend between a traditional bank-secured loan and a subordinated loan such as a second-lien and/or mezzanine loan.

Specifically, the purpose of structuring unitranche debt is to divide portions of the structured debt vehicle into tranches in one agreement. Each tranche is structured with its own class designation. The underwriter of this structure will determine and document all of the terms of each tranche including details on its interest payments, interest rate, duration, and seniority.

Payment seniority based on "waterfall" liquidation is typically the primary factor taken into account when structuring the terms of each tranche level. Underwriters will structure the tranches by seniority with the lowest-risk tranches having the highest seniority for repayment. These measures are taken to ensure stability of the facility in case of default of one or multiple loans. The strategies behind tranche-debt vehicles often follow connotations ranging from the "first-out" tranche (highest seniority) to the "last-out" tranche (lowest seniority). A typical analysis to determine the amounts of each tranche is based on the leverage ratio of each tranche amount compared to the company's last reported EBITDA. The best candidates for unitranche loans are companies in less cyclical industries with business models that have significant levels of recurring and stable revenue.

Unitranche loans serving middle-market companies are typically structured as non-amortizing loans. In many cases, these are made to riskier borrowers with the structure possibly utilizing a PIK-interest toggle as well as equity kickers. A PIK or paid-in-kind interest toggle is a mechanism that allows the interest payment to be converted to a form of cash paid subsequently to finance-deferred payments. Equity kickers are mechanisms that allow investors to obtain equity at different points during the loan term.

There are two types of unitranche loans:

- **Straight unitranche** are loans that are provided by one lender or a syndicate of lenders. A straight unitranche loan represents a senior stretch loan. The name "stretch loan" comes from the idea that the lender stretches the seniority to leverage ratios of total debt to EBITDA of five to six times instead of breaking up the facilities into senior and junior loans.
- **Bifurcated unitranche** are structures that separate the principal into first-out and last-out tranches, as discussed.

OTHER TYPES OF BANK LOANS

There are other types of bank loans that are offered primarily from banks based on the purpose of the loan. These include Debt-in-possession loans for distress companies, bridge loans for helping the companies bridge their financing to a public offering takeout, swing loans provided by one bank on behalf of the other syndicated banks and many more. These are described as follows:

Debt-In-Possession Loan (DIP)

Debtor-in-possession financing (DIP financing) is a special type of financing that aids and gears companies for the process of either filing for bankruptcy or a reorganization. Those companies that are considered financially distressed will generally seek additional financing to cover short-term liquidity while the rest of the debt is restructured post-bankruptcy.

The facility is therefore a bridge to facilitate the short-term needs of the company until post-reorganization and bankruptcy. DIP financing has immediate priority of payment over existing debt, equity, and other claims.

Chapter 11 filing was established by regulators to protect workers during bankruptcy proceedings. It is therefore encouraged by the courts to allow such financing to come into play and be placed ahead of existing debt. This is done for the purpose of giving the company enough liquidity to continue paying employees, vendors, and suppliers. In debt-or-in-possession financing, the court must approve the financing plan that is consistent with the protection granted to run the business.

Once the company secures DIP financing, it lets its vendors, suppliers, and customers know that the company will continue business as usual. Given the financing, the company is now provided with enough liquidity to pay for inventory and services. This will also give the existing lenders time to reorganize the company into a better strategic entity without completely losing out on existing business. If this is the case, investors prefer that the company continues to operate and hope to add value post-bankruptcy, avoiding straight liquidation (refer to chapter 7). During the financial crisis, the two bankrupt U.S. automakers (General Motors and Chrysler) used DIP facilities to reorganize their existing debt, which was ultimately financed by the government. DIP facilities greatly aided these companies and allowed them to continue to stay open and fully operate their business.

Typically, DIP financing is structured as term loans—fully funded throughout the bankruptcy—basically sitting in cash on the balance sheet. Many years ago, and sometimes today, DIP facilities are structured as revolving lines of credit and therefore require the company to send notices to providers requesting additional funding as they go. This type of arrangement was often preferred by borrowers because it offered more flexibility and would cost much less since much of the facility could stay unfunded. Market demand has pushed this new arrangement to the forefront, attempting to entice institutional investors to invest in this category, which was traditionally dominated by commercial banks.

Bridge Loans

Bridge loans are short-term loans that are used for cash until the company can secure more permanent financing. Bridge loans are designed so that the company is able to close on a specific transaction that requires quick funding and execution, such as an acquisition or leveraged buyout (LBO). Bridge loan participants charge high fees and interest rates once funded and could insist on interest rate escalation if the bridge objective is not accomplished within the expected time frame. Bridge loans are very popular when the company is in the process of raising public debt or equity for a specific transaction. Since such public offerings can take a long time to close and fund, the bridge facility provides the financing that enables the company to close the transaction. Once the public raising is done, the proceeds will be used to repay the bridge loan. Typically, the fees are 1–1.5% upfront and 2–2.5% on the back end via a bond offering.

Swing Loans

This is a loan that is offered by the lead syndication arranger that includes all the terms of the loan in the credit agreement. **The swing loan, which has a maximum cap, is used as a quick liquidity loan for the company to manage same day working capital needs**. In a large syndication with multiple lending banks, implementing a revolver could be a bureaucratic nightmare. It is tedious to have all the banks fund their share of a revolver. Therefore, as compensation, the administrative bank is asked to fund the working capital on behalf of the other lenders. The swing facility is usually repaid shortly thereafter (within a few days), so there is no real incentive to having additional banks involved in the financing. Even to arrange for the small possibility of default risk, if the company delays payment, notices for funding are sent to the syndicate members requiring them to cover their share of the swing loan—with the proceeds of this funding being used to pay the administrative bank. If the company files for bankruptcy, then every bank is responsible to pay its share back to the administrative bank on a pro-rata basis.

Project Finance Loans

Project loans are used to finance infrastructure and industrial projects. **A project loan is structured to include the interest payment during construction and is repaid with a more permanent loan after the project is completed or rolled over into a permanent-term debt facility.** The facility is then paid back with the cash flow generated by the project. Project financing is a loan structure that relies primarily on the project's cash flow as repayment and is secured by the project's assets.

A project loan is a non-recourse loan and is structured to finance three distinct phases of a project's initiation process; the three phases draw the connotation BOT standing for build, operate, and transfer. Project loans finance the BOT projects via a special purpose vehicle (SPV). The riskiest period of the loan for both the borrower and the lender is during the construction phase. The expected repayment in this phase relies on an off-take contract or a power purchase agreement in the case of an energy project.

RATING CORPORATE LOANS

The company obtaining a loan is not required to get a rating since these are private loans provided by sophisticated financial institutions or banks. **In a larger syndicated transaction involving a facility known as a broadly syndicated loan (BSL), typically raised in tandem with the bond issue, the agencies rate the bonds and the underwriter will also ask for ratings to be assigned to the associated loans**. The ratings for loans are desired in order to make these loans more marketable to funds like CLOs who will purchase and trade these securities in the leveraged loan market. These CLOs, discussed in later chapters, are structured for the most part to only buy rated securities and loans from dependable agencies such as S&P and Moody's. Like in the case of bonds, the rating that is assigned to loans, primarily term loan B, is measuring the likelihood of default. The rating is usually one or two notches higher than the public bonds given the seniority in the structure. The rating agencies' primary concern is measuring the risk of default for these loans. The agency issues a rating for the company that specifically issues the loans and the bonds as well as for the individual loans and bonds themselves. All three rating measurements focus on the credit strength of the company and likelihood of paying back its debt, this debt of course being composed of the aforementioned bonds payable and the term loan. Figure 8.3 shows the corporate bond rating system and the symbols assigned and is then broken down into five

FIGURE 8.3 CORPORATE LOAN RATING AGENCIES' SCALES

Description		Standard & Poor's	Moody's	Fitch
Highest Quality (Risk Free)	INVESTMENT GRADE	AAA	Aaa	AAA
High Quality	INVESTMENT GRADE	AA+ AA AA-	Aa1 Aa2 Aa3	AA+ AA AA-
Strong Payment Capacity	INVESTMENT GRADE	A+ A A-	A1 A2 A3	A+ A A-
Adequate Payment Capacity	INVESTMENT GRADE	BBB+ BBB BBB-	Baa1 Baa2 Baa3	BBB+ BBB BBB-
Likely to fullfill Obligations	NON-INVESTMENT GRADE (LEVERAGE)	BB+ BB BB-	Ba1 Ba2 Ba3	BB+ BB BB-
High-risk Obligations	NON-INVESTMENT GRADE (LEVERAGE)	B+ B B-	B1 B2 B3	B+ B B-
Current Vulnarable to Default	DISTRESS	CCC+ CCC CCC- CC C	Caa1 Caa2 Cas3 Ca C	CCC
Default	DEFAULT	D	D	RD/D

descending categories of risk, described later in this chapter. These include AAA risk-free grade, investment grade, non-investment grade, and distressed and default grades. The initial issuance usually starts at investment grade or non-investment grade. As the rating agency monitors the ratings in conjunction with the company's available cash flow, it will upgrade or downgrade the company based on ongoing intrinsic credit risk.

After an initial rating is granted, rating agencies will continue to monitor loans, bonds, and issuers that they have rated. As the issuer releases the financials or announces major changes, the rating agencies may announce they are reviewing a credit rating and comment they are in the process of downgrading or upgrading the proposed company. When such an announcement is made, the issuer or issue (bonds and corporate loans) is said to be under credit watch. The description of each of the bonds and loans were described in the last chapter (chapter 7).

TYPES OF LOAN SYNDICATION

There are three types of underwriting agreements used when syndicating loans. These are fully underwritten loans, best-efforts loans and club loans as described below:

FULLY UNDERWRITTEN

This is where the loan underwriters or arrangers of the loans guarantee the entire commitment, then syndicate the loan to reduce their exposure. Similar to a bond underwriting, if the arrangers cannot fully subscribe the loan, they are forced to absorb the difference and take full market risk. The incentive for the arrangers to take such market risk is embedded in the transaction. A fully underwritten loan can be a very competitive tool for arrangers to win a mandate. Also, the arranger requires higher fees and can profit off the spread it charges over its associated cost. Over the years due to a few failed syndications, arrangers have begun to add "flex language" in their agreements. This flex language that is spelled out in detail in the underwriting agreement includes pricing (pricing flex) and structural (structural flex) adjustments that the arranger can implement to sell the loan in the syndication just in case the market demand for the loan diminishes. This protection is sometimes necessary because there is a lot of time between the announcement of a certain acquisition or levered buyout and the time the deal materializes. During this time period pricing as well as other influences surrounding the agreement could change. Flex pricing is typically negotiated upfront and set around 1–2% above the all-in current yield. This means the adjustments can be based on spread pricing or the OID (as described earlier). Structural flex language could include an option for the underwriter to change the structure of the deal so that it can become more marketable in the secondary market. This could include a change in the capital structure such as lowering the bank loan and replacing it with more bond issuance. One would incorporate such a strategy if market demand is higher for the raising of bonds rather than bank loans. In extreme cases, structural flex language could include an option to add more equity and reduce the debt if the market thinks the transaction is too levered. Having too much debt can add substantial priority of payment and cash flow risk. As such, to prevent a deal from being too rigid with respect to ongoing investor continuity, lending parties will incorporate this structural flex language into their deals. Another language found recently in underwriting agreements is the memorandum of understanding (MOU) between the syndicate arrangers for selling their exposure on their own without consulting the underwriter. This MOU is to coordinate the sell once sourced and the price is controlled for at least some agreed-on period (90–180 days), especially if the syndication failed.

BEST-EFFORTS SYNDICATION

This is where the underwriter or arranger commits to underwriting less than the entire amount of the loan. If the loan is undersubscribed, the deal may not close unless the terms/pricing/structure are changed (revisiting the terms). Best-efforts syndications are used for risky borrowers or for complex transactions.

CLUB DEAL

This arrangement is a very typical financing arrangement for smaller and middle-market transactions and involves a pre-marketed offering to a group of issuers or equity sponsors called relationship lenders. The arranger is generally a first among equals, and each lender gets a full cut of the fees.

THE LOAN SYNDICATION PROCESS

The loan syndication process starts from a handful of arrangers who solicit bids to win the mandate of a specific deal. These arrangers provide the company or the sponsor with information including an outline of their syndication strategy and their view on the way the loan will be priced in market.

After all the solicitation processes are completed by the potential arrangers, the following process is executed:

- The issuer gives the mandate to one or more arrangers (co-arrangers).
- The arranger will prepare an information memo (IM) describing the terms of the transactions. The IM typically will include the following:
    - Executive summary
    - Investment considerations
    - Summary of terms and conditions (term sheet)

  - Transaction overview
  - Company
  - Management and equity sponsor overview
  - Industry overview
  - Financial model
  - Timing for commitments, closing, as well as fees on level of commitments

- A bank meeting is scheduled at which potential lenders hear from the management and the investor group.
- A deadline is given for the banks to send their commitment levels that are subject to final documentation.
- Each bank analyzes the deal's credit and assesses the pricing (RORA). Each issuer is assigned an internal rating.
- The arranger collects all commitments, different amounts from each bank.
- Allocations are given and legal documentation is sent for final review.
  - If the deal is oversubscribed, the allocation of each bank will most likely be reduced
  - If the deal is undersubscribed, depending on the FLEX language, the pricing could be flexed up
- After review and signatures of legal documents by each lender, the deal closes and is funded.

FIGURE 8.4 LOAN SYNDICATION PROCESS

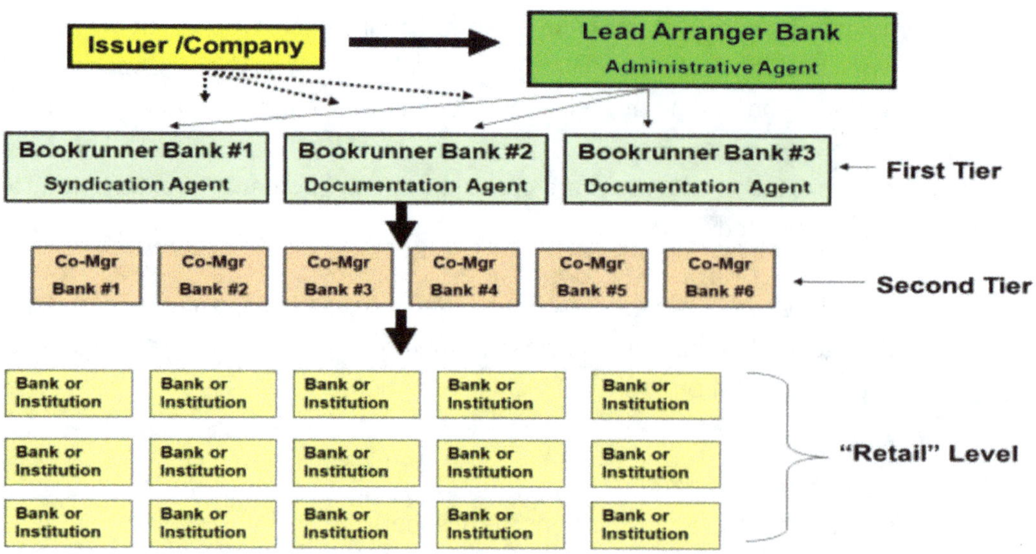

TYPICAL INTERNAL ANALYSIS PROCESS BY EACH BANK

Each bank or financial institution (commercial bank or CLO, respectively), that is invited to participate in the financing has its own internal analysis and application that is sent to its respected investment or credit committees. A typical application includes the following analysis:

1. The requested amount committed to the deal that is within the rating parameters for each bank
2. Recommended amounts by tranche (revolving credit/term loans or pro-rata)
3. Term and conditions of the loans (includes pricing, structure, and covenants)
4. Profitability analysis (return on return on asset (RORA) and risk-adjusted return on capital (RAROC))
5. The syndication strategy: who is the left lead arranger and how many banks were invited
6. Transaction discussion including sources and uses and capital structure
7. Company discussion including historical performance and outlook
8. Corporate structure including holding company, subsidiaries, and any guarantors of the loans
9. Management biographies/equity sponsor profile
10. Collateral analysis
11. Industry analysis
12. Financial analysis (projections model)
13. Internal rating analysis
14. Internal legal review
15. KYC (know your customer) and compliance review

Each bank runs its own internal rating process, which is in line with the rating agency's external ratings, though the analysis is done independently.

This rating analysis, typically a 10-rating score card ("1" being equivalent to A+/A/A- and "10" being in default) is determined with the two following approaches.

QUANTITATIVE ANALYSIS

The quantitative analysis for establishing the internal rating, which measures the probability of default, is based on the following parameters (each component is weighted at a specific level of importance):

- **Leverage ratio:** The relationship between debt and earnings (i.e., debt/EBITDA)
- **Capitalization ratio**: The relationship between the bank debt and the rest of the capital (capital leases, bonds, equity)

- **Coverage ratio**: Issuer's cash flow covering its debt obligations (interest and principal payments)
- **Variance of projections:** Based on the projections, the model typically assumes a certain haircut (10–30%) to the management's projections and tests its ability to pay its debt obligations
- **Industry adjustments:** The quantitative approach adjusts up or down based on industry characteristics (recession resistance, cyclical, or event driven)

QUALITATIVE ANALYSIS

The qualitative analysis is subjective based on each bank's internal policy. The analysis includes strength of management, support from the private equity sponsor, recovery analysis (asset collateral), and outlook.

TERMS AND CONDITIONS OF CORPORATE LOANS (MONEY AND NON-MONEY TERMS)

Loans are governed by the credit agreement. The money terms cover the amount, interest rate, maturity or term, and scheduled principal payments. These four characteristics are relevant for every loan vehicle; however, other non-money terms such as covenants and others can vary substantially.

PARTIES TO THE CREDIT AGREEMENT

Borrower or the obligor is the company that is directly responsible for paying back the loan.

Holding company: The parent company of the borrower. It's important to know if the holding company is guaranteeing the loan when the borrower fails to service the debt. By listing the holding company in the credit agreement, it does not necessarily mean that they are guaranteeing the loan. To obtain this information the analyst needs to see if they are listed in the guarantor section of the agreement.

Guarantor/parent and subsidiaries' guarantee: These are the parties that guarantee the loans when the borrower fails to service the debt. In many LBO financing structures the holding company and operating subsidiaries are listed as the guarantors.

Agent banks: These banks are listed on the term sheet and/or the credit agreement. One or multiple banks have many duties that are listed based on their official designation as follows:

- **Administrative agent:** This is the bank that is responsible for communicating the borrower's announcements, financial statements, compliance certificates or other information to the syndicate of banks after the agreement is signed, basically, being a liaison between the borrower and the syndicate member banks. The administrative agent is paid an annual fee by the borrower for that role.

- **Collateral agent:** This is the bank that is responsible for listing the collateral of the borrower that is part of the security agreement including the fixed assets, inventory, cash, receivables, and other assets that are pledged in the agreement. If the loan is an asset-based loan (ABL) it will need constant auditing of the company's assets to ensure the basis of the borrower's assets. The collateral agent is responsible to list these assets for every notice of borrowing and run advanced rates that are used for funding.
- **Syndication agent:** This is the bank that is responsible for "building the book" during syndication. The syndication bank is the bank that coordinates the syndication and communicates the demand to the borrowers and other co-arrangers.
- **Documentation agent:** Though this is known in the syndication world as a courtesy title, this bank is responsible for making sure all the documents are in order for closing and funding. It is important to make sure that the "condition precedents are met at closing," which could mean a completion for an environmental report as an example.
- **Law firms:** The law firms that are representing the borrower and the syndicate banks are listed in the terms sheet and/or the credit agreement.

Description of the transaction/purpose of the loan(s): The first item on the term sheet and/or the credit agreement is a description of the specific financed transaction and lists in detail the purpose of the financing. For example, atypical language for a loan agreement would be "The purpose of the loan is to finance the acquisition of Colorado Dental LLC and provide financing for the Company's working capital" ("Company" is capitalized so it will define the exact company as the borrower).

Money terms: The money terms in a credit agreement need 100% approval by the syndicated members to amend. Basically, any requests to change the following terms usually triggers refinancing and recommitment by the existing lenders:

- **Amount/tranches**
- **Pricing** including the interest rate, spread over LIBOR, and revolver commitment fees on the unfunded portion
- **Maturity dates**
- **Amortization schedule** (set principal payments)

Non-money terms: The non-money terms in a debt agreement include financial covenants, negative covenants, and affirmative covenants. These are terms in the credit agreement that need majority or 51% approval by the syndicated members to amend after close and funding of the transaction.

- **Financial covenants:** In many loan agreements that include financial covenants, they are set to measure the borrower's financial condition during the term of the loan. In the last few years, most of the broadly syndicated loans (BSL) in the leveraged loan market have very few or no covenants. These terms are often referred to as "covenant-lite" or "covy-lite." When loans have covenants in the cases of smaller and middle-market companies, the most popular covenants used are the following:
    - Maximum leverage ratio (total debt/EBITDA)
    - Maximum senior leverage ratio (bank debt/EBITDA)
    - Minimum coverage ratio (EBITDA/Interest)
    - Minimum fixed charge ratio (EBITDA - Capex - taxes)/(interest + principal payments)
    - Maximum capital expenditures
    - Minimum tangible net worth
- **Negative covenants:** These are set restrictions and limitations that the company needs to comply with during the life of the loan. They are called negative because they refer to items that the borrower cannot do during the life of the loan.
    - Limitations on additional debt
    - Limitations on asset sales/mergers and acquisitions/sale/leaseback transactions
    - Limitations of dividends/investments
    - Limitation on liens/negative pledges
    - Limitations of change of ownership
- **Affirmative covenants:** These covenants are set instructions and timetables for the company to provide ongoing reporting. The reporting information, typically every 3 months, could include the following:
    - Financial reporting (audited annual reports and quarterly financial statements)
    - Covenant compliance
    - Annual budgets
    - Maintenance of corporate existence
    - Collateral analysis (for ABL loans)

Other terms and conditions: Credit agreements include other terms that address various events and situations that, when triggered, give direction to the company on how to address them. These are the following:

- **Mandatory prepayments:** This term requires the company to mandatorily make payments toward the loan when, for example, they receive proceeds from selling assets or proceeds from equity investment and other cash that is received by the company.
- **Optional prepayments/call protection:** When the company voluntarily chooses to repay the loan there could be certain conditions such as prepayment penalties or call provisions (similar to the bond indenture).
- **Events of default:** This section gives instructions if the company triggers an event of default, which includes a missed interest or principal payment. The instructions could give time to remedy the situation before the banks send a notification for accelerating the full repayment of the loan.
- **Cross-default cross-acceleration:** This section addresses a situation where the company can continue to make contractual payments toward the loan but miss payments on other facilities that are not governed by this agreement. This could entail actions such as missing a bond payment. When this occurs it also triggers the bank loan's event of default. This is to protect the banks and ensure they put their claims ahead of the bonds. This is outlined in a timetable set typically 30 days prior to the bond accelerating the payment (triggering cross-acceleration).
- **Assignments and participations/secondary sales:** This section of the credit agreement addresses the process of selling or buying the loan in the secondary market via assignment. Any sales or purchases between existing banks that are on record as the original lenders do not need an approval by the company. However, the company needs to approve all new lenders that buy the loans in the secondary markets.
- **Waivers and amendments:** This section describes the process of requesting to amend the credit agreement. Since there are varying numbers of banks in each syndicate, the percentage required to make an amendment could be different for different terms spelled out in this section. Most non-money sections of a credit agreement require a 51% vote across facilities or 51% per facility. Some other sections could require 67% to amend, and others up to 100%.
- **Excess cash sweep:** Some credit agreements, especially ones that include highly leveraged companies or small- to middle-market companies, require that any excess cash remaining after the scheduled principal is paid as additional payment to subsidize the loan. Typically, the excess cash is tied to a leverage ratio such as total debt to EBITDA and is based on a percentage of excess cash. For example, a 50%

excess cash sweep requires that if the company has $20 million excess cash after the scheduled payment is made, $10 million (50%) must be applied to repay the loan further.

Other terms and conditions before close: These terms apply primarily during the syndication process and before closing and funding:

- **Representation and warranties:** This section is to protect the representing lenders in that any statements or information given to them is true and correct.
- **Conditions precedent at closing:** This is to make sure that by closing the loan all conditions are met. In many cases there is a list of conditions that the borrower needs to meet before close, including receiving an environmental report, for example, or a list of the collateral or getting all the necessary regulatory approvals.
- **Indemnification:** Like the reps and warranties, this section protects the borrower for any burden, loss, or damage. The lender can sue for damages on items for which the company was indemnified prior to closing. For example, the company could list potential liabilities such as pending lawsuits or environmental costs that they are planning to pay in the future. If these are listed, then the lender is taking the risk by indemnifying the borrower for these items.
- **Material adverse clause (MAC):** This is a major event that might happen prior to closing that enables the prospective lender to free itself from the obligation of committing and funding the loan. For example, on large transactions a long period of time between is often required between the actual agreement and the closing. In many acquisitions the acquirer is applying to obtain governmental or regulatory approvals. If the approvals are not granted or new instructions are given by the government to make changes, such as selling a division, that will affect the transaction, then the acquirer could exercise the MAC to get out of the deal.

Pricing, fees, and expenses on separate documents: There other separate agreements outside the loan agreement that the underwriter and the company need to sign prior to closing. These agreements are purposely kept separate from the credit agreement so the details on the fees and expense the lead bank is paid for their services are confidential.

Other schedules attached to the credit agreement include the intercreditor agreement, purchase agreement, and hedging arrangement.

PROBLEMS

1. Explain the revolver facility and its usefulness for the borrower.
2. What are the pros and cons for the company that obtains ABL facility?
3. Who are the major secondary loan buyers for the term loan B facility?
4. Calculate the initial annual loan yield for the term loan B priced with OID of 98.5 and a spread of 3.5%. LIBOR is currently at 2.0%.
5. What are the main characteristics of second lien loans and mezzanine loans?
6. What is the origin of unitranche facilities and what problem did they solve during the financial crisis?
7. When does a company seek to raise DIP financing, and what are the main characteristics of such a loan facility?
8. What's the main use of bridge loans?
9. Explain project finance loans and their use.
10. What are the differences between firm commitments, best effort commitments, and club deal commitments in a loan syndication process?
11. What are the roles for each of the agent banks that are assigned the following titles?
    a. Administrative agent
    b. Collateral agent
    c. Syndication agent
    d. Documentation agent
    e. Law firms
12. What are the five quantitative parameters the credit analyst uses to grade the company's ability to pay its debt obligation?
13. In addition to the quantitative approach, what qualitative review does the credit analyst perform in approving a corporate loan?
14. Define the four money terms of a loan agreement and explain the use of each term.
15. Explain each of the following restrictions found in the credit agreement:
    a. Financial covenants
    b. Negative covenants
    c. Affirmative covenants

ONLINE TEMPLATES

The Excel spreadsheets used in the chapter can be accessed online via Cognella Active Learning platform.

CHAPTER 9

Transaction Analysis: LBOs, M&As, and other Capital Market Deals

This chapter will introduce substantive **case studies** that highlight the application of different approaches to raising capital in the primary market. Many of the methods covered are outlined in the earlier chapters of this unit. The case studies include a public-to-private leveraged buyout (LBO); private-to-private leveraged buyout; a merger between two strategic companies, both a stock purchase and an asset purchase; a buyout of a distressed company; and an initial public offering (IPO) private to public.

LEARNING OBJECTIVES

After reading this chapter, students will be able to do the following

- Understand the various types of financing used for various capital transactions
- Analyze each transaction and recommend the right structure to be used based on market, credit, and investment return expectations
- Learn the sequence and approach of financing various structures

TRANSACTION ANALYSIS: AN OVERVIEW

In the last four chapters, this textbook has described in detail the processes and concepts behind all the capital available in the markets. A company needs to decide either to raise equity or debt, or both, and that constitutes a transaction. Every transaction that involves accessing the capital markets for successful execution is unique. Whether a private equity firm is tendering 100% of the shares of publicly traded company, or a company is seeking to merge with another company, the capital market raised has different "shapes and sizes." The common goal, of course, is meeting or exceeding return expectation. Since each investor, debt or equity, that is participating in the transaction has different objectives, it's important that the transaction is structured to meet everyone's expectations.

AUTHOR'S NOTES

I worked on many of the earlier transactions in the late 1980s including the famous or infamous $31 billion LBO of RJR Nabisco by KKR that was made into a movie and a book (Barbarians at the Gate) *(Burrough, & Helyar, 1990), the management buyout of Viacom by Sumner Redstone, and the acquisition of Warner by Time (known today as Time Warner). In those days, many of the transactions were motivated by various tax loopholes that would enhance a financier's overall return. In turn, different methods of financial engineering were established to meet the needs of these intricate strategies, including the outset of high-yield bonds. Introduced by Michael Milken, (a well-known leveraged-buyout investment banker who worked for a boutique investment bank, Drexel Lambert, at the time), these bonds were used to finance many of the massive LBO deals of the period. Thinking back, many of the tax-skimming transactions that I had worked on as an analyst for Bank of America would not be allowed by today's standards. Another method was put into practice by a well-known investment banker, Paul Bilzerian. The high-profile transactions he was often involved in shared a similar scheme and belief: The sum of parts was worth more than the value of the whole company. Mr. Bilzerian would target his investments with the purpose of buying the company and selling each of its subsidiaries separately. By doing so, he was able to avoid any tax on the capital gain from the sale of each subsidiary. Following the execution, he would create various subsidiaries on his own, called at the time "mirror subsidiaries." His associate Paul Singer would create companies that "mirrored" the companies he bought but as revived and improved strategic entities. He would then allocate the acquisition deal's debt to each of these companies and use that as a substantial capital infusion for startup costs. Another deal that I worked on was the private LBO of Fairfield Gear Manufacturing, which was acquired by three investors, Peter Joseph, Angus Littlejohn, and Paul Levy, who founded a private equity firm called JLL. These investors aimed to take advantage of a $29-million net-operating loss tax carryforward (NOL) that they inherited from another company they owned. Basically, JLL used the $29 million NOL as a tax shield to offset tax payments on their acquired profitable companies. These companies, such as Fairfield Gear Manufacturing Company, would inherit a portion of the deferred tax asset from JLL via a tax sharing agreement. Since then, a lot of the tax rules have changed and there is no longer the same type of tax shields offered to companies. Despite tighter rules surrounding the relevant tax laws regarding restrictions on capital gain tax shields and NOL carryovers, modern-day LBOs continue to benefit from elements of the tax code, the most important being the tax deductibility of interest expense.*

KEY TAKEAWAYS

- Debt-capacity analysis, investment considerations, and company expectations need to all balance in order to form deal continuity in a constantly evolving debt and equity market.
- In general, the target company in any transaction is valued based on who is buying it:
  - Strategic investors focus on either revenue and revenue multiples or gross profit and gross profit multiples, as they are focused on the company's ability to generate customers and deliver their product to consumers.
  - Private equity firms focus on the target companies EBITDA and EBITDA multiples as they are interested in the future cash flows of the company as a means to realize their return on investment (realized gain).
  - IPO investors will focus on net income and earnings per share (EPS) as they interested in stock appreciation primarily based on earnings growth.
  - Distress investors base the company's value on its future cash flows post-bankruptcy or after a reorganization net the amount of cash infusion required to generate their intended cash flow.

ONE TRANSACTION, MULTIPLE EXPECTATIONS: THE ANALYSIS

A transaction includes multiple parties that are needed for a successful execution such as private, strategic, and public investors; investment bankers and underwriters; commercial bankers who provide bank loans; bond investors; target companies; government regulators; and rating agencies. Each transaction, whether an LBO, M&A, IPO, or restructuring, depends heavily on the market dynamics of the period and environment. At times, one party could be forced to be more conservative or more aggressive based on their market's economic environment and intracompany objectives. As a result, the success rate and possibility of the transaction can shift based on intrinsic expectations of these environments. The parties involved in a transaction such as an LBO or an M&A have the following expectations at different periods of their business cycle in their respective markets:

- **Private equity firms (PE firms): Private equity firms, also known as financial sponsors, are investment companies financed by third-party investors such as pension funds, insurance companies, and high net-worth individuals.** These firms have a limited or general partnership fund structure. When investing in a PE fund, investors require high-end equity returns due to the nature of these funds' investment strategies. Typical minimum expected returns run from 20–35% depending on market conditions. Usually, PE funds invest in riskier companies and implement more complex/demanding investment techniques to finance large-scale and worthwhile deals. They will often target companies that have a high likelihood of cash flow growth and stability. This becomes a requirement for these deals as they tend to use large amounts of leverage to finance the deal and fund the immediate objectives of the business plan. However, while doing so, the owners of the company (now the PE fund) are simultaneously taking on a large liability (amortizing loan) for the company to deal with following execution. If the public equity markets are bullish and overvalued, PE firms can have problems finding opportunities that meet their minimum returns and are forced to look elsewhere for value. Their analysis depends heavily on finding the right financial structure to balance the buyout's debt and equity. The valuation and debt capacity depend on the target company's future cash flows and cost savings implementation following execution.

- **Investment bankers and underwriters:** An investment banker plays a key role in any transaction that requires capital raising. Investors rely heavily on investment bankers to assist them in raising capital such as loans, bonds, and equity to successfully close and fund their largest transactions. Investment bankers also advise the investors or company by supplying valuations and structuring the financing. Investment bankers' expectation is to receive fees for their advice or increase their market exposure and risk-return profile. The latter is done by underwriting loans and/or bonds that eventually result in an underwriter spread and are syndicated to reduce their exposure back to a more reasonable level (discussed in previous chapters). **As a direct investor and holder of loans or bonds, the expectation is to price the risk given the probability of default for each transaction.** In risk-on market cycles when liquidity is strong, bankers have historically and consistently taken more risk and structured the transactions more aggressively (e.g., 2003–2007). In comparison, during risk-off market cycles with limited liquidity, transactions have been structured far more conservatively (2008–2010).
- **Commercial banks and institutional investors:** These groups of investors provide most of the capital in the form of a loan called a bank debt. These loans are a big part of any LBO or M&A financing as well as distress situations where the company is seeking liquidity during bankruptcy. For large transactions that require a large amount of bank debt, the banks can underwrite these loans and syndicate (sell) their exposure to other banks or financial institutions. The financial institutions that invest in bank loans have set up special purpose vehicles such as collateralized loan obligations (CLOs) in order to maximize their loan portfolios capabilities. The return expectation for these banks and financial institutions is primarily at a much lower

rate (6–10%) than bonds or equity. **The most important component for these institutions that invest in bank loans is minimizing the probability of loan default by using an extensive credit and debt capacity analysis for each transaction.**

- **Public bond and private note investors:** These investors provide part of the capital for an LBO or M&A transaction. These fixed-income investors will purchase high-yield bonds for an LBO or investment-grade bonds for a large M&A transaction. These investors include pension funds, insurance companies, mutual funds, hedge funds, and collateral bond obligations (CBO). The return expectation for these investors are higher than the bank loan returns due to the higher risk. It is important to mention that their analysis is focused largely on the stability of cash flows to be able to service the debt. The return expectation is based on the credit agency ratings that measure probability of default and recovery.
- **Target company:** The target company is the company that the investor is interested in buying outright or investing in the existing ownership. These companies could be publicly traded or privately owned. The companies could hire a buy-side advisor to prepare the company to seek its best possible offer. The existing ownership expectation is to get the highest possible price for the company. In anticipation of such a transaction, the buy-side advisor will value the company to build the expectation of return. Some transactions might require the existing ownership to rollover a portion of its investment into the newly owned company.
- **Government:** The government, through regulation, has in many cases impacted the LBO and M&A markets in reaction to major market swings. For example, following the 2008 financial crisis the Office of the Controller of the Currency (OCC), the board of governors of the Federal Reserve System (Board), and the Federal Deposit Insurance Corporation (FDIC) issued lending guidance for financing LBOs with details on how much debt the banks can provide to specific transactions. So, if a regulated bank is in the process of financing an LBO, the amount of debt that can be used is limited and can impact the equity return expectation as a whole. As a result, an equity investor will need to invest a higher amount in order to win the deal. Another example is the Securities Exchange Commission's (SEC) objective of warning public investors of the risks of investing in high-yield bonds. Included in these guidelines are regulations that require the issuer to do certain reporting, which can delay the transaction and ultimately have an impact on the pricing or execution of the transaction. Many M&A transactions require extensive regulatory approvals by the government.
- **Rating agencies:** As discussed in previous chapters, the rating agencies such as S&P and Moody's play a major role in an LBO or M&A transaction as it is typically required by the SEC to rate the risk of bonds and the issuer. The loans are also rated

to be more marketable to the CLOs. The rating will impact the pricing of these bonds and loans. When structuring the debt facilities, the investment banker advises on the structure based on the expected risk rating. The rest of the chapter will go over specific case studies addressing various transactions, including a public-to-private LBO, private-to-private LBO, stock purchase M&A, asset purchase M&A, buying a company out of bankruptcy (distress buyout) and initial public offering (IPO).

CASE STUDY

LEVERAGED BUYOUT TRANSACTION (LBO), PUBLIC TO PRIVATE (HYPOTHETICAL): AK STEEL

As mentioned, an LBO needs cooperation from all the parties involved, including the private equity investor, bank loan, and bond providers. The following is a hypothetical LBO analysis of a randomly picked company: AK Steel. Let's assume a private equity fund or a strategic entity that is in the steel industry is interested in buying a publicly traded company such as AK Steel. The LBO of such a company is analyzed next.

AK STEEL: COMPANY OVERVIEW (DESCRIPTION TAKEN OUT OF THE 2018 10K)

AK Steel Corporation (AK Steel) is a leading producer of flat-rolled carbon, stainless, and electrical steel products primarily for the automotive, infrastructure and manufacturing, and electrical power generation and distribution markets. AK's holding subsidiaries also provide customer solutions with carbon and stainless-steel tubing products, tool design, and hot-and-cold-stamped steel components and assemblies.

According to the company's annual report, AK Steel's 2018 breakdown of sales was 65% to the automotive market, 16% to infrastructure and manufacturing, and 19% to distributors and convertors. Since the automotive industry is their core market, the company will be looked at by investors and bankers as a cyclical company in addition to be a commodity player—not an ideal candidate for an LBO given the potential volatility of their revenue and income. However, there are a few strong characteristics that could be considered by the acquirers when bidding for the company. This includes elements such as the technological innovation of their new product, a hybrid, third-generation, high-strength steel. This innovative technology is intended to be used by automotive manufacturers for surface-critical light-weight components.

Figure 9.1 shows AK Steel's 4-year selective historical financial information.

TRANSACTION

It's Friday, March 1, 2019 at 4:00 p.m. AK Steel's (AKS) stock price just closed at $3.00. H&H Capital Partners (H&H), a PE firm, is interested in announcing first thing on Monday morning, March 4, 2019, a tender offer (TO) by filing with the SEC an intention to buy 100% of AKS's stock (currently, AKS has 316.31 million shares outstanding). Before the announcement is made, H&H approached JPJ, an investment bank, to see how they could advise them on the structure of the deal and help them raise bank loans and bonds, which will be used as part of the LBO financing. Given the quick turnaround, the investment bank has invited three other banks to co-underwrite the debt before they ultimately sell a large

FIGURE 9.1 AK STEEL (INCOME STATEMENT)

($ millions)	2015	2016	2017	2018
Income Statement Summary				
Net Sales	6,692.9	5,882.5	6,080.5	6,818.2
Growth		*-12.1%*	*3.4%*	*12.1%*
Cost of Goods Sold	6,032.0	5,064.7	5,359.7	5,911.0
Gross Profit	660.9	817.8	720.8	907.2
Groaa Margin	9.9%	13.9%	11.9%	13.3%
EBIT	86.7	230.2	220.0	364.4
EBIT % of Net Sales	1.3%	3.9%	3.6%	5.3%
Cash Flow Summary				
Depreciation & Amortization	237.2	235.0	250.1	252.2
Capital Expenditures	(99.0)	(127.6)	(152.5)	(152.0)
Balance Sheet Summary				
Total Debt		1,857.9	2,150.2	2,354.1

part of their exposure to other banks via syndication. These co-underwriters will need to work all weekend to analyze H&H's business plan and form a syndication strategy. The plan is that by Monday morning before the stock market opens, they will need to get the approval to fully underwrite the deal. It is important that the deal has the right structure so it can be first supported by the loan and bond market; second, it must meet H&H's target return of at least 30%; and third, it must ensure the purchase price of the stock is attractive enough (30%-plus premium of the current stock) that the main shareholders are able to secure the majority of the shareholders who are willing to sell their stock for cash without a significant proxy fight.

Based on public financial information and H&H's projections, the maximum leverage that underwriters are willing to underwrite for both the bank loans and bonds are 2x and 3x senior and total leverage or bank debt/EBITDA and total debt/EBITDA at 2x and 3x, respectively. These debt capacity multiples are what is recommended to be the advisable leverage, along with what the co-underwriters are comfortable underwriting given AKS's cyclical and commodity-like business. As a point of reference, a steadier type of company that has strong and stable cash flows can be leveraged up to 6x total debt/EBITDA. The transaction sources and uses that represent data concerning the recommended structure is shown in Figure 9.2.

Figure 9.2 satisfies first the debt holders (bank loans and corporate bonds) with the debt capacity multiple being met. Second, it satisfies the existing shareholders who expect to sell

FIGURE 9.2 AK STEEL (TRANSACTION SOURCES & USES)

Transaction Sources & Uses

Transactions Uses	Current Stock Price	Desired Premium	Purchase Stock Price Feb 28, 2019	Shares Outstanding (millions)	Total Amount ($ millions)	% Total Uses	EBITDA Multiple
Purchase of 100% Shares	$ 3.00	33%	$ 4.00	316.31	1,265	33.78%	
Refinance Short-Term & Long Term Debt					2,354	62.84%	
Transaction Fees & Expenses	3.50%				127	3.38%	
Total Cost of Transaction (Uses)					3,746	100.00%	6.08x

Transactions Sources	EBITDA Multiple (Capacity)	Interest Rate / Expected Return	Total Amount ($ 000's)	% Capital
Revolver Loan ($200 million)	0.00x	L+4.0%	-	0.00%
Term Loan B	2.00x	L+4.0%	1,233	32.91%
Corporate Bonds	1.00x	8.5%	617	16.47%
Total Debt	3.00x		1,850	49.39%
Equity	3.08x		1,896	50.61%
Total Sources	6.08x		3,746	100.00%

Tax Rate =	36.0%

EBIT =	364.4
Plus Deprec. & Amort.=	252.2
EBITDA =	616.6

their shares at a healthy 33% premium offer of $4 per share. Using this structure, the equity capital will need to contribute to the balance of financing needed in order to purchase all the shares of AKS at $4 per share, refinance all the existing debt, and pay transaction fees and expenses (calculated at 3.5% of the total enterprise value). The balance of $1.9 million represents 50.6% of the capital structure. For this significant portion of the capital needed to be raised in equity, the expected return for such equity could be very challenging for investors to meet the 30% targeted return. which is the challenge to meet the 30.

Figure 9.3 shows the debt and credit adjustments of AKS's balance sheet post LBO. Basically, the transaction's sources, which now include the new bank loans and unsecured notes, as well as the new cash equity, are the starting liabilities and equity of the new company under new ownership, respectively. The current equity and debt are zeroed out and the difference is goodwill. Goodwill represents the premium paid for the book equity. In this case the book equity is $256 million and the market value, as a result of this LBO, is $1,256 million, representing $4 per share found on the transaction uses (goodwill in $ millions = $1,010 = $1,256 − 256). The $125 million transaction fees in the transaction's uses is debited as capitalized fees and amortized over the life of the loans.

Figure 9.4 shows the debt schedule, H&H's main product analysis that is highly negotiated during the preparation for the deal. It will be used as the main source of data for the contractual obligations that the target company will need to meet on a non-recourse arrangement with H&H. The bank term loan for this deal (term loan B) is structured as a 7-year term loan priced at LIBOR + 4.0% at an increasing scheduled amortization rate. The corporate bonds are structured as 8-year securities priced with a 8.5% fixed rate and no scheduled amortization for 7 years with all principal repayment being on the eighth year. Before H&H runs their return analysis test to see if their expectation is met, the

FIGURE 9.3 HYPOTHETICAL ACQUISITION OF AK STEEL BY STEEL DYNAMICS

BALANCE SHEET	AKS Pre-Transaction 2018	LBO Purchase Adjustments Debit	LBO Purchase Adjustments Credit	PROFORMA AKS Post-Transaction 2018
ASSETS				
Cash and Cash Equivalents	49			49
Accounts Receivable	636			636
Inventory	1,420			1,420
Oher Current Assets	97			97
Total Current Assets	2,201			2,201
Property Plant & Equipment	1,912			1,912
Lont-Term Investments	81			81
Goodwill	255	1,213		1,468
Capitalized Expenses	-	127		
Intangibe Assets	44			44
Oher Long Term Assets	23			23
Total Assets	4,516			5,729
LIABILITIES				
Accounts Payable	801			801
Other Curret Liabilities	15			15
Current Portion of LTD	-			-
Total Current Liabilities	816			816
Existing Long Term Debt	2,354	2,354		-
Revolver Loan			-	-
Term Loan B			1,233	1,233
Senior Unsecured Notes			617	617
Total Long Term Debt	2,354			1,850
Other Liabilities	964			964
Minority Interest	330			330
Total Liabilities	4,464			3,960
SHAREHOLDER'S EQUITY				
Common Stock	3	3	1,896	1,896
Treasury Stock	(106)	(106)		-
Capital Surplus	2,895	2,895		-
Retained Earnings	(2,740)	(2,740)		-
Total Shareholder Equity	52			1,896
Total Liabilities 7 Shareholder's Equity	4,516	3,746	3,746	5,856

FIGURE 9.4 AK STEEL (DEBT SCHEDULES)

Debt Schedules

Debt Schedule	Years	Rate	31/12/18	31/12/19	31/12/20	31/12/21	31/12/22	31/12/23	31/12/24	31/12/25	31/12/26
Bank Loan - Term Loan B	7	L+4.0%									
Outstanding			1,233.0	1,183.0	1,108.0	1,008.0	883.0	733.0	533.0	-	-
Scheduled Principal Payments (P)				**50.0**	**75.0**	**100.0**	**125.0**	**150.0**	**200.0**	**533.0**	-
Interest Payments (I)				83.2	85.8	91.4	83.2	72.8	60.5	44.0	-
Total Payments (P+I)				133.2	160.8	191.4	208.2	222.8	260.5	577.0	-
LIBOR			2.25%	2.75%	3.25%	4.25%	4.25%	4.25%	4.25%	4.25%	4.25%
LIBOR Increase				0.50%	0.50%	1.00%	0.00%	0.00%	0.00%	0.00%	0.00%
Spread				4.00%	4.00%	4.00%	4.00%	4.00%	4.00%	4.00%	4.00%
Interest Rate				6.75%	7.25%	8.25%	8.25%	8.25%	8.25%	8.25%	8.25%
Corporate Bonds	8	8.5%									
Outstanding			617.0	617.0	617.0	617.0	617.0	617.0	617.0	617.0	-
Scheduled Principal Payments (P)				-	-	-	-	-	-	-	617.0
Interest Payments (I)				52.4	52.4	52.4	52.4	52.4	52.4	52.4	52.4
Total Payments (P+I)				52.4	52.4	52.4	52.4	52.4	52.4	52.4	669.4
Interest Payments				135.7	138.2	143.9	135.6	125.3	112.9	96.4	52.4
Principal Payments				50.0	75.0	100.0	125.0	150.0	200.0	533.0	617.0
Total Debt Payments				185.7	213.2	243.9	260.6	275.3	312.9	629.4	669.4
Total Debt Outstanding				1,800.0	1,725.0	1,625.0	1,500.0	1,350.0	1,150.0	617.0	-

underwriters have presented the terms and conditions of bank loans and corporate bonds, including the debt schedule, shown in Figure 9.4. LIBOR was conservatively projected to increase 0.5% per year for the next 2 years, 1.0% the third year, and stay flat for the life of the loan.

Figure 9.5 shows H&H's projected cash flow based on its plan after it owns the company. The growth rates are projected to be moderate at 4.0% with the cost of goods sold kept as a constant percentage of net sales at 87% and operating expenses similarly as a percentage of sales at 8%, with the terminal value averaging $5.4 billion using two methods, including

FIGURE 9.5 AK STEEL (EQUITY RETURN)

Equity Reurn Analysis

($ millions)				year =			1	2	3	4	5	6
	HISTORICAL				Historical Assumptions Average	Projections Assumptions	PROJECTIONS				EXIT YEAR	
	31/12/15	31/12/16	31/12/17	31/12/18			31/12/19	31/12/20	31/12/21	31/12/22	31/12/23	31/12/24
Net Sales	6,693	5,883	6,081	6,818			7,091	7,375	7,670	7,976	8,295	8,627
Net Sales Growth		-12.1%	3.4%	12.1%	1.1%		4.0%	4.0%	4.0%	4.0%	4.0%	4.0%
Cost of Goods Sold	(6,032)	(5,065)	(5,360)	(5,911)	87.8%	87.0%	(6,169)	(6,416)	(6,673)	(6,939)	(7,217)	(7,506)
Operating Expenses (Excl. Non-rec.)	(574)	(588)	(501)	(543)	8.7%	8.0%	(567)	(590)	(614)	(638)	(664)	(690)
EBIT	87	230	220	364			355	369	383	399	415	431
Less Interest							136	138	144	136	125	113
EBT							490	507	527	534	540	544
Less Taxes (tax rate x of EBIT)						36.0%	(176)	(182)	(190)	(192)	(194)	(196)
Net Income							314	324	337	342	346	348
Plus Depreciation & Amortization	237.2	235.0	250.1	252.2	3.8%	3.8%	271	282	293	305	317	330
Plus Capitalized Fee Amortization						7 Years	18	18	18	18	18	18
Less Capex	(99.0)	(127.6)	(152.5)	(152.0)	2.1%	2.1%	(148)	(154)	(160)	(166)	(173)	(180)
Cash Flow Before Principal Payment							**455**	**471**	**489**	**499**	**508**	**517**
Debt Principal Payment							(50)	(75)	(100)	(125)	(150)	(200)
Equity Cash Flows							405	396	389	374	358	317
EBITDA				**617**			**626**	**651**	**677**	**704**	**732**	**761**
Debt							**1,800**	**1,725**	**1,625**	**1,500**	**1,350**	**1,150**
Terminal Value				**Growth**	**Assumptions**							
EBITDA Multiple Method					6.08x		(EBITDA x EBITDA Multiple)				4,448	
Perpetuity Method				4.00%	10.00%	(before Tax)	Next Year's CF adj for IE / (Disc. Rate - Growth)				6,728	
Average											5,588	
Less Debt Outstanding (at Exit)											(1,350)	
Plus Cash (at Exit)											-	
Equity Value at Terminal											4,238	
Desired Equity Return =					**30%**							
Equity Cash Flows						**(1,896)**	**405**	**396**	**389**	**374**	**4,596**	
					PV @30%		**312**	**234**	**177**	**131**	**1,238**	
				PV of CF =	**2,092**							
				Initial Invest=	(1,896)							
				NPV =	196							
				IRR =	**33.4%**							

the EBITDA multiple method (5.73x initial multiple) and the perpetuity method using a 10% discount rate and 4% growth. The perpetuity method terminal value is calculated by taking next year's equity cash flow of $317 million divided by a 10% discount rate minus the 4% growth rate. The expected return based on these cash flows is calculated to be 33.4%, which in turn generates a slightly positive net present value (NPV) just north of the 35% expected target return.

In this case, since all parties have met their respective expectations, the-public-to-private LBO transaction of AK Steel will most likely be successfully completed. As a summary, the first group of lenders have met their credit and market risk expectation of keeping a conservative lending structure of a maximum 3x total leverage (total debt/EBITDA), decreasing the probability of default on getting repaid. Also, at these levels of leverage and pricing, the co-underwriters feel comfortable reducing their exposure through syndications, thus mitigating the market risk of holding the paper after the close of the transaction. Furthermore, the target company's shareholders have met their expectation showing that that the $4-per-share offering represents more than the 30% premium on the stock (actual 33%). This also represents the time that the $4 stock has been the highest in more than 2 years, plus the stock momentum has been negative. The third party who is satisfied is the buyers, the PE firm, in this case H&H, that set their target return at 35%. Based on the projected cash flows, the expected return is calculated to be 37% at a $4 per share of the offering price.

LEVERAGED BUYOUT TRANSACTION (LBO), PRIVATE TO PRIVATE: CELERITY TECHNOLOGY, INC.

The seller and purchaser of a private company will use primarily the discount cash flow (DCF) and LBO methods to value the target, respectively. These methods are referred to as methods 6 & 7, respectively, and are discussed in detail in chapter 17. The DCF method (method 6) is a method where the seller wants to find the intrinsic value of the company that could possibly include a staple financing. The purchaser uses the LBO model (method 7) to derive a bid price by calculating the desired equity return. Both are based on the company's future cash flows.

One of the most effective ways to value a private company is to dive into the company's projections, use them as a basis, and change the assumptions based on the seller's and purchaser's views on how the revenue will grow and at what cost (revenue growth rate, COGS, and OPEX). Since there is no stock price that trades actively enough to give the investor a direct indication of what the company is worth (market value), an important method that is used by valuation analysts is the discount cash flow (DCF) method, which measures the company's intrinsic value.

Let's assume Celerity Technology is in the process of finding a seller for the company. The sell-side advisor will prepare a valuation analysis for management, which is based on the future cash flows of the company and includes an assumed financing based on market parameters. He or she will also prepare a selling information memorandum (SIM) that will be shared with prospective buyers. The SIM could include committed financing, called "stapled financing," named as an addendum that is stapled to the SIM. In this case, we assume there was staple financing available, but the seller has run the projections including only the existing debt structure to calculate the value of the company.

Figure 9.6 shows the valuation of the Celerity Technology Inc. is approximately $3 billion or 7x current EBITDA based on the company's projections.

The cash flows were built on base case projections, including a modest growth rate and flat operating costs as a percentage of revenues as well as other expenses including working capital and capital expenditures. The terminal value is calculated based on two methods: (1) using 7.5x EBITDA multiple, and (2) using the perpetuity method (next year's cash flow/(discount rate – growth)). The discount rate used is 10% and the growth rate is 5%; these are basic "rule-of-thumb" levels, but a more comprehensive approach would include a discount rate at the weighted average cost of capital (WACC) and a historically derived growth rate.

The buyer, a private equity firm, will use the SIM to run its own analysis and either choose to go with the stapled financing provided by the seller or structure its own financing. The buyer will run a valuation model (LBO valuation method) derived from its equity

FIGURE 9.6 CELERITY TECHNOLOGY (DCF ANALYSIS)

Discount Cash Flow Valuation Method (000's)

			PROJECTED				
						EXIT YEAR	
	Year -1	**Year 0**	**Year 1**	**Year 2**	**Year 3**	**Year 4**	**Year 5**
Revenues	960,000	1,110,000	1,228,140	1,344,200	1,442,919	1,529,268	1,605,161
Cost of Revenues	(345,000)	(420,000)	(463,078)	(506,823)	(544,053)	(576,709)	(605,474)
Operating Expenses	(230,000)	(257,000)	(271,501)	(289,448)	(306,442)	(322,900)	(338,999)
EBITDA	**385,000**	**433,000**	**493,561**	**547,928**	**592,424**	**629,659**	**660,688**
Less Depreciation & Amortization	(60,000)	(65,000)	(73,688)	(80,652)	(86,575)	(91,756)	(96,310)
EBIT	325,000	368,000	**419,872**	**467,276**	**505,849**	**537,902**	**564,378**
Less Taxes			(129,769)	(147,070)	(156,960)	(158,461)	(162,851)
EAT			**290,103**	**320,206**	**348,889**	**379,441**	**401,527**
Plus Depreciation & Amortization			73,688	80,652	86,575	91,756	96,310
Less Working Capital			2,870	(4,548)	(3,869)	(3,384)	(2,974)
Less Capital Expenditures and Investments			(193,626)	(211,923)	(227,487)	(241,101)	(253,066)
Cash Before Financing Payments			**173,036**	**184,386**	**204,109**	**226,713**	**241,796**
Less Debt Service (Principal + Interest)			(125,450)	(129,600)	(153,450)	(201,750)	(237,250)
Free Cash Flow			**47,586**	**54,786**	**50,659**	**24,963**	**4,546**
TERMINAL VALUE (TV)		**TV Assumptions**					
Terminal Value using EBITDA Multiple Method		EBITDA Multiple = **7.5x**				4,722,439	
Terminal Value using Perpetuity Method		Discount Rate = **10%**				4,835,926	
Average Terminal Value		Growth = **5%**				4,779,182	
Less Debt						(1,030,000)	
Equity Value at Exit Year						3,749,182	
Equity Cash Flows		Equity Expected Return = **20%**	47,586	54,786	50,659	3,774,145	
Present Value of Equity		1,927,111	39,655	38,046	29,316	1,820,093	
Plus Debt		1,190,000					
Less Cash		(65,800)					
Firm Enterprise value		**3,051,311**					
Enteprise Value / EBITDA		7.0x					

expectation or rate of return. It will assume a structure that includes debt to get the highest possible return. The debt obtained by banks and institutional investors is evaluated based on a debt capacity analysis (discussed in detail in chapter 18). The debt capacity is typically derived as a multiple of current EBITDA. The new debt level and its debt service is integrated into the company's projections and is the first step to determining the new valuation of the company.

Figure 9.7 shows that the valuation for Celerity Technology Inc., using the LBO valuation method, is approximately $4 billion or 10x EBITDA. In this case, the private equity investors expect a 25% return on investment after the debt capacity is imbedded in the capital structure; at this time the debt is structured at a maximum of 6x EBITDA. This $4 billion will be at the highest negotiating level that the buyers of Celerity Technology Inc. anticipate they can get to. According to the seller, $3 billion will be the lowest acceptable bid. Integrating both models, run from different perspectives and based on negotiations, it turns out that Celerity Technology could end up being purchased at a price between $3 to $4 billion.

FIGURE 9.7 CELERITY TECHNOLOGY (LBO METHOD ANALYSIS)

LBO Method (000's)

TRANSACTION SOURCES & USES

Sources	Capacity EBITDA x	Amount	% Capital	Inter. / Exp. Ret.	WACC	Uses		Purchase EBITDA Multiple	Amount
Bank Loan	3.5x	1,515,500	33.8%	5.0%	1.1%	Purchase Enteprise Value		10.0x	4,330,000
Corporate Bonds	2.5x	1,082,500	24.2%	8.0%	1.2%	Fees (% EV)	3.50%		151,550
Total Debt	6.0x	2,598,000	58.0%		0.0%				
Equity		1,883,550	42.0%	25.0%	10.5%				
Total Sources		4,481,550	100.0%		10.5%				4,481,550

Tax Rate = 36%

DEBT SCHEDULES

	Years	Interest	Year 0	Year 1	Year 2	Year 3	EXIT YEAR Year 4	Year 5
Bank Loal - Outstanding	5	5.0%	1,515,500	1,363,950	1,212,400	1,060,850	909,300	-
Bank Loan - Principal Incr./Decr.				151,550	151,550	151,550	151,550	909,300
Bank Loan - Interst Payment				75,775	68,198	60,620	53,043	45,465
Bonds - Outstanding	10	8.0%	1,082,500	1,082,500	1,082,500	1,082,500	1,082,500	1,082,500
Bonds - Principal Incr./Decr.				-	-	-	-	-
Bonds - Interst Payment				86,600	86,600	86,600	86,600	86,600

CASH FLOW PROJECTIONS

	Year -1	Year 0	Year 1	Year 2	Year 3	EXIT YEAR Year 4	Year 5
Revenues	960,000	1,110,000	1,228,140	1,344,200	1,442,919	1,529,268	1,605,161
Cost of Revenues	(345,000)	(420,000)	(463,078)	(506,823)	(544,053)	(576,709)	(605,474)
Operating Expenses	(230,000)	(257,000)	(271,501)	(289,448)	(306,442)	(322,900)	(338,999)
EBITDA	**385,000**	**433,000**	**493,561**	**547,928**	**592,424**	**629,659**	**660,688**
Less Depreciation	(60,000)	(65,000)	(73,688)	(80,652)	(86,575)	(91,756)	(96,310)
Less Amortization			(30,310)	(30,310)	(30,310)	(30,310)	(30,310)
EBIT	325,000	368,000	**389,562**	**436,966**	**475,539**	**507,592**	**534,068**
Less Taxes			(140,242)	(157,308)	(171,194)	(182,733)	(192,265)
EAT			**249,320**	**279,658**	**304,345**	**324,859**	**341,804**
Plus Depreciation & Amortization			103,998	110,962	116,885	122,066	126,620
Less Working Capital			2,870	(4,548)	(3,869)	(3,384)	(2,974)
Less Capital Expenditures and Investments			(193,626)	(211,923)	(227,487)	(241,101)	(253,066)
Cash Before Financing Payments			**162,563**	**174,149**	**189,874**	**202,441**	**212,383**
Less Debt Service (Principal + Interest)			(125,450)	(129,600)	(153,450)	(201,750)	(237,250)
Free Cash Flow			**37,113**	**44,549**	**36,424**	**691**	**(24,867)**

TERMINAL VALUE (TV)	**TV Assumptions**		Year 1	Year 2	Year 3	EXIT YEAR Year 4
Terminal Value using EBITDA Multiple Method	EBITDA Multiple =	**10.0x**				6,296,585
Terminal Value using Perpetuity Method	Discount Rate =	**10.5%**				3,856,429
Average Terminal Value	Growth =	**5.0%**				5,076,507
Less Debt						(1,030,000)
Equity Value at Exit Year						4,046,507
Equity Cash Flows	Equity Expected Return =	**25%**	37,113	44,549	36,424	4,047,197
Present Value of Equity	1,734,583		29,690	28,511	18,649	1,657,732
Plus Debt	2,598,000					
Less Cash	-					
Firm Enterprise value	**4,332,583**					
Enteprise Value / EBITDA	10.0x					

STOCK PURCHASE MERGERS AND ACQUISITION (M&A): STEEL DYNAMICS ACQUISITION OF AK STEEL (HYPOTHETICAL)

A successful execution in an M&A transaction consists of meeting the expectations of both the acquirer and the target company, in this case, the banks that will be asked to finance a portion of the cost for an acquisition. However, given the credit strength of the acquiror, Steel Dynamics (STLD), the financing will be more of a concern than in the previous cases. The credit capacity of the company is measured by expected investment-grade ratings after the acquisition of the target company, AK Steel (AKS).

Before any analysis is done, STLD needs to qualify and define the merger strategy outlined in the following steps:

1. State the objective: Post transaction revenue growth, cost efficiencies, and synergies
2. Identify the business model and markets: Technology/product
3. Define price range expectation and capital accessibility (debt-equity balance)
4. Begin the preliminary analysis: Valuation, accretion, and return analysis

Following the steps for an M&A transaction outlined in Chapter 6, the hypothetical merger of STLD and AKS is described next.

STEP I: VALUATION ANALYSIS

STLD hires an investment banker (IB) to advise on the potential merger between STLD and AKS. The IB's job is to evaluate the target company using various methods, including identifying the universe of comparable companies to be used for trading comps. The IB first searches his or her own database to see if a relevant set of comparable acquisitions exists. The IB will also search various M&A databases, which are merger proxies of comparable companies that include fairness opinions. It's important for the IB to learn as much as possible regarding the target company and all the circumstances surrounding the transaction. Once the peer or comparable companies are identified, the banker gathers as much information as possible for these companies including financial statements, related acquisitions, and press releases. Since the analysis will eventually be publicly disclosed to justify the fairness opinion to the target company's shareholders, it's important to note that the banker only discloses information that is publicly available. The IB then spreads all the information of these companies and determines the multiple's ratios such as enterprise value to EBITDA, enterprise value to revenue, or even enterprise value to net income. Figure 9.8 shows a comprehensive trading comparable analysis for steel companies. The average EBITDA multiple on five public trading companies including STLD is 5.30x. Using this multiple puts AKS's stock price at the approximate level that is trading ($3.05 vs $3.00).

FIGURE 9.8 AK STEEL (AVG INDUSTRY TRADING MULTIPLES)

CORPORATE VALUATIONS

Average EBITDA Industry Trading Multiples

Company	Symbol	Stock Price	Stocks Outstanding ($000)	Equity Value ($000)	Debt (ST&LT) ($000)	Cash ($000)	Enterprise Value ($000)	EBITDA ($mm)	EBITDA Multiple	Beta
		SP	SO	SP * SO = EQ	D	C	EQ + D - C = E	E	EV / E	
United Steel	X	$ 22.93	177,270	4,064,801	2,500,000	1,340,000	5,224,801	1,360,000	3.84x	4.04x
Steel Dynamics	STLD	$ 35.12	229,550	8,061,796	2,370,000	999,320	9,432,476	1,860,000	5.07x	1.50x
Reliance Steel Industries	RS	$ 79.99	70,430	5,633,696	2,070,000	112,100	7,591,596	1,180,000	6.43x	1.08x
Schtzer Steel Industries	SCHN	$ 26.66	25,690	684,895	107,380	4,700	787,575	195,020	4.04x	0.78x
Olympic Steel	ZEUS	$ 18.19	11,010	200,272	304,480	4,270	500,482	70,450	7.10x	2.52x
AK Steel Holding Corp. (AKS)	AKS	$ 3.00	315,540	946,620	2,354,100	48,600	3,252,120	616,600	5.27x	2.91x
EBITDA * Average Multiple	616,600	5.30x						Average	5.30x	2.14x

Enteprise Value	3,266,630
Less Debt	(2,354,100)
Plus Cash	48,600
Equity Values	961,130
Shares Outstanding (SO)	315,540
Stock Price (Equity Value / SO)	$ 3.05
Premium %	1.533%

The $3.05 comparable stock price should give some comfort to the IB and STLD that any premium paid over that should be acceptable to the majority shareholders. The next set of valuation analyses is to compare the target company to other acquisition-related transactions in the steel business. Figure 9.9 shows recent acquisitions of steel companies. Based on this analysis, the average acquisition EBITDA multiple is at 6.26x, which puts the stock price at $4.93, a 64.3% premium on top of the current $3 stock trading price.

FIGURE 9.9 AK STEEL (AVG ACQUISITION MULTIPLES)

CORPORATE VALUATIONS

Using Averge EBITDA Transaction Multiples (M&A Comparable Method)

Target	Acquirer	Acquisition Price /Share	Shares Outstanding	Equity Value ($000)	Total Net Debt ($ 000)	Enterprise Value (EV)	EBITDA ($ 000)	EBITDA Multiple
	Calculations	AP	SO	AP * SO = EQ	ND	EQ + ND = EV	E	EV / E
ZS Steel	Archimedes PE	$ 47.50	24,000,000	$ 1,140,000	$ 1,500,000	$ 2,640,000	$ 350,000	7.54x
Celerity Steel Manufacturing	AZM Steel & Aliminum	$ 34.00	123,000,000	$ 4,182,000	$ 2,500,000	$ 6,682,000	$ 1,100,000	6.07x
Yes Steel & Aluminum Co.	Kingtom Steel	$ 45.00	13,500,000	$ 607,500	$ 450,000	$ 1,057,500	$ 190,000	5.57x
HI Steel Manufacturing Inc.	Excel Steel	$ 22.00	234,000,000	$ 5,148,000	$ 1,400,000	$ 6,548,000	$ 1,230,000	5.32x
Precision Steel	MW Inc.	$ 12.00	85,000,000	$ 1,020,000	$ 1,200,000	$ 2,220,000	$ 320,000	6.94x
Ross West Steel	Greenstone Capital	$ 8.00	45,000,000	$ 360,000	$ 240,000	$ 600,000	$ 98,000	6.12x
							Average	6.26x

Enteprise Value	3,860,606	616,600	6.26x
Less Debt	(2,354,100)		
Plus Cash	48,600		
Equity Values	1,555,106		
Shares Outstanding (SO)	315,540		
Stock Price (Equity Value / SO)	$ 4.93		
Premium %	64.3%		

At this level, the anticipated acceptance from the current shareholders is if STLD decides to offer that price it will sound excessive compared to the shareholder's expectation of 30%-plus, as described in the LBO case study.

The mean (average) multiples for both analytical approaches will be used to value AKS. Figures 9.8 and 9.9 show that the averages of the steel sector between trading EBITDA comparable multiples and acquisition EBITDA comparable multiples' EBITDA multiples are 5.30x and 6.26x, respectively. These multiples show a range of the stock price between $3 to $5. STLD will first assume in their return calculations an average target price of $4 before they decide to increase or decrease this assumption.

STEP II: ACCRETION AND DILUTION ANALYSIS

STLD's shareholders expect to receive an accretion and dilution analysis describing to what extent their ownership holdings will be diluted following the merger. The acquirer (with the expected backing of its shareholders) will be reluctant to pursue a deal if it will result in excessive dilution to the existing shareholders' ownership. As a result, the bid price is often guided by the EPS accretion and dilution analysis. Figure 9.10 shows the analysis for

FIGURE 9.10 HYPOTHETICAL ACQUISITION OF AK STEEL BY STEEL DYNAMICS ACCREETION & DILUTION

Accretion and Dilution Analysis

Acquirer:	Steel Dynamics	
Revenue	$ 11,821.8	million
EBIT	$ 1,722.4	
Interest	$ 126.6	
Shares Outs	224.1	million

Target:	Ak Steel (AKS)	
Revenue	$ 6,818.2	million
EBIT	$ 364.4	

Combined Synergies	
EBIT	$ 125

Transaction Assumptions

Purchase Price	($ mm)
Purchase Price @ $4 per share	1,262
% Stock Consideration	50%
% Cash Consideration	50%
EBIT Multiple x	3.5x

Financing		
Shares Issued by Acquirer	30	million
Debt Financing	$ 600	million
Cost of Debt	5.00%	(Interest Rate)

	Assumption Growth	Historical Year 0	Year 1	Year 2	Year 3	Year 4
			Projection Period ($ mm)			
EBIT						
Steel Dynamics	5.0%	$ 1,722.4	$ 1,808.5	$ 1,899.0	$ 1,993.9	$ 2,093.6
Ak Steel (AKS)	5.0%	$ 364.4	$ 382.6	$ 401.8	$ 421.8	$ 442.9
Combined Synergies			$ 125.0	$ 125.0	$ 125.0	$ 125.0
Proforma Combined EBIT		**$ 2,086.8**	**$ 2,316.1**	**$ 2,425.7**	**$ 2,540.7**	**$ 2,661.5**
Standalone Net Interest Expense		126.6	126.6	126.6	126.6	126.6
Incremental Net Interest Expense			30.0	30.0	30.0	30.0
Total Interest Expenses			156.6	156.6	156.6	156.6
EBT			2,159.5	2,269.1	2,384.1	2,504.9
Taxes		36%	777.4	816.9	858.3	901.8
Proforma Combined NI			**1,382.1**	**1,452.2**	**1,525.8**	**1,603.1**
Acquire's Standalone Net Income			**1,076.4**	**1,134.3**	**1,195.1**	**1,258.9**
Standalone Fully Diluted Shares			224	224	224	224
Net New Shares issued in the Transaction			30	30	30	30
Proforma Fully Dillluted Shares Outstanding			254	254	254	254
Proforma Combined Diluted EPS (Proforma NI / Proforma Fully Diluted Shares)			**$ 5.44**	**$ 5.72**	**$ 6.00**	**$ 6.31**
Acquirer's Standalone Dilluted EPS (Standalone NI / Standalone Fully Diluted Shares)			**$ 4.80**	**$ 5.06**	**$ 5.33**	**$ 5.62**
Accretion / (Dillution) - $ (Proforma Combined EPS - Acquirer's Standalone EPS)			**$ 0.64**	**$ 0.65**	**$ 0.67**	**$ 0.69**
Accretion / (Dillution) - % (Proforma Combined EPS / Acquirer's Standalone EPS - 1)			**13.2%**	**12.9%**	**12.6%**	**12.3%**
Accretive / Dilutive			**Accretive**	**Accretive**	**Accretive**	**Accretive**
Breakeven Pre-Tax synergies / (Cushion) (Accretion or Dillution per share x Proforma Shares) / (1 - tax rate)			**(252.5)**	**(259.5)**	**(266.9)**	**(274.6)**

the merger between STLD and AKS assuming a $4-per-share purchase, a 50/50% stock and cash consideration, $600 million in new financing, and $125 million in combined EBIT synergies that the buy-side advisor, IB, and STLD have identified.

The accretion and dilution analysis is based on a forward-looking basis considering AKS's future expected earnings, including synergies as a result of the merger. EBIT is projected to grow 5% per year for both companies. The projected synergies of $125 million include duplication of operating expenses ($80 million), economies of scale ($20 million), and other plant implementation and rationalization programs for combining the companies ($25 million). According to the analysis, STLD is showing that the merger will result in an accretion of approximately 64–69 cents or 12.3–13.2% of the stock per year.

Though AKS does not have access to this analysis, it could run its own version, putting it in a better position to negotiate a price. Figure 9.10 shows a breakeven pre-tax synergies line of $252.5 million in value that gives AKS some ammunition to negotiate a maximum price.

STEP III: BIDDING FOR THE TARGET COMPANY

Assuming this is a friendly merger of equals, STLD files a proxy statement with the SEC that describes the deal, which is 50% cash and 50% stock exchange at an estimated combined value of $4 per share, a 33% premium of the current $3 traded share price. After the SEC reviews and approves the statement, the statement is then sent to the shareholders along with a proxy card that needs to be filed by the shareholders and sent back within 20 days. The transaction is voted on at a special shareholder meeting before the final decision is made. If the transaction is hostile, then STLD needs to file a tender offer (TO) announcing the purchase of 100% of AKS stock at $4 with cash and 50% stock. The SEC will review the TO prior to the announcement since there is a stock-for-stock component of the transaction. If the transaction was all cash, then the SEC would not have a chance to review the deal. In a hostile case, the seller would immediately retain a sell-side investment banker to prepare a fairness opinion and possibly run an accretion/dilution analysis to compare if the $4 offer price is at fair value. If it's a friendly merger, the two parties will exchange information that will be reviewed and used by their respective boards of directors. The information could include all the benefits of the merger between the companies including the management succession plan and other implementation plans after the merger. Most mergers, friendly or not, include some resistance from the target company's shareholders, which could result in a shareholder proxy fight.

ASSET PURCHASE MERGERS AND ACQUISITION (M&A): STEEL DYNAMICS (STLD) ACQUISITION OF AK STEEL (AKS) (HYPOTHETICAL)

The purchase of AK Steel's assets by STLD will include a different analysis than the previous example of purchasing purely the equity of AKS outright. The asset sale by the target company refers to an M&A transaction where the acquirer purchases all or some of the target's assets. In this arrangement, the target company legally remains in existence after the transaction. The buyer purchases the assets, assumes some liabilities, but does not acquire the stock (ownership) of the company. In most situations where the company is still profitable and set to remain that way, obtaining the ownership of the other company, along with the assets, is usually a better option. In some cases where the target company's performance is deteriorating, the asset sale could be the only option to get proceeds (cash flow) into the company and pay down the debt. The asset sale may also provide tax benefits for the buyer, such as when the market value of these assets is higher than the book value and the difference could be tax deductible. This difference, called the stepped-up portion, is depreciable, amortizable over the years, and deducted from EBITDA, resulting in a realizable cash benefit for the buyer.

Figure 9.11 shows the tax benefit of buying AK Steel via an asset purchase. The example shows the same purchase price of $3.7 billion as the previous example. The difference between the market value purchase price of $3.7 billion and the $1.9 billion book value of AKS's fixed assets is the step-up investment that can be amortized, in this case, over 8 years, generating $440.4 million in savings.

The surviving entity will probably use the $3.7 billion proceeds to repay the debt and other liability obligations, excluding all the obligations that are assumed by the buyer.

FIGURE 9.11 AK STEEL (ANNUAL VALUE TAX SAVINGS)

Annual Value of Annual Tax Savings for Step-up Assets due to acquisition

Assumptions ($ millions)					
Purchase Price of Assets	3,746		Tax Rate		36%
Asset Basis	1,912		Annual Tax Savings (Tax Rate x Annual Depr.)	$	83
Asset Set-up	1,834		Discount Rate		10%
Amortization Years	8	years			
Annual Depreciation (Asset Set-up / Years)	$ 229.31				

Year	1	2	3	4	5	6	7	8
Annual Tax Savings	$ 82.55	$ 82.55	$ 82.55	$ 82.55	$ 82.55	$ 82.55	$ 82.55	$ 82.55
Present Value of Annual Tax Savings	$ 75.05	$ 68.22	$ 62.02	$ 56.38	$ 51.26	$ 46.60	$ 42.36	$ 38.51

Present Value - Savings	$ 440.40 million

DISTRESS BUYOUT OF PRIVATE COMPANY: SOUTHSTAR APPAREL MANUFACTURING INC.

Estimating the purchase price of a distressed company is probably one of the toughest tasks for private equity investors. There are few private equity investors that specialize in the stress/distress buyout area. The biggest asset these private equity firms have when analyzing a company that has gone into bankruptcy is the ability to successfully project the cash flows after purchase. While attempting to get a favorable purchase price considering the state of the proposed company's capital structure, they often integrate a detailed operating plan that is followed as an addendum to their influx of new capital. The success of these firms relies on the expertise of operating and reorganizing a company that has been declining for numerous years and has been led into bankruptcy. The first 18 months to 2 years are critical for the success of a buyout. The probability success numeral can be priced into the bid price and should determine the restructuring of the existing debt. The valuation used for the Southstar Apparel Manufacturing (SAM) case study is described in detail in chapter 17, method #8. Since the cash flow is negative and anticipated to remain negative for the next 2 years, the methodology used to determine the firm and the equity valuation is the Black-Scholes option pricing model. Basically, companies that are in distress with negative cash flows, representing out-of-the-money options can still be valued using the option pricing methods. The equity value, is out of the money today but expected to be in the money in 5 years, assuming the implementation of the cash recovery is successful.

Figure 9.12 shows a full valuation and return analysis of the SAM. The private equity firm runs its discount cash flow analysis showing cash needs to support recovery after 2 years (called the "Death Valley" period). In this case, the Black-Scholes model is used as a probability method to price the present value of equity so the investors can negotiate with the debt holders who have taken over the company.

Figure 9.12 shows the calculation of the standard deviation for both equity and debt based on pre-bankruptcy volatility of the company's earnings representing equity and debt prices in the secondary market. The analysis is based on a 5-year period with a terminal value based on a 5x multiple (a multiple expansion from the current bid of 3.1x (see uses of transaction). Based on the Black-Scholes option pricing model, the current debt is priced at 63% of the outstanding debt; this is used for the private equity as a negotiating tool to take out the debt. Typically, the buyer will raise a revolver-type line of credit based on the assets of the company for working capital purposes. In this case, the PE firm was able to raise $50 million in an asset-based loan (ABL) but used it in entirety as part of the transaction ($0 on day one).

FIGURE 9.12 SOUTHSTAR APPAREL MANUFACTURER

Buyout of Distress Company

TRANSACTION SOURCES & USES

Sources	Commited	Amount	% Capital	Inter. / Exp. Ret.
Asset Based Lending	50.0	-	0.0%	0.0%
Mezzanine Debt		-	0.0%	0.0%
Total Debt		-	0.0%	
Equity		76.6	100.0%	25.0%
Total Sources		76.6	100.0%	

Uses		Debt Discount	Purchase EBITDA Multiple (year 3)	Amount
Purchase of Equity			3.1x	49.7
Refinance Existing Debt		62.9%		25.2
Fees (% EV)	3.50%			1.7
				76.6

DEBT ASSUMPTIONS (At Bankruptcy)

Existing Debt Outstanding (at Bankruptcy)=	40 million
Remaining Term	5 years
WACC=	20.0% (Equity Return Heavy)
Tax Rate =	36.0%

VALUE ASSUMPTIONS (Pre-bankruptcy)

Volatility of Book Value of Equity measured by earnings (Variance)	3.15%
Volatility of Debt in the secondary market (Variance)	2.16%
Correlation between Equity (Earnings) /Debt	0.25
Debt proportion (5 years)	88.30%

DISCOUNT CASH FLOW ANALYSIS ($ millions)

	Year 0	Year 1	Year 2	Year 3	Year 4	Year 5
Sales		125.0	113.8	111.5	125.0	140.0
Cost of Goods Sold		(98.0)	(81.0)	(70.0)	(69.6)	(72.3)
Operatinhg Expenses		(72.0)	(45.0)	(20.6)	(21.4)	(22.3)
EBITDA		(45.0)	(12.3)	20.9	34.0	45.4
Less Depreciation		(5.0)	(5.0)	(5.0)	(5.0)	(5.0)
EBIT		**(50.0)**	**(17.3)**	**15.9**	**29.0**	**40.4**
Less Taxes		**18.0**	**6.2**	**(5.7)**	**(10.5)**	**(14.5)**
Net Income		**(32.0)**	**(11.0)**	**10.2**	**18.6**	**25.9**
Add Depreciation		5.0	5.0	5.0	5.0	5.0
Less Maintenance Capex (Depreciation Levels)		(5.0)	(5.0)	(5.0)	(5.0)	(5.0)
Less W/C	2%	(2.5)	(2.3)	(2.2)	(2.5)	(2.8)
Cash Flow		(34.5)	(13.3)	7.9	16.1	23.1
Terminal Value assumption	5.0x	EBITDA				227.0
EV (PV) of the firm	**$74.9**	**(34.5)**	**(13.3)**	**7.9**	**16.1**	**250.1**
EV (PV) of the Equity	**$56.5**	(34.5)	(13.3)	7.9	16.1	250.1
Return Analysis	(49.7)	(34.5)	(13.3)	7.9	16.1	250.1
IRR =	**27.2%**					

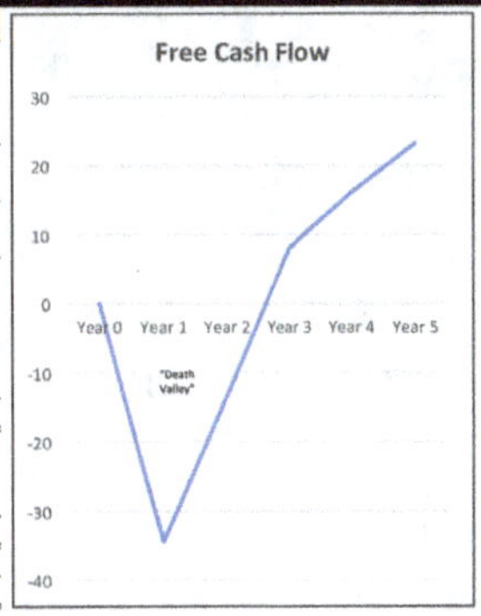

DISTRESS CASH FLOW ANALYSIS USING BLACK-SCHOLES OPTION PRICING MODEL

Step 1 - Find the annualized in Retained (Equity) and Debt prices:

Annualized Variance in Retained Earnings σ^2 =	0.37812 (annual)	St. Dev.=	0.61491463
Annualized Variance in Debt Price σ^2 =	0.2592 (annual)	St. Dev.=	0.50911688

Step 2 - Find the annualized variance in firm value

(we^2 x σe^2) + (wb^2 x σb^2) + 2. (we x wd x ped x σe x σd). C

We= 11.70% C= 0.25

Wd= 88.30%

Annualized Variance in firm value 0.211314335

The five-year bond rate (corresponding to the weighted average duration of 5.1 years) is 6.0%

Stet 3 - Find the value of call based upon the following parameters of equity as a call option

Value of the underlying Enteprise Value = S = Value of the firm =	$74.9
Exercise Price = X = Face Value of outstanding debt =	$40.0
Life of the option = t = Weighted average duration of debt=	5 years
Variance in the value of the underlying asset = σ^2 =	0.2113
Riskless Rate = I = T-Bond for option life =	6.00%

d1=	1.4154	N (d1) =	0.9215
d2=	0.3875	N (d2) =	0.6508

Value of the call (Equity) = 49.674

INITIAL PUBLIC OFFERING: DROUSSIA BEACH HOTEL COMPANY

The IPO process described in detail in chapter 6 shows the following steps before the actual IPO priced is finalized:

- Step 1: Selecting the investment company/underwriter
- Step 2: Preparing the documents for the IPO
- Step 3: SEC registration and approval
- Step 4: Marketing the IPO
- Step 5: Indication of interest
- Step 6: Closing, funding, and free to trade

Let's assume that Droussia Beach Hotel Company (DBH), a private company, is in the process of accessing the public markets for the first time primarily to payout a portion of the existing owners' stake in the company; in this case 40% of the stock issued will be held by the public holders. As mentioned in previous chapter, the success of an IPO is mainly dependent on favorable market conditions. The company also needs to have all the characteristics of an IPO including visibility of stable cash flows, a high probability of growth, and a demonstration of niche industry characteristics. Typically, the process takes 3–6 months depending on the condition of the market and size of the IPO.

An advisor is selected by the company to assist with the IPO and support the trading post IPO, along with a few other underwriters. The duty of the advisor is to prepare all the necessary information, including financial statements, that will be disclosed for official registration. After this information is filed with the SEC, called the "preliminary prospectus" or "red hearing," the SEC makes an announcement that the registration is effective. The SEC will then continue to work with the underwriter to gain additional supplemental information and make the necessary corrections for the registration to be approved. The investment bankers who were selected to underwrite the IPO start marketing the shares. The marketing involves presentations and various pitches that are sent to large-scale investors such as financial institutions and corporations. A fairness opinion on the estimated value of the company is included in the prospectus using the summary of various methods.

Figure 9.13 shows the summary of the proposed IPO priced based on three methods described later in this chapter. According to the valuation presented in Figure 9.13, it suggests the price per share, assuming 40 million shares are issued, will be between $16–$19. Using a 10% discount to the average $17.9, the proposed IPO price will be offered at $16. The discount is arranged in order to give the stock a nice momentum when it is ready to trade.

The three methods of valuation described in figure 9.13 include the hotel industry comparable EBITDA trading multiples, the hotel industry EBITDA acquisition multiples, and a

FIGURE 9.13 DROUSSIA HOTEL COMPANY (IPO ANALYSIS)

CORPORATE VALUATIONS

IPO - EQUITY VALUATION ANALYSIS			
Methodology	**Equity Value**	**Shares Outstanding (000's)**	**IPO Stock Price Offered**
Average EBITDA Industry Trading Multiples	775,437	40,000	$ 19.39
Using Averge EBITDA Transaction Multiples	728,602	40,000	$ 18.22
Discount Cash Flow Valuation Analysis	646,893	40,000	$ 16.17
Average of other methods	**716,977**		**$ 17.92**
Discount to the value			10.00%
Price Offered (Rounded)			$ 16.00

	IPO Stock Price Offered (000's)	**% of Public Offering to Total Value**	**Shares Offered to Public (000's)**	**Funds (000's)**
Equity Value (IPO Price x Shares Issued)	640,000	40%	16,000	256,000
Plus Debt	2,100,000			
Less Cash	(250,000)			
Enteprise Value	2,490,000			
EBITDA	180,000			
EV / EBITDA	13.83x			

DCF analysis. The valuation methodologies, representing method 4, 5, and 6, respectively are discussed in detail in chapter 17.

Figure 9.14 shows that based on the average EBITDA hotel industry trading multiples of 14.59x, the equity value and offering IPO price is estimated to be $775.4 million or $19.39 per share, respectively.

Figure 9.15 shows that based on the average EBITDA hotel industry acquisition multiples of 14.33x, the equity value and offering IPO price is estimated to be at $728.6 million or $18.22, respectively.

Figure 9.16 shows that based on the discount cash flow method using specific assumptions to run the company's projections and estimated terminal value in year 6, the equity value and offering IPO price is estimated to be $646.9 million or $16.17 per share, respectively.

At the end of the day, the final IPO price is based on supply and demand. How the underwriter interprets the environment will determine the market price for the IPO stock,

FIGURE 9.14 DROUSSIA HOTEL COMPANY (AVG INDUSTRY TRADING EBITDA MULTIPLES)

CORPORATE VALUATIONS

Average EBITDA Industry Trading Multiples

		SP	SO	SP * SO = EQ	D	C	EQ + D - C = EV	E	EV / E	
Company	**Symbol**	**Stock Price**	**Stocks Outstanding ($000)**	**Equity Value ($000)**	**Debt (ST&LT) ($000)**	**Cash ($000)**	**Enterprise Value ($000)**	**EBITDA ($mm)**	**EBITDA Multiple**	**Beta**
Choice Hotels International	CHH	$ 83.20	56,572	4,706,804	796,200	37,150	5,465,854	335,560	16.29x	1.13x
Hilton Worldwide Holdings Inc.	HLT	$ 80.96	298,190	24,141,462	7,580,000	423,000	31,298,462	1,760,000	17.78x	1.45x
Hyatt	HOT	$ 77.93	117,448	9,152,748	1,440,000	879,000	9,713,748	657,000	14.79x	1.18x
Intercontinental Hotel	IHG	$ 62.58	190,000	11,890,200	2,040,000	233,000	13,697,200	843,000	16.25x	1.59x
Marcus Corporation	MCS	$ 40.80	19,680	802,944	317,420	18,070	1,102,294	139,930	7.88x	0.32x
Marriott International	MAR	$ 130.90	346,990	45,420,991	8,990,000	366,000	54,044,991	2,850,000	18.96x	1.36x
Park Hotels & Resorts Inc.	PK	$ 32.89	201,180	6,616,810	3,080,000	421,000	9,275,810	734,000	12.64x	
Wyndham Worldwide	WYN	$ 136.73	108,640	14,854,347	8,310,000	1,500,000	21,664,347	1,790,000	12.10x	1.33x
								Average	14.59x	1.19x

EBITDA * Average Multiple	180,000	14.59x
Droussia Beach Hotel Enteprise Value	**2,625,437**	
Less Total Debt	(2,100,000)	
Plus Cash	250,000	
Equity Value	**775,437**	
Stock Issued	40,000	
Suggested Stock IPO Price	**$ 19.39**	

FIGURE 9.15 DROUSSIA HOTEL COMPANY (AVG TRANSACTION EBITDA MULTIPLES)

CORPORATE VALUATIONS

Using Averge EBITDA Transaction Multiples (M&A Comparable Method)

	Calculations	AP	SO	AP * SO = EQ	ND	EQ + ND = EV	E	EV / E
Target	**Acquirer**	**Acquisition Price /Share**	**Shares Outstanding**	**Equity Value ($mm)**	**Total Net Debt ($mm)**	**Enterprise Value (EV)**	**EBITDA (last reported)**	**EBITDA Multiple**
Hilton Hotels	Blackstone Group	$ 47.50	390,400,000	$ 18,544	$ 6,180	$ 24,724	$ 1,680	14.72x
Four Seasons*	Kingtom Hotels Int'l / Gates' Cascade	$ 82.00	33,078,000	$ 2,712	$ 279	$ 2,991	$ 94	31.90x
Fairmont/Rafles	Kingtom Hotels Int'l	$ 45.00	73,335,000	$ 3,300	$ 124	$ 3,424	$ 187	18.29x
Hilton International	Hilton Hotels Corp.			$ 5,578	$ -	$ 5,578	$ 504	11.07x
Starwood Hotels	Host Marriott					$ 4,096	$ 315	13.00x
La-Quinta Corp	Blackstone Group	$ 12.22	203,000,000	$ 2,481	$ 926	$ 3,406	$ 230	14.83x
Wynham Int'l	Blackstone Group	$ 1.15	172,053,000	$ 198	$ 2,682	$ 2,880	$ 275	10.47x
John Q. Hammons Hotels	JQH Acquisition LLC	$ 24.00	19,583,000	$ 470	$ 765	$ 1,235	$ 123	10.04x
Societe du Louvre	Starwood Capital					$ 1,029	$ 91	11.30x
Intercontinental Hotels	LRG					$ 981	$ 107	9.20x
Boca Resorts	Blackstone Group	$ 24.00	40,284,000	$ 967	$ 217	$ 1,184	$ 90	13.15x
Prime Hospitality	Blackstone Group	$ 12.25	44,808,000	$ 549	$ 244	$ 792	$ 55	14.38x
Extended Stay	Blackstone Group	$ 19.93	95,077,000	$ 1,895	$ 1,232	$ 3,126	$ 225	13.90x
							Average	14.33x

EBITDA * Average Multiple	180,000	14.33x
Droussia Beach Hotel Enteprise Value	**2,578,602**	
Less Total Debt	(2,100,000)	
Plus Cash	250,000	
Equity Value	**728,602**	
Stock Issued	40,000	
Suggested Stock IPO Price	**$ 18.22**	

FIGURE 9.16 DROUSSIA HOTEL COMPANY (DCF ANALYSIS

CORPORATE VALUATIONS

DISCOUNT CASH FLOW									
Company Projections ($ 000'S)	**Operating Assump.**	**Entry Year 2018**	Year 1 **2019**	Year 2 **2020**	Year 3 **2021**	Year 4 **2022**	Year 5 **2023**	**Exit Year 2024**	Year 7 **2025**
Revenues	5.0%	growth	400,000	420,000	441,000	463,050	486,203	510,513	536,038
Cost of Revenues	35.0%	% of Revenue	(140,000)	(147,000)	(154,350)	(162,068)	(170,171)	(178,679)	(187,613)
Operating Costs	20.0%	% of Revenue	(80,000)	(84,000)	(88,200)	(92,610)	(97,241)	(102,103)	(107,208)
EBITDA	45.0%		**180,000**	**189,000**	**198,450**	**208,373**	**218,791**	**229,731**	**241,217**
Less Depreciation	3.00%	% of Revenue	(12,000)	(12,600)	(13,230)	(13,892)	(14,586)	(15,315)	(16,081)
Less Amortization of Intagibles			-	-	-	-	-	-	
EBIT			168,000	176,400	185,220	194,481	204,205	214,415	225,136
Less Interest			(30,000)	(28,500)	(27,075)	(25,721)	(24,435)	(23,213)	
EBT			138,000	147,900	158,145	168,760	179,770	191,202	225,136
Less Taxes (adj out Interest Exp)	36.0%	% of EBT	(60,480)	(63,504)	(66,679)	(70,013)	(73,514)	(77,190)	(81,049)
Plus Depreciation & Amortization			12,000	12,600	13,230	13,892	14,586	15,315	16,081
Less Working Capital	1.00%	% of Revenue	(4,000)	(4,200)	(4,410)	(4,631)	(4,862)	(5,105)	(5,360)
Less Capex	3.00%	% of Revenue	(12,000)	(12,600)	(13,230)	(13,892)	(14,586)	(15,315)	(16,081)
Cash Flow Before Financing (CFBF)			**73,520**	**80,196**	**87,056**	**94,116**	**101,394**	**108,907**	**138,727**
Less Principal Financing			(20,000)	(35,000)	(50,000)	(65,000)	(80,000)	(95,000)	(110,000)
Equity Cash Flows			53,520	45,196	37,056	29,116	21,394	13,907	28,727
Terminal Value									
EBITDA Multiple Method (Industry Average)	**Growth**	**8.0x**						1,837,845	
Perpetuity Method (using WACC + growth)	**3.50%**	**12.00%**						1,632,079	
Average Terminal Value								**1,734,962**	
Debt Outstanding								(750,000)	
Equity Value (TV - Debt)								984,962	
Equity Cash Flows			**53,520**	**45,196**	**37,056**	**29,116**	**21,394**	**998,869**	
			x	x	x	x	x	x	
$ 1 PV Table (Expected Equity Rate)		12.00%	*0.8929*	*0.7972*	*0.7118*	*0.6355*	*0.5674*	*0.5066*	
PV Table (Expected Equity Rate)		**646,893**	47,786	36,030	26,376	18,504	12,140	506,058	
Stock Issued		40,000							
Suggested Stock IPO Price		**$ 16.17**							

the number of initial shares being offered, and the date open trading will begin. The underwriter then announces the price, in this case $16 per share, the number of shares issued (40 million), and number of shares that are floating in the market (16 million), shown in figure 9.13. It then determines that the trade process has been established. It takes approximately 3 days (T+3) for the IPO exchange to close. The stock is then delivered, and the company receives the proceeds (net of underwriting fees) from its sale. The underwriter's obligation, designated as the market makers (SEC definition), is to monitor the stock's price for a few months post IPO and exercise the right to purchase or sell shares to make sure the stock stabilizes.

ONLINE TEMPLATES

The Excel spreadsheets used in the chapter can be accessed online via Cognella Active Learning platform.

PART III

Secondary Markets: Investments and Derivatives

CHAPTER 10
Stock Investments, Analysis, and Valuation

CHAPTER 11
Corporate Bond Investment, Analysis, and Valuation

CHAPTER 12
Credit and Alternative Investments: Leveraged Loans, CLOs, and Structured Finance

CHAPTER 13
Derivative Investments: Option Strategies, Analysis, and Valuation

CHAPTER 14
Derivative Investments: Futures, Forwards, Swaps, Swaptions, CDAs, FRAs, and Other Derivatives

PART III of the textbook complements the material that was introduced in Part I and Part II. This part introduces the four main corporate capital market asset classes including stock, bonds, loans, and derivatives. Each chapter gives an overview of the secondary markets that these asset classes trade, how investors trade, and how the performance is measured. Each asset class is sensitive to economic cycles at various degrees and each are impacted by risk factors such as volatility, interest rates, liquidity, and credit. Part III also devotes two chapters on the derivative markets including options, futures, swaps, and others.

RAISING CAPITAL THROUGH THE COMPANY'S BUSINESS CYCLE

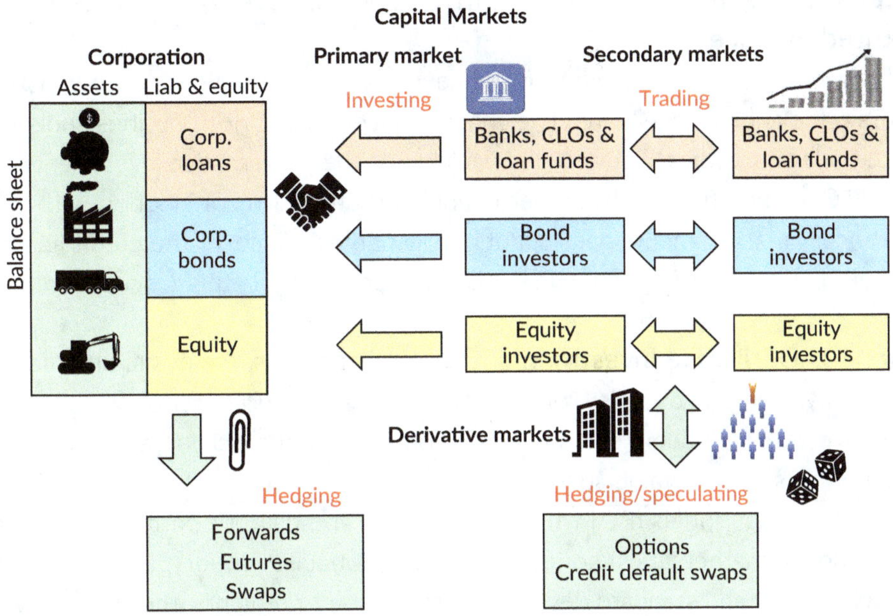

The line-up and brief description of Part III's chapters are as follows:

Chapter 10: Stock Investments, Analysis, and Valuation

This chapter will give an overview of the U.S. stock exchange markets and the regulations of these exchanges and will discuss various market indices such as the Dow Jones Industrial Average (DJIA), Standard & Poor's index, and others. It will also cover how investors trade stock and define all the parties involved in these transactions. This chapter will revisit a portion of the concepts introduced in chapters 1 and preview concepts that will be introduced in chapter 17 regarding return analysis and the time-value of money to help analyze and value stock investments. The chapter will also cover various techniques and scenarios analyses for recommending, buying, or selling a stock using fundamental, technical, and behavioral finance analysis.

Chapter 11: Corporate Bond Investments, Analysis, and Valuation

This chapter will give an overview of the secondary bond market and how investors trade bonds. It will repeat a few of the concepts introduced in chapter 1 regarding return analysis and the time value of money to analyze and value various investments in bonds and securitized bond vehicles. Entailed in the analysis includes a risk evaluation of the present factors including impacts of interest rate fluctuations, credit rating upgrades and downgrades, and refinancing risk. It will also cover various scenario analyses to determine factors such as duration and convexity.

Chapter 12: Credit and Alternative Investments: Leveraged Loans, CLOs, and Structured Finance

This chapter will give an overview of the secondary loan market and how institutional investors trade and manage loans. The chapter will discuss various entities and structures set up to trade and manage a portfolio of bank loans. These alternative investment portfolios include CLOs, credit funds, and lender finance structures. In conjunction with analyzing the secondary market and its participants, this chapter will cover the credit analysis that should take place prior to investing in loans; chapter 18 revisits this process in more detail.

Chapter 13: Derivative Investments: Option Strategies, Analysis, and Valuation

This chapter will give an overview of the options market. It will describe various strategies used by investors for hedging or speculating on significant stock increase or decrease. It will then discuss how to value such options including various methods such as the binomial option pricing models (BOPM), Black-Scholes, and call-put parity. The chapter will first reintroduce mathematical concepts such as probability theory, normal distribution, natural logarithms, and standard deviation as the basis of predicting the stock movements.

Chapter 14: Derivative Investments: Futures, Forwards, Swaps, Swaptions, CDAs, FRAs, and Other Derivatives

This chapter will give an overview of the futures exchange markets, cover forward contracts, and describe other derivatives such as swaps, swaptions, credit default swaps, and forward rate agreements. It will describe various strategies used by investors for hedging against interest rate, market price movements, foreign currency, and commodity increase or decreases.

Credits

CHAPTER 10

Stock Investments, Analysis, and Valuation

This chapter will give an overview of the U.S. stock exchange markets and the regulations of these exchanges and discuss various market indices such as the Dow Jones Industrial Average (DJIA), Standard & Poor's index, and others. It will also cover how investors trade stock and define all the parties involved in these transactions. This chapter will revisit a portion of the concepts introduced in chapter 1 and preview concepts that will be introduced in chapter 17 regarding return analysis and the time value of money to help analyze and value stock investments. The chapter will also cover various techniques and scenario analyses for recommending, buying, or selling a stock using fundamental, technical, and behavioral finance analysis.

LEARNING OBJECTIVES

After reading this chapter, students will be able to do the following

- Understand how exchange markets work and how securities are traded
- Obtain knowledge from the different trading platforms
- Understand long and short selling and how to obtain margins to purchase stocks
- Explain the different parties involved in the exchange markets including brokers and dealers, institutional and personal investors, and the role of the Securities and Exchange Commission for trading stock
- Understand the difference between fundamental, technical, and behavioral analysis

TRADING STOCKS: AN OVERVIEW

Buying and selling stock is probably the most common activity for an individual that is investing for the first time. It is, after all, an investment that triggers anyone's curiosity and excitement. The most common question of someone looking to invest is, "What company do you think I should invest in?" Everyone has the basic understanding that if I buy the stock of a company today, I am assuming that the value of such stock will go up based on their success in business. Investing in companies that have a good business or a good product is expected, but the most sophisticated investors add a few other measurement criteria before they make a recommendation. These include the risk they are taking, how long to hold the stock, how the stock is performing against a risk-free investment, and how the stock is performing against the overall market. All these questions need to be addressed by professionals when recommending a stock.

AUTHOR'S NOTES

A great book to read is Scott Patterson's (2010) The Quants: How a New Breed of Math Whizzes Conquered Wall Street and Nearly Destroyed It. *It's fun to read and it covers many of the investment concepts described in this textbook, such as the capital asset pricing model (CAPM), the formula that analysts use to set their return expectation on a stock while adjusting for the market beta. The book discusses, using a lot of humor, four math geniuses called the quants that set up quantitative funds aimed at taking advantage of inefficiencies in the equity markets: Peter Muller, a mathematician; Ken Griffin, the founder of Citadel investments; Cliff Asness, the founder of AQR Capital Management; and Boaz Weinstein, chess master and card counter who traded derivatives at Deutsche Bank. All these math wizards used pure technical analytics that involved mathematical formulas to predict the movement of stocks based on the prices' trading activity. Then you have Warren Buffet. One of the richest men in the world who throughout his entire life has used fundamental analysis to invest in companies that made good products and services. These fundamental drivers translate to healthy profits and thus higher stock prices. I always look forward to reading his famous annual letters to Berkshire Hathaway's (n.d.) shareholders. Included is always a healthy dose of valuable insight and a scope into how he thinks. His letter for the 2018 annual report starts with the statement "Focus on the Forest—Forget the Trees" and ends with the statement "At Berkshire, the whole is greater—consistently greater—than the sum of the parts." Considering these methods, you have two very different and isolated approaches to viewing the same environment (the market) and yet each has been successful in growing the practitioner's wealth. As a college student studying finance, I was taught that stock prices followed an unpredictable pattern, that stocks followed a so-called random walk; that is, that the changes in stock price are random and unpredictable. On the same token, I was always very impressed with the story of the Scottish botanist Robert Brown, who in 1827 was studying how pollen particles immersed in water would move in a random fashion. After many months, he still could not explain what caused their movement. His thorough analysis was used by a French mathematician, Louis Bachellier, to create a model called the stochastic process, a model used to predict stock prices. More mathematicians jumped on the bandwagon to create models that would predict stock movements, one being the famous Black-Scholes option pricing model. I spend a lot of time reading the Fama-French three-factor model that measures market values as compared to book values. I have bought into the idea that the market is efficient and that stock prices move based on new information. Then again, if that is the case why do they continue move with no information available? All those questions awaken my appreciation of the analysis done by the many scholars who have a stake including mathematicians, statisticians, computer engineers, graphists, investment fundamentalists, stock behavioralists, and investment strategists—all with the purpose of beating the market, all seeking alpha because achieving beta is good enough. The moral to this story is that even though many investors are seeking mathematical methods to take advantage of the stock market, we often find investors fall back to the Warren Buffet approach. Whatever your approach for picking the right stock, at the end of the day, after many lessons I learned for years as a banker, it's easier to pick a stock of company that had good products and services. It's much easier to defend your investment than trying to explain why your bitcoin investment did not do well.*

KEY TAKEAWAYS

- There is a reason that brokers, dealers, and investment advisors need a license to operate and are required to take frequent exams. The stock market can be very tempting for participants to knowingly or unknowingly cut corners to make money, so knowing the rules, regulations, and procedures are very important.

- Remember, one investor sells his or her stock and someone else buys it, but they are both smart. Who is right? The reasons and views for buying or selling a stock varies and that's why we have a market.
- The many methods of analyzing and valuating a company's stock price to assess its fair value generally fall into three categories:
  - Technical analysis
  - Fundamental analysis
  - Behavioral analysis

SECONDARY TRADING MARKETS: AN OVERVIEW

In the United States, secondary market trading takes place in exchanges and over-the-counter markets.

Exchange markets: **National exchanges serve a broad base of investors and require that the stock of traded companies meet certain standards called listing requirements.** Companies that are listed on national exchanges tend to be large and well established. The following two national exchanges are where most stocks are traded:

- **New York Stock Exchange (NYSE):** The NYSE is the largest U.S. stock exchange, as measured by the market value of all its listed firms. Some transactions at the NYSE are still completed on the trading floor. Traders are directed to the exchange floor by telephone or electronically, and a broker matches interested buyers and sellers. This process is known as the auction marketplace. Most of the stocks that are traded in NYSE are large companies based on capital and are often called blue-chip stocks. In 2000 the exchange launched Direct +, which could automatically cross smaller trades without human intervention, and in 2004, it began eliminating the size restrictions on Direct + trades. To more effectively compete with new exchanges, the NYSE now executes transactions through its hybrid markets, which allow brokers to send orders either for immediate electronic execution or to the specialists who seek price improvement from another trader.
- **NASDAQ:** The NASDAQ stock market lists approximately 3,000 firms. It has steadily introduced even more sophisticated trading platforms. NASDAQ has three levels of subscribers. The highest, level 3 subscribers are registered market makers (MM). These MMs trade large amounts of securities, maintain inventories, post bids, and ask prices to support the trades. Level 2 subscribers receive all bid and ask quotes

but do not post their own quotes. Level 2 subscribers basically can see which market makers are offering the best prices and bid on them. Level 1 subscribers receive only inside quotes and are restricted from seeing how many shares are being offered. The NASDAQ is typically known as a high-tech market and attracts many firms that deal with Internet and electronics such as Facebook.

Over-the-counter markets (OTC): OTC refers to stocks that do not trade on a national exchange such as NASDAQ or the NYSE. These markets generally have fewer regulations and requirements than the national exchanges. OTC markets rely on market makers who stand ready to buy or sell shares. The stocks that trade in OTC markets are often issued by small companies or companies that no longer meet the listing requirements of the NYSE or NASDAQ. The two primary OTC markets are the OTC Bulletin Board and OTC Pink ("Pink Sheets").

Third and fourth markets: In addition to the national exchanges and OTC markets, there are two additional markets for securities trading:

- **The third market** is a negotiated-price trading market. This market provides liquidity to NYSE and NASDAQ securities.
- **The fourth market** involves the direct trading of large blocks of securities between institutions and retail investors. These trades are done through electronic networks referred to as electronic communication networks (ECN).

Indices and tracking market performance: **A stock market index is a method of measuring the performance of a specific segment of the stock market or economy.** Financial analysts use these indices as a benchmark to compare the performance of their portfolios or their individual stocks to the indices. For example, mutual funds are frequently compared to an index to measure and pin funds' performance against the overall markets. There are two types of indices that are classified based on methods used to determine the price.

- **Price weighted:** In a price-weighted index, like the Dow Jones Industrial Average (DJIA), the price of each stock (30 stocks) is the basis for determining the index's value. Price fluctuations on even a single stock can have a large influence on the index's value regardless of the actual size of the company. For example, in March 2019 after a Boeing 737 Max crashed in Ethiopia due to an alleged computer glitch, the tragedy resulted in the grounding of all 737 Max's by all airlines. Boeing's stock dropped more than 10%, heavily influencing the DJIA, considering Boeing is one of the 30 companies in the index. Basically, a price-weighted index is an arithmetic mean of all the stock's current prices. The formula to derive the DJIA index is as follows:

$$DJIA_t = \sum_{i=1}^{30} \frac{P_{it}}{D}$$

where DJIA is the value of the DJIA index on day t, Pit is the closing price of stock I on day t, and D is the division of the day adjusted for stock splits.

- **Capitalization weighted:** The capitalization-weighted index, also known as the market value–weighted index, reflects the size of the company. Each company's value is calculated by multiplying the share price by the number of shares outstanding of the public company. Standard & Poor's 500 (S&P 500) is such an index, representing the 500 biggest companies in the United States. The S&P 500 index uses "freely floating shares" that exclude shares held by insiders. The calculation of the index number is as follows:

$$\text{Index} = \frac{\sum Pt.Qt}{\sum Pb.Qb} \text{ . beginning index value}$$

where index is the value of day, Qt is the number of outstanding freely floating shares on a day t, Pb is the ending price for stocks on the base day, and Qb is the number of outstanding or freely floating shares on the base day.

HOW TO TRADE STOCKS

This section will give an overview where, how and when an investor trades stock in the secondary market.

TYPES OF ORDERS

When you call your broker to place an order, there are two basic types of orders, with some room for variation within each category:

Market Orders

Market orders are BUY or SELL orders that need to be executed immediately at the current market price. The prices constantly fluctuate so the order will go in and be executed at the next bid price if it's to sell and the next asking price if it's to buy. For example, if you call the broker and the broker tells you that the best **BID** price available is $112.50 and the best **ASK** price is $112.75 and if the order gets executed to **BUY AT MARKET** 100 shares immediately, the price is locked at $112.75. If the order gets executed to **SELL AT MARKET** 100 shares immediately, the price is locked at $112.50. The $0.25 differential is the **BID/**

FIGURE 10.1 ABC COMPANY (STOCK)

NASDAQ REAL TIME PRICES

112.50 ↑ **1.2** **1.07%**

ORDER BOOK

Market Maker	Bid	Ask	Size (100's) Bid/Ask
MLCO	112.50	112.75	10/12
MHMY	112.53	112.79	16/25
SALD	112.58	112.81	10/15
WEED	112.65	112.84	15/19

ASK spread. It gets a little complicated when the volume order to buy, for example, is more than the volume available at the asking price. In that case, the first number of shares will be executed at the best available ask price and the balance will be executed at the next best asking price. The designated market makers (DMM) that support the specific stock that you are interested in buying will list both the bid and ask and the volume at these prices. As the orders come in and fulfill the first layer of volume at the best price available, the next set of order volume is executed at the next layer of volume and so forth until all the orders are completed. Figure 10.1 shows how the order book is set up. It lists all the market makers.

Figure 10.1 shows MLCO is willing to buy up to 1,000 shares at $112.50 and sell up to 2,000 shares at $112.75; MHMY is willing to buy up to 1,600 shares at 112.53 and sell up to 2,500 shares at 112.79; SALD is willing to buy up to 1,000 shares at 112.58 and sell up to 1,500 shares at 112.81; and so on. If a block order came in to buy 3,000 shares at market, then the first 1,000 shares will be bought at the first asking price of $112.75 per share, the 1,600 shares will be bought at $112.79, and the balance of 400 shares will be bought at $112.81.

Price-Contingent Orders or Limit Orders

Investors may place an order with an instruction to buy or sell at a specific price regardless what the market prices are. If the bid and ask prices are not available at these specific prices, the orders will not be fulfilled. The market orders are also listed in the bid/ask inventory, called the limit-order book, and need to be refreshed every day.

Stop Order (Stop-Loss Orders or Stop-Buy Orders)

A stop order is like a limit order with a condition to buy or sell at a certain price but differing on the mechanics. The stop order has a condition to buy or sell at a certain price, and when the stock hits that stop price, it activates a market order. Once the price is triggered, the order automatically becomes a market order and is listed on the market book. It's important to know that the stop order is not a limit order. It takes two steps to execute: First, it triggers the specific price that the stop order was set up and then it gets traded at the next best available market price. For example, the investor instructs his or her broker to sell Facebook once Facebook's stock drops to $150. If Facebook drops below that price, then the stop order is triggered and is sold at the next available price, which could be below $150. This arrangement is designed to protect the profit or prevent a loss if the stock begins to move the wrong direction, but the stop order price is not a guarantee. These orders are canceled if they do not participate in the closing trade of the day.

TYPES OF MARKETS

The most common type of markets are the brokered and dealer markets.

Brokered Markets

This is when an investor will call or go online to set-up an account with a brokerage firm in order to trade stocks. This is a fully licensed broker who is in the business of matching the seller and buyer for a trade and collects a commission on the transaction. The brokers could also be accessed online such as discount brokers like Ameritrade, or Charles Swab where you put in an order to sell or buy the stock. The brokers, based on their license, are restricted to carry any inventory of stocks to trade; they are basically middlemen to accommodate all the trades between buyers and sellers, like the real estate brokers where the seller will engage a broker to sell his or her home and will collect a percentage of the purchase price.

Dealer Markets

The difference between a broker and a dealer is that the dealer can hold his or her own inventory of stocks in addition to brokering the trades. Dealers buy stocks in the primary or secondary markets and sell them for a profit from their inventory.

TRADING STRATEGIES

Institutional and individual investors use lots of strategies to enhance their investment returns. This can often include financial engineering methods such as leveraging their investment, short selling for speculation, behavioral motives, hedging their holdings, and program trading by using mathematical algorithms to take advantage of the market movements.

BUYING ON MARGIN STRATEGY

Buying on margin is when an investor is leveraging the purchase of a company's stock or borrowing part of the initial investment from a bank or broker. For example, buying on

FIGURE 10.2 BUYING ON MARGIN

	Initial Purchase of Stock			Margin Loan			Investment
Year 0	Purchase Stock Price @	Number of Shares Purchased	Total Cost	Margin Percentage %	Obtaining Margin Loan	Annual Interest on Margin Loan (Cost) %	Initial Cash by Investor
Buying on Margin	$ 100.00	100	$ (10,000)	50.00%	$ 5,000	5.00%	$ (5,000)
Buying with on Margin	$ 100.00	100	$ (10,000)	0%	$ -		$ (10,000)

		Final Sale of Stock			Profit				HPR%
	Year 1	Sell Stock Price @	Number of Shares Purchased	Total Proceeds	Payment of Margin Loan	Payment of Interest Expense	Net Proceeds After Loan Payment	Net Profit Less Initial Cash by Investor	Profit / Initial Investment
Selling @ a gain	Buying on Margin	$ 120.00	100	$ 12,000	$ (5,000)	$ (250)	$ 6,750	**$ 1,750**	**35.00%**
	Buying with on Margin	$ 120.00	100	$ 12,000	$ -	$ -	$ 12,000	**$ 2,000**	**20.00%**
Selling @ a loss	Buying on Margin	$ 80.00	100	$ 8,000	$ (5,000)	$ (250)	$ 2,750	**$ (2,250)**	**-45.00%**
	Buying with on Margin	$ 80.00	100	$ 8,000	$ -	$ -	$ 8,000	**$ (2,000)**	**-20.00%**

a 50% margin means that the investor puts down 50% and borrows the other 50% to purchase the stock. The stock is pledged to the lender as collateral. The buying power refers to the total dollar amount of purchases an investor has including the margin, or loan capacity. As with any loan, when investors buy stock on margin, they must pay back the money they borrow plus interest on the loan.

Using leverage, or buying on margin, can significantly boost the returns of an investment if it is doing well while simultaneously increasing the risk profile of the investment and portfolio. Buying on leverage though can also be harmful when an investment is not doing well and increases the required floor return for the investment to remain profitable. Figure 10.2 compares the benefits and risks of buying on margin versus buying without a margin. It shows that an investor, using a 50% margin, buys 100 shares of a stock for $100. Basically, the investor funds half the purchase price with his or her own money and the other half he or she buys on margin, making his or her initial cash investment $5,000. Figure 10.2 shows two scenarios. In one the stock goes up from $100 to $120 in one year and in the other the stock drops from $100 to $80 in the same period. Let's assume that in both cases the investor sells the stock at market price. The return gets a boost when buying on margin (20% to 35%), assuming the stock goes up ($100 to $120), and a significant loss (-20% to -45%) when the stock goes down ($100 to $80).

Based on the investor's credit score, the broker sets the minimum or initial margin (minimum 50%, basically down payment of up to 50%). The broker will also set a maintenance margin (typically using the initial margin for stocks). Maintenance margin is the minimum amount of money that must be in the account before the investor must deposit more money to cover the maintenance percentage. For example, suppose an investor deposits $100,000 and the maintenance margin is 50%, or $50,000. As soon as the investor's investment portfolio value (based on mark to market) dips below 50% of the original $100,000, the investor will receive a margin call. The broker will call the investor and will demand that the investor either deposit money in his or her account or sells stocks to meet the required maintenance margin level.

SHORT-SELLING STRATEGY

Short selling is the process where an investor borrows the stock and then sells it immediately at the current price and will profit when the stock price declines. When it declines, the investor or short seller will then buy the stock at that lower price and release the stock back the original owner. The motivation is purely speculative or used as a hedging mechanism to protect the downside risk of a long position in the same stock or a related one. To open a short position, the investor must have a margin account that carries interest on the value of the borrowed shares while the position is open. To close a short position, as mentioned, the investor buys the shares back from the market and returns them to the lender.

Figure 10.3 shows various scenarios where the short seller can profit when the stock drops and can lose money when the stock price rises. In this case the investor borrows 100 shares and sells them at the current price of $100. The $10,000 is credited in his or her account. He or she then buys the shares back at the market price and profits when the stock is lower than $100 and experiences losses when the stock is higher than $100 (excluding interest payment on margin loan).

FIGURE 10.3 SHORT SELL

	Initial Short Sale			Buying the Stock / Cover Short Sale			
	Short Sell Stock Price	Shares Borrowed	Credit on Short Sale	Stock Price	Payment to Purchase New Shares	Profit/Loss	HPR%
Selling Short	$ 100.00	100	$ 10,000	$ 50	$ (5,000)	$ 5,000	50.0%
Selling Short	$ 100.00	100	$ 10,000	$ 60	$ (6,000)	$ 4,000	40.0%
Selling Short	$ 100.00	100	$ 10,000	$ 70	$ (7,000)	$ 3,000	30.0%
Selling Short	$ 100.00	100	$ 10,000	$ 80	$ (8,000)	$ 2,000	20.0%
Selling Short	$ 100.00	100	$ 10,000	$ 90	$ (9,000)	$ 1,000	10.0%
Selling Short	$ 100.00	100	$ 10,000	$ 100	$ (10,000)	$ -	0.0%
Selling Short	$ 100.00	100	$ 10,000	$ 110	$ (11,000)	$ (1,000)	-10.0%
Selling Short	$ 100.00	100	$ 10,000	$ 120	$ (12,000)	$ (2,000)	-20.0%
Selling Short	$ 100.00	100	$ 10,000	$ 130	$ (13,000)	$ (3,000)	-30.0%

The total volume of all short selling is available to the public. Two metrics used by portfolio managers to track the short-selling activity on a stock are the following:

- **Short interest ratio (SIR),** or sometimes referred to as "short float," measures the ratio of shares that are currently shorted compared to the number of shares available or "floating" in the market. A very high SIR shows the percentage of the stocks that are falling to the total stock that are traded, appearing that they are overvalued.
- **Short interest to volume ratio** or "days to cover" measures the total shares held short divided by the average daily trading volume of the stock. This will basically measure the day that the short seller must cover the shorts. A high short-interest-to-volume-ratio shows a bearish sentiment for a stock.

Both ratio metrics can be very useful. They measure the bearish sentiment of the specific stock, which can give outlook into the company and stocks' overall health. It is important to remember that selling short is very risky. If the stock price continues to go up, for the short seller to cover the shorts he or she will rapidly need to put an order in to buy the stock at the current market price before the stock goes up more. These orders by the short sellers to buy the stock back could cause the stock to rise even more. This phenomenon is called a **"short squeeze."**

Short sellers are always criticized by bullish investors or the companies themselves, potentially contributing to the decline of the stock. However, short selling provides liquidity to markets and can help prevent non-performing companies' stock price from rising on hype and over-optimism.

PROGRAM TRADING STRATEGIES

Program trading strategies are more frequent these days than even 5 years ago due to trader's ability to spend money on high-speed computer software and hardware programs. These tech-heavy and high startup cost strategies involve large-volume trading made by computers based purely on a stock's movements. Patents without emotion can be highly profitable.

Algorithmic Trading

Algorithmic trading is based on complex mathematical formulas built on powerful computers. These algebraic formulas are built based on historical stock movements to predict the direction of a given stock. Many of these trades make money on very small discrepancies in the stock prices and make money on large volumes. A typical program is built to buy the stock at the bid price and rapidly sell it at the ask price. In his best-selling book, *Flash*

Boys, Wall Street author Michael Lewis (2014) expresses the need for traders to beat other traders to specific trades. He emphasizes the importance of time. In addition to building massive computers, they spend money laying special fiber-optic cables in the ground, providing the most direct connection possible. While it provides advantages for traders to get the market price, because of the volume of trading orders it can also cause flash crashes and loss of liquidity. The flash crash of May 2010, where the stock market dropped more than 1,000 points in about 30 minutes, has been blamed on algorithmic trading.

High-Frequency Trading

High-frequency trading, a subset of algorithmic trading, is a type of trading done by state-of-the-art fast computers. A high-frequency trader makes profits on the bid-ask spread and cross-market arbitrage strategies, even at very small differentials. Trade execution times for high-frequency trading is now measured with milliseconds. This induced many traders to open locations close to the exchanges so the execution could be even faster.

Dark Pools

Dark pools are trading programs that are set up by large broker-dealers for their clients or for its proprietary traders with the purpose of trading in private. Many traders seek anonymity for block trading by institutional investors who do not wish to impact the markets with their large orders and affect the prices for their trades. The dark pools that are registered with the SEC are from broker and dealers, agents, and electronic market makers.

STOCK ANALYSIS

The stock analyst's goal is to find a company whose stock is undervalued. The stock prices of good companies are not necessarily good investments. After analyzing the company's financial performance and understanding the revenue and earnings drivers, the analyst needs to compute the intrinsic value of the stock versus the market value (the current trading value). It might sound counter-intuitive, but assessment of a company's performance cannot directly translate to a similar assessment of the stock of the company. For example, the stock of a growth company is not necessarily a growth stock.

FUNDAMENTAL ANALYSIS

Fundamental analysis includes the following observations:

Growth, Income, or Value Investing

Investors typically break down stocks into three categories: growth stocks, income stocks, and value stocks. Each stock contributes different investment objectives.

Growth Companies and Growth Stocks

Growth companies are companies that consistently experience above-average increases in revenues and earnings. These companies tend to have a higher beta and higher WACC and expect to have a higher equity rate of returns. Investors with high return expectations expect the companies' revenues and earnings to grow faster than those of similar risk firms and the overall economy. Growth companies include newer companies that are still investing heavily in their innovative products or services that are expected to have an impact in the future. Growth companies tend to be focused in areas such as technology, biotech, and pharmaceuticals, to name a few.

Value Companies and Value Stocks

Value companies are companies that have been well established with proven a business model and tend to have good steady products with relatively high demand. Value stocks trade at a lower price to book or price earnings than the market average. Value stocks may also carry high dividend payout ratios. Typically, the analyst will attempt to identify value stocks that have a temporary drop-in value due to behavioral reasons. These events are generally triggered by changes in public perception that have little to do with the company's business.

Income Companies and Income Stocks

Income companies are well-established blue-chip companies that pay constant dividends. Investors seek these stocks to strengthen their fixed-income portfolios with dividend yields that typically exceed other assets such as bonds. Examples are utility companies that have their stock price relatively flat for a long period of time but pay dividends that contribute to healthy returns. Even though income stocks can be an attractive alternative for investors, their values can decline when an interest rates rise.

Defensive Companies and Stocks

Defense companies are companies whose future earnings are likely to tolerate an economic downturn. Analysts expect that these companies have relatively low business risk. Typical examples are public utilities, grocery chains, and healthcare providers. Defensive stocks tend to have a beta with less than 1 that can result in a lower CAPM, so the expected return is lower than the overall market return. A defensive stock is expected to provide constant dividends and stable earnings regardless of the state of the stock market. Defensive stocks perform better than the broader market during recessions and perform below the market during economic expansion.

Cyclical Companies and Stocks

Cyclical stocks are highly correlated to economic cycles. A cyclical company's revenues and earnings significantly fluctuate between economic peaks and valleys, creating significant market exposure and risk. Examples of cyclical companies are in the steel, auto, or heavy manufacturing industries. Such companies expect to do well during economic expansion and poorly during economic contraction due to their relative products. A cyclical stock will experience changes in its rate of return greater than the overall market's return; having a higher CAPM and higher Beta translates to a higher return expectation on the stock when the market is doing well. Most investors who invest in cyclical stocks are attempting to time the market by buying the stock at a low point in the business cycle and selling at the high point. In a portfolio of stocks, an investor will usually add some cyclical stock holdings because they tend to outperform the market during periods of economic strength. Long-term investors aiming for long-term growth with managed volatility seek to balance their portfolios with a mix of cyclical stocks and defensive stocks who are more stable during economic downturn.

Speculative Companies and Stocks

A speculative company is one whose assets involve great risk but also have a possibility of great return. A good example of a speculative company is in the oil and gas exploration industry. A speculative stock enjoys a high probability of low or negative rates of return and a low probability of normal or high rates of return. A speculative company, such as an emergency company, has a significant percentage of its business tied up in projects in which the probability of failure is high. However, should a project succeed, the returns can be very significant.

Another good example of a speculative company could be a biotech company that is investing heavy amounts of resources into the research and development of a new drug. These types of companies can often experience many failures before a project succeeds and tend to face hurdles such as regulatory approvals. However, in the case of pharmaceuticals, if a drug is produced and approved by the FDA, the potential returns for investing before the event occurs can be significant. Although most speculative stocks are associated with early-stage companies, a large established company could become a speculative stock, especially if it's going through tough times. These companies are known as "fallen angels" and may offer the investor an opportunity to make a good return on his or her speculation that the business will turn around. It can become very difficult to value these companies since most of the time their income and cash is negative, rendering the traditional price-earnings ratios useless.

TECHNICAL ANALYSIS

Technical analysis is used by analysts to predict stock patterns. The analysis uses a lot of historical charts and tables to predict future movements of stocks or industry sectors. A few concepts for technical analysis include **trendlines, resistance levels, support levels, and momentum indicators** techniques. Figure 10.4 shows a few examples of technical analysis for the same stock.

Trendline Analysis

A trendline is a straight line that is drawn over the high and low fluctuations to show direction of price. Trendlines are a visual representation of support and resistance levels. They also show direction and the speed of price.

Figure 10.4a shows that the stock price as of end of September starts at $62 and moves to $67 in October, a brief drop to $65 in November, and an uptick in December and January 2019 to $70 and $72, respectively. The analyst has now five points to plot on a chart, starting at $62, then moving to, in 5 months, t $72. The technical analyst, or the chartist in this case, draws a line between all five price points, showing an upward trendline. The trendline shows a positive slope and is therefore telling the analyst to buy in the direction of the trend. If stock price was going down, then trendline has a negative slope and the analyst should sell in the direction of the trend.

FIGURE 10.4 TECHNICAL ANALYSIS

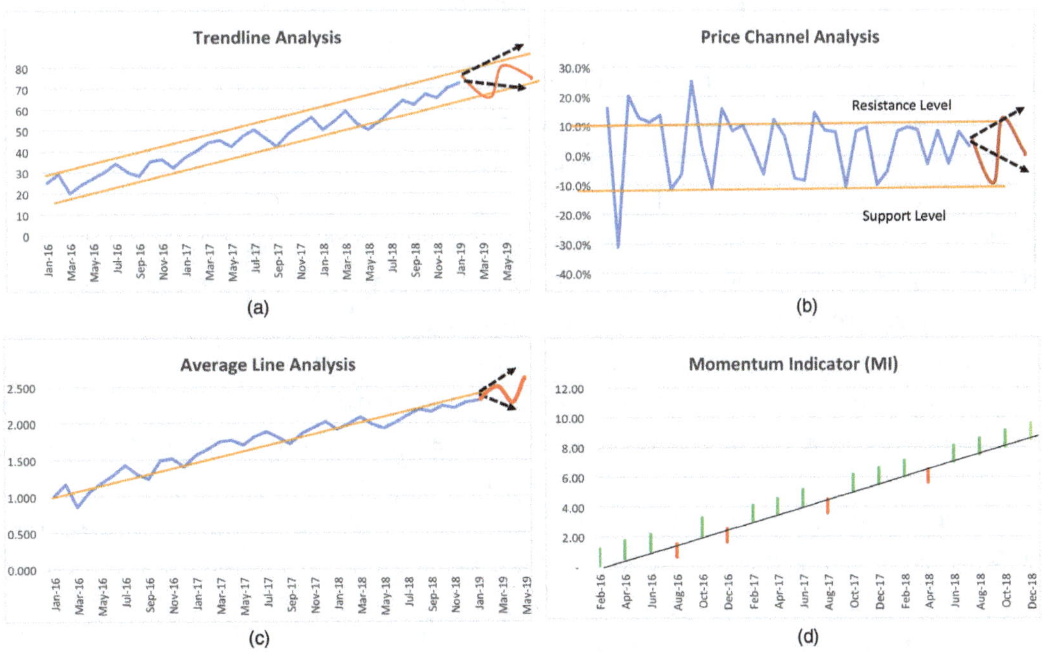

Price Channel

This technical method analyzes the percentage change of the stock and use the peaks and troughs over time to predict the future resistance and support level of the stock. The analyst buys the stock at the support level and sells it at the resistance level. Using channel analysis is best suited for low-volatile stocks. Analysts consider the stock bullish when the price jumps above the upper trendline and bearish when the stock drops below the lower trendline.

Average-Line Analysis

This analysis shown in figure 10.4c is plotting the cumulative increase in stock around the average line and analyzing the upward and downward fluctuations of the stock price as compared to the average line. This is a very similar method that is used in options through the binomial option pricing model (BOPM).

Momentum Indicators Analysis (MI)

MI is the measurement of the speed or velocity of price changes. Momentum analysis assesses the rate of the rise or fall in stock prices. Momentum is calculated as a ratio of today's price to the price n periods ago:

$$MI = \frac{\text{close (i)}}{\text{close (i} - \text{n)}} \times 100$$

where close (i) is the close price of the current bar and close (i − n) is the close price n days ago. The MI compares the current price in relation to where the price was in the past. If the current price is higher than the price in the past, then MI is positive. When the current price is lower than the price in the past, then the MI is negative. When the stock approaches its peak, there is a sharp increase of the MI ratio. The analysts recognize the point of momentum and continue to buy or sell the stock when the price passes the peak or the trough, respectively. In graph terms, assuming zero line indicates of the peak or trough and any crossing of the zero line implies that the price of the stock, future, or currency pair is reversing course, either by having bottomed out or by breaking out above recent highs; this is typically viewed as a bullish signal called "bullish divergence." If MI crosses below the zero line, it can generally mean two things: the future, currency pair, or stock's price has topped out and is reversing or the price has broken below recent lows, which gives the analyst bearish signals or bearish divergence.

Figure 10.4c shows an example of momentum indicators (MI) green and red bars reflecting bullish and bearish divergences of the stock.

BEHAVIORAL FINANCE ANALYSIS

"Animal spirits" is the term that John Maynard Keynes used in his 1936 book *The General Theory of Employment, Interest and Money* to describing the emotion or affect that human behavior influenced. This is measured today known as "consumer confidence."

The original passage by Keynes (1936) reads:

> Even apart from the instability due to speculation, there is the instability due to the characteristic of human nature that a large proportion of our positive activities depend on spontaneous optimism rather than mathematical expectations, whether moral or hedonistic or economic. Most, probably, of our decisions to do something positive, the full consequences of which will be drawn out over many days to come, can only be taken as the result of animal spirits—a spontaneous urge to action rather than inaction, and not as the outcome of a weighted average of quantitative benefits multiplied by quantitative probabilities. (pages 161–162)

Keynes seems to be referencing term for spontaneous action or the animal spirit., which is the spirit that drives human thought, feeling, and action for various spontaneous decisions, in this case buying or selling the stock and ignoring fundamental and/or technical analysis.

Lots of textbooks include concepts of behavioral finance that have impacted many stock market movements in the past. The basic concept is how humans interpret and process the information. Specific concepts used in behavioral finance are concepts such **forecasting errors, overconfidence, and conservativism.** Behavioral biases concepts include **framing, mental accounting, and regret avoidance.**

> **Forecasting errors** represent how humans justify their expectation, positive or negative, when analyzing the could-ignore signs that do not reflect their beliefs and only use the variables that meet their expectation. For example, the valuation process includes many variables including comparing the existing company EBITDA multiple to the industry segment. If they are a few outliers that that show high multiples but statistically speaking need to come, the analyst could keep them in if the outcome results to a higher average, hence a higher value of the company.
>
> **Overconfidence** includes how people overestimate. Overconfidence is seen a lot on Wall Street and can affect how humans make decisions, including how they invest affecting the value of stocks and assets.
>
> **Conservatism** reflects that is someone is conservative with the decision of buying or selling and can be too slow as he or she is analyzing all the risks associated with

such decision. This is the basis of one of the technical analyses called **momentum indicator (MI).**

Framing, a behavioral bias concept, describes how decisions are made based how the choices are framed. Sometimes analysts can frame the risks differently that others based on bias assumptions—a concept that the SEC constantly measures as part of their investigation into a specific filing or trade.

Mental accounting, a behavioral bias, describes how decisions are segregated. For example, an investor may make a different decision with one investment than another even though he or she could have the risks due to bias on the one versus the other.

Regret avoidance, a behavioral bias, describes when investors make decisions that turn out to be unsuccessful, they blame themselves more that a decision that was more conventional. For example, if the investor invests in a startup that goes bad, then he or she will blame him or herself but if an investment is made in a blue-chip company, he or she will blame the market.

STOCK VALUATION

Chapter 17 gives a comprehensive analytical approach of valuating a company by using eight different methods. Most valuation techniques used in the primary are very similar to secondary markets. Most analysts who follow stocks are constantly testing the current prices by using various technical and fundamental techniques. Of course, if you are an analyst who is actively trading certain stocks you develop a sense of another type of analysis: behavioral.

CASE STUDY

HYATT HOTELS CORPORATION (H)

The following methodologies addresses both the technical and fundamental analysis of testing if the current stock is trading at fair price. We will use Hyatt Hotels Corporation (H), a publicly traded company, as an example. The analyst's challenge is to recommend whether the current stock price of Hyatt of \$71.00 is traded fairly. Figure 10.5 shows that the average stock price is estimated at \$80 based on three valuation methods discussed later in the chapter.

The following three methods are used to value Hyatt's stock, as illustrated.

INTRINSIC VALUE METHOD

The formula for the intrinsic value is

$$V_0 = \frac{D_1 + P_1}{1+k}$$

where D1 is the dividend expected to receive within a year, P1 is the expected stock price a year from now, and k is the discount rate or expected rate of return.

Figure 10.6 shows that Hyatt's stock price using the intrinsic value and CAPM method is estimated at \$81.88 based on the average analyst expectation that the stock will be at \$90 by next year (P1=\$90) and dividends of \$1.80 per share expected to be paid within the year. To calculate the stock price using this method, we first need to calculate the expected equity return. This expected rate of 12.12% using CAPM, is based on Hyatt's stock beta of 1.18x, risk-free rate of 1.50%, and a given market premium of 9.0% (historical market premium return for this size company).

DIVIDEND DISCOUNT MODEL (DDM)

This second technical method for valuing the company can only be used if the company is a frequent payer of dividends. The value of the stock is basically the present value of

FIGURE 10.5 HYATT HOTELS (SUMMARY OF STOCK VALUATION)

Stock Price		
Book Value Equity	\$	31.46
Market Value / Using the Stock Price	\$	71.00
Intrinsic Value	\$	81.88
Dividend Discount Model (DDM)	\$	93.40
Average EBITDA Industry Trading Multiples	\$	73.28
Discount Cash Flow Valuation Analysis	\$	66.69
Average of other methods	**\$**	**78.81**

FIGURE 10.6 HYATT HOTELS (INTRINSIC VALUE)

Intrinsic Value

Using CAPM = k = Rf + (Beta * Premium)	
Risk Free =	1.50%
Beta =	1.18x
Premium=	9.00%
Market Return (Rf + Premium)=	10.50%
RoR =	12.12%

Intrinsic Value = V0 = [E(D1) + E (P1)] / (1+k)		
D1=	$1.80	
Analyst Est.	$1.64	(Average Earnings per share)
PE Multiple	17.00x	
Exp (P1)=	$90.00	(Avg Target by Analysts for 9/19)
k=	12.1%	
V0 (Stock Price)=	$ 81.88	

the dividend to be received at the end of the first year, assuming the buyer will hold the stock for a year. To calculate such value using the DDM method, the analyst needs the expected price of the stock a year from now, the expected dividend per share paid within the year, and a discount rate, which is derived using the capital asset pricing model (CAPM):

$$V = \frac{D1}{k - g}$$

where D1 is the expected dividend, k is the discount rate, and g is the expected growth rate.

Figure 10.7 shows that the stock price is valued at $93.40. The price is calculated assuming a dividend of $1.80 per share, a 12.12% discount rate using CAPM (calculated in method #2) and 10% dividend growth.

Using Comparable Trading EBITDA Multiples

This method, most used by mergers and acquisitions professionals, looks at the ratio of the enterprise value to earnings before interest, taxes, depreciation and amortization (EV/EBITDA) for each of the pier companies and applies the average to measure the company's value. The average multiple provides a benchmark, which the analyst can establish as the basis for valuating both private and publicly traded companies. The basic idea is that as the company increases its earnings based on either favorable economic conditions or management decisions from year to year, then the value should also follow in a

FIGURE 10.7 HYATT HOTELS (DIVIDEND DISCOUNT MODEL)

Dividend Discount Model (DDM)

Constant-Growth DDM (Gordon Model) V0 = D1 / (k-g)	
D1 =	$1.80
Expected Equity Return (k)=	12.12%
Expected Growth (g) =	10.00%
V0 (Stock Pice) =	$ 93.40

Expected HPR = E 9r) = [E (d1) + (E(p1) - P0) / P0		
Dividend (d1)	$1.80	(No growth)
P1 = P0+D	$72.80	
P0	$ 71.00	
Exp. HPR=	5.07%	

FIGURE 10.8 HYATT HOTELS (EBITDA TRADING MULTIPLE)

Average EBITDA Industry Trading Multiples (Hotels)

		SP	SO	SP * SO = EQ	D	C	Q + D - C = E	E	EV / E	
Company	**Symbol**	**Stock Price**	**Stocks Outstanding ($000)**	**Equity Value ($000)**	**Debt (ST&LT) ($000)**	**Cash ($000)**	**Enterprise Value ($000)**	**EBITDA ($000)**	**EBITDA Multiple**	**Beta**
Choice Hotels International	CHH	$83.20	56,572	4,706,804	796,200	37,150	5,465,854	335,560	16.29x	1.13x
Hilton Worldwide Holdings Inc.	HLT	$80.96	298,190	24,141,462	7,580,000	423,000	31,298,462	1,760,000	17.78x	1.45x
Intercontinental Hotel	IHG	$62.58	190,000	11,890,200	2,040,000	233,000	13,697,200	843,000	16.25x	1.59x
Marcus Corporation	MCS	$40.80	19,680	802,944	317,420	18,070	1,102,294	139,930	7.88x	0.32x
Marriott International	MAR	$130.90	346,990	45,420,991	8,990,000	366,000	54,044,991	2,850,000	18.96x	1.36x
Park Hotels & Resorts Inc.	PK	$32.89	201,180	6,616,810	3,080,000	421,000	9,275,810	734,000	12.64x	1.28x
Belmond (A/K Orient Express Hotels Ltd)	BEL	$17.00	102,960	1,750,320	785,170	162,010	2,373,480	103,750	22.88x	1.61x
Wyndham Worldwide	WYN	$136.73	108,640	14,854,347	8,310,000	1,500,000	21,664,347	1,790,000	12.10x	1.33x
Hyatt	HOT	$71.00	117,448	8,338,808	1,440,000	879,000	8,899,808	585,000	15.21x	1.18x

EBITDA * Average Multiple	585,000	15.67x	**Average**	15.60x	1.24x
			Outliers	15.67x	

Hyatt's Enteprise Value	**9,167,303**
Less Debt	(1,440,000)
Plus Cash	879,000
Equity Price	8,606,303
Shares Outstanding	117,448
Stock Price	$ 73.28

relatively consistent way. In general, industries with higher growth characteristics enjoy higher multiples of earnings. Companies in the same industry have the same economic factors and conditions and should have similar valuations.

In figure 10.8, the average EBITDA multiple, after taking out the high and low as outliers, is 15.67x, representing slightly higher than Hyatt's current EBITDA multiple of 15.21x. Using the 15.67 times Hyatt's last reported EBITDA of $585 million, Hyatt's enterprise value is calculated at $9.17 billion representing a stock price of $73.28.

DISCOUNT CASH FLOW METHOD (DCF)

This method is the most fundamental method that is used to value many types of companies. This method, called the DCF method, that is broadly used by many investors, advisors, banks, and academics is premised on the principle that the value of a company can be derived by the present value of its projected free cash flow (FCF). We will learn later that this FCF is derived from various assumptions, starting from revenue and subtracting operating and capital costs.

To value the company using the DCF method the analyst needs to derive the following four items:

1. Setting up a stream of cash flows
2. Identifying an exit year
3. Calculating the value at exit year (terminal value)
4. Using the appropriate discount rate to value the present value of the firm

Stream of Cash Flows

The first requirement for valuating a privately owned company is to calculate the projected equity cash flow of the company. The spreadsheet is based on certain information from the income statement, cash flow, and balance sheet. Following the last chapter where we learn how to build projections, we continue to apply this projection to value the company using this method. In chapter 17 the projection assumptions are run on revenue expectations in the next 5–6 years, then subtracting cost of revenues and operating expenses to get to EBITDA. After the EBITDA is set, the analysis subtracts depreciation, amortization and interest so it will recalculate the tax expense and then add back those items to get to a cash flow before other cash outflows, including working capital expense and capital expenditures. The cash flow of the firm before debt services represents the first line of the cash outflow, assuming the company is unlevered—an important line for calculating the terminal value. The free cash flow (FCF) represents the equity cash flow after the debt service obligations, including the payments of principal and interest. Then, this stream of cash flow is used for calculating the present value of the equity and the company. To complete the DCF analysis, in addition to calculating the 5–6-year cash outlay, the analyst needs to identify the exit year, estimate the terminal value, and use a discount rate to calculate the present value of the stock price.

Exit Year

Once the stream of cash flows is determined, we then need to choose an exit year. To complete the DCF method, the analyst must assume that there is an exit strategy set up, so the value of the firm will include a value at the exit year even if the investor is not planning to sell the company in 4 or 5 years. This is to artificially establish a realization or return on investment. Typically, the exit year is between 4–6 years.

Terminal Value

The third item that the analyst needs to quantify is the terminal value of the firm at the exit year. This value is basically the expected enterprise value or the value at which the current owner is expected to sell the company in 4–6 years. There are many methods to calculate the terminal value. The most common ones used on Wall Street are the EBITDA multiple and perpetuity growth methods. Our example for Hyatt (figure 10.9) assumes a terminal value using the current EBITDA multiple benchmark of 15.3x multiplied by company's exit year's EBITDA, resulting in approximately $12.3 billion. The second method to calculate the terminal value, as shown in figure 10.9, shows a terminal value of $21.7 billion. The formula of this method, using the perpetuity growth method, is to take next year's cash flow before debt service and divide it by the difference of the firm's discount rate and growth rate. The discount rate used is the weighted average capital cost (WACC).

Discount Rate

The fourth item that the analyst needs to quantify after the stream of cash flow is established, the exit year is determined, and the terminal value is calculated is the discount rate. The combined amounts of the yearly future free cash flows and terminal value after the outstanding debt is subtracted in the exit year represents the expected equity cash flow, or the cash flow that the investor is projecting to receive while owning the company. The present value of these cash flows is based on what the equity is expecting to return on its initial investment.

Figure 10.9 shows the calculation of the four items including the stream of cash flows, the exit year, the terminal value, and the discount rate. The average terminal value at the exit year is approximately $15.3 billion, derived by the two methods of EBITDA multiples and perpetuity. Using the 9.86% WACC as a discount rate as calculated, Hyatt's enterprise value using this method is estimated at $7.8 billion representing a stock price of $66.69 or approximately 9.0% below the current price.

FIGURE 10.9 HYATT HOTELS (DCF ANALYSIS)

Discount Cash Flow Valuation Analysis

			year =	1	2	3	4	5	6
Discout Cash Flow Valuation Analysis	Historical Assumptions	Projected Assumptions	Input Actual 12/31/2019	12/31/2020	12/31/2021	12/31/2022	12/31/2023	EXIT YEAR 12/31/2024	12/31/2025
Revenues			4,763,000	4,905,890	5,249,302	5,616,753	6,009,926	6,430,621	6,945,071
Revenue Growth				3.0%	7.0%	7.0%	7.0%	7.0%	8.0%
Cost of Revenues (CoGS)	82.0%	82.0%	(3,905,660)	(4,022,830)	(4,304,428)	(4,605,738)	(4,928,139)	(5,273,109)	(5,694,958)
Operating Expenses (Excl. Non-rec.)	13.4%	13.0%	(636,340)	(637,766)	(682,409)	(730,178)	(781,290)	(835,981)	(902,859)
EBIT			221,000	245,295	262,465	280,838	300,496	321,531	347,254
Less Taxes (tax rate x of EBIT)		22.0%	-	(53,965)	(57,742)	(61,784)	(66,109)	(70,737)	(76,396)
Plus Depreciation	7.6%	7.5%	364,000	367,942	393,698	421,257	450,744	482,297	520,880
Less Working Capital	0.0%	0.0%		-	-	-	-	-	-
Less Capex	7.8%	7.5%	(369,999)	(367,942)	(393,698)	(421,257)	(450,744)	(482,297)	(520,880)
Cash Flow			215,001	191,330	204,723	219,053	234,387	250,794	270,858
EBITDA			585,000	613,236	656,163	702,094	751,241	803,828	868,134
Debt (assuming 5% reduction of intial principal per year)			1,440,000	1,368,000	1,296,000	1,224,000	1,152,000	1,080,000	1,008,000
Terminal Value	Assumptions		Growth						
EBITDA Multiple Method	15.67x			(EBITDA x EBITDA Multiple)				12,596,464	
Perpetuity Method	9.86%		8.00%	Next Year's Cash Flow / (Discount Rate - Growth)				14,558,739	
Average			(80% of WACC)					13,577,601	
Less Debt Outstanding (at Exit)								(1,080,000)	
Plus Cash (at Exit)								-	
Equity Value at Terminal								12,497,601	
		PV (for $1)							
Equity Cash Flows	12.1%			191,330	204,723	219,053	234,387	12,748,396	
	PV (1) =	0.8919015	$170,647						
	PV (2) =	0.7954883	$162,855						
	PV (3) =	0.7094973	$155,418						
	PV (4) =	0.6328017	$148,321						
	PV (5) =	0.5643968	$7,195,154						
	PV=		$7,832,394						

Enterprise Value =	PV of Equity + PV of Debt
PV of Equity =	$7,832,394
Shares Outstanding	117,448
Stock Price	$ 66.69

Cost of Equity Calc	
Risk Free Rate (5 year)	1.50%
Premium based on MC =	9.00%
Hyatt Beta =	1.18x
Expected Equity Return =	12.1%

Interest 12/19 ($ 000s)
75,000
5.21% Rate

WACC Calc:		% Cap	AT RoR	WACC
Debt	1,440,000	28.0%	4.063%	1.139%
BV Equity	3,695,000	72.0%	12.120%	8.721%
		100.0%		9.860%

PROBLEMS

1. What companies are qualified to be listed in the national exchanges?
2. Name two national exchange markets where most of the stocks are traded in the U.S.
3. List a few differences between the exchange and over-the-counter markets.
4. What are the third and fourth markets?
5. Name at least two indices and their use.
6. What is the difference between price-weighted and capitalized-weighted indices?
7. What is the difference between a limit order and a market order?
8. What is the difference between brokered markets and dealer markets?
9. Why will someone buy stocks on margin?
10. Suppose that ZX Inc. is currently selling at $50 per share. You buy 200 shares, using $5,000 of your own money and borrowing the remainder of the purchase price from your broker. The rate on the margin loan is 5%.
    a. What is the percentage increase in the net worth of your brokerage account if the price of ZX Inc. changes to (i) $54, (ii) $50, (iii) $46?
    b. If the maintenance margin is 25%, how low can ZX Inc.'s price fall before you get a margin call?
    c. How would your answer to (b) change if you had financed the initial purchase with only $2,000 of your own money?
    d. What is the rate of return on your margined position (assuming again that you invest $5,000 of your own money) if ZX Inc. is selling after one year at (i) $54, (ii) $50, (iii) $46?
    e. Continue to assume that a year has passed. How low can ZX Inc.'s price fall before you get a margin call?
    f. Suppose that you sell short 400 shares of ZX Inc., currently selling for $50 per share what will your rate of return be after one year if ZX Inc. stock is selling at (i) $54, (ii) $50, (iii) $46? Assume that ZX Inc. pays no dividends.
11. Name a few program trading strategies and explain their objectives.
12. What is the difference between fundamental, technical, and behavioral analysis?
13. What is the investor's objective if they invest in the following type of stocks?
    a. Growth stocks
    b. Income stocks
    c. Value stocks
14. What is the difference between defensive companies and cyclical companies?
15. What are speculative companies?
16. List a few technical analysis concepts and explain their use.

ONLINE TEMPLATES

The Excel spreadsheets used in the chapter can be accessed online via Cognella Active Learning platform.

CHAPTER 11

Corporate Bond Investments, Analysis, and Valuation

This chapter will give an overview of the secondary bond market and how investors trade bonds. It will repeat a few of the concepts introduced in chapter 1 regarding return analysis and the time value of money to analyze and value various investments in bonds and securitized bond vehicles. Entailed in the analysis includes a risk evaluation of the present factors including impacts of interest rate fluctuations, credit rating upgrades and downgrades, and refinancing risk. It will also cover various scenario analyses to determine factors such as duration and convexity.

LEARNING OBJECTIVES

After reading this chapter, students will be able to do the following:

- Understand how the secondary bond markets work and how these securities are traded
- Understand various type of corporate bonds and how they are structured
- Understand all the risks involved investing in corporate bonds
- Analyze various yield results including current yield (CY), yield to maturity (YTM), yield to call (YTC), and yield to worse (YTW)
- Calculate the market price, invoice price, duration, and convexity of a corporate bond

TRADING BONDS: AN OVERVIEW

In general, investing in bonds is safer than investing in stocks. The return is expected to be fixed, assuming the investor holds the bonds until the contractual maturity, thus the risk is estimated to be lower than the equity's investment risk. What gets a little complicated with holding corporate bonds is that the market value of these bonds could fluctuate due to many factors, such as interest rates, credit risk, market liquidity, and refinancing, as will be described later in this chapter.

AUTHOR'S NOTES

When I was a junior analyst in the late 1980s working for Bank of America's leveraged finance department, I was fascinated by how deals could be strategically structured and priced, no matter how much risk the company and transaction carried. My manager at the time always used to say, "Any deal can get done as long as you can price it right." For many of the transactions, the odds were that of pulling an ace of hearts out of a deck of 52 cards. However, if people believe they can get paid $52 for a $1 bet; there will always be a game—no matter the odds of losing being 51 out of 52. I remember specifically the investment bank Drexel Burnham Lambert and one of their most successful managers, Michael Milken, being able to get some of the toughest deals I had ever seen financed and executed. I reviewed many of these deals and was stunned by how they would always manage to find a structure that worked. If the company could not pay interest, no problem: The deal was engineered to include deferred interest bonds, ironically called paid-in-kind (PIK) bonds. I remember, as a young analyst, I was so fascinated by Drexel, Michael Milken, and their famous annual convention held at the Beverly Hilton Hotel in Los Angeles. The event was later tokened the Predator's Ball, featuring speakers categorized as some of the nation's most prominent corporate raiders, private equity firm managers, and financiers such as Ron Perelman, Carl Icahn, and Henry Kravis with KKR—all Drexel's clients. These conventions became the place to go if an analyst or investor wanted to learn how to financially engineer leveraged buyouts and hostile takeovers using this new innovative financing, at the time called high-yield bonds or "junk" bonds. The convention also attracted major banks and institutional investors in high-yield bonds as well as management teams from companies involved in leveraged buyouts. This famous convention became the title of the book, The Predators' Ball: The Inside Story of Drexel Burnham and the Rise of the Junk Bond Raiders. *Since then a lot of similar conventions are organized by many major investment banks called high-yield and leveraged finance conferences that I attended in places like Miami Beach, Las Vegas, and the Bahamas—all the high-energy places where you are comfortable signing risky deals over a margarita drink. Despite the bad publicity, high volatility, and high risk, these high-yield bonds will always dominate the corporate bond market. Issuers continue to turn to high-yield bonds, which investors are happy to actively purchase and trade.*

KEY TAKEAWAYS

- The risk characteristics of investing in bonds are much different than investing in stocks. Initial bond investors don't have much upside and primarily seek stability on both ends: high and low. If the company does very well, the stockholders get the benefit and the bond holders will most likely be refinanced out. If the company does very badly, then the bond holders will get stuck holding a security that will be valued at a discount.
- Where stock investors focus on volatility as the main risk, bond investor focus on interest rates and duration as the main risk.
- Bonds are referred to as fixed-income securities because of the interest payment or coupon payments they receive. It is important to factor in that these payments could be cut short of the intended duration (bought out). The analysis therefore needs to incorporate the possibility of early retirement or redemption and how it can affect the expected returns.
- Yield to maturity (YTM) is not the only return measurement of a bond. If the company redeems or calls the bonds early, the return measurement will be Yield-to-Call (YTC). In any case, the analyst needs to run all the scenarios including YTM and YTC and report the worst-case scenario: yield to worse (YTW).
- Given the sensitivity to interest rate fluctuations, especially holding a fixed-rate security, the analyst will also need to run and asses other performance measurements such as duration and convexity.

SECONDARY BOND MARKETS: AN OVERVIEW

In the United States, the secondary market for publicly traded bonds takes place in over-the-counter transactions. Like stocks, brokers and dealers of bonds need to register with the SEC and report all secondary trading activities in a centralized reporting platform called TRACE, which stands for trade reporting and compliance engine. Specifically, it requires that all brokers and dealers who are member firms of the Financial Integrity Regulatory Authority (FINRA) report transactions in corporate bonds to TRACE including the volume and price, advances and declines, and the 10 most active investment-grade, high-yield, and convertible bonds.

Bonds that are privately placed are exempt from registration with the SEC. Many private placements and other 144A bonds trade in the secondary markets among institutional investors. The secondary market's bond prices are not publicized but rather shared between institutions, similar to bank loans, discussed in the next chapter.

As it was discussed in detail in the primary market section of this textbook, the bonds are rated, as required by the SEC, by two independent rating agencies before they are issued. As a precaution, they continue to be monitored for upgrades or downgrades, a very important factor for valuing the bonds in the secondary market. The rating that is assigned to the bond security is an estimation on the probability of default. **The rating agencies' sole objective when measuring the risk of default for bonds is to protect the public investor who is not sophisticated enough to analyze the risk of the company, raise debt, nor measure the probability of default.** The rating agencies such as Standard & Poor's (S&P), Moody's, and Fitch assign two to three separate ratings: One rating is for the company that is specifically issuing the bonds, one is for the bonds themselves, and in many cases the rating agency will issue a rate for large syndicated bank loans that are being bought by an array of funds.

Figure 11.1 shows the corporate bond rating system and the symbols assigned and is broken down into five categories of risk, described in chapter 7, including AAA risk-free grade, investment grade, non-investment grade, and distress and default grades.

Bonds are basically traded in two separate markets: investment grade and non-investment grade (high yield). Investment and commercial banks are organized to have two separate departments ranging from corporate finance to trading activities. Investment-grade bonds are rated from BBB up to AA. Non-investment-grade bonds are rated from BB down to CCC (speculative grade). A summary review, taken out of chapter 7's discussion on bonds, is described next.

INVESTMENT GRADE BONDS (BBB TO AA)

A bond is considered investment grade (IG) if the rating is BBB- or Baa3 and higher by S&P and Moody's, respectively. The designation of IG is sometimes a very important intended outcome for the companies that are in the process of raising bonds in the bond markets. Not only can the issuer's interest rate or coupon rate be substantially lower with an investment grade rating, but also certain capital structures become available. In addition, these structures have less restrictive terms and conditions integrated in the bond indenture. Typical IG bonds tend to have more flexibility in terms of refinancing these bonds with no penalties, as exampled by various non-investment grade bonds that include call prices. These call prices (discussed later in the chapter) are designed to discourage the issuer from early repayment of the bonds. The high price and redemption level are often set to be significantly higher than the par value in the case of non-investment grade versus investment grade. For example, a call price or redemption price of 105 suggests that the issuer desires to repay or call the bonds; the repayment is set at 105% of par or

FIGURE 11.1 CORPORATE BOND RATING

Description		Standard & Poor's	Moody's	Fitch
Highest Quality (Risk Free)	INVESTMENT GRADE	AAA	Aaa	AAA
High Quality	INVESTMENT GRADE	AA+ AA AA-	Aa1 Aa2 Aa3	AA+ AA AA-
Strong Payment Capacity	INVESTMENT GRADE	A+ A A-	A1 A2 A3	A+ A A-
Adequate Payment Capacity	INVESTMENT GRADE	BBB+ BBB BBB-	Baa1 Baa2 Baa3	BBB+ BBB BBB-
Likely to fullfill Obligations	NON-INVESTMENT GRADE (HIGH YEILD)	BB+ BB BB-	Ba1 Ba2 Ba3	BB+ BB BB-
High-risk Obligations	NON-INVESTMENT GRADE (HIGH YEILD)	B+ B B-	B1 B2 B3	B+ B B-
Current Vulnarable to Default	DISTRESS	CCC+ CCC CCC- CC C	Caa	CCC
Default	DEFAULT	D	D	DDD,DD,D

5% penalty—a very steep arrangement. Most IG bonds are not structured that way, giving flexibility to the issuer to refinance earlier if, for example, the rates drop or the issuer gets upgraded and can get a better coupon rate with a new bond. Another benefit an IG issuer can enjoy is a more flexible covenant package where there are less restrictions on business actions such as paying dividends to shareholders or structuring the bonds as unsecured (no pledge of collateral).

Typical IG bond structures include a "make-whole" call premium provision to address a situation where the issuer repays the bonds earlier than maturity. This feature allows an issuer to entirely avoid the call structure issue (which is typically included in non-investment grade structures; discussed in the next section). The make-whole premium is made up of penalty fees that the issuer pays over the market value of the bonds.

NON-INVESTMENT-GRADE BONDS OR HIGH-YIELD BONDS (CCC TO BB+)

Non-investment-grade high-yield bonds are debt securities issued by corporations with ratings of BB- and Ba1 or lower by S&P and Moody's, respectively. The primary purpose of a high-yield bond is to finance companies that are seeking money for growth (i.e., M&A or LBO), working capital, recapitalization, refinancing existing debt, or other cash flow purposes.

Since these issuers are viewed as riskier given their low ratings and methods for financing, as compensation these bonds offer a higher interest rate and, in most cases, have additional investor-friendly structural features. The high-yield market was originally developed in the late 80s by Michael Milken, also referred to as the "junk bond king," while he was at Drexel Lambert, an investment bank. This type of corporate bond was developed to finance the mega leveraged buyout (LBO) deals in the 80s such as the KKR buyout of RJR Nabisco, illustrated in the satiric book and movie *Barbarians at the Gate*. Though these bonds are sometimes called junk bonds (typical B, B-, and CCC+ rated bonds) and have given the asset class some negative connotation over the years, this asset class has matured into a solid 25% of the overall corporate bond market, according to Bond Market Association estimates.

High-yield bond indentures typically include call protection limits or provisions. This gives the issuer the ability to call the bond for redemption. Typically, it is at the half term of the bonds. For example, 10-year bonds will carry 5 years of call protection. Using the 10-year example, the call prices or redemptions could be set at 105, 104, 103, 102, and 101 for years 1, 2, 3, 4, and 5 from issuance, respectively. That means if the issuer decides to call (refinance) the bonds by the third anniversary from the issuance, he or she needs to repay the bonds at 103% of par, representing a 3% penalty for early termination. Some high-yield bonds are structured as 7-year (non-call 3) paper or 8-year (non-call 5) bonds. These bonds are not callable, which means that if the issuer for some reason needs to terminate the bonds during the non-call period, he or she will have to pay all the future interest for the non-callable period. In this case, the repayment amount is calculated by the present value of all future coupons that would have been paid through the non-call period.

BOND INVESTMENT CONCEPTS: REINTRODUCED

The following concepts will be used to explain the secondary trading of bonds and the various factors bond research analysts focus on when evaluating bonds. Since bonds are debt instruments, as discussed in earlier chapters, there are four important **money terms** that are relevant in every bond contract: initial and secondary price values, interest rates and pricing, days, and contractual payments.

BOND VALUE CONCEPTS

1. **Face value (par value):** The face value, or par value, of a bond is the amount the issuer pays at maturity and the starting point for calculating the coupon rate (e.g., 5% coupon rate pays 5% of \$1,000 or \$50 per year). Each bond is basically valued at \$1,000 or par (100% of \$1,000), and this is the basis for what the issuer receives as initial proceeds per bond before any fee adjustments are netted out in a form of original issue discount (OID), which represents the below-par original issue price. However, the face value of \$1,000 still represents what the issuer will pay to holders at maturity.
2. **Market value/market price (clean price):** Secondary pricing starts on the day of issuance until the bonds are refinanced. When they say that the market price of a bond is trading at either a discount, at par, or at a premium, it indicates the bond can be bought below a percentage of \$1,000, at \$1,000, or above \$1,000 per bond, respectively. For example, a bond that is trading at 98 means that you can trade it in the secondary market at 98% of a \$1,000 or \$980. This bond is considered to be trading at a discount. If a bond is trading at 103, then the secondary market value is 103% of \$1,000, or \$1,030 market price. This is sometimes referred to as the clean price, as compared to the dirty price, discussed later, that includes accrued interest. The other possibility is for the stock to be trading at par or 100% of \$1,000; in such case the secondary market price would be \$1,000. If the investor is expecting a higher yield on the bond, then the market value of the bond will decrease to a discount level that meets the expected yield. The formula for calculating the market value and price when the yield to maturity is known can be calculated as follows:

$$MV = \sum_{1}^{n} \frac{CP}{(1+YTM)^{n}} + \frac{\$1{,}000}{(1+YTM)^{n}} \text{ and } MV/10 = MP$$

where MV is the market value of the bond, CP is the coupon payment, YTM is the yield to maturity, and n is the number of years remaining until maturity. The market price (MP) or the trading price can be calculated by dividing the market value of the bonds by a factor of 10, considering that we are analyzing 10-year

FIGURE 11.2 MARKET PRICE

	B	C	D	E	F	G	H	I	J
2	**MARKET PRICE**								
3	**USING EXCEL FORMULAS**				**USING PRESENT VALUE CALCULATIONS**				
4									
5	Face Value =		1,000		**# Pmts**	**Coupon Dates**	**Coupon Payment (CP)**	**Present Value of (CP)**	
6	Settlement Date=		15/01/19		0	15/01/19			=+$D$8/2*$D$5
7	Maturity Date=		15/01/24		1	15/07/19	21.25	20.76	=+H7/((1+$D$9/2)^F7)
8	Coupon Rate=		4.250%		2	15/01/20	21.25	20.28	or =PV($D$9/2,F7,0,H7)
9	**Yield to Maturity=**		**4.740%**		3	15/07/20	21.25	19.81	
10	Redemption value %=		100		4	15/01/21	21.25	19.35	
11	Frequency (Coupon Pmts per year)=		2		5	15/07/21	21.25	18.90	
12					6	15/01/22	21.25	18.46	
13	Market Price (% Par)		**97.841**		7	15/07/22	21.25	18.04	
14					8	15/01/23	21.25	17.62	
15			=PRICE(D5,D6,D7,D8,D9,D10)		9	15/07/23	21.25	17.21	
16			=PRICE(SD,MD,CR,YTM,R,F)		**10**	**15/01/24**	**1,021.25**	**807.99**	
17									
18			**=+$D$8/2*$D$5+$D$5**				Market Value =	978.41	=SUM(I7:I16)
19							Market Price =	**97.841**	=+I18/10
20									

bonds. Using the information shown in figure 11.2, the market value of the bond is calculated as follows:

$$MV = \sum_{1}^{10} \frac{21.25}{(1+0.0474/2)^{10}} + \frac{\$1{,}000}{(1+.0474)^{10}} = 170.42 + 807.99 = 978.41$$

$$MP = \frac{978.41}{10} = 97.841$$

Figure 11.2 shows that the coupon rate is 4.25% and the trading yield or yield to maturity (YTM) is at 4.74%. The calculated market price of 97.841 or market value of $978.41 per bond is calculated using both Excel formulas and the present value of the semi-annual coupon payments using the yield as a discount rate.

The reasons bond prices move up or down in the secondary market after the original issuance could be based on the following:

Change of risk-free rate: Movement of the risk-free rate such as the treasury rate after the federal government increases or decreases the fed funds rate can affect bonds' secondary market value. If the risk-free rate moves up as a result of the increasing rates, the risk premium between the risk-free rate and the fixed rate squeezes. As a result, if someone is looking to buy a bond, the rate hike/discount will be priced into the bond's bid price to get the same premium. He or she will therefore be buying at a discount to make up for the shortfall. All new issuances are priced off the treasury rate and set until maturity. The sensitivity of interest rates is one of the most important tools used by analysts to value bonds (discussed in detail later).

Rating downgrade/upgrade: Any rating agency action (upgrade or downgrade) will almost always affect the bond's price. The downgrade of a bond's rating by an agency, let's assume from BB to BB-, will also negatively affect the bond's price. The market prices on bonds shift from that of BB to BB- and thus demand a higher coupon rate. The discount price of such a bond is calculated so that the rate of return or yield expectation of the buyer will be in line with a BB- rating bond. The relationship between yield and market price will be discussed in the valuation section of this chapter.

Refinancing: The market price of bonds will be affected up or down, if for example the company announces an early retirement or early redemption of bonds prior to maturity. A few relevant scenarios include a merger and acquisition announcement that will trigger the refinancing of the existing bonds. Another example is an unexpected upgrade of bonds' rating, attracting the company to refinance the debt securities with a lower coupon payment. Also, if the bonds are cleared to be refinanced after the bond call period is over, which means they come with an "early repayment penalty," it will be enticing for the company to take advantage of favorable markets and replace the bonds with newer, cheaper ones.

3. **Invoice price (dirty price): The invoice price or "dirty price" is the total price of the bond including the market price and accrued interest.** This is the amount that you would pay or receive if you purchase or sell the bond. Basically, the invoice price is equal to the market price (discussed previously) plus the accrued interest (discussed later). An example shown in figure 11.3 shows the calculation of the invoice price. Corporate bonds (and municipal bonds) are based on a 360-day year when calculating the accrued interest. In other words, every month has 30 days (day-count basis)—even February has 30 days when calculating the accrued interest. Figure 11.3 shows that the market price of the bond is 98.50 or $985.00. The 7.5% F&A corporate bond will pay $37.50 (7.5%/2 x $1,000) in interest on February 28 and August 31 every year. Another important input item that is needed for calculating the days since the last coupon payment is the settlement date—the date that the investor settles or owns the bond. The "regular way trade" (per SEC definition) is T+3 business days (trade day + 3 days) to calculate the settlement day. In this example in figure 11.3, since the trade was executed on Thursday, January 17, the settlement day will be on the following

FIGURE 11.3 MARKET PRICE / INVOICE PRICE

Manual Example:

Bought (Traded) F&A the 7.50% Corporate Bond at 98.50 on Thursday, January 17, 2019

INPUT

Trading Date	Thursday, 17 January 19
Settlement Date (T+3 Business Days)	Tuesday, 22 January 19
Market Price	98.50
Coupon Rate	7.500%
Coupon Dates	F&A (Feb 28 and Aug 31)
Semi-Annual Coupon Payment	$37.50
Face Value	$1,000
Accrued Basis	360 Days

OUTPUT

Market Price Paid	$985.00	$98.50 x 10
Accrued Expenses	$29.58	37.50 x (142 / 180) = $29.58
Invoice Price	$1,014.58	

Total Days	142

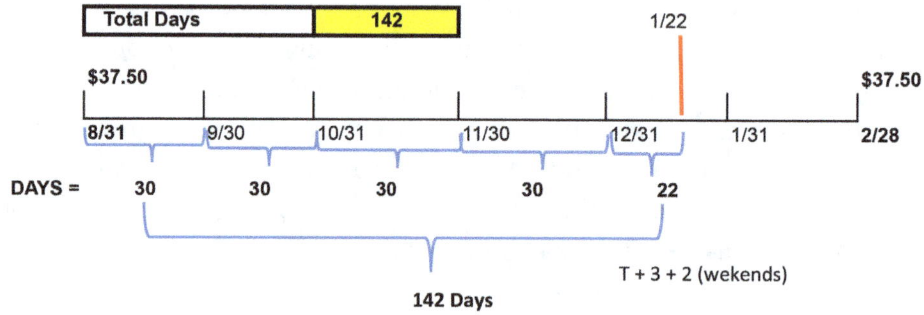

Tuesday, January 22 (T+3 business days + 2 weekend days). The days since the last coupon payment is calculated at 142 days (30 days in September + 30 days in October + 30 days in November + 30 days in December + 17 days in January through the trade days + 5 days = 142 days). This means that the investor who bought the bonds on January 17 and owned them on January 22 needs to pay back accrued interest of $29.50 representing 142 days that he/she did not own. That is 142 days out of 180 days between two coupon payments of $37.50. The $29.50 accrued interest is calculated as 142/180 x $40 = $29.50. The invoice price is calculated $1,042.58, calculated as $985.00 + $29.50 = $1,014.58.

Accrued interest can also be calculated using Excel formulas, shown in Figure 11.4.

4. **Redemption price:** The redemption price represents the bond repayment that the issuer gives to the investor on, usually, the date of maturity. The redemption is expressed as percentage of the face value of the bond. Most term bonds have a redemption price of 100 at maturity, which means that the issuer pays 100% of $1,000 for each bond. If the issuer decides to pay the bond early, assuming there

FIGURE 11.4 MARKET PRICE VS INVOICE PRICE

	B	C	D	E	F
2	**MARKET PRICE & INVOICE PRICE CALCULATION**				
3					
4	CALCULATING THE PRICE				
5	Settlement Date=		15/03/15		
6	Maturity Date=		15/01/25		
7	Coupon Rate=		4.250%		
8	**Yield to Maturity=**		**4.740%**		
9	Redemption value %=		100		
10	Coupon Pmts per year=		2		
11					
12	**Market Price =**		**96.179**		=PRICE(D5,D6,D7,D8,D9,D10)
13					
14	**Market Value =**		**$ 961.79**		=+D12*10
15					
16	Day since last coupon=		60		=COUPDAYBS(D5,D6,D10,0)
17	Days in coupon period=		180		=COUPDAYS(D5,D6,D10,0)
18	Accrued Interest=		$ 7.08		=(D16/D17)*D7*1000/2
19					
20	**Invoice Price=**		**$ 968.87**		=+D18+D14
21					

are no early repayment penalties (call provisions), the redemption price is 100 or 100% of $1,000 bond. Zero-coupon bonds (explained later) carry no coupon payments and are structured so that the initial price starts priced at a discount, depending on the deferred coupon rate, and reaches a redemption of 100.

5. **Call price/call premium:** Some indentures (bond agreements) are structured to have call provisions. These provisions allow the issuer to demand the bondholder sell the bonds back to the issuer usually for its face value, plus a set percentage as a "penalty" for early retirement. For example, for an indenture with a call price of 105 if the bonds are repaid or "called" within 2 years from issuance, the redemption price will then be 105% of face value, or $1,050 for each bond. **Depending on how the terms are structured, that premium may decrease as the bond matures.** A typical high-yield bond is structured to have 105, 104, 103, 102, 101, and 100 call prices if the issuer repays the bonds in the first, second, third, fourth, fifth, and sixth year from issuance, respectively. These arrangements are made either by design by the investor to discourage the issuer from early repayment because of hefty "penalties" or pushed by the issuer to have more flexibility of repayment on the debt. Some bonds are non-callable for a period of time, meaning the issuer cannot refinance the bonds for a certain duration unless he or she pays for all the future interest owed (make-whole provision). Once a bond has been called, the issuer has no legal obligation to make any interest payments after the call date.

6. **Original issuance discount (OID):** An original issue discount (OID) is the percentage discount from par value on the issuance date, hence the original issue discount. **It is the difference between the stated redemption price of 100 and the actual issue price, basically representing the upfront fee.** For example, if the OID is set at 98, the difference of 2 points from the face value (100–98) represents 2% of fees or $20 per bond to the investor as he or she will receive a redemption price of 100 or $1,000 plus the paid coupon rate (interest) that is set based on the $1,000. The OID going to the secondary market sets the secondary price 1 day before it trades up or down from there. A typical press announcement will say that "on day one the bond is trading above the OID level." The OID that is set in the primary market is part of the overall pricing of the bond. A bond that has an OID below a 100 when issued, by definition, will come with a bond yield higher than the coupon or nominal rate. For example, an 8% bond issued with a 98 OID will have an opening yield of 8.163% (annual coupon payment/market price = $80/980 = 0.08163 = 8.163%). Current yield is discussed later in the chapter.

BOND INTEREST AND YIELDS CONCEPTS

1. **Nominal yield (coupon rate): This is the contractual interest rate (typically a fixed rate) that the issuer needs to pay the bond holder until the bonds mature or gets repaid.** For example, an 8% bond pays $80 per year (8% x $1,000) per bond or $40 every 6 months (typically, bonds pay on a semi-annual basis).
2. **Accrued interest: This is the interest payment owed by the buyer and earned by the seller if the settlement day (the day the investor owns the bond) is between coupon.** Figure 11.2 shows the calculation of the accrued interest of $29.50. In Figure 11.2 shows an example of a 7.5% F&A corporate bond that pays $37.50 (7.5%/2 x $1,000) on February 28 and August 31 every year. Another important input item that is needed for calculating the days since the last coupon payment is the settlement date—the date that the investor settles or owns the bond. The "regular way trade" (per SEC definition) is T+3 business days (trade day + 3 days) to calculate the settlement day. In this example, in figure 11.2 since the trade was executed on Thursday, January 17, the settlement day will be on the following Tuesday, January 22 (T+3 business days + 2 weekend days). The days since the last coupon payment is calculated to be 142 days (30 days in September + 30 days is October + 30 days in November + 30 days in December + 17 days in January through the trade days + 5 days = 142 days). This means that the investor who bought the bonds on January 17 and owns them on January 22 needs to pay back accrued interest of $29.50, representing 142 days that he or she did

not own the bond. Therefore, with 142 days out of 180 days being the accrued period between two coupon payments of $37.50, the $29.50 of accrued interest is calculated as 142/180 x $40 = $29.50. Accrued interest can also be calculated using Excel formulas. Figure 11.4 shows the formulas for calculating the accrued interest on a different example.

3. **Yield to maturity (YTM):** This is the interest rate that is equal to the present value of a bond's cash flow to its current price. YTM assumes that the bond will be held until maturity and that all coupon payments representing the cash flows of the bond investment will be reinvested at a rate equal to the yield to maturity, though the formula for YTM is complicated to measure and therefore most analysts use Excel (shown in figure 11.5); however, the following is the rule of thumb method used in the FINRA license exams:

$$\frac{\text{Annual coupon or interest payment} \pm \left[\dfrac{\text{Discount or premium}}{\text{Years to maturity}}\right]}{\text{Average price of bonds}}$$

For example, using Figure 11.5 input numbers, the annual coupon payment is $42.50 (4.25% x $1000); the discount is $38.21 (1,000 - 961.79); estimated

FIGURE 11.5 YIELD TO MATURITY CALCULATIONS

	B	C	D	E	F	G	H	I
2								
3	**Yield to Maturity Calculation**							
4								
5	CALCULATING THE YTM					**# pmts**	**Remaining Dates**	**Cash Flow**
6	Settlement Date (SD) =		**15/01/18**					
7	Maturity Date (MD) =		15/01/25			0		(961.79)
8	Coupon Rate (CR) =		4.250%			1	15/07/18	21.25
9	**Market Price (MP) =**		**96.179**			2	15/01/19	21.25
10	Redemption value % (R) =		100			3	15/07/19	21.25
11	Coupon Pmts per year (Frequency (F) =		2			4	15/01/20	21.25
12						5	15/07/20	21.25
13	Yield to Maturity (YTM) =		**4.902%**	**=YIELD(D6,D7,D8,D9,D10,D11)**		6	15/01/21	21.25
14				**= YIELD (SD,MD,CR,MP,R,F)**		7	15/07/21	21.25
15						8	15/01/22	21.25
16						9	15/07/22	21.25
17						10	15/01/23	21.25
18						11	15/07/23	21.25
19						12	15/01/24	21.25
20						13	15/07/24	21.25
21						14	15/01/25	1,021.25
22								
23							IRR =	**4.902%**
24								**=IRR(I7:I21)*2**

years to maturity is 7 years (1/15/2018 today and 1/15/2025 is maturity); and the average price of the bonds is between $1,000 and $961.79 since issuance. Then, the rule of thumb yield to maturity is calculated as follows:

$$\frac{42.50+\left[\frac{38.21}{7}\right]}{(961.79+1{,}000)/2}=\frac{42.50+5.46}{980.90}=0.04889=4.9\%$$

Please note that the discount price amount (1,000 - 961.79) is added to the coupon payment on the numerator. If the bond is trading at a premium, then premium price amount is subtracted from the coupon payment.

Figure 11.5 shows an example of calculating the yield given the market price by using both bond yield Excel formulas and the internal rate of return methods.

4. **Yield to call (YTC): This is the yield on a bond assuming the bond is redeemed by the issuer at the first call date.** Yield to call differs from yield to maturity in that yield to call uses a bond's call date as the final maturity date (most often, the first call date). Figure 11.6 shows a yield to call calculation using both the Excel formulas and internal rate of return method (IRR). The call redemption prices shown are 105, 104, 103, 102, 101 for repayment of 1, 2, 3, 4, and 5 years from maturity.
5. **Yield to worst (YTW):** After calculating the YTM and YTC, the YTW represents the lowest yield generated between the YTM and the YTC. Figure 11.6 shows that the yield to worse is 8.249%, representing the lowest possible yield. (Please note that the current yield of 8.1218% should not be included.)
6. **Current yield (CY): This measures a quick annual rate of return for the investor who is planning to buy the bond in the secondary market**. The calculation is same as the holding period return (HPR), discussed in earlier chapters, which equals the expected cash flows from the investment divided by the initial investment (CF/I). The current yield (CY) formula is as follows:

$$\text{Current bond yield}=\frac{\text{Annual coupon or interest payment}}{\text{Market price}}$$

Figure 11.6 shows a $1,000 bond that is selling for $985 and paying an 8% coupon rate. The current yield is calculated as follows:

$$\text{Current bond yield}=\frac{\$80.00}{\$985.00}=0.08122=8.122\%$$

BOND DATES AND GENERAL TIMING CONCEPTS

1. **Issuance date:** This is the day the bonds get issued in the primary market and set the coupon payment dates on a semi-annual basis thereafter. Using the

FIGURE 11.6 YIELD TO MAURITY (YTM), YIELD TO CALL (YTC), YIELD TO WORSE (YTW) AND CURRENT YIELD (CY)

	B	C	D	E	F	G	H	I	J	K	L
2	**YIELD TO MAURITY (YTM), YIELD TO CALL (YTC), YIELD TO WORSE (YTW) and CURRENT YIELD (CY)**										
3	**EXCEL FORMULAS**										
4				**YTM**			**YTC1**	**YTC2**	**YTC3**	**YTC4**	**YTC5**
5	Issuance Date =			16/01/17			16/01/17	16/01/17	16/01/17	16/01/17	16/01/17
6	Trading Date =			Wednesday, 11 July 18			11/07/18	11/07/18	11/07/18	11/07/18	11/07/18
7											
8	**Settlement Date (T+3) (SD)**			Monday, 16 July 18			**16/07/18**	**16/07/18**	**16/07/18**	**16/07/18**	**16/07/18**
9	**Maturity Date / Call Date (MD)**			**16/01/27**			**16/01/18**	**16/01/19**	**16/01/20**	**16/01/21**	**16/01/22**
10	**Coupon Rate (CR)**			**8.00%**			**8.00%**	**8.00%**	**8.00%**	**8.00%**	**8.00%**
11	**Market Price (MP)**			**98.50**			**98.50**	**98.50**	**98.50**	**98.50**	**98.50**
12	**Redemption (Final payment % of Par) (R)**			**100.00**			**105.00**	**104.00**	**103.00**	**102.00**	**101.00**
13	**Frequency (payments per year) (F)**			**2**			**2**	**2**	**2**	**2**	**2**
14											
15	**Call Provision**						105.00	104.00	103.00	102.00	101.00
16											
17			**YTM=**	**8.249%**		**YTC=**	**NA**	**19.289%**	**11.006%**	**9.415%**	**8.757%**
18											
19			**YTW=**	**8.249%**		**CY=**	**8.1218%**				
20									**=YIELD(J9,J9,J11,J12,J13)**		
21	**Face Value**			**$1,000**					**=YIELD(SD,MD,CR,MP,R,F)**		
22	**Coupon Payment $**			**$40**	**=+E10*E21/2**						
23	**Years (Term)**			**10 Years**							
24											
25	**INTERNAL RATE OR RETURN METHOD**										
26											
27		**# Pmts**	**Coupon Dates**	**YTM**			**YTC1**	**YTC2**	**YTC3**	**YTC4**	**YTC5**
28				**(985.00)**				**(985.00)**	**(985.00)**	**(985.00)**	**(985.00)**
29		1	**16/01/19**	40.00				**1,080.00**	40.00	40.00	40.00
30		2	16/07/19	40.00					40.00	40.00	40.00
31		3	16/01/20	40.00					**1,070.00**	40.00	40.00
32		4	16/07/20	40.00						40.00	40.00
33		5	16/01/21	40.00						40.00	40.00
34		6	16/07/21	40.00						**1,060.00**	40.00
35		7	16/01/22	40.00							40.00
36		8	16/07/22	40.00			**=+$E$10/$E$13*$E$21+K12*10**				**1,050.00**
37		9	16/01/23	40.00							
38		10	16/07/23	40.00				**Payment $40**			
39		11	16/01/24	40.00				**Redemption $1020**			
40		12	16/07/24	40.00							
41		13	16/01/25	40.00							
42		14	16/07/25	40.00							
43		15	16/01/26	40.00							
44		16	16/07/26	40.00							
45		17	16/01/27	1,040.00							
46	**IRR =**			**8.249%**			**N/A**	**19.289%**	**11.006%**	**9.177%**	**8.666%**
47				**=IRR(E28:E45)*2**				**=IRR(I28:I45)*2**			

example in Figure 11.6, showing that the issuance date is January 16, 2017, the coupon payments are paid on January 16 and July 16 every year until maturity. The maturity day is also set. In this example, this a 10-year bond, so it matures exactly 10 years from January 16, 2017 with the maturity date shown in figure 11.4 of January 16, 2027. On issuance day, the company receives the money from the investors (net of fees or OID) and the bonds are free to trade in the secondary market.

2. **Maturity date:** This is the last day, contractually, that the bonds come due. If the bond is structured as a term bond (all of the principal payment is paid on the last day) paid on maturity day, the issuer pays the last coupon payment and the redemption price—typically the face value of $1,000 per bond or redemption of 100.
3. **Coupon dates:** Coupon payments are the dates that the issuer, contractually, needs to make the coupon payments. Typical corporate bonds are paid semi-annually,

and the first coupon date is set at exactly 6 months from date of issuance. All future payments are set to be every 6 months thereafter until maturity. In figure 11.6 the coupon dates are January 16 and July 16. Most bond desks will use the abbreviation J&J16 to indicate that the coupon payments are paid on January 16 and July 16. Coupon payment abbreviations are J&J for January and July, F&A for February and August, M&S for March and September, A&O for April and October, M&N for May and November, and J&D for June and December.

4. **Call dates:** These dates that are set contractually are the optional "maturity dates" that the issuer can call the bonds or repay at a set call price. Figure 11.6 shows that the five call dates are set 1 year to 5 years from the issuance at 1/16/2018, 1/16/2019, 1/16/2020, 1/16/2021, 1/16/2022. If the company calls the bonds on or before those dates the redemption prices are 105, 104, 103, 102, and 101, respectively.
5. **Trading day:** This is the day the investor buys or sells the bonds at the market price.
6. **Settlement day:** This is the day that the investor officially owns the bonds after he or she purchases them, typically 3 days before settlement. Typically, the "regular way" settlement is T+3, which means the investor buys or sells the bonds on trade day (T) and settles in 3 business days. Please note for a trade that happens on a Wednesday, Thursday, or Friday, the settlement is 3 business day later or 5 calender days. Also, it is important to know the holidays before calculating the settlement day. As mentioned, the settlement day is the day the investor takes possession of the bond (the bonds are delivered) and is therefore entitled to receive the next coupon payment as well as the principal repayment on the date of maturity. The coupon repayment portion since the last coupon date that is paid back to the previous owner is calculated by number of days during the period at a pro-rated amount for these days, called accrued interest.
7. **Day-count basis:** These are the number of days since the last coupon payment, and they are used as the basis to calculate the accrued interest, which will be part of the invoice price. Figure 11.3 shows that there are 142 days since the last coupon that the new investor needs to pay accrued interest on back to the previous investor.

BOND PAYMENT CONCEPTS

1. **Coupon payments:** These are the contractual payments that the issuer must pay to the investor, typically every 6 months. The annual coupon payment is calculated by taking the interest rate times the face value of the bond ($1,000). For example, an 8% bond pays $80 per year (8% x $1,000) or $40 every 6 months.

2. **Frequency of payments:** This is the number of times the coupon payment is paid per year. Most bond coupons are paid on a semi-annual basis with a frequency (F) of 2. For annually the F is 1, quarterly is 4, monthly is 12, and so on.
3. **Principal payments:** This refers to the face value of the bond, which is typically $1,000 per bond. The principal payment, which is different than the coupon or interest payment, can be paid back based on the structure of the bond as follows:
    - Term bond, the most popular, refers to the bond that pays all its principal amount at maturity. For example, for a 5-year bond the principal payments for years 1–5 are 0, 0, 0, 0, 1000.
    - Serial bond refers to the bond that pays all its principal amount equally across maturity. For example, for a 5-year bond the principal payments for years 1–5 are 200, 200, 200, 200, 200.
    - Bullet bond refers to the bond that pays a partial amount of the principal upfront and the balance at maturity. For example, for a 5-year bond the principal payments for years 1–5 are 50, 50, 50, 50, 800.

BOND INVESTMENT VALUATION CONCEPTS

Bond analysis lives by the fundamental concept that the value of the bonds in the secondary market go up and down based on the return expectation for the investor looking to buy these bonds. The investor knows that this type of security includes a contractual payment that the issuer needs to make every 6 months. The question for an investor who is looking to buy such a bond is to assess if the fixed payment (coupon payment) is enough to justify the risk. If it's not, then investors will be bidding for the bond at a discount to make up that shortfall expectation. Therefore, the expected return or yield affects the value of the bonds. Figure 11.7 shows the inverse relationship between bond values and yield.

Bond price calculation: See the description of the **market value** and how is derived. The bond price or market price is the quoted trading price expressed as percentage of market value. In Figure 11.4 the market price is calculated at 96.179, representing 96.179% of the face value of $1,000 and calculating the market value at $961.79. The formula to derive to a bond price or market price (MP) is as follows:

$$MV = \sum_{1}^{n} \frac{CP}{(1+YTM)^n} + \frac{\$1{,}000}{(1+YTM)^n} \text{ and } MP = \frac{MV}{10}$$

where MV is the market value of the bond, CP is the coupon payment, YTM is the yield to maturity, and n is the number of years remaining until maturity. The market price (MP) or the trading price can be calculated by dividing the market value of the bonds by a factor of 10.

FIGURE 11.7 MARKET PRICES VS YIELDS CHRISTAKIS DROUSSIOTIS

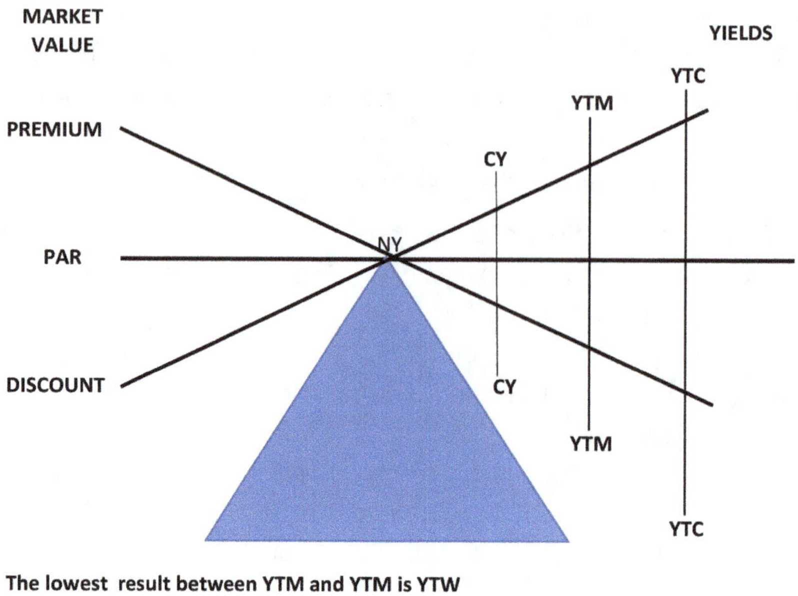

Duration (D) calculation: This is a measurement the price sensitivity of the bond and/or bond funds to changes with interest rates. They are two types of duration measurement:

- The **Macaulay duration**, expressed in years, identifies how many years it will take to recover the initial investment (market value) by calculating the weighted average of each present value of future coupon payments using the yield as a discount rate times the payment year. The formula to calculate the Macaulay duration is as follows:

$$Dm = \frac{\sum_{1}^{n} \frac{CF}{(1+y)^t}.t}{MV}$$

Where Dm is the Macaulay duration, t is the time period, CF is the cash flow payment or the coupon payment, y is the periodic yield, n is the number is periods, and MV is the market value of the bond (market price x 10).

- The **modified duration**: This duration, expressed in percentages, measures the average percentage of movement of the bond price for every 1% movement of the interest rate. For example, the price of a bond with a duration of 5 would be expected to move 5% for every 1% move in interest rates. The formula for calculating the modified duration is as follows:

$$\text{Modified Duration} = \frac{Dm}{1+\frac{y}{n}}$$

Where Dm is the Macaulay duration, y is the periodic yield, and n is the number is periods.

- **Convexity (C) calculation:** Like the modified duration, convexity is a further measurement of the relationship between the value of the bond and a movement of interest rates. It also measures the sensitivity of the bond price to 1% movement of the interest rates, but it's calculated on non-linear relationships. Duration can be a good measure of how bond prices may be affected due to sudden fluctuations in interest rates. Nevertheless, the relationship between bond prices and yields has more of a sloped or convex relationship. It is represented as a derivative to the duration. The formula for calculating the convexity is as follows:

$$\text{Convexity} = \frac{\frac{1}{(1+y)^2} \sum_{1}^{n} \frac{CF}{(1+y)^t}(t^2+t)}{MV \,.\, f^2}$$

Where y is the periodic yield, t is the time period, CF is the cash flow payment or the coupon payment, n is the number is periods, and *f* is the frequency of payments per year.

Figure 11.8 shows the calculation of all three including market price/market value, duration, and convexity.

FIGURE 11.8 BOND PRICE, DURATION & CONVEXITY

1	B	C	D	E
2	BOND PRICE, DURATION & CONVEXITY			
3	Sensitivity to interest rate movements			
4				
5	Face Value	1,000		
6	Coupon Rate	8.00%		
7	Life in Years	5		
8	Yield	10.00%		
9	Frequency	2		
10	Bond Price	$922.78	=-PV(E9/E10,E8*E10,E7*E6/E10,E6)	
11				
12	Macaulay Duration	4.18		
13				
14	Modified Duration	4.1%	=+E13/(1+E9/E8)/100	
15				
16	Convexity	17.83	1.93%	=+E17/E11
17				

Row	Period	Cash Flow	PV Cash Flow		Weighted	Duration Calc		Factor years	Convexity Calc	
18										
19	0	($922.78)								
20	1	40.00	38.10	=+C21/(1+($E$9/2))^B21	4.128%	0.04128	=+F21*B21	2.000	76.19	=+I21*D21
21	2	40.00	36.28		3.932%	0.07863		6.000	217.69	
22	3	40.00	34.55		3.744%	0.11233	=+B21+B21^2	12.000	414.64	
23	4	40.00	32.91		3.566%	0.14265		20.000	658.16	
24	5	40.00	31.34		3.396%	0.16982		30.000	940.23	
25	6	40.00	29.85		3.235%	0.19408		42.000	1,253.64	
26	7	40.00	28.43		3.081%	0.21564		56.000	1,591.93	
27	8	40.00	27.07		2.934%	0.23471		72.000	1,949.30	
28	9	40.00	25.78		2.794%	0.25148		90.000	2,320.59	
29	10	1,040.00	638.47		69.190%	6.91896		110.000	70,231.68	
30					100.000%	8.35959	=SUM(G21:G30)		79,654.05	=SUM(J20:J30)
31										
32		PRICE	922.78	=SUM(D20:D30)	DURATION	4.18	=+G31/2	CONVEXITY	17.83	=+((J31/((1+E9)^2))/(D33*E10^2))
33										

CASE STUDY

HERTZ GLOBAL HOLDINGS (HTZ)

Company Description (Source: Yahoo Finance)

Hertz Global Holdings, Inc. (Hertz) provides airport and off-airport vehicle rental and leasing services. It operates through three segments: U.S. rental car, international rental car, and all other operations. The company rents cars, vans, crossovers, and light trucks under the Hertz, Dollar, Thrifty, Firefly, and Flexicar brands from approximately 12,400 corporate and franchisee locations in North America, Europe, Latin America, Africa, Asia, Australia, the Caribbean, the Middle East, and New Zealand. It rents vehicles on an hourly, daily, weekend, weekly, monthly, or multi-month basis. The company also sells value-added services and vehicles, as well as offers car- and van-sharing membership services. In addition, the company offers vehicle and lease financing; acquisition and remarketing; license, title, and registration; vehicle maintenance consultation; fuel, accident, and toll management; telematics-based location, and driver performance and scorecard reporting; and fleet management services. As of December 31, 2019, it operated a rental fleet of approximately 567,600 vehicles in the United States and 204,000 vehicles in international operations. The company serves business and leisure customers. Hertz Global Holdings, Inc. was founded in 1918 and is headquartered in Estero, Florida.

Bond Issuance Information

On October 15, 2015, Hertz raised $500 million of bonds with the purpose of refinancing existing debt that was maturing the next year. The summary terms of the bond are as follows:

Bond Description	Hertz, 6.25% 15oct2025, USD		
Issuance Date:	October 15, 2015		
Face Value:	$1,000		
Amount:	$500 million		
Maturity Date:	October 15, 2025		
Coupon Rate:	6.25%		
Ratings:	B3/B-		
Coupon Dates:	April 15, October 15 (if it falls on a weekend or holiday, the payment will be made the day before)		
Call Dates/Price:	**Call Event**	**Call Dates**	**Call Prices**
	Non-Callable	Oct 15, 2015–Oct 15, 2018	Make-Whole
	First Call (last day)	Oct 15, 2019	103
	Second Call (last day)	Oct 15, 2020	102
	Third Call (last day)	Oct 15, 2021	101
	Callable	Oct 16 - 2021–Oct 15, 2025	100
Joint Bookrunners:	BARC/BAML/BMO/BNP/CA/GS/JPM/RBC		
Managers:	ONE/DB/MIZ/NATIXIS/RBS/SCOTIA/UNICREDIT		

BOND Trading Information

Trading Day:	Thursday, March 12, 2020
Settlement Day:	Regular Way (T + 3)
Market Price	97.50

Project

1. Calculate the market value and invoice price.
2. Construct a table that shows the semi-annual cash flows of the bond until maturity, and calculate YTM, YTC for each call date, YTW and current yield.
3. Calculate duration and convexity.
4. Let's assume the bonds were downgraded from B3/B− to CCC+/Caa1, and the average yield for comparable bonds with this rating is 9.75%. Calculate the price, duration, and convexity.

Project
Question 1 (Figure 11.9)

Figure 11.9 shows the calculation of both the market value of each bond and the invoice price. Since the trading day was on Thursday, the T+3 includes two weekend days. The accrued interest is calculated at $26.56 and is based on 153 days, representing the days since the last coupon payment was paid.

Question 2 (Figure 11.10)

Figure 11.10 shows the expected fixed income case flows from the bond. Use the Excel yield formula = yield (settlement date, maturity date, coupon rate, market price, redemption, frequency) to calculate yield to maturity (YTM) and all the yield to call (YTC) using the Excel formula. The lower of the yields represents the yield to worse (YTW). The current yield is calculated using the annual coupon payment divided by the market value of each bond.

Question 3 (Figure 11.11)

Figure 11.11 shows the price (slightly different due to timing), the duration, and the convexity based on the market information.

Question 4 (Figure 11.12)

Figure 11.12 shows the Price (slightly different due to timing), the Duration and Convexity based on the new yield required for a CCC+/Caa1 rated corporate bond.

FIGURE 11.9 MARKET AND INVOICE PRICE

INPUT

Trading Date	Thursday, 12 March 20
Settlement Date (T+3 Business Days)	Tuesday, 17 March 20
Market Price	97.50
Coupon Rate	6.250%
Coupon Dates	April 15, October 15
Semi-Annual Coupon Payment	$31.25
Face Value	$1,000
Accrued Basis	360 Days

OUTPUT

Market Price Paid	$975.00	$97.50 x 10
Accrued Expenses	$26.56	31.25 x (153 / 180) = $26.56
Invoice Price	$1,001.56	

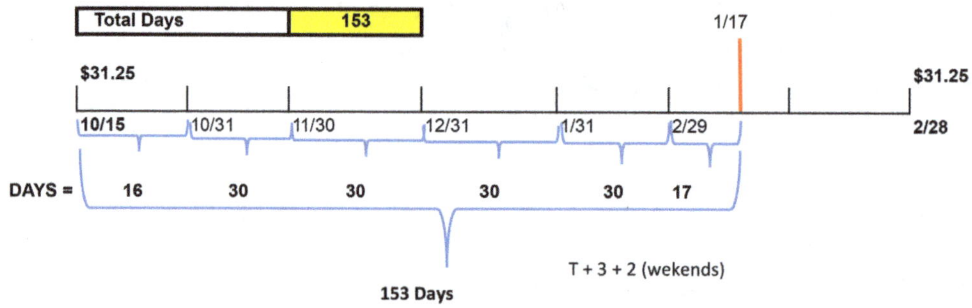

FIGURE 11.10 YIELD TO MAURITY (YTM), YIELD TO CALL (YTC), YIELD TO WORSE (YTW) AND CURRENT YIELD (CY)

	B	C	D	E	F	G	H	I	J	K	L
2	YIELD TO MAURITY (YTM), YIELD TO CALL (YTC), YIELD TO WORSE (YTW) and CURRENT YIELD (CY)										
3	EXCEL FORMULAS										
4				YTM			Non-Collable	YTC1	YTC2	YTC3	YTM
5	Issuance Date =			15/10/15			15/10/15	15/10/15	15/10/15	15/10/15	15/10/15
6	Trading Date =			Thursday, 12 March 20			12/03/20	12/03/20	12/03/20	12/03/20	12/03/20
7											
8	Settlement Date (T+3) (SD)			Tuesday, 17 March 20			17/03/20	17/03/20	17/03/20	17/03/20	17/03/20
9	Maturity Date / Call Date (MD)			15/10/25			15/10/18	15/10/19	15/10/20	15/10/21	15/10/25
10	Coupon Rate (CR)			6.25%			6.25%	6.25%	6.25%	6.25%	6.25%
11	Market Price (MP)			97.50			97.50	97.50	97.50	97.50	97.50
12	Redemption (Final payment % of Par) (R)			100.00			-	103.00	102.00	101.00	100.00
13	Frequency (payments per year) (F)			2			2	2	2	2	2
14											
15	Call Provision							103.00	102.00	101.00	100.00
16											
17			YTM=	6.794%		YTC=	NA	NA	14.328%	8.577%	6.794%
18											
19			YTW=	6.794%		CY=	6.4103%				
20									=YIELD(J9,J9,J11,J12,J13)		
21	Face Value			$1,000					=YIELD(SD,MD,CR,MP,R,F)		
22	Coupon Payment $			$31.25	=+E10*E21/2						
23	Years (Term)			10 Years							
24											
25											

FIGURE 11.11 BOND PRICE, DURATION & CONVEXITY

1	B	C	D	E	F	G	H	I	J	K	L
2	**BOND PRICE, DURATION & CONVEXITY**										
3	**Sensitivity to interest rate movements**										
4											
5	Face Value	**1,000**									
6	Coupon Rate	**6.25%**									
7	Remaining Years	**5.5836**	125.8767123	*(Maturity -Setlment Date)/365 days)*							
8	Yield	**6.79%**									
9	Frequency	2									
10	**Bond Price**	**$975**	=-PV(E9/E10,E8*E10,E7*E6/E10,E6)								
11											
12	**Macaulay Duration**	**4.36**									
13											
14	Modified Duration	4.3%	=+E13/(1+E9/E8)/100								
15											
16	**Convexity**	**20.05**	**2.06%**	=+E17/E11							
17											
18	**Period**	**Cash Flow**	**PV Cash Flow**			**Weighted**	**Duration Calc**		**Factor years**	**Convexity Calc**	
19	0	($975.05)									
20	1	31.25	30.22	=+C21/(1+($E$9/2))^B21		3.093%	0.03093	=+F21*B21	2.000	60.45	=+I21*D21
21	2	31.25	29.23			2.991%	0.05982		6.000	175.38	
22	3	31.25	28.27			2.893%	0.08678	=+B21+B21^2	12.000	339.24	
23	4	31.25	27.34			2.798%	0.11191		20.000	546.82	
24	5	31.25	26.44			2.706%	0.13529		30.000	793.28	
25	6	31.25	25.57			2.617%	0.15702		42.000	1,074.10	
26	7	31.25	24.73			2.531%	0.17717		56.000	1,385.08	
27	8	31.25	23.92			2.448%	0.19582		72.000	1,722.31	
28	9	31.25	23.14			2.367%	0.21306		90.000	2,082.15	
29	10	1,031.25	738.37			75.557%	7.55567		110.000	81,220.83	
30						100.000%	8.72348	=SUM(G21:G30)		89,399.64	=SUM(J20:J30)
31											
32		PRICE	977.24	=SUM(D20:D30)		DURATION	4.36	=+G31/2	CONVEXITY	20.05	
33											=+((J31/((1+E9)^2))/(D33*E10^2))

FIGURE 11.12 BOND PRICE, DURATION & CONVEXITY

1	B	C	D	E	F	G	H	I	J	K	L
2	**BOND PRICE, DURATION & CONVEXITY**										
3	**Sensitivity to interest rate movements**										
4											
5	Face Value	**1,000**									
6	Coupon Rate	**6.25%**									
7	Remaining Years	**5.5836**	125.8767123	*(Maturity -Settment Date)/365 days)*							
8	Yield	**9.75%**									
9	Frequency	2									
10	**Bond Price**	**$852**	=-PV(E9/E10,E8*E10,E7*E6/E10,E6)								
11											
12	**Macaulay Duration**	**4.31**									
13											
14	Modified Duration	4.2%	=+E13/(1+E9/E8)/100								
15											
16	**Convexity**	**18.71**	**2.20%**	=+E17/E11							
17											
18	**Period**	**Cash Flow**	**PV Cash Flow**			**Weighted**	**Duration Calc**		**Factor years**	**Convexity Calc**	
19	0	($851.99)									
20	1	31.25	29.80	=+C21/(1+($E$9/2))^B21		3.449%	0.03449	=+F21*B21	2.000	59.59	=+I21*D21
21	2	31.25	28.41			3.288%	0.06577		6.000	170.47	
22	3	31.25	27.09			3.135%	0.09406	=+B21+B21^2	12.000	325.10	
23	4	31.25	25.83			2.990%	0.11959		20.000	516.64	
24	5	31.25	24.63			2.851%	0.14254		30.000	738.94	
25	6	31.25	23.49			2.718%	0.16309		42.000	986.43	
26	7	31.25	22.39			2.592%	0.18143		56.000	1,254.11	
27	8	31.25	21.35			2.471%	0.19771		72.000	1,537.47	
28	9	31.25	20.36			2.356%	0.21208		90.000	1,832.50	
29	10	1,031.25	640.68			74.149%	7.41494		110.000	70,475.30	
30						100.000%	8.62569	=SUM(G21:G30)		77,896.56	=SUM(J20:J30)
31											
32		PRICE	864.05	=SUM(D20:D30)		DURATION	4.31	=+G31/2	CONVEXITY	18.71	
33											=+((J31/((1+E9)^2))/(D33*E10^2))

PROBLEMS

1. What is TRACE?
2. What is the rating agency's objective for rating the bonds?
3. Why does the Securities Exchange Commission rate bonds?
4. What is the highest rating possible?
5. What is the minimum grade needed to be an investment-grade company?
6. What is the difference between face value and market value?
7. List three reasons why the market value of the bonds value fluctuates up and down.
8. What is the difference between the market price and invoice price?
9. On Monday, May 15, you bought (traded) the XZX, Inc. 8.25% corporate bonds with a trading value of $96.50 price. The coupon payments are paid on March 31 and September 30. Using the 360-day accrual basis, calculate the market price per bond and invoice price of the bond. Please use T+3 to calculate the settlement day.
10. On Thursday, July 22, you bought (traded) the FG, Inc. 6.75% corporate bonds for $101.25. The coupon payments are paid on May 31 and November 30. Using the 360-day accrual basis, calculate the market price and invoice price of the bonds. Please use T+3 to calculate the settlement day.
11. Explain what the redemption price is.
12. What are callable and non-callable bonds?
13. What is the definition of OID?
14. On Monday, February 20, you bought (traded) the 7.5% Saturn Tech Company's corporate bonds for $98.75. The maturity date is June 30, 2030, the redemption price is 100, and the coupons are paid twice a year. Calculate the yield to maturity.
15. Calculate the price, duration, and convexity given the following information:
    Face value = $1,000
    Coupon rate = 7.75%
    Yield = 8.25%
    Remaining years = 4
    Redemption = 100
    Frequency = 2

ONLINE TEMPLATES

The Excel spreadsheets used in the chapter can be accessed online via Cognella Active Learning platform.

CHAPTER 12

Credit and Alternative Investments: Leveraged Loans, CLOs, and Structured Finance

This chapter will give an overview of the secondary loan market and how institutional investors trade and manage loans. The chapter will discuss various entities and structures set up to trade and manage a portfolio of bank loans. These alternative investment portfolios include CLOs, credit funds, and lender finance structures. In conjunction with analyzing the secondary market and its participants, this chapter will cover the credit analysis that should take place prior to investing in loans; chapter 18 revisits this process in more detail.

LEARNING OBJECTIVES

After reading this chapter, students will be able to do the following:

- Understand how the secondary loan market works as well as the various securities that are traded and managed for both investment-grade and non-investment-grade loans or leveraged loans
- Understand the various types of corporate loans including the revolver facility and term loan A, called pro-rata facilities, and the term loan B, called an institutional loan facility
- Understand the pricing, terms, and conditions that are used in the secondary loan market such as the conventional calculation of loan yields and secondary loan syndication conditions. Secondary conditions surrounding loans and the securities that underlie them include the Most Favored Nation (MFN) clause, loan "flex" language, "sunset" provisions, and other conditions

SECONDARY LOAN MARKETS—AN OVERVIEW

The secondary loan market sprung up in the late 1990s and early 2000s with the creation of the institutional loan market, also referred to as term loan B market, since the traditional term loan (term loan A) was financed by commercial banks. The growth came from the establishment of collateralized loan obligations (CLO) that became the majority of the syndication market. These loans evolved into many types, depending on the purpose of the loan, the investor providing the loan, and the market demand supply dynamics. Also, when Standard & Poor's and Moody's expanded their rating services to loans from bonds, the secondary market opened, and many funds were created that were designed to frequently trade these loans.

AUTHOR'S NOTES

The concept of loan syndication was created in the 1980s to finance the mega deals of the time such as the aforementioned $31-billion buyout of RJR Nabisco by KKR. When I was at Bank of America, I worked closely with our syndication department. Their job for a large and high-risk loan transaction such as RJR Nabisco LBO was to find a strategy that would enable them to sell such a large amount of debt to investors. In order to entice investment in the deal's debt, these bankers would "work the phones" with other commercial banks including large international banks. The composition of banks that committed and funded the $31 billion RJR Nabisco transaction consisted of many of the large Japanese banks that had an average hold of $1 billion each—a very risky proposition, even in today's environment. Having $1 billion of exposure on a single company that would have been rated a B/B- is no easy sell as a syndicator, nor a sure proposition for the investor (in this case, the Japanese banks). The syndication department was focused on building a book that included the support of banks that would commit and hold large investments; it didn't help that there was no organized secondary market at the time. Today's syndication process has changed significantly. Today, the syndication department that arranges the transaction acts more like a bond shop. The analysts will try to richly price the transaction in order to increase the possibility and level of a successful sell down, keeping in mind their clientele will be price-sensitive institutional investors such as CLOs. Because many of these CLO funds of loans are structured to achieve a minimum required set pricing based on the company's credit rating, syndicators' selling strategies in some instances must be tailored to their price point.

KEY TAKEAWAYS

- The risk characteristics of investing in loans are very different than investing in bonds and stocks. Loans typically provide the lowest risk on the corporate structure and the lowest volatility in the secondary market and expect to have the highest recovery rates in a bankruptcy.
- Most loans are structured as floating rate notes based on a floating index such LIBOR versus corporate bonds that are typically structured with a fixed rate; that difference changes the analysis between a bonds vulnerability to interest rate fluctuations versus a loan's, where rates move directly up and down based on interest rates.
- The primary source of repayment for loans is income and cash from operations. Secondary sources of repayments are the sale of the entire or partial company (enterprise value) and/or the current and non-current assets of the company.

THE BANK LOAN OR CREDIT MARKETS

The secondary loan market is divided into two distinct markets: investment-grade (IG) and non-investment-grade or leverage loan (LevFin) markets. The IG secondary market consists primarily of commercial banks trading with one another to reduce or increase exposure on certain borrowers. In the case of non-investment-grade and leveraged transactions, the parties that trade these loans consist of financial companies and institutional investors such as collateralized loan obligations (CLOs), loan mutual funds (LMF), business development companies (BDCs) and other direct lenders and hedge funds. Since the IG secondary market involves trading between commercial banks whose cost of capital is relatively low, the pricing is not as important as the LevFin secondary market. These commercial banks, often called relationship banks, are more interested in providing other banking products to the company. Thus, they see the transaction as a source of increasing their exposure to obtain customers or up-tier their relationship with the company. The participants in LevFin secondary market, on the other hand, care more about the loan's price based on the credit quality of the issuer and their personal risk appetite.

THE CASE OF LOANS

The leveraged loan asset class has been relatively attractive for many portfolio managers due to the following investment characteristics:

- **Insulation from interest rate risk**: Both the revenues and cost of the CLO is based on floating rate interest (LIBOR based) that is reset at least every 90 days, so even if the interest rate rises for the CLO's loan obligations, the rates will also rise at the same level for the individual portfolio of companies, enabling natural arbitrage for the CLO manager.

- **Low price volatility**: In general, leverage loans experience reduced volatility resulting from a low correlation and covariance with other assets. The floating rate nature of leveraged loans contributes to its low correlation with other security types. Only short-term treasury bills (considered risk free) consistently exhibit lower volatility.
- **Defensive strategy**: Senior loan funds have historically provided consistent, higher risk-adjusted returns compared to other asset classes, which may make them attractive to investors during volatile markets.

PRICING AND LOAN YIELDS

The Loan Syndication and Trading Association (LSTA) was established in the mid 1990s to develop liquidity and transparency in the secondary market for bank loans. LSTA provides dealer-secondary quotes based on market-to-market and other relevant information including the most volatile loans, the list of the biggest price movers, and the listing of the newest deals.

As discussed previously in chapter 8, the arrangers responsible for raising the initial loans in the primary market must first approach a few investors to gauge their appetite for credit. Based on this feedback, the arrangers adjust the pricing and even use their option to flex the price to meet market demand. Then the pricing is set based on an initial spread over a base rate (usually LIBOR) at set original issuance discount (OID), which represents the additional "fee" the investor receives. The loan yield formula is as follows:

$$Annual\ loan\ yield = LIBOR + spread + \frac{\left(\frac{100 - OID}{4\ years}\right)}{100}$$

Please note that this conventional formula is based on 4 years' average life of the loan. A typical press announcement from the lead arranger bank will be as follows:

"The term loan B price is set at LIBOR + 4.5% at 99.0 OID and is now free to trade."

Based on this example and assuming the starting LIBOR is 2.50%, the initial loan yield is then calculated as follows:

$$Annual\ loan\ yield = 2.5\% + 4.5\% + \frac{\left(\frac{100 - 99}{4\ years}\right)}{100} = 2.5\% + 4.5\% + 0.25\% = 7.25\%$$

FIGURE 12.1 SECONDARY LOAN MARKET

LIBOR (3M)=	2.25%

Companies	Corporate Rating	Facility	Spread bps	Remaining Avg Life Years	OID %	Secondary Bid Price %	Secondary Ask Price %	Difference to OID	Current Yield %
Axell Corporation	B+/B1	TL B	400	3.50	98.500%	97.500%	97.625%	-1.000%	6.964%
Buzz Tech. Corp.	B/B2	TL B	475	3.75	99.000%	99.500%	99.525%	0.500%	7.133%
Cite Inc.	B+/B1	TL A	375	4.00	99.500%	99.750%	99.850%	0.250%	6.063%
Delmon Company	B-/B3	TL B	525	2.50	97.000%	100.500%	101.100%	3.500%	7.300%
Excelent Hotel Corp.	B+/B2	TL B	450	2.25	98.250%	97.500%	98.000%	-0.750%	7.861%
Filarmo Inc.	B-/B2	TL B	545	3.50	98.250%	97.500%	97.750%	-0.750%	8.414%
Gray Tech Inc.	B+/B2	TL B	425	2.00	99.250%	97.500%	98.000%	-1.750%	7.750%
Holifas Saas Co.	B/B1	TL B	400	1.75	98.750%	97.500%	97.750%	-1.250%	7.679%
Intergem Inc.	B/B2	TL B	475	2.00	99.250%	97.500%	97.875%	-1.750%	8.250%
Jasminsen Corp.	BB-/Ba3	TL B	325	3.25	99.750%	97.500%	98.000%	-2.250%	6.269%
Kapko Company	B+/B1	TL B	425	3.50	99.000%	97.500%	97.750%	-1.500%	7.214%

The LSTA, in conjunction with Standard & Poor's Leveraged Commentary & Data (LCD), has developed a LevFin index as a benchmark representing a weighted average of the 100 largest loan facilities. The index, S&P/LSTA Index is a total return index of the leverage loans. Loan portfolio managers use this as a benchmark to compare the portfolio performance and other asset class to the market. A list of loan secondary trading level examples is shown in figure 12.1.

SECONDARY LOAN TERMS

The following are some of the secondary loan trading and loan syndication concepts:

1. **Loan participation: A loan participation, sometimes called "silent participation," is an agreement between two or more lenders in which a primary lender sells specific rights in a loan to other lenders (participants).** In this participation arrangement the primary lender is the only bank that has contact with the borrower and is listed in the credit agreement as the lender of record. The purpose of this arrangement is for the primary bank to transfer the risk to other banks to "hide" their exposure deficit and need for support as sometimes the borrower expects the primary bank to have adequate exposure as a relationship bank. The participant has no direct obligations to the borrower and is therefore "along for the ride." The participants only look to the participation agreement to understand its rights—and not the underlying loan documents with the borrower. There could be some specific language in the participating agreement that allows the conversion from participation to assignment, for example in case of bankruptcy or event of default. Sometimes this type of arrangement can cause some problems when the company, for example, is asking the primary bank to amend money terms in the

credit agreement including pricing, maturity, or scheduled payments. In this case, since there is 100% approval, the primary bank could buy back the participation since it doesn't have the right to amend such a major term and condition per the participation agreement. Any non-money terms in the credit agreement require only majority vote (51%) and the primary bank could make changes without the consent of the participating bank.

2. **Loan assignments:** Defined in the credit agreement, assignments are the sale or transfer of all or portion of the loan from one bank (assignor) to another bank (assignee). With the purchase, the assignee has the same rights and obligations as all the other banks listed in the agreement as a lender of record. Basically, upon completion of the loan assignment, the assignee will step into the same shoes as the assignor for those rights assigned. The assignee has a direct contractual relationship with the borrower, controlled by the initial loan documentation. New assignees that were not part of the initial transaction (primary market) need to be signed off by the lead bank and the borrower. Trading the loans between banks that both already own the loan do not need the consent of the borrower.
3. **Most-favored nation:** Most agreements for leverage loans include "most-favored nation" (MFN) pricing protection. This is a rare provision providing that if the pricing (yield) of any incremental term loan is to be raised after the initial loan was priced, the price should be the same as the original or have a maximum threshold expressed in basis points. For example, let's assume that the MFN provides a 50-basis point threshold. If the new incremental loan is priced 100 basis points more than the original loan, then the original loan will be adjusted by 50 basis points to be in line within the threshold.
4. **Sunset provision:** A sunset provision is a clause in the loan agreement that would allow the MFN protection to expire after a set period, typically 90–180 days.

COLLATERALIZED LOAN OBLIGATIONS (CLOS)

Collateralized loan obligations (CLOs) are funds created with a pool of corporate loans. Typically, these corporate loans are comprised of leveraged loans with lower credit ratings with higher expected returns. In exchange for taking on higher risk, the investor in a CLO is offered higher diversity and better-than-average returns.

A typical CLO fund will include a portfolio of 100–250 first-lien bank loans that the manager of such funds is actively buying and selling in the secondary loan market. To fund the initial purchase of these loans, the CLO raises funds from outside investors in structures called tranches. Each tranche is ranked with a priority of payment when and if the CLO fund liquidates. The tranches are comprised of debt and equity investments. The investments in the debt tranches are rated by Moody's based on risk of default, where the equity investments in CLOs are not ranked and are the last to get paid in a liquidation. Investors who are paid out first have lower overall risk, but they receive smaller interest payments as a result. Investors who are in later tranches, referred to as equity tranches, are paid last, and thus expect higher interest payments. The highest priority tranches, referred to as debt tranches, are treated just like bonds and have credit ratings as well as set coupon payments. These debt tranches are structured and rated in a specific pecking order.

STRUCTURING THE TRANCHES OF CLOS

CLO funds are structured to meet certain criteria set by the credit agencies such as Moody's including portfolio diversification factors by industry, company and credit ratings discussed further in this chapter. These loans are primarily leveraged loans given the higher yield characteristics.

Intermediate Investing: Warehouse Financing

Typically, before raising the capital, the CLO manager obtains a warehouse facility. This is basically a credit facility obtained by a commercial bank (typically by the underwriter for the intended new-issue CLO). This will serve as a short-term financing for the purchase (or warehousing) of leverage loans before the launch of the CLO. Especially with new issuance of CLOs, companies need to show their success of ramping up the portfolio before they obtain more permanent financing. Also, since the permanent financing requires diversification, this arrangement is built toward securing that.

The terms and conditions of the warehouse facility are relatively straightforward. Such facility, similar to revolving credit facility, could have several classes of loans with differing seniority levels, and the short-term equity during the ramp up is typically funded by the CLO manager or affiliates. The borrower is often the special purpose vehicle or entity (e.g., Metanext CLO Fund IV Ltd.) that will raise the permanent financing shortly after a significant percentage of the ramp up has occurred. This borrower will pledge the corporate loans purchased as security to the warehouse lenders. This credit agreement (warehouse facility agreement) typically has specific criteria of what loan can be purchased.

The most significant risk to a manager who provides the warehouse facility is market risk, a loss that various commercial banks experienced during the financial crisis of 2008/2009 when the secondary loan market plummeted due lack of liquidity. Given the potential fluctuations of the secondary loan markets, these loans are vulnerable to price movements. To mitigate this market risk, a typical warehouse lender requires that the manager who provides the short-term equity maintain a pre-negotiated level of loan-to-value ratio, so if the market value of loans decreases above the set loan-to-value ratio, the manager must provide additional funding to maintain the required level of loan-to-value ratio stated in the agreement (similar to a margin loan).

In recent years, a lot of seasoned CLO managers have successfully launched new-issue CLOs without relying on a warehouse facility, as it seems very costly for the equity investor in a ramp-up stage.

Banks have been very innovative in creating various structures that encourage the manager to use these warehouse facilities by using various cash flow techniques such as higher overcollateralization during the ramp up. Overcollateralization ratio tests (OC tests) are used to maintain a par amount of the warehouse portfolio, in aggregate, instead secondary market value-based tests.

Capital Raising

Once the ramp up is successful (typically 70% of the fund used), the manager moves to raise a more permanent finance for the CLO investments (typical 10–14 years). The CLO manager will reach out to an advisor (typically the provider of the warehouse facility) to assist with capital raising for the next CLO portfolio. The capital raising includes the debt and equity. As mentioned, the debt is divided by tranche based on probability of default assigned by third-party rating agency for each tranche. Typically, each tranche is raised by different investors based on their risk appetite. Historically, commercial banks invest in the AAA- and AA-rated tranches, and any tranches below that (BBB–BB) involve other institutional investors such as insurance companies, pension funds, and hedge funds.

Investing the Capital Raised

Moody's and Standard Poor's set various parameters for CLO managers to follow when building a portfolio of investments including certain diversification levels across companies, industries, and ratings levels. The typical investment is between $5–$15 for a $500-million loan.

CLO PORTFOLIO ANALYSIS

CLOs generate relatively attractive returns due to leverage where the investor expects to receive a healthy rate of return even after expected losses of the portfolio. For example, if the investor assumes that 3% of the portfolio will default with a recovery rate of 70%, the loss-given default (LGD) is calculated to at 0.9% where LGD = 3.0% × (1 − 0.70) = 0.9%.

BANK LOAN FUNDS (BLF)

These are closed-end funds that trade leveraged loans. BLFs are sometimes called floating rate funds because the loans in these funds are LIBOR or prime rate based on floating rate loans. These funds trade based on the market value of the individual loans that create BLFs' net asset value and are structured like CLOs except they provide daily information such as liquidity and diversification across borrowers and industries. The market values in these funds may fluctuate based on individual loan and industry performance. These loans are typically repaid without penalty at any time and cause the expected income stream to end before the stated maturity. Such prepayment is caused by an upgrade of the rating of the borrower, a declining interest rate environment, and favorable market conditions.

BUSINESS DEVELOPMENT COMPANY (BDC)

A business development company (BDC) is a firm that also invests in leveraged loans. To qualify as a business development company, a company must be registered in compliance with Section 54 of the Investment Company Act of 1940. Many financial institutions are set up to have both CLOs and BDC structures. A major difference between a BDC and a CLO fund is that BDCs allow smaller, non-accredited investors to invest in these funds. The other difference is that BDCs have a maximum leverage of 1:1 equity and debt. Due to lower leverage than CLOs, many BDCs invest in junior debt that carries higher yields.

BDC funds are typically closed-end funds that make investments in middle-market companies. BDCs provide the investors with exposure to debt and equity investments in predominantly privately owned companies. Because BDCs are regulated investment companies, they must distribute over 90% of their profits to shareholders, which results in above-average dividend yields.

CREDIT ANALYSIS OF LEVERAGED LOANS "INTERAGENCY GUIDANCE ON LEVERAGED LENDING"

Based on the March 21, 2013 letter by the board of governors of the Federal Reserve Systems (FED), the Federal Deposit Insurance Corporation (FDIC), and the Office of the Comptroller of the Currency (OCC) with the subject "Interagency Guidance on Leveraged Lending" to the banking institutions, the banks that underwrite and manage leveraged loans need to establish a comprehensive assessment of financial, business, industry, and management risks including, whether:

1. cash flow analyses rely on overly optimistic or unsubstantiated projections of sales, margins, and merger and acquisition synergies.
2. liquidity analyses include performance metrics appropriate for the borrower's industry, predictability of the borrower's cash flow, measurement of the borrower's operating cash needs, and ability to meet debt maturities.
3. projections exhibit an adequate margin for unanticipated merger-related integration costs.
4. projections are stress tested for one or more downside scenarios, including a covenant breach;

5. transactions are reviewed at least quarterly to determine variance from the plan, the related risk implications, and the accuracy of risk ratings and accrual status, and from inception the credit file should contain a chronological rationale for an analysis of all substantive changes to the borrower's operating plan and variance from expected financial performance;
6. enterprise and collateral valuations are independently derived or validated outside of the origination function, are timely, and consider potential value erosion.
7. collateral liquidation and asset sale estimates are based on current market conditions and trends; potential collateral shortfalls are identified and factored into risk ratings and accrual decisions, contingency plans anticipate changing conditions in debt, or equity markets when exposures rely on refinancing or the issuance of new equity; and,
8. the borrower is adequately protected from interest rate and foreign exchange risk.

CASE STUDY

METANEXT CLO FUND IV (MCLO)

Figure 12.2 illustrates the structure of a CLO and demonstrates the cash flow arbitrage created from the cash inflow to cash outflow. In this example, Metanext CLO Fund IV (MCLO) has raised $500 million to set up their fourth CLO. In this case, $450 million out of the $500 million capital raised is debt divided by four tranches (details discussed later) with a weighted average cost of debt being LIBOR + 2.5% (L+2.5%). The remaining $50 million raised is from equity investors that are looking to make a return based on natural cash flow arbitrage. The loan portfolio of investments returns on average LIBOR + 5.0% (L+5.0%) and even after management of the portfolio gets its return, which adds to the cost the equity an amount of 0.5%, the resulting return translates to $11.5 million in annual income or 23% ROE ($11.5 mm/$50 mm) before any portfolio losses.

After the CLO raises its initial capital in the primary market, it becomes an actively managed instrument. The investment and portfolio management company's job are to actively buy and sell individual bank loans to generate gains and minimize losses.

Capital Raising

Figure 12.3 shows that Metanext CLO Fund IV (MCLO) raised $500 million with a leverage of equity/total fund of 1/10 or 10% equity and 90% debt. The debt tranches are rated by

FIGURE 12.2 METANEXT CLO FUND IV CLO STRUCTURE

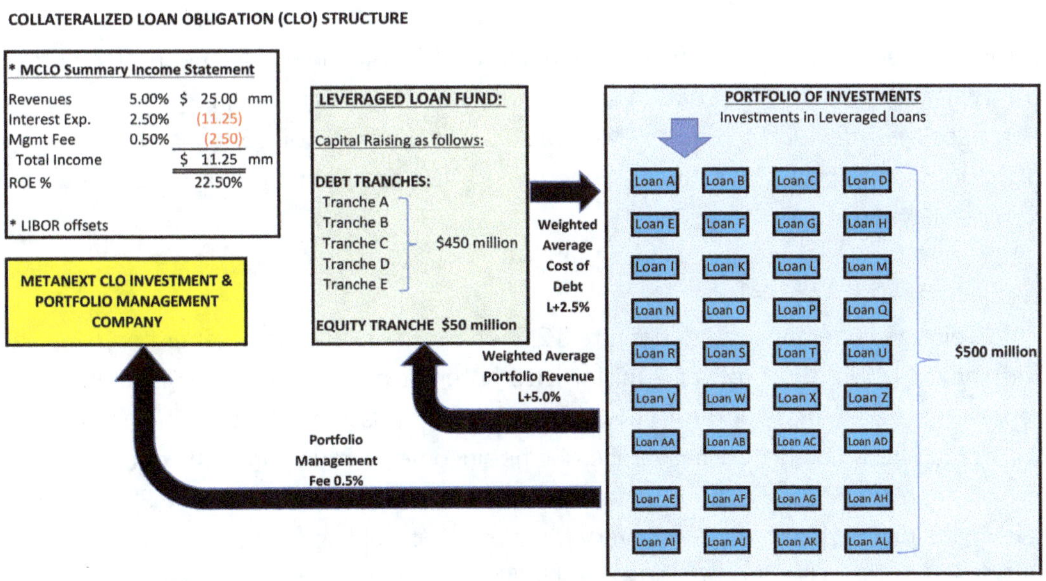

FIGURE 12.3 METANEXT CLO FUND IV ARBITRAGE CASH FLOW CLO MODEL

Arbitrage Cash Flow CLO Model

Capital Structure

Tranches	Par amount	% Cap	% Debt	Rating S&P/M	Coupon Libor+ Spread	WACD Libor +
Tranche A	335.0	67.0%	74.4%	AAA/Aaa	178	132.51
Tranche B	41.0	8.2%	9.1%	AA/Aa2	300	27.33
Tranche C	30.0	6.0%	6.7%	A/A2	400	26.67
Tranche D	27.0	5.4%	6.0%	BBB/Baa2	600	36.00
Tranche E	17.0	3.4%	3.8%	BB/Ba2	730	27.58
Total Debt	**450.0**	**90.0%**	100.0%			
Equity	50.0	10.0%		NR		
	500.0	**100.0%**				**250.1**

S&P and Moody's and are priced based on the probability of default and recovery. The average cost of debt is calculated at 250 basis points or 2.5%. Tranche A representing 67% of the capital is rated AAA, the highest possible rating. The reason for getting such a high rating is that the probability of expected default is almost zero. Since tranche A is at the top of the pecking order in payment priority, or at 67% of the capital, it means that 33% of the entire portfolio has to experience total loss before the AAA tranche is affected—a very unrealistic scenario, especially since the portfolio companies that expect to default have some percentage recovery value.

Investing the Capital Raised

Figure 12.4 shows a sample version of a portfolio (25 companies). As mentioned before, the typical investment is between $5-$15 for a $500-million loan, but for illustration purposes Metanext CLO Fund IV (MCLO) shows a purchase of 25 loans at an average of $20 million per loan investment, generating 500 basis points or 5% of revenue on a $500-million portfolio.

CLO Portfolio Analysis

The arbitrage is demonstrated in figure 12.5 where the net income generated form the Metanext CLO Fund IV of $11.2 million after interest payments and management fees represents a 22.5% rate of return (ROE). If the investor assumes that 3% of the portfolio will default based on historical average, the net income to equity after the default is $6.7 million, representing a 13.5% return on the investment. Please note that the 3% defaulted leveraged loans typically have recovery rates of 70%, yielding a loss-given default (LGD) of 0.9% of $500 million, as demonstrated in figure 12.5.

FIGURE 12.4 METANEXT CLO FUND IV ARBITRAGE CASH FLOW CLO MODEL

Arbitrage Cash Flow CLO Model

Capital Structure

Tranches	Par amount ($ millions)	% Cap	% Debt	Rating S&P/M	Coupon Libor+ Spread	WACD Libor +
Tranche A	335.0	67.0%	74.4%	AAA/Aaa	178	132.51
Tranche B	41.0	8.2%	9.1%	AA/Aa2	300	27.33
Tranche C	30.0	6.0%	6.7%	A/A2	400	26.67
Tranche D	27.0	5.4%	6.0%	BBB/Baa2	600	36.00
Tranche E	17.0	3.4%	3.8%	BB/Ba2	730	27.58
Total Debt	**450.0**	**90.0%**	100.0%			
Equity	50.0	10.0%		NR		
	500.0	**100.0%**				**250.1**

Portfolio of Leveraged Loans

	Par amount ($ millions)	% of Total	Rating S&P	Discount margin Libor+	Annual Income (excluding LIBOR)	Weighted Average Interest Income (bps)
Company 1	15.0	3.0%	B+	425	637,500	12.75
Company 2	30.0	6.0%	B-	525	1,575,000	31.50
Company 3	20.0	4.0%	B	475	950,000	19.00
Company 4	12.0	2.4%	B+	450	540,000	10.80
Company 5	25.0	5.0%	B+	425	1,062,500	21.25
Company 6	12.0	2.4%	BB-	350	420,000	8.40
Company 7	16.0	3.2%	B+	425	680,000	13.60
Company 8	15.0	3.0%	B	425	637,500	12.75
Company 9	12.0	2.4%	B-	600	720,000	14.40
Company 10	25.0	5.0%	CCC	850	2,125,000	42.50
Company 11	21.0	4.2%	B+	425	892,500	17.85
Company 12	23.0	4.6%	B-	625	1,437,500	28.75
Company 13	27.0	5.4%	B-	525	1,417,500	28.35
Company 14	15.0	3.0%	B+	425	637,500	12.75
Company 15	30.0	6.0%	B+	400	1,200,000	24.00
Company 16	27.0	5.4%	BB	330	891,000	17.82
Company 17	26.0	5.2%	B+	450	1,170,000	23.40
Company 18	14.0	2.8%	B-	500	700,000	14.00
Company 19	12.0	2.4%	B-	550	660,000	13.20
Company 20	15.0	3.0%	B	500	750,000	15.00
Company 21	14.0	2.8%	B-	575	805,000	16.10
Company 22	22.0	4.4%	B	475	1,045,000	20.90
Company 23	20.0	4.0%	B	500	1,000,000	20.00
Company 24	25.0	5.0%	B-	600	1,500,000	30.00
Company 25	27.0	5.4%	B-	575	1,552,500	31.05
	500.0	100.0%			25,006,000	500.12
Average	20.0					

FIGURE 12.5 METANEXT CLO FUND IV ARBITRAGE CASH FLOW CLO MODEL

Arbitrage Cash Flow CLO Model

EXPECTED EQUITY CASH FLOW ANALYSIS		Average Interest Assumptions	
CLO Interest Income		5.00%	25,006,000
Less Management Fee		0.50%	2,500,000
CLO Income after Management Fees			22,506,000
Less Interest Expenses:			
Tranche A	335,000,000	1.78%	5,963,000
Tranche B	41,000,000	3.00%	1,230,000
Tranche C	30,000,000	4.00%	1,200,000
Tranche D	27,000,000	6.00%	1,620,000
Tranche E	17,000,000	7.30%	1,241,000
Total Interest Expense	450,000,000	2.50%	11,254,000
Equity Cash Flow (before Loss Given Default)			**11,252,000**
Portfolio Amount			500,000,000
Debt Investment			450,000,000
Equity Investment			50,000,000
ROE			**22.5%**

EXPECTED EQUITY CASH FLOW ADJUSTED FOR LOSS		
Equity Cash Flow (before Loss Given Default)		11,252,000
Less Loss Given Default (LGD) -Assumptions		
Default Rate	3.00%	
Recovery	70.00%	
LGD rate	0.900%	
Total Portfolio Value	$ 500.00 million	
Less Loss Given Default		**4,500,000**
Risk Adjusted Income on Capital		6,752,000
RAROC %		**13.50%**

BREAK EVEN ANALYSIS	
Default Rate	**7.50%**
Recovery	70.00%
LGD rate	2.250%
Break Even LGD	11,252,000

Figure 12.5 shows a breakeven scenario analysis. According to the break event (BE) analysis, the default rate needs to raise to 7.5% before the equity's capital is affected. In other words, $37.5 million out of the $500-million portfolio needs to default before the initial equity cash flow is zero.

PROBLEMS

1. Name the two different secondary loan markets and what distinguishes them.
2. What are some of the benefits for an investor to invest in the loan markets?
3. Assuming LIBOR is 1.5%, OID is 98, and the spread is 300 basis points, calculate the initial loan yield.
4. What is the difference between "silent participation" and loan assignment?
5. Explain the terms "most-favored nation" and "sunset" provisions.
6. Define CLO and explain how it is set up.
7. Explain the benefits of investing in a CLO as compared to other asset classes, such as equity or bonds.
8. What is "warehouse financing" and what is its use?
9. What is the most significant risk to a manager who provides the warehouse facility, and why?
10. What is Moody's rating agency focused on before rating a new CLO?
11. Assuming a CLO manager is projecting a 4% default rate (DR) and 75% recovery, what is the expected loss given default (LGD)?
12. Use the following capital structure of a $600 million CLO fund to complete these tasks.
    a. Calculate the weighted average cost of debt.
    b. Assuming the weighted average gross income is 6.0%, calculate the gross equity return.
    c. Assuming the default rate is 2.0% and the recovery rate is 70%, calculate the LGD in percentage and amount.
    d. Given the information above, calculate the net risk adjusted equity return.
    e. Given the information above, calculate the breakeven default rate for this CLO fund.

TRANCHES	AMOUNT $	SPREAD %
Tranche A	420,000,000	1.500
Tranche B	60,000,000	2.750
Tranche C	30,000,000	3.125
Tranche D	20,000,000	4.500
Tranche E	10,000,000	6.750
Total Debt	$540,000,000	
Equity	60,000,000	
Total Fund	$600,000,000	

ONLINE TEMPLATES

The Excel spreadsheets used in the chapter can be accessed online via Cognella Active Learning platform.

CHAPTER 13

Derivative Investments: Option Strategies, Analysis, and Valuation

This chapter will give an overview of the options market. It will describe strategies used by investors for hedging or speculating on significant increases or decreases in stock price using derivatives. It will then discuss how to value options including various methods such as the binomial option pricing models (BOPM), Black-Scholes, and the call-put parity. The chapter will re-introduce mathematical concepts such as probability theory, normal distributions, natural logarithms, and standard deviation as the basis of predicting the stock's price movements.

LEARNING OBJECTIVES

After reading this chapter, students will be able to do the following:

- Understand how the options market works and how these types of investments are traded and managed as part of an overall investment strategy
- Understand various option strategies including buying and selling covered and uncovered (naked) options
- Understand how option prices are valued and calculated using various methods including the binomial option pricing models (BOPM), Black-Scholes, call-put parity, hedge, and leverage methods

OPTION MARKETS: OVERVIEW

Options play a significant role in the financial markets. These types of securities' values are derived from other securities such as stocks or bonds. Options and futures (futures are discussed in the next chapter) are derivative securities, meaning their payoff is dependent on other securities' price movements. Option contracts are traded in many exchange markets such as the Chicago Board Option Exchange (CBOE) and over-the-counter markets. These option contracts include two types of options: call options and put options. Each type can be used in conjunction with the other for-certain strategies. The strategies described in this chapter can be used for buying or selling "uncovered" or "covered" option contracts. Uncovered or "naked" options are speculative strategies and entail buying or selling options without owning the underlying investment or stock. Covered strategies involve buying or selling option securities in conjunction with owning the underlying stock.

AUTHOR'S NOTES

I didn't know it at the time, but my very first "finance" book was Dr. Seuss's (Geisel, 1947) McElligot's Pool. *I was 4 years old and I was so fascinated with the story. I read this to my daughter, Amanda, when she was 2 years old and she still remembers it after all these years. Now, at the age of 30, she is an elementary school art teacher and told me that she reads the book to the class of second graders.* McElligot's Pool *is of course a children's book written by Dr. Seuss. It's about a boy named Marco who is sitting by a small 6-foot pool with a fishing rod, waiting there patiently for 3 hours to catch a fish. The very first page of the book sets the mood. It shows a farmer laughing at Marco and saying, in Dr. Seuss's brilliant rhymed way,*

"Young man … you are sort of a ***fool****! You'll never catch fish in McElligot's* ***Pool****!*

The pool is too small. And, you might as well ***know it****, when people have junk, here is where they* ***throw it****.*

You might catch a boot, or you might catch a can. You might catch a bottle, but listen, young man. … If you sat fifty years with your worms and your ***wishes****, you'd grow a long beard, long before you'd catch* ***fishes****!"*

Marco strongly believed that this pool was connected to an underground brook that lead to a river and eventually the sea. Marco imagines a school of fish from the sea heading up the river into McElligot's pool. There were all kinds of fish, including ones with a checkerboard stomach, an eel with heads on both ends, and an imaginary dogfish that's chasing the catfish as they make their way to McElligot's pool. The imagination and beauty of the fish make it a very entertaining children's book. The book ends with the boy saying,

"Oh, the sea is so full of a number of fish, if a fellow is patient, he might get his wish!

And that's why I think, that I'm not such a fool, when I sit here and fish in McElligot's Pool!"

This children's story illustrated brilliantly by Dr. Seuss represents many investors who are hoping an unlikely event will happen in the future, usually expecting a large payoff. Some are willing to bet or buy out of the money options today, banking that someday they will pay huge returns. Similar to betting for the collapse of the housing market, as is depicted in the book (and movie) by Michael Lewis, The Big Short, *where a few investors tried to position themselves for a large payoff. The position of course, was to profit if the mortgage-backed securities defaulted as the housing market defaulted in the 2008/2009 financial crisis. The derivatives market, which includes options, futures, forwards, and swaps are all types of investments that expect a large payoff in the future. Since I joined Kinisis Ventures after 30-plus years in banking, I have devoted many hours to valuing start-up companies that have zero revenues and are hoping one day their innovative product will turn out to be profitable. How do you value a company that has negative cash flow? Using many option valuation techniques is one way of setting up such a scenario and outcome model.*

KEY TAKEAWAYS

- Future events such as a significant rise or fall in stock price, movements of interest rates, or a specific default of a bond can be measured with probability theory, found in many of the methodology models such as the binomial option pricing model and Black-Scholes.
- Many option strategies are designed to either protect the underlying investments or enhance the overall exposure to a future event for maximum profit. Other option strategies, such as spreads, are designed to minimize the upfront cost of premiums.
- An investor who trades options will gain a better understanding of stock movements and patterns.

OPTION MARKETS

There are two types of option contract structures: American and European. The American option contract is structured such that the buyer of the option can exercise his or her right to buy or sell the stock anytime from the day the contract is signed until expiration. The European option contract is structured as such that the investor can only exercise the option on the expiration day. The investor can get out of both options anytime by selling his or her contract at the market premium anytime until expiration. Given the difference, the price of each type of structure is priced as such. The valuation methods discussed later in the chapter take into consideration each of these structures.

UNCOVERED (NAKED) OPTION TRADING STRATEGY CONTRACTS

Uncovered options, also known as "naked" option strategies, are buying or selling options primarily on speculation where the investor does not hold any ownership in the underlying asset, in this case stock, from which the option premium is derived. The following three strategies including buying and selling call options, put options, and straddles.

BUYING CALL OPTION

A call option is a contract that gives the holder the right, not the obligation, to buy 100 shares at a set price, called the exercise price (X), at and before the set date, referred to as the expiration date, no matter what happens to the stock. Of course, if the holder has the right to buy the stock at a set price, he or she is hoping that the stock price will go up significantly. The holder can then profit from the difference, representing a **bullish view** on the stock. For example, a May call option on shares of Facebook with an exercise price of $165 entitles its owner to buy 100 shares of Facebook at price of $165 at any time up until the third week of May (contract expiration date). If the Facebook stock goes to $180 before the third week of May, the option holder will exercise the right to buy Facebook at $165 and then turn around and sell the stock to the market at $180, profiting from the $15 difference. If the stock of Facebook goes below $165, the option holder will let the contract expire without exercising. To purchase the option, the investor needs to pay upfront a set price per share called a premium. Figure 13.1 shows the payoff, profit, return (HPR), and break even (BE) of Facebook stock during various scenarios and stock prices (using a range of $155–$190).

Figure 13.1 shows that if the price of the stock is below $165, the call option is not exercisable since the stock (S) minus the exercise price (X) will be negative, indicating an out-of-the-money option. At $165, where the stock (S) is equal to the exercise price (X) the call option is at the money and exercisable since there is zero payoff (S – X = 0). If the stock is higher than $165, the call option is not exercisable and is therefore an in-the-money option. It's important to note that being in the money does not necessarily mean that the option is profitable. It means that there is a payoff if exercised. Using the example in Figure 13.1, it shows that if the stock is at $170 on the last day, then the investor needs to exercise the option. In that case, the payoff per share is $5 (S – X = payoff or $170 – $165 = $5) and the investor will always exercise the option even though the transaction is not profitable. Since the investor paid a $10.65 premium for the option, if exercised at any price in the money, he or she can recover some of the initial loss (premium paid). Instead of losing the entire

FIGURE 13.1 UNCOVERED (NAKED) OPTION STRATEGIES BUYING A CALL OPTION

FB	CALLS		
Exercise Price (X)	MARCH	APRIL	MAY
150	20.00	21.50	23.00
155	15.50	16.25	17.75
160	12.50	12.85	13.50
165	8.10	9.00	10.65
170	5.20	6.30	8.50
175	3.25	4.25	5.75
180	2.50	3.40	4.45

ACTION

Buy Call @ Exercise (X) = $ 165.00
Pay Premium (p) = $ 10.65

Break Even = $ 175.65
Max Loss = $ (10.65)
Max Gain = Unlimited

(light yellow)	Out-of-the-money Option
(white)	On-the-money Option
(light blue)	In-of-the-money Option

INPUT		
	X	p
ACTION	Exercise Price (X)	Premium Per Share (p)
Buy May	$ 165.00	$ (10.65)
Buy May	$ 165.00	$ (10.65)
Buy May	$ 165.00	$ (10.65)
Buy May	$ 165.00	$ (10.65)
Buy May	$ 165.00	$ (10.65)
Buy May	$ 165.00	$ (10.65)
Buy May	$ 165.00	$ (10.65)
Buy May	$ 165.00	$ (10.65)

WHAT IF SCENARIO
S
Stock Price (S)
$ 155.00
$ 160.00
$ 165.00
$ 170.00
$ 175.00
$ 180.00
$ 185.00
$ 190.00

OUTPUT				
	O = max (0,S-X)	(π) = O - p	HPR % = π / p	X + p
Exercise Y/N?	Payoff (O)	Profit (π)	HPR (%)	Break Even Stock
No	$ -	$ (10.65)	-100.0%	$ 175.65
No	$ -	$ (10.65)	-100.0%	$ 175.65
No	$ -	$ (10.65)	-100.0%	$ 175.65
Yes	$ 5.00	$ (5.65)	-53.1%	$ 175.65
Yes	$ 10.00	$ (0.65)	-6.1%	$ 175.65
Yes	$ 15.00	$ 4.35	40.8%	$ 175.65
Yes	$ 20.00	$ 9.35	87.8%	$ 175.65
Yes	$ 25.00	$ 14.35	134.7%	$ 175.65

premium of $10.65, by exercising the call option at $170, the investor recovers the $5 back, netting to a total loss of $5.65 per share. The rule is that the investor always exercises the option if the option is in the money or $S - X > 0$.

The following formulas are used for calculating the output when buying a call option:

Call option payoff = Maximum (0, stock price − exercise price), max (0, S − X)

Call option profit = Payoff − premium

Holding period return % = Profit/premium

Break-even stock price for call option = Exercise price + premium

Maximum loss on buying a call option = Premium

Maximum gain on buying a call option = Unlimited

BUYING PUT OPTION

A put option is a contract that gives the holder the right, not the obligation, to sell 100 shares at a set price, called the exercise price (X), at and before the set date, referred to as the expiration date, no matter what happens to the stock. Of course, if the investor has the right to sell the set number of shares at a set price, he or she is then hoping that the stock goes down significantly and can profit from the difference, representing a **bearish view** on the stock. For example, a March put option on shares of Facebook with an exercise price of $170 entitles its owner to sell 100 shares of Facebook at price of $170 at any time up until the third week of March (contract expiration date). If Facebook's stock goes down to $155 before the third week of March, the option holder can buy the stock from the market at $155 and exercise the right to sell at $170, profiting from the $15 difference. If the stock of Facebook goes above $170, the option holder will let the contract expire without exercising. To purchase the option the investor needs to pay an upfront set price per share called a premium. Figure 13.2 shows the payoff, profit, return (HPR), and break-even (BE) stock of Facebook at various scenarios of the stock (using a range of $155–$190).

Figure 13.2 shows that if the range of the stock is above $170, the put option is not exercisable since the exercise price (X) minus the stock price (S) is negative, representing the out-of-money option. At $170, where the stock (S) is equal to the exercise price (X), the call option is at the money and not exercisable since there is zero payoff (X – S = 0). If the stock is lower than $170, the put option is exercisable or an in-the-money option. It's important to note that being in the money does not necessarily mean that the option is profitable. It means that there is a payoff. Using the example in Figure 13.2, it shows that if the stock is at $165 on the last day, then the investor needs to exercise the option with the payoff per share being $5 (X – S = payoff or $170 – $165 = $5). The investor will still exercise this option even though the transaction is not profitable since he or she paid $9.40 for the option. By exercising the option, the investor at least recovers some of the premium paid, in this case $5, calculating the net loss to be $4.40 per share instead of the entire premium of $9.40. The rule is that the investor always exercises the option if the option is in the money or X – S > 0.

The following formulas are used for calculating the output when buying a put option:

Put option payoff = Maximum (0, exercise price – stock price), max (0, X – S)

Put option profit = Payoff – premium

Holding period return % = Profit/premium

Break-even stock price for put option = Exercise price – premium

Maximum loss on buying a put option = Premium

Maximum gain on buying a put option = Exercise price – premium at stock = 0

FIGURE 13.2 UNCOVERED (NAKED) OPTION STRATEGIES BUYING A PUT OPTION

FB	PUTS		
Exercise Price (X)	MARCH	APRIL	MAY
150	3.00	3.50	4.45
155	4.10	4.90	5.90
160	5.30	6.00	6.80
165	7.00	8.00	9.20
170	9.40	10.75	12.45
175	13.00	14.30	14.20
180	15.00	16.10	17.75

ACTION

Buy Put @ Exercise (X) = $ 170.00

Pay Premium (p) = $ 9.40

Break Even = $ 160.60

Max Loss = $ (9.40)

Max Gain = X - Premium at S=0

(yellow)	Out-of-the-money Option
(white)	On-the-money Option
(blue)	In-of-the-money Option

INPUT			WHAT IF SCENARIO	OUTPUT				
	X	p	S		O = max (0,X-S)	(π) = O - p	HPR % = π / p	X + p
ACTION	Exercise Price (X)	Premium Per Share (p)	Stock Price (S)	Exercise Y/N?	Payoff (O)	Profit (π)	HPR (%)	Break Even Stock
Buy May	$ 170.00	$ (9.40)	$ 155.00	Yes	$ 15.00	$ 5.60	59.6%	$ 160.60
Buy May	$ 170.00	$ (9.40)	$ 160.00	Yes	$ 10.00	$ 0.60	6.4%	$ 160.60
Buy May	$ 170.00	$ (9.40)	$ 165.00	Yes	$ 5.00	$ (4.40)	-46.8%	$ 160.60
Buy May	$ 170.00	$ (9.40)	$ 170.00	No	$ -	$ (9.40)	-100.0%	$ 160.60
Buy May	$ 170.00	$ (9.40)	$ 175.00	No	$ -	$ (9.40)	-100.0%	$ 160.60
Buy May	$ 170.00	$ (9.40)	$ 180.00	No	$ -	$ (9.40)	-100.0%	$ 160.60
Buy May	$ 170.00	$ (9.40)	$ 185.00	No	$ -	$ (9.40)	-100.0%	$ 160.60
Buy May	$ 170.00	$ (9.40)	$ 190.00	No	$ -	$ (9.40)	-100.0%	$ 160.60

SELLING CALL AND PUT OPTIONS

Selling call and put options are contracts where the seller has the obligation to sell or buy 100 shares when the buyer exercises his or her option at the exercise price. The seller of an option receives the premium and is hoping that the stock remains out of the money until expiration, so he or she can keep the premium. Selling uncovered or naked call options is the most dangerous play since the loss could be unlimited if the stock significantly rises above the exercise price. Selling uncovered or naked puts is also very dangerous if the stock goes down to zero. It's usually advised to sell call or put options in conjunction with either holding the stock (covered later in this chapter) or in combination with a buy of a call option (covered later in this chapter).

The following formulas are used for calculating the output when selling call and put options:

Call option payoff = Stock price − exercise price

Break-even stock price for call option = Exercise price + premium

Maximum loss on selling a call option = Unlimited

Maximum gain on selling a call option = Premium

Put option payoff = Exercise price − stock price

Break-even stock price for put option = Exercise price − premium

Maximum loss on selling a put option = Exercise price − premium at stock = 0

Maximum gain on selling a put option = Premium

BUYING AND SELLING STRADDLES

A straddle contract involves a buy of both calls and puts at the same exercise price. This is a contract that gives the holder the right, not the obligation, to buy or sell 100 shares at a set exercise price (X) at and before the set date, referred to as the expiration date, no matter what happens to the stock. The strategy for buying both call and put options represents the view of buying against the stock's volatility. This is a strategy where the investor expects that the stock will move significantly (scenario based) up or down based on a coming announcement. As an example, take a pharmaceutical company announcing that the only drug it sells is approved or disapproved by the Federal Drug Administration (FDA). If it's approved, the stock price is expected to increase significantly, and the straddle holder will be exercising the option (supported by call option side of the straddle) to buy 100 shares of the stock at the exercised price (X). If the company announces that the FDA did not approve the drug to be sold to the market, the stock is expected to significantly decline, especially if the company does not have any cash left to continue its research and development for another round. The seller of a straddle is hoping that the news will not have as much as an effect on the stock price and that it will stay within the break-even points. Of course, the best-case scenario of the seller of straddles and the worst-case scenario of the buyer of straddles is when the stock expires at the exercise price (S = X). For example, let's assume that the May call and put options on shares of Facebook with an exercise price of $165 entitles its owner to buy or sell 100 shares of Facebook at price of $165 at any time up until the third week of May (contract expiration date). If Facebook's stock goes above or below $165 by the expiration day, the straddle option holder will exercise the right to buy or sell Facebook, at $165, respectively, and get paid the difference. To purchase the straddle option, the investor needs to pay both call and put premiums upfront. Figure 13.3 shows the payoff, profit, return (HPR), and two

FIGURE 13.3 UNCOVERED (NAKED) OPTION STRATEGIES BUYING A STRADDLE

FB	CALLS			PUTS		
Exercise Price (X)	MARCH	APRIL	MAY	MARCH	APRIL	MAY
150	20.00	21.50	23.00	3.00	3.50	4.45
155	15.50	16.25	17.75	4.10	4.90	5.90
160	12.50	12.85	13.50	5.30	6.00	6.80
165	8.10	9.00	10.65	7.00	8.00	9.20
170	5.20	6.30	8.50	9.40	10.75	12.45
175	3.25	4.25	5.75	13.00	14.30	14.20
180	2.50	3.40	4.45	15.00	16.10	17.75

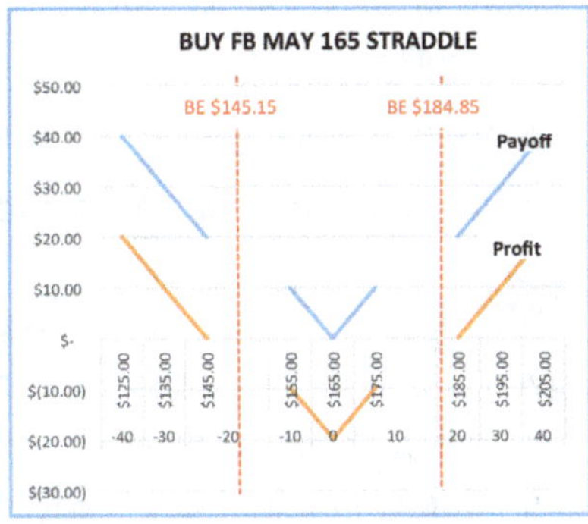

ACTION

Strategy: Buying a Call and Put at the same X

Buy Call & Put @ (X) = $ 165.00

Pay both Total Prem. (p) = $ 19.85 (10.65+9.20)

Two Break Evens = $ 184.85 $ 145.15

Max Loss = $ (19.85)

Max Gain = Unlimited

On-the-money Option

In-of-the-money Option

INPUT			WHAT IF SCENARIO	OUTPUT						
	X	p	S		O = (S-X) or (X-S)	(π) = O - p	HPR % = π / p	X + p	X -p	
ACTION	Exercise Price (X)	Premium Per Share (p)	Stock Price (S)	Exercise Y/N?	Payoff (O)	Profit (π)	HPR (%)	Break Even Stock 1	Break Even Stock 2	
Buy May	$ 165.00	$ (19.85)	$ 125.00	Yes	$ 40.00	$ 20.15	101.5%	$ 184.85	$ 145.15	
Buy May	$ 165.00	$ (19.85)	$ 135.00	Yes	$ 30.00	$ 10.15	51.1%	$ 184.85	$ 145.15	
Buy May	$ 165.00	$ (19.85)	$ 145.00	Yes	$ 20.00	$ 0.15	0.8%	$ 184.85	$ 145.15	
Buy May	$ 165.00	$ (19.85)	$ 145.15	Yes	$ 19.85	$ -	0.0%	$ 184.85	$ 145.15	Breakeven
Buy May	$ 165.00	$ (19.85)	$ 155.00	Yes	$ 10.00	$ (9.85)	-49.6%	$ 184.85	$ 145.15	
Buy May	$ 165.00	$ (19.85)	$ 165.00	No	$ -	$ (19.85)	-100.0%	$ 184.85	$ 145.15	
Buy May	$ 165.00	$ (19.85)	$ 175.00	Yes	$ 10.00	$ (9.85)	-49.6%	$ 184.85	$ 145.15	
Buy May	$ 165.00	$ (19.85)	$ 184.85	Yes	$ 19.85	$ -	0.0%	$ 184.85	$ 145.15	Breakeven
Buy May	$ 165.00	$ (19.85)	$ 185.00	Yes	$ 20.00	$ 0.15	0.8%	$ 184.85	$ 145.15	
Buy May	$ 165.00	$ (19.85)	$ 195.00	Yes	$ 30.00	$ 10.15	51.1%	$ 184.85	$ 145.15	
Buy May	$ 165.00	$ (19.85)	$ 205.00	Yes	$ 40.00	$ 20.15	101.5%	$ 184.85	$ 145.15	

break evens (BE1 and BE2) of Facebook's stock during various scenarios of stock price performance (Range: \$125–\$205).

Figure 13.3 shows that if the range of the stock is above or below \$165, the straddle option is in the money and exercisable with the payoff being S – X or X – S. At \$165, where the stock (S) is equal to the exercise price (X), the call option is at the money and not exercisable since there will be zero payoff (X – S = 0). Looking at Figure 13.3, let's assume the stock significantly increases to \$205 by the expiration date. The straddle holder will exercise the right to buy the stock at \$165, calculating a payoff of \$40 (S – X = \$205 – \$165). With the \$40 payoff, the profit will be \$20.15 (payoff – total premiums for both call and put options = \$40.00 – \$19.85). In general, the straddle holder will always exercise except in the unlikely event that the stock is equal to the exercise price, basically no volatility.

The following formulas are used for calculating the output when buying a straddle option:

Straddle option payoff = Exercise price – stock price or stock price – exercise price

Straddle option profit = Payoff – both call and put premiums

Holding period return % = Profit/both call and put premium

Both break-even stock price for straddle option = Exercise price − premium and exercise + premium

Maximum loss on buying a straddle option = Premium (assuming S − X = 0)

Maximum gain on buying straddle option = Unlimited

COVERED OPTION TRADING STRATEGY CONTRACTS

Covered option strategies are buying or selling options primarily for hedging purposes. The strategy called a covered option is typically a strategy where the investor buys or sells options in conjunction with buying or selling the underlying stock from which the option's premium prices are derived. Another reason to use this covered strategy is to enhance the overall exposure by maximizing the gain on both the underlying stock and option securities. The following three strategies including protective puts, covered calls, and a combination of the two called collars.

PROTECTIVE PUT STRATEGY

A protective put is a strategy where the investor buys or owns the underlying stock and simultaneously buys put options to hedge his or her holdings in case the stock drops. This is like buying insurance on a stock. If the stock drops in price, the price is protected by exercising the option to sell the stock at X price. For example, let's assume the investor buys 100 shares of Facebook at the current price of $163.00 (February 20), investing $16,300 ($163 x 100 shares). The investor is concerned that the stock will drop in the next few months, so he buys the $165 May call option, paying a premium of $9.20 per share for 100 shares, or $920.00. The total cost of the investment including the option is $17,220 ($16,300 + 920.00). Figure 13.4 shows the protective put strategy on various stock price scenarios assuming the investor sells the stock at the market price. The output shows the profit and loss as well as the holding period return on the strategy. Figure 13.4 shows that the maximum loss on selling the stock at any price below $165 is capped at $720. If the stock was not hedged by setting a protective put or if the stock drops to $125, the loss will be $3,800 ($163 − 125 = $38 loss x 100 shares). By having the protective put option, the maximum loss is capped at $720, as the investor exercises the right to sell the stock at $165 no matter what. If the stock increases to $205, the investor could sell the stock and record the gain on the stock, as demonstrated in Figure 13.4, showing $3,280 of profit net of premium. At $205, the investor will let the put expire.

COVERED CALL STRATEGY

A covered call strategy is a strategy where the investor buys or owns the underlying stock and simultaneously sells a call option of the same stock. This is a popular strategy

FIGURE 13.4 COVERED OPTION STRATEGIES PROTECTIVE PUT

FB	PUTS		
Exercise Price (X)	MARCH	APRIL	MAY
150	3.00	3.50	4.45
155	4.10	4.90	5.90
160	5.30	6.00	6.80
165	7.00	8.00	9.20
170	9.40	10.75	12.45

Strategy: Buying or holding the Stock and Buying Put Option at X

ACTION	Exercise (X)	Stock (S)/ Premium (p)	Number of Shares	Investment (I)
Buy the Stock =		$163.00	100	$ (16,300)
Buy Put at X =	$ 165.00			
Pay Prem. (p) =		$ 9.20	100	$ (920)

Total Initial Investment =	$ (17,220)

INPUT					OUTPUT							
	STOCK INVEST	OPTION SECURITY		WHAT IF SCENARIO	STOCK INVEST	OPTION SECURITY		BOTH STOCKS AND OPTIONS				
	So	X	p	S	CG = S - So	O	π - p	(π - p + CG)	(π - p + CG) x Sh	I	NP / I
STRATEGY	Stock Purchase per share	Exercise Price (X)	Paid Premium Per Share (p)	Market Price Stock Price (S)	Stock Capital Gain/ (Loss)	Put Option Payoff (Hedging)	Profit from the Option per share	Net Profit per share	Net Profit (Total $) (NP)	Initial Investment	HPR%
Buy Stock & May Puts	$163.00	$ 165.00	$ (9.20)	$ 125.00	$ (38.00)	$ 40.00	$ 30.80	$ (7.20)	$ (720.00)	$ 17,220	-4.18%
Buy Stock & May Puts	$ 163.00	$ 165.00	$ (9.20)	$ 135.00	$ (28.00)	$ 30.00	$ 20.80	$ (7.20)	$ (720.00)	$ 17,220	-4.18%
Buy Stock & May Puts	$ 163.00	$ 165.00	$ (9.20)	$ 145.00	$ (18.00)	$ 20.00	$ 10.80	$ (7.20)	$ (720.00)	$ 17,220	-4.18%
Buy Stock & May Puts	$ 163.00	$ 165.00	$ (9.20)	$ 155.00	$ (8.00)	$ 10.00	$ 0.80	$ (7.20)	$ (720.00)	$ 17,220	-4.18%
Buy Stock & May Puts	$ 163.00	$ 165.00	$ (9.20)	$ 165.00	$ 2.00	$ -	$ (9.20)	$ (7.20)	$ (720.00)	$ 17,220	-4.18%
Buy Stock & May Puts	$ 163.00	$ 165.00	$ (9.20)	$ 175.00	$ 12.00	$ -	$ (9.20)	$ 2.80	$ 280.00	$ 17,220	1.63%
Buy Stock & May Puts	$ 163.00	$ 165.00	$ (9.20)	$ 185.00	$ 22.00	$ -	$ (9.20)	$ 12.80	$ 1,280.00	$ 17,220	7.43%
Buy Stock & May Puts	$ 163.00	$ 165.00	$ (9.20)	$ 195.00	$ 32.00	$ -	$ (9.20)	$ 22.80	$ 2,280.00	$ 17,220	13.24%
Buy Stock & May Puts	$ 163.00	$ 165.00	$ (9.20)	$ 205.00	$ 42.00	$ -	$ (9.20)	$ 32.80	$ 3,280.00	$ 17,220	19.05%

and commonly referred to as writing cover calls. It is a low-risk hedge strategy. What's interesting is that selling uncovered calls is the riskiest option strategy with possible unlimited losses but selling calls while you own the stock is thought of as the most conservative strategy. An example of who would be using such a strategy is an investor who is planning to sell the stock soon at a higher than market level; so instead of setting up a limit order that instructs his or her broker to sell the stock when that higher price is met, he or she could sell the equivalent shares in call options, receiving the premium at a set future price. If the stock hits that higher price, instead of paying the difference between the exercise price and the market price as a seller of calls, he or she can deliver the stock at that price or sell the stock in the market and cover the call option obligation from the profit made as a result of selling the stock. For example, let's assume the investor holds 100 shares of Facebook. At the current price of $163.00 (February 20) the investment is worth $16,300 ($163 x 100 shares). The investor is expected to sell the stock when the price gets to $180. Instead of putting in a limit order, he or she enters into a cover call contract at the $180 level where he or she will be obliged to pay the difference between the market value above $180 and the exercise price of $180 (S – X). In return, he or she will receive a premium of $4.45. If the stock goes above $180, he or she will either sell the stock at the market price or deliver the stock to the buyer of the call option. If the stock goes to $180 exactly (on the money), the option will not be exercised. The investor holding the stock could sell it at $180 and record the gain in

FIGURE 13.5 COVERED OPTION STRATEGIES COVERED CALL

FB	CALLS		
Exercise Price (X)	MARCH	APRIL	MAY
150	20.00	21.50	23.00
155	15.50	16.25	17.75
160	12.50	12.85	13.50
165	8.10	9.00	10.65
170	5.20	6.30	8.50
175	3.25	4.25	5.75
180	2.50	3.40	4.45

Strategy: Holding the Stock and Selling Call Option at X

ACTION	Exercise (X)	Stock (S)/ Premium (p)	Number of Shares	Investment (I)
Own the Stock (So) =		$163.00	100	$ (16,300)
Sell Call at (X) =	$ 165.00			
Pay Prem. (p) =		$ (4.45)	100	$ 445
			Total Initial Investment =	$ (15,855)

INPUT				
	STOCK INVEST	OPTION SECURITY		WHAT IF SCENARIO
	So	X	p	S
STRATEGY	Market Price	Exercise Price (X)	Received Premium Per Share (p)	Market Price Stock Price (S)
Buy Stock & Sell May Calls	$163.00	$ 180.00	$ 4.45	$ 180.00
Buy Stock & Sell May Calls	$163.00	$ 180.00	$ 4.45	$ 190.00
Buy Stock & Sell May Calls	$163.00	$ 180.00	$ 4.45	$ 200.00
Buy Stock & Sell May Calls	$163.00	$ 180.00	$ 4.45	$ 210.00
Buy Stock & Sell May Calls	$163.00	$ 180.00	$ 4.45	$ 220.00

OUTPUT						
STOCK INVEST	OPTION SECURITY		BOTH STOCKS AND OPTIONS			
CG = S -So	O	π - p	(π - p + CG)	(π - p + CG) x Sh	I	NP / I
Stock Capital Gain/ (Loss)	Call Option Payoff (Hedging)	Profit from the Option per share	Net Profit per share	Net Profit (Total $) (NP)	Initial Investment	HPR%
$ 17.00	$ -	$ 4.45	$ 21.45	$ 2,145.00	$ 15,855	13.53%
$ 27.00	$ (10.00)	$ (5.55)	$ 21.45	$ 2,145.00	$ 15,855	13.53%
$ 37.00	$ (20.00)	$ (15.55)	$ 21.45	$ 2,145.00	$ 15,855	13.53%
$ 47.00	$ (30.00)	$ (25.55)	$ 21.45	$ 2,145.00	$ 15,855	13.53%
$ 57.00	$ (40.00)	$ (35.55)	$ 21.45	$ 2,145.00	$ 15,855	13.53%

addition to the premium he or she received. The strategy is basically giving up a sudden upside of the stock, but the investor has no need to complain if the stock jumps higher than $180. The alternative was that he or she would have to sell the stock at the $180 mark, being a limit order. Figure 13.5 shows that the profit is capped at $2,145 at any stock price above $180.00.

COLLARS

A collar option strategy is one where holders of stock want to hedge their downside by giving up the upside. In previous sections that discussed protective puts, the investor obtained a protective put to hedge his or her investment in case the stock declines, but it costs money to buy put options. The collar option strategy is customized to minimize or eliminate the premiums paid to buy puts by selling calls at a much higher level of stock. Basically, collars are a combination of protective puts and covered calls. Figure 13.6 shows an example where the investor holding 100 shares of Facebook with a current price of $163 wants to set up a floor to cap his losses at $150 by buying the May puts. The May puts cost $4.45 per share or $445 on 100 shares. The investor scans the pricing page and finds that the May $180 calls are also $4.45. Given that the premiums match, he enters into a collar option contract where he buys the May $150 puts and sells the $180 calls, netting the premiums at zero since he pays for the put premium by receiving premiums from the calls. Figure 13.6 shows the payoff, profit, and overall return (HPR) of Facebook at various scenarios of the stock (using a range of $120–$210).

FIGURE 13.6 COVERED OPTION STRATEGIES COLLARS

FB	CALLS			PUTS		
Exercise Price (X)	MARCH	APRIL	MAY	MARCH	APRIL	MAY
150	20.00	21.50	23.00	3.00	3.50	4.45
155	15.50	16.25	17.75	4.10	4.90	5.90
160	12.50	12.85	13.50	5.30	6.00	6.80
165	8.10	9.00	10.65	7.00	8.00	9.20
170	5.20	6.30	8.50	9.40	10.75	12.45
175	3.25	4.25	5.75	13.00	14.30	14.20
180	2.50	3.40	4.45	15.00	16.10	17.75

Collars Strategy: Own Stock, Buy Put, Sell Calls (combination of Protective Puts and Covered Calls) - the intention is to minimize or eliminate the premium
Action: Own 100 shares of Facebook (current price at $163)
Buy the May 150 Puts -pay $4.45 premium
Sell (Write) the May 180 Calls - receive $4.45 premium

INPUT				
	STOCK INVEST	OPTION SECURITY		
	So	X puts	X calls	p
STRATEGY	Market Price M2M	Exercise Call Price (X1)	Exercise Put Price (X2)	Net Premium Paid Per Share (p)
Collars 150 Puts/180 Calls May	$163.00	$ 150.00	$ 180.00	$ -
Collars 150 Puts/180 Calls May	$163.00	$ 150.00	$ 180.00	$ -
Collars 150 Puts/180 Calls May	$163.00	$ 150.00	$ 180.00	$ -
Collars 150 Puts/180 Calls May	$163.00	$ 150.00	$ 180.00	$ -
Collars 150 Puts/180 Calls May	$163.00	$ 150.00	$ 180.00	$ -
Collars 150 Puts/180 Calls May	$163.00	$ 150.00	$ 180.00	$ -
Collars 150 Puts/180 Calls May	$163.00	$ 150.00	$ 180.00	$ -
Collars 150 Puts/180 Calls May	$163.00	$ 150.00	$ 180.00	$ -
Collars 150 Puts/180 Calls May	$163.00	$ 150.00	$ 180.00	$ -
Collars 150 Puts/180 Calls May	$163.00	$ 150.00	$ 180.00	$ -

OUTPUT								
WHAT IF SCENARIO	STOCK INVEST	OPTION SECURITY			BOTH STOCKS AND OPTIONS			
S	CG = S - So	O1	O2	π - p	(π - p + CG)	(π - p + CG) x Sh	I	NP / I
Market Price Stock Price (S)	Stock Capital Gain/ (Loss)	Put Option Payoff	Call Option Payoff	Profit from the Option per share	Net Profit per share	Net Profit (Total $) (NP) 100 shares	Based on original February 20 Date	HPR%
$ 120.00	$ (43.00)	$ 30.00	$ -	$ 30.00	$ (13.00)	$ (1,300.00)	$ 16,300	-7.98%
$ 130.00	$ (33.00)	$ 20.00	$ -	$ 20.00	$ (13.00)	$ (1,300.00)	$ 16,300	-7.98%
$ 140.00	$ (23.00)	$ 10.00	$ -	$ 10.00	$ (13.00)	$ (1,300.00)	$ 16,300	-7.98%
$ 150.00	$ (13.00)	$ -	$ -	$ -	$ (13.00)	$ (1,300.00)	$ 16,300	-7.98%
$ 160.00	$ (3.00)	$ -	$ -	$ -	$ (3.00)	$ (300.00)	$ 16,300	-1.84%
$ 170.00	$ 7.00	$ -	$ -	$ -	$ 7.00	$ 700.00	$ 16,300	4.29%
$ 180.00	$ 17.00	$ -	$ -	$ -	$ 17.00	$ 1,700.00	$ 16,300	10.43%
$ 190.00	$ 27.00	$ -	$ (10.00)	$ (10.00)	$ 17.00	$ 1,700.00	$ 16,300	10.43%
$ 200.00	$ 37.00	$ -	$ (20.00)	$ (20.00)	$ 17.00	$ 1,700.00	$ 16,300	10.43%
$ 210.00	$ 47.00	$ -	$ (30.00)	$ (30.00)	$ 17.00	$ 1,700.00	$ 16,300	10.43%

ADVANCED OPTION TRADING STRATEGIES

Advanced option strategies involve simultaneously buying and selling multiple options. The strategies that entail buying and selling at different exercise prices but keeping the same expiration dates are called vertical spreads or money spreads and the buying and selling of options across different expiration dates with the same exercise price are called horizontal spreads or time spreads. Spread options typically involve two or more options where the investor buys one option and pays a premium and sells another and receives a premium. The objective of spread strategies is to minimize the net premium paid. Figure 13.7 shows the differences between vertical spreads or money spreads and horizontal spreads or time spreads. Choosing vertical spreads as an option strategy, the investor buys and sells call or put options at different exercise prices with the same date, in this case April is the chosen expiration day and the exercise prices are listed vertically. Choosing horizontal spreads as an option strategy, the investor buys and sells options choosing the same exercise price at different dates; in this case, the exercise price is $165, and the chosen dates are listed horizontally.

An investor can be bullish or bearish on a stock, so he or she uses a combination of spreads to take advantage of his or her view. The spread strategies include vertical bull and bear spreads for both calls and puts and are described in detail next (please note

FIGURE 13.7 VERTICAL AND HORIZONTAL SPREADS

FB	CALLS			PUTS		
Exercise Price (X)	MARCH	APRIL	MAY	MARCH	APRIL	MAY
150	20.00	21.50	23.00	3.00	3.50	4.45
155	15.50	16.25	17.75	4.10	4.90	5.90
160	12.50	12.85	13.50	5.30	6.00	6.80
165	8.10	9.00	10.65	7.00	8.00	9.20
170	5.20	6.30	8.50	9.40	10.75	12.45
175	3.25	4.25	5.75	13.00	14.30	14.20
180	2.50	3.40	4.45	15.00	16.10	17.75

HORIZONTAL SPREAD (TIME SPREADS)

VERTICAL SPREADS (MONEY SPREADS)

VERTICAL SPREADS (MONEY SPREADS)

that the chapter will not cover horizontal or time spreads, which are not as popular as the vertical or money spreads).

BULL CALL VERTICAL SPREADS

Bull call spreads are vertical spreads that involve the buying of a call option with a low exercise price and selling the call option with a high exercise price with the same expiration date. To remember this strategy, think of an investor who is bullish on the stock. He or she will be buying the stock at its low price, anticipating selling it at a higher price in the future; the same is the case for bull call spreads. The investor buys the low exercise call price and sells the high exercise price in the hopes that the stock price will go up. Spread strategies such as bull call spreads are conservative strategies with maximum profit and maximum loss because an investor is giving up the significant upside to be protected on the downside. Figure 13.8 shows a bull call spread strategy where the investor buys the 155 May calls and pays $17.75 premium and sells the 165 May calls and receives $10.65 premium, calculating a net premium paid of $7.10. The investor in this case is bullish, expecting the stock to go up higher than $165 to maximize the $2.90 per share. Obviously if the stock drops below $155, the maximum loss will be capped at $7.10. The break-even stock is calculated at $162.10. Figure 13.8 shows the payoff and profit at various stock prices.

BEAR PUT VERTICAL SPREADS

Bear put spreads are vertical spreads that involve the buying of a put option with a high exercise price and selling the put option with a low exercise price with the same

FIGURE 13.8 ADVANCED OPTION STRATEGIES CALL BULL SPREADS

FB	CALLS			PUTS		
Exercise Price (X)	MARCH	APRIL	MAY	MARCH	APRIL	MAY
150	20.00	21.50	23.00	3.00	3.50	4.45
155	15.50	16.25	17.75	4.10	4.90	5.90
160	12.50	12.85	13.50	5.30	6.00	6.80
165	8.10	9.00	10.65	7.00	8.00	9.20
170	5.20	6.30	8.50	9.40	10.75	12.45
175	3.25	4.25	5.75	13.00	14.30	14.20
180	2.50	3.40	4.45	15.00	16.10	17.75

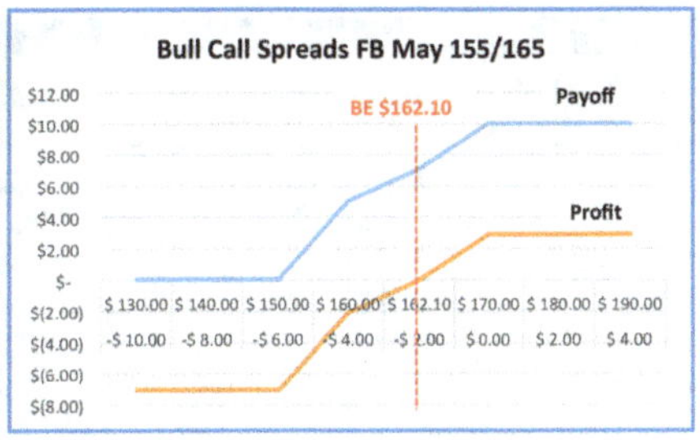

Bull Call Strategy: Buy the Low Exercise Call Price and sell the high Call Exercise Price at the same expiration date (Vertical Spread)
Action Example: Buy the May Call 155 -pay $17.75 premium
Sell the May 165 Calls - receive $10.65 premium

INPUT							OUTPUT			
	Low X	p1	High X	p2	p	S	S - X1 + X2			
STRATEGY	Buy Exercise Call (X1)	Premium Paid Per Share (p1)	Sell Exercise Call (X2)	Premium Received Per Share (p2)	Net Premium Paid Per Share	Market Price Stock Price (S)	Net Payoff	Net Profit	Maximum Profit	Maximum Loss
Buy Low and Sell High Call	$ 155.00	$ (17.75)	$ 165.00	$ 10.65	$ (7.10)	$ 130.00	$ -	$ (7.10)		$ (7.10)
Buy Low and Sell High Call	$ 155.00	$ (17.75)	$ 165.00	$ 10.65	$ (7.10)	$ 140.00	$ -	$ (7.10)		$ (7.10)
Buy Low and Sell High Call	$ 155.00	$ (17.75)	$ 165.00	$ 10.65	$ (7.10)	$ 150.00	$ -	$ (7.10)		$ (7.10)
Buy Low and Sell High Call	$ 155.00	$ (17.75)	$ 165.00	$ 10.65	$ (7.10)	$ 160.00	$ 5.00	$ (2.10)		$ (7.10)
Buy Low and Sell High Call	**$ 155.00**	**$ (17.75)**	**$ 165.00**	**$ 10.65**	**$ (7.10)**	**$ 162.10**	**$ 7.10**	**$ -**		Breakeven
Buy Low and Sell High Call	$ 155.00	$ (17.75)	$ 165.00	$ 10.65	$ (7.10)	$ 170.00	$ 10.00	$ 2.90	$ 2.90	
Buy Low and Sell High Call	$ 155.00	$ (17.75)	$ 165.00	$ 10.65	$ (7.10)	$ 180.00	$ 10.00	$ 2.90	$ 2.90	
Buy Low and Sell High Call	$ 155.00	$ (17.75)	$ 165.00	$ 10.65	$ (7.10)	$ 190.00	$ 10.00	$ 2.90	$ 2.90	

expiration date. To remember this strategy, think of an investor who is bearish on the stock; he or she will be shorting or selling the stock at its high price today and buying the stock back at a lower price in the future; the same is the case for bear put spreads. The investor buys the high exercise put price and sells the low exercise price in the hopes that the stock price will drop. Spread strategies such as bear put spreads are conservative strategies with maximum profit and maximum loss because an investor is giving up the significant upside of the stock going down to be protected on the downside if the stock goes. Figure 13.9 shows a put bear spread strategy where the investor buys the 170 April puts and pays $10.75 premium and sells the 160 April puts and receives a $6.00 premium, calculating a net premium paid of $4.75. The investor in this case is bearish, expecting the stock to drop lower than $160 to maximize the $5.25 per share. Obviously if the stock increases above $170, the maximum loss will be capped at $4.75. The break-even stock is calculated at $165.25. Figure 13.8 shows the payoff, profit maximum profit, and maximum loss at various stock prices.

BULL PUT VERTICAL SPREADS

Bull put spreads are vertical spreads that involve the buying of a put option with a low exercise price and selling a put option with a high exercise price with the same expiration date. Like the bull call spreads previously discussed, this strategy is bullish even though

FIGURE 13.9 ADVANCED OPTION STRATEGIES PUT BEAR SPREADS

FB	CALLS			PUTS		
Exercise Price (X)	**MARCH**	**APRIL**	**MAY**	**MARCH**	**APRIL**	**MAY**
150	20.00	21.50	23.00	3.00	3.50	4.45
155	15.50	16.25	17.75	4.10	4.90	5.90
160	12.50	12.85	13.50	5.30	6.00	6.80
165	8.10	9.00	10.65	7.00	8.00	9.20
170	5.20	6.30	8.50	9.40	10.75	12.45
175	3.25	4.25	5.75	13.00	14.30	14.20
180	2.50	3.40	4.45	15.00	16.10	17.75

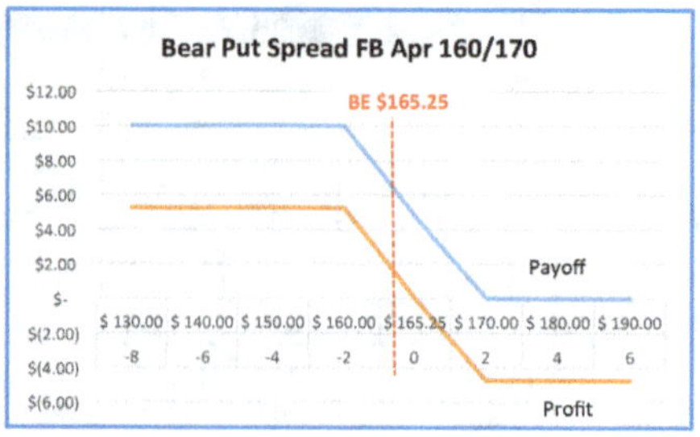

Bear Put Strategy: Buy the High Exercise Put Price and sell the Low Put Exercise Price at the same expiration date (Vertical Spread)
Action Example: Buy the Apr 170 Puts -pay $10.75 premium
Sell the Apr 160 Puts - receive $6.00 premium

INPUT							OUTPUT				
	High X	p1	Low X	p2	p	S	X1 - X2 -S				
STRATEGY	**Buy Exercise Put (X1)**	**Premium Paid Per Share (p1)**	**Sell Exercise Call (X2)**	**Premium Received Per Share (p2)**	**Net Premium Paid Per Share**	**Market Price Stock Price (S)**	**Net Payoff**	**Net Profit**	**Maximum Loss**	**Maximum Profit**	
Buy High and Sell Low Put	$ 170.00	$ (10.75)	$ 160.00	$ 6.00	$ (4.75)	$ 130.00	$ 10.00	$ 5.25		$ 5.25	
Buy High and Sell Low Put	$ 170.00	$ (10.75)	$ 160.00	$ 6.00	$ (4.75)	$ 140.00	$ 10.00	$ 5.25		$ 5.25	
Buy High and Sell Low Put	$ 170.00	$ (10.75)	$ 160.00	$ 6.00	$ (4.75)	$ 150.00	$ 10.00	$ 5.25		$ 5.25	
Buy High and Sell Low Put	$ 170.00	$ (10.75)	$ 160.00	$ 6.00	$ (4.75)	$ 160.00	$ 10.00	$ 5.25		$ 5.25	
Buy High and Sell Low Put	**$ 170.00**	**$ (10.75)**	**$ 160.00**	**$ 6.00**	**$ (4.75)**	**$ 165.25**	**$ 4.75**	**$ -**			**Breakeven**
Buy High and Sell Low Put	$ 170.00	$ (10.75)	$ 160.00	$ 6.00	$ (4.75)	$ 170.00	$ -	$ (4.75)	$ (4.75)		
Buy High and Sell Low Put	$ 170.00	$ (10.75)	$ 160.00	$ 6.00	$ (4.75)	$ 180.00	$ -	$ (4.75)	$ (4.75)		
Buy High and Sell Low Put	$ 170.00	$ (10.75)	$ 160.00	$ 6.00	$ (4.75)	$ 190.00	$ -	$ (4.75)	$ (4.75)		

the investor is buying put options. Bull put spreads sound like mixed thinking, as typically an investor who buys puts has a more pessimistic view on the stock while the spread is called bull, which represents an optimistic strategy. The strategy here though is still bullish. The investor is hoping that the stock stays high so the options are not exercised, and the investor can keep the net premium received. In all spread strategies where there is contradiction between puts and bulls or calls with bears, the net proceeds are received by the investor. Figure 13.10 shows a bull put spread strategy where the investor buys the 155 March puts, pays $4.10 premium, sells the 165 May calls, and receives a $7.00 premium, calculating a net premium paid of $2.90. The investor in this case is bullish, expecting the stock to go up higher than $165 to keep the $2.90 per share proceeds he or she received. Obviously if the stock drops below $155, the maximum loss will be capped at $7.10. The break-even stock is calculated at $162.10. Figure 13.8 shows the payoff and profit at various stock prices.

BEAR CALL VERTICAL SPREADS

Bear call spreads are vertical spreads that involve the buying of a call option with a high exercise price and the selling of a call option with a low exercise price with the same expiration date. Bear call spreads sound like mixed thinking, as typically an investor who buys calls has a more optimistic view on the stock while the spread is called bear, which

FIGURE 13.10 ADVANCED OPTION STRATEGIES PUT BULL SPREADS

FB	CALLS			PUTS		
Exercise Price (X)	MARCH	APRIL	MAY	MARCH	APRIL	MAY
150	20.00	21.50	23.00	3.00	3.50	4.45
155	15.50	16.25	17.75	4.10	4.90	5.90
160	12.50	12.85	13.50	5.30	6.00	6.80
165	8.10	9.00	10.65	7.00	8.00	9.20
170	5.20	6.30	8.50	9.40	10.75	12.45
175	3.25	4.25	5.75	13.00	14.30	14.20
180	2.50	3.40	4.45	15.00	16.10	17.75

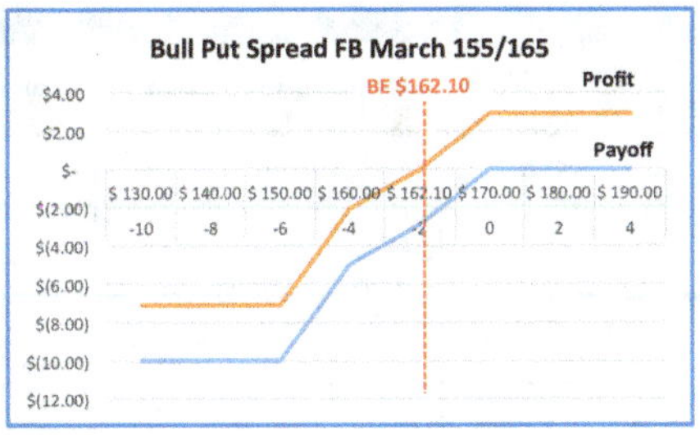

Bull Put Strategy: Buy the Low Exercise Put Price and sell the high Exercise Put Price at the same expiration date (Vertical Spread)
Action Example: Buy the March 155 Puts -pay $4.10 premium
Sell the March 165 Puts - receive $7.00 premium

INPUT						S	OUTPUT				
	Low X	p1	High X	p2	p	S	S - X1 + X2				
STRATEGY	Buy Exercise Puts (X1)	Premium Paid Per Share (p1)	Sell Exercise Puts (X2)	Premium Received Per Share (p2)	Net Premium Received Per Share	Market Price Stock Price (S)	Net Payoff	Net Profit	Maximum Profit	Maximum Loss	
Buy Low and Sell High Put	$ 155.00	$ (4.10)	$ 165.00	$ 7.00	$ 2.90	$ 130.00	$ (10.00)	$ (7.10)		$ (7.10)	
Buy Low and Sell High Put	$ 155.00	$ (4.10)	$ 165.00	$ 7.00	$ 2.90	$ 140.00	$ (10.00)	$ (7.10)		$ (7.10)	
Buy Low and Sell High Put	$ 155.00	$ (4.10)	$ 165.00	$ 7.00	$ 2.90	$ 150.00	$ (10.00)	$ (7.10)		$ (7.10)	
Buy Low and Sell High Put	$ 155.00	$ (4.10)	$ 165.00	$ 7.00	$ 2.90	$ 160.00	$ (5.00)	$ (2.10)		$ (7.10)	
Buy Low and Sell High Put	**$ 155.00**	**$ (4.10)**	**$ 165.00**	**$ 7.00**	**$ 2.90**	**$ 162.10**	**$ (2.90)**	**$ (0.00)**			**Breakeven**
Buy Low and Sell High Put	$ 155.00	$ (4.10)	$ 165.00	$ 7.00	$ 2.90	$ 170.00	$ -	$ 2.90	$ 2.90		
Buy Low and Sell High Put	$ 155.00	$ (4.10)	$ 165.00	$ 7.00	$ 2.90	$ 180.00	$ -	$ 2.90	$ 2.90		
Buy Low and Sell High Put	$ 155.00	$ (4.10)	$ 165.00	$ 7.00	$ 2.90	$ 190.00	$ -	$ 2.90	$ 2.90		

represents a pessimistic strategy. The strategy here though is bearish. The investor is hoping that the stock price stays low and the options are not exercised so he or she can keep the net premium received. In all spread strategies that have that contradiction between calls and bears or puts with bulls, as discussed earlier, the net proceeds are received by the investor. Figure 13.11 shows a put bear spread strategy where the investor buys the 170 April puts, pays $10.75 premium, sells the 160 April puts, and receives a $6.00 premium, calculating a net premium paid of $4.75. The investor in this case is bearish, expecting the stock to drop lower than $160 to maximize the $5.25 per share. Obviously if the stock increases above $170, the maximum loss will be capped at $4.75. The break-even stock is calculated at $165.25. Figure 13.8 shows the payoff, profit, maximum profit, and maximum loss at various stock prices.

LONG AND SHORT BUTTERFLY CALL SPREADS

Long butterfly call spreads are vertical spreads that involve the buying of call options with both the high and low exercise prices and selling the average of the two call options twice with the same expiration date. The investor could also short the butterfly spread, representing the reverse strategy: selling the high and low exercise call prices and buying the average of the two prices twice with the same expiration date. The long butterfly call investor is expecting that the stock will not have any volatility. Figure 13.12 shows the

FIGURE 13.11 ADVANCED OPTION STRATEGIES CALL BEAR SPREADS

FB	CALLS			PUTS		
Exercise Price (X)	MARCH	APRIL	MAY	MARCH	APRIL	MAY
150	20.00	21.50	23.00	3.00	3.50	4.45
155	15.50	16.25	17.75	4.10	4.90	5.90
160	12.50	12.85	13.50	5.30	6.00	6.80
165	8.10	9.00	10.65	7.00	8.00	9.20
170	5.20	6.30	8.50	9.40	10.75	12.45
175	3.25	4.25	5.75	13.00	14.30	14.20
180	2.50	3.40	4.45	15.00	16.10	17.75

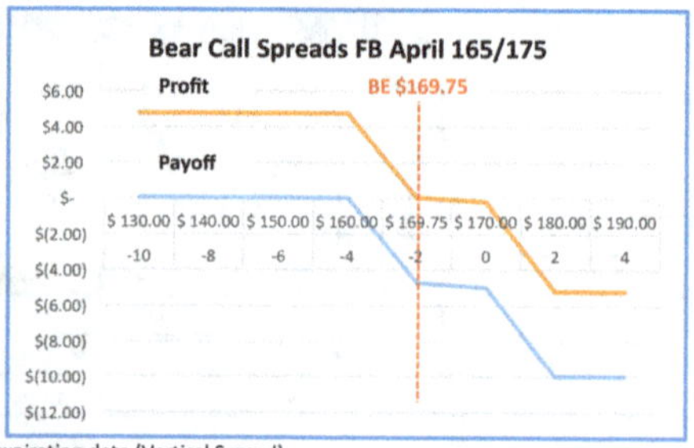

Bear Call Strategy: Buy the high Exercise Call Price and sell the low Exercise Call Price at the same expiration date (Vertical Spread)
Action Example: Buy the April 175 Calls -pay $4.25 premium
Sell the April 165 Calls - receive $9.00 premium

INPUT							OUTPUT				
	High X	p1	Low X	p2	p	S	S - X1 + X2				
STRATEGY	Buy Exercise Call (X1)	Premium Paid Per Share (p1)	Sell Exercise Call (X2)	Premium Received Per Share (p2)	Net Premium Received Per Share	Market Price Stock Price (S)	Net Payoff	Net Profit	Maximum Loss	Maximum Profit	
BuyHigh and Sell Low Call	$ 175.00	$ (4.25)	$ 165.00	$ 9.00	$ 4.75	$ 130.00	$ -	$ 4.75		$ 4.75	
BuyHigh and Sell Low Call	$ 175.00	$ (4.25)	$ 165.00	$ 9.00	$ 4.75	$ 140.00	$ -	$ 4.75		$ 4.75	
BuyHigh and Sell Low Call	$ 175.00	$ (4.25)	$ 165.00	$ 9.00	$ 4.75	$ 150.00	$ -	$ 4.75		$ 4.75	
BuyHigh and Sell Low Call	$ 175.00	$ (4.25)	$ 165.00	$ 9.00	$ 4.75	$ 160.00	$ -	$ 4.75		$ 4.75	
BuyHigh and Sell Low Call	**$ 175.00**	**$ (4.25)**	**$ 165.00**	**$ 9.00**	**$ 4.75**	**$ 169.75**	**$ (4.75)**	**$ -**			**Breakeven**
BuyHigh and Sell Low Call	$ 175.00	$ (4.25)	$ 165.00	$ 9.00	$ 4.75	$ 170.00	$ (5.00)	$ (0.25)	$ (5.25)		
BuyHigh and Sell Low Call	$ 175.00	$ (4.25)	$ 165.00	$ 9.00	$ 4.75	$ 180.00	$ (10.00)	$ (5.25)	$ (5.25)		
BuyHigh and Sell Low Call	$ 175.00	$ (4.25)	$ 165.00	$ 9.00	$ 4.75	$ 190.00	$ (10.00)	$ (5.25)	$ (5.25)		

FIGURE 13.12 ADVANCED OPTION STRATEGIES LONG CALL BUTTERFLY SPREADS

FB	CALLS			PUTS		
Exercise Price (X)	MARCH	APRIL	MAY	MARCH	APRIL	MAY
150	20.00	21.50	23.00	3.00	3.50	4.45
155	15.50	16.25	17.75	4.10	4.90	5.90
160	12.50	12.85	13.50	5.30	6.00	6.80
165	8.10	9.00	10.65	7.00	8.00	9.20
170	5.20	6.30	8.50	9.40	10.75	12.45
175	3.25	4.25	5.75	13.00	14.30	14.20
180	2.50	3.40	4.45	15.00	16.10	17.75

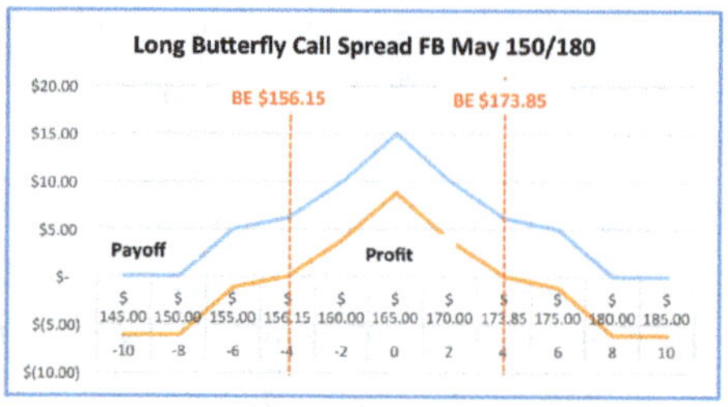

Long Butterfly Call Strategy: Buy the Low Exercise Call Price, Buy the High Exercise Price and sell the average Call Exercise Price twice at the same expiration date (Vertical Spread)
Action Example: Buy the May Call 150 -pay $23 premium
Buy the May 180 Calls - pay $4.45 premium
Sell the May 165 Calls - receive $10.65 premium
Sell the May 165 Calls - receive $10.65 premium

INPUT										OUTPUT			
	Low X1	p1	High X2	p2	2 x Avg X3	2 x p3	p	S		S - X1 + X2			
STRATEGY	Buy Exercise Call (X1)	Premium Paid Per Share (p1)	Buy Exercise Call (X2)	Premium Paid Per Share (p2)	Sell Exercise Call (X2)	Premium Received Per Share (p3)	Net Premium Paid Per Share	Market Price Stock Price (S)		Net Payoff	Net Profit	Maximum Profit	Maximum Loss
Buy Low, High and Sell Avg Call	$ 150.00	$ (23.00)	$ 180.00	$ (4.45)	$ 165.00	$ 21.30	$ (6.15)	$ 140.00		$ -	$ (6.15)		$ (6.15)
Buy Low, High and Sell Avg Call	$ 150.00	$ (23.00)	$ 180.00	$ (4.45)	$ 165.00	$ 21.30	$ (6.15)	$ 145.00		$ -	$ (6.15)		$ (6.15)
Buy Low, High and Sell Avg Call	$ 150.00	$ (23.00)	$ 180.00	$ (4.45)	$ 165.00	$ 21.30	$ (6.15)	$ 150.00		$ -	$ (6.15)		$ (6.15)
Buy Low, High and Sell Avg Call	$ 150.00	$ (23.00)	$ 180.00	$ (4.45)	$ 165.00	$ 21.30	$ (6.15)	$ 155.00		$ 5.00	$ (1.15)		
Buy Low, High and Sell Avg Call	$ 150.00	$ (23.00)	$ 180.00	$ (4.45)	$ 165.00	$ 21.30	$ (6.15)	$ 156.15	BE	$ 6.15	$ 0.00		
Buy Low, High and Sell Avg Call	$ 150.00	$ (23.00)	$ 180.00	$ (4.45)	$ 165.00	$ 21.30	$ (6.15)	$ 160.00		$ 10.00	$ 3.85		
Buy Low, High and Sell Avg Call	$ 150.00	$ (23.00)	$ 180.00	$ (4.45)	$ 165.00	$ 21.30	$ (6.15)	$ 165.00		$ 15.00	$ 8.85	$ 8.85	
Buy Low, High and Sell Avg Call	$ 150.00	$ (23.00)	$ 180.00	$ (4.45)	$ 165.00	$ 21.30	$ (6.15)	$ 170.00		$ 10.00	$ 3.85		
Buy Low, High and Sell Avg Call	$ 150.00	$ (23.00)	$ 180.00	$ (4.45)	$ 165.00	$ 21.30	$ (6.15)	$ 173.85	BE	$ 6.15	$ 0.00		
Buy Low, High and Sell Avg Call	$ 150.00	$ (23.00)	$ 180.00	$ (4.45)	$ 165.00	$ 21.30	$ (6.15)	$ 175.00		$ 5.00	$ (1.15)		
Buy Low, High and Sell Avg Call	$ 150.00	$ (23.00)	$ 180.00	$ (4.45)	$ 165.00	$ 21.30	$ (6.15)	$ 180.00		$ -	$ (6.15)		$ (6.15)
Buy Low, High and Sell Avg Call	$ 150.00	$ (23.00)	$ 180.00	$ (4.45)	$ 165.00	$ 21.30	$ (6.15)	$ 185.00		$ -	$ (6.15)		$ (6.15)
Buy Low, High and Sell Avg Call	$ 150.00	$ (23.00)	$ 180.00	$ (4.45)	$ 165.00	$ 21.30	$ (6.15)	$ 190.00		$ -	$ (6.15)		$ (6.15)

long butterfly call spread of Facebook buying the May 150 and May 180 call options and selling the May 165 call options twice—basically four options (buy, buy, sell, and sell). The net premium paid is $6.15. The investor in this case is expecting no volatility on the stock and the best-case scenario with the maximum amount of profit is when the stock gets to an average price of $165. At $165, the investor will exercise the low call exercise price in order to get the maximum payoff, in this case $15 per share, yielding a profit of $8.85 per share. In butterfly spreads there are two break-even points at expiration; in this case the stock prices are $156.15 and $173.85, as shown in figure 13.12. The figure also shows the payoff and profit levels at various stock prices.

LONG AND SHORT BUTTERFLY PUT SPREADS

Like the long butterfly call spreads, long butterfly put spreads have the same strategy. Basically, it's a vertical spread that involves the buying of put options for both high and low exercise prices and selling the average of the two put options twice with the same expiration date. The investor could also short the butterfly spread, representing the reverse strategy: selling the high and low exercise put prices and buying the average of the two prices twice with the same expiration date. The long butterfly put investor is expecting that the stock will not have any volatility. Figure 13.12 shows the long butterfly put spread of Facebook buying the April 155 and April 175 call options and selling the April 165 put options twice—basically four options (buy, buy, sell, and sell). The net premium paid is $3.20. The investor in this case is expecting no volatility on the stock and the best-case scenario with the maximum profit is when the stock gets to the average price of $165. At $165, the investor will exercise the high put exercise price in order to get the maximum payoff, in this case $10 per share, yielding a profit of $6.80 per share. While using butterfly spreads there are two break-even points; in this case the stock prices are $158.20 and $171.80 to expiration, as shown in figure 13.13. The figure also shows the payoff and profit levels at various stock prices.

OPTION VALUATION METHODS

So far, the chapter covered various option strategies that the investor can use to benefit based on his or her view on the direction of the stock. Using the right option strategy, based on the view of how the stock will perform in the future, the investor used two input variables including the exercise price (X) and premium (p) to determine the potential payoff (O), profit (π), and holding period return (HPR%) at various stock prices (S) by expiration day (t) or stock at expiration (St). For the call option buyer, the payoff is either $S - X$ or 0 if the $X > S$, and for the put option buyer, the payoff is either $X - S$ or 0 if the

FIGURE 13.13 ADVANCED OPTION STRATEGIES LONG PUT BUTTERFLY SPREADS

FB	CALLS			PUTS		
Exercise Price (X)	MARCH	APRIL	MAY	MARCH	APRIL	MAY
150	20.00	21.50	23.00	3.00	3.50	4.45
155	15.50	16.25	17.75	4.10	4.90	5.90
160	12.50	12.85	13.50	5.30	6.00	6.80
165	8.10	9.00	10.65	7.00	8.00	9.20
170	5.20	6.30	8.50	9.40	10.75	12.45
175	3.25	4.25	5.75	13.00	14.30	14.20
180	2.50	3.40	4.45	15.00	16.10	17.75

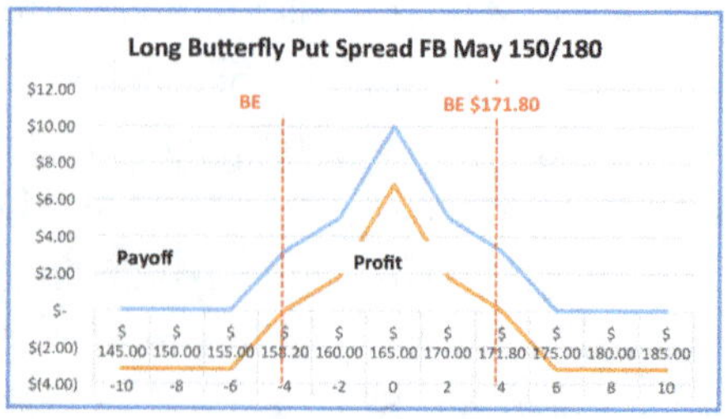

Long Butterfly Put Strategy: Buy the Low Exercise Put Price, Buy the High Exercise Put Price and sell the average Put Exercise Price twice at the same expiration date (Vertical Spread)
Action Example: Buy the Apr 155 Puts -pay $4.90 premium
Buy the Apr 175 Puts - pay $14.30 premium
Sell the Apr 165 Puts - receive $8.00 premium
Sell the Apr 165 Puts - receive $8.00 premium

INPUT										OUTPUT			
	Low X1	p1	High X2	p2	2 x Avg X3	2 x p3	p	S		X1 + X2 - S			
STRATEGY	Buy Exercise Call (X1)	Premium Paid Per Share (p1)	Buy Exercise Call (X2)	Premium Paid Per Share (p2)	Sell Exercise Call (X2)	Premium Received Per Share (p3)	Net Premium Paid Per Share	Market Price Stock Price (S)		Net Payoff	Net Profit	Maximum Profit	Maximum Loss
Buy Low, High and Sell Avg Put	$ 155.00	$ (4.90)	$ 175.00	$ (14.30)	$ 165.00	$ 16.00	$ (3.20)	$ 140.00		$ -	$ (3.20)		$ (3.20)
Buy Low, High and Sell Avg Put	$ 155.00	$ (4.90)	$ 175.00	$ (14.30)	$ 165.00	$ 16.00	$ (3.20)	$ 145.00		$ -	$ (3.20)		$ (3.20)
Buy Low, High and Sell Avg Put	$ 155.00	$ (4.90)	$ 175.00	$ (14.30)	$ 165.00	$ 16.00	$ (3.20)	$ 150.00		$ -	$ (3.20)		$ (3.20)
Buy Low, High and Sell Avg Put	$ 155.00	$ (4.90)	$ 175.00	$ (14.30)	$ 165.00	$ 16.00	$ (3.20)	$ 155.00		$ -	$ (3.20)		$ (3.20)
Buy Low, High and Sell Avg Put	$ 155.00	$ (4.90)	$ 175.00	$ (14.30)	$ 165.00	$ 16.00	$ (3.20)	$ 158.20	BE	$ 3.20	$ (0.00)		
Buy Low, High and Sell Avg Put	$ 155.00	$ (4.90)	$ 175.00	$ (14.30)	$ 165.00	$ 16.00	$ (3.20)	$ 160.00		$ 5.00	$ 1.80		
Buy Low, High and Sell Avg Put	$ 155.00	$ (4.90)	$ 175.00	$ (14.30)	$ 165.00	$ 16.00	$ (3.20)	$ 165.00		$ 10.00	$ 6.80	$ 6.80	
Buy Low, High and Sell Avg Put	$ 155.00	$ (4.90)	$ 175.00	$ (14.30)	$ 165.00	$ 16.00	$ (3.20)	$ 170.00		$ 5.00	$ 1.80		
Buy Low, High and Sell Avg Put	$ 155.00	$ (4.90)	$ 175.00	$ (14.30)	$ 165.00	$ 16.00	$ (3.20)	$ 171.80	BE	$ 3.20	$ (0.00)		
Buy Low, High and Sell Avg Put	$ 155.00	$ (4.90)	$ 175.00	$ (14.30)	$ 165.00	$ 16.00	$ (3.20)	$ 175.00		$ -	$ (3.20)		$ (3.20)
Buy Low, High and Sell Avg Put	$ 155.00	$ (4.90)	$ 175.00	$ (14.30)	$ 165.00	$ 16.00	$ (3.20)	$ 180.00		$ -	$ (3.20)		$ (3.20)
Buy Low, High and Sell Avg Put	$ 155.00	$ (4.90)	$ 175.00	$ (14.30)	$ 165.00	$ 16.00	$ (3.20)	$ 185.00		$ -	$ (3.20)		$ (3.20)
Buy Low, High and Sell Avg Put	$ 155.00	$ (4.90)	$ 175.00	$ (14.30)	$ 165.00	$ 16.00	$ (3.20)	$ 190.00		$ -	$ (3.20)		$ (3.20)

S > X. To obtain such an option, the investor needs to pay a premium (p), representing the upfront money or the bet per share and hoping the stock by expiration day (St) covers the original bet.

This section of the chapter will focus on various valuation methods to calculate the fair premium that the investor should pay to receive such a payoff. The thinking and calculations should be very similar to betting on a game of chance. Using probability concepts, for example, someone who bets on a coin toss with two outcomes represents a 50% chance of winning and a 50% chance of losing. In this simple example, let's assume that the payoff is $20 if the coin turns up to be heads (H) and $0 if the coin turns out to be tails (T). On a toss of the dice the winner will be paid $60 if the dice turns out to be a 6. The likelihood (probability) that on one single throw the dice will turn out to be 6 is one in six (1/6) and the probability of not getting a 6 is five out of six (5/6). To evaluate what a fair bet would be based on these games of chance, the formula starts with the following decision tree, shown in figure 13.14.

FIGURE 13.14 CALCULATING THE FAIR BET ...

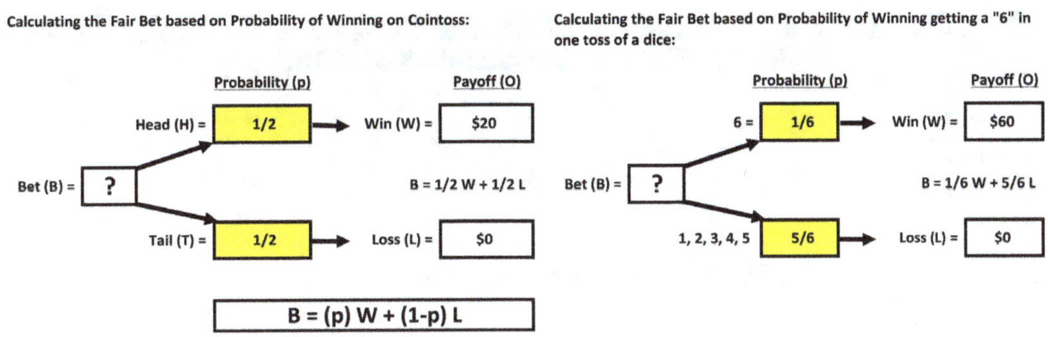

Figure 13.14 shows that the winnings or payoffs as \$20 and \$60 for the coin toss and dice throwing, respectively. Using the probability formulas derived from the decision tree, the bets are calculated as follows:

$$\text{Coin toss bet} = \frac{1}{2}(\$20) + \frac{1}{2}(\$0) = \$10$$

$$\text{Dice toss bet} = \frac{1}{6}(\$60) + \frac{5}{6}(\$0) = \$10$$

The wins or losses of these games of chance represent the option payoff and the outcome from the toss of a coin and a dice represent the stock price. This probability formula concept can be used to determine the fair bet that the player needs to pay up front to enter this game. This fair bet represents the premium that the investor needs to pay upfront to have the right to exercise such option when there is a positive payoff outcome. The challenge is to derive such probabilities when the investor is betting on the direction of the stock in the future. Such direction is measured by historical stock movements, expressed in statistics as the variance (σ^2) of the stock or standard deviation (σ). A few such valuation models that use stock variances and standard deviations are the binomial option pricing model and Black-Scholes.

BINOMIAL OPTION PRICING MODEL: SINGLE-PERIOD PROBABILITY METHOD

The binomial option pricing model (BOPM) is a model that continuously measures the two possible outcomes of the stock, up or down, from any point in time until expiration. As the stock goes up, the probability it will continue to go up can change versus the probability of going down from that new level. The up (u) and down (d) values are derived from historical experiences and are used in the BOPM to derive such probabilities. The probability of the stock going up or down is ultimately measured to be the fair bet or the

FIGURE 13.15 ONE-PERIOD BINOMIAL OPTION CALCULATING THE CALL PREMIUM

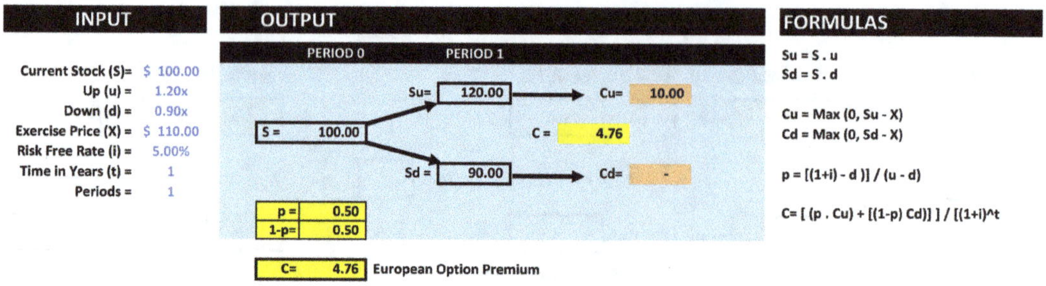

premium an investor is willing to pay to meet his or her expectation. Figure 13.15 uses an example on how to calculate the premium using BOPM.

Figure 13.15 shows there is a 50% probability that the stock will go up from its current level \$100 to \$120 and a 50% probability that the stock will go down to \$90 within the measurable period, in this case one year. The probability calculation is as follows:

$$p = \frac{[(1+i)-d]}{u-d} = \frac{[(1+0.05)-0.90]}{1.20-0.90} = \frac{1.05-0.90}{1.20-0.90} = \frac{0.15}{0.30} = 0.5 \text{ and } i-p=0.5$$

If the stock goes up to \$120, the call option payoff will be \$10 (C = max (0, S − X) = max (0, 120 − 110). If the stock goes down to \$90, the call option will be out of the money and the payoff will be \$0 based on C = max (0, S − X) = max (0, \$110 − \$120). Given the binomial outcome of 50%, in this case, the payoff is \$10 and the 50% payoff is \$0, using the probability theory explained next the fair bet or premium should be at \$5, representing 50% × \$10 + 50% × \$0. If we present value the \$5 back to today's value, since it is what are we paying today for the future outcome, the value is calculated to be \$4.76 based on the present-value calculation of PV = FV/[(1 + i)^t] or 5/[(1 + .05)^1] = 4.76.

Figure 13.16 calculates the put option premium using the same probabilities.

FIGURE 13.16 ONE-PERIOD BINOMIAL OPTION CALCULATING THE PUT PREMIUM

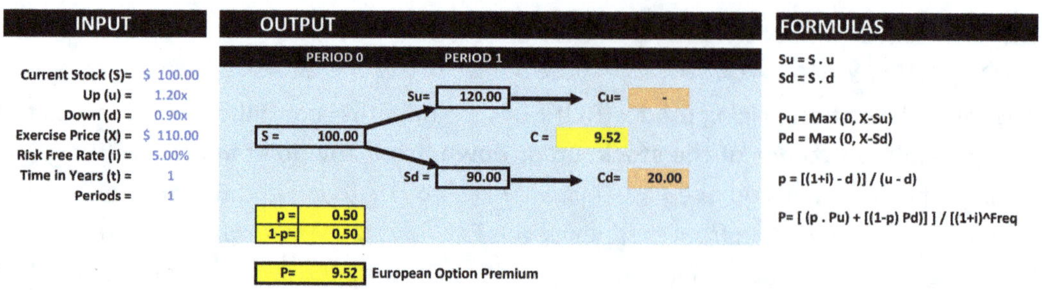

Please notice that the put option price calculated at $9.52 is below the X – S intrinsic value of $10, which at the offset does not make sense because the investor can buy the put option at $9.54, exercise immediately, and receive $10, recording a profit of $0.08. The method, however, calculates a European structure, which the investor can only exercise at expiration day. It's deep in the money but that can change within a year, as the probability forces signal an increase of the stock (1.2x or 20% increase) versus the down factor of 0.90x or 10% decline).

BINOMIAL OPTION PRICING MODEL: TWO-PERIOD PROBABILITY METHOD

The binomial option pricing model (BOPM) using two periods measures four possible outcomes of the stock, up and then up, up and the down, down and then up and down and then down again from any point in time until expiration. The four outcomes illustrated in figure 13.17 show three possible payoffs since the stock that is going up and then down (Sud) is the same as the stock that is going down and then up (Sdu) unless there are dividends paid between these periods (examine that phenomenon later in the chapter). Like before with the single-period BOPM, the up (u) and down (d) values are derived from historical experiences and are used to derive such probabilities. This probability of the stock going up or down ultimately measures the fair bet or the premium an investor is willing to pay to meets his or her expectation. Figure 13.17 uses an example of how to

FIGURE 13.17 TWO-PERIOD BINOMIAL OPTION PRICING MODEL CALL AND PUTS OPTIONS

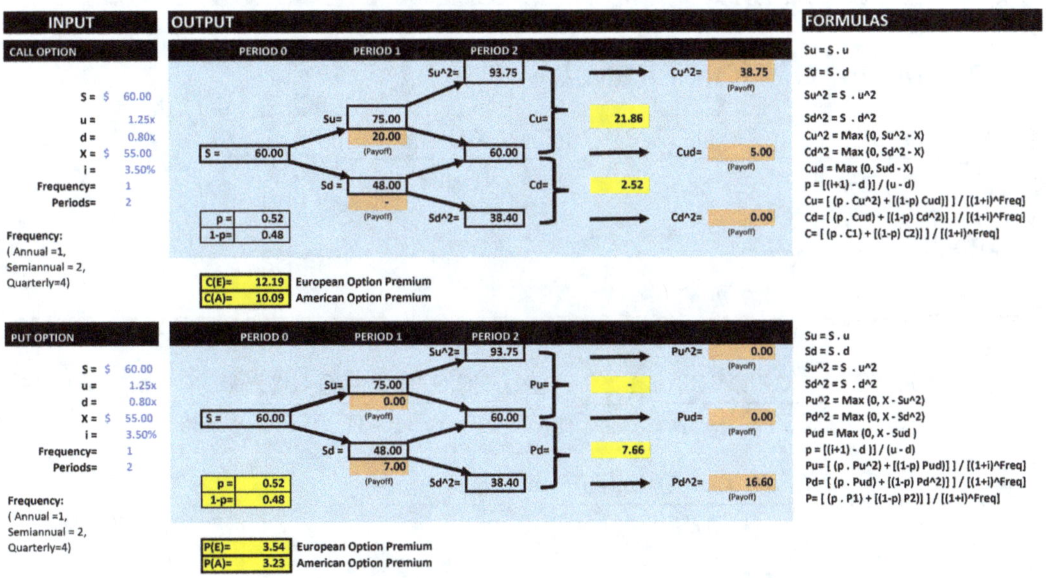

calculate the premium for both call and put options using two-period BOPM. The example calculates both the European and American structures.

Option Premium Calculations Based on European Structure

The probability calculations for both the call and put option premiums are the same. After the investor calculates the call and put option payoffs for the second period, the probability is applied to the upper/upper, upper/lower, and lower/lower payoffs as follows:

CALL OPTION PREMIUM

$$Cu = \frac{[p(Cu^2) + (1-p)(Cud)]}{(1+i/f)} \text{ and } Cd = \frac{[p(Cud) + (1-p)(Cd^2)]}{(1+i/f)} \textbf{\textit{ and then}}$$

$$C = \frac{[p(Cu) + (1-p)(Cd)]}{(1+i/f)}$$

$$Cu = \frac{[0.52(38.75) + (0.48)(5)]}{(1+0.035/1)} = 21.86 \text{ and } Cd = \frac{[0.52(5) + (0.48)(0.0)]}{(1+0.035/1)} = 2.52$$

$$\textit{and then } C(E) = \frac{[0.52(21.86) + (0.48)(2.52)]}{(1+0.035/1)} = 12.19$$

PREMIUM OPTION PREMIUM

$$Pu = \frac{[p(Pu^2) + (1-p)(Pud)]}{(1+i/f)} \text{ and } Pd = \frac{[p(Pud) + (1-p)(Pd^2)]}{(1+i/f)} \textbf{\textit{ and then}}$$

$$P = \frac{[p(Pu) + (1-p)(Pd)]}{(1+i/f)}$$

$$Pu = \frac{[0.52(0.0) + (0.48)(0.0)]}{(1+0.035/1)} = 0.0 \text{ and } Cd = \frac{[0.52(0.0) + (0.48)(16.60)]}{(1+0.035/1)} = 7.66$$

$$\textit{and then } C(E) = \frac{[0.52(0.0) + (0.48)(7.66)]}{(1+0.035/1)} = 3.54$$

Option Premium Calculations Based on American Structure

The probability calculations for both the call and put option premiums are the same. After the investor calculates the call and put option payoffs for the first period, the probability is applied to the upper and lower payoffs as follows:

CALL OPTION PREMIUM

$$C = \frac{[p(C\ higher\ payoff) + (1-p)(C\ lower\ payoff)]}{(1 + i / f)}$$

$$C(A) = \frac{[0.52(20.00) + (0.48)(0.00)]}{\left(1 + \frac{0.035}{1}\right)} = 10.09$$

PUT OPTION PREMIUM

$$P = \frac{[p(P\ lower\ payoff) + (1-p)(P\ higher\ payoff)]}{(1 + i / f)}$$

$$C(A) = \frac{[0.52(0.0) + (0.48)(7.00)]}{(1 + 0.035 / 1)} = 3.23$$

BINOMIAL OPTION PRICING MODEL: TWO-PERIOD PROBABILITY METHOD WITH DIVIDENDS

When the company announces that it will be paying dividends, the stock will most likely drop by a percentage equal to the current dividend yield as the investor is pricing in the dividend paid, affecting the present value of the stock. In option pricing, dividends make the calculation of premium more challenging. In valuing the premium of an option to stock that pays dividends using the BOPM, the analysis needs be adjusted during the predicted binomial up or down of the stock. The four outcomes illustrated in figure 13.18 show the yield adjustments prior to calculating the Su^2 and Sd^2. Figure 13.18 uses an example on how to calculate the premium for a call option using two-period BOPM adjusting for dividend

FIGURE 13.18 TWO-PERIOD BINOMIAL OPTION PRICING MODEL WITH DIV. CALL OPTIONS

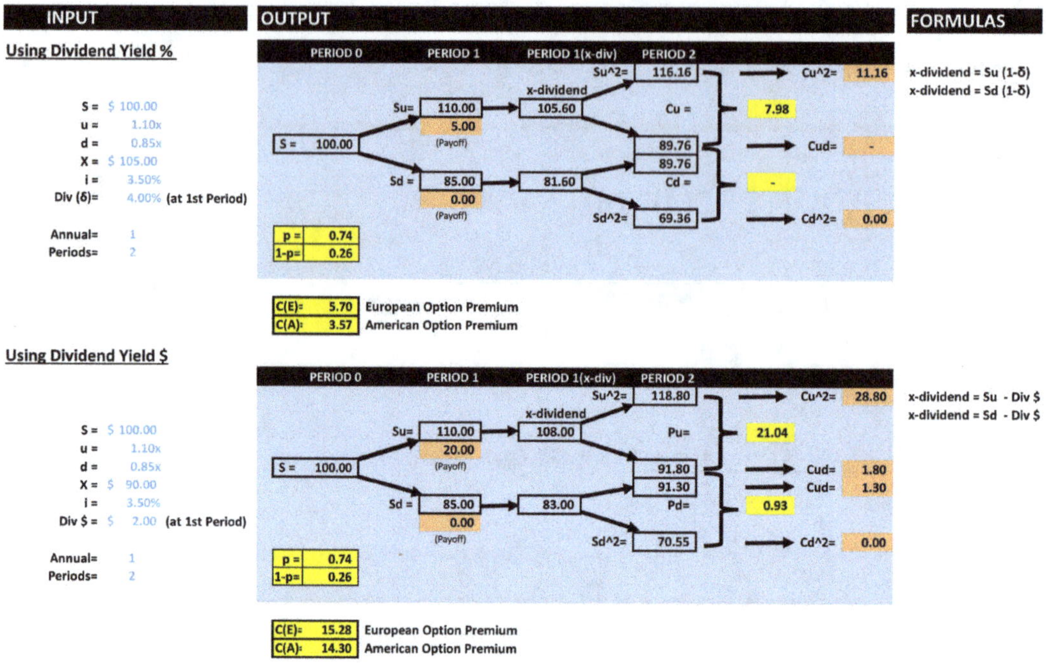

yield and dividend amount paid per share. The example also calculates both the European and American structures. Suppose that the dividend yield is 4%; then the stock after the first period is adjusted to be 4% less or 96% of the upper and lower stock prices.

BLACK-SCHOLES-MERTON (BSM) MODEL

Black-Scholes-Merton model (BSM), also referred to in short as Black-Scholes, is one of the first pricing models that was used to calculate the fair price for a call or a put option premium based on five variables including current stock price, strike price, volatility, time, and risk-free rate. If the company pays dividends on underlying stock, the price is adjusted by the dividend yield, similar to the BOPM that was previously discussed. Before the Black-Scholes formula is stated, the chapter will focus on these five variables and other statistical concepts.

Five Variables

All option valuation methods are consistent of using the same five variables including the current stock price as the underline asset, the exercise or future price, the variance or standard deviation representing the volatility, time and the risk-free rate described below:

1. Current Stock Price (S_0)

Like the BOPM, the current price of the underlying stock is one the most important variables in determining the intrinsic value of the expected option payoff in the future. As mentioned earlier, the relationship between the current stock price to the future exercise price is the first natural comparison to determine how high the stock needs to go to exceed the exercise price for a call option and how low the stock needs to go below the exercise price for a put option. The value, or intrinsic value of S – X and X – S for the call option and put option payoffs, respectively, is the basis of the Black-Scholes formula.

2. Exercise Price (X)

This is the future price of the underlying stock at expiration of the option. This price is constant, and the investor is constantly comparing the current stock price (S) to the exercise price as the expiration time comes near and the intrinsic value of S – X or X – S is expanding or contracting to calculate the call option and put option payoff, respectively.

3. Volatility and Standard Deviation (σ)

This is the volatility measured by the standard deviation of the historical underlying stock price as it changes from day to day or week to week or month to month. Bigger swings in stock price translate to higher volatility and a higher standard deviation. Basically, this swing determines how probable it is for the stock to go higher or lower than the constant exercise price. The higher the standard deviation, the most likely the stock will be in the money with positive intrinsic value of S – X or X – S for the call and put option, respectively. The higher the standard deviation, the higher the expected option premium.

4. Time (t)

Time to maturity or time to option expiration is an important variable to measure the value of the option. In general, the premium paid to buy the option is higher if there is more time to exercise. It also gives a higher chance for the stock to reach the exercise price.

5. Risk-Free Rate (i)

Use the risk-free rate to calculate the present value of the exercise price. The rate used should be the annualized rate and be adjusted for maturity. The other adjustment is compounding.

Other Statistical Concepts

It's important to reintroduce some mathematical concepts that are essential for valuating options including the natural logarithms, probability theory and normal distribution.

Compounding Using Exponential (e)

The number **e** is a mathematical constant 2.7182 that is the base of the natural logarithm and is equal to one. The future value calculation discussed in the first chapter is calculated based on the following formula:

$$FV = PV\left(1+\frac{i}{f}\right)^{t}$$

where PV is the present value, i is the interest, t is the time, and f is the frequency or compounding payment per year.

As the frequency increases from annual to semi-annual, to quarterly, to monthly, and to infinite, compounding the future value will increase, but it won't get higher than 2.718 times the original present value, as illustrated in figure 13.19.

The infinite compounding e is used in the Black-Scholes model to calculate the present value of the exercise price (X) as e^{-it} and is derived based on the following mathematical calculation:

$$e = PV\ (1+i)^{t} \text{ then } PV = \frac{e}{(1+i)^{t}} \text{ then } PV = e^{-it}$$

Natural Logarithm (ln)

The model assumes stock prices follow a lognormal distribution because asset prices cannot be negative (they are bounded by zero). This is also known as a Gaussian distribution.

FIGURE 13.19 COMPOUND INTEREST USING E

Present Value =	$	1.00
Interest =		10%
Years =		10

Description	Compound per year Freguency (f)	Future Value Compunded
Annual	1	2.5937425
Semi	2	2.6532977
Quarterly	4	2.6850638
Monthly	12	2.7070415
Daily	365	2.7179096
Hourly	8,760	2.7182663
By Minute	525,600	2.7182816
By Second	31,536,000	2.7182819
Infinite	e	2.7182818

Often, asset prices are observed to have significant right skewness and some degree of kurtosis (fat tails). This means high-risk downward moves often happen more often in the market than a normal distribution predicts. The assumption of lognormal underlying asset prices should thus show that implied volatilities are similar for each strike price according to the Black-Scholes model.

Normal Probability Distribution (N)

The normal probability distribution in a bell-shaped curve gives the probability that a standard normal random variable will be less than equal to a given value. Figure 13.20 shows that the normal distribution graph represents a standard normal distribution with mean $\mu = 0$ and standard deviation $\sigma = 1$. For example, if the stock has a standard deviation of 10%, that means that the stock "swings" either way of 10% from the average, representing that a stock with an average of $100 in the upper and lower limits within the period is between $90–$110 (–10% to +10%). Within one standard deviation, the probability that the stock will stay at 10% is 64%. In a game of chance, the investor will bet $6.40 to get a $10 payoff for the stock to move within 10%.

The values of N (d) are given by Figure 13.20. The value of d is between negative infinite and positive infinite, but for valuation purposes showing 3 decimals the levels are basically between −3.00 and 3.00 for almost ~100% of the normal distribution of positive values between zero and one. For example, if d = 1.3, the normalized value is 0.903. The table is used in the Black-Scholes model to determine the normal probability of the stock to determine the fair value of the premium.

The formulas for calculating the probability distribution to be used in the calculation of the intrinsic value of S − X or X − S for the call and put options, respectively using

FIGURE 13.20 NORMAL PROBABILITY DISTRIBUTION

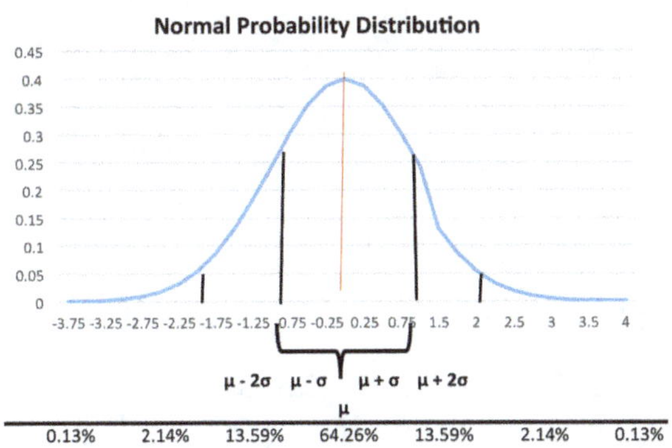

NORMAL DISTRIBUTION TABLE									
d	N(d)	d	N(d)	d	N(d)	d	N(d)	d	N(d)
3.200	0.999	1.900	0.971	0.600	0.726	-0.700	0.242	-2.000	0.023
3.100	0.999	1.800	0.964	0.500	0.691	-0.800	0.212	-2.100	0.018
3.000	0.999	1.700	0.955	0.400	0.655	-0.900	0.184	-2.200	0.014
2.900	0.998	1.600	0.945	0.300	0.618	-1.000	0.159	-2.300	0.011
2.800	0.997	1.500	0.933	0.200	0.579	-1.100	0.136	-2.400	0.008
2.700	0.997	1.400	0.919	0.100	0.540	-1.200	0.115	-2.500	0.006
2.600	0.995	1.300	0.903	0.000	0.500	-1.300	0.097	-2.600	0.005
2.500	0.994	1.200	0.885	-0.100	0.460	-1.400	0.081	-2.700	0.003
2.400	0.992	1.100	0.864	-0.200	0.421	-1.500	0.067	-2.800	0.003
2.300	0.989	1.000	0.841	-0.300	0.382	-1.600	0.055	-2.900	0.002
2.200	0.986	0.900	0.816	-0.400	0.345	-1.700	0.045	-3.000	0.001
2.100	0.982	0.800	0.788	-0.500	0.309	-1.800	0.036	-3.100	0.001
2.000	0.977	0.700	0.758	-0.600	0.274	-1.900	0.029	-3.200	0.001

the Black-Scholes model N(d1) which is the probability of the stock being in the money and N(d2) representing the probability of being out-of-the-money, are follows:

$$d1 = \frac{\ln\left(\frac{S}{X}\right) + \left(i + \frac{\sigma^2}{2}\right)t}{\sigma\sqrt{t}} \text{ and } d2 = d1 - \sigma\sqrt{t}$$

where S is the current price, X is the exercise price, i is the risk-free rate, t is time to expiration, and σ is the standard deviation.

The Black-Scholes formula for the call option (C) and put option (P) are as follows:

$$C = SN(d1) - Xe^{-it}N(d2) \text{ and } P = Xe^{-it}[1 - N(d2)] - S[1 - N(d1)]$$

For example, let's assume that the that the current stock price (S) is $100 and the future exercise price (X) that expires in 6 months is $110. This out-of-the-money call option and in-the-money put option have a standard deviation (σ) of 0.40. Given the risk-free rate of 5%, what is the fair value for both call and put option premiums?

Input

S = $100

X = $110

t = 0.50 (6 months)

i = 5.0%

σ = .40

Formulas

$$d1 = \frac{\ln\left(\frac{100}{110}\right) + \left(0.05 + \frac{.4^2}{2}\right)0.50}{0.40\sqrt{0.5}} = \frac{\ln(0.9091) + (0.05 + 0.08)\ 0.50}{(0.40)(0.7071)} = \frac{-0.0953 + 0.065}{0.2828}$$

$d1 = -0.1071$

and

$d2 = -0.1071 - 0.2828 = -0.3899$

N (d1) = N (−0.1071) = 0.4573

N (d2) = N (−0.3899) = 0.3482

The call option for the call option is calculated using the Black-Scholes formula:

$$C = 100(0.4573) - 110\ e^{-(0.05)(0.5)}(0.3482) = 45.73 - 110(0.9753)(0.3482)$$
$$= 45.73 - 37.36 = 8.37$$

C = 8.37

The put option is calculated as follows:

$$P = 110\ e^{-(0.05)(0.5)}[1-(0.3482)] - 100[1-0.4573]$$
$$= 110\ (0.9753)(0.6518) - 100(0.5427) = 69.93 - 54.27 = 15.66$$

P = 15.66

BLACK-SCHOLES-MERTON (BSM) MODEL: ADJUSTING FOR DIVIDENDS

As mentioned previously, in general, stocks fall by the amount of the dividend payment on the ex-dividend date. Since the dividend is important in the mathematics of the pricing of the option, the Black-Scholes formula can be modified to reflect such payment. Since, theoretically, the stock should drop by the amount of the dividend, the current stock price needs to be adjusted to anticipate the future dividend. The current stock price (S), which is part of the Black-Scholes equation, is modified to $Se^{-\delta t}$, reflecting the present of value the stock using a dividend yield (δ). The Black-Scholes formula is modified to include the dividend as part of calculating the d1 (note that if they are no dividends with $\delta = 0$ the $Se^{-\delta t}$ will be written Se^{0}, which equals to S as $e^{0} = 1$).

$$d1 = \frac{\ln\left(\frac{S}{X}\right) + \left(i - \delta + \frac{\sigma^2}{2}\right)t}{\sigma\sqrt{t}} \text{ and } d2 = d1 - \sigma\sqrt{t}$$

where S is the current price, X is the exercise price, i is the risk-free rate, t is time to expiration, σ is the standard deviation, and δ is the dividend yield.

The Black-Scholes formula for the call option (C) and put option (P) are as follows:

$$C = Se^{-\delta t}\ N(d1) - Xe^{-it}N(d2) \text{ and } P = Xe^{-it}[1-N(d2)] - Se^{-\delta t}[1-N(d1)]$$

For example, let's assume that the that the current stock price (S) is \$100 and the future exercise price (X) that expires in 6 months is \$110. This out-of-the-money call option and in-the-money put option have a standard deviation (σ) of 0.40. The dividend yield (δ) is 3%. Given the risk-free rate of 5%, what is the fair value of both the call and put option premium?

Input

S = \$100
X = \$110
t = 0.50 (6 months)
i = 5.0%
σ = .40
δ = 3.0%

Formulas

$$d1 = \frac{\ln\left(\frac{100}{110}\right) + \left(0.05 - 0.03 + \frac{.4^2}{2}\right)0.50}{0.40\sqrt{0.5}} = \frac{\ln(0.9091) + (0.02 + 0.08)0.50}{(0.40)(0.7071)}$$

$$= \frac{-0.0953 + 0.050}{0.2828}$$

$$d1 = -0.1602$$

and

d2 = -0.1602 - 0.2828 = -0.4430

N (d1) = N (-0.1602) = 0.4364

N (d2) = N (-0.4430) = 0.3289

The call option for the call option is calculated using the Black-Scholes formula:

$$C = 100\ e^{-(0.03)(0.5)}(0.4364) - 110\ e^{-(0.05)(0.5)}(0.3289)$$
$$= 100\ (0.9851)(0.4364) - 110(0.9753)(0.3289)$$
$$= 42.99 - 35.28 = 7.71$$

C = 7.71

The put option is calculated as follows:

$$P = 110\ e^{-(0.05)(0.5)}[1 - (0.3482)] - 100\ e^{-(0.03)(0.5)}[1 - 0.4573]$$
$$= 110\ (0.9753)(0.6518) - 100\ (0.9851)(0.5427) = 69.93 - 53.46 = 16.47$$

P = 16.47

The call option calculations using Excel is shown in figure 13.21 (assuming zero dividends). The put option calculations using Excel is shown in figure 13.22.

FIGURE 13.21 BLACK-SCHOLES VALUATION CALL OPTION

CALL OPTION

A	B	C	D	E	F	G	H	I
4								
5	INPUT				OUTPUT			FORMULAS
6								
7		Standard Deviation (σ) =	0.4		d1 =	-0.107		=(LN(D11/D12)+(D10-D13+(D8^2)/2)*D9)/(D8*SQRT(D9))
8		Expiration (in years) (T) =	0.5		d2 =	-0.390		=+G8-D8*SQRT(D9)
9		Risk-Free Rate (Annual) (i) =	0.05		N(d1) =	0.457		=NORMSDIST(G8)
10		Stock Price (S) =	100		N(d2) =	0.348		=NORMSDIST(G9)
11		Exercise Price (X) =	110					
12		Dividend Yield (annual) (δ) =	0		C =	8.3696		=+D11*EXP(-D13*D9)*G10-D12*EXP(-D10*D9)*G11
13								

FIGURE 13.22 BLACK-SCHOLES VALUATION PUT OPTION

PUT OPTION

A	B	C	D	E	F	G	H	I
4								
5	INPUT				OUTPUT			FORMULAS
6								
7		Standard Deviation (σ) =	0.4		d1 =	-0.107		=(LN(D11/D12)+(D10-D13+(D8^2)/2)*D9)/(D8*SQRT(D9))
8		Expiration (in years) (T) =	0.5		d2 =	-0.390		=+G8-D8*SQRT(D9)
9		Risk-Free Rate (Annual) (i) =	0.05		N(d1) =	0.457		=NORMSDIST(G8)
10		Stock Price (S) =	100		N(d2) =	0.348		=NORMSDIST(G9)
11		Exercise Price (X) =	110					
12		Dividend Yield (annual) (δ) =	0		P =	15.6537		=D11*EXP(-D9*D8)*(1-G10)-D10*EXP(-D12*D8)*(1-G9)
13								

PUT CALL PARITY

Either the investor needs to calculate the call option or the put option and given that the probability concepts used are the same pricing for the same period, the call price should be in parity of the put price. The difference between the call premium to the put premium should equal the intrinsic value S − X or X − S, with the exception that the X will be adjusted to represent the present value, since by definition the exercise price is in the future. The call put parity is as follows:

$$C - P = S - PV(X) \text{ or } C - P = S - Xe^{-it}$$

If an investor knows the call price and needs to determine the put price and vice versa, the formulas translate to the following:

$$C = S - Xe^{-it} + P \text{ and } P = Xe^{-it} - S + C$$

Using this example where the stock is \$100 and the future exercise price (X) that expires in 6 months is \$110, the call option is priced at \$8.37. Given the risk-free rate of 5%, what is the fair value of the put option premium? Using the call put parity formula, calculate the put option as follows:

$$P = Xe^{-it} - S + C = 110\,e^{-(0.05)(0.5)} - 100 + 8.37 = 110(0.9753) - 100 + 8.37 = 15.66$$

P = **15.66**

HEDGE RATIO (H) AND LEVERAGE (BORROWING) METHODS: USING BOPM

There is another method that can be used to determine the option pricing. This method is like the binomial option pricing model (BOPM) discussed earlier, but instead of using the probability, the values can be derived by using the leverage method. This leverage method is important when the investor is using the BOPM valuation to determine the fully

FIGURE 13.23 BINOMIAL OPTION PRICING MODEL

LEVERAGE (BORROWING) METHOD - Call option

Parameters	Current Stock Price	Increase / Decrease Factors (u and d)	Stock x (Su) and (Sd)	Call Option Payoff (Cu) and (Cd)	h
Current Price (So)=	$ 100.00				
Up factor (u) =		1.2x	$ 120.00	$ 10.00	
Down factor (d) =		0.9x	$ 90.00	$ -	
Ranges (Su - Sd) and (Cu-Cd) =			$ 30.00	$ 10.00	1/3

Exercise Option =	$ 110.00	
Exercise time =	1	year
Interest Rate =	5%	annual compounding
Step 1: (Su - Sd) =	$ 30.00	Range between Upper and Lower Stock
Step 2: (Cu - Cd) =	$ 10.00	Range between Upper and Lower Payoff
Step 3: h = (Cu - Cd) / (Su - Sd) =	1/3	Hedge Ratio (Buy 1 Stock / Sell 3 Calls)
Step 4: (PV of Sd)	$ 85.71	Present Value of the Stock - Borrowing)
Step 5: (So - PV(Sd))	$ 14.29	Intrinsic Value (S - Expected X)
Step 6: ([So - PV(Sd)] x h) =	$ 4.76	Intrinsic Value times the hedge ratio
Premium =	**$ 4.76**	
Break Even =	**$ 114.76**	Stock Price + Premium
Distance to BE ($) =	$ 14.76	Break Even $116.06 - Current Stock $100
Distance to BE (%) =	14.76%	Break Even / Stock Price - 1

CALL-PUT PARITY ERROR CHECK
$ 9.52

LEVERAGE (BORROWING) METHOD - Put Option

Parameters	Current Stock Price	Increase / Decrease Factors (u and d)	Stock x (Su) and (Sd)	Put Option Payoff (Pu) and (Pd)	h
Current Price (So)=	$ 100.00				
Up factor (u) =		1.2x	$ 120.00	$ -	
Down factor (d) =		0.9x	$ 90.00	$ 20.00	
Ranges (Su - Sd) and (Cd-Cu) =			$ 30.00	$ 20.00	2/3

Exercise Option =	$ 110.00	
Exercise time =	1	year
Interest Rate =	5%	annual compounding
Step 1: (Su - Sd) =	$ 30.00	Range between Upper and Lower Stock
Step 2: (Pu - Pd) =	$ 20.00	Range between Upper and Lower Payoff
Step 3: h = (Pu - Pd) / (Su - Sd) =	2/3	Hedge Ratio (Buy 2 Stocks / Buy 3 Puts)
Step 4: (PV of Su)	$ 114.29	Present Value of the Stock - Borrowing)
Step 5: (So - PV(Su))	$ 14.29	Intrinsic Value (Expected X-S)
Step 6: ([PV(Su) - S0] x h) =	$ 9.52	Intrinsic Value times the hedge ratio
Premium =	**$ 9.52**	
Break Even =	**$ 100.48**	Stock Price - Premium
Distance to BE ($) =	$ 0.48	Break Even $96.36 - Current Stock $100
Distance to BE (%) =	0.48%	Break Even / Stock Price - 1

hedged position for option strategies such as covered calls and protective puts. The method to calculate the call price is demonstrated. This six-step method shown in figure 13.23 determines first the hedge ratio and then, using a leverage component, calculates the fair value of both call and put options.

Figure 13.23 shows that the European call option should be priced at $4.76 and the put option at $9.52, with hedge ratios of 1/3 and 2/3, respectively. Let's assume that the call option is mispriced versus our calculation. Instead of $4.76, the market quotes the call option at $5.25. This represents an arbitrage opportunity, demonstrated in figure 13.24.

Figure 13.24 calculates an arbitrage opportunity of the call option that is trading at $5.25 while the BOPM suggested value is $4.76. Since the current price is higher, then the investor should take advantage of the mispriced call option and enter a cover call by selling the option by using the hedge ratio that is calculated at 1/3. With the hedge ratio 1/3, the investor should buy one share at $100 and sell three call options at $5.25 each, for a total cost of $15.75, and borrow the difference at 5%. If the stock goes to $90, then the investor will sell the stock at $90 and pay off the loan, which is projected to be at $88.46, including the original loan of $84.25 and 5% interest. At $90, the call options will not be exercised since the price (S) is lower than the exercise price (X). The proceeds of selling the stock will be $1.54 per share with no risk. The same is shown if the stock goes to the upper level of $120. The investor will sell the stock, receive $120, and pay $30 to cover the three call options ((X – S) × # of call options = ($120 – 110) × 3 = $10 × 3 = $30). The net proceeds of $90 will more than cover the loan of $88.46, including interest. Since $1.54 is a future payment, the investor needs to discount that back to determine today's

FIGURE 13.24 BINOMIAL OPTION PRICING MODEL MISPRICED SECURITY

Mispriced Security: Arbitrage Opportunity

Assume Call option is mispriced at	**$ 5.25**
Calculated the Call option price using BOPM =	$ 4.76
Current Stock Price	$ 100.00
Using the Hedge ratio you get to the following strategy	1/3
Exerecise Price	$ 110.00
Borrowing Interest Rate	5.0%
Time to expiration (years)	1

Sequence	**Strategy**	**Initial CF**	**At Stock $ 90.00**	**At Stock $ 120.00**
FIRST	Write 3 Calls ($5.25 x 3) at cost =	$ 15.75	$ -	$ (30.00)
SECOND	Buy one share ($100 x 1)=	$ (100.00)	$ 90.00	$ 120.00
THIRD	Borrow the difference at 5% =	$ 84.25	$ (88.46)	$ (88.46)
Total		**$ -**	**$ 1.54**	**$ 1.54**
Present Value =			$ 1.46	$ 1.46
Per option profit =			$ 0.49	$ 0.49

Note : Exactly the amount that the option is mispriced $5.25 - $4.76 = $ 0.49

arbitrage price at a 5% discount rate, calculated at $1.46. The $1.46 represents today's arbitrage price per share for three call options. If you divide $1.46 by three call options, the mispriced opportunity per option is $49, which represents the difference between the calculated $4.76 using the BOPM and the $5.25 current misprice.

CASE STUDY

USING OPTION STRATEGY TO HEDGE AGAINST THE COVID-19 CORONAVIRUS—MARCH 2020

Synopsis: The coronavirus (Covid-19) outbreak was first identified in Wuhan, Hubei, China, in December 2019, and was recognized as a pandemic by the World Health Organization (WHO) on March 11, 2020. This pandemic had spread throughout the United States by mid-March, had a major economic impact, and created unprecedented market volatility. On Friday, February 28, 2020 after seeing the major impact in China and Europe, especially in Italy, you were asked to hedge your existing portfolio of U.S. stock against further deterioration of the stock market, specifically the S&P 500 Index. A direct way of using the S&P 500 is to buy or sell options of the ETF called SPY. The tables below show the put option prices for April 13 on March 10 and the cash value of the index (actual value of the SPY EDF).

APRIL 13 PUTS	X	PREMIUM			10-MAR
SPY200413P00275000	275	6.50	SPY200413P00275001	-262	(530.50)
SPY200413P00280000	280	13.63	-6.21	-31.30%	47.57%
SPY200413P00285000	285	20.60	10.91	112.59%	0.00%
SPY200413P00289000	289	21.33	21.33	-	0.00%
SPY200413P00290000	290	23.44	11.94	103.83%	0.00%
SPY200413P00295000	295	13.35	0	–	0.00%
SPY200413P00300000	300	22.96	-3.84	-14.33%	43.13%
SPY200413P00305000	305	17.96	0	-	0.00%
SPY200413P00315000	315	26.55	0	-	0.00%
SPY200413P00325000	325	30.48	0	-	0.00%

	CASH MARKETS	
	10-Mar-20	284.33
Monday	9-Mar-20	274.23
	6-Mar-20	297.46
	5-Mar-20	302.46
	4-Mar-20	312.86
	3-Mar-20	300.24
	2-Mar-20	309.09
Friday	28-Feb-20	296.26
	27-Feb-20	297.51
	26-Feb-20	311.50
	25-Feb-20	312.65

Option Strategy: On February 28, the April 300 put option premiums were trading at $10.35 and the April 275 put option premiums were trading at $4.14. On that day, the investor entered a vertical bear put spread option in which he bought the April 300 puts and sold the April 275. He has a choice of the following:

1. Sell the puts in the secondary market, since there was a significant decline in the S&P Index as the coronavirus significantly spread in the United States and had a tremendous impact in the markets.
2. Hold on to the options until expiration if he thinks that the coronavirus will continue to get worse.

The profit/loss is calculated as follows:

CORONAVIRUS HEDGE (FEB 28) USING OPTIONS				
Bear Put April 13 Spread	**X**	**Premium**	Return	
Buy	300	(10.35)	Profit	10.25
Sell (Bear market -20%)	275	4.14	HPR%	265.06%
Paid		(6.21)	100 shares	1,025
Trade today (Mar 10)	**X**	**Premium**		
	300	22.96		
	275	(6.50)		
		16.46		

The investment per share was $6.21 or $621 for 100 shares, calculated by paying $10.35 for buying the put option with X = $300, and receiving $4.14 for selling the put option with X = $275. On March 10, shown in the table, the April 300 puts were trading at $22.96 and the April 275 were trading at $6.50, netting out $16.46 profit if unwinding the options in the market. If the investor exercises the option, the profit will be calculated as follows:

CORONAVIRUS HEDGE (FEB 28) USING OPTIONS						
Bear Put April 13 Spread	**X**	**Premium**				
Buy	300	(10.35)				
Sell (Bear market -20%)	275	4.14				
Paid		(6.21)				
	X	**Stock**	**Premium**	**Payoff**	**Profit**	**HPR%**
Exercise	300	274.23	(10.35)	25.77		
Exercise	275	274.23	4.14	(0.77)		
			(6.21)	25.00	18.79	302.58%

PROBLEMS

1. Calculate the payoff, profit/loss, and BE price of the stock:

ACTION	OPTION	EXERCISE PRICE	PREMIUM	STOCK PRICE	PAYOFF	PROFIT/ LOSS	BE STOCK
Buy	Call	140.00	9.00	165.00			
Buy	Call	62.00	5.00	59.00			
Buy	Put	46.00	5.00	38.00			
Buy	Put	66.00	9.00	66.00			
Sell	Put	132.00	11.00	126.00			
Sell	Put	127.00	9.00	128.00			
Sell	Call	156.00	6.00	152.00			
Sell	Call	143.00	8.00	145.00			
Sell	Straddle	120.00	21.00	135.00			
Buy	Straddle	95.00	13.00	125.00			

2. Using the options table below, answer questions 2a. and 2b.

	CALL			PUT		
EXERCISE PRICE (X)	MARCH	APRIL	MAY	MARCH	APRIL	MAY
150	20.00	21.50	23.00	3.00	3.50	4.45
155	15.50	16.25	17.75	4.10	4.90	5.90
160	12.50	12.85	13.50	5.30	6.00	6.80
165	8.10	9.00	10.65	7.00	8.00	9.20
170	5.20	6.30	8.50	9.40	10.75	12.45
175	3.25	4.25	5.75	13.00	14.30	14.20
180	2.50	3.40	4.45	15.00	16.10	17.75

a. Calculate payoff, profit/loss, breakeven stock price, and HPR%, if applicable.

ACTION	DATE	OPTION	EXERCISE PRICE	STOCK PRICE	PAYOFF	PROFIT/ LOSS	BE (STOCK)	HPR %
Buy	March	Call	150.00	175.00				
Buy	April	Call	165.00	165.00				
Buy	May	Put	170.00	160.00				
Buy	March	Put	180.00	162.00				
Sell	May	Put	165.00	125.00				
Sell	April	Put	175.00	165.00				

Sell	May	Call	155.00	180.00
Sell	April	Call	150.00	165.00
Sell	May	Straddle	175.00	200.00
Buy	March	Straddle	180.00	185.00

b. Calculate payoff and profit/loss for the spread option strategies below.

ACTION	DATE	OPTION	EXERCISE PRICE	STOCK PRICE	TOTAL PAYOFF	TOTAL PROFIT/ LOSS
Buy	March	Bull Call Spread	150	170		
Buy	April	Bull Put Spread	160	162		
Buy	May	Bear Put Spread	170	150		
Buy	April	Bear Call Spread	160	170		
Buy	March	Butterfly Call Spread	150	165		
Sell	May	Butterfly Call Spread	170	200		

3. Using the options table below, answer questions 3a., 3b., 3c., and 3d.

	CALLS			PUTS		
ABC, INC.	APR-19	MAY-19	JUN-19	APR-19	MAY-19	JUN-19
125	12.65	12.80	13.40	5.30	6.00	6.80
130	8.10	9.00	10.65	7.00	8.00	9.00
135	5.20	6.30	8.50	9.40	10.75	12.45
140	3.25	4.25	5.75	13.00	14.30	16.20

a. On March 12, 2019, John bought 100 shares of ABC, Inc. at $135, expecting it to go up soon. Assuming he is right, he wants to protect his investment, so that by June 2019 his investment won't go below $13,500 (excluding premium costs). Using the options market to protect this floor ($13,500), what would you recommend John do to protect his investment for the next 3 months (until June 2019)? He does not mind paying for premium if he is fully protecting his investment.

b. If the stock goes up to $165 and he decides to sell, please calculate John's profit and holding period rate of return (HPR) since his purchase, including the cost of the option contract he entered.

c. If the stock goes down to $125 and he decides to sell it at that level, please calculate John's profit and holding period rate of return (HPR) since his purchase, including the cost of the option contract he entered.

4. Consider the following binomial option pricing problem involving a call. This call has one period to go before expiring. Its stock price is $45, and its exercise price is $49.50. The risk-free rate is 0.05%, the value of u is 1.25, and the value of the d is .95. Construct the 1-period binomial tree model and find the value of the call premium using the leverage (6-step, Method 1) and probability method (Method 2).
5. Consider the following binomial option pricing problem involving a call. This call has two periods to go before expiring. Its stock price is $65, and its exercise price is $60. The risk-free rate is 0.05%, the value of u is 1.20, and the value of the d is .95. Construct the 2-period binomial tree model and find the value of the European call premium.
6. Consider the following binomial option pricing problem involving a put. This put has two periods to go before expiring. Its stock price is $100, and its exercise price is $110. The company expects to pay dividends after the first period. The dividend yield is 7%, the risk-free rate is 0.05%, the value of u is 1.15, and the value of the d is .90. Construct the 2-period binomial tree model and find the value of the European put premium.
7. Calculate the value of the call and put options using the Black Scholes model, assuming the option expires in one year's time, standard deviation (σ) is 0.3, risk-free rate is 1.0%, a stock price of 95, and an exercise price of 115. Assume no dividend is expected to be paid.
8. Calculate the value of a one-year put option if the one-year call option is priced at $13, the stock price is $65, the exercise price is $60, and the risk-free rate is 2.0%, using the call-put parity method.

ONLINE TEMPLATES

The Excel spreadsheets used in the chapter can be accessed online via Cognella Active Learning platform.

CHAPTER 14

Derivative Investments: Futures, Forwards, Swaps, Swaptions, CDAs, FRAs, and Other Derivatives

This chapter will give an overview of the futures exchange markets, cover forward contracts, and describe other derivatives such as swaps, swaptions, credit default swaps, and forward rate agreements. It will describe various strategies used by investors for hedging against interest rate and market price movements as well as foreign currency and commodity increases or decreases.

LEARNING OBJECTIVES

After reading this chapter, students will be able to do the following:

- Understand how the future exchange market works and how these types of investments are traded and managed as part of an overall investment strategy
- Understand the various hedging strategies against interest rate, foreign currency rate, and commodity price movements
- Learn about other types of derivatives such as swaptions, credit default swaps, and forward rate contracts

FORWARDS, FUTURES SWAP CONTRACTS: OVERVIEW

The main difference between option contracts, described in the previous chapter, and other derivatives such as forwards and futures contracts, is that the buyer of an option pays upfront to obtain the right to exercise the option in the future and buy or sell the underlying stock. In the case of forward and future contracts, the parties are both obliged to sell or buy from each other on a specific date for a specific price. Swaps are also different than options as they are contracts in which the parties agree to exchange cash flows based on a set interest and currency rate today. Forwards, futures, and swaps are types of securities that are derived by the direction of other securities such as interest rates, currency rates, commodity prices, or index levels.

AUTHOR'S NOTES

It would be great if we could read tomorrow's newspaper, see which stocks would do well, buy today, and guarantee ourselves a healthy gain. It would be great to know tomorrow's lottery drawings or next week's main news so we could position ourselves today to take advantage of future events. The problem is, of course, that we can't predict the future, and what happens in the future is impossible to know for certain. We know that everyone will die at some point, but we don't know when. We pay for life insurance just in case. Life insurance is basically a future contract where the two parties, the insurance company and the policy holder, place a side bet; if the policy holder dies, the insurance will pay the policy holder's beneficiaries $1 million; however, for every month the policy holder "loses" the bet, he or she will pay $150 per month in premiums. In addition, every month after the $150 is made, the bet is reset for next month. I was always fascinated how insurance companies could price someone's life at $150 per month for a $1 million payoff. The actuarial science behind premium pricing is based on the probability of life expectancy given someone's age and health condition. The core analysis of investments, finance, and credit (the title of this textbook) is to quantify future return given an investment's risk expectation.

The number-one New York Times *bestselling book* The Big Short, *written by Michael Lewis (2010), which later became a successful Hollywood movie, describes a few investors who waited very patiently to benefit from the collapse of the mortgage markets. The book writes about a hedge fund manager named Michael Burry who visited many of the major investment banks, asking them to structure an instrument that would allow him to benefit from the potential collapse of the housing market. These banks were happy to create such a vehicle, using a structure called a credit default swap (CDS) that would allow Michael Burry to short the housing market. There is a scene in the movie where representatives from the various investment banks are laughing and mocking the stupidity of such an idea. The CDS was structured like a life insurance policy. The investors in the CDS would be paying monthly premiums and the payoff ("death benefit") would be based on the event of default of collateralized debt obligations (CDOs) that included mortgage-backed securities, secured by subprime mortgages, and funded by various tranches of debt that are rated by the rating agencies. These fund's structures start at the top, with the highest-quality tranches including AAA securities, then AA, and all the way down to the risky BB security tranches. One of my favorite scenes is when the actor Ryan Gosling, playing an investment banker, pulls blocks from a Jenga tower showing how the debt tranches work in mortgage-backed securities. He explains how, by pulling the blocks from the lower part of the tower, the top-rated securities at the top would fall too.*

Profiting, hedging, or exiting your investment today based on future events such as the movement of interest and currency rates or the price of coffee have become the main analytical objective of every analyst on Wall Street. Portfolio managers use the futures markets to secure or strengthen their investment in case of certain unexpected price movements or events.

KEY TAKEAWAYS

- The difference between options and futures is that option investors have the right or option to buy or sell securities in the future whereas futures investors have the obligation to buy or sell securities in the future.
- Many future and forward strategies are designed to either protect or hedge the underlying investments or enhance the overall exposure to a future event for maximum profit.
- An investor who trades futures gains a better understanding of how interest or currency rates move and what the investor is pricing into the bonds based on default expectation in the future.

FORWARDS, FUTURES SWAP CONTRACTS

When comparing contracts between options and futures, it is important to note that they have the same input characteristics including a future price (letters "X" in options and "K" in futures), an underlying asset such as a stock or commodity (both represent letter "S" for stock and spot for options and futures, respectively), and an expiration date (delivery day for forwards). The difference is the obligation that comes with future contracts, as well as the fact that options contracts carry a premium (p) while futures and forwards do not.

FORWARD CONTRACTS

A forward contract is a private and highly customized contract between two parties to buy or sell a specific asset at a pre-agreed price on a specific future date. Typically, these contracts are between large institutions; the public does not usually get involved in these forward transactions. However, they can access these types of opportunities in the futures market. The terms and conditions of a forward contract will include the description of the asset such as the specific commodity, the price of the asset, the delivery date, and the volume to be traded. Forwards are used primarily for hedging purposes. Typical forward contracts are usually on commodities that could include precious metals, agricultural products, and natural gas and oil. A forward contract settlement can occur on a cash or delivery basis. The cash basis is receiving or paying the difference between the future price and the spot price. The delivery basis is paying for receiving the delivery of the actual asset and receiving payment if you deliver the asset to the buyer.

Consider a perfect real example that both parties can benefit from: a delivery basis forward contract. Assume a farmer who produces wheat sells his stock primarily to a local bread company. This farmer's cash flow is primarily dependent on wheat prices. The farmer knows the market prices for wheat will tend to fluctuate from the time the farmer harvests the wheat until it is delivered it to the bread company. The farmer, wanting to secure his revenues, looks for a way to ensure the amount he'll receive for his inventory. This could be especially important for the farmer if he has debt payments such as a mortgage on his farm or leases on his equipment. Securing his revenue is essential if he wishes to predict what he can pay toward his loans and still profit in order to stay in business. In this case, the farmer will seek to enter a contract with the bread company to lock in the delivery price, volume, and date for his sale. Along the same lines, the bread company oddly enough is faced with the same problem as the farmer. The bread company needs to lock in its expenses in order to accurately predict its profit. For the bread company, wheat cost represents the highest and potentially variable cost component in its income statement. The forward contract between the wheat farmer and the bread company will include the volume, price, date, volume, and will be delivered as follows:

Buyer: Bread company
Seller: Wheat Farms Inc.
Volume: One million bushels
Price: $4.45
Delivery date: 03/15/20xx (6 months from today)

Two different views: The seller is concerned about a potential decline in the price of wheat and the buyer is concerned that the wheat's prices will increase by the time one million bushels of wheat is delivered. With the contract in place, no matter what happens to wheat prices the seller is promised to be paid $4.45 per bushel or $4.45 million and the buyer is obliged to pay $4.45 per bushel or $4.45 million on delivery date as the one million bushels are satisfied.

This contract can also be done with a financial institution on a cash basis to hedge the farmer's position as a derivative to wheat's current spot price. In this case, the farmer signs a short price contract because he is hedging against a decline in wheat prices. The bread company can also reach out to a financial institution to hedge its cost via a derivative forward contract. In this case, the bread company signs a long contract since it is hedging against any increase in price. Both contracts (direct) between the farmer and the bread company and indirect derivative contract between the parties, separately, as well as the financial institutions, are illustrated in figure 14.1.

For the derivative contract between the parties and the financial institutions, the parties will pay or receive the contract depending on the spot price upon expiration day. Figure 14.1 shows three possibilities of the wheat spot price at expiration day.

If it's exactly $4.45 per bushel (contract price), no money is owed by the farmer or the bread company to the financial institution and the contract is closed. If the spot price is lower than the contract price ($3.95), the bread company will pay the lower price to buy the wheat in its course of doing business, but also pay the cash difference between the contract price and the spot price ($0.50 x 1 million bushels). The wheat company will receive lower revenues by its customers for selling wheat at $3.95 per bushel, or $3,950,000. However, it will make up the difference from the lower price by also receiving $500,000 from the derivative contract ($0.50 x 1 million bushels). At a higher spot price, the bread company will pay its suppliers $4,950,000, or 4.95 a bushel, but will receive $500,000 from the derivative contract to offset the higher prices. The farmer will receive higher revenues for selling his wheat at a higher spot price but will be asked to pay for the derivative contract, resulting in net proceeds of $4,450,000.

FIGURE 14.1 FORWARD CONTRACTS

Direct Contracts and Indirect Derivative Contracts

DIRECT PRIVATE FORWARD CONTRACT BETWEEN TWO PARTIES (Not using the financial institution)	
BUYER:	Bread Company
SELLER:	Wheat Farms Inc.
VOLUME:	1,000,000 bushels
PRICE:	$ 4.45 per bushel
TOTAL COST	$ 4,450,000
DATE:	3/15/20XX (6 months)
TYPE:	Delivery Basis

Bread Company

Income Statement	3/15/20XX
Revenues	
Cost of Goods Sold - Wheat Expenses	(4,450,000)

Wheat Farms Inc.

Income Statement	3/15/20XX
Revenues	4,450,000
Cost of Goods Sold - Wheat Expenses	

INDIRECT (DERIVATIVE)FORWARD CONTRACT BETWEEN EACH PARTY (LONG & SHORT) WITH FINANCIAL INSTITUTION

PARTY A	
LONG:	Bread Company
CONTRACT:	5,000 bushels
VOLUME:	1,000,000 bushels
NO OF CONTRACTS:	200.00 (1,000,000/5,000)
PRICE:	$ 4.45
EXP. DATE:	3/15/20XX (6 months)
TYPE:	Cash Basis

PARTY B	
SHORT:	Wheat Farms Inc.
CONTRACT:	5,000 bushels
VOLUME:	1,000,000 bushels
NO OF CONTRACTS:	200.00 (1,000,000/5,000)
PRICE:	$ 4.45
EXP. DATE:	3/15/20XX (6 months)
TYPE:	Cash Basis

Bread Company

Transaction on Delivery/Expiration Day	WHEAT PRICES ON DELIVERY DAY		
Increase/Decrease in Spot Prices	-$ 0.50	$ 0.00	$ 0.50
Scenarios - Spot Prices	$ 3.95	$ 4.45	$ 4.95
Cost of Wheat Purchases at Spot Prices	(3,950,000)	(4,450,000)	(4,950,000)
+ Profit/Loss form Forward Contract	(500,000)	-	500,000
Net Payment	(4,450,000)	(4,450,000)	(4,450,000)

Fully Hedged

Wheat Farms Inc.

Transaction on Delivery/Expiration Day	WHEAT PRICES ON DELIVERY DAY		
Increase/Decrease in Spot Prices	-$ 0.50	$ 0.00	$ 0.50
Scenarios - Spot Prices	$ 3.95	$ 4.45	$ 4.95
Revenue from Wheat Sales at Spot Price	3,950,000	4,450,000	4,950,000
+ Profit/Loss form Forward Contract	500,000	-	(500,000)
Total Proceeds	4,450,000	4,450,000	4,450,000

Fully Hedged

Risks with Forward Contracts

The market for forward contracts is huge since many of the world's biggest corporations use it to hedge currency and interest rate risks. However, since the details of forward contracts are restricted to the buyer and seller—and are not known to the general public—the size of this market is difficult to estimate.

The large size and unregulated nature of the forward contracts market makes it susceptible to a cascading series of defaults in the worst-case scenarios. While banks and financial corporations mitigate this risk by being very careful in their choice of counterparty, the possibility of large-scale default does exist.

FUTURE CONTRACTS: COMMODITIES

Futures contracts have the same characteristics as forward contracts, with the exception being that futures trade in the exchange markets that the public can invest in. Most transactions are on a cash basis but there is an option, rarely used, to receive the actual delivery of the asset. Figure 14.2 shows the future trading prices (expiring 1 or 2 months from today).

Typically, the future markets are divided into five major commodity sections: agriculture, precious metals and industrial metals, energy, currency futures, and index futures. Each asset also has a customized number of units per contract. For example, figure 14.2 shows

FIGURE 14.2 FUTURES MARKETS - EXCHANGE PRICE

April

AGRICULTURE	Volume per Contract	Units	Future Price	$ Change	% Change	Delivery Day (Future)
Cocoa (ICE)	10	USD/MT	2,342.00	(30.00)	-1.26%	May
Coffee 'C' (ICE)	37,500	USd/lb.	92.85	(0.05)	-0.05%	May
Corn (CBOT)	5,000	Cents/bu.	364.50	(2.75)	-0.75%	May
Cotton #2 (ICE)	50,000	USd/lb.	78.37	0.10	0.13%	May
Lean Hogs (CME)	40,000	USd/lb.	94.23	(2.52)	-2.61%	May
Live Cattle (CME)	40,000	USd/lb.	121.50	(1.17)	-0.96%	May
Oats (CBOT)	5,000	Cents/bu.	279.50	1.25	0.45%	May
Orange Juice (ICE)	15,000	USd/lb.	109.80	(0.35)	-0.32%	May
Rough Rice (CBOT)	2,000	USD/cwt	10.69	0.02	0.14%	May
Soybean (CBOT)	60,000	Cents/bu.	891.75	(2.50)	-0.28%	May
Sugar #11 (ICE)	112,000	USd/lb.	12.77	(0.21)	-1.62%	May
Wheat (CBOT)	5,000	Cents/bu.	441.25	(7.00)	-1.56%	May

Precious Metals & Industrial Metals	Volume per Contract	Units	Price	$ Change	% Change	Delivery Day (Future)
Aluminum (LME)	25	USD/MT	6,476.00	(80.00)	-1.22%	May
Copper (Comex)	25,000	USD/lb	291.10	(1.55)	-0.53%	May
Gold (Comex)	100	USD/t oz.	1,277.50	1.50	0.12%	May
Silver (Comex)	5,000	USD/t oz.	15.06	0.02	0.11%	May

Energy	Volume per Contract	Units	Price	$ Change	% Change	Delivery Day
Brent Crude (ICE)	1,000	USD/bbl.	74.20	2.23	3.10%	May
Heating Oil (Nymex)	42,000	Cents/gal.	211.35	4.26	2.06%	May
Natural Gas (Nymex)	10,000	USD/MMBtu	2.52	0.03	1.24%	May
WTI Crude Oil (Nymex)	1,000	USD/bbl.	65.75	1.75	2.73%	May

Interest Rate Funds	Volume per Contract	Units	Price	$ Change	% Change	Delivery Day
Treasury Bonds (CBT)	100,000	pts 32nds of 100%.	145-080	15.00	0.10%	June
Treasury Notes (CBT)	100,000	pts 32nds of 100%.	122-050	12.50	0.25%	June
5-yr Tresury Notes (CBT)	100,000	pts 32nds of 100%.	114-195	6.50	1.24%	June
30-Day Fed Funds (CBT)	5,000,000	Daily Avg	97.60	-	0.00%	May
1-Month Libor (CME)	3,000,000	pts of 100%	97.49	0.01	0.00%	May

Currency Futures	Volume per Contract	Units	Price	$ Change	% Change	Delivery Day
Japanese Yen (CME)	¥12500000	$ per 100 ¥	97.2900	-	0.00%	June
Canadian Dollar (CME)	100,000	$ per CAD	0.7351	0.001	0.14%	June
Euro (CME)	€125,000	$ per €	1.1523	0.011	0.95%	June

Index Futures	Volume per Contract	Units	Price	$ Change	% Change	Delivery Day
S&P 500 Index (CME)	250	$USD x Index	2,505.20	19.20	0.77%	June
Mini Nasdaq 100 (CME)	20	$USD x index	6,333.30	40.00	0.63%	June
Mini Russel 2000 (CME)	50	$USD x index	1,349.00	8.10	0.60%	June

that Silver's one contract is 5,000 troy ounces, so buying the Silver futures at $15.06 per troy ounce will cost $75,300. The brokers will ask the investor to deposit 10% of that amount, or $7,530 (initial margin), and at expiration day, the settlement will be set up on cash basis and will be expected to be paid or the difference received between the original future price and current price, which should converge to the spot price on delivery day. A delivery basis contract gives the investor the right to buy 5,000 ounces at $15.06, no matter what happens to the price.

There are two following reasons for the investor to enter a futures contract:

1. **Speculation:** This is when investors enter futures contracts if they believe the underlying asset such as a commodity price, interest rate, or market index will increase or decrease based on specific events. If the investor anticipates an increase in the price of an underlying asset in the future, he or she could potentially profit by purchasing the asset at a set price via entering a futures contract and selling it later at a higher price in the spot market through cash settlement. However, if the underlying asset declines, he or she could lose the difference between the future price they locked in and the spot price.
2. **Hedging:** The purpose of hedging, like the example used in the forward contract, is not to profit from any favorable price movements but to prevent losses from selling or buying the underlying asset as a course of business (see example of the farmer and wheat companies shown in figure 14.1).

For an investor to set up a futures contract account, most brokers will ask the investors to deposit 10–15% of the potential delivery amount (future price x volume) times the number of contracts. The prices are settled every day and a mark to market tracks the account to see if the investor needs to deposit additional funds to cover the original margin (10–15%). Figure 14.3 shows an example of the original deposit and the mark-to-market daily settlement until expiration.

The basis is the difference between the futures price and spot price. In general, when the underlying asset's price moves up, the futures should move up as well. However, the movement could be inconsistent, potentially creating an arbitrage opportunity. Speculators can take advantage of this and speculate on the **basis, which is the differential between the future price and the spot price K-S or S-K.** The basis risk is the risk associated with imperfect hedging. Under these conditions, the spot price of the asset, and the futures price, do not converge on the expiration date of the future. The amount by which the two quantities differ measures the value of the basis risk.

FIGURE 14.3 FUTURES AND FORWARDS

Silver (COMEX) 5,000 USD/troy oz. April

Precious Metals & Industrial Metals	Volume per Contract	Units	Price	$ Change	% Change	Delivery Day (Future)
Aluminum (LME)	25	USD/MT	6,476.00	(80.00)	-1.22%	May
Copper (Comex)	25,000	USD/lb	291.10	(1.55)	-0.53%	May
Gold (Comex)	100	USD/t oz.	1,277.50	1.50	0.12%	May
Silver (Comex)	5,000	USD/t oz.	15.06	0.02	0.11%	May

Daily Mark-to-Market - 5/15/20xx

Day			Futures Price	Profit (loss) per ounce	USD / Unit Contract contract		Deposit (Initial Invest.)	10% Balance *	Balance	Profit	HPR%
5/10	Wednesday	Today	$ 15.06				(7,530)	7,530	75,300		
5/11	Thursday		$ 15.26	$ 0.20	1,000.00	Credit		8,530			
5/12	Friday		$ 15.36	$ 0.10	500.00	Credit		9,030			
5/15	Monday		$ 15.06	$ (0.30)	(1,500.00)	Debit		7,530			
5/16	Tuesday		$ 14.90	$ (0.16)	(800.00)	Debit		6,730			
5/17	Wednesday		$ 15.00	$ 0.10	500.00	Credit		7,230			
5/18	Thursday		$ 14.65	$ (0.35)	(1,750.00)	Debit		5,480			
5/19	Friday		$ 14.79	$ 0.14	700.00	Credit		6,180			
5/22	Monday		$ 15.04	$ 0.25	1,250.00	Credit		7,430			
5/23	Tuesday	Delivery	$ 15.39	$ 0.35	1,750.00	Credit		9,180			
				sum=	1,650.00					1,650	21.9%

EXAMPLE OF SPECULATING ON THE BASIS

An investor is holding 100 ounces of gold, who is short one gold futures contract. Suppose that gold today (April) sells for $1,247 an ounce, and the futures price for May delivery is $1,277 an ounce, as shown in figure 14.3. Therefore, the basis is currently $30 ($1,277 - $1,247). Tomorrow, the spot price might increase to $1,257, while the futures price might increase to $1,282, so the basis narrows to $25 ($1282 - $1,257). The investor's gains and losses are as follows:

Gain on selling of gold (per ounce) is $1,257 - 1,247 = $10 and loss on gold futures position (per ounce) is $1,282 - 1,277 = $5, which is used for hedging purposes, netting a gain of $5 per ounce.

Optimal Hedge Ratio

The hedge ratio is a measurement of the size of the position taken in futures contracts to the size of the exposure as follows:

$$h = \rho \frac{\sigma S}{\sigma K}$$

where ρ is the correlation between the spot price (S) and the future price (K), σS is the standard deviation of the spot price, and σK is the standard deviation of the futures price.

EXAMPLE OF USING THE OPTIMAL RATIO

A company knows that it will buy one million gallons of jet fuel in 3 months. The standard deviation of the change in the price per gallon of jet fuel over a 3-month period is calculated to be 0.032 (3.2%). The company chooses to hedge its market exposure by buying futures contracts on heating oil. The standard deviation of the change in the futures price over a 3-month period is 0.040 (4.0%) and the coefficient of correlation between the 3-month change in the price of jet fuel and 3-month change in the futures price is 0.8. The optimal hedge ratio is therefore

$$h = \rho \frac{\sigma S}{\sigma K} = 0.80 \frac{0.032}{0.040} = 0.64$$

One heating oil futures contract is on 42,000 gallons (see figure 14.3 under energy futures and heating oil showing 42,000 per contract). The company should therefore buy 0.64 × (1,000,000/42,000) = 15.2 contracts (~15 contracts).

FUTURES: INTEREST RATES

The interest rate future contract is a contract between the buyer and seller (financial institution) agreeing to a set interest rate in the future. The interest rate future can be based on underlying assets such as treasury bills, fed funds, or the 1-month LIBOR traded on the Chicago Mercantile Exchange (CME). Interest rate futures are used mostly for hedging purposes and sometimes speculation purposes. They can be bought and sold on exchanges such as Intercontinental Exchange (ICE) Futures, Europe.

Take treasuries, for example. Each future contract size for treasuries is $100,000. Each contract trades in handles of $1,000, but these handles are split into 30 seconds or increments of $31.25 ($1,000/32). Figure 14.2 shows the June 5-year treasury notes on a contract that is listed as 114–195. This means that the total price of the contract is the face value, plus one handle, plus 19.5/32s of another handle, or

$$122'5 \text{ price} = \$100{,}000 + 1{,}000 + \left(1{,}000 \times \frac{19.5}{32}\right) = \$101{,}609.37$$

Each futures contract party has a different view on interest rates and depending on its view it buys or sells futures contracts. **The seller of the interest rate future contract is obliged to borrow money and pay interest. The buyer of the interest rate future contract is obliged to deposit money and has the right to receive interest.** The price of a futures contracts is derived from the underlying rate of interest (spot rate) and fluctuates along with interest rates. Like bond prices, it is important to understand that as interest rates rise, the market price of futures contracts falls.

For example, let's assume that a particular futures contract allows borrowers and lenders to pay or receive interest at 3%, which is the current market rate of interest available. Let's assume interest rates increase by 1% to 4%. The 4% futures contract has become less attractive to buy because depositors can earn 4% at the market rate but only 3% under the futures contract. The price of the futures contract must fall. Also, borrowers will now have to pay 4%, but if they sell the future contract, they must pay only 3%, so the market will have many sellers, and this reduces the selling price until a buyer-seller equilibrium price is reached.

The hedging mechanism works as follows:

An investor of a floating rate loan that earns interest is concerned that interest rates such as LIBOR will fall, thus reducing their income. If interest rates fall, futures prices will rise. If the investor is smart, he or she will buy futures contracts (long position) now and sell later. The gain on futures can be used to offset the lower interest earned.

On the other hand, the borrower is concerned that interest rates will rise and increase his or her expense. If interest rates rise, futures prices will fall, so the borrower could sell the futures contracts now (short position) and buy later at the lower price.

FUTURES: FOREIGN CURRENCY RATES

The foreign currency future contract is a contract between the buyer and seller (financial institution) agreeing to a set specific currency rate in the future. The foreign currency future can be based on underlying assets such as the Japanese yen (¥,) Canadian dollar, European euros (€) or any other foreign currencies. Currency futures are used mostly for hedging and speculation purposes and can be bought and sold on exchanges such as the Chicago Mercantile Exchange (CME). Each futures contract party has a different view on currency rates and depending on his or her view he or she buys or sell futures contracts.

For example, let's assume an importer of European goods is vulnerable to currency risk as he needs to convert the U.S. dollar to euros to pay for goods. In order to hedge his position, he buys (long) the euros at the current exchange rate of 1.15 $/€ and locks it in (see figure 14.4). This importer is scheduled to receive a shipment that requires a €1 million equivalent payment, so he locks in the currency at 1.15x so the most he can pay is $1,150,000. Each

FIGURE 14.4 FUTURES AND FORWARDS

Currency Futures					
	Volume per Contract	Units	Price	$ Change	% Change
Japanese Yen (CME)	¥12,500,000	$ per 100 ¥	97.2900	-	0.00%
Canadian Dollar (CME)	100,000	$ per CAD	0.7351	0.001	0.14%
Euro (CME)	€125,000	$ per €	1.1523	0.011	0.95%

Purhase Goods in € =	€ 1,000,000
Lock in Exchange Rate - futures =	1.1523x

Transaction on Delivery/Expiration Day	Contracts	EXCHANGE RATES $/€		
Increase/Decrease in Spot Prices		0.10x	0.00x	-0.10x
Scenarios - Spot Prices		1.25x	1.15x	1.05x
Cost of purhasing at the European good at the spot Prices		1,252,300	1,152,300	1,052,300
+ Profit/Loss form Forward Contract	8	(100,000)	-	100,000
Net Payment for the European Goods		1,152,300	1,152,300	1,152,300

Fully Hedged

futures contract is $125,000. For $1,150,000 he should buy eight contracts at the exchange rate of 1.15 (€1,000,000/€125,000 per contract). Figure 14.4 shows the hedging helps the importer predict the payment at various scenarios of the exchange rate.

INTEREST RATES SWAPS

Interest rate swaps are contracts between two parties via a financial intermediary who agree to exchange (swap) one set of cash flows for another. Since swaps trade over the counter (OTC), the contracts are between two or more parties and are customized based on each circumstance. There are three different types of interest rate swaps: fixed to floating, floating to fixed, and float to float.

1. **Fixed to floating:** For example, let's assume a company issued bonds at a fixed interest rate. The company's management feels that it can reduce the payments by entering into a swap agreement that swaps its fixed rate with a net floating rate supporting its view that rates will stay low for a while. In this case, the issuer of bonds can enter into a swap with a counterparty bank in which the company receives a fixed rate to offset its bond coupon payment and pay a floating rate. The swap is structured to match the maturity and cash flow of the fixed-rate bond and these two fixed-rate payments are netted.
2. **Floating to fixed:** A company that is currently a borrower of a LIBOR floating rate loan and needs access to a fixed-rate loan because of concern that the rates will go up can enter a swap to achieve a fixed rate.

FIGURE 14.5 INTEREST RATE SWAP

Company A	
Fixed Rate	5.00%
Float (L+)	0.30%
IR View:	Low
Choose:	Fixed
Cash Flow:	
Pay	-5.00%
Pay	-LIBOR
Receive	4.95%
Net Pay	L + 5 bps
Savings	0.25%

Company B	
Fixed Rate	6.20%
Float (L+)	1.00%
IR View	High
Choose:	Float
Cash Flow:	
Pay	-(L+1.0%)
Pay	-4.95%
Receive	+ L
Net Pay	-5.95%
Savings	0.25%

SWAP AGREEMENT - TERMS	
Notional Amount	**100,000,000**
Swap Rate:	**4.95%**
Years	**5**

Figure 14.5 shows an example of two parties with two different views on interest rates who seek advice from their investment advisor on how to use the swap market to get a better-priced loan. This is a case where two parties (A&B) have approached a bank to borrow a $100 million loan. The bank gives them a choice of fixed rate or floating rate, shown in figure 14.5.

In this case, Party A was given a choice to borrow either 5% fixed or LIBOR + 0.30%. Separately, Party B was given a choice to borrow either 6.20% fixed rate or LIBOR + 1.0%. Party A's view is that rates will stay low, so it intends to choose the floating rate while Party B's view is that the rates will go up so it's natural that it should lock in the fixed rate. The investment advisor is recommending that both parties choose the opposite option and enter into a swap agreement to not only achieve their view but also to save on cash flow.

Figure 14.5 shows that despite their view, Party A chose the fixed-rate option and Party B chose the floating-rate option. Party A will pay the 5% fixed rate to the bank it is borrowing from, receive a swap rate of 4.95% from the swap dealer, and pay LIBOR to the swap dealer, so Party A's net pay is LIBOR + 5 bps derived from 5.0% + LIBOR – 4.95%. Party B will pay the floating rate LIBOR + 1% to the bank that it is borrowing from and receive LIBOR from the swap dealer as well as pay a swap rate of 4.95%. Party A's net pay comes to be the 5.95% fixed payment derived from LIBOR + 1% – LIBOR + 4.95% (LIBOR offsets to derive a fixed rate of 5.95%). Both parties benefited from the swap agreement by 25 basis points. Without the swap agreement and going with its view, Party A would have chosen LIBOR + 0.30% instead of paying LIBOR + .05% and Party B would have chosen a fixed rate of 6.20%, which is higher than the swap agreement at a net fixed rate of 5.95%.

3. **Float to float:** Companies sometimes enter into a swap to address different maturities that have different floating rates, known as a basis swap. A company can swap from 1e-month LIBOR to 3-month LIBOR because the rate is more attractive, or it matches other payment flows.

CROSS-CURRENCY SWAPS

Cross-currency swaps, or simply, currency swaps, are exchange contracts of interest across different currencies. Interest payments are exchanged at specific set dates through the life of the contract. Companies that have their businesses abroad often use currency swaps to hedge their currency exposure and get more favorable interest rates by borrowing in local markets and using them to swap their payment exposure to the home currency.

Figure 14.6 shows an example of a U.S. company that obtains a loan in Europe to build a manufacturing plant. However, since it will be servicing a loan to start the construction and it is abroad, it will have to convert its debt payments in U.S. dollars to euros. In such a case where payments such as debt payments will be large expenses, the company will be exploring ideas of how to hedge its currency and lock in its expected expenses.

Figure 14.6 shows that despite the higher fixed interest rate charged (from 6% to 7%), by swapping from euro to U.S. dollar today, the U.S. company expects to yield a benefit of an estimated $2.37 million, of course, assuming that the euro-versus-dollar ratio will increase, showing levels from 1.15x to 1.21x in 3 years.

Like interest rate swaps, currency swaps have three variations on the exchange of interest rates: fixed-to-fixed rate; floating-to-floating rate; or fixed-to-floating rate. The cross-currency swap opportunity offered to an investor weighs the difference between taking higher or lower interest rate today to hedge the higher or lower movement in the currency exchange.

CREDIT-DEFAULT SWAPS (CDS)

A credit-default swap (CDS) is a contract that allows the investor to swap the investor's credit risk with another investor. If an investor who holds bonds is concerned that the bonds will be defaulted, the investor will buy CDS to offset or swap the risk when the bonds do default. The investor who agrees to sell the CDS and receives a premium is obliged to reimburse the investor if the bonds default; this is structured similar to a life insurance policy where the insured pays a monthly payment or premium to the insurance company who does not expect that the insured will die anytime soon. In this case, the

FIGURE 14.6 CROSS-CURRENCY SWAP

US COMPANY (Business in Europe)

BOND INFORMATION

Construction Note - Face Value (€)=	€ 100.00 million (Euros)
Euro-denominated Fixed Rate=	6.00%
Years (Term) =	3 years

SWAP INFORMATION

Spot Exchange Rate=	1.15x $ per €
Nominal Amount in $	$ 115 million
Dollar-denominated Fixed Rate =	7.00%

UNHEDGED - WITH A AN EXCHNAGE FUTURE ASSUMPTION

Time	Unhedged Euro Cash Flow (€)	Forward Exchange Rate $/€	Hedges Dollar Cash Flow ($)	Present Value of the unhedged Cash Flows ($)
1	-6.00	1.1500	-6.9	$6.51
2	-6.00	1.1700	-7.02	$6.25
3	-106.00	1.2100	-128.26	$107.69
				$120.45

Benefit = $2.37

HEDGED VIA SWAP CONTRACT

Time	Cash Flow ($)	Hedges Dollar Cash Flow ($)	Present Value of the hedged Cash Flows ($)
1	-8.05	-8.05	$7.59
2	-8.05	-8.05	$7.16
3	-123.05	-123.05	$103.32
			$118.07

event is the death of the insured before the payment is made. In a CDS, the event is the default of the bonds.

A credit-default swap is the most common form of credit derivative for most bonds, including municipal bonds, sovereign bonds, corporate loans and bonds, or mortgage-backed securities—a popular asset class written for the 2008–2009 crisis in the book written by Michael Lewis (2010) *The Big Short*. Depending on the contract, most CDS contracts are designed so that the buyer of a credit-default swap is entitled to receive the par value of the bonds, along with any unpaid interest, if the issuer defaults on the bond payments. CDS are priced very close to their probability of default. Some investors use CDS to price equivalent bonds.

FIGURE 14.7 CREDIT DEFAULT SWAP

LOAN AGREEMENT TERMS:

Loan Amount: 100,000,000

Interest Rate: LIBOR + 3.00%

Maturity/Term 5 years

CDS Contract

Notional Amou 100,000,000 million

Time (six months)	Lender A receives LIBOR SPREAD	Lender A pays CDS Rate based on Forward Rates	Cash Flow Received from borrower	CDS Cost paid to Counter party	Cash Flow Recived
0					
1	3.00%	2.00%	3,000,000	(2,000,000)	1,000,000
2	3.00%	2.40%	3,000,000	(2,400,000)	600,000
3	3.00%	3.25%	3,000,000	(3,250,000)	(250,000)
4	3.00%	4.00%	3,000,000	(4,000,000)	(1,000,000)
5	3.00%	4.00%	3,000,000	(4,000,000)	(1,000,000)
Total					(650,000)

Figure 14.7 shows an example where a lender or an investor in corporate loans that holds $100 million in floating rate loans is receiving a rate of LIBOR + 3%. The investor in this loan has a few concerns that the loan could potentially be in default and thus enters into a CDS contract to hedge the risk. The CDS rates offered escalate from 2–4% as the maturity increases from 1 to 5 years, calculated based on a duration (not shown here). In this case, the borrower initially receives L + 3% and pays out 2% on a notional amount of the $100 million that matches the direct exposure of the loan. Despite a negative cash flow that the borrower is scheduled to receive in years 3, 4, and 5, the preservation of capital is more important. In this case, the borrower expects a refinancing at par soon or the worst-case scenario of a bankruptcy will give the borrower the right to receive par (100%) of $100 million from the swap contract. Please note that the actual LIBOR that the borrower receives is not included in the cash flow, assuming that the borrower's cost of capital is LIBOR offsetting that income.

VALUING CREDIT-DEFAULT SWAPS (CDS): JOHN HALL'S METHOD

Most derivative models used for valuing options, futures, forwards, swaps, and other derivatives have two items in common: quantifying the payoff based on a probability of an event to incur and then calculating the fair price or the bet today that is in line with such expectation. The Black-Scholes or the binomial option pricing model, for example, discussed in the last chapter, are modeling examples that are used to value options or

FIGURE 14.8 VALUATION OF CREDIT DEFAULT SWAPS - JOHN HALL'S METHOD

Valuation of Credit Default Swap (CDS) - John Hall's method

INPUT

Notional (N)=	$	100 million
Risk Free Rate (Rf)=		3%
Prob. Of Default (d)=		3%
Recovery Rate (Rec)=		70%

PV of Payments = PV of Payoff

Payments by CDS Buyer (Buyer of protection) | **Payoffs by CDS seller (protection seller)**

PAYMENT

Expected Payments					Expected Accrual		Expected Payoff			
Time	Discount Factor (comp. e) e^{-it}	Prob of Survival (p = $(1\text{-def})^t$	PV of Exp. Payments		Expected Accrual adj of 1/2 year	PV of Exp. Acrrual	Probability of Default p.(d)	Discount Factor (comp. e)	% of Notional p(d) (1-Rec)	PV of:
0.5					1.50%	0.015	3.00%	0.988	0.90%	0.009
1.0	0.975	97.0%	0.946	=+D16*C17						
1.5					1.46%	0.014	2.91%	0.963	0.87%	0.008
2.0	0.951	94.1%	0.895							
2.5					1.41%	0.013	2.82%	0.939	0.85%	0.008
3.0	0.928	91.3%	0.847							
3.5					1.37%	0.013	2.74%	0.916	0.82%	0.008
4.0	0.905	88.5%	0.801							
4.5					1.33%	0.012	2.66%	0.894	0.80%	0.007
5.0	0.882	85.9%	0.758							
		TOTAL=	4.247	=SUM(E15:E24)	TOTAL=	0.066				0.040
		Plus Accrued	0.066	0.066					Per $1 Notional	
		Total	4.313	=+E25+E26						

Exp. Payments =	4.313	=+E27
Exp. Payoff =	0.040	=+O25
Solve spread (s) (Exp. Pmt x Spread = Exp./ Payoff)=	0.009250214	=+E30/E29
CDS Premium (Insurance) Payment	**92.50**	**bps**

future events. There are various methods of valuing CDS. One that directly addresses the fair value of premiums that an investor is willing to pay today to protect the investment capital in the future is one of John Hall's many simplified credit risk methods. John Hall, an author of various articles and books in the area of derivatives, specialized in credit risk and probability of default concepts.

Figure 14.8 shows the Excel version of John Hall's methodology of valuing CDS in an example with a notional amount of $100 million. Discussed in chapters 9 and 17, the credit risk of an investment is measured by two main variables: probability of default and recovery rate. These are used extensively to calculate the actual loss or loss-given default (LGD) assuming a 3% default rate and 70% recovery. As illustrated in figure 14.8, the LGD and probability of survival are used to measure the premium that the investor needs to pay to enter a CDS Contract. In the example, the CDS annual premium rate, exponentially compounded (e) and paid on a semi-annul basis, is calculated at 92.5 basis points for the next 5 years.

OTHER DERIVATIVES

The main difference between option contracts, described in the previous chapter, and other derivatives such as forwards and futures contracts, is that the buyer of option securities pays upfront to obtain the right to exercise the option in the future to either buy or sell the underlying asset, where in the forward and future contracts the parties are both obliged to sell or buy from each other at a specific date for a specific price. Swap contracts are also different than options as they are contracts that the parties agree to exchange cash flows based on a set interest rate and currency rate today. Forwards, futures, and swaps are types of securities that are derived from the direction of other securities such as interest rates, currency rates, commodity prices, or index levels.

FORWARD-RATE AGREEMENTS (FRAS)

Forward-rate agreements (FRAs) are contracts between two parties that agree on a future rate today and in the future, depending what the market rate is, pay or receive the net difference between the contract rate and the floating rate in the market, called the reference rate.

The formula for determining the FRA is as follows:

$$\text{FRA} = \text{Notional}\left[\frac{(\text{LIBOR} - \text{agreed rate})\left(\frac{m}{360}\right)}{1 + \text{LIBOR}\left(\frac{m}{360}\right)}\right]$$

The agreed rate is the upfront LIBOR rate (reference rate) that the contract locks in today, and the payoff is calculated at expiration day. "m" represents the reference rate expiration before a reset. Suppose Party A takes a long position (receives floating) in an FRA based on a 3-month (90-day) LIBOR that expires in 30 days. The notional amount is $10 million. If the agreed rate is 3% today, then, in 30 days, the payoff to the holder of the long position will calculate as follows:

$$\text{FRA} = \$10{,}000{,}000\left[\frac{(\text{LIBOR} - 0.03)\left(\frac{90}{360}\right)}{1 + \text{LIBOR}\left(\frac{90}{360}\right)}\right]$$

If the 90-day LIBOR at expiration is 2%, then the payoff is calculated as follows:

$$\text{FRA} = \$10{,}000{,}000\left[\frac{(.02 - 0.03)\left(\frac{90}{360}\right)}{1 + 0.02\left(\frac{90}{360}\right)}\right] = 10{,}000{,}000\left(\frac{-0.0025}{1.005}\right) = -24{,}876$$

If the 90-day LIBOR at expiration is 4% then the payoff is calculated as follows:

$$\text{FRA} = \$10{,}000{,}000\left[\frac{(.04-0.03)\left(\frac{90}{360}\right)}{1+0.04\left(\frac{90}{360}\right)}\right] = 10{,}000{,}000\left(\frac{0.0025}{1.0100}\right) = 24{,}752$$

The party that is long receives $24,752 when LIBOR is at 4% (The long investor expects that LIBOR will go up). The short position will receive 24,876 when LIBOR is at 2% (1.0% lower than the agreed rate). Figure 14.9 shows the positive and negative payoff for the long position.

Figure 14.9 shows that if a long position buyer such as the borrower enters into an FRA to lock in the interest rate today (agreed rate of 3%), he or she must believe that rates will rise in the future. The cash difference between the FRA and the 90-day LIBOR rate (reference rate) or floating rate is settled on the value date, in this case 30 days. An increase in rates could be based on the view that the Federal Reserve Bank is in the process of hiking U.S. interest rates based on their monetary policy.

FIGURE 14.9 HEDGING AND ANTICIPATED LOAN W FORWARD RATE AGREEMENT

Nominal Value=	$ 10,000,000
Spread =	3.00%
Agreed Rate (LIBOR)	3.00%

LIBOR on Day 30 (%)	FRA PAYOFF ON DAY 30 ($)	FRA PAYOFF COMPOUND TO DAY 90 ($)	AMOUNT DUE ON LOAN ON DAY 120 ($)	TOTAL AMOUNT PAID ON DAY 120 ($)	EFFECTIVE RATE ON LOAN (%) based on 365 days	EFFECTIVE RATE WITHOUT FRA (%)
1.00%	$ (49,875)	$ (50,000)	$ 10,100,000	$ 10,150,000	6.22%	4.12%
1.50%	$ (37,360)	$ (37,500)	$ 10,112,500	$ 10,150,000	6.22%	4.64%
2.00%	$ (24,876)	$ (25,000)	$ 10,125,000	$ 10,150,000	6.22%	5.17%
2.50%	$ (12,422)	$ (12,500)	$ 10,137,500	$ 10,150,000	6.22%	5.69%
3.00%	$ 0	$ 0	$ 10,150,000	$ 10,150,000	6.22%	6.22%
3.50%	$ 12,392	$ 12,500	$ 10,162,500	$ 10,150,000	6.22%	6.76%
4.00%	$ 24,752	$ 25,000	$ 10,175,000	$ 10,150,000	6.22%	7.29%
4.50%	$ 37,083	$ 37,500	$ 10,187,500	$ 10,150,000	6.22%	7.82%
5.00%	$ 49,383	$ 50,000	$ 10,200,000	$ 10,150,000	6.22%	8.36%
5.50%	$ 61,652	$ 62,500	$ 10,212,500	$ 10,150,000	6.22%	8.90%
6.00%	$ 73,892	$ 75,000	$ 10,225,000	$ 10,150,000	6.22%	9.44%
6.50%	$ 86,101	$ 87,500	$ 10,237,500	$ 10,150,000	6.22%	9.99%
7.00%	$ 98,280	$ 100,000	$ 10,250,000	$ 10,150,000	6.22%	10.53%
7.50%	$ 110,429	$ 112,500	$ 10,262,500	$ 10,150,000	6.22%	11.08%
8.00%	$ 122,549	$ 125,000	$ 10,275,000	$ 10,150,000	6.22%	11.63%
8.50%	$ 134,639	$ 137,500	$ 10,287,500	$ 10,150,000	6.22%	12.18%
9.00%	$ 146,699	$ 150,000	$ 10,300,000	$ 10,150,000	6.22%	12.74%

FIGURE 14.10 PRICING AND VALUATIONOF FORWARD RATE AGREEMENTS

	B	C	D	E
2	**PRICING AND VALUATION OF FORWARD RATE AGREEMENTS**			
3				
4	**INPUT:**			
5	**Description**	**Symbol**		
6	Notional Amount		$ 10,000,000	
7	**LIBOR (spot of h) lets call La**	**L(h)**	**2.50%**	
8	LIBOR (Reference Days)	m	90	days
9	LIBOR (Days FRA exp)	h	30	days
10	**LIBOR (spot of h+m) lets call Lb**	**L(m+h)**	**2.75%**	
11	LIBOR (Days m+h)	m+h	120	days
12	Basis		360	days
13				
14	Days into its life	g	20	days
15	Days remaining (h-g)	h-g	10	days
16	Days of Reference + Remaining	m+g	100	days
17	**LIBOR (spot of h-g) lets call Lc**	**L(h-g)**	**2.25%**	
18	**LIBOR (spot of h+m-g) lets call Ld**	**L(h+m-g)**	**2.45%**	
19				
20	**OUTPUT:**			
21		**Formula**	**Result**	**Excel Formula**
22	**STEP 1 - Solving for the rate of FRA:**			
23	Numerator (N)	**1+(Lb*((m+h)/360)**	1.009166667	=1+(D10*(D11/D12))
24	Denominator (D)	**1+(La*(h/360)**	1.002083333	=1+(D7*(D9/D12))
25	**FRA Calculation**	**(N/D-1)*(360/m)**	**2.83%**	=+((D22/D23)-1)*(D12/D8)
26				
27	**STEP 2 - Valuing FRA durinng its Life**			
28	**Adj for Days Remain (A)**	**1/(1+Lc*((h-g)/360))**	0.99937539	=1/(1+(D17*(D15/D12)))
29				
30	**STEP 3 -FRA Rate Calc**			
31	Numerator (N)	**(1+(step1*(m/360)**	1.007068607	=1+(D25*(D8/D12))
32	Deenominator (D)	**(1+(Ld*(h+m-g)/360)**	1.006805556	=1+(D18*(D16/360))
33	FRA Rate Calc	**N/D**	1.000261273	=+D31/D32
34				
35	**Value FRA (VFRA)**		**$ (8,858.83)**	=+(D28-D33)*D6
36				

PRICING AND VALUATION OF FRAS (VFRA)

The method to price and value these FRAs is illustrated in Excel format using the example in figure 14.10.

The example in figure 14.10 assumes that the following inputs:

Notional amount:	$10 million
Reference index:	90-day LIBOR
Days to expiration:	30 days
Days into its life:	20 days
Days remaining:	10 days
Market LIBOR spot rates:	10 Days: 2.25%

20 Days: 2.45%

30 Days: 2.50%

90 Days: 2.65%

120 day: 2.75%,

The FRA is calculated at 2.83% and adjusted for the 10 days remaining in the contract; the contract is valued (VFRA) at $8,858.83 on $10 million notional amount.

SWAPTIONS

A swaption is basically structured like an FRA with the exception that the investor has the option and not the obligation to exercise the right to enter an FRA. Like an option, there is a premium paid upfront, strike price, and expiration day. It can be structured as an American option, which allows the investor to exercise an any-time or a European-style option, which allows the investor to exercise the option at expiration day. Like options, there are call and put swaptions. Call investors become the receiver of swaption and put investors become the payer of the swaption.

The buyer of a call swaption has a view that the interest rates will fall and uses swaptions to swap from a fixed to a floating rate while the buyer of put swaption expects the interest rates to increase and uses swaptions to swap the floating rate to fixed at expiration.

Figure 14.11 illustrates an example where the investor enters into a swaption for a $10 million notional amount at an 11.5% exercise price. The 11.5% is the rate that the investor can swap out and receive a floating rate of LIBOR instead. The analysis shows that the annual premium payments the investor needs to make to keep the swaption is effective based on 3-year forward rates.

FIGURE 14.11 SWAPTIONS

	B	C	D	E	F	G
2	**SWAPTIONS**					
3						
4	**INPUT**					
5	Notional Amount:	10,000,000				
6	Exercise Rate (X) =	11.50%	Swap to pay and receive LIBOR			
7	1 year (360-Day) Rate=	12.00%				
8	2 year (720-Day) Rate=	13.28%				
9	3 Years (1080-Day) Rate=	14.51%				
10						
11	**OUTPUT**					
12	**Term Days**	**Rate (INPUT)**	**Discount Bond Price**		**R**	
13	360	12.00%	0.892857143	=1/(1+(C13*(B13/360)))	12.000%	=+((1-D13)/SUM($D$13:D13))*360/360
14	720	13.28%	0.790139064	=1/(1+(C14*(B14/360)))	12.469%	=+((1-D14)/SUM($D$13:D14))*360/360
15	1080	14.51%	0.696718456	=1/(1+(C15*(B15/360)))	12.744%	=+((1-D15)/SUM($D$13:D15))*360/360
16						
17	3 Year Swap Rate =		12.744%	=+F15	Swap to pay LIBOR and receive	
18	Less Exerice Price (X)		-11.500%	=-C6		
19	The Net Effect =		1.2444%	=+D17+D18		
20						
21	Payments		$ 124,445	=+C5*D19	per year	
22	PV Payments		$ 296,144	=+D21*(D13+D14+D15)	This what the Swaption is worth at Expiration	
23						

CASE STUDY

USING THE FUTURES MARKETS FOR HEDGING STRATEGIES

Synopsis: ZZZ Airline Inc., an airline company, operates 10 charter flights from New York–area airports including JFK, LaGuardia, and Newark. The charter flights are only scheduled during spring break (March and April) and during the winter holidays (December) from New York to Miami.

Commodity Futures

Since jet fuel is one of the largest direct costs for operating the charter flights, the CFO is looking for opportunities to "lock-in" fuel prices for the months of March and April. Based

FIGURE 14.12 FUTURES MARKETS

Energy	Volume per Contract	Units	Price	$ Change	% Change	Delivery Day
Brent Crude (ICE)	1,000	USD/bbl.	74.20	2.23	3.10%	April
Heating Oil (Nymex)	42,000	Cents/gal.	211.35	4.26	2.06%	April
Natural Gas (Nymex)	10,000	USD/MMBtu	2.52	0.03	1.24%	April
WTI Crude Oil (Nymex)	1,000	USD/bbl.	65.75	1.75	2.73%	April

FUTURES CONTRACT		
LONG:	ZZZ Airlines, INC.	
CONTRACT:	42,000	gallons
VOLUME:	420,000	gallons
NO OF CONTRACTS:	10	(420,000/42,000)
PRICE:	$ 4.26	
EXP. DATE:	April	
TYPE:	Cash Basis	

100% Hedge			
Transaction on Delivery/Expiration Day	HEATING OIL PRICES ON DELIVERY DAY		
Increase/Decrease in Spot Prices	-$ 0.50	$ 0.00	$ 0.50
Scenarios - Spot Prices	$ 3.76	$ 4.26	$ 4.76
Cost of Jet Fuel Purchases at Spot Prices	(1,579,200)	(1,789,200)	(1,999,200)
+ Profit/Loss form Forward Contract	(210,000)	-	210,000
Net Payment	(1,789,200)	(1,789,200)	(1,789,200)

Fully Hedged

Optimum Method		
LONG:	ZZZ Airlines, INC.	
CONTRACT:	42,000	gallons
VOLUME:	420,000	gallons
NO OF CONTRACTS:	5	(420,000/42,000 * H)
PRICE:	$ 4.26	
EXP. DATE:	April	
TYPE:	Cash Basis	
Monthly Stand. Dev. (σ) for Spot Price (S)	1.67%	
Monthly Stand. Dev. (σ) for Future Price (K)	2.61%	
Corelation between S and K	0.8100	
Optimal Hedge Ratio (H)	**0.520**	

Heating Oil Historical Prices		
Month	Monthly % Changes	
	Spot	Futures
April	1.0%	2.0%
May	0.5%	1.3%
June	-1.0%	-1.0%
July	0.4%	1.0%
August	1.8%	2.4%
September	-1.2%	-2.3%
October	3.0%	3.2%
November	1.0%	-2.0%
December	-1.0%	2.0%
January	2.0%	4.0%
February	0.5%	2.0%
March	-0.5%	3.5%
April	-3.0%	-6.0%
May	-0.5%	1.0%
June	0.8%	1.2%
July	2.0%	3.0%
August	-1.1%	-1.0%
September	-2.6%	-2.4%
October	1.2%	2.2%
November	1.4%	2.1%
December	-2.5%	-4.0%
January	-0.8%	-2.0%
February	-1.1%	-1.0%
March	3.0%	3.0%
Stand. Dev	1.67%	2.61%
Correlation	0.8100	

on new booking projections and the number of flights scheduled for March and April, the company will consume 420,000 gallons of jet fuel. Using the futures market table below, calculate the following options that the CFO has in his possession to hedge against jet fuel price increases, thus impacting ZZZ Airline's profitability.

1. Prepare a 100% fully hedged strategy using the April heating oil future prices.
2. Using the optimum hedge ratio method, how many future contracts should the CFO enter to optimize ZZZ Airline's hedging?

ZZZ Airlines Inc. knows that it will buy 420,000 gallons of jet fuel in few months. The standard deviation of the change in the price per gallon of jet fuel over a 1-month period is calculated over the last two years to be 1.67%. The company chooses to hedge its market exposure by buying futures contracts in heating oil. The standard deviation of the change in the futures price over a 1-month period is calculated over the last two years to be 2.61% (EXCEL FORMULA: = STDEV(DATA)). The coefficient of correlation between the 1-month change in the price of jet fuel and 1-month change in the futures price for the last 2 years is calculated at 0.81 (EXCEL FORMULA: = CORR (Array 1, Array 2)). The optimal hedge ratio is therefore

$$h = \rho \frac{\sigma S}{\sigma K} = 0.81 = \frac{0.0167}{0.0261} = 0.51$$

One heating oil futures contract is on 42,000 gallons. The company should therefore buy 0.51 × (420,000/42,000) = 5.1 contracts (~5 contracts).

PROBLEMS

1. Luxury Cotton ("Luxury"), an independent distributor of cotton, is planning to sell 4.0 million pounds of cotton in March 2017 at the spot price on delivery day. In order to hedge against a possible decline in cotton prices, Luxury wants to enter a futures contract and lock in the price. The standard deviation of the change in the price per pound is calculated as 0.04 (4.0%), the standard deviation of the change in the futures is 0.035 (3.5%), and the coefficient of correlation between the price of cotton and change in the futures price is 0.80.
   a. Looking at the future's contract table below, how many contracts should Luxury optimize so that **2/3** of its exposure is hedged for its March 2017 delivery? Show your calculation.

Cotton (ICE-US) 50,000 pounds; cents per pound

DATE	OPEN	HIGH	LOW	SETTLE	CHANGE	OPEN INTEREST
Dec	62.29	63.63	62.10	62.79	.50	94.584
Mar 17	61.73	62.25	61.53	61.91	.21	68,686

   b. After entering into the March 2017 contracts for 100% of its delivery exposure, suppose that there are only three possible price moves for cotton in March: stay at the same level, increase by 5 cents, and decrease by 10 cents. Show the profit and loss from the futures contracts as well as the total proceeds for Luxury.

	UNITS	$6.81	$6.91	$6.96
Revenue from Sales				
Profit/Loss on Futures				
Total Proceeds				

2. Today (April) the May 20xx ethanol future price was settled at $1.97 per gallon. Suppose that when the contract matures in May 20xx, the price of ethanol turns out to be $2.07 per gallon.
   a. What will be the profit or (loss) for the long position trader who entered the contract at the futures price?
   b. If each contract calls for delivery of 29,000 gallons, what would the dollar profit/(loss) be to the long position trader?
3. Goldman Sachs Investment Bank has two companies as customers who are in the process of raising funds and each has different views on the interest rate

movements in the future. Company A thinks that interest rates will stay low and Company B feels that rates will rise.

Company A offered either a fixed rate of 7.0% or float LIBOR + 75 bps.
Company B offered either a fixed rate of 8.25% or float LIBOR + 150 bps.

Given the different views, the broker recommends that Company A and Company B get into a swap agreement with a 6.50% swap price.

a. Show the net interest pay.
b. Show the benefits for both parties.

4. Company XYZ Inc. raised a EURO 200 million fixed rate annual bond paying 7.0% fixed rate for 4 years per the indenture, but wants to explore the possibility of entering into a currency swap with the notional amount equal to the bond amount ($150 million). If the currency swap exchange rate is 1.25× $/Euro with 8.5% rate, run the two different scenarios of (a) not entering into the currency swap and projecting the exchange rate using the forward rates below, and (b) entering into the currency swap. Of these two scenarios, which is one more beneficial? (Tip: Use the 7.0% as your discount rate for both.)

TIME	FORWARD EXCHANGE RATE	HEDGES DOLLAR CASH FLOW ($)	PRESENT VALUE OF THE UNHEDGED CASH FLOWS ($)	TIME	CASH FLOW ($)	HEDGES DOLLAR CASH FLOW ($)	PRESENT VALUE OF THE HEDGED CASH FLOWS ($)
1	1.2500						
2	1.2500						
3	1.2500						
4	1.2500						

Benefit =	

ONLINE TEMPLATES

The Excel spreadsheets used in the chapter can be accessed online via Cognella Active Learning platform.

PART IV

Company-Specific Analysis: Corporate Finance, Valuations, and Credit Analysis

CHAPTER 15
Financial Statement Analysis

CHAPTER 16
Projections Analysis

CHAPTER 17
Valuation Analysis

CHAPTER 18
Credit Analysis and Debt-Capacity Analysis

PART IV of the textbook provides the tools and techniques required to perform a financial and credit analysis, as well as basic valuation techniques on private and publicly traded companies. Every investment decision to determine the expected return or the decision to lend money to a company starts with good fundamental analysis. Part IV will first give an overview of basic accounting, from the finance analyst perspective, and introduce various performance metrics to assess performance trends, provide comparative analysis to piers, and set up expectations for projecting the company's earnings in the future. Part IV will then introduce various techniques used for projecting a company's performance, including revenue drivers and cost assumptions. The projections will then help facilitate two important analytical frameworks: valuation analysis and credit analysis, both covered in chapter 17 and 18, respectively.

COMPANY SPECIFIC ANALYSIS

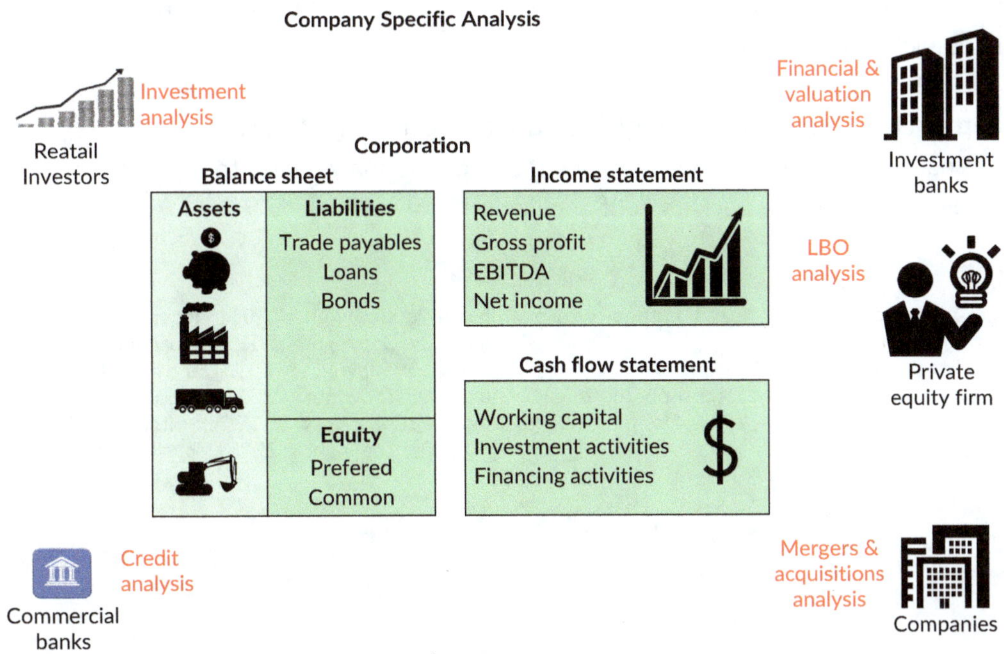

The lineup and brief description of Part IV's chapters are as follows:

Chapter 15: Financial Statement Analysis

In this chapter, you will learn about the information that is included in each financial statement, the correct term for every item in each statement, and how to read and understand the three types of statements. By looking at examples of statements, you will see how the information is provided and how the information is used to perform the analysis to get an overall picture of a company's performance.

Chapter 16: Projections Analysis

This chapter will focus on using the historical information from the financial statements and ratio analysis, as described from the last chapter, to build the projections. The projections will be based on drivers and assumptions that are customized by standard industry parameters. After setting the company's base projections (base case), the chapter will then discuss the process of sensitizing such cases based on the analyst's view (downside and upside cases).

Chapter 17: Valuation Analysis

This chapter will cover eight different methods of valuating a firm's worth. These are methods that are currently used on Wall Street to determine the values for both the private and publicly traded companies.

Chapter 18: Credit Risk Analysis and Debt-Capacity Analysis

This chapter will cover various methods that a credit analyst uses to measure the ability of the company to pay back its debt applications.

CHAPTER 15

Financial Statement Analysis

In this chapter, you will learn about the information that is included in each financial statement, the correct term for every item in each statement, and how to read and understand the three types of statements. By looking at examples of statements, you will see how the information is provided and how the information is used to perform the analysis to get an overall picture of a company's performance.

LEARNING OBJECTIVES

After reading this chapter, students will be able to do the following

- Understand and interpret the company's income statement, balance sheet, and statement of cash flows
- Learn how to build an entire cash flow statement based on 2-year balance sheet information
- Learn how to calculate standard measures of the company's liquidity, solvency, and operating efficiency
- Understand the difference between income and cash flows
- Understand book value versus market value and real assets versus financial assets

FINANCIAL STATEMENTS OVERVIEW

There are three primary financial statements: income statements, balance sheets, and cash flow statements. Public traded companies are required to include audited financial statements in their annual and quarterly reports. The Securities Exchange Commission (SEC) requires the public traded companies to file one 10K and three 10Q reports per year representing their annual and quarterly performance, respectively. These detailed statements can be found on the company's filings in the SEC's EDGAR system. They are also usually available on the company's website under "Investor Relations" and other financial websites such as www.finance.yahoo.com and www.google.com/finance. In addition to the statements, the company discusses its performance found in the "Management, Discussion, and Analysis" (MD&A) section as well as provides detailed footnotes to each of the statements.

AUTHOR'S NOTES

What makes a perfect financial analysis?

To get a perfect financial analysis done when reviewing the financial statements, the analyst needs to answer the following three questions:

1. *How is the company performing versus last year or the last few years (chronological analysis)?*
2. *How is the company performing versus its peers or versus the benchmark (peer analysis)?*
3. *How is the company performing versus analyst expectations (expectation analysis)?*

KEY TAKEAWAYS

- The income statement represents the measurement of profit and loss over period of time.
- The "top line" is the company's sales and the "bottom line" is the company's net income.
- Revenue (sales) less expenses = Profit or loss.
- The balance sheet shows us on a snapshot of the wealth of a company.
- The balance sheet statement is set up in order of liquidity.
- It's called the balance sheet because the left side, representing the assets, shows what the company processes and the right side represents how a company paid for these processions.
- The cash flow statement shows a company's cash inflow and outflow activities over a certain period.

- The differences between income statements and cash flow statement are the following:
  - Timing differences (working capital activities)
  - Capital expenses versus operating expenses (investment activities)
  - Financing expenses not included in the income statement (financing activities)
- The cash flow statement represents the changes from last year's balance sheet to this year's balance sheet
  - Asset goes up = Cash negative
  - Asset goes down = Cash positive
  - Liability goes up = Cash positive
  - Liability goes down = Cash negative
  - Owner's equity goes up = Cash positive
  - Owner's equity goes down = Cash negative

In building the cash flow statement spreadsheet, the following rules apply regarding the balance sheet changes between two periods:

- If the asset items increase between two periods, then the cash is recorded in the cash flow statement as outflow (negative)
- If the asset items decrease between two periods, then the cash is recorded in the cash flow statement as inflow (positive)
- If the liability items increase between two periods, then the cash is recorded in the cash flow statement as inflow (positive)
- If the liability items decrease between two periods, then the cash is recorded in the cash flow statement as outflow (negative)
- If the shareholder's items increase between two periods, then the cash is recorded in the cash flow statement as inflow (positive)
- If the shareholder's items decrease between two periods, then the cash is recorded in the cash flow statement as outflow (negative)

UNDERSTANDING FINANCIAL STATEMENTS

To evaluate publicly traded companies, analysts who represent different investors need uniform financial standards that are consistent, accurate, and complete. Public accounting organizations around the world have set up global accounting standards. The biggest organization, the International Financial Reporting Standards (IFRS), is gradually replacing country-specific standards. Developed by the Financial Accounting Standard Board (FASB), the United States still recognizes generally accepted accounting principles (GAAP) regulated by the SEC. However, the United States is gradually unifying to the IFRS standards.

INCOME STATEMENT

The income statement is a summary of the company's profit or loss over a period. It reports the revenues, expenses, and net profit or net loss over a quarter or a full year. It's also referred to as a profit and loss statement or "P&L." The income statement drives the company's reported quarterly earnings per share (EPS). It is usually accompanied by a statement of comprehensive income, which reconciles the income statement to account for investments made by owners of the company.

The income statement is very useful when comparing revenues, expenses, and profits for the period and for one or more prior periods. For example, this quarter's results can be compared to two prior quarters or the same quarter from last year (this is called "year over year" or "YoY").

The income statement demonstrated in figure 15.1 is basically broken down into top-line revenues and two types of expenses, including cost of revenues and operating expenses.

FIGURE 15.1 CELERITY TECHNOLOGY FINANCIAL STATEMENT—INCOME STATEMENT.

Celerity Technogy Inc. ("CTI")
Financial Statement Analysis

	Income Statement (000's)	Year 1	Year 2	Operating Ratios for Year 2	
8	**Revenues by Geography**			Rev. Growth	% Breakdown
9	U.S.	800,000	920,000	15.0%	82.9%
10	Europe	120,000	140,000	16.7%	12.6%
11	Asia	40,000	50,000	25.0%	4.5%
12	Total Revenue	960,000	1,110,000	15.6%	100.0%
14	**Cost of Revenues by Geography**			Gross Margin	Gross Profit
15	U.S.	293,000	350,000	62.0%	570,000
16	Europe	39,000	50,000	64.3%	90,000
17	Asia	13,000	20,000	60.0%	30,000
18	Total Cost of Revenue	345,000	420,000	62.2%	690,000
20	Gross Profit	615,000	690,000		
22	**Operating Expenses**			As % of Sales	
23	Administrative & General	145,000	165,000	14.9%	
24	Marketing Expenses	75,000	80,000	7.2%	
25	Other Operating Expenses	10,000	12,000	1.1%	
26	Total Operating Expenses	230,000	257,000	23.2%	
28	**EBITDA**	385,000	433,000	39.0%	(EBITDA Margin)
30	**Depreciation**	60,000	65,000	5.9%	Deprec.as % of Revenues
32	**EBIT**	325,000	368,000	33.2%	EBIT Margin
34	**Interest Expense**	130,000	120,000	10.0%	Interest Rate
36	EBT	195,000	248,000	Interest Exp. / (Avg Debt incl. LT and ST)	
38	**Taxes**	78,000	99,200	40.0%	Tax Rate
40	Net Income	117,000	148,800	13.4%	NI Margin

The difference between revenues and these expenses the company's income from operations is calculated before other expenses such as interest and taxes. Net income or the company's bottom line is derived after these expenses are subtracted.

Revenues

Revenue (or sales) is the first line item on the income statement. **Revenues represent the total dollar amount realized by companies for the sale of products and services at a given period.** Revenues could be itemized by product, segment, division, or geographical location. In analyzing revenues, an analyst looks at the drivers of such revenues. The drivers could be volume, price, or contractual obligations. These drivers will be discussed in later chapters.

Expenses

Expenses reported in the income statement are generally broken down into two parts:

1. Direct cost or cost of revenue or cost of goods sold (COGS)
2. Indirect cost or operating expenses or selling, general, and administrative expenses (SG&A)

Cost of Revenues

Cost of revenues (or cost of goods sold (COGS)) includes the direct costs of selling the goods of the company. These expenses include raw material, labor, and overhead (MLO). Cost of revenues captures expenses that are variable based on sales volume or units sold.

Operating Expenses

Operating expenses include the fixed costs of running a company that are not directly related to the sales volume or number of units sold. Operating expenses are also referred to as selling, general, and administrative expenses (SG&A). SG&A includes administrative costs such as the CEO's salary, marketing costs such as advertising, and general costs such as office supplies and other office expenses. In addition to the SG&A expenses, publicly traded companies include non-cash expenses such as depreciation and amortization.

Operating Income or EBIT

Revenues minus operating expenses result to operating income or earnings before interest and taxes (assuming the depreciation and amortization expenses are included in the "Operating Expense" section). Usually private companies exclude depreciation and amortization expenses from the "Operating Expense" section resulting in earnings before interest, taxes, depreciation, and amortization (EBITDA).

Earnings Before Interest, Taxes, Depreciation, and Amortization or EBITDA

For publicly traded companies, earnings before interest, taxes, depreciation, and amortization (EBITDA) is not usually found in the income statement. This is calculated by adding back depreciation and amortization (D&A) to EBIT or operating income. This income line is commonly used to estimate the operating cash flow of the company. EBITDA is used in various methods to estimate the value of the firm and is discussed in later chapters.

Net Income

Net income represents the bottom-line profit or loss of the company after tax and interest expenses and after other non-ordinary expenses such as dividends and one-time or non-recurring expenses. Net income or earnings after taxes represent the value added to last year's earnings.

BALANCE SHEET STATEMENT

The balance sheet represents the wealth or the financial condition of the company. Unlike the income statement, which measures company performance over a quarter or a year, the balance sheet is a snapshot of all a company's assets, representing everything the company owns (cash, equipment, investments, etc.); liabilities, representing what the company owes against those assets and the company's net worth; and shareholder's equity, representing what the owners keep or earned, taken at a moment in time, as demonstrated in figure 15.2.

Assets

This section of the balance sheet gives a list of the assets of the company. The statement is formatted to start from the most liquid assets to the least liquid. The first section is current assets, representing assets that should turn to cash within the next 12 months. These are followed by non-current assets that includes tangible and intangible assets such as goodwill.

FIGURE 15.2 A = L + NW IMAGE IN WORKSHEET

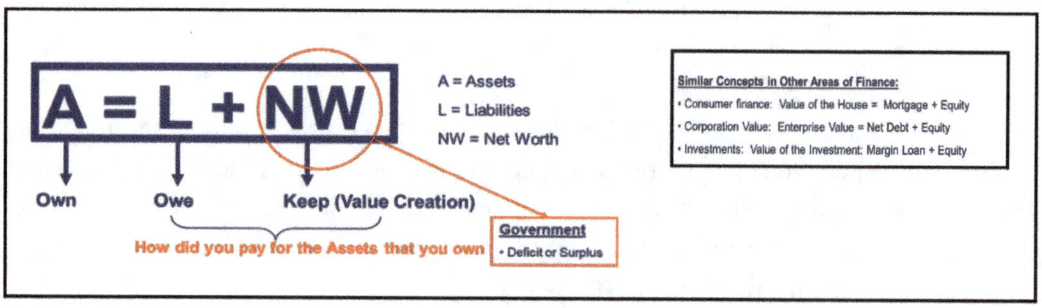

Current Assets

Current assets include cash and cash equivalents, accounts receivable, inventory and other current assets.

- **Cash and cash equivalents:** Cash and cash equivalents represent the deposit account and/or short-term investments of the company. This cash is accessible within a day or two.
- **Accounts receivable:** Accounts receivable represent the money owed to the company by the customer and are considered the second-most liquid item on the balance sheet as the customers typically have 30–60 days to pay the company for goods they bought.
- **Inventory:** Inventory represents the cost of raw materials, work in process (WIP), and finished goods that are ready to be shipped. Inventory will usually turn into cash in 30–120 days, depending of the type of the inventory the company buys, develops, and sells.
- **Other current assets:** Other current assets include money owed to the company for reasons other than customers. It also includes prepaid expenses, which are expenses that are prepaid upfront such as insurance fees and annual license fees.

Non-Current Assets

Non-current assets include both tangible and non-tangible assets. Tangible assets include property, plant, and equipment; long-term investments; and other long-term assets. Intangible assets include goodwill and other intangible assets such as patterns and trademarks.

- **Gross property, plant, and equipment (PP&E):** PP&E represent tangible assets such as buildings, land, equipment, cars, and trucks at their book value. The balance sheet ignores any appreciation in asset value. Sometimes the company reports the net PP&E, which represents the value of these assets after all depreciation is subtracted from the gross amount.
- **Long-term investments:** These could be investments such as joint ventures or other long-term investments.
- **Goodwill**: Goodwill is created when the company is acquired for a price greater than book value. The difference between the acquisition price and book value is recorded as goodwill.

LIABILITIES

This section of the balance sheet gives a list of the liabilities of the company. The statement is formatted to start from the most liquid to the least liquid. The first section is current liabilities, representing the obligations that the company should pay within the next 12 months. These are followed by long-term liabilities, which are obligations that extend further that a year into the future.

Current Liabilities

Current liabilities include outstanding payments to suppliers, short-term debts and obligations due within one year such as accounts payable, short-term interest and tax payables, current portions of long-term debt, and other accrued expenses.

- **Accounts payable:** These are payment obligations due by the company to suppliers, primarily for purchasing inventory or raw material.
- **Income tax accruals:** These are short-term income-related taxes that are payable within a year.
- **Accrued expenses:** These are expenses that needed to be paid within a year. These accrued expenses do not include any obligations owed to suppliers.
- **Current portion of long-term debt:** This is the company's debt obligations that are due within a year.

Long-Term Liabilities

- **Long-term debt:** Any debt including loans, bonds, or mortgages that are due more than a year are included in this section.
- **Deferred taxes:** These are taxes that are deferred, due, and payable in more than a year.
- **Other liabilities:** Other liabilities include long-term obligations such as contingent liabilities. These include potential payments due to lawsuits, environmental obligations, and/or insurance payments.

Net Worth or Shareholder's Equity

Shareholder's equity measures the amount by which a company's assets exceed its liabilities at snapshot in time; basically if one sold all that the company owns after paying all the obligations against these assets, the balance left is what the ownership will keep (figure 15.2). Shareholder's equity is also referred to as net worth or book value of equity. Included in this section are common stock, preferred stock, treasury stock, paid-in capital, and other equity and retained earnings.

- **Common stock:** This represents the original issuance of equity by the owners and it will go down when the company buys back shares.

- **Preferred stock:** This could be an issuance by a third-party investor who expects the company to pay certain fixed dividends (like debt obligations).
- **Treasury stock:** Recorded as a negative number on the balance sheet, treasury stock represents shares that have been issued in the past but were repurchased by the company. The amount repurchased will reduce both par value and capital surplus on the balance sheet if the company decides to permanently retire the stock that was repurchased. If the company decides to re-issue the stock sometime in the future, the treasury stock will be set up at a separate account, reducing common stock and shareholder's equity.
- **Paid-in capital:** This represents proceeds from any additional equity investments invested in the company.
- **Retained earnings:** Retained earnings represent the cumulative income net of loses over time. The retained earnings could also be reducing if the company pays out dividends to shareholders or records loses.

IMAGE 15.1 CALCULATION OF RETAINED EARNINGS

Calculation of Retained Earnings				
$ millions	**Year 1**	**Year 2**	**Year 3**	**Year 4**
Retained Earnings Beginning	$ 250.0	$ 263.0	$ 240.0	$ 233.0
Plus Net Income	25.0	(20.0)	(5.0)	45.0
Less Dividends Paid	(12.0)	(3.0)	(2.0)	(13.0)
Retained Earnings Ending	$ 263.0	$ 240.0	$ 233.0	$ 265.0

As the example shows, it is possible for companies to continue paying dividends even in years that the company shows losses. These will of course reduce the retained earnings.

Figure 15.3 shows an example of a balance sheet: total assets equal to total liabilities plus net worth (hence it is called the "balance" sheet statement).

CASH FLOW STATEMENT

The cash flow statement represents the cash inflow and outflow of the company. The cash statement is like the income statement when it comes to measuring performance over a period of time. However, it focuses on the actual cash generated or spent by the business. In a perfect world you might not need both the income and cash flow statements. A perfect scenario is described in figure 15.4 where we use an example of a 9-year old setting up a lemonade stand. In this humorous example the young 9-year old Joey decides to set up a lemonade stand in front of his house. His dad helps him with $20 to start his lemonade

FIGURE 15.3 CELERITY TECHNOLOGY FINANCIAL STATEMENT—BALANCE SHEET STATEMENT

Celerity Technogy Inc. ("CTI")
Financial Statement Analysis

	Balance Sheet (000's)	**Year 1**	**Year 2**	**$ Change**	**% Change**
7	**Current Assets**				
8	Cash	45,000	65,800	20,800	46.2%
9	Accounts Receivable	45,000	60,000	15,000	33.3%
10	Inventories	35,000	40,000	5,000	14.3%
11	Prepaid Expenses	10,000	9,000	(1,000)	-10.0%
12	Total Current Assets	135,000	174,800	39,800	29.5%
14	**Property and Equipment**				
15	Land	2,500,000	2,500,000	-	0.0%
16	Building	450,000	550,000	100,000	22.2%
17	Furniture & Equipment	50,000	75,000	25,000	50.0%
18	Total Gross P&E	3,000,000	3,125,000	125,000	4.2%
19	Less Accumulated Depreciaition	(300,000)	(365,000)	(65,000)	21.7%
20	Net P&E	2,700,000	2,760,000	60,000	2.2%
22	Long-Term Investments	200,000	250,000	50,000	25.0%
24	Total Assets	3,035,000	3,184,800	149,800	4.9%
26	**Liabilities and Owners Equity**				
28	**Current Liabilities**				
29	Accounts Payable	35,000	40,000	5,000	14.3%
30	Accrued Income Taxes	12,000	10,000	(2,000)	-16.7%
31	Accrued Expenses	10,000	8,000	(2,000)	-20.0%
32	Current Portion of Long Term Debt	20,000	10,000	(10,000)	-50.0%
33	Total Current Liabilities	77,000	68,000	(9,000)	-11.7%
35	Long-Term Debt:	1,200,000	1,180,000	(20,000)	-1.7%
37	Deferred Income Taxes	12,000	17,000	5,000	41.7%
39	Total Liabilties	1,289,000	1,265,000	(24,000)	-1.9%
41	**Owners' Equity**				
42	Common Stock	1,000,000	1,000,000	-	0.0%
43	Paid-in-Capital	-	25,000	25,000	
44	Retained Earnings	746,000	894,800	148,800	19.9%
45	Total Owners' Equity	1,746,000	1,919,800	173,800	10.0%
47	Total Liabilities & Owner's Equity	3,035,000	3,184,800	149,800	4.9%

business. Joe uses the full $20 to buy a box of 100 cups ($5), a lemonade-concentrated juice ($5), and 4 gallons of bottled water ($10). In this story, we assume that he sells all his lemonade and uses all 100 cups (no inventory left). Assuming he sold each lemonade for $1, after the end of the day, Joey will set up an income statement to show his profit. Revenues are recorded at $100 ($1 x 100 cups), minus his cost of $20, showing a profit of $80. This should match his cash on hand. In this case his simple income statement will be the same as his cash flow statement since every transaction was done with all cash. See both statements (figure 15.4).

IMAGE 15.2 LEMONADE STAND—VECTOR

FIGURE 15.4 INCOME VS CASH (TIMING DIFERENCE) THE PEREFECT WORLD: CASH = INCOME

A not so perfect world: Cash is different than income

if every business is run like a lemonade stand by a 9-year old

Income Statement		
Lemonade Sales:		
Sold 100 cups @ $1 each		$ 100.00
Expenses:		
Box of 100 Cups	$ 5.00	
Lemonade Concetrate Juice	$ 5.00	
4 Gallons of Water	$ 10.00	
Total Expenses		$ 20.00
Net Income		$ 80.00

Cash Flow Statement		
Net Income		$ 80.00
Cash Flows:		
Plus money that we owe	$ -	
Less money owed to us	$ -	
Net Working Capital		$ -
Cash		$ 80.00

If we slightly change the story, you will see a need for creating both the income and cash flow statements. Suppose that while Joey was selling his lemonade, his friend Billy bought a lemonade but did not have any money to pay for it. He was very thirsty, he explained, so Joey allowed Billy to have a lemonade and expect to get his $1 later. At the end of the day, Billy has not showed up. Now if Joey had to build both his income and cash flow statement to keep up with the difference between what he earned and what cash he has,

FIGURE 15.5 INCOME VS CASH (TIMING DIFERENCE) THE NOT SO PEREFECT WORLD: CASH IS DIFFERENT.

A not so perfect world: Cash is different than income

if every business is run like a lemonade stand by a 9-year old

Income Statement		
Lemonade Sales:		
Sold 100 cups @ $1 each		$ 100.00
Expenses:		
Box of 100 Cups	$ 5.00	
Lemonade Concetrate Juice	$ 5.00	
4 Gallons of Water	$ 10.00	
Total Expenses		$ 20.00
Net Income		$ 80.00

Cash Flow Statement		
Net Income		$ 80.00
Cash Flows:		
Plus money that we owe	$ -	
Less money owed to us	$ (1.00)	
Net Working Capital		$ (1.00)
Cash		$ 79.00

as is demonstrated in the figure 15.5, Joey's income statement will show a profit of $80 since he sold all his lemonade, but when he looks at his cash flow statement he notices a cash profit of $79. The difference of course is the $1 owed (earned because Joey should eventually get his $1 from Billy). This $1 will be recorded as accounts receivable and it will be adjusted in the cash flows statement to reflect the timing difference between income and cash. This timing difference is basically the definition of working capital, as described later in this chapter. We are living is non-perfect world—a world of IOUs.

The cash flow statement also reflects the fact that the company receives and spends cash other than its primary business (these transactions are not recorded in the income statement which represents the company's direct or primary operations). For example, a company may spend money on new equipment, conduct improvements of manufacturing facilities, or decide to issue bonds in the capital markets.

The company's cash position per period (going up or down) does not necessarily represent the company's operating health. For example, the company might decide to use extra cash to repay debt. This decision will result in a lower cash outflow, even though it may be positive over time, reducing interest obligations.

The cash flow statement, which represents the change in position from one period to the next, has three primary sections:

1. Cash Flow from Operating Activities
2. Cash Flow from Investment Activities
3. Cash Flow from Financing Activities

It is important to realize that one could build an entire cash flow statement by looking at 2 years of balance sheets. The difference of each item on the balance sheet from one year to the next represents the activity for that year and can been seen on the cash flow statement.

Building the Cash Flow Statement Spreadsheet

The cash flow statement can be fully constructed by using addressing every item of two sequential balance sheets. By the taking the difference of this year's balance sheet to last year's representing this year's activities can be used to build the cash flow statement.

Forming the Cash Flow Statement

The cash flow statement was built to reconcile income to cash. The first line of the statement is net income and the last line is free cash flow. The balance sheet statement is presented the same way except the first line on the balance sheet is the cash balance and the last line is retained earnings. The changes of these balance sheet items represent free cash flow and net income, respectively.

Starting from net income we first need to add any non-cash items that are included in the income statement, moving upward. This includes depreciation, amortization, deferred taxes, or even deferred interest, representing the cash portion of net income before any timing differences in cost of goods sold and revenue.

As you can see in this example, we add depreciation and deferred taxes to net income; both items can be found on the balance sheet, as demonstrated in figure 15.6. After adding or subtracting these items we calculate cash income. Net income can also be found on the balance sheet as the difference in retained earnings from one year to the next.

FIGURE 15.6 CASH FLOW (LINES 2-11)

Celerity Technogy Inc. ("CTI")
Financial Statement Analysis

	Balance Sheet (000's)	Year 1	Year 2	$ Change	% Change
7	**Current Assets**				
8	Cash	45,000	65,800	20,800	46.2%
9	Accounts Receivable	45,000	60,000	15,000	33.3%
10	Inventories	35,000	40,000	5,000	14.3%
11	Prepaid Expenses	10,000	9,000	(1,000)	-10.0%
12	Total Current Assets	135,000	174,800	39,800	29.5%
14	**Property and Equipment**				
15	Land	2,500,000	2,500,000	-	0.0%
16	Building	450,000	550,000	100,000	22.2%
17	Furniture & Equipment	50,000	75,000	25,000	50.0%
18	Total Gross P&E	3,000,000	3,125,000	125,000	4.2%
19	Less Accumulated Depreciaition	(300,000)	(365,000)	**(65,000)**	21.7%
20	Net P&E	2,700,000	2,760,000	60,000	2.2%
22	Long-Term Investments	200,000	250,000	50,000	25.0%
24	Total Assets	3,035,000	3,184,800	149,800	4.9%
26	**Liabilities and Owners Equity**				
28	**Current Liabilities**				
29	Accounts Payable	35,000	40,000	5,000	14.3%
30	Accrued Income Taxes	12,000	10,000	(2,000)	-16.7%
31	Accrued Expenses	10,000	8,000	(2,000)	-20.0%
32	Current Portion of Long Term Debt	20,000	10,000	(10,000)	-50.0%
33	Total Current Liabilities	77,000	68,000	(9,000)	-11.7%
35	Long-Term Debt:	1,200,000	1,180,000	(20,000)	-1.7%
37	Deferred Income Taxes	12,000	17,000	**5,000**	41.7%
39	Total Liabilties	1,289,000	1,265,000	(24,000)	-1.9%
41	**Owners' Equity**				
42	Common Stock	1,000,000	1,000,000	-	0.0%
43	Paid-in-Capital	-	25,000	25,000	
44	Retained Earnings	746,000	894,800	**148,800**	19.9%
45	Total Owners' Equity	1,746,000	1,919,800	173,800	10.0%
47	Total Liabilities & Owner's Equity	3,035,000	3,184,800	149,800	4.9%

Cash Flow Statement (000's)	Year 2
Net Income	148,800
Plus Depreciation	65,000
Plus/Less Deffered Taxes	5,000
Cash Income	218,800

Once the cash flow statement is adjusted for any non-cash expense addbacks, as described, the statement is broken down to three different activities representing different parts of the balance sheet as follows:

1. **Cash flow from operating activities (figure 15.7)**, or working capital, represent changes in current assets and current liabilities on the balance sheet. Out of these sections of the balance sheet we omit cash balances and current-portion long-term debt, as these are included in other sections of the activity sectors.
2. **Cash flow from investment activities (figure 15.8)** are activities that represent the balance sheet changes between two periods in long-term assets such as property, plant, and equipment, long-term investments, and other assets. Goodwill and intangibles are not included in this section. The changes in PP&E are called capital expenditures (Capex). If the company decides to sell assets, a new line could be created called "Asset Disposition," or sometimes the Capex is net of asset sales.
3. **Cash flow from financing activities (figure 15.9)** are activities that represent the balance sheet changes between two periods in long-term liabilities and shareholder's equity (except for retained earnings).

FIGURE 15.7 CASH FLOW (LINES 2–21)

Celerity Technogy Inc. ("CTI")
Financial Statement Analysis

	Balance Sheet (000's)	Year 1	Year 2	$ Change	% Change
7	**Current Assets**				
8	Cash	45,000	65,800	20,800	46.2%
9	Accounts Receivable	45,000	60,000	15,000	33.3%
10	Inventories	35,000	40,000	5,000	14.3%
11	Prepaid Expenses	10,000	9,000	(1,000)	-10.0%
12	Total Current Assets	135,000	174,800	39,800	29.5%
14	**Property and Equipment**				
15	Land	2,500,000	2,500,000	-	0.0%
16	Building	450,000	550,000	100,000	22.2%
17	Furniture & Equipment	50,000	75,000	25,000	50.0%
18	Total Gross P&E	3,000,000	3,125,000	125,000	4.2%
19	Less Accumulated Depreciaition	(300,000)	(365,000)	(65,000)	21.7%
20	Net P&E	2,700,000	2,760,000	60,000	2.2%
22	Long-Term Investments	200,000	250,000	50,000	25.0%
24	Total Assets	3,035,000	3,184,800	149,800	4.9%
26	**Liabilities and Owners Equity**				
28	**Current Liabilities**				
29	Accounts Payable	35,000	40,000	5,000	14.3%
30	Accrued Income Taxes	12,000	10,000	(2,000)	-16.7%
31	Accrued Expenses	10,000	8,000	(2,000)	-20.0%
32	Current Portion of Long Term Debt	20,000	10,000	(10,000)	-50.0%
33	Total Current Liabilities	77,000	68,000	(9,000)	-11.7%
35	Long-Term Debt	1,200,000	1,180,000	(20,000)	-1.7%
37	Deferred Income Taxes	12,000	17,000	5,000	41.7%
39	Total Liabilties	1,289,000	1,265,000	(24,000)	-1.9%
41	**Owners' Equity**				
42	Common Stock	1,000,000	1,000,000	-	0.0%
43	Paid-in-Capital	-	25,000	25,000	
44	Retained Earnings	746,000	894,800	148,800	19.9%
45	Total Owners' Equity	1,746,000	1,919,800	173,800	10.0%
47	Total Liabilities & Owner's Equity	3,035,000	3,184,800	149,800	4.9%

Cash Flow Statement (000's)	Year 2
Net Income	148,800
Plus Depreciation	65,000
Plus/Less Deffered Taxes	5,000
Cash Income	218,800
Working Capital Activities	
Change in Accounts Receivable	(15,000)
Change in Inventory	(5,000)
Change in Prepaid Expenses	1,000
Change in Accounts Payable	5,000
Change in Accrued Income Taxes	(2,000)
Change in Accrued Expenses	(2,000)
Total Change in Working Capital	(18,000)
Operating Cash Flow (OCF)	200,800

FIGURE 15.8 CASH FLOW (LINES 2–29)

Celerity Technogy Inc. ("CTI")
Financial Statement Analysis

	Balance Sheet (000's)	Year 1	Year 2	$ Change	% Change
7	**Current Assets**				
8	Cash	45,000	65,800	20,800	46.2%
9	Accounts Receivable	45,000	60,000	15,000	33.3%
10	Inventories	35,000	40,000	5,000	14.3%
11	Prepaid Expenses	10,000	9,000	(1,000)	-10.0%
12	Total Current Assets	135,000	174,800	39,800	29.5%
14	**Property and Equipment**				
15	Land	2,500,000	2,500,000	-	0.0%
16	Building	450,000	550,000	100,000	22.2%
17	Furniture & Equipment	50,000	75,000	25,000	50.0%
18	Total Gross P&E	3,000,000	3,125,000	**125,000**	4.2%
19	Less Accumulated Depreciaition	(300,000)	(365,000)	(65,000)	21.7%
20	Net P&E	2,700,000	2,760,000	60,000	2.2%
22	Long-Term Investments	200,000	250,000	**50,000**	25.0%
24	Total Assets	3,035,000	3,184,800	149,800	4.9%
26	**Liabilities and Owners Equity**				
28	**Current Liabilities**				
29	Accounts Payable	35,000	40,000	5,000	14.3%
30	Accrued Income Taxes	12,000	10,000	(2,000)	-16.7%
31	Accrued Expenses	10,000	8,000	(2,000)	-20.0%
32	Current Portion of Long Term Debt	20,000	10,000	(10,000)	-50.0%
33	Total Current Liabilities	77,000	68,000	(9,000)	-11.7%
35	Long-Term Debt:	1,200,000	1,180,000	(20,000)	-1.7%
37	Deferred Income Taxes	12,000	17,000	5,000	41.7%
39	Total Liabilties	1,289,000	1,265,000	(24,000)	-1.9%
41	**Owners' Equity**				
42	Common Stock	1,000,000	1,000,000	-	0.0%
43	Paid-in-Capital	-	25,000	25,000	
44	Retained Earnings	746,000	894,800	148,800	19.9%
45	Total Owners' Equity	1,746,000	1,919,800	173,800	10.0%
47	Total Liabilities & Owner's Equity	3,035,000	3,184,800	149,800	4.9%

Cash Flow Statement (000's)	Year 2
Net Income	148,800
Plus Depreciation	65,000
Plus/Less Deffered Taxes	5,000
Cash Income	218,800
Working Capital Activities	
Change in Accounts Receivable	(15,000)
Change in Inventory	(5,000)
Change in Prepaid Expenses	1,000
Change in Accounts Payable	5,000
Change in Accrued Income Taxes	(2,000)
Change in Accrued Expenses	(2,000)
Total Change in Working Capital	(18,000)
Operating Cash Flow (OCF)	200,800
Investment Activities	
Capital Expenditures	(125,000)
Investments (Change)	(50,000)
Total Financing Activities	(175,000)
Cash Available Before Financing Activities	25,800

FIGURE 15.9 CASH FLOW (LINES 2–41)

Celerity Technogy Inc. ("CTI")
Financial Statement Analysis

	Balance Sheet (000's)	Year 1	Year 2	$ Change	% Change
7	**Current Assets**				
8	Cash	45,000	65,800	20,800	46.2%
9	Accounts Receivable	45,000	60,000	15,000	33.3%
10	Inventories	35,000	40,000	5,000	14.3%
11	Prepaid Expenses	10,000	9,000	**(1,000)**	-10.0%
12	Total Current Assets	135,000	174,800	**39,800**	29.5%
14	**Property and Equipment**				
15	Land	2,500,000	2,500,000	-	0.0%
16	Building	450,000	550,000	**100,000**	22.2%
17	Furniture & Equipment	50,000	75,000	**25,000**	50.0%
18	Total Gross P&E	3,000,000	3,125,000	**125,000**	4.2%
19	Less Accumulated Depreciaition	(300,000)	(365,000)	**(65,000)**	21.7%
20	Net P&E	2,700,000	2,760,000	**60,000**	2.2%
22	Long-Term Investments	200,000	250,000	**50,000**	25.0%
24	Total Assets	3,035,000	3,184,800	**149,800**	4.9%
26	**Liabilities and Owners Equity**				
28	**Current Liabilities**				
29	Accounts Payable	35,000	40,000	**5,000**	14.3%
30	Accrued Income Taxes	12,000	10,000	(2,000)	-16.7%
31	Accrued Expenses	10,000	8,000	(2,000)	-20.0%
32	Current Portion of Long Term Debt	20,000	10,000	(10,000)	-50.0%
33	Total Current Liabilities	77,000	68,000	(9,000)	-11.7%
35	Long-Term Debt:	1,200,000	1,180,000	(20,000)	-1.7%
37	Deferred Income Taxes	12,000	17,000	5,000	41.7%
39	Total Liabilties	1,289,000	1,265,000	(24,000)	-1.9%
41	**Owners' Equity**				
42	Common Stock	1,000,000	1,000,000	-	0.0%
43	Paid-in-Capital	-	25,000	25,000	
44	Retained Earnings	746,000	894,800	148,800	19.9%
45	Total Owners' Equity	1,746,000	1,919,800	173,800	10.0%
47	Total Liabilities & Owner's Equity	3,035,000	3,184,800	149,800	4.9%

Cash Flow Statement (000's)	Year 2
Net Income	148,800
Plus Depreciation	65,000
Plus/Less Deffered Taxes	5,000
Cash Income	218,800
Working Capital Activities	
Change in Accounts Receivable	(15,000)
Change in Inventory	(5,000)
Change in Prepaid Expenses	1,000
Change in Accounts Payable	5,000
Change in Accrued Income Taxes	(2,000)
Change in Accrued Expenses	(2,000)
Total Change in Working Capital	(18,000)
Operating Cash Flow (OCF)	200,800
Investment Activities	
Capital Expenditures	(125,000)
Investments (Change)	(50,000)
Total Financing Activities	(175,000)
Cash Available Before Financing Activities	25,800
Financing Activities	
ST Debt Payments	(10,000)
LT Debt Payments	(20,000)
Equity Contribution	25,000
Total Financing Activities	(5,000)
Free Cash Flow	20,800
Beginning Cash	45,000
Ending Cash	65,800

The book *The Four Cornerstones of Corporate Finance Value*, written by Tim Koller, Richard Dobbs, and Bill Huyett (2011) discusses the importance for a company create value (value creation). In one of the chapters of the book the authors elaborate how important it is for management to seek revenue growth and return on invested capital (ROIC) and compare this to the use of cash to achieve such growth. "Disaggregating cash flow into revenue growth and ROIC clarifies the underlying drivers of the company's performance," they stated (Koller, Dobbs, & Huyett, 2011, p. 17). The book goes on to say that "this doesn't tell us much about its economic performance since an increase of cash flow come[s] from many sources, including revenue growth or reduction in capital spending, or a reduction in marketing expenses. But if we [were] told the company was growing at 7% per year and would earn ROIC of 15%, you could then evaluate its performance" (p. 17). Basically, management needs to invest more in Capex today, so it could achieve higher revenue growth in the future. This relationship between Capex and revenues is one that the analyst needs to address in the analysis.

FINANCIAL RATIO ANALYSIS

Understanding how to interpret financial statements does not purely involve looking at the trends between years such as revenue growth to determine how the company is performing. Though this approach is usually the first line of every financial analysis, the analyst needs to get deeper in the analysis to determine specific results that should enhance the assessment of the company's performance. For example, by combining a few items from the income statement and the balance sheet, or by comparing cash flow statement and income statement lines, the analyst could better interpret the company's performance. This process is called ratio analysis and is designed to give the analyst a better story about the performance of the company. Ratio analysis is broken down into liquidity ratios, solvency ratios, operating ratios, and profitability ratios (figure 15.10).

LIQUIDITY RATIOS

Liquidity ratios measure how the company manages cash. This of course is more relevant when the company is in distress and having liquidity is its top priority. The following ratios are considered liquidity ratios (figure 15.11).

> **Current ratio:** Current assets/current liabilities. This ratio measures the ability of the company to pay off its short-term obligations such as payment to vendors or accrued taxes by liquidating its current assets, basically using the cash balances and proceeds from turning receivable and inventory into cash. Companies with lower than 1x current ratio, by definition, do not have enough liquidity to cover their short-term obligations. The example shows that the current ratio improves from 1.75x in 2016 to 2.57x in

FIGURE 15.10 CELERITY TECHNOLOGY FINANCIAL STATEMENT—RATIO ANALYSIS

Celerity Technogy Inc. ("CTI")
Financial Statement Analysis

		Year 1	Year 2	Definition
7	**Trend Analysis Ratios**			
8	Revenue Growth		15.6%	This Year's Revenue / Last Year's Revenue - 1
9	Stock one-year Return (HPR)		25.0%	This Year's SP/ Last Year's SP -1
11	**Liquidity Ratios**			
12	Current Ratio	1.75x	2.57x	CA/CL
13	Quick ratio	1.17x	1.85x	(Cash + A/R) / CL
14	Cash ratio	0.58x	0.97x	Cash / CL
15	Accounts Receivable Turnover (ART)		21.14x	Revenue/Avg AR
16	Accounts Receivable Days		17.26	365 / ART
18	**Solvency Ratios**			
19	Debt/Equity Ratio	68.7%	61.5%	LTD / Equity
20	LTD / Total Capitalization	40.7%	38.1%	LTD / (LTD + Equity)
21	**EBITDA / Interest (Coverage Ratio)**	2.96x	3.61x	EBITDA / Interest
22	EBIT / Interest	2.50x	3.07x	EBIT / Interest
23	Fixed Charge Coverage Serv./Debt Serv.		2.05x	(EBITDA - Capex)/(Int.+ ST + LT Pmts)
24	Cash Avail. For Debt Serv. / Debt Serv.		0.97x	(CABFA + Int.) / (int. + ST + LT Pmts)
25	LTD / EBITDA (Leverage Ratio)	3.12x	2.73x	LTD / EBITDA
27	**Activity Ratios / Operating Ratios**			
28	Inventory Ratio (IR)		11.20x	Cost of Revenues/Avg Inventory
29	Inventory Ratio - Days		32.59	365 / IR
30	Fixed Asset Turnover Ratio		0.407x	Rev / Avg of FA
31	Asset Turnover Ratio		0.36x	Rev / Avg of Total Assets
33	**Profitability Ratios**			
34	Gross Margin	64.1%	62.2%	Gross Margin / Revenues
35	EBITDA Margin	40.1%	39.0%	EBITDA / Revenue
36	EBIT Margin	33.9%	33.2%	EBIT / Revenue
37	Return on Assets (ROA)		4.8%	NI / Avg Assets
38	Gross Return on Assets		11.8%	EBIT / Avg Assets
39	Return on Equity (ROE)		8.1%	NI / Avg Equity
50	**Other Ratios**			
51	Altma's Z-score	2.15x	2.67x	
53	**Z Formula**			
54	Z = 1.2x(WC/TA) + 1.4x(RE/TA)+3.3x(EBIT/TA)+0.6x(MVE/Liabilities) + 0.99x(Sales/TA)			
56	WC = Working Capital			
57	TA=Total Assets			
58	RE=Retained Earnings			
59	MVE=Market Value of Equity			
61	**Z-Score**			**Bankruptcy**
62	1.8x or less			Likely
63	Between 1.8 - 3.0			Uncertain
64	3.0 or above			Not likely

FIGURE 15.11 LIQUIDITY RATIOS

		Year 1	Year 2	Definition
5	**Liquidity Ratios**			
6	Current Ratio	1.75x	2.57x	CA/CL
7	Quick ratio	1.17x	1.85x	(Cash + A/R) / CL
8	Cash ratio	0.58x	0.97x	Cash / CL
9	Accounts Receivable Turnover (ART)		21.14x	Revenue/Avg AR
10	Accounts Receivable Days		17.26	365 / ART

2017, showing that even if the company's liquidity is cut in half it has enough cash left to cover its short-term obligations. This indicates the ability to avoid insolvency for the near future.

Quick ratio: (Cash and cash equivalents + accounts receivable)/current liabilities. This ratio, also known as acid test ratio, has the same denominator as the current ratio but better represents the immediate liquidity of the company. Sometimes, converting inventory to cash is more challenging. In distressed companies where liquidity is the most important assessment of insolvency, inventory is usually sold at a discount to what is reported in the books. In this case the current ratio could be overestimating the company's liquidity position.

Accounts receivable turnover (ART) and days: ART = Revenue/average receivables and ART/365 days. This ratio is called a mixed ratio as it combines items from the income statement and balance sheet. In most cases when an analyst combines items from the income statement and balance sheet, he or she needs to use the average approach for the balance sheet due to the application of periodic information to snapshot information. ART takes the revenue divided by the average receivable amounts between periods found on the balance sheet. This ratio represents how many times a year the receivables convert to cash revenue. Taking that result further, someone can calculate how often the receivables are paid. In the example (figure 15.11), the company shows that the receivables turned 21 times per year or every 17.3 days.

SOLVENCY RATIOS

Solvency ratios measure how a company manages debt. Debt can be a friend or a foe. Using the right amount of debt to grow your business is considered good and effective management. Debt though, a lot of it, can put a lot of pressure on the company's performance. Solvency ratios include debt to equity **capitalization ratio** or long-term debt to total capitalization; **coverage ratio** or EBITDA to interest expenses, EBIT to interest expenses, fixed charge coverage, cash flow available for debt service to debt service; and **leverage ratio** of long-term debt to EBITDA. All these are important ratios that gives the analyst a clear understanding of the company's solvency status (figure 15.12).

Debt to equity: Debt/equity. This ratio is generally used for comparing the strength of the equity as it compares to its debt, essentially for investment-grade companies (BBB+ and better under Standards & Poor's grading system) that have a debt-to-equity ratio of less than 1x, showing that the composition of book value of equity is higher

FIGURE 15.12 SOLVENCY RATIOS

		Year 1	Year 2	Definition
5	**Solvency Ratios**			
6	Debt/Equity Ratio	68.7%	61.5%	LTD / Equity
7	LTD / Total Capitalization	40.7%	38.1%	LTD / (LTD + Equity)
8	**EBITDA / Interest (Coverage Ratio)**	2.96x	3.61x	EBITDA / Interest
9	EBIT / Interest	2.50x	3.07x	EBIT / Interest
10	Fixed Charge Coverage Serv./Debt Serv.		2.05x	(EBITDA - Capex)/(Int.+ ST + LT Pmts)
11	Cash Avail. For Debt Serv. / Debt Serv.		0.97x	(CABFA + Int.) / (int. + ST + LT Pmts)
12	LTD / EBITDA (Leverage Ratio)	3.12x	2.73x	LTD / EBITDA

than the value of debt. Companies with higher than 1x are considered riskier as the debt is higher than the equity.

Capitalization ratios: Total debt/(Total debt + shareholders' equity) or long-term debt/(Long-term debt + shareholders' equity): This ratio measures the proportion of debt in the company's capital structure. This ratio is a very common ratio to measure balance sheet leverage, an important measurement for a company to effectively access the capital markets.

Coverage ratios: EBITDA/interest expense and EBIT/interest, Both ratios could be found in many loan agreements as financial covenant. This covenant measures how much cushion a company needs to be able to make its periodical debt obligations such as interest expenses. Other coverage ratios are **fixed-charge coverage and cash flow available for debt service to debt service**. These ratios are more specific to the ability of the company to make its debt obligations, both principal and interest payments.

Leverage ratio: Total debt/EBITDA or long-term debt/EBITDA: This one of the most popular solvency ratios. This ratio is typically included as a covenant in many loan agreements, primarily for companies that are non-investment grade (BB- or below rated by Standard & Poor). It's also a market benchmark for raising debt in the loan and bond markets. Even the government, after the financial crisis, implemented guidelines to discourage regulated banks to lend money to companies that had a ratio higher than 6x. In 2013, the federal government published the Leveraged Lending Guidelines to guide banks to run debt capacity measurements before providing credit. This ratio measures how long it will take a company to pay off its debt. In a later chapter regarding debt capacity, this ratio is one of the ratios that we will use to derive debt capacity at certain transactions.

> **Altman's Z-score:** Altman's Z-score measures the credit strength of a publicly traded manufacturing company that faces bankruptcy. The five combined ratios, as illustrated, measure the strength of the company's cash collateral and the likelihood of bankruptcy. Four out of the five ratios have total assets as the denominator, putting emphasis on the relationship between income and cash flow to the collateral of the company, a special relevant factor when a company is facing bankruptcy. These ratios include working capital/total assets, retained earnings/total assets, EBIT/total assets, and sales/total assets. The other ratio, market value of equity/total liabilities, measures the company's market value of the equity in relationship to the total liabilities. In most distress situations where the company is facing bankruptcy, the stock price will significantly decline and simultaneously the liability increases. As a result, the company finances it loses by accessing its credit facilities (figure 15.13).

Each ratio that makes the combined five-ratio formula called Z-Score has different weights assigned to calculate the credit strength of the company. If the company's Z-score is less than 1.8x, the likelihood of bankruptcy is high. Between 1.8x and 3.0x results in uncertainty; in this case what is most important is the negative or positive trend to or away from bankruptcy. The likelihood of bankruptcy is remote if the Z-score is calculated at 3x or above, indicating that the numerator number of each ratio has a relationship to with collateral that is healthy.

ACTIVITY OR OPERATING RATIOS

These ratios measure how well and efficiently the company manages the overall business operations including inventory, working capital, revenue, and cost. For example, the hotel

FIGURE 15.13 OTHER SOLVENCY RATIOS

		Year 1	Year 2	
5	**Other Ratios**			
6	Altma's Z-score	2.15x	2.67x	
8	**Z Formula**			
9	Z = 1.2x(WC/TA) + 1.4x(RE/TA)+3.3x(EBIT/TA)+0.6x(MVE/Liabilities) + 0.99x(Sales/TA)			
11	WC = Working Capital			
12	TA=Total Assets			
13	RE=Retained Earnings			
14	MVE=Market Value of Equity			
16	**Z-Score**			**Bankruptcy**
17	1.8x or less			Likely
18	Between 1.8 - 3.0			Uncertain
19	3.0 or above			Not likely

FIGURE 15.14 ACTIVITY RATIOS

		Year 1	Year 2	Definition
5	**Activity Ratios / Operating Ratios**			
6	Inventory Ratio (IR)		11.20x	Cost of Revenues/Avg Inventory
7	Inventory Ratio - Days		32.59	365 / IR
8	Fixed Asset Turnover Ratio		0.407x	Rev / Avg of FA
9	Asset Turnover Ratio		0.36x	Rev / Avg of Total Assets

sector uses occupancy ratio (OR), which represents the percentage amount of rooms booked divided by the total available rooms. It is a perfect example to measure how active the hotel is with less vacancies. The restaurant sector uses turnover ratio, which represents how often tables are turned over or reused during a lunch shift. For a manufacturing company, **inventory turnover** measures how well the company manages inventory (figure 15.14).

> **Inventory turnover:** Cost of revenues/average inventory: This is a ratio that measures how effectively inventory is managed compared to cost of goods that are sold. The result shows how many times a year inventory is turned. The example shows 11.2x, the inventory as it moves from raw material to work in process, to being finished goods stored in the warehouse, and eventually to being sold is done approximately 11 times per year.
>
> **Inventory days:** 365 days/inventory turnover: Using the example, the inventory is turned every 32.6 days; the inventory, as it moves from raw material to work in process, then to finished good stored in the warehouse, and to eventually sold, is done every 32.6 days before new inventory goes though the cycle.
>
> **Fixed asset turnover ratio and total asset turnover:** Revenue/average fixed assets or revenue/total assets. Both ratios measure how well the business is using its long-term assets, primarily plant and equipment, to generate revenue. A declining ratio would show that the business is overinvested in plant and equipment or other assets to yield the revenues. This is a good ratio to demonstrate how the company is trending from year to year and how it compares versus its peers that manufacture the same products.

PROFITABILITY RATIOS

These ratios measure how profitable the companies are. These ratios are very popular for pier comparison and trend analysis. These ratios include gross margin ratios expressed in percentage, EBITDA or EBIT margin ratios, return of assets, and return of equity (figure 15.15).

FIGURE 15.15 PROFITABILITY RATIOS

		Year 1	Year 2	Definition
5	**Profitability Ratios**			
6	Gross Margin	64.1%	62.2%	Gross Margin / Revenues
7	EBITDA Margin	40.1%	39.0%	EBITDA / Revenue
8	EBIT Margin	33.9%	33.2%	EBIT / Revenue
9	Return on Assets (ROA)		4.8%	NI / Avg Assets
10	Gross Return on Assets		11.8%	EBIT / Avg Assets
11	Return on Equity (ROE)		8.1%	NI / Avg Equity

Gross margin: Gross profit/revenues: This is one of the most common profitability ratios. This ratio, usually expressed as a percentage, measures what the direct profit of a unit of sale is. In figure 15.15, a gross margin of 62.2% (2017) is stating that every $1 of unit sale yields 62.2 cents of gross profit.

EBITDA margin and EBIT margin: EBITDA/revenues and EBIT/revenues: These ratios measure the percentage profit after operating expenses for every single unit of sale. EBITDA represents profit before depreciation and amortization, reflecting as close to cash profit as possible.

Return on assets (ROA) and gross return on Assets: Net income/average total assets and EBIT/total assets: This ratio represents the percentage of income that the company generates from the all the assets it owns. Based on figure 15.15 the ROA is 4.8%, which basically means that if the company decides to sell its assets at book value of an average $3 billion and deposit it at a bank, they would do better than 4.8% return.

Return on equity (ROE): Net income/average total shareholder's equity: This ratio takes the ROA one step further. Since the value of the assets are offset by liabilities, the net difference, which is owner's equity, represents the book value of the investment in the company. ROE measures the return on the shareholders' equity or how much net income the company generates for every $1 of investment value.

Credit

CASE STUDY

HYATT HOTELS

Profile (Source: Yahoo Finance): Hyatt Hotels Corporation, a hospitality company, develops, owns, operates, manages, franchises, licenses, or provides services to hotels, resorts, and other properties. It operates through four segments: Owned and Leased Hotels, Americas Management and Franchising, ASPAC Management and Franchising, and EAME/SW Asia Management and Franchising. The company operates its properties under the Park Hyatt, Miraval, Grand Hyatt, Alila, Andaz, The Unbound Collection by Hyatt, Destination, Hyatt Regency, Hyatt, Hyatt Ziva, Hyatt Zilara, Thompson Hotels, Hyatt Centric, Caption by Hyatt, Hyatt House, Hyatt Place, tommie, Hyatt Residence Club, Hyatt Residences, Exhale, World of Hyatt, and Hyatt Resorts brands. As of December 31, 2019, its hotel portfolio consisted of 913 hotels in 65 countries. It primarily serves corporations; national, state, and regional associations; specialty market accounts, including social, government, military, educational, religious, and fraternal accounts; travel agency and luxury organizations; and a group of individual consumers. Hyatt Hotels Corporation has a strategic alliance with Small Luxury Hotels to provide benefits to the members of World of Hyatt loyalty program by providing additional stay opportunities at luxury hotels primarily in Europe. The company was formerly known as Global Hyatt Corporation and changed its name to Hyatt Hotels Corporation in June 2009. Hyatt Hotels Corporation was founded in 1957 and is headquartered in Chicago, Illinois.

Financial Statements

Hyatt's balance sheet and income statement for 2019, 2018, 2017, and 2016 are as follows:

HYATT HOTELS CORPORATION (H)
INCOME STATEMENT (December 31)

(000S)	2019	2018	2017	2016
Total Revenue	**5,042,000**	**4,474,000**	**4,685,000**	**4,429,000**
Cost of Revenue	4,099,000	3,495,000	3,638,000	3,473,000
Gross Profit	943,000	979,000	1,047,000	956,000
Total Operating Expenses	746,000	647,000	745,000	657,000
EBIT (Operating Income or Loss)	197,000	332,000	302,000	299,000
Interest Expense	75,000	76,000	80,000	76,000
EBT & Other Income/Expenses	122,000	256,000	222,000	223,000
Other Income/Expenses Net	884,000	695,000	351,000	66,000
EBT	1,006,000	951,000	573,000	289,000
Income Tax Expense	240,000	182,000	323,000	85,000
Net Income	766,000	769,000	250,000	204,000

BALANCE SHEET STATEMENT (December 31)

(000S)	2019	2018	2017	2016
Assets				
Current Assets				
Cash and Cash Equivalents	929,000	570,000	503,000	482,000
Other Short-Term Investments	32,000	116,000	49,000	56,000
Total Cash	961,000	686,000	552,000	538,000
Net Receivables	421,000	427,000	350,000	304,000
Inventory	12,000	14,000	14,000	28,000
Total Current Assets	1,394,000	1,127,000	916,000	870,000
Non-Current Assets				
Gross Property, Plant, and Equipment	6,098,000	5,847,000	6,332,000	6,634,000
Accumulated Depreciation	-2,149,000	-2,239,000	-2,298,000	-2,364,000
Net Property, Plant, and Equipment	3,949,000	3,608,000	4,034,000	4,270,000
Long-Term Investments	1,784,000	1,513,000	883,000	787,999
Goodwill	326,000	283,000	150,000	125,000
Intangible Assets	437,000	628,000	683,000	599,000
Other Long-Term Assets	527,000	484,000	1,006,000	1,098,000
Total Non-Current Assets	7,023,000	6,516,000	6,756,000	6,879,999
Total Assets	**8,417,000**	**7,643,000**	**7,672,000**	**7,749,999**
Liabilities				
Current Liabilities				
Accounts Payable	150,000	151,000	175,000	162,000
Accrued Liabilities	283,000	339,000	540,000	520,000
Deferred Revenues	200,000	238,000	540,000	407,000
Current Portion of Long-Term Debt	11,000	11,000	11,000	119,000
Total Current Liabilities	644,000	739,000	1,266,000	1,208,000
Non-Current Liabilities				
Long-Term Debt	1,612,000	1,623,000	1,440,000	1,445,000
Deferred Taxes Liabilities	47,000	54,000	62,000	57,000
Deferred Revenues	421,000	300,000	746,000	1,131,999
Total Non-Current Liabilities	2,080,000	1,977,000	2,248,000	2,633,999
Total Liabilities	2,724,000	2,716,000	3,514,000	3,841,999

Stockholders' Equity				
Common Stock	1,000	1,000	1,000	1,000
Retained Earnings	5,692,000	4,926,000	4,157,000	3,907,000
Total Stockholders' Equity	5,693,000	4,927,000	4,158,000	3,908,000
Liabilities & Stockholders' Equity	8,417,000	7,643,000	7,672,000	7,749,999

Building the Summary Cash Flow Statements and Financial Analysis

In building Hyatt's summary cash flow statement, the challenge is to breakdown the balance sheet items into activities that can be allocated in the cash flow statement. The summary cash flow and ratio analysis below was prepared based on the income and balance sheet statements.

SUMMARY CASH FLOW ANALYSIS (December 31)

(000S)	2019	2018	2017
Net Income	766,000	769,000	250,000
Depreciation	-90,000	-59,000	-66,000
Amortization (Intangibles)	-191,000	-55,000	84,000
Deferred Taxes	-7,000	-8,000	5,000
ST Deferred Revenue	-38,000	-302,000	133,000
Cash Income	440,000	345,000	406,000
Working Capital Activity			
Net Receivables	6,000	-77,000	-46,000
Inventory	2,000	00	14,000
Accounts Payable	-1,000	-24,000	13,000
Accrued Liabilities	-56,000	-201,000	20,000
Total Working Capital	**-49,000**	**-302,000**	**1,000**
Operating Cash Flow (OCF)	**391,000**	**43,000**	**407,000**
Investment Activities			
Capital Expenditure	-251,000	485,000	302,000
Long-Term Investment	-271,000	-630,000	-95,001
Other Long-Term Assets	296,000	499,000	-101,000
Total Investment Activities	**-226,000**	**354,000**	**105,999**
Cash Flow Before Financing	**165,000**	**397,000**	**512,999**

Financing Activity			
ST Debt	00	00	-108,000
LT Debt	-11,000	183,000	-5,000
LT Deferred Revenue	121,000	-446,000	-385,999
Other Long-Term Liabilities	00	00	00
Total Financing Activities	**110,000**	**-263,000**	**-498,999**
Free Cash Flow	**275,000**	**134,000**	**14,000**
Allocation Cash and Cash Equivalents	359,000	67,000	21,000
Allocation Other Short-Term Investments	-84,000	67,000	-7,000
Beginning Cash	**686,000**	**552,000**	**538,000**
Allocation Cash and Cash Equivalents	570,000	503,000	482,000
Allocation Other Short-Term Investments	116,000	49,000	56,000
Ending Cash	**961,000**	**686,000**	**552,000**
Allocation Cash and Cash Equivalents	929,000	570,000	503,000
Allocation Other Short-Term Investments	32,000	116,000	49,000

FINANCIAL RATIO ANALYSIS

	2019	**2018**	**2017**
EBITDA ($ 000s)	**618,000**	**707,000**	**658,000**
TREND ANALYSIS			
Revenue Growth	12.7%	-4.5%	5.8%
LIQUIDITY RATIOS			
Current Ratio	2.2×	1.5×	0.7×
Quick Ratio	2.1×	1.5×	0.7×
Accounts Receivable Turnover	11.9×	11.5×	14.3×
Accounts Receivable Days	30.69	31.69	25.48
SOLVENCY RATIOS			
Total Debt/Total Capitalization (Cap Ratio)	22.2%	24.9%	25.9%
EBITDA/Interest (Coverage Ratio)	8.2×	9.3×	8.2×
Total Debt/EBITDA (Leverage Ratio)	0.4×	0.4×	0.5×
PROFITABILITY RATIO			
Gross Profit	18.7%	21.9%	22.3%
EBITDA Margin	12.3%	15.8%	14.0%
ROA	9.5%	10.0%	3.2%
ROE	3.6%	4.2%	1.5%

PROBLEMS

1. Based on the information below, complete the spreadsheet that includes a brief cash flow statement, balance sheet, and ratios.

INPUT	2018	2019
Sales	250,000	300,000
Cost of Good Sold	120,000	150,000
Cash	40,000	
Depreciation	36,000	40,000
Amortization	5,000	5,000
Interest Expense	8,000	9,000
Tax Rate	28.0%	28.0%
SG&A	50,000	55,000
Long Term Debt	240,000	230,000
Cash Taxes		10,000
Initial Equity Investment	150,000	150,000
Paid in Capital	-	-
Accounts Receivable	40,000	42,000
Inventory	15,000	14,500
Gross Fixed Assets	800,000	820,000
Accumulated Depreciation	(350,000)	
Accounts Payable	35,000	36,000
Retained Earnings	100,000	
Defered Taxes	50,000	
Capitalized Fees (Amort)	30,000	

OUTPUT

Income Statement

	2018	2019
Sales		
COGS		
Gross Profit		
SG&A		
EBITDA		
Depreciation		
Amortization		
EBIT		
Interest		
EBT		
Taxes		
NI		

Balance Sheet

	2018	2019
Cash		
Account Receivable		
Inventory		
Total C/A		
Capitalized Fees (Amortiz)		
Gross Fixed Assets		
Accumulated Depreciation		
Net Fixed Assets		
Total Assets		
Accounts Payable		
Long Term Debt		
Defered Taxes		
Total Liabilities		
Initial Equity Investment		
Paid in Capital		
Retained Earnings		
Total Equity		
Total Liability + Equity		

Cash Flow

		2019
	NI	
	Depreciation	
	Amortization	
	Deffered Taxes	
WC	Cash Income	
	Change in A/R	
	Change in Inventory	
	Change in A/P	
	Change Working Capital	
Inv	Operating Cash Flow	
	Capex	
	CFBFA	
Fin	Debt	
	Equity Pmt/Contribution	
	Fin Activity	
	Cash Flow	
	Beginning Cash Flow	
	Ending Cash Flow	

Financial Ratios

Gross Margin %	
Accounts Receivable Days	
Inventory Turnover Days	
ROA	
ROE	

2. Complete the cash flow statement based on the 2-year balance sheet and income statements provided below.

Balance Sheet (000's)	2016	2017
Current Assets		
Cash	67,500	86,100
Accounts Receivable	67,500	87,000
Inventories	52,500	65,000
Prepaid Expenses	15,000	13,000
Total Current Assets	202,500	251,100
Property and Equipment		
Land	3,750,000	3,750,000
Building	675,000	800,000
Furniture & Equipment	75,000	100,000
Total Gross P&E	4,500,000	4,650,000
Less Accumulated Depreciaition	(450,000)	(550,000)
Net P&E	4,050,000	4,100,000
Long-Term Investments	300,000	400,000
Total Assets	4,552,500	4,751,100
Liabilities and Owners Equity		
Current Liabilities		
Accounts Payable	52,500	65,000
Accrued Income Taxes	18,000	15,000
Accrued Expenses	15,000	10,000
Current Portion of Long Term Debt	30,000	30,000
Total Current Liabilities	115,500	120,000
Long-Term Debt:	1,800,000	1,700,000
Deferred Income Taxes	18,000	22,000
Total Liabilties	1,933,500	1,842,000
Owners' Equity		
Common Stock	1,500,000	1,500,000
Paid-in-Capital	-	30,000
Retained Earnings	1,119,000	1,379,100
Total Owners' Equity	2,619,000	2,909,100
Total Liabilities & Owner's Equity	4,552,500	4,751,100

Income Statement (000's)	2016	2017
Revenues by Geography		
U.S.	1,200,000	1,400,000
Europe	180,000	210,000
Asia	60,000	75,000
Total Revenue	1,440,000	1,685,000
Cost of Revenues by Geography		
U.S.	330,000	405,000
Europe	150,000	172,500
Asia	37,500	52,500
Total Cost of Revenue	517,500	630,000
Gross Profit	922,500	1,055,000
Operating Expenses		
Administrative & General	217,500	247,500
Marketing Expenses	112,500	120,000
Other Operating Expenses	15,000	18,000
Total Operating Expenses	345,000	385,500
EBITDA	577,500	669,500
Depreciation	90,000	100,000
EBIT	487,500	569,500
Interest Expense	144,000	136,000
EBT	343,500	433,500
Taxes	137,400	173,400
Net Income	206,100	260,100

Cash Flow Statement (000's)	**2017**
Net Income	
Plus Depreciation	
Plus Deffered Taxes	
Cash Income	
Working Capital Activities	
Change in Accounts Receivable	
Change in Inventory	
Change in Prepaid Expenses	
Change in Accounts Payable	
Change in Accrued Income Taxes	
Change in Accrued Expenses	
Total Change in Working Capital	
Operating Cash Flow (OCF)	

Investment Activities	
Capital Expenditures	
Investments (Change)	
Total Investment Activities	
Cash Available Before Financing Activities	
Financing Activities	
ST Debt Payments	
LT Payments	
Equity Contribution	
Total Financing Activities	
Free Cash Flow	
Beginning Cash	
Ending Cash	

Ratio Analysis	**2017**	**2018**
Total Revenue Growth		
LTD / Total Capitalization		
EBITDA / Interest (Coverage Ratio)		
Total Debt / EBITDA (Leverage Ratio)		
Inventory Days		
Accounts Receivable Days		
Total Company Gross Margin		
US Business Gross Margin		
EBITDA Margin		
Return on Assets (ROA)		
Return on Equity (ROE)		

3. Download the financial statements for any publicly traded company from websites such as www.finance.yahoo.com and www.google.com/finance and calculate the following ratios.

Ratio Analysis	2017	2018
Total Revenue Growth		
LTD / Total Capitalization		
EBITDA / Interest (Coverage Ratio)		
Total Debt / EBITDA (Leverage Ratio)		
Inventory Days		
Accounts Receivable Days		
Total Company Gross Margin		
US Business Gross Margin		
EBITDA Margin		
Return on Assets (ROA)		
Return on Equity (ROE)		

ONLINE TEMPLATES

The Excel spreadsheets used in the chapter can be accessed online via Cognella Active Learning platform.

CHAPTER 16

Projections Analysis

This chapter will focus on using the historical information from the financial statements and ratio analysis, as described from the last chapter, to build the projections. The projections will be based on drivers and assumptions that are customized by standard industry parameters. After setting the company's base projections (base case), the chapter will then discuss the process of sensitizing such cases based on the analyst's view (downside and upside cases).

LEARNING OBJECTIVES

After reading this chapter, students will be able to do the following:

- Use historical assumptions and trends to drive the projections
- Know what must be considered before setting up projective revenue drivers
- Differentiate between organic and inorganic revenue growth
- Understand the different assumptions used for start-up companies and mature companies as well as companies with revenues based on contractual obligations
- Once the revenues are established, you will learn how to build the company's cost structure
- Understand how to run different sensitivity cases including a downside case, a break-even case, and an equity upside case

PROJECTIONS OVERVIEW

The main role of both the financial analyst and credit analyst is to measure the future income and cash flow of the firm. The financial analyst, representing the equity investors, is trying to determine the value the corporation based on the future cash flows. The credit analyst, representing the debt holder, is trying to determine if the current debt is high or low based on the future cash flows. Also, the credit analyst is measuring how much debt the company can handle for a given transaction. This measurement, called debt capacity, will be covered on chapter 18.

AUTHOR'S NOTES

I started my career at Bank of America in the late 80s building financial models for the leveraged buyout financing area of the bank. I had a heavy Greek accent, originally from Cyprus, so they asked me to sit in the corner on the trading floor and run numbers. Given my accent, they didn't want me to talk directly to clients and asked me to focus on building the financial models. So, I accepted my role and that's what I did all day and night; as the analyst, I needed to be quick and consistent with my analysis, so I developed various methods to be more efficient. For example, my input numbers such as operating assumptions were shown in blue, any downloaded numbers from any other databases (edgar.gov) such as the 10K and 10Q financial statements were in red and all the output formulas showing the results were in black. This will help the reader in suggesting any changes to the model. I learned over the years that to build an efficient financial model, someone needs to consider the following three factors:

1. *The model needs to be easy to follow (set clearly the input and output sections).*
2. *The assumptions that drive the projections need to be realistic, defensible, and logical.*
3. *The model needs to be flexible for quick changes.*

KEY TAKEAWAYS

- There are two approaches for setting up your projections: the top-to-bottom approach and the bottom-to-top approach.
- The income statement projections are primarily built first on revenue growth trends and then the operating cost assumptions that are based on these projected revenues.

- Some companies are striving to generate cash flow instead of focusing on profit and others are focusing on profit targets instead of cash based on where they are in their business growth cycle.
- Equity analysts and credit analysts focus on different performance criteria when analyzing companies.
- There are three performance measurements that the analysts use for reviewing management's projections: the projected cash or profit when compared to historical results, when compared to the company's piers, and when compared to the analysts' expectations.

PROJECTIONS—BUILDING THE FINANCIAL MODEL

All analysts, including the credit analyst, equity financial analyst, or the company that is in the process of raising capital, start with the base case. The base case is the first approach to building the financial model. Since this model will be shared with all the stakeholders, including bankers, investors, and management, the case needs to be simple, reasonable, and basic before any adjustments that need to be made to run other scenarios, such as the upside case, downside case and breakeven case.

BUILDING THE BASE CASE

The base case is the first projected scenario that the analyst sets up before making any of his or her own customized adjustments. Depending on the circumstances, the assumptions to build this case are either given directly by management as part of the plan to raise capital or the analyst independently builds it to determine the value of the company, as later described in chapter 18. When building this case, it is important for the analyst to arrange the revenue drivers or the cost assumptions so that are in line with industry standards and so the proper comparison can be made for follow-up adjustments.

Revenue Drivers

The revenue drivers are customized based on the industry performance measurements that the company competes in. This makes it easier to compare the results versus the industry operating benchmarks. For example, the assumptions used for a hotel company could be based on the average daily rate (ADR) representing what the customer will pay to rent the room for a night; the number of rooms available per property; and the occupancy rate (OR), which represents the rooms that are rented as a percentage of total available rooms. A common benchmark that is used in the hotel business is revenue per available room (RevPAR), calculated by multiplying the ADR by OR. For manufacturing companies,

FIGURE 16.1 REVENUE ASSUMPTIONS (BASE CASE)

Celerity Technogy Inc. ("CTI")
Operating Assumptions

	HISTORICAL		PROJECTED				
BASE CASE	**Year -1**	**Year 0**	**Year 1**	**Year 2**	**Year 3**	**Year 4**	**Year 5**
Revenues by Geography							
Volume Growth							
U.S.		7.50%	5.00%	4.50%	3.00%	2.50%	2.00%
Europe		10.87%	10.00%	8.00%	6.00%	4.00%	2.00%
Asia		21.95%	20.00%	18.00%	15.00%	12.00%	8.00%
Total Volume Growth		15.63%	10.64%	9.45%	7.34%	5.98%	4.96%
Volume Sold (000's Units)							
U.S.	16,000	17,200	18,060	18,873	19,439	19,925	20,323
Europe	2,300	2,550	2,805	3,029	3,211	3,340	3,406
Asia	820	1,000	1,200	1,416	1,628	1,824	1,970
Total Volume	19,120	20,750	22,065	23,318	24,278	25,088	25,699
Price Increase							
U.S.		6.98%	4.00%	3.50%	3.00%	2.50%	2.50%
Europe		5.23%	5.00%	4.50%	4.00%	3.00%	2.50%
Asia		2.50%	3.00%	3.00%	3.00%	3.00%	2.50%
Total Price Increase			4.05%	3.57%	3.10%	2.56%	2.47%
Sales Price per Unit ($)							
U.S.	$ 50.00	$ 53.49	$ 55.63	$ 57.57	$ 59.30	$ 60.78	$ 62.30
Europe	$ 52.17	$ 54.90	$ 57.65	$ 60.24	$ 62.65	$ 64.53	$ 66.14
Asia	$ 48.78	$ 50.00	$ 51.50	$ 53.05	$ 54.64	$ 56.28	$ 57.68
Average Price	$ 50.21	$ 53.49	$ 55.66	$ 57.65	$ 59.43	$ 60.96	$ 62.46
Revenue Growth							
U.S.		15.00%	9.20%	8.16%	6.09%	5.06%	4.55%
Europe		16.67%	15.50%	12.86%	10.24%	7.12%	4.55%
Asia		25.00%	23.60%	21.54%	18.45%	15.36%	10.70%
Total Price Increase		15.63%	10.64%	9.45%	7.34%	5.98%	4.96%

the revenues are typically driven by volume and price. The analyst will assume a volume growth and price increase/decrease assumption to drive the future revenue. The best starting approach of setting up these assumptions is to use historical growth rates and extend them going forward. Then the analyst can use discretion to adjust these numbers based on expectation. In figure 16.1, Celerity Technology Company shows a breakdown of revenues by geography. Each region then is projected based on historical average unit volume growth and price increases per unit. In this case, despite the 2-year historical assumptions that show high total revenue growth rates of 15.6%, the analyst is adjusting these numbers for the future to lower revenue growth rates to perhaps show a more moderate rate of growth (from 9.45% down to 4.96% in year 5).

In setting up the projected revenue drivers the following assumptions are typically needed to be considered:

- **Historical averages:** One of the better approaches for building the revenue forecast is using historical averages to extend the revenue going forward. This approach is typically a good starting point. This projection that is built based on historical averages is typically called the base case.

- **Future assumptions/views:** The financial analysts may then adjust the base case to reflect their view more going forward. The views could be based on future economic conditions such as economic cycles that could positively or negatively affect the revenues. The views could also be firm specific. For example, the product could be at its early stage and should experience higher volume than typically seen.
- **Industry drivers–based demand and supply:** Another approach that is typically used for new companies that do not have much historical information is to look at the industry and assume how much market share the company could capture. For example, if the analyst is building the revenues of a newly established company in the oncology diagnostics business and the total industry is $8 billion per year, the drivers could be a potential market share percentage (e.g., projecting $400 million assuming 5% market share). It's very important for the analyst to look for trend changes in the industry including regulation governing the product, any structural changes, product obsoletion and replacement, and overall demand of the product.
- **Organic and inorganic volume growth:** The forecasted unit volume growth could be derived from the existing business and/or acquired business or new products. The growth derived from the existing business or the sale of the company's current products is referred to as "organic" growth. For companies in the retail space, as an example, the analyst needs to separate the organic growth, sometimes referred to as "same-store sales," and the inorganic growth representing the opening or acquiring of new stores. Since the growth rates are different it essential to separate them so the analyst can make the necessary adjustments to derive to the overall revenue.
- **Price assumptions:** The unit price increase is depended on market conditions, demand and supply dynamics, and other specific drivers including expected volatility in the commodity prices such the distribution of oil and gas or chemical products. An important assumption that the analyst needs to consider when the company's main expense is the purchasing of commodity raw material that experiences significantly price fluctuations. The analysis is how the company is able to pass-through the increase to their customers to mitigate some of the revenue cyclicality.
- **Contractual revenues:** If the company shows that the revenue is tied to specific contracts with its customers on volume and/or prices, the analyst needs to make a case of predictability of revenue generation in the future. Certain companies break up the revenues by firm orders and non-firm orders to show that some of the volume is expected and some is not.
- **Cyclical revenues:** Cyclical businesses like appliances and auto parts industries that are less stable and dependent on economic cycles are important considerations when projecting the revenue forecasts.

- **Newly Established Companies:** Typically, companies at their early stage of development have erratic sales growth. It's important to reasonably estimate the correct assumptions based on where the company is in their product life cycle, from early development stage to mature to stabilization and decline stages.

Revenue Segments (Subsidiaries, Product/Services, Geographical, Departments)

As mentioned, the revenue drivers can be built based on acceptable industry parameters, as demonstrated in the figure 16.2.

Cost Assumptions

The analysts typically rely on historical cost amounts in relationship to revenues. The projected revenue is the basis for estimating the company's total costs going forward. The premise is that as the company grows, the cost will probably grow at the same pace as revenues. Direct costs, such as cost of goods sold, which includes labor, materials, and overhead expenses, are expected to grow at the same percentage of revenues. Indirect costs though, such as selling, general, and administrative expenses, expect to grow from year to year at a higher or lower growth rate than revenues, depending on where the

FIGURE 16.2 REVENUE ASSUMPTION DRIVERS BY INDUSTRY

Industry	Revenue Drivers	Revenue Formula	Comments
Airline	Revenue Passenger Mile (RPM); Miles Travelled (MT) per Day, Available Seat Miles (ASM)	Revenue = RPM x MT x 365 days	MT as % of ASM to indicate the activity of the airline during certain periods - an indusry benchmark used to compare between seasonal and non-seasonal periods and versus com pany peers.
Consumer Communications, Digital Media and Networking	Average Revenue per User (ARPU) per month, Number of Users (NofU)	Revenue = ARPU x NofU x 12 months	ARPU could be recorded per month, or per year. The Numbe rof Users could be broken down by existing and new users.
Hotel	Average Daily Rates (ADR); Occupancy Rate (OR); Numbers of Rooms (NofR); Revenue Per Available Room (RevPAR)	Revenue = ADR x OR x NofR x 365 days RevPar = ADR x OR Total Yearly Rooms = NofR x 365 days, so Revenues = RevPAR x Total Yearly Rooms	For more detailed analysis the ADR and OR could be broken down into weekdays and weekends. A typical benchmark used in the industry is RevPAR.
Manufacturing	Volume (V); Price (P)	Revenue = Unit Volume x Price per Unit	Companies with multiple products could share the unit prices and volumes so the analyst could better project the revenues
Restaurant	Average Check (AC); Turnover (TO) per day; Number of Seats (NofS)	Revenue = AC x TO x NofS x 365 days	For more detailed analysis the AC and TO could be broken down into different shifts (Breakfast, Lunch, Dinner) a well as weekdays and weekends
Retail	Average sales Price per Square Footage (APSF); Total Square Footage; Total Stores (TS); Average Square Footage Per Store (ASFPS); Number of Customers per store per year (C)	Revenue = APSF x TS x ASFPS x C	
Shipping/Transportation/Freight	Revenue Ton-Mile (RTM); Gross Ton Mile (GTM)		
Software as a Service (SaaS)	Net Monthly Recurring Revenue (MRR); Number of Bookings (NofB); Churning Rate (CR);		
Utilities			

company stands in its promotional cycle. New companies spend more on up-front SG&A as they are positioning the company to grow in the future. Mature companies' SG&A typically grow at a slower pace than revenue, contributing to higher EBITDA margins from the year before. For conservative purposes though, is not unusual to see that the analysts assume that these indirect operating expenses for a mature company grow at the same rate as revenues; therefore, they are running these costs as a percentage of revenues. Of course, it's important for the analyst to understand which costs are fixed and which ones are variable before running the projections to better reflect the cost structure of the company. In some cases where the analyst runs the projections based on a specific event, such as the buyout of the company, the costs could be adjusted down to reflect specified savings identified by the investor buying the company. These savings could be reductions in cost of labor if the investor announces a labor reduction or a plant closure and implementation.

In setting up the projected cost drivers, the following assumptions typically need to be considered:

- **Cost of goods sold:** The cost of goods sold (COGS) includes the labor costs, material costs, and overhead costs. A detailed analysis would include the number of workers per shift, number of shifts, number of shifts per day, and average wages per worker to determine the cost of labor. A detailed analysis would also include the cost of inventory as a raw material and the energy costs that are spent to produce the manufacturing units (overhead expenses). Most of the analysts though don't have such detailed information, so it is typical to use the historical COGS as percentage of revenue to run the projections. Sometimes, the COGS are given by segment or by product, which will be helpful to project the cost going forward and being able to make different assumptions based on each segment dynamics. In a typical transaction that the company is seeking financing, the management lays its cost strategy, which could include cost savings that need to be incorporated in the projections. Other information that is useful for the analyst is the capacity utilization. This is measured as a percentage of the actual volume output per year to the maximum yearly output, assuming 100% of the manufacturing facility is running at its peak. In figure 17.3, for example, the company provided its COGS by geography. As you can see the European operations produce higher gross margins than the United States and Asia (65% versus 62% and 60% compared to the United States and Asia, respectively); this is important information when projecting the gross profitability per region going forward.
- **Operating expenses:** The operating expenses include the selling or the expenses to market the company's products, administrative expenses for indirectly supporting the

FIGURE 16.3 INCOME STATEMENT COST ASSUMPTIONS (BASE CASE)

Celerity Technogy Inc. ("CTI")
Income Statement Cost Assumptions

	HISTORICAL		PROJECTED				
BASE CASE	**Year -1**	**Year 0**	**Year 1**	**Year 2**	**Year 3**	**Year 4**	**Year 5**
Cost of Revenues as % of Revenue by Geography							
U.S.	36.63%	38.04%	38.00%	38.00%	38.00%	38.00%	38.00%
Europe	32.50%	35.71%	35.00%	35.00%	35.00%	35.00%	35.00%
Asia	32.50%	40.00%	40.00%	40.00%	40.00%	40.00%	40.00%
Total Cost of Rev. as % of Total Revenue	35.94%	37.84%	37.71%	37.70%	37.71%	37.71%	37.72%
Gross Margin by Geography							
U.S.	63.38%	61.96%	62.00%	62.00%	62.00%	62.00%	62.00%
Europe	67.50%	64.29%	65.00%	65.00%	65.00%	65.00%	65.00%
Asia	67.50%	60.00%	60.00%	60.00%	60.00%	60.00%	60.00%
Total Cost of Rev. as % of Total Revenue	64.06%	62.16%	62.29%	62.30%	62.29%	62.29%	62.28%
Operating Expenses Assumptions							
Administrative & General Increase %		13.79%	5.00%	5.00%	5.00%	5.00%	5.00%
Marketing Expenses as % of Total Revenue	7.81%	7.21%	7.00%	7.00%	7.00%	7.00%	7.00%
Other Operating Expenses as % of Total Rev.	1.04%	1.08%	1.00%	1.00%	1.00%	1.00%	1.00%
Total Operating Expenses as % of Total Rev.	23.96%	23.15%	22.11%	21.53%	21.24%	21.11%	21.12%
Depreciation Expense % of Total Revenue	6.25%	5.86%	6.00%	6.00%	6.00%	6.00%	6.00%

company's business, and any other general expenses that are not directly expenses based on the company's revenues. Other expenses in this category could include research and development expenses very important expenses, especially for companies that spend a lot of money to support the growth of the company. This segment could be looked at as separating the fixed costs and variable costs. If the company is positively growing at a healthy pace, the fixed costs could contribute higher margins, but if the company shows revenue declines, the fixed cost has a reverse impact to operating margins. The analyst needs to be aware of the sensitivity of the fixed expenses to revenue, especially the factors influencing the largest cost line items. For conservative purposes, analysts typically run the operating assumptions as a percentage of revenue. The better approach for general and administrative expenses is to assume a growth rate, so if the revenues decline, these expenses continue to grow, causing a problem for the company that needs to manage these expenses during tough periods. The selling or marketing expenses are typically run as percentages of revenues since these expenses directly support the revenue growth of the company. Figure 16.3 shows the growth rate used for the general and administrative expenses is lower than the average revenue growth, contributing to an increase in EBITDA margins (5% growth versus average revenue growth, seen in figure 16.3 of ~5–10%).

- **Depreciation expenses:** Depreciation expense, which is a non-cash expense, is typically projected based on the company's fixed assets using an average life. A lot of the analysis, though, since depreciation is not significant, is done using the same approach as any other expense: by calculating the depreciation as percentage of revenue, as seen in figure 16.3. It's not perfectly correct, but the argument is that since revenue grows so does the need to invest in capital to sustain the growth, hence the growth of depreciation at the same rate. It's important to compare the depreciation to the capital expenditures (Capex) found in the cash flow statement, as it need to be in line. Since depreciation expense is used primarily for tax benefits, it's important to make sure the amount is not excessively high, especially as it relates to capital expenditures. Typically for valuation purposes, depreciation is assumed to be equal with Capex, representing the minimum capital expenditures the company needs to spend to keep up with the devaluation of its assets or depreciation.

Cash Flow Expenditures Assumptions

As mentioned previously, the cash flow statement represents all the other activities in which the company is engaged to run the business including the management of working capital, its investment activity, and its financing activity. To project the cash flow statement, these activities needed to be addressed separately.

- **Working capital activities:** Working capital activity recorded in the cash flow statement is driven directly by year-to-year changes of the current assets minus current liability changes, as shown on the balance sheet statement. The current asset includes the accounts receivable, inventory, and other current assets such as prepaid expenses. The current liabilities include accounts payable and other current liabilities such as accrued income taxes and accrued expenses. The assumptions that drive these items are shown in figure 16.4.
    - **Accounts receivable:** The accounts receivable (AR) on the balance sheet are based on accounts receivable days (ARD) and accounts receivable turnover (ART) calculations. In figure 16.4 the projected ARD used for the projections is based on historical average of 17.26 days or the average length of time that the customers pay starting from the day they are charged to pay for the merchandise. The formula is
        - ***AR = [(ARD/365) × revenues]***
    - **Inventory:** The inventory (Inv) on the balance sheet is based on inventory turnover (ITO) and inventory days (ID) calculations. In figure 16.4 the projected ID used for the projections used is based on the historical average of 11.20 days or the average length of time that the raw material bought from the suppliers turns into a finished good and a cash sale. The formula is
        - ***Inv = [(ID/365) × COGS]***

FIGURE 16.4 WORKING CAPITAL ASSUMPTIONS (BASE CASE)

Celerity Technogy Inc. ("CTI") Working Capital Assumptions	HISTORICAL				PROJECTED		
BASE CASE	Year -1	Year 0	Year 1	Year 2	Year 3	Year 4	Year 5
Accounts Receivable							
Accounts Receivable Turnover		21.14x	21.14x	21.14x	21.14x	21.14x	21.14x
Accounts Receivable Days		17.26	17.26	17.26	17.26	17.26	17.26
Inventory							
Inventory Turnover		11.20x	11.20x	11.20x	11.20x	11.20x	11.20x
Inventory Days		32.59	32.59	32.59	32.59	32.59	32.59
Prepaid Expenses							
Prepaid Expenses as % of Revene	0.81%	0.81%	0.81%	0.81%	0.81%	0.81%	0.81%
Accounts Payable							
Accounts Payable Turnover		11.20x	11.20x	11.20x	11.20x	11.20x	11.20x
Accounts Payable Days		32.59	32.59	32.59	32.59	32.59	32.59
Accrued Income Taxes							
Accrued Income Taxes as % of Revenues	1.25%	0.90%	0.90%	0.90%	0.90%	0.90%	0.90%
Accrued Expenses							
Accrued Expenses as % of Revenues	1.04%	0.72%	0.72%	0.72%	0.72%	0.72%	0.72%

- **Other current assets:** For projection purposes, other current assets are based as a percentage of revenue. In figure 16.4 the projected prepaid expenses are calculated based on last year's percentage of revenues of 0.81%.
- **Accounts payable:** The accounts payable (AP) on the balance sheet are based on accounts payable days (APD) and accounts payable turnover (APT) calculations. In figure 16.4, similar to inventory, the projected APD that is used to calculate the projections is based on the historical average of 11.20 days or the average length of time that the company pays its bills to the vendors or suppliers the inventory. The formula is
  - ***AP = [(APD/365) × COGS]***
- **Other current liabilities:** For simplistic purposes, all other current liabilities on the balance sheet are calculated based on percentage of revenue. In figure 16.4 both the accrued income taxes and accrued expenses are based on percentage of revenues at 0.90% and 0.72%, respectively.

- **Investment Activities Assumptions:** For simplistic purposes, unless there are specific plans to spend a major one-time manufacturing plant improvements or major purchases of the truck fleet, the **Capital Expenditures** (Capex) and **Long-Term Investments** (LTI) are projected to grow at the same level as the revenues calculated as percentage of revenues—this is sometimes called "Maintenance Capex". In the Figure 16.5 below the Capex and LTI are estimated at 11.26% and 4.50% respectively (historical levels). One approach for the analyst is to run the Capex at the same percentage of Depreciation to Revenue representing low maintenance

FIGURE 16.5 INVESTMENT ACTIVITY ASSUMPTIONS (BASE CASE)

Celerity Technogy Inc. ("CTI") Investment Activity Assumptions	HISTORICAL		PROJECTED				
BASE CASE	Year -1	Year 0	Year 1	Year 2	Year 3	Year 4	Year 5
Capital Expenditures							
Capital Expenditures as % of Revenue		11.26%	11.26%	11.26%	11.26%	11.26%	11.26%
Long Term Investments							
Long Term Investments as % of Revenues		4.50%	4.50%	4.50%	4.50%	4.50%	4.50%

growth and any additional percentage of Capex to revenue should contribute directly to higher growth.

- **Financing activities assumptions:** The financing activities shown in the cash flow statement consists of debt activities of borrowing or paying down the debt as well any equity activities including any distributions or issuance of new equity. The debt assumptions include the borrowing and repayment of debt, which are based on the contractual obligation between the company and its creditors. The equity component of the cash flow statement is based on specific plans for the company to make equity distributions to the existing investors or to raise new equity via public issuance or private placement offering. The repayment of debt shown on the cash flow statement is driven from the debt schedule table (figure 16.6) and described under the Debt Schedule Assumptions.

Debt Schedule

The debt schedule is built based on the four basic input criteria, also called money terms, typically seen in the credit agreements and bond indentures: amount borrowed (outstanding); the cost of borrowing (interest payment); the principal payment (scheduled or amortized debt payments); and the term of the debt facility representing how many years it takes to pay the loan. The debt outstanding drives the balance sheet, the interest payments drive the income statement, and the principal payment drives the cash flow statement. The interest rate charged could be set as fixed or floating and the principal payments are based on a set scheduled payment found in the agreement. Figure 16.6 shows that the short-term and long-term debt interest payment is based on floating rate index London Inter Bank Offering Rate (LIBOR) starting at 2% plus a spread rate of 3%. LIBOR is a rate that most banks use as an interest rate benchmark, which represents the cost of a bank's borrowing from other banks. In this example, the projections assume an increase in LIBOR by 0.5% per year for the next 3 years and another 1% increase in year 4 before it stabilizes at that level. Please note that the interest payment is calculated based

FIGURE 16.6 DEBT SCHEDULE

Celerity Technogy Inc. ("CTI")
Debt Schedule

	HISTORICAL		PROJECTED				
	Year -1	**Year 0**	**Year 1**	**Year 2**	**Year 3**	**Year 4**	**Year 5**
Interest Rate Forward Assumptions- LIBOR		2.00%	2.50%	3.00%	3.50%	4.50%	4.50%
LIBOR Incr./ (Decr.)			0.50%	0.50%	0.50%	1.00%	0.00%
Short-Term Debt							
Spread Pricing (L + Spread)			3.00%	3.00%	3.00%	3.00%	3.00%
Interest Rate			5.50%	6.00%	6.50%	7.50%	7.50%
Outstanding	20,000	10,000	-				
Principal Payment			10,000	-	-	-	-
Interest Payment			550	-	-	-	-
Total Payment			10,550	-	-	-	-
Long-Term Debt							
Spread Pricing (L + Spread)			3.00%	3.00%	3.00%	3.00%	3.00%
Interest Rate			5.50%	6.00%	6.50%	7.50%	7.50%
Outstanding	1,200,000	1,180,000	1,160,000	1,130,000	1,090,000	1,030,000	950,000
Principal Payment			20,000	30,000	40,000	60,000	80,000
Interest Payment			64,900	69,600	73,450	81,750	77,250
Total Payment			84,900	99,600	113,450	141,750	157,250
Total Debt	1,220,000	1,190,000	1,160,000	1,130,000	1,090,000	1,030,000	950,000
Outstanding			30,000	30,000	40,000	60,000	80,000
Principal Payment			65,450	69,600	73,450	81,750	77,250
Interest Payment			95,450	99,600	113,450	141,750	157,250
Total Payment			160,900	169,200	186,900	223,500	234,500

on last year's outstanding, conservatively assuming that the principal payment is paid on the last day of each year.

Tax Schedule

The tax schedule is set up to estimate the yearly tax expenses going forward. These expenses are typically calculated by multiplying the tax rate to the earnings before taxes (EBT). A portion of this expense could be the actual taxes paid in cash and the remaining will be deferred. Figure 16.7 shows that 4% of the tax expenses are deferred (historical estimate) and the other 96% is paid in cash. The tax rate used in this case is 40%. The

FIGURE 16.7 TAX SCHEDULE (BASE CASE)

Celerity Technogy Inc. ("CTI")
Tax Schedule

	HISTORICAL		PROJECTED				
BASE CASE	**Year -1**	**Year 0**	**Year 1**	**Year 2**	**Year 3**	**Year 4**	**Year 5**
EBT			324,422	367,676	392,399	396,152	407,128
Tax Rate			40.00%	40.00%	40.00%	40.00%	40.00%
Tax Expenses			129,769	147,070	156,960	158,461	162,851
Tax Deffered			5,191	5,883	6,278	6,338	6,514
Tax Paid (Cash)			124,578	141,188	150,681	152,123	156,337
Tax Deferred as % of Taxes			4.00%	4.00%	4.00%	4.00%	4.00%

deferred tax is added to the net income in the cash flow statement, similar to the depreciation expense.

Balance Sheet Assumptions

The balance sheet flows entirely as an output. The income statement builds the retained earnings (RE) found in the bottom of the balance sheet by adding the net income to last year's income, and the cash flow statement builds the cash (C) found on the top of the balance sheet by adding the free cash flow to last year's cash. All the balance sheet items in between the cash and retained earnings are driven primarily by the cash flow statement activities.

Other balance sheet items such as other intangible and tangible long-term assets, as well as other liabilities, are projected based on either set asset schedules or as percentage of revenues. In later chapters we will discuss these assets such as goodwill that are generated based on new transactions involving the acquisition of the company or initial public offering. The example used, **Celerity Technology Inc.** does not show any other assets or liabilities at the moment. In later chapters, we will examine the generation of goodwill and other intangibles based on an assumed leveraged buyout (LBO) or an acquisition of the company by another strategic investor.

The Finished Product: "Base Case" Spreadsheet: Balance Sheet, Income, and Cash Flow Statements

The finished product that should be included in the analyst's presentation is sometimes called "the deliverable." The presentation typically starts with a summary of results (figure 16.8) followed by the three core statements.

FIGURE 16.8 SUMMARY OF RESULTS (BASE CASE)

Celerity Technogy Inc. ("CTI")
Summary of Results

	HISTORICAL		PROJECTED				
BASE CASE	Year -1	Year 0	Year 1	Year 2	Year 3	Year 4	Year 5
Revenues	960,000	1,110,000	1,228,140	1,344,200	1,442,919	1,529,268	1,605,161
Revenue Growth		15.6%	10.6%	9.5%	7.3%	6.0%	5.0%
EBITDA	385,000	433,000	493,561	547,928	592,424	629,659	660,688
EBITDA Margin							
Interest Expense			95,450	99,600	113,450	141,750	157,250
Tax Expense			129,769	147,070	156,960	158,461	162,851
Working Capital			(2,870)	4,548	3,869	3,384	2,974
Capex			138,304	151,374	162,491	172,215	180,761
Cash on Balance Sheet	45,000	65,800	118,577	179,246	236,183	267,484	278,544
Total Debt	1,220,000	1,190,000	1,160,000	1,130,000	1,090,000	1,030,000	950,000
Equity Ownerhip	1,746,000	1,919,800	2,114,453	2,335,059	2,570,498	2,808,190	3,052,467
EBITDA / Interest (Coverage Ratio)	3.0x	3.6x	5.2x	5.5x	5.2x	4.4x	4.2x
Total Debt / EBITDA (Leveraged Ratio)	3.1x	2.7x	2.4x	2.1x	1.8x	1.6x	1.4x
Debt Capitalization	41.1%	38.3%	35.4%	32.6%	29.8%	26.8%	23.7%

FIGURE 16.9 BALANCE SHEET STATEMENT (BASE CASE)

Celerity Technogy Inc. ("CTI")
Balance Sheet (000's)

	HISTORICAL		PROJECTED				
BASE CASE	**Year -1**	**Year 0**	**Year 1**	**Year 2**	**Year 3**	**Year 4**	**Year 5**
Current Assets							
Cash	45,000	65,800	118,577	179,246	236,183	267,484	278,544
Accounts Receivable	45,000	60,000	58,088	63,577	68,246	72,330	75,920
Inventories	35,000	40,000	41,346	45,252	48,576	51,492	54,060
Prepaid Expenses	10,000	9,000	9,958	10,899	11,699	12,399	13,015
Total Current Assets	135,000	174,800	227,969	298,974	364,704	403,706	421,539
Property and Equipment							
Land	2,500,000	2,500,000					
Building	450,000	550,000					
Furniture & Equipment	50,000	75,000					
Total Gross P&E	3,000,000	3,125,000	3,263,304	3,414,678	3,577,169	3,749,384	3,930,145
Less Accumulated Depreciaition	(300,000)	(365,000)	(438,688)	(519,340)	(605,916)	(697,672)	(793,981)
Net P&E	2,700,000	2,760,000	2,824,616	2,895,338	2,971,253	3,051,712	3,136,164
Long-Term Investments	200,000	250,000	305,322	365,871	430,868	499,753	572,058
Total Assets	3,035,000	3,184,800	3,357,906	3,560,182	3,766,825	3,955,171	4,129,761
Liabilities and Owners Equity							
Current Liabilities							
Accounts Payable	35,000	40,000	41,346	45,252	48,576	51,492	54,060
Accrued Income Taxes	12,000	10,000	11,064	12,110	12,999	13,777	14,461
Accrued Expenses	10,000	8,000	8,851	9,688	10,399	11,022	11,569
Current Portion of Long Term Debt	20,000	10,000	-	-	-	-	-
Total Current Liabilities	77,000	68,000	61,262	67,050	71,975	76,291	80,090
Long-Term Debt:	1,200,000	1,180,000	1,160,000	1,130,000	1,090,000	1,030,000	950,000
Deferred Income Taxes	12,000	17,000	22,191	28,074	34,352	40,690	47,204
Total Liabilties	1,289,000	1,265,000	1,243,453	1,225,123	1,196,327	1,146,981	1,077,294
Owners' Equity							
Common Stock	1,000,000	1,000,000	1,000,000	1,000,000	1,000,000	1,000,000	1,000,000
Paid-in-Capital	-	25,000	25,000	25,000	25,000	25,000	25,000
Retained Earnings	746,000	894,800	1,089,453	1,310,059	1,545,498	1,783,190	2,027,467
Total Owners' Equity	1,746,000	1,919,800	2,114,453	2,335,059	2,570,498	2,808,190	3,052,467
Total Liabilities & Owner's Equity	3,035,000	3,184,800	3,357,906	3,560,182	3,766,825	3,955,171	4,129,761
Error Check	-	-	-	-	-	-	-

The balance sheet (figure 16.9) shows the base case results assuming the company continues to grow on all fronts, generating higher cash balances every year as retained earnings continue to grow.

The income statement (figure 16.10) shows a normalized growth and flat costs as percentage of revenue.

The cash flow statement (figure 16.11) shows the buildup of free cash flow resulting from continuous growth of the income statement. The base case assumes working capital and investment activities are in line with the revenue growth. The financing activities are based on the debt schedule obligations including interest payments calculated on an assumed increase in floating rate (LIBOR) and set scheduled principal payments.

FIGURE 16.10 INCOME STATEMENT (BASE CASE)

Celerity Technogy Inc. ("CTI")
Income Statement (000's)

		HISTORICAL		PROJECTED				
BASE CASE		**Year -1**	**Year 0**	**Year 1**	**Year 2**	**Year 3**	**Year 4**	**Year 5**
Revenues by Geography								
U.S.		800,000	920,000	1,004,640	1,086,594	1,152,767	1,211,126	1,266,232
Europe		120,000	140,000	161,700	182,495	201,182	215,506	225,312
Asia		40,000	50,000	61,800	75,112	88,970	102,636	113,618
Total Revenue		960,000	1,110,000	1,228,140	1,344,200	1,442,919	1,529,268	1,605,161
Total Revenue Growth			*15.6%*	*10.6%*	*9.5%*	*7.3%*	*6.0%*	*5.0%*
Cost of Revenues by Geography								
U.S.		293,000	350,000	381,763	412,906	438,051	460,228	481,168
Europe		39,000	50,000	56,595	63,873	70,414	75,427	78,859
Asia		13,000	20,000	24,720	30,045	35,588	41,054	45,447
Total Cost of Revenue		345,000	420,000	463,078	506,823	544,053	576,709	605,474
Gross Profit		615,000	690,000	765,062	837,377	898,866	952,558	999,687
Total Margin			*62.2%*	*62.3%*	*62.3%*	*62.3%*	*62.3%*	*62.3%*
Operating Expenses								
Administrative & General		145,000	165,000	173,250	181,913	191,008	200,559	210,586
Marketing Expenses		75,000	80,000	85,970	94,094	101,004	107,049	112,361
Other Operating Expenses		10,000	12,000	12,281	13,442	14,429	15,293	16,052
Total Operating Expenses		230,000	257,000	271,501	289,448	306,442	322,900	338,999
EBITDA		385,000	433,000	493,561	547,928	592,424	629,659	660,688
EBITDA Margin %		*40.1%*	*39.0%*	*40.2%*	*40.8%*	*41.1%*	*41.2%*	*41.2%*
Depreciation		60,000	65,000	73,688	80,652	86,575	91,756	96,310
Amortization		-	-	-	-	-	-	-
EBIT		325,000	368,000	419,872	467,276	505,849	537,902	564,378
EBITA Margin %		*33.9%*	*33.2%*	*34.2%*	*34.8%*	*35.1%*	*35.2%*	*35.2%*
Total Interest Expense				95,450	99,600	113,450	141,750	157,250
EBT				324,422	367,676	392,399	396,152	407,128
Taxes	40%			129,769	147,070	156,960	158,461	162,851
Net Income				194,653	220,606	235,439	237,691	244,277

Part of the "deliverable" presentation, a summary of the results, is a good way of showing a snapshot of the main results taken by each of the statements and analyzed in a ratio analysis (figure 16.12).

BUILDING THE WHAT-IF SCENARIO CASES

The what-if scenario analysis could include a downside case, an upside case, a break-even case, or any other sensitivity case customized for the analyst that challenges the base case. The equity analyst could run the upside case including potential cost savings or enhanced revenue assumptions resulting from a new product launch or a significant price increase or an acquisition. The debt analyst could run a downside case measuring how resistant the company is if revenue declines and/or cost increases. The management could run a break-even case scenario to measure how low the revenue can go so a few of the obligations such as short-term and long-term debt services are not met.

FIGURE 16.11 CASH FLOW STATEMENT (BASE CASE)

Celerity Technogy Inc. ("CTI")
Cash Flow Statement (000's)

BASE CASE	Year 0	Year 1	Year 2	PROJECTED Year 3	Year 4	Year 5
Net Income	148,800	194,653	220,606	235,439	237,691	244,277
Plus Depreciation	65,000	73,688	80,652	86,575	91,756	96,310
Plus Deffered Taxes	5,000	5,191	5,883	6,278	6,338	6,514
Cash Income	218,800	273,532	307,140	328,293	335,786	347,101
Working Capital Activities						
Change in Accounts Receivable	(15,000)	1,912	(5,489)	(4,669)	(4,084)	(3,590)
Change in Inventory	(5,000)	(1,346)	(3,906)	(3,324)	(2,916)	(2,568)
Change in Prepaid Expenses	1,000	(958)	(941)	(800)	(700)	(615)
Change in Accounts Payable	5,000	1,346	3,906	3,324	2,916	2,568
Change in Accrued Income Taxes	(2,000)	1,064	1,046	889	778	684
Change in Accrued Expenses	(2,000)	851	836	711	622	547
Total Change in Working Capital	(18,000)	2,870	(4,548)	(3,869)	(3,384)	(2,974)
Operating Cash Flow (OCF)	**200,800**	**276,403**	**302,592**	**324,424**	**332,402**	**344,126**
Investment Activities						
Capital Expenditures	(125,000)	(138,304)	(151,374)	(162,491)	(172,215)	(180,761)
Investments (Change)	(50,000)	(55,322)	(60,550)	(64,996)	(68,886)	(72,305)
Total Financing Activities	(175,000)	(193,626)	(211,923)	(227,487)	(241,101)	(253,066)
Cash Available Before Financing Activities	25,800	82,777	90,669	96,937	91,301	91,060
Financing Activities						
ST Debt Payments	(10,000)	(10,000)	-	-	-	-
LT Debt Payments	(20,000)	(20,000)	(30,000)	(40,000)	(60,000)	(80,000)
Equity Contribution	25,000					
Total Financing Activities	(5,000)	(30,000)	(30,000)	(40,000)	(60,000)	(80,000)
Free Cash Flow	20,800	52,777	60,669	56,937	31,301	11,060
Beginning Cash	45,000	65,800	118,577	179,246	236,183	267,484
Ending Cash	65,800	118,577	179,246	236,183	267,484	278,544

FIGURE 16.12 FINANCIAL RATIOS (BASE CASE)

Celerity Technogy Inc. ("CTI")
Financial Ratios

	HISTORICAL			PROJECTED			
BASE CASE	Year -1	Year 0	Year 1	Year 2	Year 3	Year 4	Year 5
Liquidity Ratios							
Current Ratio	1.8x	2.6x	3.7x	4.5x	5.1x	5.3x	5.3x
Quick ratio	1.2x	1.9x	2.9x	3.6x	4.2x	4.5x	4.4x
Accounts Receivable Turnover (ART)		21.1x	20.8x	22.1x	21.9x	21.8x	21.7x
Accounts Receivable Days		17.3x	17.5x	16.5x	16.7x	16.8x	16.9x
Solvency Ratios							
LTD / Total Capitalization	40.7%	38.1%	35.4%	32.6%	29.8%	26.8%	23.7%
EBITDA / Interest (Coverage Ratio)	3.0x	3.6x	5.2x	5.5x	5.2x	4.4x	4.2x
LTD / EBITDA (Leverage Ratio)	3.1x	2.7x	2.4x	2.1x	1.8x	1.6x	1.4x
Altma's Z-score (used Book Value of Equity)	2.2x	2.7x	2.3x	2.5x	2.8x	3.0x	3.3x
Activity Ratios / Operating Ratios							
Inventory Ratio (IR)		11.2x	11.4x	11.7x	11.6x	11.5x	11.5x
Inventory Ratio - Days		32.6	32.1	31.2	31.5	31.7	31.8
Profitability Ratios							
Gross Margin	64.1%	62.2%	62.3%	62.3%	62.3%	62.3%	62.3%
EBITDA Margin	40.1%	39.0%	40.2%	40.8%	41.1%	41.2%	41.2%
Return on Assets (ROA)		4.8%	6.0%	6.4%	6.4%	6.2%	6.0%
Return on Equity (ROE)		8.1%	9.7%	9.9%	9.6%	8.8%	8.3%

Revenue drivers: For example, the downside case (figure 16.13) for Celerity Technology Inc. shows lower revenue growth assumptions, perhaps to illustrate a potential recession that might occur in year 2, slower growth expectations in year 1, and very slow recovery post-recession years. The lower revenue growth and declines are adjusted by region including volume and price.

Cost assumptions: This case will also assume an increase in costs on both the direct and indirect expenses (figure 16.14) resulting in lower margins, profit, and cash flow.

Working capital assumptions: The working capital assumptions (figure 16.15) were kept at the same levels as the base case though there could be an argument that the company manages the receivables and payables differently in recession years as it is trying to squeeze more cash given the income declines.

Investment activities: The capital expenditures and annual investments are typically the first expenses that management is able to cut when facing recessionary pressures, lower revenues, and/or higher operating costs. This downside case though

FIGURE 16.13 REVENUE ASSUMPTIONS (DOWNSIDE CASE)

Celerity Technogy Inc. ("CTI")
Revenue Assumptions

	HISTORICAL		PROJECTED				
DOWNSIDE CASE	**Year -1**	**Year 0**	**Year 1**	**Year 2**	**Year 3**	**Year 4**	**Year 5**
Revenues by Geography							
Volume Growth							
U.S.		7.50%	2.00%	-1.00%	1.00%	2.00%	2.00%
Europe		10.87%	5.00%	-2.00%	2.00%	2.00%	2.00%
Asia		21.95%	10.00%	3.00%	5.00%	5.00%	5.00%
Total Volume Growth		15.63%	10.64%	9.45%	7.34%	5.98%	4.96%
Volume Sold (000's Units)							
U.S.	16,000	17,200	17,544	17,369	17,542	17,893	18,251
Europe	2,300	2,550	2,678	2,624	2,676	2,730	2,785
Asia	820	1,000	1,100	1,133	1,190	1,249	1,312
Total Volume	19,120	20,750	21,322	21,126	21,408	21,872	22,347
Price Increase							
U.S.		6.98%	1.00%	1.00%	1.00%	2.00%	2.00%
Europe		5.23%	2.00%	2.00%	3.00%	3.00%	2.50%
Asia		2.50%	2.00%	2.00%	2.00%	2.00%	2.50%
Total Price Increase			7.68%	10.47%	5.93%	3.74%	2.73%
Sales Price per Unit ($)							
U.S.	$ 50.00	$ 53.49	$ 54.02	$ 54.56	$ 55.11	$ 56.21	$ 57.34
Europe	$ 52.17	$ 54.90	$ 56.00	$ 57.12	$ 58.83	$ 60.60	$ 62.11
Asia	$ 48.78	$ 50.00	$ 51.00	$ 52.02	$ 53.06	$ 54.12	$ 55.47
Average Price	$ 50.21	$ 53.49	$ 57.60	$ 63.63	$ 67.40	$ 69.92	$ 71.83
Revenue Growth							
U.S.		15.00%	9.20%	8.16%	6.09%	5.06%	4.55%
Europe		16.67%	15.50%	12.86%	10.24%	7.12%	4.55%
Asia		25.00%	23.60%	21.54%	18.45%	15.36%	10.70%
Total Price Increase		15.63%	10.64%	9.45%	7.34%	5.98%	4.96%

FIGURE 16.14 INCOME STATEMENT COST ASSUMPTIONS (DOWNSIDE CASE)

Celerity Technogy Inc. ("CTI")
Income Statement Cost Assumptions

	HISTORICAL		PROJECTED				
DOWNSIDE CASE	**Year -1**	**Year 0**	**Year 1**	**Year 2**	**Year 3**	**Year 4**	**Year 5**
Cost of Revenues as % of Revenue by Geography							
U.S.	36.63%	38.04%	40.00%	39.00%	39.00%	39.00%	39.00%
Europe	32.50%	35.71%	36.00%	36.00%	36.00%	36.00%	36.00%
Asia	32.50%	40.00%	40.00%	40.00%	40.00%	40.00%	40.00%
Total Cost of Rev. as % of Total Revenue	35.94%	37.84%	37.71%	37.70%	37.71%	37.71%	37.72%
Gross Margin by Geography							
U.S.	63.38%	61.96%	60.00%	61.00%	61.00%	61.00%	61.00%
Europe	67.50%	64.29%	64.00%	64.00%	64.00%	64.00%	64.00%
Asia	67.50%	60.00%	60.00%	60.00%	60.00%	60.00%	60.00%
Total Cost of Rev. as % of Total Revenue	64.06%	62.16%	62.29%	62.30%	62.29%	62.29%	62.28%
Operating Expenses Assumptions							
Administrative & General Increase %		13.79%	5.00%	5.00%	5.00%	5.00%	5.00%
Marketing Expenses as % of Total Revenue	7.81%	7.21%	8.00%	8.00%	8.00%	8.00%	8.00%
Other Operating Expenses as % of Total Rev.	1.04%	1.08%	1.00%	1.00%	1.00%	1.00%	1.00%
Total Operating Expenses as % of Total Rev.	23.96%	23.15%	22.11%	21.53%	21.24%	21.11%	21.12%
Depreciation Expense % of Total Revenue	6.25%	5.86%	6.00%	6.00%	6.00%	6.00%	6.00%

FIGURE 16.15 WORKING CAPITAL ASSUMPTIONS (DOWNSIDE CASE)

Celerity Technogy Inc. ("CTI")
Working Capital Assumptions

	HISTORICAL		PROJECTED				
DOWNSIDE CASE	**Year -1**	**Year 0**	**Year 1**	**Year 2**	**Year 3**	**Year 4**	**Year 5**
Accounts Receivable							
Accounts Receivable Turnover		21.14x	21.14x	21.14x	21.14x	21.14x	21.14x
Accounts Receivable Days		17.26	17.26	17.26	17.26	17.26	17.26
Inventory							
Inventory Turnover		11.20x	11.20x	11.20x	11.20x	11.20x	11.20x
Inventory Days		32.59	32.59	32.59	32.59	32.59	32.59
Prepaid Expenses							
Prepaid Expenses as % of Revene	0.81%	0.81%	0.81%	0.81%	0.81%	0.81%	0.81%
Accounts Payable							
Accounts Payable Turnover		11.20x	11.20x	11.20x	11.20x	11.20x	11.20x
Accounts Payable Days		32.59	32.59	32.59	32.59	32.59	32.59
Accrued Income Taxes							
Accrued Income Taxes as % of Revenues	1.25%	0.90%	0.90%	0.90%	0.90%	0.90%	0.90%
Accrued Expenses							
Accrued Expenses as % of Revenues	1.04%	0.72%	0.72%	0.72%	0.72%	0.72%	0.72%

FIGURE 16.16 INVESTMENT ACTIVITY ASSUMPTIONS (DOWNSIDE CASE)

Celerity Technogy Inc. ("CTI")
Investment Activity Assumptions

	HISTORICAL		PROJECTED				
DOWNSIDE CASE	**Year -1**	**Year 0**	**Year 1**	**Year 2**	**Year 3**	**Year 4**	**Year 5**
Capital Expenditures							
Capital Expenditures as % of Revenue		11.26%	11.26%	11.26%	11.26%	11.26%	11.26%
Long Term Investments							
Long Term Investments as % of Revenues		4.50%	4.50%	4.50%	4.50%	4.50%	4.50%

FIGURE 16.17 BALANCE SHEET STATEMENT (DOWNSIDE CASE)

Celerity Technogy Inc. ("CTI")
Balance Sheet Statement (000's)

	HISTORICAL		PROJECTED				
DOWNSIDE CASE	**Year -1**	**Year 0**	**Year 1**	**Year 2**	**Year 3**	**Year 4**	**Year 5**
Current Assets							
Cash	45,000	65,800	436,210	812,904	1,163,688	1,482,200	1,790,591
Accounts Receivable	45,000	60,000	54,573	54,700	56,157	58,593	61,115
Inventories	35,000	40,000	100	(53)	56	121	130
Prepaid Expenses	10,000	9,000	9,355	9,377	9,627	10,045	10,477
Total Current Assets	135,000	174,800	500,238	876,928	1,229,529	1,550,959	1,862,313
Property and Equipment							
Land	2,500,000	2,500,000					
Building	450,000	550,000					
Furniture & Equipment	50,000	75,000					
Total Gross P&E	3,000,000	3,125,000	3,254,935	3,385,173	3,518,880	3,658,388	3,803,900
Less Accumulated Depreciaition	(300,000)	(365,000)	(453,586)	(574,620)	(644,981)	(691,271)	(726,574)
Net P&E	2,700,000	2,760,000	2,801,349	2,810,553	2,873,900	2,967,117	3,077,326
Long-Term Investments	200,000	250,000	301,974	354,069	407,552	463,355	521,560
Total Assets	3,035,000	3,184,800	3,603,562	4,041,550	4,510,980	4,981,431	5,461,199
Liabilities and Owners Equity							
Current Liabilities							
Accounts Payable	35,000	40,000	100	(53)	56	121	130
Accrued Income Taxes	12,000	10,000	10,395	10,419	10,697	11,161	11,641
Accrued Expenses	10,000	8,000	8,316	8,335	8,557	8,929	9,313
Current Portion of Long Term Debt	20,000	10,000	-	-	-	-	-
Total Current Liabilities	77,000	68,000	18,811	18,702	19,310	20,210	21,084
Long-Term Debt:	1,200,000	1,180,000	1,160,000	1,130,000	1,090,000	1,030,000	950,000
Deferred Income Taxes	12,000	17,000	29,674	41,832	55,049	68,803	83,320
Total Liabilties	1,289,000	1,265,000	1,208,485	1,190,534	1,164,359	1,119,013	1,054,404
Owners' Equity							
Common Stock	1,000,000	1,000,000	1,000,000	1,000,000	1,000,000	1,000,000	1,000,000
Paid-in-Capital	-	25,000	25,000	25,000	25,000	25,000	25,000
Retained Earnings	746,000	894,800	1,370,077	1,826,016	2,321,622	2,837,418	3,381,796
Total Owners' Equity	1,746,000	1,919,800	2,395,077	2,851,016	3,346,622	3,862,418	4,406,796
Total Liabilities & Owner's Equity	3,035,000	3,184,800	3,603,562	4,041,550	4,510,980	4,981,431	5,461,199
Error Check	-	-	-	-	-	-	-

FIGURE 16.18 INCOME STATEMENT (DOWNSIDE CASE)

Celerity Technogy Inc. ("CTI")
Income Statement (000's)

		HISTORICAL		PROJECTED				
DOWNSIDE CASE		**Year -1**	**Year 0**	**Year 1**	**Year 2**	**Year 3**	**Year 4**	**Year 5**
Revenues by Geography								
U.S.		800,000	920,000	947,784	947,689	966,738	1,005,794	1,046,428
Europe		120,000	140,000	149,940	149,880	157,464	165,432	172,959
Asia		40,000	50,000	56,100	58,939	63,123	67,605	72,760
Total Revenue		960,000	1,110,000	1,153,824	1,156,508	1,187,325	1,238,831	1,292,147
Total Revenue Growth			*15.6%*	*3.9%*	*0.2%*	*2.7%*	*4.3%*	*4.3%*
Cost of Revenues by Geography								
U.S.		293,000	350,000	-	-	-	-	-
Europe		39,000	50,000	-	-	-	-	-
Asia		13,000	20,000	1,122	(589)	631	1,352	1,455
Total Cost of Revenue		345,000	420,000	1,122	(589)	631	1,352	1,455
Gross Profit		615,000	690,000	1,152,702	1,157,097	1,186,694	1,237,479	1,290,692
Total Margin			*62.2%*	*99.9%*	*100.1%*	*99.9%*	*99.9%*	*99.9%*
Operating Expenses								
Administrative & General		145,000	165,000	165,000	165,000	165,000	165,000	165,000
Marketing Expenses		75,000	80,000	-	-	-	-	-
Other Operating Expenses		10,000	12,000	11,538	11,565	11,873	24,777	25,843
Total Operating Expenses		230,000	257,000	176,538	176,565	176,873	189,777	190,843
EBITDA		385,000	433,000	976,164	980,532	1,009,821	1,047,702	1,099,849
EBITDA Margin %		*40.1%*	*39.0%*	*84.6%*	*84.8%*	*85.1%*	*84.6%*	*85.1%*
Depreciation		60,000	65,000	88,586	121,034	70,361	46,291	35,303
Amortization		-	-	-	-	-	-	-
EBIT		325,000	368,000	887,578	859,498	939,460	1,001,411	1,064,546
EBITA Margin %		*33.9%*	*33.2%*	*76.9%*	*74.3%*	*79.1%*	*80.8%*	*82.4%*
Total Interest Expense				95,450	99,600	113,450	141,750	157,250
EBT				792,128	759,898	826,010	859,661	907,296
Taxes	40%			316,851	303,959	330,404	343,865	362,918
Net Income				475,277	455,939	495,606	515,797	544,378

(figure 16.16), takes a conservative approach by showing that capital expenditures and long-term investments as percentage of revenues remain the same as the base case.

The downside case results shown in each core statement (balance sheet in figure 16.17, income statement in figure 16.18, and cash flow statement figure 16.19, are better captured in the ratio analysis.

FIGURE 16.19 CASH FLOW STATEMENT (DOWNSIDE CASE)

Celerity Technogy Inc. ("CTI")
Cash Flow Statement (000's)

DOWNSIDE CASE	Year 0	Year 1	Year 2	PROJECTED Year 3	Year 4	Year 5
Net Income	148,800	475,277	455,939	495,606	515,797	544,378
Plus Depreciation	65,000	88,586	121,034	70,361	46,291	35,303
Plus Deffered Taxes	5,000	12,674	12,158	13,216	13,755	14,517
Cash Income	218,800	576,537	589,131	579,183	575,842	594,197
Working Capital Activities						
Change in Accounts Receivable	(15,000)	5,427	(127)	(1,458)	(2,436)	(2,522)
Change in Inventory	(5,000)	39,900	153	(109)	(64)	(9)
Change in Prepaid Expenses	1,000	(355)	(22)	(250)	(418)	(432)
Change in Accounts Payable	5,000	(39,900)	(153)	109	64	9
Change in Accrued Income Taxes	(2,000)	395	24	278	464	480
Change in Accrued Expenses	(2,000)	316	19	222	371	384
Total Change in Working Capital	(18,000)	5,783	(105)	(1,208)	(2,018)	(2,089)
Operating Cash Flow (OCF)	**200,800**	**582,319**	**589,026**	**577,975**	**573,824**	**592,108**
Investment Activities						
Capital Expenditures	(125,000)	(129,935)	(130,237)	(133,708)	(139,508)	(145,512)
Investments (Change)	(50,000)	(51,974)	(52,095)	(53,483)	(55,803)	(58,205)
Total Financing Activities	(175,000)	(181,909)	(182,332)	(187,191)	(195,311)	(203,717)
Cash Available Before Financing Activities	25,800	400,410	406,694	390,784	378,512	388,391
Financing Activities						
ST Debt Payments	(10,000)	(10,000)	-	-	-	-
LT Debt Payments	(20,000)	(20,000)	(30,000)	(40,000)	(60,000)	(80,000)
Equity Contribution	25,000					
Total Financing Activities	(5,000)	(30,000)	(30,000)	(40,000)	(60,000)	(80,000)
Free Cash Flow	20,800	370,410	376,694	350,784	318,512	308,391
Beginning Cash	45,000	65,800	436,210	812,904	1,163,688	1,482,200
Ending Cash	65,800	436,210	812,904	1,163,688	1,482,200	1,790,591

FIGURE 16.20 FINANCIAL RATIOS (DOWNSIDE CASE)

Celerity Technogy Inc. ("CTI")
Financial Ratios

DOWNSIDE CASE	HISTORICAL Year -1	Year 0	Year 1	Year 2	PROJECTED Year 3	Year 4	Year 5
Liquidity Ratios							
Current Ratio	1.8x	2.6x	3.2x	3.5x	3.3x	2.6x	1.6x
Quick ratio	1.2x	1.9x	2.4x	2.6x	2.5x	1.8x	0.8x
Accounts Receivable Turnover (ART)		21.1x	20.8x	22.1x	21.9x	21.8x	21.7x
Accounts Receivable Days		17.3x	17.5x	16.5x	16.7x	16.8x	16.9x
Solvency Ratios							
LTD / Total Capitalization	40.7%	38.1%	35.4%	32.6%	29.8%	26.8%	23.7%
EBITDA / Interest (Coverage Ratio)	3.0x	3.6x	4.4x	4.3x	3.8x	3.2x	3.0x
LTD / EBITDA (Leverage Ratio)	3.1x	2.7x	2.8x	2.7x	2.5x	2.3x	2.0x
Altma's Z-score (used Book Value of Equity)	2.2x	2.7x	2.3x	2.5x	2.8x	3.0x	3.3x
Activity Ratios / Operating Ratios							
Inventory Ratio (IR)		11.2x	11.4x	11.7x	11.6x	11.5x	11.5x
Inventory Ratio - Days		32.6	32.1	31.2	31.5	31.7	31.8
Profitability Ratios							
Gross Margin	64.1%	62.2%	62.3%	62.3%	62.3%	62.3%	62.3%
EBITDA Margin	40.1%	39.0%	40.2%	40.8%	41.1%	41.2%	41.2%
Return on Assets (ROA)		4.8%	6.0%	6.4%	6.4%	6.2%	6.0%
Return on Equity (ROE)		8.1%	9.7%	9.9%	9.6%	8.8%	8.3%

CASE STUDY

LBO OF COLORADO DENTAL LLP

Company Overview

Colorado Dental operates 480 locations across 30 states, primarily in the Northeast and Midwest. The dentists supported by Colorado Dental in 2016 served 2 million patients.

Transaction

Heinz Ward & Co (HW), a private equity firm, signed an agreement to acquire Colorado Dental LLP ("Colorado Dental") for an aggregate of $1.1 billion (before transaction expenses). The $1.1 billion acquisition includes a purchase of equity of $780 million and $320 million of refinancing of existing debt. Transaction fees are $50 million.

Capital Raising

HW is in the process of raising the necessary funds to cover the purchase price, refinance Colorado Dental's existing debt, and pay the transaction fees. The proposed structure is as follows:

Equity

HW will invest $600 million of equity.

Bank Debt

Spring Bank approved a loan based on the company's last year's EBITDA. The money terms were as follows:

Revolver: $100 million ($0 funded on day one)—assume no unfunded expense

TERM LOAN A

AMOUNT	1.8X YEAR 0 EBITDA*
Interest	LIBOR + 3.5%
Term	7 years
Scheduled Payments	Year 1: 5%, Year 2: 5%, Year 3: 8%, Year 4: 10%, Year 5: 12%, Year 6: 15%, Year 7: 45%

TERM LOAN B

AMOUNT	2.0X YEAR 0 EBITDA*
Interest	LIBOR + 4.0%
Term	7 years
Scheduled Payments	Year 1: 1%, Year 2: 1%, Year 3: 1%, Year 4: 1%, 5: 1%, Year 6: 1%, Year 7: 94%

LIBOR Assumptions

Starting LIBOR at 1.0%, increasing 0.5% in Year 1, 0.5% in Year 2 and 1.0% in Year 3

Senior Unsecured Notes

Morgan Stanley, an investment bank, managed to raise the senior unsecured notes. The money terms were as follows:

AMOUNT	THE BALANCE OF THE FINANCING (AFTER BANK LOANS & EQUITY)
Interest	7.5%
Term	8 years
Scheduled Payments	Year 1–Year 7: 0%, Year 8: 100% (bullet payment)

Last Year's Operation Assumptions (Year 0)

- Average revenue per patient per visit (ARPV): $250
- Average number of visits per patient per year: 2 visits
- Number of patients in Year 0: 2 million
- Cost of revenue as 60% of revenue
- Operating expenses as 30% of revenue
- Depreciation as 5% of revenue

Projections' Assumptions (Years 1–8)

- ARPV: Increase of 6% per year
- Average number of visits per patient per year: 2
- Patients annual growth rate: 2%
- Cost of revenue: 55% of revenues
- Operating expense: 30% of revenues
- Depreciation: 5% of revenues
- Amortization of fees—use 7 years
- Tax rate at 34%
- Deferred taxes as % of tax expense: 5%
- Accounts receivables days: 30 days
- Inventory days: 65 days
- Accounts payable days: 20 days
- Other current assets as % of revenues: 1.0%
- Other current liabilities as % of revenues: 1.5%
- Capex: 5% of revenues per year

Financial Model

The first approach is to calculate Year 0 EBITDA as it is needed to build the transaction sources and uses, since the debt raised is approved based on last year's EBITDA using the leverage ratio (debt/EBITDA).

FIGURE 16.21 EBITDA CALCULATION

	B	C	D	E
5	**EBITDA CALCULATION**			
6				**Historical**
7	**INCOME STATEMENT ASSUMPTIONS**			**Year 0**
8	**Revenue Worksheet Assumptions**			
9	Average Revebue Per Patient (ARPV)			250.00
10	Average number of Visits per year			2
11	Number of visitors			2,000
12	**Total Revenue**			1,000,000
13				
14	Cost of Revenue as % of Revenue			60.0%
15	Cost of Revenue			600,000
16				
17	Operating Expenses as % of Revenue			30.0%
18	Operating Expenses			300,000
19	EBITDA			100,000

The uses of the transaction that represent the use of capital to pay for 100% of the current stock, refinance the existing debt, and pay closing fees, such as financing fees.

FIGURE 16.22 TRANSACTION SOURCES AND USES

	Q	R	S
24	**TRANSACTION SOURCES & USES**		
25	**Uses**		**Amount ($ 000's)**
26	**Cash**		-
27	**Purchase of Equity (100% shares**		780,000
28	**Refinance Existing Debt**		320,000
29	**Transaction Fees & Expenses**		50,000
30	**Total Uses**		**1,150,000**

The transaction sources are then built based on the maximum equity committed and the debt that is approved. The bank loan portion that includes revolver (working capital facility), term loan A, and term loan B is based on the leverage ratio of total debt/EBITDA and the senior unsecured note makes the balance of the financing.

FIGURE 16.23 TRANSACTION SOURCES AND USES

	B–G	H	I	J	K	L	M	N
24	**TRANSACTION SOURCES & USES**							
25	**Sources**	**Princing / Expected Return**	**Funded ($ 000's)**	**% Cap**	**EBITDA x**	**Interest Rate / Expected Return**	**After Tax IR / ER**	**Calc WACC**
26	**Revolver ($100 million)**	*=+K27*$H$178*	-			*=+L27*(1-$H$37)*		
27	**Term Loan A**	LIBOR + 3.5%	180,000	15.7%	1.80x	6.0%	3.8%	0.6%
28	**Term Loan B**	LIBOR + 4.0%	200,000	17.4%	2.00x	6.6%	4.2%	0.7%
29	**Total Bank Debt**		380,000	33.0%	3.80x		*=IRR(I73:Q73)*	
30	**Senior Unsecured / Subordinated Notes**	10% FIXED	170,000	14.8%	1.70x	10.0%	6.4%	0.9%
31	**Total Debt**		**550,000**	47.8%	5.50x			
32	**Cash Equity**	Based On CAPM	600,000	52.2%	6.0x	18.0%	18.0%	9.4%
33	**Total Sources**		**1,150,000**	100.0%	11.5x			
34							**WACC=**	**11.7%**
35	**Acquisition Target 2018 Year 0 EBITDA =**	**100,000**	**Calculate EBITDA**					
36	**Tax Rate =**	36.00%						
37								
38		**Risk Free Rate (Rf)**	**Equity Market Return (Rm)**	**Equity Market Risk Premium (Rp = Rm - Rm)**	**Industry Beta (β)**	**CAPM = Rf + B .Rp**		
39	**Return Calculation based on CAPM =**	2.00%	10.00%	8.00%	2.00x	**18.00%**		
40							*=+H39+(K39*J39)*	

The debt schedule is built to include each facility's debt outstanding, scheduled contractual principal payments, and interest payments based on the LIBOR, plus a contractual spread for the bank loan and a fixed rate for the unsecured notes. The outstanding amount will be included in the balance sheet; the principal payments will be included in cash flow statement as cash outflow; and the interest payments will be included in the income statement.

FIGURE 16.24 DEBT SCHEDULES

41	B	E	F	H	I	J	K	L	M	N	O	P	Q
42													
43	DEBT SCHEDULES / ANALYSIS												
44	($ 000's)				Historical				PROJECTED				
45					Year 0	Year 1	Year 2	Year 3	Year 4	Year 5	Year 6	Year 7	Year 8
46	Interest Rate Assumptions												
47	LIBOR Rate				1.00%	1.50%	2.00%	3.00%	3.00%	3.00%	3.00%	3.00%	3.00%
48	LIBOR Iincrease / Decrease					0.5%	0.5%	1.0%					
49													
50	Revolver ($100 million)			COMMITMENT	FUNDED								
51	Outstanding			100,000	-	-	-	-	-	-	-	-	-
52	Increase / (Decrease)					-	-	-	-	-	-	-	-
53	Interest Payment												
54	Unfunded Fee												
55	Spread												
56	Interest rate												
57					% Amort								
58	Term Loan A												
59	Outstanding				180,000	171,000	162,000	147,600	129,600	108,000	81,000	-	-
60	Increase / (Decrease)			=+$I$59*J67 →		9,000	9,000	14,400	18,000	21,600	27,000	81,000	-
61	Interest Payment			=+I59*J65 →		9,000	9,405	10,530	9,594	8,424	7,020	5,265	-
62	Total Payment (Interest + Principal)	IRR=	6.0%		(180,000)	18,000	18,405	24,930	27,594	30,024	34,020	86,265	-
63													
64	Spread					3.50%	3.50%	3.50%	3.50%	3.50%	3.50%	3.50%	3.50%
65	Interest rate					5.00%	5.50%	6.50%	6.50%	6.50%	6.50%	6.50%	6.50%
66													
67	Schedule Repayment based on Percentage %					5.00%	5.00%	8.00%	10.00%	12.00%	15.00%	45.00%	
68													
69	Term Loan B												
70	Outstanding				200,000	198,000	196,000	194,000	192,000	190,000	188,000	-	-
71	Increase / (Decrease)					2,000	2,000	2,000	2,000	2,000	2,000	188,000	-
72	Interest Payment					11,000	11,880	13,720	13,580	13,440	13,300	13,160	-
73	Total Payment (Interest + Principal)	IRR=	6.6%		(200,000)	13,000	13,880	15,720	15,580	15,440	15,300	201,160	-
74													
75	Spread					4.00%	4.00%	4.00%	4.00%	4.00%	4.00%	4.00%	4.00%
76	Interest rate					5.50%	6.00%	7.00%	7.00%	7.00%	7.00%	7.00%	7.00%
77													
78	Schedule Repayment based on Percentage %					1.00%	1.00%	1.00%	1.00%	1.00%	1.00%	94.00%	
79													
80	Senior Unsecured / Subordinated Notes												
81	Outstanding				170,000	170,000	170,000	170,000	170,000	170,000	170,000	170,000	-
82	Increase / (Decrease)					-	-	-	-	-	-	-	170,000
83	Interest Payment					17,000	17,000	17,000	17,000	17,000	17,000	17,000	17,000
84	Total Payment (Interest + Principal)	IRR=	10.0%		(170,000)	17,000	17,000	17,000	17,000	17,000	17,000	17,000	187,000
85													
86	Interest rate					10.00%	10.00%	10.00%	10.00%	10.00%	10.00%	10.00%	10.00%
87													
88	Total Interest Payment					37,000	38,285	41,250	40,174	38,864	37,320	35,425	17,000
89	Total Scheduled Payment					11,000	11,000	16,400	20,000	23,600	29,000	269,000	170,000
90	Total Payment (Interest + Principal)					48,000	49,285	57,650	60,174	62,464	66,320	304,425	187,000
91	Total Debt Outstanding					539,000	528,000	511,600	491,600	468,000	439,000	170,000	-
92	Total Senior Debt					369,000	358,000	341,600	321,600	298,000	269,000	-	-

The financial statements, such as the balance sheet, income statements, and cash flow are built based on the projected operating assumptions provided. The opening or proforma post transaction Year 0 balance sheet is calculated based on the transaction sources and uses, reflecting the new financing replacing both the debt and equity, and the retained earnings reset to $0.

FIGURE 16.25 BALANCE SHEET

94	B	C	D	E	F	G	H	I	J	K	L	M	N	O	P
95															
96	**BALANCE SHEET**														
97	**($ 000's)**														
98		Pre-Transaction		Debit	Credit		Post - Transaction								
99		Year 0					Year 0	Year 1	Year 2	Year 3	Year 4	Year 5	Year 6	Year 7	Year 8
100	**Current Assets**														
101	Cash	50,000					50,000	82,681	114,480	144,265	177,008	213,342	252,137	59,584	(15,835)
102	Accounts Receivable	80,000					80,000	88,866	96,082	103,883	112,319	121,439	131,300	141,962	153,489
103	Inventory	105,000					105,000	105,898	114,497	123,794	133,847	144,715	156,466	169,171	182,907
104	Other Current Assets	10,000					10,000	10,812	11,690	12,639	13,665	14,775	15,975	17,272	18,674
105	**Total Current Assets**	245,000					245,000	288,257	336,749	384,582	436,839	494,271	555,877	387,988	339,235
106															
107	Goodwill	-		310,000			310,000	310,000	310,000	310,000	310,000	310,000	310,000	310,000	310,000
108	Capitalized Fees	-		50,000			50,000	42,857	35,714	28,571	21,429	14,286	7,143	(0)	(0)
109	Net PP&E	150,000					150,000	150,000	150,000	150,000	150,000	150,000	150,000	150,000	150,000
110	Invesment in JV	450,000					450,000	450,000	450,000	450,000	450,000	450,000	450,000	450,000	450,000
111	**Total Assets**	845,000					1,205,000	1,241,115	1,282,464	1,323,153	1,368,267	1,418,557	1,473,020	1,297,988	1,249,235
112															
113	**Current Liabilities**														
114	Accounts Payable	30,000					30,000	32,584	35,230	38,091	41,184	44,528	48,143	52,053	56,279
115	Other Current Liabilities	15,000					15,000	16,218	17,535	18,959	20,498	22,163	23,962	25,908	28,012
116	**Total Current Liabilities**	45,000					45,000	48,802	52,765	57,049	61,682	66,690	72,106	77,961	84,291
117															
118	Existing Long Term Debt	320,000		320,000			-	-	-	-	-	-	-	-	-
119	Revolver ($100 million)				-		-	-	-	-	-	-	-	-	-
120	Term Loan A				180,000		180,000	171,000	162,000	147,600	129,600	108,000	81,000	-	-
121	Term Loan B				200,000		200,000	198,000	196,000	194,000	192,000	190,000	188,000	-	-
122	Senior Unsecured / Subordinated Notes				170,000		170,000	170,000	170,000	170,000	170,000	170,000	170,000	170,000	-
123	Total Long Term Debt	320,000					550,000	539,000	528,000	511,600	491,600	468,000	439,000	170,000	-
124															
125	Other Liabilities / Deferred Taxes	10,000					10,000	11,088	12,303	13,629	15,147	16,877	18,837	21,049	23,935
126	**Total Liabilities**	375,000					605,000	598,890	593,067	582,278	568,429	551,567	529,942	269,010	108,226
127															
128	**Shareholder's Equity**														
129	Common Stock	260,000		260,000	600,000		600,000	600,000	600,000	600,000	600,000	600,000	600,000	600,000	600,000
130	Retained Earnings	210,000		210,000			-	42,225	89,396	140,875	199,838	266,989	343,078	428,978	541,009
131	**Total Shareholder's Equity**	470,000					600,000	642,225	689,396	740,875	799,838	866,989	943,078	1,028,978	1,141,009
132															
133	**Total Liabilities & Equity**	845,000		1,150,000	1,150,000		1,205,000	1,241,115	1,282,464	1,323,153	1,368,267	1,418,557	1,473,020	1,297,988	1,249,235
134							-	-	-	-	-	-	-	-	-

The operating assumptions are laid out to build the projections for all the statements. The revenues are based on growth rates of both volume and price. The cost of revenues and operating expenses are based on percentage of revenue, except for administrative expenses that are based on inflationary growth rate. Taxes are based on tax rate times the earnings before tax (EBT). Other assumptions include the amortization of financing fees, which are based on the term of the loan (in this case, 7 years).

The balance sheet projections are also based on certain assumptions. The accounts receivables, accounts payables, and inventory are based on days calculation provided. All other assets and liabilities are based on percentage of revenues.

FIGURE 16.26 INPUT OPERATING ASSUMPTIONS

135	B	C	D	E	F	G	H	I	J	K	L	M	N	O	P
136															
137	**INPUT OPERATING ASSUMPTIONS**														
138							Historical	PROJECTED							
139	**INCOME STATEMENT ASSUMPTIONS**						Year 0	Year 1	Year 2	Year 3	Year 4	Year 5	Year 6	Year 7	Year 8
140	**Revenue Worksheet Assumptions**														
141	Average Revebue Per Patient (ARPV)						250.00	265.00	280.90	297.75	315.62	334.56	354.63	375.91	398.46
142	Increase %							6.00%	6.00%	6.00%	6.00%	6.00%	6.00%	6.00%	6.00%
143	Average number of Visits per year						2	2	2	2	2	2	2	2	2
144	Number of visitors						2,000	2,040	2,081	2,122	2,165	2,208	2,252	2,297	2,343
145	Patience Annual Growth Rate							2.00%	2.00%	2.00%	2.00%	2.00%	2.00%	2.00%	2.00%
146															
147	**Total Revenue**						1,000,000	1,081,200	1,168,993	1,263,916	1,366,546	1,477,509	1,597,483	1,727,199	1,867,447
148															
149	Cost of Revenue as % of Revenue						60.0%	55.0%	55.0%	55.0%	55.0%	55.0%	55.0%	55.0%	55.0%
150	Operating Expenses as % of Revenue						30.0%	30.0%	30.0%	30.0%	30.0%	30.0%	30.0%	30.0%	30.0%
151	Depreciation as % of Revenue							5.0%	5.0%	5.0%	5.0%	5.0%	5.0%	5.0%	5.0%
152	Tax Rate							34.0%	34.0%	34.0%	34.0%	34.0%	34.0%	34.0%	34.0%
153															
154	**CASH FLOW STATEMENT ASSUMPTIONS**														
155	Capital Expenditures as % of Revenue							5.0%	5.0%	5.0%	5.0%	5.0%	5.0%	5.0%	5.0%
156	Deferred Taxes as % of Taxes							5.0%	5.0%	5.0%	5.0%	5.0%	5.0%	5.0%	5.0%
157															
158	**BALANCE SHEET ASSUMPTIONS**														
159	Accounts Receivable Days							30	30	30	30	30	30	30	30
160	Inventory Days							65	65	65	65	65	65	65	65
161	Other Current Assets % of Revenues							1.0%	1.0%	1.0%	1.0%	1.0%	1.0%	1.0%	1.0%
162	Accounts Payable Days							20	20	20	20	20	20	20	20
163	Other Current Liabilities as % of Revenues							1.5%	1.5%	1.5%	1.5%	1.5%	1.5%	1.5%	1.5%

The income statement is built based on the operating assumptions provided.

FIGURE 16.27 INCOME STATEMENT

165	B	C	D	E	F	G	H	I	J	K	L	M	N	O	P
166															
167	**INCOME STATEMENT**														
168	**($ 000's)**						Historical	**PROJECTED**							
169							Year 0	Year 1	Year 2	Year 3	Year 4	Year 5	Year 6	Year 7	Year 8
170	**REVENUE**						1,000,000	1,081,200	1,168,993	1,263,916	1,366,546	1,477,509	1,597,483	1,727,199	1,867,447
171	Sales Growth							8.1%	8.1%	8.1%	8.1%	8.1%	8.1%	8.1%	8.1%
172															
173	**COST OF SALES (excl. Deprec.)**						600,000	594,660	642,946	695,154	751,600	812,630	878,616	949,959	1,027,096
174	**Gross Profit**						400,000	486,540	526,047	568,762	614,946	664,879	718,867	777,239	840,351
175	Gross Margin						40.0%	45.0%	45.0%	45.0%	45.0%	45.0%	45.0%	45.0%	45.0%
176															
177	**Selling, General & Administrative Expenses**						300,000	324,360	350,698	379,175	409,964	443,253	479,245	518,160	560,234
178	**EBITDA**						100,000	162,180	175,349	189,587	204,982	221,626	239,622	259,080	280,117
179	% Sales							15.0%	15.0%	15.0%	15.0%	15.0%	15.0%	15.0%	15.0%
180															
181	Depreciation							54,060	58,450	63,196	68,327	73,875	79,874	86,360	93,372
182	**EBITA**							108,120	116,899	126,392	136,655	147,751	159,748	172,720	186,745
183	Amort. of Fees							7,143	7,143	7,143	7,143	7,143	7,143	7,143	
184	**EBIT**							100,977	109,756	119,249	129,512	140,608	152,605	165,577	186,745
185															
186	**INTEREST EXPENSE (INCOME):**														
187	Revolver ($100 million)							-	-	-	-	-	-	-	-
188	Term Loan A							9,000	9,405	10,530	9,594	8,424	7,020	5,265	-
189	Term Loan B							11,000	11,880	13,720	13,580	13,440	13,300	13,160	-
190	Senior Unsecured / Subordinated Notes							17,000	17,000	17,000	17,000	17,000	17,000	17,000	17,000
191	Total Interest Expense							37,000	38,285	41,250	40,174	38,864	37,320	35,425	17,000
192															
193	EBT Taxes							63,977	71,471	77,999	89,338	101,744	115,285	130,152	169,745
194	Tax Rate							34.0%	34.0%	34.0%	34.0%	34.0%	34.0%	34.0%	34.0%
195	Tax Expense							21,752	24,300	26,520	30,375	34,593	39,197	44,252	57,713
196	**NET INCOME (LOSS)**							42,225	47,171	51,479	58,963	67,151	76,088	85,900	112,032

The cash flow statement is based on the operating assumptions provided, and most of it is built on the balance sheet results.

FIGURE 16.28 CASH FLOW STATEMENT

198										
199	**CASH FLOW STATEMENT**									
200	**($ 000's)**					**PROJECTED**				
201		Year 0	Year 1	Year 2	Year 3	Year 4	Year 5	Year 6	Year 7	Year 8
202	Net Income (Loss)		42,225	47,171	51,479	58,963	67,151	76,088	85,900	112,032
203	Depreciation		54,060	58,450	63,196	68,327	73,875	79,874	86,360	93,372
204	Amortization of Fees		7,143	7,143	7,143	7,143	7,143	7,143	7,143	-
205	Deffered Taxes		1,088	1,215	1,326	1,519	1,730	1,960	2,213	2,886
206	**Cash Income (CI)**		104,515	113,979	123,144	135,952	149,899	165,065	181,616	208,290
207										
208	**WORKING CAPITAL ACTIVITIES:**									
209	Change in Accounts Receivable		(8,866)	(7,216)	(7,802)	(8,435)	(9,120)	(9,861)	(10,662)	(11,527)
210	Change in Inventory		(898)	(8,599)	(9,297)	(10,052)	(10,868)	(11,751)	(12,705)	(13,737)
211	Change in Other Current Assets		(812)	(878)	(949)	(1,026)	(1,110)	(1,200)	(1,297)	(1,402)
212	Change in Accounts Payable		2,584	2,646	2,861	3,093	3,344	3,616	3,909	4,227
213	Change in other Current Liabilities		1,218	1,317	1,424	1,539	1,664	1,800	1,946	2,104
214	**Total Working Capital Activities**		(6,774)	(12,730)	(13,764)	(14,881)	(16,090)	(17,396)	(18,809)	(20,336)
215										
216	**Operating Cash Flow (OCF)**		97,741	101,249	109,380	121,070	133,809	147,669	162,807	187,953
217										
218	**INVESTMENT ACTIVITIES:**									
219	Capital Expenditures		(54,060)	(58,450)	(63,196)	(68,327)	(73,875)	(79,874)	(86,360)	(93,372)
220	Investments in the JV		-	-	-	-	-	-	-	-
221	**Total Investment Activivites**		(54,060)	(58,450)	(63,196)	(68,327)	(73,875)	(79,874)	(86,360)	(93,372)
222										
223	**Cash Available for Debt Service (CAFDS)**		43,681	42,799	46,184	52,743	59,934	67,795	76,447	94,581
224										
225	**FINANCING ACTIVITIES (Pmts/Borrowings):**									
226	Revolver ($100 million)		-	-	-	-	-	-	-	-
227	Term Loan A		(9,000)	(9,000)	(14,400)	(18,000)	(21,600)	(27,000)	(81,000)	-
228	Term Loan B		(2,000)	(2,000)	(2,000)	(2,000)	(2,000)	(2,000)	(188,000)	-
229	Senior Unsecured / Subordinated Notes		-	-	-	-	-	-	-	(170,000)
230	**Total Debt Payments**		(11,000)	(11,000)	(16,400)	(20,000)	(23,600)	(29,000)	(269,000)	(170,000)
231										
232	Equity Contribution		-	-	-	-	-	-	-	-
233	**Total Financing Activivites**		(11,000)	(11,000)	(16,400)	(20,000)	(23,600)	(29,000)	(269,000)	(170,000)
234										
235	Free Cash Flow		32,681	31,799	29,784	32,743	36,334	38,795	(192,553)	(75,419)

PROBLEMS

1. Prepare Green Landscape projections using the following information.

Company Overview

GLS is a provider of residential landscape services in 30 states, primarily in the Northeast and Midwest. In 2015 GLS served approximately 2 million customers.

Last Year's Operation Assumptions (Year 0)

- Average revenue per service (ARPS): $60
- Average number of services per customer per year: 10 visits
- Number of total customers: 2 million
- Cost of revenue as 50% of revenue
- Operating expenses as 30% of revenue

Projections' Assumptions (Years 1–8)

- ARPS: Increase of 6% per year
- Average number of services per customer per year: 10 visits
- Total services annual growth rate: 2%
- Cost of revenue: 45% of revenues
- Operating expense: 30% of revenues
- Depreciation: 5% of revenues
- Tax rate at 34%
- Deferred taxes as % of tax expense: 5%
- Working capital is 1% revenue
- Capex: 6% of revenues per year

2. Prepare Alexandria Hotel projections using the following information.

First Year of Operation Assumptions:

- Revenue of $40 million
- Cost of revenue as % of revenue is 35%
- Operating expenses as % of revenue is 15%
- Depreciation as % of revenue is 3%
- Taxes are 36%

- Working capital is 1% of revenue
- Capital expenditures as % of revenue is 3%

Projections' Assumptions (Year 2 and thereafter)

- Revenue growth: 5%
- Cost of room: Keep the same 35% of revenues
- Operating expense: Keep the same 15% of revenues
- Depreciation: Keep the same 3% of revenues
- Tax rate at 36%
- Working capital is 1% revenue
- Capex: Keep the same 3% of revenues per year

3. Prepare Expo Hotel Corporation projections using the following information.

Company Overview

Expo Hotel Corporation operates as a hotel franchisor worldwide. The company franchises lodging properties under the brand names of Beautiful Inn, Beautiful Suites, Expo, and Experience Suites. As of December 31, Year 0, the company had approximately 6,900 franchised hotels with 56,000 rooms in approximately 40 countries and territories.

LBO Transaction

Whitestone Partners (PW), a private equity firm, signed an agreement to acquire Expo Hotel Corporation ("Expo"), a publicly traded company, for $37.50 per share. Total acquisition cost includes the purchase of 100% of Expo's 100 million shares and the refinancing of $750 million of existing debt. In addition to the acquisition, there will be transaction fees of $100 million.

Transaction Overview

PW is in the process of raising the necessary funds to cover the purchase all the shares of the company, refinance Expo's existing debt, and pay the transaction fees. The proposed structure is as follows:

Bank Debt: JPP Bank approved a 2-tranch loan (revolver, term loan B) based on the company's last year EBITDA (Year 0). The money terms were as follows:

Revolver: $200 million ($0 funded on day one)—assume no unfunded expense

TERM LOAN B

AMOUNT	3.0x YEAR 0 EBITDA
Interest	LIBOR + 4.0%
Term	7 years
Scheduled Payments	Year 1: 1%, Year 2: 1%, Year 3: 1%, Year 4: 1%, Year 5: 1%, Year 6: 1%, Year 7: 94%

LIBOR Assumptions

Starting LIBOR at 2.5%, increasing 0.5% in 2019, 0.5% in 2020, and 1.0% in 2021

Senior Unsecured Notes

Morgan Stanley, an investment bank, managed to raise the senior unsecured notes. The money terms were as follows:

AMOUNT	2.5x YEAR 0 EBITDA
Interest	8%
Term	8 years
Scheduled Payments	Year 1–7: 0%, Year 8: 100% (bullet payment)

Equity

The balance of the financing. The expected equity return is calculated based on CAPM where the risk-free rate is 2.0%, the market return is 12%, and the industry beta is 2.0x.

Last Year's Operation Assumptions (Year 0)

- Average daily rate (ADR): $140
- Occupancy rate: 67%
- Cost of revenue as 50% of revenue
- Operating expenses as 20% of revenue

Projections' Assumptions (Years 1–8)

- ADR increase of 5% per year
- Occupancy rate stays at 67%
- No growth on the number of rooms
- Cost of revenue: 50% of revenues
- Operating expense: 30% of revenues

- Depreciation: 5% of revenues
- Amortization of fees—use 7 years
- Tax rate at 34%
- Deferred taxes as % of tax expense: 5%
- Accounts receivables days: 30 days
- Inventory day (assume no inventory)
- Accounts payable days: 20 days
- Other current assets as % of revenues: 1.0%
- Other current liabilities as % of revenues: 1.5%
- Capex: 5% of revenues per year

ONLINE TEMPLATES

The Excel spreadsheets used in the chapter can be accessed online via Cognella Active Learning platform.

CHAPTER 17

Valuation Analysis

This chapter will cover eight different methods of valuating the firm's worth. These are methods that are currently used on Wall Street to determine the values for both the private and publicly traded companies.

LEARNING OBJECTIVES

After reading this chapter, students will be able to do the following:

- Prioritize the sections of the financial statement to be used for building projections and determining the value of the company
- Learn the eight different methods to value a company
- Learn the difference between the discount cash flow (DCF) and LBO methods for analyzing privately owned companies
- Use the Black-Scholes option pricing model to determine a value of the equity and the firm when the company is in distress or bankruptcy

VALUATION OVERVIEW

The chapter will introduce the following eight methods of valuating the company's enterprise value:

Method 1: Using the current stock price as a basis of valuation
Method 2: Intrinsic value and capital asset pricing model (CAPM)
Method 3: Dividend discount model (DDM)
Method 4: Comparable method using trading EBITDA multiples
Method 5: Comparable method using acquisition EBITDA multiples
Method 6: Discount cash flow method (DCF)

Method 7: Leveraged buyout private equity expectation model (LBO)
Method 8: Black-Scholes option pricing model

All the eight methods are currently used on Wall Street by various investors (sophisticated and unsophisticated), financial analysts, mergers and acquisition specialists and advisors, and creditors. Each of the methods is more relevant depending on who is analyzing the company. For publicly traded companies, for example, for the investor who is interested in buying the stock and wants to assess whether the current stock price is fair he or she could use methods 1–6. For the investment banker who is interested in pricing a private company that is issuing shares through an initial public offering it is very common to use methods 4–6 in the assessment of that initial market value. For private equity firms who are in the process of buying 100% of a publicly traded company's shares or buying a privately-owned company (private to private) it will use methods 4–7, especially method 7 that attempts to derive value from the equity return expectation. An existing shareholder of the company who is going through restructuring or reorganization on pre- or post-bankruptcy stages can use method 8 to find some value of its equity in the future, similar to pricing an equity option.

AUTHOR'S NOTES

Valuing the company or the investor's equity will be highly subjective. There is a lot of interpretation of the data used for the valuation methods. Although there are several methods to value a company, the valuation is both art and science. There is some judgement that goes in choosing the data. Naturally, the buyer has a different perspective than the seller and therefore the valuation assessment could be derived differently.

As a junior analyst working for Bank of America in the late 80s, I consulted many times with the Mergers & Acquisition Department on various companies that our private equity client wanted to acquire. One of my favorite stories on valuations is when I asked one of my colleagues to help me value a company. He asked me if I wanted the 3-day analysis, the 1-day analysis or the 1-second analysis. He went on, "The 3-day valuation analysis involves an extensive comparable data analysis of many of their company's piers ..." Before he continued, I stopped him I said, "Okay. I see. Just curious, what is the one-second analysis?" He turned and said, "Six times EBITDA," referring to multiples of the company's reported earnings before interest taxes, depreciation, and amortization. Most manufacturing companies at the time were quoted trading at 6x their EBITDA and that was the basis to start your valuation. The point is that we can spend hours and days analyzing the value of the company but at the end of the day the value of anything is what someone is willing to pay.

KEY TAKEAWAYS

- There are many methods for valuing the firm, and the results could be very different.
- Ultimately, the value of the firm is the price that a buyer is willing to pay and not necessarily what the seller is asking.
- Typically, different acquirers focus on valuing the target company using different sections of the of the firm's income statement:
  - The strategic buyer is focusing more on the firm's **top line revenues**—acquiring new customers and implementing its own structure.
  - The private equity buyer is focused more on the firm's **earnings before interest taxes, depreciation, and amortization (EBITDA)**—acquiring the firm's cash flow.
  - The public investors who are investing by buying the stock of the company care more about the firm's **net income**—a number that is used for valuing *the stock price like earnings per share (EPS) or price earnings multiple (PE multiple).*

VALUATION METHODS

The following methods of valuation are the most common methods used on Wall Street:

METHODS 1–6: VALUATION OF PUBLIC TRADED COMPANIES

The chapter will first focus on how to value a publicly traded company using the first six methods. The chapter then will cover extensively methods 6 and 7, valuing a privately held company using the projections described in the last chapter. The chapter will then conclude with method 8, which is a unique way to measure the enterprise value of a company when it is in default of its debt obligations or going through restructuring and reorganization.

METHOD 1: USING THE STOCK PRICE AS THE BASIS OF VALUATION

The stock price represents the value of the company. The price of the stock trades every minute of the day as investors buy and sell their holdings. Scholars over the years have spent a lot of time writing about this continuous movement in stock price. How can the price of a stock go up and down when there is little to no information given about the company on a minute-by-minute basis? **The company issues financial statements every 3 months and other non-financial information as it comes up, so how does the stock price behave like this? It is said that the stock price moves based on technical, fundamental, and behavioral reasons and there are plenty of analytical approaches that back each**

FIGURE 17.1 HYATT HOTELS CORPORATION METHOD 1 - MARKET VALUE/USING THE STOCK PRICE

CORPORATE VALUATIONS

METHOD #1 - Market Value / Using the Stock Price

Calculations→		SP	SO	SP * SO = EQ	D	C	EQ + D - C = EV
Company	**Symbol**	**Stock Price**	**Stocks Outstanding ($000)**	**Equity Value ($000)**	**Debt (ST&LT) ($000)**	**Cash ($000)**	**Enterprise Value ($000)**
Hyatt	H	$ 72.00	117,448	8,456,279	1,440,000	879,000	9,017,279

of these three reasons. To simplify our approach to value, we will start with the current price of the stock as our basis of value, called method 1. All other methods that follow are attempting to test if the traded price of the stock is fair. The formula to value the firm or the enterprise value (EV) is as follows:

$$EV = MVE + D - C,$$

where EV is enterprise value, MVE is the market value of the equity, D is the total debt outstanding, and C is the cash and cash equivalents of the company.

The stock price that represents the market value of each share when multiplied by the shares outstanding will give us the market value of the equity.

$$MVE = (SP \times SO),$$

where MVE is the market value of the equity, SP is the stock price and SO is the shares outstanding.

The shares outstanding represent all the shares that a publicly traded company has issued since its initial public offering including any follow-up secondary offerings. Figure 17.1 shows Hyatt Hotels' current stock market, which translates to the company's enterprise value. The current stock price of $77.93, when multiplied by its 117.4 million shares outstanding, gives a market value of equity of $9.2 billion. Finally, adding the equity to the last reported debt minus the last reported cash results in an enterprise value of $9.7 billion.

METHOD 2: INTRINSIC VALUE AND CAPM

One of the first technical methods to value a firm is measuring the future stock price based on return expectation and applying basic time-value techniques. We conduct this method in order to value the stock price and enterprise value today. For example, if you expect the stock to be a $100 in a year, at what price do you need to buy it today when the expected return is 10%? Using finance 101 where $PV = FV/(1 + r)^t$, where PV is present value, FV is future value, r is the return, and t is time, the stock should have been at $90 or 90 = 100/(1 + 0.10)[1]. The expected return is calculated by applying the capital asset pricing model (CAPM):

$$\mathbf{E_r = Rf_r + \beta(M_r - Rf_r)}$$

where E_r is the expected return, R_{fr} is the risk-free rate, β is the beta of the company that is analyzed, and M_r is market return.

The stock price expectation is based on various analysts' stock predictions. These can be found on various financial websites including finance.yahoo.com.

The formula for today's intrinsic value is

$$V_0 = \frac{D_1 + \rho_1}{1 + k}$$

where D_1 is the dividend expected to receive within a year, P_1 is the expected stock price a year from now, and k is the discount rate or expected rate of return.

Figure 17.2 shows that the stock price using the intrinsic value and the CAPM method is estimated at $81.88. To calculate the stock price using this method, we first need to calculate the expected equity return. This expected rate of 12.1% using CAPM is based on Hyatt's stock beta of 1.18x, risk-free rate of 1.50%, and a given market premium of 9%.

FIGURE 17.2 HYATT HOTELS CORPORATION METHOD 2 - INTRINSIC VALUE

Hyatt Hotels Corporation
CORPORATE VALUATIONS

METHOD #2- Intrinsic Value

Using CAPM = k = Rf + (Beta * Premium)		Intrinsic Value = V0 = [E(D1) + E (P1)] / (1+k)		
Risk Free =	1.50%	D1=	$1.80	
Beta =	1.18x	Analyst Est.	$1.64	(Average Earnings per share)
Premium=	9.00%	PE Multiple	14.55x	
Market Return (Rf + Premium)=	10.50%	Exp (P1)=	$90.00	(Avg Target by Analysts for 9/19)
		k=	12.1%	
RoR =	12.1%	V0=	$ 81.88	
Hyatt's Enteprise Value	10,177,265			

METHOD 3: DIVIDEND DISCOUNT MODEL (DDM)

This technical method for valuing the company can only be used if the company is a frequent payer of dividends. The value of the stock is basically the present value of the dividend to be received at the end of the first year—assuming the buyer will hold the stock for a year. To calculate such value using the DDM method, the analyst needs the expected price of

FIGURE 17.3 HYATT HOTELS CORPORATION METHOD 3 - DIVIDDEND DISCOUNT METHOD (DDM)

Hyatt Hotels Corporation
CORPORATE VALUATIONS

METHOD #3- Dividend Discount Model (DDM)

Constant-Growth DDM (Gordon Model) V0 = D1 / (k-g)			Expected HPR = E 9r) = [E (d1) + (E(p1) - P0) / P0		
D1 =		$1.80	Dividend (d1)	$1.80	(No growth)
Expected Equity Return (k)=		12.1%	P1 = P0+D	$73.80	
Expected Growth (g) =		10.0%	P0	$ 72.00	
V0=	**$**	**93.40**	**Exp. HPR=**	**5.00%**	
Hyatt's Enteprise Value		**11,530,230**			

the stock a year from the date of the analysis, the expected dividend per share paid within the year, and a discount rate, which derived using the capital asset pricing model (CAPM).

$$V = \frac{D1}{k - g}$$

where D_1 is the expected dividend, k is the discount rate, and g is the expected growth rate.

Figure 17.3 shows that the stock price is valued at $93.40. The price is calculated assuming a dividend of $1.80 per share and a 12.1% discount rate using CAPM, method #2.

METHOD 4: USING COMPARABLE TRADING EBITDA MULTIPLES

This method, most commonly used by mergers and acquisitions professionals, looks at the ratio of the enterprise value to earnings before interest, taxes, depreciation, and amortization (EV/EBITDA) for each of the peer companies and applies the average to measure the company's value. The average multiple provides a benchmark, which the analyst can establish as the basis for valuating both private and publicly traded companies. The basic idea is that as the company increases its earnings based on either favorable economic conditions or management decisions from year to year, then the value should also follow at a relatively consistent way. In general, industries with higher growth characteristics enjoy higher multiples of earnings. Similar companies that compete with the company being valued give similar business and financial characteristics.

In figure 17.4, the average EBITDA multiple, after taking out the high and low as outliers, is 15.67x, representing slightly higher than Hyatt's current EBITDA multiple of 15.41x. Using the 15.67x, Hyatt's last reported EBITDA, Hyatt's enterprise value is calculated at $9.0 billion.

FIGURE 17.4 HYATT HOTELS CORPORATION METHOD 4 - AVERAGE EBITDA INDUSTRY TRADING MULTIPLES)

CORPORATE VALUATIONS

METHOD #4 -Average EBITDA Industry Trading Multiples

		SP	SO	SP * SO = EQ	D	C	EQ + D - C = EV	E	EV / E	
Company	**Symbol**	**Stock Price**	**Stocks Outstanding ($000)**	**Equity Value ($000)**	**Debt (ST&LT) ($000)**	**Cash ($000)**	**Enterprise Value ($000)**	**EBITDA ($mm)**	**EBITDA Multiple**	**Beta**
Choice Hotels International	CHH	$ 83.20	56,572	4,706,804	796,200	37,150	5,465,854	335,560	16.29x	1.13x
Hilton Worldwide Holdings Inc.	HLT	$ 80.96	298,190	24,141,462	7,580,000	423,000	31,298,462	1,760,000	17.78x	1.45x
Intercontinental Hotel	IHG	$ 62.58	190,000	11,890,200	2,040,000	233,000	13,697,200	843,000	16.25x	1.59x
Marcus Corporation	MCS	$ 40.80	19,680	802,944	317,420	18,070	1,102,294	139,930	7.88x	0.32x
Marriott International	MAR	$ 130.90	346,990	45,420,991	8,990,000	366,000	54,044,991	2,850,000	18.96x	1.36x
Park Hotels & Resorts Inc.	PK	$ 32.89	201,180	6,616,810	3,080,000	421,000	9,275,810	734,000	12.64x	
Belmond (A/K Orient Express Hotels Ltd)	BEL	$ 17.00	102,960	1,750,320	785,170	162,010	2,373,480	103,750	22.88x	1.51x
Wyndham Worldwide	WYN	$ 136.73	108,640	14,854,347	8,310,000	1,500,000	21,664,347	1,790,000	12.10x	1.33x
Hyatt	HOT	$ 72.00	117,448	8,456,279	1,440,000	879,000	9,017,279	585,000	15.41x	1.18x
EBITDA * Average Multiple	585,000	15.67x					**Average**		15.60x	1.23x
							Outliers		15.67x	
Hyatt's Enteprise Value	**9,167,303**									

METHOD 5: USING COMPARABLE ACQUISITION EBITDA MULTIPLES

Like the trading multiples for method 4, method 5 establishes a similar benchmark to what the companies in the same industry are being bought at based on multiples of their EBITDA. This method is very similar to what real estate professionals use. To determine the selling price of someone's home, the real estate agent researches other similar-in-size homes that are sold in the neighborhood. Like the real estate method, corporate values using this method are determined based on other companies in the same business that are recently sold to either strategic investors or private equity firms. The mergers and acquisition professional searches for other companies in the same business that were sold to either strategic investors or private equity firms and establishes a benchmark based on average multiples over time. That average acquisition multiple of the purchase price to EBITDA is then used as a measurement to value the company in question.

Figure 17.5 shows that the average acquisition EBITDA multiples for the hotel sector is 13.19x (after the high and low multiples are taken out). Using the 13.19x multiple, Hyatt's enterprise value of $7.7 billion.

METHOD 6: USING THE DISCOUNT CASH FLOW METHOD (DCF)

This method is the most fundamental method that is used to value many types of companies, especially companies that are tough to find any trading and acquisition multiple comparables. This method, called the DCF method, that is broadly used by many investors, advisors, banks, and academics is premised on the principal that the value of a company can be derived by the present value of its projected free cash flow (FCF). We

FIGURE 17.5 HYATT HOTELS CORPORATION METHOD 5 - AVERAGE EBITDATRANDACTION MULTIPLES

CORPORATE VALUATIONS

METHOD #5 - Using Averge EBITDA Transaction Multiples (M&A Comparable Method)

	Calculations	AP	SO	AP * SO = EQ	ND	EQ + ND = EV	E	EV / E
Target	**Acquirer**	**Acquisition Price /Share**	**Shares Outstanding**	**Equity Value ($mm)**	**Total Net Debt ($mm)**	**Enterprise Value (EV)**	**EBITDA (last reported)**	**EBITDA Multiple**
Hilton Hotels	Blackstone Group	$ 47.50	390,400,000	$ 18,544	$ 6,180	$ 24,724	$ 1,680	14.72x
Four Seasons*	Kingtom Hotels Int'l / Gates' Cascade	$ 82.00	33,078,000	$ 2,712	$ 279	$ 2,991	$ 94	31.90x
Fairmont/Rafles	Kingtom Hotels Int'l	$ 45.00	73,335,000	$ 3,300	$ 124	$ 3,424	$ 187	18.29x
Hilton International	Hilton Hotels Corp.			$ 5,578	$ -	$ 5,578	$ 504	11.07x
Starwood Hotels	Host Marriott					$ 4,096	$ 315	13.00x
La-Quinta Corp	Blackstone Group	$ 12.22	203,000,000	$ 2,481	$ 926	$ 3,406	$ 230	14.83x
Wynham Int'l	Blackstone Group	$ 1.15	172,053,000	$ 198	$ 2,682	$ 2,880	$ 275	10.47x
John Q. Hammons Hotels	JQH Acquisition LLC	$ 24.00	19,583,000	$ 470	$ 765	$ 1,235	$ 123	10.04x
Societe du Louvre	Starwood Capital					$ 1,029	$ 91	11.30x
Intercontinental Hotels	LRG					$ 981	$ 107	9.20x
Boca Resorts	Blackstone Group	$ 24.00	40,284,000	$ 967	$ 217	$ 1,184	$ 90	13.15x
Prime Hospitality	Blackstone Group	$ 12.25	44,808,000	$ 549	$ 244	$ 792	$ 55	14.38x
Extended Stay	Blackstone Group	$ 19.93	95,077,000	$ 1,895	$ 1,232	$ 3,126	$ 225	13.90x
							Average	**14.33x**
Havtt's Enteprise Value	**7,718,401**			585,000	13.19x		Adjust. Outlier	**13.19x**

will learn later that this FCF is derived from various assumptions, starting from revenue and subtracting operating and capital costs.

To value the company using the DCF method the analyst needs to derive the following four items:

1. Setting up a stream of cash flows
2. Identifying an exit year
3. Calculating the value at exit year (terminal value)
4. Using the appropriate discount rate to value the present value of the firm

Stream of Cash Flows

The first requirement for valuating a privately own company is to calculate the projected equity cash flow of the company. The spreadsheet is based on certain information from the income statement, cash flow, and balance sheet. Following last chapter where we learn how to build projections, we continue to apply this projection to value the company using this method. Showed in previous chapter how the ds projections were built by starting from revenues and then subtracting cost of revenues and operating expenses to get to EBITDA. After the EBITDA is set, we subtract depreciation, amortization, and interest so we can recalculate the tax expense and then add back those items to get to a cash flow before other cash outflows including working capital expense and capital expenditures. The cash flow of the firm before debt services represents the first line of the cash outflow assuming the company is unlevered—an important line for calculating the terminal value.

The free cash flow (FCF) represents the equity cash flow after the debt service obligations, including the payments of principal and interest. Then, this stream of cash flow is used for calculating the present value of the equity and the company.

Exit Year

Once the stream of cash flows is determined, we then need to choose an exit year. To complete the DCF method, the analyst must assume that there is an exit strategy set up, so the value of the firm will include a value at the exit year even if the investor is not planning to sell the company in 4 or 5 years. This is to artificially establish a realization or return on investment. Typically, the exit year is between 4–6 years.

Terminal Value

The third item that the analyst needs to quantify is the terminal value of the firm at the exit year. This value is basically the expected enterprise value or the value that the current owner is expected to sell the company in 4–6 years. There are many methods to calculate the terminal value. The most common ones used on Wall Street are the EBITDA multiple and perpetuity growth methods. Our example for Hyatt (figure 17.6) assumes a terminal

FIGURE 17.6 HYATT HOTELS CORPORATION METHOD 6 - DISCOUNT CASH FLOW VALUATION ANALYSIS

CORPORATE VALUATIONS

METHOD #6 - Discount Cash Flow Valuation Analysis

Discout Cash Flow Valuation Analysis	Historical Assumptions	Projected Assumptions	Input Actual 12/31/2019	12/31/2020	12/31/2021	12/31/2022	12/31/2023	EXIT YEAR 12/31/2024	12/31/2025
year =				1	2	3	4	5	6
Revenues			4,763,000	4,905,890	5,249,302	5,616,753	6,009,926	6,430,621	6,945,071
Revenue Growth				3.0%	7.0%	7.0%	7.0%	7.0%	8.0%
Cost of Revenues (CoGS)	82.0%	82.0%	(3,905,660)	(4,022,830)	(4,304,428)	(4,605,738)	(4,928,139)	(5,273,109)	(5,694,958)
Operating Expenses (Excl. Non-rec.)	13.4%	13.0%	(636,340)	(637,766)	(682,409)	(730,178)	(781,290)	(835,981)	(902,859)
EBIT			221,000	245,295	262,465	280,838	300,496	321,531	347,254
Less Taxes (tax rate x of EBIT)		22.0%	-	(53,965)	(57,742)	(61,784)	(66,109)	(70,737)	(76,396)
Plus Depreciation	7.6%	7.5%	364,000	367,942	393,698	421,257	450,744	482,297	520,880
Less Working Capital	0.0%	0.0%		-	-	-	-	-	-
Less Capex	7.8%	7.5%	(369,999)	(367,942)	(393,698)	(421,257)	(450,744)	(482,297)	(520,880)
Cash Flow			215,001	191,330	204,723	219,053	234,387	250,794	270,858
EBITDA			585,000	613,236	656,163	702,094	751,241	803,828	868,134
Debt (assuming 5% reduction of intial principal per year)			1,440,000	1,368,000	1,296,000	1,224,000	1,152,000	1,080,000	1,008,000

Terminal Value	Assumptions	Growth		EXIT YEAR
EBITDA Multiple Method	15.67x		(EBITDA x EBITDA Multiple)	12,596,464
Perpetuity Method	9.86%	8.00%	Next Year's Cash Flow / (Discount Rate - Growth)	14,558,739
Average		(80% of WACC)		13,577,601
Less Debt Outstanding (at Exit)				(1,080,000)
Plus Cash (at Exit)				-
Equity Value at Terminal				12,497,601

		PV (for $1)		1	2	3	4	5
Equity Cash Flows	12.1%			191,330	204,723	219,053	234,387	12,748,396
	PV (1) =	0.8919015	$170,647					
	PV (2) =	0.7954883	$162,855					
	PV (3) =	0.7094973	$155,418					
	PV (4) =	0.6328017	$148,321					
	PV (5) =	0.5643968	$7,195,154					
	PV=		$7,832,394					

Enterprise Value =	PV of Equity + PV of Debt
PV of Equity =	$7,832,394
+ PV of Debt =	1,440,000
+ PV of Cash =	(879,000)
Hyatt's Enterprise Value	8,393,394

Cost of Equity Calc	
Risk Free Rate (5 year)	1.50%
Premium based on MC =	9.00%
Hyatt Beta =	1.18x
Expected Equity Return =	12.1%

Interest 12/19 ($ 000s)	
75,000	
5.21%	Rate

WACC Calc:		% Cap	AT RoR	WACC
Debt	1,440,000	28.0%	4.063%	1.139%
BV Equity	3,695,000	72.0%	12.120%	8.721%
		100.0%		9.860%

value using the current EBITDA multiple benchmark of 15.67x multiplied by company's exit year's EBITDA, resulting in approximately $12.6 billion. The second method to calculate the terminal value, as shown in figure 17.6, shows a terminal value of $14.6 billion. The formula of this method, using the perpetuity growth method, is done by taking next year's cash flow before debt service and dividing it by the difference of the firm's discount rate and growth rate. The discount rate used is the weighted average capital cost (WACC).

Discount Rate

The fourth item that the analyst needs to quantify after the stream of cash flow is established, the exit year is determined, and the terminal value is calculated is the discount rate. The combined amounts of the yearly future free cash flows and terminal value after the outstanding debt is subtracted in the exit year represents the expected equity cash flow, or the cash flow that the investor is projected to receive while owning the company. The present value of these cash flows is based on what the equity is expecting to return on its initial investment.

Figure 17.6 shows the calculation of the four items including the stream of cash flows, the exit year, the terminal value, and the discount rate. The average terminal value at the exit year is approximately $13.6 billion, derived by the two methods of EBITDA multiples and perpetuity. Using the 9.86% WACC as a discount rate, Hyatt's enterprise value using this method is estimated at $8.4 billion.

METHOD 7: USING THE LEVERAGED BUYOUT MODEL (LBO) METHOD

This method is very similar to method 6 (DCF method), which is based on future free cash flows except the projected debt, WACC, and expected return. While the DCF analysis is used for determining today's value of the company based on future cash flows, **the value of the company using this LBO method is determined based on investor expectation, which means return determines the acquisition price of the firm**. In other words, the analyst needs to determine first the equity expected rate of return and then back into a present value of the firm that meets that expectation. The equity investment amount is determined after assuming that most of the financing will be via debt. This method is unique because it uses the capital markets to engineer the financing of the buyout, so the equity return expectation is met via the use of leverage. This method starts step by step, starting first with the maximum debt the private equity can raise based on the target's cash flow. These steps are highlighted next, starting with the debt and equity financing to running the company's projections, including servicing this new debt to ultimately calculating the return. If the return is not met using the current market price, then the company is overvalued. If the return is more than the expectation, then the stock price will be adjusted to determine the level that it can be bought at to meet such expectation. The expected return of the investor, which is based on the projections, determines the intrinsic value per share. This is the value that the private equity is willing to pay for the company. The difference between this intrinsic value and the current trading value of the stock is called premium. This is expressed as a percentage of the current price of the stock. This premium sets the level of negotiation that the investor announces the tendering offer to acquire 100% of the stock.

Building the Transactions Sources and Uses

Building the transaction sources and uses is the first statement built when analyzing an LBO transaction.

Transaction Sources

Calculating debt capacity: Typically, in an LBO transaction the debt comprised between 60–70% of the transaction and the remaining 30–40% is equity. The most common measurement of how much debt a transaction can handle is based on the ability of the borrower to service such debt. In a traditional LBO where the borrower has relatively stable cash flow, there is an ability to raise debt up to six to seven times the company's EBITDA, though it has varied based on credit cycles. In building the LBO valuation case, the analyst needs first to calculate the maximum debt capacity in order to determine the expected equity needed to invest and complete the hypothetical leveraged buyout of the publicly traded company. Figure 17.7 shows that both the source of debt, including bank loan and corporate bonds, allowed leverage or total debt to EBITDA multiple up to 6x, or total debt made of the bank loan at 3.5x and corporate bonds at 2.5x EBITDA.

Equity makes the balance of the transaction sources: Since the debt capacity is at 6x for Hyatt, the rest of the capital that needed to be raised to cover the current trading enterprise value's equity or 11.51x.

Transaction Uses

To set-up the transaction uses, first, the analyst needs to calculate the purchase price or enterprise value by taking the current stock price, times the shares outstanding and adding the debt plus any estimated transaction expenses. The implied purchase price of the company is the enterprise value divided by the company's EBITDA represent the acquisition multiple. In figure 17.7, the acquisition cost is $10.24 billion or 17.51x last reported EBITDA multiple. The LBO model first assumes that the private equity buys Hyatt for $10.96 billion with 0% premium over the current stock.

Setting up the Debt Schedules

The debt raised for the LBO includes the amount, which is calculated based on maximum capacity; the interest rate, representing the cost of borrowing; and the scheduled amortization that is given by the banker or the corporate bond holder. These scheduled principal payments represent the contractual repayment or reduction of the outstanding debt over the life of the loan. The bank loan tends to have a set annual schedule amortization and

FIGURE 17.7 HYATT HOTELS CORPORATION METHOD 7 - LBO ANALYSIS (TRANSACTION SOURCES & USES, DEBT SCHEDULES)

CORPORATE VALUATIONS

METHOD #7 - Leveraged Buyout (LBO) Analysis

Transactions Uses	Current Stock Price	Premium	Purchase Stock Price	Shares Outstanding (millions)	Total Amount ($ 000's)	% Total Uses	EBITDA Multiple
Purchase of 100% Shares	$ 72.00	0%	$ 72.00	117,448	8,456,279	82.56%	14.46x
Refinance Short-Term & Long Term Debt					1,440,000	14.06%	2.46x
Transaxtion Fees & Expenses	3.50%				346,370	3.38%	0.59x
Total Cost of Transaction (Uses)					10,242,649	100.00%	17.51x

Transactions Sources	EBITDA Multiple (Capacity)	Interest Rate / Expected Return	After Tax Interest Rate Adjustments	WACC Calc	Total Amount ($ 000's)	% Capital
Bank Loan	3.50x	5.0%	3.90%	0.780%	2,047,500	19.99%
Corporate Bonds	2.50x	8.0%	6.24%	0.891%	1,462,500	14.28%
Total Debt	6.00x				3,510,000	34.27%
Equity	11.51x	12.1%	12.1%	7.967%	6,732,649	65.73%
Total Sources	17.51x			9.637%	10,242,649	100.00%

Cost of Equity Calc	
Risk Free Rate (5 year)	1.50%
Premium based on MC =	9.00%
Hyatt Beta =	1.18x
Expected Equity Return =	12.1%

Debt Schedule	Years	Rate	12/31/2019	LTM 12/31/2020	12/31/2021	12/31/2022	12/31/2023	12/31/2024	12/31/2025	1/1/2027	1/1/2028
Bank Loan	7	5.0%									
Outstanding			2,047,500	2,047,500	1,947,500	1,822,500	1,672,500	1,472,500	1,222,500	872,500	-
Scheduled Principal Payments (P)				-	100,000	125,000	150,000	200,000	250,000	350,000	872,500
Interest Payments (I)				102,375	102,375	97,375	91,125	83,625	73,625	61,125	43,625
Total Payments (P+I)				102,375	202,375	222,375	241,125	283,625	323,625	411,125	916,125
Corporate Bonds	10	8.0%									
Outstanding			1,462,500	1,462,500	1,462,500	1,462,500	1,462,500	1,462,500	1,462,500	1,462,500	1,462,500
Scheduled Principal Payments (P)				-	-	-	-	-	-	-	-
Interest Payments (I)				117,000	117,000	117,000	117,000	117,000	117,000	117,000	117,000
Total Payments (P+I)				117,000	117,000	117,000	117,000	117,000	117,000	117,000	117,000
Total Debt Payments				219,375	319,375	339,375	358,125	400,625	440,625	528,125	1,033,125
Total Debt Outstanding				3,510,000	3,410,000	3,285,000	3,135,000	2,935,000	2,685,000	2,335,000	1,462,500

the bonds are structured to have a balloon payment at the last year of maturity. Figure 17.7 shows the scheduled payments.

Calculating the Expected Equity Return

Typically, if the PE firm does not have a set expectation as part of its investment policy, for example the policy might say that minimum expected return is 25%, then the expected return could be measured using the capital asset pricing model (CAPM). The CAPM formula, as mentioned in method #2, is as follows:

$$\mathbf{E_r = Rf_r + \beta(M_r - Rf_r)}$$

where E_r is the expected return, Rf_r is the risk-free rate, β is the beta of the company that is analyzed, and M_r is market return.

Figure 17.7 shows that the expected return is calculated at 12.1% based on a risk-free rate of 1.5%, market return premium of 9%, and company beta of 1.18x.

Running Projections

The projections are basically the same as method 6, starting with the revenue growth rates and building the cost assumptions based on revenue. The main difference is that the projections under the LBO method use the new debt raised to buy the target company.

FIGURE 17.8 HYATT HOTELS CORPORATION METHOD 7 - LBO ANALYSIS CASH FLOW AND RETURN ANALYSIS

CORPORATE VALUATIONS

METHOD #7 - Leveraged Buyout (LBO) Analysis

			year =	1	2	3	4	5	6
Discout Cash Flow Valuation Analysis	Historical Assumptions	Projected Assumptions	Input Actual 12/31/2019	LTM 12/31/2020	12/31/2021	12/31/2022	12/31/2023	EXIT YEAR 12/31/2024	12/31/2025
Revenues			4,763,000	5,239,300	5,763,230	6,166,656	6,598,322	7,060,205	7,625,021
Revenue Growth				10.0%	10.0%	7.0%	7.0%	7.0%	8.0%
Cost of Revenues (CoGS)	82.0%	81.0%	(3,905,660)	(4,243,833)	(4,668,216)	(4,994,991)	(5,344,641)	(5,718,766)	(6,176,267)
Operating Expenses (Excl. Non-rec.)	13.4%	12.0%	(636,340)	(628,716)	(691,588)	(739,999)	(791,799)	(847,225)	(915,003)
EBIT			221,000	366,751	403,426	431,666	461,883	494,214	533,751
Less Interest				(219,375)	(219,375)	(214,375)	(208,125)	(200,625)	(190,625)
EBT			221,000	147,376	184,051	217,291	253,758	293,589	343,126
Less Taxes (tax rate x of EBIT)		22.0%	-	(32,423)	(40,491)	(47,804)	(55,827)	(64,590)	(75,488)
Net Income			221,000	114,953	143,560	169,487	197,931	229,000	267,639
Plus Depreciation	7.6%	7.5%	364,000	392,948	432,242	462,499	494,874	529,515	571,877
Plus Amortization		7 Years		49,481	49,481	49,481	49,481	148,444	
Less Working Capital	0.0%	0.0%		-	-	-	-	-	-
Less Capex	7.8%	7.0%	(369,999)	(366,751)	(403,426)	(431,666)	(461,883)	(494,214)	(533,751)
Cash Flow Before Principal Payment			**215,001**	**190,631**	**221,857**	**249,802**	**280,404**	**412,745**	**305,764**
Debt Principal Payment				-	(100,000)	(125,000)	(150,000)	(200,000)	(250,000)
Equity Cash Flows			215,001	190,631	121,857	124,802	130,404	212,745	55,764
EBITDA			**585,000**	**759,699**	**835,668**	**894,165**	**956,757**	**1,023,730**	**1,105,628**
Debt			**1,440,000**	**3,510,000**	**3,410,000**	**3,285,000**	**3,135,000**	**2,935,000**	**2,685,000**
Terminal Value	**Assumptions**		**Growth**						
EBITDA Multiple Method	15.67x			(EBITDA x EBITDA Multiple)				16,042,461	
Perpetuity Method	9.64%		8.00%	Next Year's Cash Flow / (Discount Rate - Growth)				18,675,462	
Average								17,358,961	
Less Debt Outstanding (at Exit)								(2,935,000)	
Plus Cash (at Exit)								-	
Equity Value at Terminal								14,423,961	
		PV (for $1)							
Equity Cash Flows	**12.1%**			**190,631**	**121,857**	**124,802**	**130,404**	**14,636,706**	
	PV (1) =	**0.8919015**	**$170,024**						
	PV (2) =	**0.7954883**	**$96,936**						
	PV (3) =	**0.7094973**	**$88,546**						
	PV (4) =	**0.6328017**	**$82,520**						
	PV (5) =	**0.5643968**	**$8,260,910**						
	PV=		**$8,698,937**						
	Enterprise Value =		**PV of Equity + PV of Debt**						
	PV of Equity =		**$8,698,937**						
	+ PV of Debt =		**1,440,000**						
	+ PV of Cash =		**(879,000)**						
Hyatt's Enterprise Value			**9,259,937**						

In figure 17.8 the stream of free cash flows is calculated based on revenue growth of approximately 10% per year, and the costs are set flat as percentage of revenue. The debt service, including the interest and principal payment, are then laid (see figure 17.7) to determine the final free cash flows. Sometimes, the private equity firm that is interested in buying the target company might run its own set of projections based on its equity plan, which could include cost savings or revenue enhancements.

Determining the Terminal Value

The terminal value is derived similarly to method 6: using two methods including the EBITDA trading method and perpetuity method. In figure 17.8, the EBITDA multiple used is 15.67x (as determined by method 4, average pier multiple). The perpetuity method for determining the terminal value uses a 9.64% WACC and 8.0% growth rate.

Determining the Value of the Firm

Since the equity return expectation is set, the future cash flows are then present valued back using the minimum equity return. In figure 17.8 the minimum equity return is 12.1%.

FIGURE 17.9 HYATT HOTELS CORPORATION ENTEPRISE VALUATION ANALYSIS—SUMMARY

CORPORATE VALUATIONS

ENTERPRISE VALUATION ANALYSIS	EV	Debt	Cash	Eq Value	Shares Outs	Stock Price
Book Value Equity	4,256,000	1,440,000	879,000	3,695,000	117,448	$ 31.46
METHOD #1 - Market Value / Using the Stock Price	9,017,279	1,440,000	879,000	8,456,279	117,448	$ 72.00
METHOD #2- Intrinsic Value	10,177,265	1,440,000	879,000	9,616,265	117,448	$ 81.88
METHOD #3- Dividend Discount Model (DDM)	11,530,230	1,440,000	879,000	10,969,230	117,448	$ 93.40
METHOD #4 -Average EBITDA Industry Trading Multiples	9,167,303	1,440,000	879,000	8,606,303	117,448	$ 73.28
METHOD #5 - Using Averge EBITDA Transaction Multiples	7,718,401	1,440,000	879,000	7,157,401	117,448	$ 60.94
METHOD #6 - Discount Cash Flow Valuation Analysis	8,393,394	1,440,000	879,000	7,832,394	117,448	$ 66.69
METHOD #7 - LBO Analysis	9,259,937	1,440,000	879,000	8,698,937	117,448	$ 74.07
Average of other methods	**9,333,979**	**1,440,000**	**879,000**	**8,772,979**		**$ 69.21**

Using 12.1% as the discount rate on the future free cash flow and terminal value, the value of Hyatt is estimated at $9.3 billion.

Putting All the Values Together

Taking all the enterprise values for methods 1–7 and calculating the per share price will give the analyst a range of the value per share to compare to the current market price and book value price. Figure 17.9 shows that method 4 and methods 6 and 7 (intrinsic values) calculates stock price which is higher than the currently traded price of $72.00. This will result to a "BUY" recommendation if these are the only methods used.

METHODS 6–7: VALUATION OF PRIVATE COMPANIES

For valuating private companies, the analyst uses various methods that are similar to valuations used for publicly traded companies. Methods 4 and 5 of valuing the company based on EBITDA multiples of comparable publicly traded companies and companies that have been acquired are very common methods. These methods can be found in the offering memorandum or prospectus of an IPO where the investment bank gives an opinion to what the value of the private to public company should be based on other comparable companies. The most effective methods for valuing a private company, though, is finding the intrinsic value by using the methods 6 and 7. These methods are both based on the company's future cash flow. Method 6, the discount cash flow method, and method 7, the leveraged buyout (LBO) method, are described next.

Method 6: Discount Cash Flow Method for Private Companies

One of the most effective ways to value a private company is to dive into the company's projections and change the assumptions based on the investor's view of how the revenue will grow and at what cost. Since there is no stock price that trades, which gives the investor a direct indication of what the company is worth (market value), an important method used by professionals is the discount cash flow (DCF) method, which measures the company's intrinsic value. This method that is broadly used by investors, advisors, banks, and academics is premised on the principal that the value of a company can be derived by the present value of its projected cash flow. The conduction of this method, as it was discussed earlier in the chapter, is to calculate the first the equity cash flows, identify the exit year, estimate the terminal value in the exit year, and use the expected equity return as the discount rate.

Figure 17.10 shows the valuation of the Celerity Technology is approximately $3 billion or 7x current EBITDA based on projections found in chapter 16. The cash flows were built on the base case projections, including a modest growth and flat operating costs as percentage of revenues and other expenses including working capital and capital expenditures. The terminal value is calculated based on two methods: using 7.5x EBITDA multiple and using the perpetuity method (next year's cash flow/(discount rate − growth)). The discount rate used is 10% and growth is 5%; these are basic rule-of-thumb levels, but a more comprehensive approach will include a discount rate as the weighted average cost of capital (WACC) and historical growth rate.

FIGURE 17.10 CELERITY TECHNOLOGY INC. DISCOUNT CASH FLOW METHOD

Celerity Technogy Inc. ("CTI")
Discount Cash Flow Valuation Method (000's)

			PROJECTED				
						EXIT YEAR	
	Year -1	Year 0	Year 1	Year 2	Year 3	Year 4	Year 5
Revenues	960,000	1,110,000	1,228,140	1,344,200	1,442,919	1,529,268	1,605,161
Cost of Revenues	(345,000)	(420,000)	(463,078)	(506,823)	(544,053)	(576,709)	(605,474)
Operating Expenses	(230,000)	(257,000)	(271,501)	(289,448)	(306,442)	(322,900)	(338,999)
EBITDA	**385,000**	**433,000**	**493,561**	**547,928**	**592,424**	**629,659**	**660,688**
Less Depreciation & Amortization	(60,000)	(65,000)	(73,688)	(80,652)	(86,575)	(91,756)	(96,310)
EBIT	325,000	368,000	**419,872**	**467,276**	**505,849**	**537,902**	**564,378**
Less Taxes			(129,769)	(147,070)	(156,960)	(158,461)	(162,851)
EAT			**290,103**	**320,206**	**348,889**	**379,441**	**401,527**
Plus Depreciation & Amortization			73,688	80,652	86,575	91,756	96,310
Less Working Capital			2,870	(4,548)	(3,869)	(3,384)	(2,974)
Less Capital Expenditures and Investments			(193,626)	(211,923)	(227,487)	(241,101)	(253,066)
Cash Before Financing Payments			**173,036**	**184,386**	**204,109**	**226,713**	**241,796**
Less Debt Service (Principal + Interest)			(125,450)	(129,600)	(153,450)	(201,750)	(237,250)
Free Cash Flow			**47,586**	**54,786**	**50,659**	**24,963**	**4,546**
TERMINAL VALUE (TV)		TV Assumptions					
Terminal Value using EBITDA Multiple Method		EBITDA Multiple = **7.5x**				4,722,439	
Terminal Value using Perpetuity Method		Discount Rate = **10%**				4,835,926	
Average Terminal Value		Growth = **5%**				4,779,182	
Less Debt						(1,030,000)	
Equity Value at Exit Year						3,749,182	
Equity Cash Flows		Equity Expected Return = **20%**	47,586	54,786	50,659	3,774,145	
Present Value of Equity		1,927,111	39,655	38,046	29,316	1,820,093	
Plus Debt		1,190,000					
Less Cash		(65,800)					
Firm Enterprise value		**3,051,311**					
Enteprise Value / EBITDA		7.0x					

Method 7: Leveraged Buyout (LBO) Method for Private Companies

Similar to valuing a publicly traded company where the valuation analysis starts from what the investor is willing to pay to acquire the company, privately owned companies can be valued using this method as well. The equity expectation or rate of return is estimated based on the company's business, determining the risk premium the investor is seeking. For example, buying a technology company might require higher expected return as compared to a manufacturing company. The stability of cash flow should dictate the equity return expectation. The rate of return is also determined based on the acquisition structure—how much debt the business can finance. Debt capacity is typically derived as a multiple of current EBITDA. The new debt level and its debt service laid in the company's projections is the first step to determine the valuation of the company.

In figure 17.11 it shows that the valuation for Celerity Technology, using the LBO valuation method, is approximately \$4 billion or 10x EBITDA. In this case the private equity expects 25% return on its investment after the debt capacity is in bedded in the capital structure; at this time the debt is structured at 6.0x EBITDA.

METHODS 8: VALUATION OF DISTRESS FIRMS

Out of the traditional methods 1–7, the DCF analysis is the one that can be closely related to method 8. The DCF valuation is based on the present value of the future cash flows at a pre-determined discount rate that will provide an estimate of the value of the equity or the firm. Method 8 is unique because it uses an option pricing model such the Black-Scholes to value the equity for a company that is currently in distress or bankruptcy. Of course, the equity value in a company that is in bankruptcy is expected to be close to zero or negative as the liabilities reported are higher than the assets of the company. The option pricing theory values the present value of the equity and enterprise based on future cash flows post-bankruptcy.

Option Pricing Model Framework

In option pricing and specifically in call options the payoff formula or intrinsic value of the option is

$$\textbf{Option payoff} = \text{Max}(0, S - X)$$

where S is the stock price and X is the exercise price.

To calculate the enterprise value

$$EV = E + D - C \text{ or } EV = E + \text{net } D$$

where EV is the enterprise value of the firm, E is the equity value, D is the debt and C is cash. The net D is referred to as debt minus cash implied that the current debt could be paid with cash on hand.

FIGURE 17.11 CELERITY TECHNOLOGY INC. LBO METHOD

Celerity Technogy Inc. ("CTI")
LBO Method (000's)

TRANSACTION SOURCES & USES

Sources	Capacity EBITDA x	Amount	% Capital	Inter. / Exp. Ret.	WACC	Uses		Purchase EBITDA Multiple	Amount
Bank Loan	3.5x	1,515,500	35.6%	5.0%	1.1%	Purchase Enteprise Value		9.5x	4,113,500
Corporate Bonds	2.5x	1,082,500	25.4%	8.0%	1.3%	Fees (% EV)	3.50%		143,973
Total Debt	6.0x	2,598,000	61.0%		2.4%				
Equity		1,659,473	39.0%	25.0%	9.7%				
Total Sources		4,257,473	100.0%		**12.2%**				4,257,473

Tax Rate = 36%

DEBT SCHEDULES	Years	Interest	Year 0	Year 1	Year 2	Year 3	EXIT YEAR Year 4	Year 5
Bank Loal - Outstanding	5	5.0%	1,515,500	1,515,500	1,515,500	1,515,500	1,515,500	-
Bank Loan - Principal Incr./Decr.				-	-	-	-	1,515,500
Bank Loan - Interst Payment				75,775	75,775	75,775	75,775	75,775
Bank Loan - Total Payment				75,775	75,775	75,775	75,775	1,591,275
Bonds - Outstanding	10	8.0%	1,082,500	1,082,500	1,082,500	1,082,500	1,082,500	1,082,500
Bonds - Principal Incr./Decr.				-	-	-	-	-
Bonds - Interst Payment				86,600	86,600	86,600	86,600	86,600
Bonds - Total Payment				86,600	86,600	86,600	86,600	86,600
Total Debt Payments				162,375	162,375	162,375	162,375	1,677,875
Total Debt Outstanding			2,598,000	2,598,000	2,598,000	2,598,000	2,598,000	1,082,500

CASH FLOW PROJECTIONS	Year -1	Year 0	Year 1	Year 2	Year 3	EXIT YEAR Year 4	Year 5
Revenues	960,000	1,110,000	1,228,140	1,344,200	1,442,919	1,529,268	1,605,161
Cost of Revenues	(345,000)	(420,000)	(463,078)	(506,823)	(544,053)	(576,709)	(605,474)
Operating Expenses	(230,000)	(257,000)	(271,501)	(289,448)	(306,442)	(322,900)	(338,999)
EBITDA	**385,000**	**433,000**	**493,561**	**547,928**	**592,424**	**629,659**	**660,688**
Less Depreciation	(60,000)	(65,000)	(73,688)	(80,652)	(86,575)	(91,756)	(96,310)
Less Amortization			(28,795)	(28,795)	(28,795)	(57,589)	
EBIT	325,000	368,000	**391,078**	**438,482**	**477,055**	**480,313**	**564,378**
Less Taxes			(140,788)	(157,853)	(171,740)	(172,913)	(203,176)
EAT			**250,290**	**280,628**	**305,315**	**307,401**	**361,202**
Plus Depreciation & Amortization			102,483	109,446	115,370	149,345	96,310
Less Working Capital			2,870	(4,548)	(3,869)	(3,384)	(2,974)
Less Capital Expenditures and Investments			(193,626)	(211,923)	(227,487)	(241,101)	(253,066)
Cash Before Financing Payments			**162,017**	**173,603**	**189,329**	**212,261**	**201,471**
Less Debt Service (Principal + Interest)			(162,375)	(162,375)	(162,375)	(162,375)	(1,677,875)
Free Cash Flow			**(358)**	**11,228**	**26,954**	**49,886**	**(1,476,404)**

TERMINAL VALUE (TV)	TV Assumptions		Year 1	Year 2	Year 3	Year 4	Year 5
Terminal Value using EBITDA Multiple Method	EBITDA Multiple =	**9.5x**				5,981,756	
Terminal Value using Perpetuity Method	Discount Rate =	**12.2%**				9,219,164	
Average Terminal Value	Growth =	**10.0%**				7,600,460	
Less Debt						(2,598,000)	
Equity Value at Exit Year						5,002,460	
	IRR=	**32%**					
Equity Cash Flows	Equity Expected Return =	(1,659,473)	(358)	11,228	26,954	5,052,346	
Present Value of Equity	2,090,141	**25%**	(286)	7,186	13,800	2,069,441	
Plus Debt	2,598,000						
Less Cash	-						
Firm Enterprise value	**4,688,141**						
Enteprise Value / EBITDA	10.8x						

Solving for equity:

$$E = EV - \text{net } D$$

where E is the equity, EV is the enterprise value and net D is the net debt.

The equity in a firm is the residual value after the company defaults. That is, the equity is at the bottom of the waterfall from any proceeds from selling the firm. These proceeds are used to pay the debt and other financial claims first, and anything that is left over goes toward the equity. Payoff to equity on liquidation is the value minus the debt.

The Black-Scholes formula is

$$C \text{ option payoff} = Se^{-\delta.t}.N(d1) - Xe^{-i.t}.N(d2)$$

where S is the stock price, δ is the dividend yield, t is time until expiration, X is the option exercise price, i is the risk-free interest rate, and N is the normal distribution.

$$d1 = \frac{\left[\ln\left(\frac{S}{X}\right) + \left(i - \delta + \frac{\sigma^2}{2}\right).t\right]}{\sigma\sqrt{t}} \text{ and } d2 = d1 - \sigma\sqrt{t}$$

where S is the current stock price, X is the contractual exercise price, i is the risk-free interest rate, δ is the dividend yield, σ is the standard deviation, and t is time to expiration.

Putting It All Together

To calculate the present value of the equity or the firm during distress where the current equity most likely is out of the money, that is the debt is higher than the enterprise value or in option terms the $S - X < 0$, the analyst can use the Black-Scholes model to determine the present value based on future cash flows post-debt restructuring or bankruptcy.

The equity can be viewed as a call option (C) premium, the debt and other financial claims can be viewed as the exercise price (X), and the enterprise value can be viewed as the current stock price (S). Since the debt of the firm has a maturity date, the equity investors can liquidate the firm at a time prior to the maturity, similar to exercising the option any time before the option expires.

For example, let us assume that the assets of the firm are valued at $1 billion and that the standard deviation of this asset is 20%. Also assume that the book value or face value of the 5-year debt is $1,200 million. If the 5-year risk-free bond rate is 3%, how much is the equity worth? In applying the Black-Scholes option pricing model the answer is as follows:

Input:

S = Value of the firm = $1 billion
X = Exercise price = debt value = $1,200 million
σ = Standard deviation of the asset = 20%
t = Time = term of the bond = 5 years
i = Risk-free rate = 3%
δ = Dividends = cash flow paying the equity = $0
C = Equity value = E = ?

Formulas and output:

Using the formula to determine the deviations d1 and d2:

$$d1 = \frac{\left[\ln\left(\frac{S}{X}\right) + \left(i - \delta + \frac{\sigma^2}{2}\right).t\right]}{\sigma\sqrt{t}} \text{ and } d2 = d1 - \sigma\sqrt{t}$$

$d1 = .7671$ **and** $N(d1) = .7785$

$d2 = .5678$ **and** $N(d2) = .7149$

Using the Black-Sholes formula:

$$C = Se^{-\delta.t}.N(d1) - Xe^{-i.t}.N(d2)$$

$$C = \$152.0 \ million$$

Despite that the value of the current equity is negative $200 million (asset of $1,000 million – debt $1,2000 million), indicating that is out of the money, the value of equity until maturity on a present value basis is $152 million. Subtracting the $152 million equity value from the $1,000 million asset value results in $848 million of current debt value.

Therefore, the interest rate of the debt is $\left(\frac{\$1200}{\$848}\right)^{\frac{1}{5}} - 1 = 0.0719 \ or \ 7.19\%$

CASE STUDY

VALUING A DISTRESS COMPANY: AB AIR COMPANY

Case Study 17.1 shows a real-life example of SB Air Co. (changed the name and figures to protect the private information), an airline company that entered bankruptcy in 1990. At the time of the filing, the debt outstanding, representing the exercise price X, was at $600 million with a remaining life or duration of 5 years. To establish the value of equity, the enterprise value needs to be calculated. The management put together a business plan including 5 years of projections. In the first year, the company is planning to spend more money, representing restructuring costs and downsizing. Based on the 5 years' projection, the equity analyst could calculate the present value of the future cash flows, an estimated terminal value, and an assumed discount rate using the weighted average cost of capital of 10.5%.

The DCF analysis yields an enterprise value or the value of S of $934 million. Obviously with S = $934 million and X = $600 million the equity is in the money. Using the Black-Scholes option pricing model the equity or the call option C is calculated at $575 million after taking into consideration the combined variance for both debt and equity using the following formula:

$$\sigma sb^2 = Ws^2.\sigma s^2 + Wb^2.\sigma b^2 + 2(Ws.Wb.\sigma s.\sigma b).\rho$$

where σsb^2 is the combined variance of bonds and stocks, Ws is the percentage of stocks to total capitalization, σs^2 is the stock price variance prior to bankruptcy, Wb is the bond outstanding as percentage of total capitalization, σb^2 is the bond price variance prior to bankruptcy, and ρ is the correlation between the stock and bond prices.

VALUING A START-UP COMPANY: PHARMA INC.

Synopsis: Pharma Inc., a biotech firm, has a patent on a drug to treat multiple sclerosis for the next 17 years, and it plans to produce and sell the drug by itself. The drug will be priced at $46.50 per patient per day, with each patient taking it for an average of 2 years. After extensive market research, it was determined that 100,000 patients will be buying this drug immediately. The total cost of development for commercial use is estimated at $2.75 billion. Patent life is 17 years. The 17-year treasury bond rate is 3.5%. Variance in expected present values = 0.224 based on industry average firm variance for bio-tech firms.

CASE STUDY 17.1 CASE STUDY: SB AIR CO. METHOD 8

File for Bankruptcy 1990

DEBT ASSUMPTIONS		**VALUE ASSUMPTIONS (Pre-bankrupcy)**	
Debt Outstanding =	600	Stock Montly Var. (1985 - 1990) =	3.15%
Weighted Average Duration=	5 years	Bonds Monthly Var. (1985 - 1990) =	2.16%
Weighted Average maturity=	8.7 years	Correlation between Stock/Bond	0.25
WACC=	10.0%	Debt proportion (1987 - 1991) =	88.30%
Tax Rate =	36.0%		

Discount Cash Flow Analysis ($ millions)		**1991**	**1992**	**1993**	**1994**	**1995**
Revenue		1,250.0	1,137.5	1,114.8	1,159.3	1,205.7
CoGS		(980.0)	(810.0)	(668.0)	(695.6)	(723.4)
Oper. Exp.		(720.0)	(210.0)	(205.8)	(214.0)	(222.6)
EBIT		**(450.0)**	**117.5**	**241.0**	**249.7**	**259.7**
EBIT (t)		**(162.0)**	**42.3**	**86.8**	**89.9**	**93.5**
EBIT (i-t)		**(288.0)**	**75.2**	**154.2**	**159.8**	**166.2**
Less Maintenance Capex (offset by Depreciation)		-	-	-	-	-
Less W/C (assumiung $0)		-	-	-	-	-
Cash Flow		(288.0)	75.2	154.2	159.8	166.2
Terminal Value assumption	5.0x EBIT					1,298.5
EV (PV) of the firm	**$934.8**	**(288.0)**	**75.2**	**154.2**	**159.8**	**1,464.7**

Step 1 - Find the annualized in stock and bond prices:

Annualized Variance in Stock Price σ^2 =	0.37812 (annual)	St. Dev.=	0.61491463
Annualized Variance in Bond Price σ^2 =	0.2592 (annual)	St. Dev.=	0.50911688

Step 2 - Find the annualized variance in firm value

(we^2 x σe^2) + (wb^2 x σb^2) + 2. (we x wd x ped x σe x σd). C

We=	11.70%	C=	0.25
Wd=	88.30%		

Annualized Variance in firm value 0.2113143

The five-year bond rate (corresponding to the weighted average duration of 5.1 years) is 6.0%

Stet 3 - Find the value of call based upon the following parameters of equity as a call option

Value of the underlying asset = S = Value of the firm =	$934.8
Exercise Price = X = Face Value of outstanding debt =	$600.0
Life of the option = t = Weighted average duration of debt=	5 years
Variance in the value of the underlying asset = σ^2 =	0.21131434
Riskless Rate = I = T-Bond for option life =	6.00%

d1= 1.2372098	N (d1) = 0.8919954
d2= 0.2093131	N (d2) = 0.58289807

Value of the call (Equity) = 574.53638

Setting Up the Input Variables

INPUT	PROCESS
Value of the Underlined Asset (S)	PV of Cash Flows expected from the commercialization of the IP
Exercise Price on Option (X)	Cost of Development of the IP
Variance in Value of Underlined Asset (σ^2)	Variance in Cash Flows of similar assets on firm (i.e. the stock price of other companies with similar applications) or Variance in present value from capital budgeting simulation
Expiration of the Option (t)	Life of the IP patent
Dividend Yield (δ)	Cost of Delay - each year of delay translates to one less year of value-creating cash flows 1/t

CASE STUDY 17.2 PHARMA INC.

Using Black-Scholes Option Pricing Model

Number of Patients=	100,000	
Drug Price (per pill) - net of cost of producing =	$46.50	
Daily Use =	365	Days
Average Length for Usage =	2	Years
Present Value of =	$3,394,500,000	
Total Development Cost (X) =	$2,750,000,000	
IP Patent life (t)=	17	years
Cost of Delay (δ)=	5.882%	1/17 years
Risk Free Rate (i) =	4%	
Variance =	0.224	

USING BLACK-SCHOLES OPTION MODEL

INPUT		OUTPUT	
Standard Deviation (σ) =	47.33%	d1 =	0.8761
Expiration (in years) (T) =	17	d2 =	-1.0753
Risk-Free Rate (Annual) (i) =	4%	N(d1) =	0.8095
Stock Price (S) =	3,394,500,000	N(d2) =	0.1411
Exercise Price (X) =	2,750,000,000		
Dividend Yield (annual) (δ) =	5.882%	**Value=**	**796,844,462**

PROBLEMS

1. ZIP Apparel Company's stock is trading at $25 per share. The last reported total debt and cash was $150 million and $25 million, respectively. With 10 million outstanding shares, what is the enterprise value of the company?
2. Use the information below to answer problems 2a. and 2b.

Trading EBITDA Multiple =	10.00x	
Shares Outstanding =	110.00	million
Book Equity =	$1,000.00	million
Short-Term Bank Debt =	$100.00	million
Long-Term Bank Debt =	$1,150.00	million
Corporate Bonds Debt =	$250.00	million
Accounts Payable =	$50.00	million
Total Liabilities =	$1,900.00	million
Total Assets =	$2,900.00	million
Cash =	$100.00	million
EBIT =	$300.00	million
Depreciation & Amortization	$50.00	million

   a. Calculate the current stock price.
   b. Assuming the stock price is $25, what is the enterprise value?
3. Calculate the stock price given the following information:

Risk Free Rate =	2.50%	
Market Rate of Return =	10.50%	
Beta =	2.00x	
Shares Outstanding =	110.00	million

(MILLIONS $)	YEAR 1	YEAR 2	EXIT YEAR 3
Equity FCF	250.0	275.0	302.5
Firm Terminal Value			3,000.0
Debt			700.0

4. Use finance.yahoo.com to choose any publicly traded company. Download that company's 3-year financial statements and information needed to value the company using Methods 1 to 6.
5. Consider a FinTech SaaS based start-up company with an estimated subscription market opportunity of 10 million subscribers who are willing to sign up and pay $20 per month the first year. For the first year, the cost of revenue is estimated at $3 per subscriber and operating expenses, including marketing, is estimated at $2 per subscriber.

The following assumptions are for Year 2 through 10:

ASSUMPTIONS	YEARS 2-10
Monthly Subscription Price Increase per Year	5.0%
Number of Subscribers Increase per Year	2.0%
Monthly Cost of Revenue per Subscriber Increase per Year	3.0%
Monthly Operating Cost per Subscriber Increase per Year	5.0%
No Tax Assumed	
Brand Terminal Value (Year 10)—multiple of EBIT (x)	0x
IP Expected Return	25%

IP Assumptions

The present value of the development cost is initially estimated at $400 per subscription (cost per customer acquisition). The firm has the IP patent to exploit for the next 10 years.

The 10-year riskless rate is 3.0%, and the variance is 0.05, based on the stock variance of similar companies' stock price.

Given this information above, calculate the value of the IP patent using the Black-Scholes pricing method (Method #8).

ONLINE TEMPLATES

The Excel spreadsheets used in the chapter can be accessed online via Cognella Active Learning platform.

CHAPTER 18

Credit Risk Analysis and Debt-Capacity Analysis

This chapter will cover various methods that a credit analyst uses to measure the ability of the company to pay back its debt applications.

LEARNING OBJECTIVES

After reading this chapter, students will be able to do the following:

- Forecast the major value drivers that impact and could affect the company's future performance
- Understand ways to measure the ability of a company to repay its debt obligations
- Determine the appropriate financing structure based on debt capacity and propose solutions consistent with risk/reward strategy
- Understanding the five ways to assess the credit worthiness of the company
- Understand and analyze different options when the company files for bankruptcy
- Understand the rating agencies' rating scale of default and rate of recoveries
- Know other types of models that calculate the probability of defaults and rate of recoveries

CREDIT ANALYSIS OVERVIEW

The chapter follows on from previous chapters on understanding and analyzing financial statements. This works as the basis for analyzing the company that is planning to borrow. The chapter will cover in detail of how a credit analyst goes about running a risk analysis by using various methodologies. The three main areas that the chapter will go over are the following:

1. Review of financial statements and application of credit-related ratios
2. Debt capacity analysis
3. Risk and credit restructure analysis

AUTHOR'S NOTES

One of my favorite jokes that I heard many years ago goes like this: John was looking out of his window watching this government construction worker. He came every morning, exactly at 8:00 a.m., dug a big hole manually with his shovel, and left approximately at 9:00 a.m. Then around 11:00 a.m. another worker came and closed the hole with a spading fork and left around 11:30 a.m. This went on for many days. The first worker dug the hole and few hours later another worker covered the hole. John was very curious as to what's going on. It looked like each of them, for sure, were working very hard, but they weren't achieving anything meaningful. After the fourth day, John stormed out his house, went across the street, and asked the first worker: "Excuse me sir. Sorry to bother you. What's going on here? You are digging the hole and another guy comes in and covers the hole." The worker looked at John and said, "Well, my job is to dig a hole and the other guy's job is cover the hole. If the guy between us never showed up at 9:30 to plant the tree is not our fault." Lessons learn out of this funny story is that the ultimate purpose of the work done is about planting trees. Even though both workers worked extremely hard, the work was not getting done without the third person. It is the same with the credit risk analysis. Unlike the valuation methods, discussed in the previous chapter, where each method gives a different perspective in determining the value of the company, all methods used for assessing credit risk depend on each other. For example, even if the company shows strong income, the credit analyst needs to also see the strength of its cash flow before lending money to the company; both methods are needed and dependent on each other to make the right assessment, which is to determine the likelihood of the company to pay back its debt obligations.

KEY TAKEAWAYS

- There are three parties involved in the analysis of credit: borrower or issuer, lender or investor, and market.
- The difference between a credit analysis and a financial analysis is that the credit analysis is based on the likelihood of default and the expected loss if default occurs where the financial analysis is based on the expected return over the risk-free rate or measuring the risk premium.
- The credit analyst is trying first to establish a primary source of repayment such as cash and then is trying to measure the secondary source of repayment such as selling assets to recover the debt.
- Know the five Cs in completing the credit analysis: conditions, collateral, character, capacity, and capital.
- Availability of debt is based on market conditions, sometimes referred to as credit cycles or leveraged cycles. The availability is based on money supply, credit crunch where banks become very cautious in lending, and the cost of the debt that can be volatile through the cycles.
- The three independent rating agencies, Standards & Poor's, Moody's, and Fitch rate both the loans and the bonds with the intention to measure the risk of credit loss. It's important to know that these rating agencies do not intend to measure market risk or the prices of these debt facilities as they trade in the secondary market.
- For a credit analyst the most important performance measurement is cash flow, not income. This is because cash flow ultimately repays the debt.

REVIEW OF FINANCIAL STATEMENTS AND APPLICATION OF CREDIT-RELATED RATIOS

As discussed earlier, all three financial statements including the **income, balance sheet, and cash flow statements serve as the basis for assessment of both financial, equity, and credit risk analysis.** Each analyst prioritizes and focuses on different sections of these statements because his or her objectives vary. The objectives for the credit risk analysis are as follows:

- Use the various ratio analysis methods to measure how well the company manages its debt (solvency ratios), how well it manages its cash (liquidity ratios) and how profitable it is and how it will fair in economic turmoil (profitability ratios) once we run various stress case scenarios.

- Use the specific ratio analysis methods to capture asset efficiency and collateral coverage.
- Use the ratio analysis to structure the debt capacity of any company including the appropriate starting leverage and ongoing coverage of the company's contractual debt obligations.
- Build in warning signal ratios of deterioration such as the Altman Z-score credit parameter.
- Use customized ratios based on industry drivers to measure revenue growth and cost structures and change those to sensitize the company's performance during economic cycles or commodity price fluctuations.

Usefulness of Ratio Analysis

To complete the full credit risk assessment of a company, the analyst should compare ratio results:

1. With past results to establish how well they are trending
2. With the company's peers to establish how well they are performing versus the bench mark
3. With the company's budget to establish management credibility of meeting its business plan

Five Areas Where the Risk-Credit Analysis Should Focus

A lot of the commercial banks and institutions that lend money to corporations, as well as credit agencies, focus on the following five areas of analysis:

1. **Loan-to-value or debt capitalization ratio**: This ratio, expressed as a percentage, is the debt amount raised over the total capital or the amount over the total value of the asset or business that is purchased. One of the areas of the credit analysis is to assess the debt's position in capital structure in relationship to other capital raised. Figure 18.1 shows that the debt capitalization ratio starts at 35.4%, meeting Standard & Poor's BB- benchmark of 60%.
2. **Leverage ratio of debt to EBITDA:** This solvency-type ratio, well known as the leverage ratio, is one of the most popular ratios to analyze the credit of a company. Even a few government agencies, such as the board of governors of the Federal Reserve System (the "Fed Reserve"), the Federal Deposit Insurance Corporation (FDIC), and the Office of the Comptroller of the Currency (OCC), use this ratio to give guidance to banks to how much debt they should be advancing to companies in a new transaction, such as a leveraged buyout. In March 2013, four years after

FIGURE 18.1 CELERITY TECHNOLLOGY INC. CREDIT RISK ANALYSIS

Celerity Technogy Inc. ("CTI")
Credit Risk Analysis

	HISTORICAL		PROJECTED				
BASE CASE	**Year -1**	**Year 0**	**Year 1**	**Year 2**	**Year 3**	**Year 4**	**Year 5**
Revenues	960,000	1,110,000	1,228,140	1,344,200	1,442,919	1,529,268	1,605,161
Revenue Growth		15.6%	10.6%	9.5%	7.3%	6.0%	5.0%
EBITDA	385,000	433,000	493,561	547,928	592,424	629,659	660,688
EBITDA Margin							
Interest Expense			95,450	99,600	113,450	141,750	157,250
Tax Expense			129,769	147,070	156,960	158,461	162,851
Working Capital			(2,870)	4,548	3,869	3,384	2,974
Capex			138,304	151,374	162,491	172,215	180,761
Cash on Balance Sheet	45,000	65,800	118,577	179,246	236,183	267,484	278,544
Total Debt	1,220,000	1,190,000	1,160,000	1,130,000	1,090,000	1,030,000	950,000
Equity Ownerhip	1,746,000	1,919,800	2,114,453	2,335,059	2,570,498	2,808,190	3,052,467
Credit Risk Analysis							
1. Debt Capitalization			35.4%	32.6%	29.8%	26.8%	23.7%
2. Leverage Ratio : Total Debt / EBITDA			2.4x	2.1x	1.8x	1.6x	1.4x
3. Interest Ratio: EBITDA / Interest			5.2x	5.5x	5.2x	4.4x	4.2x
4. 30% EBITDA Haircut:	Haircut						
Total Debt / EBITDA (Leveraged Ratio)	30.0%		3.4x	2.9x	2.6x	2.3x	2.1x
EBITDA / Interest (Coverage Ratio)	30.0%		3.6x	3.9x	3.7x	3.1x	2.9x
Bench Mark (Target S&P BB- or higher):							
Debt Capitalization			60.0%	60.0%	60.0%	60.0%	60.0%
Total Debt / EBITDA (Leveraged Ratio)			4.0x	4.0x	4.0x	4.0x	4.0x
EBITDA / Interest (Coverage Ratio)			3.0x	3.0x	3.0x	3.0x	3.0x
5. Industry Designation (Industry Beta Sensitivity - needs to be less than 3x)							
Technology			2.5x	2.5x	2.5x	2.5x	2.5x
Credit Risk Benchmark			3.0x	3.0x	3.0x	3.0x	3.0x

the financial crisis of 2008–2009, these government agencies sent a letter to all the commercial banks with a subject "*Interagency Guidance of Leveraged Lending*" (2013). Page 7 of the letter states the following: "Credit agreement covenant protections, including financial performance (such as debt-to cash flow, interest coverage, or fixed charge coverage), reporting requirements, and compliance monitoring. Generally, a leverage level after planned asset sales (that is, the amount of debt that must be serviced from operating cash flow) in excess of 6X Total Debt/EBITDA raises concerns for most industries."

This ratio is also used by analysts to derive debt capacity, and it's incorporated in a lot of the credit agreements as a covenant ratio to measure ongoing performance of the borrower versus its projections. Figure 18.1 shows that the leverage ratio starts at 2.4x, meeting Standard & Poor's BB- benchmark of 4x.

3. **Coverage ratios including EBITDA/interest and cash flow to debt service**: While the two previous ratios focus on the debt as in relationship to value or other sources of capital or setting up the initial debt as compared to current EBITDA

and cash flow, the coverage ratios address the ongoing ability of the company to meet its annual debt obligations. These ratios, such EBITDA to interest or EBITDA minus Capex to debt payments are usually found in credit agreements as a covenant ratio. This ratio is very effective when the analyst runs various sensitivity cases to test the ability of the company to pay its debt obligations. For example, if the starting EBITDA-to-interest ratio of a transaction is 3x, assuming EBITDA of $90 million and interest expense of $30 million, then even if EBITDA drops in half, from $90 million to $45 million, the $30 million interest expenses can be covered though the risk of the company has significantly changed. In this example, the credit agreement between the company and banks that have given the loan might have a covenant restriction of 2x, which means that at 1.5x the company will have a technical default. This technical default will give the bank a reason to increase its interest rate to reflect the new risk before approving to amend a new covenant level or waiving the current level. Figure 18.1 shows that the starting coverage ratio starts at 5.2x meeting Standard & Poor's BB- benchmark of 3x.

4. **Run a 30% haircut across operating assumptions to test profitability and cash flow**: Typically, the company will give the bank a business plan, which will include financial projections before obtaining a loan. The analysts working for this bank who are in the process of approving a loan will run various sensitivity cases including a case that adjusts down the top line and bottom line income and cash flow by 30% to test how the company can meet such obligations. The 30% threshold is typically used to set up the covenants that will be incorporated in the credit or loan agreement. In Figure 18.1 the model adjusts EBITDA to be 30% lower and measured against Standard & Poor's BB- benchmark. All three previous ratios (debt capitalization, leverage, and coverage) still meet Standard & Poor's BB- benchmark.
5. **Adjust and customize operating ratios based on the company's business that can be cyclical or seasonal or depend on commodity pricing**: After the four areas of analysis are run and measured, the analyst should focus on the specific operating ratios based on the industry drivers. For example, if the credit analyst is analyzing a chemical company where a large portion of its cost of revenue is oil or an oil-related commodity such as benzine, the cost of raw material should be sensitized and adjusted for price fluctuations unless the company has hedging contracts in place to stabilize its cost of materials. In grading the company after applying the measurement ratios, including the leverage and coverage ratios, the analyst allows the adjustments (plus or minus) based on the stability or volatility of the company's revenues and/or costs. In Figure 18.1 the credit analysis benchmark shows a threshold of 3x beta business volatility as the maximum level. Celerity Technology shows that the businesses in their industry measure volatility or beta at 2.5x, thus no further adjustments need to be made to assess the credit risk.

The best approach to complete an effective credit analysis is to create a checklist and make sure you sure you check every item. Figure 18.1 shows the check points at each area of analysis.

DEBT-CAPACITY ANALYSIS

The objective of the debt capacity analysis is to measure the ability to borrow. It refers to the amount of funding that a firm can borrow up to the point where its corporate value no longer increases. There various methods of measuring debt capacity:

1. Based on maximum leverage ratio (Total Debt/EBITDA)
2. Based on loan to value (Total Debt/Enterprise value or total debt/total assets)
3. Based on debt coverage ratio (DCR)

Based on Maximum-Leverage Ratios (Total Debt/EBITDA)

This ratio, which has been one of the most controversial ratios used to measure debt capacity, has been changing every year based on risk appetite of the banks. Prior to the financial crisis of 2008, leveraged buyout transactions were structured on average of 7x times leverage. During the financial crisis, any deal that got done was done less than 5x, and after the financial crisis the leverage ratio climbed up to 6x, so on a $100-million acquisition of a company with a $10 million EBITDA, the $40 million needs to be paid with equity (40%) because the market capacity is 6 × $10 = $60 million of debt; the extra multiple (4x on a 10x acquisition multiple) needs to come from equity. If, for example, the negotiation raises the price to $120 million, the equity needs to make up the difference since the debt level has met its maximum capacity. Figure 18.2 shows that no matter what the acquisition cost is, the debt capacity stays at the same level. In this case figure 18.2 shows a maximum senior debt leverage (what a bank will be comfortable lending against EBITDA) and total debt at 6x. If the private equity firm negotiates to buy the company at the acquisition multiple of 12.0x, then the equity adjusts as percentage to the total capital raised.

As mentioned, debt capacity involves the assessment of the amount of debt that the company can repay in a timely manner without forfeiting its financial viability. It includes the determination of the appropriate limit to the amount of long-term debt that can remain outstanding at any point of time.

Based on Loan to Value (Total Debt/Total Assets or Total Debt/Enterprise Value)

Many commercial banks have developed the asset-based loan business (ABL) where the debt capacity is based on the book value of the company's assets by multiplying the latest reported assets by an assigned advanced rate or loan-to-value rate. The advanced

FIGURE 18.2 DEBT CAPACITY BASED ON LEVERAGE

DEBT CAPACITY BASED ON TOTAL LEVERAGE (6.0X)

	EBITDA Multiple X	% Capital	EBITDA Multiple X	% Capital	EBITDA Multiple X	% Capital
Cost of Acquisition	**8.00x**		**10.00x**		**12.00x**	
Senior Bank Debt	3.50x	43.8%	3.50x	35.0%	3.50x	29.2%
Corporate Bonds	2.50x	31.3%	2.50x	25.0%	2.50x	20.8%
Total Debt	6.00x	75.0%	6.00x	60.0%	6.00x	50.0%
Equity	2.00x	25.0%	4.00x	40.0%	6.00x	50.0%
Total	**8.00x**	**100.0%**	**10.00x**	**100.0%**	**12.00x**	**100.0%**

rate is determined at the time based on the company's strength of assets. For example, cash has the strongest coverage with 100% advance rate, and inventory is analyzed closely before applying an advanced rate. Raw materials could be viewed as having higher value than work-in-process inventory or lower-than-finished goods inventory. These categories of inventory are based on comfort level for each bank. The banks develop a list of these assets to loan against, sometimes referred to eligible assets. Figure 18.3 shows that Celerity Technology can borrow up to $1,642 million against the assets based on this method. Many analysts do this type of analysis to determine the strength of secondary source of repayment in addition to other debt-capacity methodologies such as using the leverage ratio or the cash flow capacity method.

Based on Debt-Coverage Ratio (DCR)

The debt-coverage ratio (DCR) method of calculating debt capacity is similar a discount cash flow (DCF) method of calculating the firm and equity values. The difference is that the stream of cash flows is before debt service and the discount rate used to calculate the present value of these cash flows is the loan rate that the bank will charge the customer based on its risk rating. Figure 18.4 shows that the maximum debt that can be supported from Celerity Technology's projected cash flows is $4.4 billion pre-adjusted and $3.5 billion adjusted. There is a 20% risk appetite cushion used.

RISK AND CREDIT RESTRUCTURE ANALYSIS

The first part of this chapter focused on credit risks and debt capacity. **These analytical methods are designed to focus primarily on the ability of the company to pay back its debt obligations in a timely fashion and are used by the bank to obtain an approval before the loan is funded.** This section of the chapter will focus on the risk analysis of

FIGURE 18.3 CELERITY TECHNOLLOGY INC. DEBT CAPACITY ANALYSIS BASED ON LOAN TO VALUE

Celerity Technogy Inc. ("CTI")
Debt Capacity Analysis based on Loan to Value

	HISTORICAL		Advanced Rates Loan/Value	Debt Capacity
BASE CASE	**Year -1**	**Year 0**		**Year 0**
Current Assets				
Cash	45,000	65,800	**100%**	65,800
Accounts Receivable	45,000	60,000	**85%**	51,000
Inventories	35,000	40,000	**50%**	20,000
Prepaid Expenses	10,000	9,000	**0%**	-
Total Current Assets	135,000	174,800		
Property and Equipment				
Land	2,500,000	2,500,000		
Building	450,000	550,000		
Furniture & Equipment	50,000	75,000		
Total Gross P&E	3,000,000	3,125,000		
Less Accumulated Depreciaition	(300,000)	(365,000)		
Net P&E	2,700,000	2,760,000	**50%**	1,380,000
Long-Term Investments	200,000	250,000	**50%**	125,000
Total Assets	3,035,000	3,184,800	**Debt Capacity =**	**1,641,800**

FIGURE 18.4 CELERITY TECHNOLLOGY INC. DEBT CAPACITY ANALYSIS BASED DEBT COVERAGE RATIO (DCR)

Celerity Technogy Inc. ("CTI")
Debt Capacity based on Debt Coverage Ratio (DCR)

		PROJECTED				
		Year 1	**Year 2**	**Year 3**	**Year 4**	**Year 5**
Total Revenue		1,228,140	1,344,200	1,442,919	1,529,268	1,605,161
Total Cost of Revenue		(463,078)	(506,823)	(544,053)	(576,709)	(605,474)
Total Operating Expenses		(271,501)	(289,448)	(306,442)	(322,900)	(338,999)
EBITDA		493,561	547,928	592,424	629,659	660,688
Less Capex		(138,304)	(151,374)	(162,491)	(172,215)	(180,761)
Less Working Capital		2,870	(4,548)	(3,869)	(3,384)	(2,974)
Less Taxes		(129,769)	(147,070)	(156,960)	(158,461)	(162,851)
Cash Flow Available for Debt Service		228,358	244,935	269,105	295,599	314,101
	EBITDA Multiple					
Terminal Value (Enteprise Value based on EBITDA Multiple)	7.0x					4,624,814
Cash Flows Available for Debt Service including Terminal Value		228,358	244,935	269,105	295,599	4,938,915
	Loan Rate					
Present Value of Cash Flows Uisng the Loan Rate	7.00%	213,419	213,936	219,670	225,511	3,521,378
Total Present Value of Cash Flows to support Debt Service		4,393,914				
	Cushion %					
Adjusting for cushion	20.00%	(878,783)				
Maximum Debt based on DCR		3,515,131				

companies that have already obtained a loan and are now having a hard time meeting their debt obligations. The credit analyst needs to continue its analysis after the transaction is closed. In many distress cases, the bank has the following options:

- Calculate the losses if it decides to sell off its debt investment to other lenders for the best possible price, possibly selling at a discount
- Calculate the losses if it decides to stay in the credit and work with the company through their tough times and hopefully have a better outcome

The objective of the risk and credit restructure analysis is to calculate these possibilities, so the bank can have the highest possible recovery described below.

Recovery Analysis

The basic assumption of any recovery analysis is to assume that if the company files for bankruptcy the debt obligations will be considered as claims. Any value that is created by a possible restructuring is first used to repay the highest-priority claim based on the certain ranking, starting from senior-secured loans such a bank loan, then second-lien loans, then subordinated debt notes, then preferred equity, and last common equity. Once the claims meet the first level of debt, the remaining residual value can then be applied to the next most-senior-level of claims, referred to as the "waterfall." Most of the time, though, since the bankruptcy process is a lengthy one and the ultimate decision of how the claims are paid is determined by the bankruptcy judge, recovery rates are not immediately known. Since time to recovery is dependent on the level of control or influence of different creditors suggesting different plan of reorganization, the enforceability of the "waterfall" of claims is speculative at best. For larger syndicated loans, since there is a secondary market, the price of the loans determines the recovery as it sets the market demand and supply of such distressed loan. The analyst might decide that is better to sell the loan at 70% of par rather than wait until a restructuring occurs post-bankruptcy or after the reorganization is approved by the creditors and the courts. Sometimes the company will not pay cash interest during the bankruptcy proceedings, so the loans will be dormant for an unknown length of time. To compare the secondary market prices to what the expectation of recovery is post-bankruptcy, the credit analysts should utilize various valuation approaches including the current enterprise value, albeit at distress levels, as well a liquidation value by measuring the fixed asset or examining the current collateral via a collateral analysis.

- **Valuing the enterprise in a distressed scenario:** If the analyst's view is that the company can continue to operate its business during distressed times and possibly come out of bankruptcy with strong growth, then the credit analyst should prepare an enterprise valuation of the company. In such a case the most likely course of action will be reorganization of the business and credit analysis should measure the business as a going concern. As it was illustrated in previous chapters of valuating the enterprise, the best approach, even in distressed times, is to compare to other companies that are in the same industry (peer analysis). Taking the average EBITDA multiple of the company's peers is fist benchmark used to determine the value of the company. The approach is to value the business, which will continue to operate during and after the restructuring or be sold as going concern. Once this enterprise is estimated using various methods, then these values are compared to the debt outstanding.

- **Collateral Analysis:** Collateral is an asset provided to secure an obligation. Traditionally, banks might require corporate borrowers to commit company assets as security for loans. Today, this practice is called secured lending or asset-based lending. Collateral can take many forms: property, inventory, equipment, receivables, oil reserves, etc. The collateral analysis is very similar to debt-capacity analysis based on loan to value. Basically, the collateral values are based on certain advanced rates that the bank is comfortable lending against (see figure 18.3 in previous section).

Cost of Capital Analysis

The credit analyst needs to review whether the business can be restructured or whether it will be sold or liquidated and closed.

- **Restructuring option**: The analyst will need to calculate both the cost of debt and cost of the equity. The cost of debt can be easily found if the debt is trading in the secondary market. This price represents the price an investor is willing to pay to take the debt out. If there is no secondary price, the analyst should assume the cost of debt is in line with what the rating expectation will be once the company emerges from restructuring. If the loan emerging out of bankruptcy is anticipated to be rated by Standard and Poor's and/or Moody's, this rating should help establish a benchmark for market price and recovery levels. If the company has different tranches of debt such as corporate loans, unsecured notes, or subordinated notes, each of these will be priced based on its specific rating. The price of debt is expected to be reduced during restructuring and, depending of what the restructuring looks like, the cost will settle at that price. This is important so the analyst can price in the expected recovery rate. The cost of equity is more difficult to measure given that, by definition, it is the last on the waterfall for receiving any payment during the restructuring. One of the methods of valuing the equity is using a call option methodology. Basically, the equity value thesis is that there is some value for ongoing business on a post-restructuring basis like a call option that is currently out of the money but anticipated that after the restructuring the value will move up from negative to be positive it will be in the money given a certain time.

- **Business sale option**: Despite the distress level that the company is in, the value of the business could be very attractive. More often than not, the company is relatively healthy if you strip out the debt. There are plenty of examples where a distress buyer has stepped in and renegotiated with the banks to buy the company at a discount and then the company not only survives after the sale but thrives in the future under new management. The credit analyst needs to run this option if the restructuring option does not work. The value of such business is calculated based on what is someone willing to pay for the business via the discount cash flow method or the comparable EBITDA multiples. Once the enterprise value is calculated, then the analyst can measure the recovery rate, which is the ratio of the enterprise value to debt.
- **Liquidation option:** When the restructuring and the sale of the business option are not feasible, the credit analyst will look then to find value in the real assets (instead of financial assets or enterprise value). Figure 18.5 shows that the maximum recovery based on Celerity Technology assets is 1x, assuming certain distressed asset-based modified advance rates (discount rates) and subtracting all the trade and tax claims. The total claims based on this analysis is $1,244 million against total debt of $1,190 million.

CORPORATE CREDIT AND RECOVERY SCORES BY RATING AGENCIES AND OTHERS

Credit rating agencies, such as Standard & Poor's, Moody's, and Fitch grade companies that raised debt in the capital markets. The rating levels represent proxies for default risk and the recovery rates issued are proxies for recovery expectation. The combination of the two represents the probabilities of default and expected loss.

Figure 18.6 shows the rating levels by each of the rating agencies. Each level represents an opinion of the creditworthiness of an obligor. Even though the symbols differ between rating agencies, the three scales are set the same.

Every year the rating agencies will publish the actual historical probability of default based on rating. As an example, AAA issuer has 0.0% probability of default and CCC has 31% for a year. The agencies also place the probability of default for longer maturities.

Standard & Poor's recover ratings focuses on expected recovery in the event of a payment default. The recovery rating is based on 1+ to 6 numerical rating that corresponds to recovery percentage of the debt outstanding, as described in Figure 18.7.

FIGURE 18.5 CELERITY TECHNOLLOGY INC. LIQUIDATION VALUES

Celerity Technogy Inc. ("CTI")
Liquidation Values

	HISTORICAL		Distress Advanced Rates Loan/Value		Debt Capacity
BASE CASE	**Year -1**	**Year 0**			**Year 0**
Current Assets					
Cash	45,000	65,800	**100%**		65,800
Accounts Receivable	45,000	60,000	**60%**		36,000
Inventories	35,000	40,000	**35%**		14,000
Prepaid Expenses	10,000	9,000	**0%**		-
Total Current Assets	135,000	174,800			
Property and Equipment					
Land	2,500,000	2,500,000			
Building	450,000	550,000			
Furniture & Equipment	50,000	75,000			
Total Gross P&E	3,000,000	3,125,000			
Less Accumulated Depreciaition	(300,000)	(365,000)			
Net P&E	2,700,000	2,760,000	**40%**		1,104,000
Long-Term Investments	200,000	250,000	**40%**		100,000
Total Assets	3,035,000	3,184,800		**Asset Coverage =**	**1,319,800**
Liabilities and Owners Equity					
Current Liabilities					
Accounts Payable	35,000	40,000	**100%**		(40,000)
Accrued Income Taxes	12,000	10,000	**100%**		(10,000)
Accrued Expenses	10,000	8,000	**100%**		(8,000)
Current Portion of Long Term Debt	20,000	10,000			
Total Current Liabilities	77,000	68,000			
Long-Term Debt:	1,200,000	1,180,000			
			Less Trade/Tax Claims =		
Deferred Income Taxes	12,000	17,000	**100%**		(17,000)
Total Liabilties	1,289,000	1,265,000			
Owners' Equity				**Trade/tax Claims**	**(75,000)**
Common Stock	1,000,000	1,000,000			
Paid-in-Capital	-	25,000		**Net Value =**	**1,244,800**
Retained Earnings	746,000	894,800			
Total Owners' Equity	1,746,000	1,919,800		Short Term Debt =	10,000
				Long-Term Debt =	1,180,000
Total Liabilities & Owner's Equity	3,035,000	3,184,800		Total Debt =	1,190,000
Error Check	-	-			
				Value/Total Debt =	**1.046x**

FIGURE 18.6 CREDIT RATING AGENCIES' SCALES

Description		Standard & Poor's	Moody's	Fitch
Highest Quality (Risk Free)	INVESTMENT GRADE	AAA	Aaa	AAA
High Quality	INVESTMENT GRADE	AA+ AA AA-	Aa1 Aa2 Aa3	AA+ AA AA-
Strong Payment Capacity	INVESTMENT GRADE	A+ A A-	A1 A2 A3	A+ A A-
Adequate Payment Capacity	INVESTMENT GRADE	BBB+ BBB BBB-	Baa1 Baa2 Baa3	BBB+ BBB BBB-
Likely to fullfill Obligations	NON-INVESTMENT GRADE (LEVERAGE)	BB+ BB BB-	Ba1 Ba2 Ba3	BB+ BB BB-
High-risk Obligations	NON-INVESTMENT GRADE (LEVERAGE)	B+ B B-	B1 B2 B3	B+ B B-
Current Vulnarable to Default	DISTRESS	CCC+ CCC CCC- CC C	Caa1 Caa2 Cas3 Ca C	CCC
Default		D	D	RD/D

The combination of the probability of default and recovery rates could be used by the credit analyst to calculate the expected losses on the outstanding debt.

The rating agencies have been publishing annual studies that analyze the behavior of rates during the year that these agencies review and publish the cumulative default rates by rating. The general takeaways from these studies that there is clear correlation between ratings and probability of default. One observation that is gathered from these studies is the migration of ratings based on the new issuer of debt versus the companies that already managed the debt few years. In other words, the probability of default in higher in the early years and it reduces in the later years.

FIGURE 18.7 STANDARD & POOR'S RECOVERY RATES

Description	Recovery Rates	Recovery % of Outstanding
Highest Exp[ectation of full recovery in the event of default	1+	100%
Expectaion of Very High	1	90%-100%
Expectaion of substantial	2	70%-90%
Expectation of Meanigful	3	50%-70%
Expectation of Average	4	30%-50%
Expectation of Modest	5	10%-30%
Expectation of Neglible	6	0%-10%

OTHER PROBABILITY OF DEFAULT AND RECOVERY MODELS

Even though the rating agencies are seen as the experts in the credit analysis, academics and risk managers have developed their own sophisticated statistical models to predict the likelihood of bankruptcy. Many commercial banks that approve large loans for their customers developed their own internal ratings based on many methodologies. Academics have also created statistical models to predict defaults and recoveries. **These statistical models include the Altman's Z-score, the Merton model, and KMV.**

Altman's Z-Score

A well-known ratio used for measuring the company's ability to manage debt, especially manufacturing companies, is Altman's Z-score. The ratio heavily tests the relationship of the primary source of repayment such as cash and income to the secondary source of repayment such as fixed assets. The Z-score, created and developed by NYU professor Dr. Edward Altman, is the measurement of the likelihood of bankruptcy. This ratio is built to include the ratios profitability, liquidity, solvency, and activity ratios.

Z-score = 1.2A + 1.4B + 3.3C + 0.6D + 1.0E

where, A is working capital/total assets; B is retained earnings/total assets; C is earnings before interest and tax/total assets; D is market value of equity/total liabilities; and E is sales/total assets. The weights used next to the individual ratios are based on historical assessment for publicly traded manufacturing companies.

The lower the score, the higher the probability of bankruptcy. If the Z-score is above 3.0 the likelihood of default is very low. If the score is less than 1.8 the likelihood of default or bankruptcy is high.

The Z-score formula for private companies was incorporated much later and is as follows:

Z-score = 0.717A + 0.847B + 3.107C + 0.420D + 0.998E

where, A is working capital/total assets; B is retained earnings/total assets; C is earnings before interest and tax/total assets; D is book value of equity/total liabilities; and E is sales/total assets. The weights used next to the individual ratios are based on historical assessment for private manufacturing companies.

For measuring the Z-score for non-manufacturing companies, Altman modified the formula to exclude the last component (E) of sales/to total assets. Taking this last component out of the Z-score formula minimizes the effects of manufacturing-intensive asset turnover.

Merton Model

The Merton model developed in 1974 uses basic option pricing that looks at the relationship between credit risk and the financial structure of the company. It assumes that the equity holders hold a call option and the debt holders hold a put option. The default happens at maturity of the debt (similar to a European-type option pricing method such Black-Scholes) if the enterprise value is lower than the strike price or debt levels. Credit analysts use the Merton model to analyze the company's risk of credit default.

The value of the asset adjusted for volatility is based on the Black Scholes Model discussed in the options section (chapter 13) is calculated as follows:

$$E = V_t N(d_1) - K_{e^{-i.t}} N(d_2) \text{ where } d1 = \frac{\ln\left(\frac{V}{K}\right) + \left(i + \frac{\sigma^2}{2}\right)t}{\sigma\sqrt{t}} \text{ and } d2 = d1 - \sigma\sqrt{t}$$

Where E is the theoretical value of the company's equity, is V_t is the value of the company's assets in period t, K is the value of the company's debt, i is the interest rate, t is maturity of the loan, and σ is the standard deviation or volatility of the stock returns, N is the cumulative standard normal distribution.

KMV Model

Similar to the Merton Model, KMV is a newer model used by banks to analyze the likelihood of default based on expected default frequency, (EDF) which is basically a probability of default mechanism to give the credit analyst a warning signal. **The hypothesis of the KMV model is that default happens when the value of the firm's assets falls somewhere between the value of short-term debt and the value of total debt**. The measurement of KMV, expressed as a suggestive Moody's rating (i.e. Ba1) and assess three factors such the value of the assets adjusted for volatility, the distance to default (DtoD) and determining the expected default frequencies (EDF).

- **Value of the Assets adjusted for volatility (A_t):** The value of the asset adjusted for volatility is based on the Black Scholes Model discussed in the options section (chapter 13) is calculated as follows:

$$E_t = A_t N(d_1) - B_{e^{-i.t}} N(d_2) \text{ where } d1 = \frac{\ln\left(\frac{A}{B}\right) + \left(i + \frac{\sigma^2}{2}\right)t}{\sigma\sqrt{t}} \text{ and } d2 = d1 - \sigma\sqrt{t}$$

Where A_t is the value of the current Asset, B is the value of the loan, i is the interest rate, t is maturity of the loan, and σ is the standard deviation or volatility of the asset value.

The standard deviation or the volatility (σ) of the asset value is derived based on the volatility of the equity value or the stock price assuming the company is publicly traded. Since the premise of the KMV is the relationship of the value of the firm to the value of the loan using the volatility of the stock price should translate to the volatility of the asset.

- **Distance to Default (DtoD)**: KMV assumes that the point of default lies between the short-term and total debt. The formula to determine the default point (DPT) is to add the current short-term debt amount and half the long-term debt amount (DPT = STD + 0.5 LTD). The distance to default (DtoD) is the number of standard deviations that the asset has to move lower from the average amount before getting to the default point (DPT). It is calculated as follows:

  $$DtoD = \frac{E(A_t) - DPT}{\sigma_A}$$

  Where $E(A_t)$ is the expected value of the assets in future time t.
  The DtoD can also be calculated using the Black-Scholes formula's d_2 as follows:

  $$DofD = \frac{\ln\left(\frac{A_0}{DPT}\right) + \left(i - \frac{\sigma^2}{2}\right)t}{\sigma\sqrt{t}}$$

  Where i is the mean of the expected asset return, A_0 is the current market value of the firm and σ is the annualized firm value volatility.
- **Expected Default Frequencies (EDF):** The determination of the expected default frequencies which basically the implied probability of default within a year. The formula for EDF is as follows:

  $$EDF_t = N(-DtoD)$$

  Where N (-DofD) is the normal distribution of the distance to default result expressed as percentage (0–100%).

Credits

Fig. 18.6: Source: Standard & Poor's and Moody's.

Fig. 18.7: Source: Standard & Poor's and Moody's.

CASE STUDY

ZACK JONES COMPANY

Synopsis: Mr. Smith, the CFO of Zack Jones Company, has been considering two options for raising $200 million that is needed for plant modernization. The two choices are as follows:

1. Borrow $200 million in a bank loan bearing a 7% fixed-rate interest.
2. Issue 5,741,000 shares of common stock at $35. The stock is now selling for $35 per share.

The plant modernization is expected to increase EBITDA by $25 million. Zack Jones Company's financial statements for 20 × 1 are given below, as well the proforma's adjusting for each financing option. The goal is to create shareholder value without compromising the balance sheet with unnecessary leverage.

Based on the proforma balance sheet and income statement for each option, the preferred option for shareholder value is the debt option. Despite adding additional debt obligations, the EPS and dividend scheduled for 50% of net income is higher than the new stock issuance option, which dilutes the existing shareholders.

Option 3: Assume that the bank can only approve a total debt/total capitalization of 40% or total debt/EBITDA no more than 3.0x, whichever is lower. What is the preferred option between this option, which is partially financed by debt and the balance by issuance of stock at the market price, or all equity issuance?

Based on proforma statements, the preferred option for shareholder value is the debt option—the maximum debt to raise is $138 million based on 3.0x maximum debt to EBITDA (leverage ratio based on debt capacity). The other criteria is to be at 40% total debt/total capitalization, which puts the new debt at approximately $186 million. Since the bank is approving the lower of the two capacity numbers, the $138 million becomes the maximum. Since the modernization requires $200 million, the balance needs to be raised by the new equity. The EPS is lower than option 1 but better than option 2, showing $1.84 based on 19.8 million shares (1.8 million shares issued).

CASE STDY 18.1 ZACK JONES COMPANY

SUMMARY BALANCE SHEET (December 31, 20X1)

		OPTION 1: DEBT OPTION			OPTION 2: EQUITY OPTION		
ASSETS	**Amount ($ mm)**	**Dr**	**Cr**	**Amount ($ mm)**	**Dr**	**Cr**	**Amount ($ mm)**
Current Assets	**220.0**			220.0			220.0
PP&E	**849.2**	$ 200.0		1,049.2	$ 200.0		1,049.2
Other Assets	**80.7**			80.7			80.7
Total Assets	**1,149.9**			1,349.9			1,349.9
LIABILITIES & EQUITY							
Current Liabilities	**120.0**			120.0			$ 120.0
Long-Term Debt (5.0%)	**300.0**		$ 200.0	500.0			$ 300.0
Shareholder's Equity	**729.9**			729.9		$ 200.0	$ 929.9
	1,149.9	200.0	200.0	1,349.9	200.0	200.0	1,349.9

SUMMARY INCOME STATEMENT (December 31, 20X1)

			OPTION 1: DEBT OPTION			OPTION 2: EQUITY OPTION	
	Amount ($ mm)		**Adjustment**	**Amount ($ mm)**		**Adjustment**	**Amount ($ mm)**
Sales	**831.00**						
Cost of Sales	**580.00**						
Gross Profit	**251.00**						
Operating Expenses	**130.00**						
EBITDA	**121.00**		25.0	146.00		25.0	146.00
Depreciation	**15.00**		(3.1)	18.10		(3.1)	18.10
EBIT	**106.00**			127.90			127.90
Interest	**21.00**		(14.0)	35.00			21.00
EBT	**85.00**			92.90			106.90
Taxes	**21.25**		(2.0)	23.23		(5.5)	26.73
Net Income	**63.75**		5.9	69.68		16.4	80.18
EPS, based on outs. shares	**$ 3.54**	18 shares	$ 0.33	**$ 3.87**	23.71	$ 0.69	**$ 3.38**
Dividends per share	**$ 1.77**	1	$ 0.16	**$ 1.94**	shares	$ 0.35	**$ 1.69**

Financing Alternatives

OPTION 1: DEBT OPTION

Obtain Debt	$ 200.0	million
Interest	7.00%	
Term	6 years	

	Pmt Sched.	Outstand.	Interest
Year 1	0.0	$ 200.0	14.0
Year 2	20.0	$ 180.0	14.0
Year 3	30.0	$ 150.0	12.6
Year 4	40.0	$ 110.0	10.5
Year 5	50.0	$ 60.0	7.7
Year 6	60.0	$ -	4.2
Total	**200.0**		

Market Information

Stock Price		$35	
Shares Outstanding		18.00	milion
Market Capitalization	$	630.0	million
Total Debt	$	300.0	million
Total Capital	$	930.0	million

OPTION 2: EQUITY OPTION

Issue Stock	$	200.0	million
Shares Issued		5.71	million
Price Issued	$	35.0	

CASE STDY 18.2A ZACK JONES COMPANY

SUMMARY BALANCE SHEET (December 31, 20X1)		OPTION 1: DEBT OPTION			OPTION 2: EQUITY OPTION		
ASSETS	**Amount ($ mm)**	**Dr**	**Cr**	**Amount ($ mm)**	**Dr**	**Cr**	**Amount ($ mm)**
Current Assets	220.0			220.0			220.0
PP&E	849.2	$ 200.0		1,049.2	$ 200.0		1,049.2
Other Assets	80.7			80.7			80.7
Total Assets	1,149.9			1,349.9			1,349.9
LIABILITIES & EQUITY							
Current Liabilities	120.0			120.0			$ 120.0
Long-Term Debt (5.0%)	300.0		$ 200.0	500.0			$ 300.0
Shareholder's Equity	729.9			729.9		$ 200.0	$ 929.9
	1,149.9	200.0	200.0	1,349.9	200.0	200.0	1,349.9

SUMMARY INCOME STATEMENT (December 31, 20X1)		OPTION 1: DEBT OPTION			OPTION 2: EQUITY OPTION		
	Amount ($ mm)		**Adjustment**	**Amount ($ mm)**		**Adjustment**	**Amount ($ mm)**
Sales	831.00						
Cost of Sales	580.00						
Gross Profit	251.00						
Operating Expenses	130.00						
EBITDA	121.00		25.0	146.00		25.0	146.00
Depreciation	15.00		(3.1)	18.10		(3.1)	18.10
EBIT	106.00			127.90			127.90
Interest	21.00		(14.0)	35.00			21.00
EBT	85.00			92.90			106.90
Taxes	21.25		(2.0)	23.23		(5.5)	26.73
Net Income	63.75		5.9	69.68		16.4	80.18
EPS, based on outs. shares	$ 3.54	18 shares	$ 0.33	$ 3.87	23.71	$ 0.69	$ 3.38
Dividends per share	$ 1.77	0.5	$ 0.16	$ 1.94	shares	$ 0.35	$ 1.69

Financing Alternatives

OPTION 1: DEBT OPTION

Obtain Debt	$ 200.0 million
Interest	7.00%
Term	6 years

	Pmt Sched.	Outstand.	Interest
Year 1	0.0	$ 200.0	14.0
Year 2	20.0	$ 180.0	14.0
Year 3	30.0	$ 150.0	12.6
Year 4	40.0	$ 110.0	10.5
Year 5	50.0	$ 60.0	7.7
Year 6	60.0	$ -	4.2
Total	200.0		

Market Information

Stock Price		$35
Shares Outstanding		18.00 milion
Market Capitalization	$	630.0 million
Total Debt	$	300.0 million
Total Capital	$	930.0 million

OPTION 2: EQUITY OPTION

Issue Stock	$	200.0 million
Shares Issued		5.71 million
Price Issued	$	35.0

CASE STDY 18.2B ZACK JONES COMPANY

OPTION 3

DEBT CAPACITY ANALYSIS

Existing Debt	300.0				
Plus Additional Debt (assume all Debt for modernization)	$ 200.0				
Total Debt	500.0				
Total Capitalization	1,229.90				
Total Debt / Total Cap	40.7%				
Maximum	40.0%				
Maximum New Loan	**186.5** approx.			**PROPOSED TRANSACTION:**	
Proforma EBITDA	146.00				
Leverage Ratio (Debt/EBITDA)	3.42	max new Debt	**138.0**	Equity	62.0
Maximum	3.00			Debt	138.0
Maximum Debt	438.00			Total	**$ 200.0**
Less Existing	300.0				
Maximum New Debt	**138.0**	Shares raised at current Market Price =			1.77 million

SUMMARY BALANCE SHEET (December 31, 20X1)

	Amount ($ mm)	OPTION 3: DEBT AND EQUITY Dr	Cr	Amount ($ mm)
ASSETS				
Current Assets	**220.0**			220.0
PP&E	**849.2**	$ 200.0		1,049.2
Other Assets	**80.7**			80.7
Total Assets	**1,149.9**			1,349.9
LIABILITIES & EQUITY				
Current Liabilities	**120.0**		62.0	182.0
Long-Term Debt (5.0%)	**300.0**		$ 138.0	438.0
Shareholder's Equity	**729.9**			729.9
	1,149.9	200.0	200.0	1,349.9

SUMMARY INCOME STATEMENT (December 31, 20X1)

	Amount ($ mm)		OPTION 1: DEBT OPTION Adjustment	Amount ($ mm)
Sales	**831.00**			
Cost of Sales	**580.00**			
Gross Profit	**251.00**			
Operating Expenses	**130.00**			
EBITDA	**121.00**		25.0	146.00
Depreciation	**15.00**		(3.1)	18.10
EBIT	**106.00**			127.90
Interest	**21.00**		(9.7)	30.66
EBT	**85.00**			97.24
Taxes	**21.25**		(3.1)	24.31
Net Income	**63.75**		9.2	72.93
EPS, based on outs. shares	**$ 3.54**	19.8 shares	$ 0.46	**$ 3.69**
Dividends per share	**$ 1.77**	0.5	$ 0.23	**$ 1.84**

PROBLEMS

1. What is debt capacity analysis and how is it used?
2. Based on the case below, please construct the transaction sources and uses and calculate the WACC.

Phatchance Hotel Properties, Inc.

Jack Von Crook, a hotel investor, is in the process of purchasing Phatchance Hotel Properties, Inc. ("PHP"). PHP operates two hotels in Miami, Florida, with total of 800 rooms. He is anticipating completing the necessary renovations on these properties by December 31, 2017, and opening their doors for business on January 1st, 2018. The estimated total cost of both properties is $400 million, plus additional renovations calculated at $100 per square foot. The size of the rooms averages 500 square feet. PHP estimated 2019E EBITDA of $50 million and outstanding debt of $100 million. Transaction expenses will be $10 million. Use tax rate = 36%.

Capital Raising

The total capital needed to purchase PHP, renovate, refinance its current debt outstanding, and pay fees will be sourced from a bank loan, and corporate bonds will be based on the 2019E EBITDA multiples, as shown below. The equity financing represents the balance needed for financing. The equity expected return is calculated based on CAPM. Assume a risk-free rate of 2.0%, a market return of 12%, and beta for the hotel sector at 2.2x.

TRANSACTION SOURCES	AMOUNT	FIXED INTEREST RATE
Bank loan 6%	Based on 4x 2019E EBITDA	Bank loan 6%
Corporate bonds 10%	Based on 2x 2019E EBITDA	Corporate bonds 10%
Equity	The balance of the financing	Based on CAPM

3. Calculate the annual debt service payments of the bank loan below based on increasing LIBOR. For 2 extra bonus points, calculate the initial loan yield.

Bank Loan Amount	$200,000
Term	5 years
Pricing (Spread)	4.50%
Starting LIBOR (Year 0)	2.25%
OID	98

LIBOR Increases
Year 1: 0.5%
Year 2: 0.5%
Year 3: 1.0%

Scheduled Amortization
Year 1: $20,000
Year 2: $30,000
Year 3: $40,000
Year 4: $50,000
Year 5: $60,000

4. Construct 5-year projections for Green Landscape & Snow Removal Services LLP (GL&S) given the following assumptions.

Company Overview

GL&S is a provider of residential landscape and snow removal services in 30 states, primarily in the Northeast and Midwest. GLS in 2018 served approximately 1.5 million customers for landscape services and 500,000 customers for snow removal services.

Last Year's Revenue Assumptions (2018)

Average revenue per services (ARPS): $60 for landscape and $70 for snow removal

Average number of services per customer per year: 8 visits for landscape and 3 visits for snow removal

Projections' Assumptions (Years 2019–2023)

ARPS: Increase of 3% per year for both services

Average number of services per customer per year: 8 visits for landscape and 3 visits for snow removal

Total services annual growth rate: 1% for both services

Cost of revenue: 45% of total revenues

Operating expense: 30% of total revenues

Depreciation: 5% of total revenues

Capitalized fees of $70 million—amortize over 7 years

5. Go to finance.yahoo.com and choose any publicly traded company. Collect the information to complete the following:
   a. You need to spread 3-year historical financials, including the balance sheet, income statement, cash flow statement, and ratio analysis.
   b. You need to build the transaction sources and uses and proforma balance sheet using the following assumptions:
      - Purchase stock price: 20% premium of the December 31, 2017 closing price

- Refinance total debt (including short term and long term)
- Total transaction fees and expenses of 3.0% of total (purchase price + debt)
- New acquisition debt should be structured as follows:
    - Senior bank debt 4.0x December 31, 2017 EBITDA
    - Subordinated bonds at additional 2.0x December 31, 2017 EBITDA (6.0x total debt)
    - The balance will be cash equity from the private equity investor

c. You need to build projections using reasonable assumptions (sales growth, margins, Capex, depreciation, working capital as % of revenues) based on historical experience. You may adjust them based on your independent work justifying the projected levels. Other assumptions will be as follows:
- Tax rate: 30%
- Bank loan interest (floating L+4.0% with Libor 50 bps escalation for the next 3 years)—use starting Libor rate of 1.0%
- Subordinated debt interest rate—fixed 8.0%
- No dividends
- No divestitures

d. You need to include projected ratio analysis.

e. Write a few bullet points of your conclusion. Will you finance this transaction given the credit analysis performed?

ONLINE TEMPLATES

The Excel spreadsheets used in the chapter can be accessed online via Cognella Active Learning platform.

PART V

Financial Models and Case Study

PART V focuses on training finance students and first-year analysts to use financial modeling for many discipline areas in investment and commercial banking. The following case models and case studies are built on Excel listed below can be accessed online via the Cognella Active Learning platform:

- **Financial Model 1** - Leveraged Buyout (LBO) Model
- **Financial Model 2** - Mergers and Acquisition Financial Model
- **Financial Model 3** - Securitization Structure (CLO) Analysis
- **Financial Model 4** - Real Estate and Real Estate Fund Equity Analysis
- **Financial Model 5** - Student Loan Structured Fund Model
- **Financial Model 6** - Start-up Cash Flow and Valuation Model
- **Financial Model 7** - Distress Company Valuation Model
- **Financial Model 8** - Portfolio of Stocks and Bonds Analysis Model

References

Alexander, C. (2001). *Market models*. John Wiley & Sons, Ltd.

Bhansali, V. (2011). *Bond portfolio investing and risk management*. The McGraw-Hill Companies, Inc.

Bodie, Z., & Kane, A. (2017). *Essentials of investments*. McGraw-Hill Education.

Bodie, Z., & Kane, A. (2017). *Investments*. McGraw-Hill Education.

Borowski, E. J., & Borwein, J. M. (1991). *Mathematics*. Harper Collins Publishers.

Bragg, S. M. (2017). *Financial analysis, a controller's guide*. John Wiley & Sons, Inc.

Burrough, B., & Helyar, J. (1990). *Barbarians at the gate, the fall of RJR Nabisco*. Harper & Row Publishers, Inc.

Chance D. M., & Brooks, R. (2016). *An introduction to derivatives and risk management*. Cengage Learning.

Damodaran, A. (1996). *Investment valuation, tools and techniques for determining the value of any asset*. Wiley Frontiers in Finance.

Damodaran, A. (2010). *The dark side of valuation*. Pearson Education, Inc.

Elton, E. J., & Gruber, M. J. (1981). *Modern portfolio theory and investment analysis*. John Wiley & Sons, Inc.

Fabozzi, F. J. (2013). *Bond markets, analysis and strategies*. Pearson Education Inc.

Fridson, M., & Alvarez, F. (2011). *Financial statement analysis*. John Wiley & Sons, Inc.

Ganguin, B., & Bilardello, J. (2005). *Fundamentals of corporate credit analysis*. The McGraw-Hill Companies, Inc.

Geisel, T. S. (1947). *McElligot's Pool*. Random House, Inc.

Investopedia. www.investopedia.com

Jordan, R. W., & Westerfield, R. W. (2019). *Fundamentals of corporate finance*. McGraw-Hill Education.

Knopman, H., & Streiff, E. (2014). *Limited Representative—Investment Banking Exam, license exam manual*. Financial Training Services, Inc.

Koller, T., Dobbs, R., & Huyett, B. (2011). *Value, the four cornerstones of corporate finance*. John Wiley & Sons, Inc.

Kricheff, R. S. (2012). *A pragmatist's guide to leveraged finance*. FT Press.

LCD News. *Leveraged Commentary & Data*. www.lcdcomps.com/lcd/f/news.html

Lewis, M. (2010). *The big short*. W.W. Norton & Company, Inc.

Lewis, M. (2014). *Flash boys, a Wall Street revolt*. W.W. Norton & Company.

Loan Syndications and Trading Association. www.lsta.org

Najarian, J., & Najarian, P. (2018). *Follow the smart money.* Paradigm Direct, LLC.

Patterson, S. (2010). *The quants.* Crown Publishing Group.

Pearson. (2009). *Derivatives and portfolio management.* Pearson Custom Publishing.

Poniachek, H. (2018). *Mergers and acquisitions, a practitioner's guide to successful deals.* World Scientific Publishing, Co. Pte. Ltd.

Rosenbaum, J., & Pearl, J. (2013). *Investment banking, valuation, leveraged buyouts, and mergers & acquisitions.* John Wiley & Sons, Inc.

Sundaram, R. K., & Das, S. R. (2016). *Derivatives, principles and practice.* McGraw-Hill Education.

Sundheim, D. (2013). *Taking smart risks, how sharp leaders win when stakes are high.* The McGraw-Hill Companies, Inc.

Ziegel, A. (2014). *Fundamentals of credit and credit analysis.* Mountain Mentors Associates.

www.ingramcontent.com/pod-product-compliance
Lightning Source LLC
La Vergne TN
LVHW080743150926
848052LV00022B/2183